MW00788221

Against All Odds

Volume I

The History of Burlington Northern Railroad's Innovative Intermodal Business: 1890s - 1988

Mark S. Cane

Copyright © 2023 by Mark S. Cane

All rights reserved. Aside from attributed Fair-Use utilization of the work, no part of this publication may be reproduced or transmitted in any form or by any means, electronic or mechanical, including photocopy, recording, or any information storage and retrieval system, without permission in writing from the copyright owner. Requests for permission to make copies of this publication should be emailed to Mark S. Cane at mcane1@outlook.com.

Great Northern Railway, Northern Pacific Railway, Burlington Route, Burlington Northern, BN, The Atchison, Topeka and Santa Fe Railway Company, Santa Fe, BNSF, BNSF Railway, and Burlington Northern Santa Fe Railway are licensed marks owned by BNSF Railway Company.

The opinions expressed by the contributors to this book are solely those of the individual contributors. They do not necessarily reflect the opinions or views of BNSF Railway Company or its affiliates.

All references to, and utilization of, fully attributed copyrighted material are for the Fair-Use purposes of criticism, comment, news reporting, scholarship and research in the context of the history of Burlington Northern Railroad's Intermodal business. It is the desire/intent of the author that such use and references will increase the interest-in, and value of, those referenced materials and advance overall historical supply chain management, Railroad Industry and Burlington Northern Railroad scholarship. To help promote such research/scholarship, a portion of proceeds related to the distribution of this book will be donated to the John W. Barriger III National Railroad Library at the University of Missouri-St. Louis and the National Railroad Hall of Fame.

Excerpts and photos from *Piggyback and Containers – A History of Rail Intermodal on America's Steel Highway*, by David J. DeBoer, are reprinted with the permission of Mr. DeBoer.

Excerpts, tables and photos from *The TTX Story, Volumes 1 and 2*, by James D. Panza, Richard W. Dawson and Ronald P. Sellberg, are reprinted with the permission of the authors.

Excerpts from *History of the Atchison, Topeka and Santa Fe Railway, New Edition*, by Keith L. Bryant, Jr., and Fred W. Frailey, are reprinted with the permission of Mr. Frailey.

Excerpts from *Riding the Rails – Inside the Business of America's Railroads*, by Robert D. Krebs, are reprinted with the permission of Indiana University Press.

Excerpts from transcripts of National Railroad Hall of Fame interviews conducted with Bill Greenwood, Darius Gaskins, Rob Krebs, Michael Haverty and Dick Davidson are utilized with the permission of Julie King and the National Railroad Hall of Fame.

Cover designed with the help of Camilla Cane and Addison Bronsted.

ISBN 979-8-9876755-0-2

Volume I Contents

Dedication x

Acknowledgments xi

Preface 1

Chapter 1 - Introduction 5

    BN Predecessor Railroads' Historic International Intermodal Orientation 5

    Railroad Industry and Market and Regulatory Backdrop through the 1950s...............7

Chapter 2 - Piggyback on the Chicago, Burlington & Quincy and the Atchison, Topeka and Santa Fe ...25

    The CB&Q and the Chicago Tunnel Company..26

    Piggyback on the Chicago, Burlington & Quincy and the Atchison, Topeka and Santa Fe (continued) . 26

Chapter 3 - The Advent of Burlington Northern Railroad's Coal Boom Conflicts with Resources Business Exploitation 33

    Railroad Investments Compete with Resource Business Opportunities 35

    Energy Transportation Systems, Inc. (ETSI) 40

    The Energy Crisis and Clean Air Act Amendments Accelerate Coal Demand and BN Coal Transportation Investments...42

    Continued Heavy Rail Capital Investments Trigger Shareholder Complaints 43

    BN Increases its All-in Commitment to Coal Transportation amid Renewed C&NW/UP Pressure While Seeking a Merger with the Frisco Railroad 46

Chapter 4 - Burlington Northern's Pre-Deregulation "Piggyback" Business Build-Up............51

    Year to Year Piggyback Progress through 1979 51

    What Inhibited Significant Piggyback Growth? 56

Chapter 5 - New Competitive Rail Industry Regulatory Challenges and Relief.................61

    Concurrent Efforts to Give the Railroad Industry Regulatory Relief.......................62

Chapter 6 - Frisco Merger, Bressler Arrival, and Momentum for the Holding Company Formation 65

    BN's Board Hires Richard Bressler as Menk's Successor....................................68

    The Motor Carrier Act of 1980 Provides Truckers Massive Additional Regulatory Relief 72

    The Staggers Rail Act of 1980 Provides the Railroad Industry its Most Significant Regulatory Relief....72

    The 1980-1981 Booz, Allen & Hamilton Study...75

Louis Menk and Norman Lorentzsen Leave BN 79

Continued Rust Belt Decline 80

Chapter 7 – 1981 and the Birth of Burlington Northern's Intermodal Business Unit (IBU) **83**

Chapter 8 - The 1981 Intermodal Task Force **95**

Life During and After the Intermodal Task Force Effort 100

Chapter 9 - Attempts to Implement Intermodal Task Force Recommendations in 1982 .... **105**

Burns, DeWitt, Trafton and Berry join the Intermodal Leadership Team 106

Walter Drexel Takes the BN Railroad Helm 110

What Might Have Been – a 1982 BN/Santa Fe Merger? 113

Barbarians Still at the Gates 114

Barbarians Within the Gates – The 1982 Organization Study 116

Northwestern University and "Marketing Myopia" 121

Darius Gaskins Arrives Just in Time 124

A New and Important Transportation Department Advocate 130

1982 Intermodal Business Unit (IBU) Performance 138

Chapter 10 - Pursuing the Three Intermodal Strategies in 1983 .... **140**

Strategy #1: Convert a Vast Network of Ramps to a Lean Network of Hubs 140

Strategy #2: Utilize New Technology Equipment in Dedicated Intermodal Trains............ 145

Strategy #3 - Customer Oriented Marketing Packages 151

Capitalizing on an Integrated IBU Focus on Equipment Productivity 153

American President Lines (APL) Prepares to Disrupt the Industry 154

The Need for International Terminal Capacity in Seattle 157

Should BN Purchase a Third Party Intermodal Marketing Company?........................... 157

RoadRailer Southwest Express... 158

Dallas Smith Trailers... 159

Stampede Pass Route Mothballed.. 161

Other Significant 1983 Events... 162

First Non-Trucker BN Hub Manager Selected for Spokane 163

1983 Performance Wrap-up 163

Chapter 11 – BN Intermodal's Positive Momentum Builds in 1984................................ **165**

The 1984 "White Paper" 165

"White Paper" Outcome 170

Relocation Impacts and Organizational Emphasis Changes 171

Hub Start-ups Continue 171

Sales and Service Reorganization... 172

BN Information Systems Deficiencies 173

APL Competitive Concerns Realized 174

Other Significant Intermodal Initiatives 175

Bill Greenwood is Promoted 177

Garland Resigns, Wood Arrives, Donahue and Reed Promoted, Wackstein Hired 177

BN's PRB Coal Monopoly is Lost, and More.. 178

More Bad 1984 Coal News 180

Intermodal's Internal Profile Rises 181

1984 Performance Wrap-Up.. 181

Chapter 12 - A Year of Disruptive 1985 Transitions..**185**

Continued Internal Promotion of Intermodal 186

Genesis of BN's Expediter Trains 187

Extensive Market Analyses 198

Seattle International Gateway (SIG) 199

BN Recaptures Sea-Land's Business.. 200

Trailer Train Buys Stack Cars but BN Objects to Conditions 201

BN's Common-User Stack Train 202

BN Works to Save RoadRailer from Bankruptcy 203

Another Crack at a Strategic Intermodal Information Systems Plan 204

Where to Locate the Dallas/Ft. Worth Hub and What to Do About Chicago? 205

BN's Chicago Neutral Chassis Pool... 206

BN Automotive Business Leadership 207

Dallas Smith Trailers.. 207

Burlington Northern Inc.'s Motor Carrier Industry Presence 208

Solicitation of Schneider National.. 210

Walter Drexel Promotes BN Intermodal 210

Darius Gaskins is Promoted 211

Bill Greenwood is Promoted Again 212

BN Intermodal Network as of August, 1985 214

BN Intermodal Train Service Growth Through 1985 215

More Expediters? 215

New BN Intermodal 800 Number 215

Highway Satellite Hub Growth 215

Stampede Pass Route Briefly Reopened and Quickly Shut Down Again 218

BNI Buys Southland Royalty Company to Expand Oil and Gas Assets 219

1985 Performance Wrap-up 219

Chapter 13 – Intermodal Advances in 1986 While Coal and Resource Business Challenges Persist 221

1986 IBU Goals 221

Information Systems Initiative – Next Steps 222

Greenwood Attempts to Hire John Gray 223

Steve Nieman Hired to Lead the IBU 224

IBU Organization Issues 225

RoadRailer Venture Transferred to Norfolk Southern 226

Chicago Hub Situation 227

IBU Organization Restructuring 228

Initiation of Lane Management 229

New Expediters and the Prospect of a Detroit Expediter and IBU Hub 230

IBU Service Performance Measurement 232

Original Expediter Continuation? End Haul-Length Restrictions? 233

Hub Capital Investments 234

BN Double Stack Service Capability 234

Jim Kelly Rejoins BN 235

Domestic Containerization? 237

Dallas Smith Trailer 238

A Strained Relationship Builds Between BN and Trailer Train 239

ICC Rejects Proposed SF-SP Merger 241

Union Pacific Buys Overnite Transportation Company 242

Competitive Situation Increases the Focus on Labor Costs 242

VCAs, Line Sales and the "Black Hole" 244

Power by the Hour Locomotives 246

BN – Santa Fe Avard Gateway 248

Chicago – Kansas City Expediter 249

Gerald Grinstein Begins BNRR Involvement 249

BNI Takes a Massive Asset and Accounting Charge Write-off.. 250

1986 BNI, BNRR and BN Intermodal Performance Recap... 251

Chapter 14 – 1987 is a Year of Continued Intermodal Growth but also Major Transitions 255

The IBU Presses Ahead Aggressively but also Reassesses 256

Domestic Marketing Organization Adjustment 257

Aggressive Expediter Service Expansion 258

Santa Fe Adopts BN's Expediter Strategy 258

BN Establishes a Detroit Hub 259

Domestic Channel Management 260

Refinement of BN Transportation Agreement Qualifications 261

Bill Greenwood Promoted Again and Don Wood "Leaves" BNRR.. 262

Information Systems Progress 262

Establishment of IBU Product Line Based Pricing Strategies 263

Change in the IBU Promotion and Advertising Strategy... 265

Strengthening BN Intermodal's Media Image 266

The Unrelenting Competitive Environment.. 266

CSX-Sea-Land Intermodal, Inc. (CSXI) is Born 267

Gerald Grinstein's Presence and BN Railroad Role Solidified 267

Interline Development Efforts 268

Dallas Smith Lawsuit 268

Trailer Train Saga Continues 269

R.C. Matney and RoadRailer 271

Santa Fe Avard Gateway Proposal 271

Murry Watson and BN Worldwide (BNWW) 274

The Rebirth of the Winona Bridge Railway Company (WBRC) 275

Montana Rail Link (MRL) is Born.. 279

BN Domestic Containerization Groundwork.. 281

Former Northern Pacific Railroad Properties are Unencumbered 285

1987 Comparative Intermodal Load Originations 286

1987 BNI, BNRR and BN Intermodal Financial Performance 286

Chapter 15 - 1988 Brings Major Disruptions Setting the Stage for Future Challenges **289**

Steve Nieman's Fate is Sealed 289

1988 IBU Strategic Direction as the Nieman Era Closes 289

Bob Ingram Replaces Steve Nieman 296

Bob Ingram Shared the IBU Strategic Vision... 297

Steve Nieman Shifts to Winona Bridge, but is Soon Replaced by Bill DeWitt 298

R.C. Matney/RoadRailer and Domestic Containerization Related Organization Restructuring 299

Comparative BNRR/Intermodal Pricing Performance 301

RoadRailer / Mark VII Initiative.. 302

Ingram Proposes Another RoadRailer Venture... 306

BN Domestic Containerization Moves to the Launching Pad 307

BN Double Stack Clearance Improvements for Domestic Containerization..................... 312

Santa Fe's Internal 1988 Challenges 313

Why Not a BN/Southern Pacific Intermodal Marriage? 314

The Only Santa Fe Joint-Venture Progress Before Year-End 316

The Steamship Size Evolution Accelerates.. 316

APL's Competitive Intermodal Market Impact 317

BN Worldwide Update 317

BN Railroad Labor Action Without a Northern Lines UTU Section 6 Notice..................... 319

BNRR Operations Department Reorganization.. 320

BN Motor Carriers is Sold... 321

BN's ETSI Anti-trust Lawsuit Settlement.. 321

Grinstein's "No-Show" in the Contentious Burlington Northern Railroad/Burlington Resources Assets Distribution Fight 323

BN's Remanufactured Locomotive Initiative 328

Coal Litigation Saga 329

1988 BNI, BR and BN Intermodal Performance 330

Comparative 1988 Originated Intermodal Loads.. 332

BN Employee and Locomotive Productivity, 1978-1988 333

Appendix 1 – October, 1981, BN Railroad's Motor Carrier Divertible Carload Business **335**

Appendix 2 – Circa 1983-1986 BN *Innovative Intermodal Service* Print Advertisements....................**337**

Appendix 3 – May, 1987 BN Intermodal Service Map **345**

Appendix 4: Unissued August 10, 1988 Draft Press Release Announcing the Formation of the BN/Santa Fe "BSF AMERICA" Joint Venture 347

Bibliography 349

Volume I Index 351

Dedication

The bulk of this three volume work focuses on what happened between 1978 and 1995 while I was employed by Burlington Northern (BN) Railroad. During that time I had the privilege of working with countless talented and selfless people inside and outside of BN who worked tirelessly to help make all aspects of BN successful. Special thanks to all of those associated with BN's Intermodal Business Unit (IBU) who I was blessed to work with. That includes the spouses and families of my former BN IBU teammates whose support helped us achieve incredible accomplishments in spite of significant internal and external obstacles. This work is dedicated to all of you.

Thanks to Bill Greenwood for the faith he had in me throughout my Burlington Northern career as he sponsored me for, and placed me in, a steady progression of challenging positions that helped me grow

 personally and professionally. The value and impact of his ethical, visionary and tireless customer-focused leadership, within BN overall, BN's Intermodal business in particular, and the railroad industry in general, against continuous impediments, is greatly underappreciated.

Special thanks to Darius Gaskins for his unrelenting drive to bring about deregulation of the railroad and trucking industries which made it possible for the global supply chain to be as efficient, effective and financially healthy as it is today. He helped make Burlington Northern Railroad the focal point for railroad industry leading customer service and shareholder-return growth, and envelope-pushing innovations, during his BN tenure. BN's Intermodal business may not have survived, and certainly would not have accomplished what it did, without his encouragement and support. (Picture at left includes Bill Greenwood, Mark Cane and Darius Gaskins, November 8, 2022, Courtesy of Julie King and the National Railroad Hall of Fame)

Finally, this work is also dedicated to my best friend and wife, Camilla and my daughters Maggie, Maureen and Michelle. They put up with many BN-era years of 70+ hour workweeks, lost weekends, and shortened and interrupted vacations. Camilla's willingness to pretty much raise our precious daughters without me enabled me to do all I could to contribute to the success of Burlington Northern Railroad and especially its Intermodal Business. Camilla's continued tolerance as I worked on this project, demanding a work-load comparable to my BN days, is also sincerely appreciated.

Mark Cane
June 8, 2023
 - The 35th birthday of my daughter Michelle whose birth, as it would have been for my other daughters, was a higher priority for me than a RoadRailer/Stack train demonstration in Birmingham. ☺

Acknowledgments

In the late 1980s, and through the 1990s, Burlington Northern (BN) Railroad utilized the consulting services of McKinsey & Company. In 1991, McKinsey's Jon Katzenbach, who led their worldwide organization performance and change practice, met with Bill Greenwood when he was BN's Chief Operating Officer. Katzenbach said he was co-authoring a book about high-performance teams. Greenwood mentioned the team that launched BN's Intermodal Business Unit (IBU) in 1981 and the challenges they faced. Katzenbach was fascinated with the story and asked Greenwood if he would assemble members of that original group to talk about their experiences. He believed the lessons learned from those experiences would add value to his new book. Greenwood agreed and Katzenbach, and his co-author Doug Smith, held several such meetings. The result of those sessions became the subject of Chapter Two of *The Wisdom of Teams – Creating the High-Performance Organization,* which was published by Harvard Business School Press in 1993.

Fast forward to 2001. Two of the original members of that Intermodal team, Ken Hoepner and Bill DeWitt, told me they would like to build on W*isdom* and tell the rest of the BN Intermodal story. Other priorities bumped the project off of their lists and it never regained traction. Former BN executive Earl Currie passed away in late 2021. He authored several books about BN's history but none of them dealt with BN's Intermodal story. Earl's passing reminded me of Hoepner's and DeWitt's 2001 desire to tell the full story about BN's Intermodal business. Unfortunately, after two decades Ken Hoepner had also passed by then. I spoke with Bill DeWitt about resuscitating the idea. He encouraged me to adopt the project "before it was too late." He said he had some material he would contribute to the effort. I also ran the idea of "telling the rest of the story" by Bill Greenwood. He offered his full support and stressed how important he thought it was that a complete, fact-based, account of BN's Intermodal story existed. Numerous other former teammates/business associates I reached out to expressed excitement and offered encouragement and their willingness to contribute to the effort.

Before proceeding, the main question I wrestled with is whether, approximately 40 years after the fact, the incredible history of Burlington Northern Railroad's Intermodal business still mattered. A statement from the late Columbia University history professor Garrett Mattingly provided perspective:

> *Nor does it matter at all to the dead whether they receive justice at the hands of succeeding generations. But to the living, to do justice, however belatedly, should matter.*[1]

Bill DeWitt's comment about how important it was to document and preserve the story of BN's Intermodal team and what they accomplished "before it was too late," combined with the support of so many former associates, provided the impetus the project needed.

Against All Odds documents the story of a team of visionary and dedicated individuals who rallied around a common cause to overcome tremendous internal and external obstacles. They helped revitalize a major corporation and revolutionize an essential component of the global supply chain. BN Railroad's Intermodal story may still matter to others who have an interest in this unique perspective about an important element of railroad history and the evolution of the global supply chain. Volume III

---

[1] Mattingly, Garrett, *The Armada*, Houghton Mifflin, Boston, 1959, p. 11.

also includes an attempt to document lessons that might be learned from BN's Intermodal experience. Because history tends to be cyclical, these lessons may have value for those who are struggling with issues similar to those confronted by BN's IBU. The lessons may also be helpful for those who are considering contemporary ways to improve corporate performance.

This chronicle, and its attempt "to do justice," would have been impossible without the help of many former BN and non-BN colleagues who still believe the story matters and generously assisted me. I hope I have justly incorporated your extensive contributions into the story. Sincere thanks to all of you.

Thank you to Katie Farmer, Steve Bobb, Zak Anderson, Matt Larseingue and Susan Green of BNSF for their assistance.

Thanks to Fred Frailey who offered encouragement and valuable material he collected, but did not use, when he compiled the Revised Edition of the *History of the Atchison, Topeka and Santa Fe Railway*. This material is located within the *Donald G. McInnes Collection* of the John W. Barriger III National Railroad Library at the University of Missouri – St. Louis (UMSL). Thanks to Don McInnes for his encouragement and the use of his archives. Thanks to curator Nick Fry and the staff of the Barriger Library for their help. Dave DeBoer graciously offered encouragement and permission to include material from his book, *Piggyback and Containers – A History of Rail Intermodal on America's Steel Highway*. Rob Krebs graciously agreed to provide his insights as well as a copy of his book, *Riding the Rails – Inside the Business of America's Railroads*. Thank you to Brian Carroll and Indiana University Press for permission to cite from Rob Krebs' book. James Panza, Richard Dawson and Ron Sellberg also generously permitted the use of material from their extraordinary two-volume book, *The TTX Story,* which was provided to me by Shannon Bagato and Liz Flores of TTX.

Julie King and the National Railroad Hall of Fame graciously granted me permission to quote from transcripts of interviews they conducted with Bill Greenwood, Darius Gaskins, Rob Krebs and Dick Davidson. As you will see, each of those interviews provided invaluable contributions that enriched the story. Julie said, "This is exactly why we do them."[2]

Special thanks to Jim Kelly, Dave Howland and Curt Richards for their willingness to critique the work and provide invaluable editing assistance and content and form suggestions.

I relied heavily on Bill Greenwood's archives, which are housed within the *William Greenwood Collection* of the Barriger National Railroad Library.

Finally, I apologize for the literary-style and editing shortcomings of the work. I never dreamed that I would ever write a book. The fact that I haven't written one before will be evident. Many areas the work are essentially personal memoirs of my BN experiences. Those first-hand experiences left me with strong beliefs that are reflected throughout the work. I have done my best to justify those beliefs with unvarnished facts. That is why I have included so many citations. Hopefully this will make it easier for the reader to explore my information sources to conduct further research or verify if accounts in the book are well-grounded. That is also why I sought out and incorporated the voices of so many people who are parts of this incredible story because it is also theirs.

Mark S. Cane

---

[2] Julie King email to Mark Cane, March 6, 2023.

Preface

Logistics companies have released their 2022 results. BNSF (Burlington Northern Santa Fe) Railroad, owned by Warren Buffet's Berkshire Hathaway, reported $5.95 billion of net income on freight revenue of $24.49 billion. Its Consumer (Intermodal and relatively smaller automotive) business accounted for 38% ($9.23 billion) of total revenue compared to 23% for Agricultural Products, 23% for Industrial Products and 16% for Coal. Year-over-year Consumer revenue growth was 11.8% compared to 12.6% for Agricultural Products, 5.6% for Industrial Products and 21.7% for Coal. Consumer revenue was 135% higher than Coal and 61% higher than Agricultural Products.[3] Average Consumer revenue-per-unit during the same time period of $1,775 was 22% higher than the same period of 2021.[4] BNSF generated a full-year operating ratio ("OR" - the cents of operating expenses required to generate $1 of revenue) of 66.8[5] and distributed a $5.0 billion cash distribution to its parent company Berkshire Hathaway.[6]

Other BNSF-affiliated intermodal companies also performed exceptionally well in 2022:

In the full year of 2022, J.B. Hunt Intermodal (JBHI), the Intermodal segment of truckload motor carrier J. B. Hunt Transport, Inc. (JBHT), which is one of BNSF's largest customers, generated $7.02 billion revenue and $800 million operating income (47% and 60% of total company revenue and operating income (OI), respectively) from 2.07 million shipments. Hunt's Intermodal segment generated an OR of 88.6% which was better than the total company's OR of 91.0%. Average Intermodal segment revenue per unit was $3,395, up 24% compared to 2021.[7]

Another large BNSF Intermodal customer, truckload motor carrier Schneider National Inc., grew their Intermodal segment revenue from $780 million in 2017 to $1.287 billion in 2022 with plans to double it by the year 2030.[8] In 2022 Schneider's Intermodal segment generated $165.1 million of OI and an OR of 87.2% with the help of a 2,848 container (11%) increase in the size of its intermodal container fleet. Intermodal revenue per unit increased 12.6% from $2,526 in 2021 to $2,845 in 2022.[9] In their earnings press release Schneider CEO Mark Rourke reiterated that Schneider, "plans to double our Intermodal offering by 2030 while providing customers more lane options and more frequent departures."[10]

---

[3] BNSF 2022 10-K, accessed from: https://bnsf.com/about-bnsf/financial-information/pdf/10k-llc-2022.pdf, on February 27, 2023.

[4] Ibid, p. 11.

[5] Ibid, p. 19.

[6] Ibid, p. 22.

[7] J.B. Hunt Transport Services, Inc., 2022 Form 8-K, January 18, 2023, accessed from: https://d18rn0p25nwr6d.cloudfront.net/CIK-0000728535/070909c4-e8b9-47f9-a2f0-e07d12037a53.pdf .

[8] Schneider National April 2022 Investors Presentation, accessed from: https://s28.q4cdn.com/901178831/files/doc_financials/2022/q1/Q1-Investor-Presentation-Print-APR2022.pdf, on May 18, 2022.

[9] Schneider National, Inc. Announces Fourth Quarter 2022 Results, February 2, 2023, accessed from: https://investors.schneider.com/news-events/financial-news/news-details/2023/Schneider-National-Inc.-Announces-Fourth-Quarter-2022-Results/default.aspx , on February 6, 2022.

[10] Ibid.

A third large BNSF customer, Intermodal Marketing Company, Hub Group generated 2022 intermodal and transportation solutions revenue of $3.3 billion (61.8% of total company revenue and 24% higher than 2021). This contributed to a total gross margin of 16.7%, OI of $474.7 million (vs. $361.2 million in 2021), net income of $356.9 million (vs. $171.5 million in 2021) and a pre-tax operating margin of 8.8%.[11]

A fourth large North American intermodal customer, XPO Logistics, announced on March 25, 2022 that it sold its intermodal brokerage, fleet of 11,000 53' domestic containers and intermodal drayage business to STG Logistics for a cash price of $710 million. STG had purchased the Pacer Stack Train operation in 2014 so this acquisition was layered onto that infrastructure.[12]

In addition, in March of 2022 J.B. Hunt announced that it:

> *... plans to increase the size of its intermodal container fleet to 150,000 units over the next three to five years. The additional capacity would expand the fleet by more than 40% from the close of 2021. J.B. Hunt's current intermodal fleet includes 109,000 53-foot containers as well as supporting chassis and tractors, making it the largest company-owned fleet in North America. Back of the envelope math suggests the additions could add another $2 billion in revenue to the nearly $5.5 billion the segment generated last year. J. B. Hunt estimates that between 7 million and 11 million loads could be moved off the highway and onto rail."[13]*

Regarding their relationship with Hunt, BNSF CEO Katie Farmer added:

> *"We will raise the bar on service to the next level through technology and innovation as we further integrate our platforms with real-time data exchanges," Katie Farmer, BNSF president and CEO, said. "We want our customers to enjoy the best of both worlds: economical and environmentally friendly service delivered by transportation's premium providers."[14]*

There are very few people in the railroad or trucking industry in the 1980s and early 1990s who would have believed facts such as those cited above would ever be possible. Given the reputation intermodal business had at the time, anyone who had said that someday Burlington Northern Railroad could generate an OR in the low to mid 60s while its Intermodal business accounted for 38% of revenue would have been dreaming. They would have been considered insane if they were to add that a low to mid-60s operating ratio would result when Agricultural Commodities and Coal would only generate 23% and 16% of company revenue, respectively, (under the ownership of Warren Buffett's Berkshire Hathaway),.

In 2010, BNSF generated OI of $4.5 billion and an operating ratio of 74.3 with a business portfolio composed of 31% intermodal/consumer, 27% coal and 22% Ag commodities. In the 1980s-1990s, it was incomprehensible for most to even speculate that BN or a successor could generate nearly a doubling of

---

[11] Hub Group, Inc. Reports Fourth Quarter and Full Year 2022 Results, February 2, 2023, accessed from: https://www.hubgroup.com/about-us/news/hub-group-inc-reports-fourth-quarter-and-full-year-2022-results/, on February 6, 2023.

[12] ttnews.com, XPO Sells Intermodal Unit to STG Logistics for $710 Million, accessed from: https://www.ttnews.com/articles/xpo-sells-intermodal-unit-stg-logistics-710-million , on March 28, 2022.

[13] Freightwaves, J.B. Hunt to expand intermodal container fleet by 40%, March 16, 2022, accessed from: https://www.freightwaves.com/news/j-b-hunt-to-expand-intermodal-container-fleet-by-40, on May 18, 2022.

[14] Ibid.

OI to $8.6 billion and a 7.5 point lower OR of 66.8 from a portfolio composed of 38% Intermodal / consumer, only 16% coal and 23% Ag commodities. Yet, that is what BNSF accomplished in 2022.

The prosperity intermodal business brought the railroad industry has been fueled by significant growth in international trade. Equally important, as evidenced by the performance of J.B. Hunt, Schneider National and Hub Group, has been the explosive growth of domestic intermodal. Anyone who would have said that someday J.B. Hunt would generate 46% of its revenue and 60% of its OI from Intermodal and have more than 100,000 containers in their intermodal container fleet, would have also been considered insane. The same applies to anyone in the late 1980s who would have said that Schneider National would even be in the intermodal business, much less eventually generating well more than $1 billion a year in revenue from intermodal at an OR of less than 88, with a plan to double its intermodal market presence from such levels within 8 years. Even the thought of an Intermodal Marketing Company like Hub Group being able to generate more than $3 billion of very profitable revenue in a year would have been considered insanity in the 1980s and early 1990s, even without having to face the headwinds of powerful competition such as that from Hunt and Schneider. Three decades after the fact, some said no such intermodal opportunity was foreseen. In 2020, when BNSF was celebrating the 25th anniversary of the BNSF merger, *Progressive Railroading* Magazine stated the following:[15]

> *Steve Bobb, BNSF's EVP and chief marketing officer, who joined BN in 1987 and has served the company for 33 years, says. "We never would have forecasted [at the time of the merger] how domestic intermodal would grow. In the late 1980s into the 1990s, international was the focus."*

In reality, that is not accurate. It is true that between 1981 and 1995 few people within Burlington Northern Railroad believed in a prosperous future for either the domestic or international Intermodal business. This three volume work provides a chronological and fact-based historical account that puts the story of BN's Intermodal business into perspective. It articulates the backdrop of major economic, competitive and transportation industry regulatory transitions as well as a continuous string of internal BN Railroad challenges that BN's Intermodal Business Unit (IBU) confronted. This incredible story is told, with the help of many former fellow former co-workers and industry associates, by someone who lived it.

It tells how the selfless people of BN's IBU were able to, *Against All Odds*, overcome multiple attempts to neutralize, or essentially kill, BN's Intermodal business between 1981 and 1995. Their collective efforts transformed it from being an "illegitimate step-child" of a railroad that couldn't decide what it wanted to be into a business that, *Against all Odds*, drove significant gains in BN shareholder value. Their efforts helped to ultimately drive BN's extraordinarily successful 1995 merger with the Atchison, Topeka & Santa Fe Railway and help make Intermodal transportation the foundation piece it has become for the U.S. railroad industry and the global supply chain. The dauntless faith and persistence of these people played a major part in making BNSF Railroad's phenomenal 2022 performance, cited above, possible. Their efforts also contributed greatly to the possibility of the above-cited 2022 performance of BNSF's current and former intermodal partners.

---

[15] Stagl, Jeff, BNSF in solid position as silver anniversary nears, *Progressive Railroading*, January 2020, Accessed from: https://www.progressiverailroading.com/bnsf_railway/article/BNSF-in-solid-position-as-silver-anniversary-nears--59427 , on January 25, 2023.

Chapter 1 - Introduction

Since the 1970 merger that created the Burlington Northern (1972 Main-Line Route Map at left), [16] much has been written about the growth of its Powder River Basin (PRB) coal carrying franchise and the rich agricultural and lumber bounty it carried. Dave DeBoer wrote a book about the history of railroad industry's intermodal business[17] but it only covered that story up to 1991. Little has been written about Burlington Northern's intermodal business. Chapter two of the 1993 book, *The Wisdom of Teams*, told part of the story of the BN team that established BN's Intermodal Business Unit (IBU) in the face of

significant internal and external adversity.[18] That, however, gave only a miniscule hint of what the IBU actually encountered, the repeated existential attacks it survived and overcame, and what it ultimately accomplished. This is an account of the history of Burlington Northern's Intermodal Business based on the contributions of numerous people who lived it.

BN Predecessor Railroads' Historic International Intermodal Orientation

The history of the BN-predecessor Chicago, Burlington & Quincy Railroad (CB&Q) goes back to the Aurora Branch Railroad in 1849.[19] The congressional land grant bill that was passed on May 31, 1864, and which became law on July 2, 1864 when President Lincoln signed it, authorized and partially financed the construction of the Northern Pacific Railroad (NP). "The land grants would, in time, become very valuable and would serve as the nucleus of Burlington Northern's land resources."[20] The "Empire Builder," James J. Hill is renowned for his courage and fortitude in building a transcontinental railroad, the Great Northern Railway (GN), without land grants.[21]

---

[16] Burlington Northern Inc., 1972 Annual Report, p. 15.

[17] DeBoer, David J., *Piggyback and Containers – A History of Rail Intermodal on America's Steel Highway*, Golden West Books, San Marino, CA, 1992.

[18] Katzenbach, John R., Smith, Douglas K., *The Wisdom of Teams – Creating the High-Performance Organization*, Harvard Business School Press, Boston, 1993, Chapter 2.

[19] Overton, Richard C., *Burlington Route – A History of the Burlington Lines*, University of Nebraska Press, Lincoln, Nebraska, 1965, p. 3.

[20] Glischinski, Steve, *Burlington Northern and Its Heritage*, Andover Junction Publications, Andover, New Jersey, 1992, p. 36.

[21] Hidy, Ralph W., Hidy, Muriel E., and Scott, Roy V., with Hofsommer, Don L. *The Great Northern Railway, A History*, Harvard Business School Press, Boston, 1988.

> *Only government lands ever received by Mr. Hill's company were those attached to 600 miles of railway in Minnesota constructed by predecessor companies and acquired by purchase.[22]*

> *Hill's railroad was a monument to its creator's daring vision and careful management. Unlike many nineteenth-century railroad men who laid tracks as a means to land grants and collateral speculations, Hill built his Great Northern as an end in itself. His road had the flattest grades, the straightest track, the lowest rates. "When we are all dead and gone," he said, "the sun will shine, the rain will fall, and this railroad will run as usual."[23]*

The NP and GN were pioneers in multi-modal transportation. In 1870, Hill launched "his Selkirk on the Red River" for freight service and then entered the passenger and freight business on the Great Lakes in 1892. "In the 1880s and 1890s, he found time to explore the development of American exports to the Orient through western ports." [24] In 1893 the NP Railroad connected with the trans-Pacific service operated by the Northern Pacific Steamship Company.

> *In 1896 Hill of the GN signed an agreement with Nippon Yusen Kaisha (NYK), the leading*

Japanese shipping company, to provide monthly service connecting the GN at Seattle with Hong Kong and Japanese ports.[25]

This service involved the exchange of both freight and passengers. Hoping to capitalize on his NYK relationship and build a greater market for American exports, especially wheat and cotton, Hill placed an order for two large ships, the *Minnesota* and the *Dakota*, which entered service in 1903 and 1904. They docked at the GN-owned Pier 91 on the Puget Sound in Seattle (see image at left with GN's Oriental Limited passing in the foreground). [26] Sailing to the Philippine, Japanese and Chinese ports, the Great Northern Steamship Company catered to both passengers and freight. Its 28,000-ton vessels were equipped with

---

[22] Great Northern Railway Company, Public Relations Department, *A Condensed History of The Great Northern Railway*, St. Paul, MN, 1953, p. 4.

[23] Minnesota Historical Society, James J. Hill Mansion Tour Brochure.

[24] Yenne, Bill, *The History of the Burlington Northern*, Bonanza Books, New York, 1991, p. 9.

[25] Donovan, Arthur, *Intermodal Transportation in Historical Perspective*, p. 14, accessed on February 14, 2022 via: https://www.du.edu/ncit/media/documents/donovan-intermodal-transportation-in-historical-perspective.pdf, p. 15.

[26] Hidy, Hidy and Scott with Hofsommer, p. 123. Public Domain image: Great Northern train and ships at Smith Cove, 1905 (MOHAI 7168).jpg, sourced from Wikipedia Commons.

elegant staterooms, electric lights and telephones.[27] It took longer to build them than Hill expected and Hill was losing interest in transpacific shipping by the time the *Minnesota* was launched in 1904.[28] As he told a Merchant Marine Commission in 1905, the steamship company 'is really an incident to our railroad enterprise, and we did not go into it with a view of entering the shipping business.' Hill clearly thought of himself as operating in the transportation industry rather than in a single mode, but experience taught him that American shipbuilding was one aspect of the industry he would do well to avoid. As he told the Commission, 'I would rather undertake to build a thousand miles of railway than to build two ships.'"

> *In 1915, the GN began maritime operations along the Pacific seaboard. The Great Northern Pacific Steamship Company, jointly held by the GN and NP, commissioned two large steamers. The Great Northern began service between Flavel (Astoria), Oregon, and San Francisco in June and the Northern Pacific followed shortly after that. Both carried freight as well as passengers, and they were sufficiently speedy to make a strong bid for coastal business. Despite supplemental winter cruises to Hawaii, the ships were not financially successful. During World War I, the federal government purchased them for use as troop transports.*[29]

Burlington Northern Railroad and its predecessors would not again directly enter the ocean shipping business until the early 1990s.

Railroad Industry and Market and Regulatory Backdrop through the 1950s

The history of the United States has been shaped by its transportation infrastructure.

> *On March 29, 1806, three years after Lewis and Clark left for the West Coast, President Jefferson approved legislation to construct the Cumberland Road (also called the National Road). He understood that by bridging the land gap between the Potomac and Ohio Rivers, the Cumberland Road would build commercial and social links that would bind the territories west of the Appalachian Mountains to the eastern States. As President Jefferson explained in his 1806 message to the 9th Congress, the most important transportation modes of his day, roads and canals, would knit the union together, facilitate defense, furnish avenues of trade, break down prejudices, and consolidate a "union of sentiment." Further, with such "great objects" as public education, roads, rivers, and canals, "new channels of communication will be opened between the states; the lines of separation will disappear, their interests will be identified, and their union cemented by new and indissoluble ties."*[30]

President Jefferson's Cumberland Road project was essentially the nation's first transportation related public works project for a country dependent on roads and waterways for commerce.

---

[27] Hidy, Hidy and Scott with Hofsommer, p. 122.
[28] Donovan, p. 16.
[29] Hidy, Hidy and Scott with Hofsommer, p. 122.
[30] Weingroff, Richard F., Moving the Goods: As the Interstate Era Begins, U.S. Department of Transportation, Federal Highway Administration, updated September 8, 2017, Accessed from: https://www.fhwa.dot.gov/interstate/freight.cfm, on February 24, 2023.

Growth of Railroads

The advent of railroad technology held out the means for the Country to accelerate development but it was a capital intensive effort and private entrepreneurs were challenged to obtain the funding necessary to build railroads.

> *The Illinois Central procured smaller land grants back in the 1850s. Small land grants were also offered in Ohio and Wisconsin in the late 1850s. While those grants were helpful to the companies involved, they were small in scope, and very much unlike the millions of acres of land given away for building transcontinental railroads.*[31]

The first major land grant was a product of 1862 legislation that stimulated the development of the transcontinental Central Pacific (which became part of the Southern Pacific Railroad) and Union Pacific Railroads between Omaha, NE and Sacramento, CA. The grants did not come without a catch. In addition to requiring the railroad to provide the United States Government reduced rates for moving government goods and passengers:[32]

> *For the land grant system to work as planned, the government hoped railroads would sell their lands to help pay for the construction costs of laying rail lines. The problem was that very few people wanted to buy any land until after rail lines were constructed. Moreover, there were severe problems with Native Americans, obviously upset at having their lands stolen. In truth, vast areas of land grants were located in barren and "worthless" parts of western states where it was nearly impossible to grow or ranch anything.*
> *When it was realized that land grants alone would never accomplish the building of transcontinental rail lines, the government decided to loan 30-year Federal bonds to railroad companies. The whole idea was that government bonds would be easier to sell than land. With an economic kickstart, companies would lay track across the continent, develop undeveloped areas and thereby sell land in the bargain. In the process, land grant laws intended that companies would ultimately repay the government loans with interest.*
>
> *As originally designed, the Federal government loaned $16,000 per mile of track across flat land. In hilly terrain, the loans jumped to $32,000 per mile and then to $48,000 per mile for mountain construction. Government bonds were doled out in 40-mile units.*
>
> *The government also required that railroad companies could not build curves sharper than 10 degrees, nor grades steeper than 116 feet per mile (a little over 2%.) Additionally, rail lines had to be built with American steel which created a serious hardship for the Central Pacific. Finally, the whole intercontinental line between Omaha and Sacramento had to be completed within fourteen years. If not completed in that time, all land, all track, all tunneling, and all labor would be forfeited!*
>
> *Oh, yes. One other thing. The government initially gave the companies the rights to use the surface of the land, **not** the minerals underneath.*

---

[31] Cox, Terry, Collectible Stocks and Bonds from North American Railroads – Railroad Land Grants, CoxRail.com, accessed from: https://www.coxrail.com/land-grants.asp, on February 24, 2023.
[32] Ibid.

Another little-understood problem was that the government required companies to use their railroad and lands as collateral for the government bond loans. In effect, the Federal government held the first mortgage on every inch of the transcontinental railroad. Contemporaneous writers suggest that the government's own first mortgage made it impossible for transcontinental railroads to sell their own corporate bonds like railroads elsewhere had done for almost 30 years.

The Railroad Act of 1864 modified the land grant law to allow the railroad to retain mineral rights, collect the government loan more rapidly and increase the size of the land grant itself. Another important feature was that it essentially removed the government from a first mortgage position by allowing the railroad to sell bonds in the market in amounts equivalent to government bonds. Land grants were then used as collateral for loans obtained from the market. In the West, such grants were used to help finance the construction of the transcontinental Union Pacific, Northern Pacific, Milwaukee Road, Atchison, Topeka and Santa Fe, and Southern Pacific Railroads.

As railroads grew they focused on moving cars that did not leave the rail. The first attempt to provide intermodal service unrelated to physically transferring commodities between cars and wagons or ships seems to have occurred in the mid 1880s:

> *In 1885 the Long Island Railroad established a short-lived service in which loaded wagons, horses and farmers were carried into Long Island City on flatcars, boxcars and a passenger coach, respectively, thus moving two transfer operations in getting the produce to market. This was by no means the earliest "piggyback" operation, so the idea of intermodal through shipments without reloading is not new.[33]*

"Piggybacking" did not gain traction and there were many years of little intermodal rail activity. The industry was doing relatively well without it. The era through the 1940s was for the most part a golden age for railroads. Yet, the industry was under growing competitive pressure.

Competitive Backdrop

The 20th Century began with railroads dominating interstate transportation of both freight and passengers. Navigable waterways were also critical to the development of the United States. Their development was one of the first salvos in the subsequent competitive transportation wars:[34]

> *Unlike the West, where irrigation became the focus of attention, the East was more concerned over hydropower development. Beginning in the early 1880s, when a plant in Appleton, Wisconsin, first used falling water to produce electricity, the construction of hydroelectric dams on the nation's waterways proliferated. These private dams threatened navigation and forced Congress, acting through the Corps of Engineers, to regulate dam construction. The Rivers and Harbors Acts of 1890 and 1899 required that dam sites and plans be approved by the secretary of war and the Corps of Engineers before construction. The General Dam Act of 1906 empowered the federal government to compel dam owners to construct, operate, and maintain navigation*

[33] Armstrong, John H., *The Railroad – What It Is, What It Does*, Simmons-Boardman Publishing Corp., Omaha, 1977, p. 177.
[34] The U.S. Army Corps of Engineers: A Brief History, Multipurpose Waterway Development, accessed from: https://www.usace.army.mil/About/History/Brief-History-of-the-Corps/Multipurpose-Waterway-Development/, On February 24, 2023.

facilities without compensation whenever necessary at hydroelectric power sites.

Private interests developed most power projects before World War I. The Corps of Engineers did install a power station substructure at Lock and Dam #1 on the upper Mississippi River. The government later leased the power facility to the Ford Motor Company. In 1919, the Corps began construction of Dam #2 later renamed Wilson Dam as a hydroelectric facility at Muscle Shoals on the Tennessee River. Support for the facility, which was intended to supply power for nitrate production, declined with the end of World War I, and its completion was threatened. However, by 1925 that project was substantially finished.

The General Dam Act of 1906 requirement that dam owners construct, operate and maintain navigation locks without compensation opened the door to more railroad competition. Water based rail competition intensified as the Corps increased its river dredging efforts.

The most significant competitive development for railroads was the growth of the United States highway network. Motor carrier competition was slow to develop because of the lack of a substantial roadway infrastructure. This started to change with the invention of low priced automobiles:[35]

The Good Roads Movement that had begun in the 1880s to promote improved roads for bicycles, took hold as the automobile began to gain power and speed. When Henry Ford introduced the low priced Model T in 1908, he transformed the landscape. Soon, the automobile would be a staple of the American family, with roads gradually improved to expand the scope of travel.

Early trucks, which could not compete in cost or speed with railroads, were most efficient in cities and transporting farm goods to rail or cities. World War I changed that. With the American entry into the European war in April 1917, the railroads were stretched beyond their capacity. For the first time, interstate transportation of freight by truck became not only possible but essential. Interstate roads were still largely dirt, and the trucks tore them up, but trucks demonstrated their value.

Recognizing the symbiotic relationship between roads and trucks, the roadbuilders and truck manufacturers agreed to limit the capacity of trucks to 7½ tons. Looking back on this period, Thomas H. MacDonald, Chief of the U.S. Bureau of Public Roads (BPR) from 1919 to 1953, explained that the compromise reflected recognition that the cost of highway transportation "is made up of the cost of the highways and the cost of operating the vehicles over the highways." The goal, he said, of road builders, vehicle manufacturers, and operators "should be to reduce the total cost of transportation rather than one or the other of the elemental costs." He explained:

"It could be proved that the number of large-capacity trucks already using some of the highways, principally those radiating from and connecting the larger cities - had already grown to the point where the combined savings in operating cost would more than balance the greater cost of providing highway service for them. As to those highways there could be little doubt of the wisdom of building a type of surface adequate for the heavy truck traffic."

---

[35] Weingroff, Richard F., Moving the Goods: As the Interstate Era Begins, U.S. Department of Transportation, Federal Highway Administration, updated September 8, 2017, Accessed from: https://www.fhwa.dot.gov/interstate/freight.cfm, on February 24, 2023.

In spite of the Great Depression, the United States Government continued to work to increase the competitiveness of the motor carrier industry:[36]

> *During the Great Depression, the Public Works Administration, part of President Franklin D. Roosevelt's New Deal program, advanced national road construction, created jobs, and improved the economy by building thousands of miles of roads. These roads were part of the U.S. Numbered Highway System, a paved network of two-lane roads, carrying a U.S. route number that crisscrossed the United States. One of the most famous highways constructed during this time was U.S. Route 66, a 2,448-mile stretch of road that linked Chicago to California. In addition to bringing farm workers to California from the Midwest, many Americans enjoyed driving on Route 66 simply for the sake of traveling and seeing the sights along the way.*

Route 66 cobbled together existing State, local and national roads between Chicago and Los Angeles creating a more competitive route versus the Santa Fe Railway. It almost perfectly paralleled the Santa Fe between Amarillo and Los Angeles. It as well as other roads that were part of the building effort were not well designed and were not located in the most advantageous locations so they were not as efficient or safe as was ideal. Funding was a major issue:[37]

> *In the Federal-Aid Highway Act of 1938, Congress asked the BPR for a report on "the feasibility of building, and cost of, superhighways ... including the feasibility of a toll system on such roads." The BPR based its report on data collected from extensive highway planning surveys that had been conducted around the country beginning in 1935. The origin-and-destination surveys showed that transcontinental traffic was limited, with traffic heaviest around cities and in interregional movements. Given the low income of most motorists, toll roads would have a traffic-repelling character. As a result, most routes would not carry enough traffic to generate sufficient revenue to pay off bonds needed to finance their construction.*

> *Instead, the BPR recommended construction of a network of toll-free express highways. The BPR's description of "A Master Plan for Free Highway Development" was its first description of what would become the Interstate System. Based on the survey data, the BPR explained that the primary justification for the network was passenger traffic, particularly congested city traffic, not interstate trucking. In fact, the report made little reference to trucks.*

> *President Franklin D. Roosevelt submitted Toll Roads and Free Roads to Congress on April 27, 1939. His transmittal letter summarized the report's conclusion:*

> *"It emphasizes the need of a special system of direct interregional highways, with all necessary connections through and around cities, designed to meet the requirements of the national defense and the needs of a growing peacetime traffic of longer range."*

---

[36] Phelps, Hailey, When Interstates Paved the Way, Econ Focus, Federal Reserve Bank of Richmond, Second/Third Quarter, 2021, Accessed from: https://www.richmondfed.org/publications/research/econ_focus/2021/q2-3/economic_history, on March 2, 2023.

[37] Ibid.

The effort was not pursued due to the start of World War II and the heavy financial strain it subjected the country to. Toward the end of the war Roosevelt made another attempt:[38]

> *President Roosevelt submitted Interregional Highways to Congress on January 12, 1944. Like its predecessor, Interregional Highways based its conclusions largely on passenger traffic, with special emphasis on the need to address traffic problems in cities as a way of reversing the trends that were causing cities to decentralize, lose their tax base, and turn to blight. With the country at war, the report also focused on the military aspects of highway development.*

> *As with the 1939 report, the 1944 study had little to say on "motor-trucks" and "tractor-trailers" or "semitrailer combinations." Much of what it did say related to the accommodation of trucks in cities, especially city terminals. Considering the visionary urban sections of the two reports, their failure to anticipate the positive impacts the Interstate System would have on trucking is surprising. The failure reflects the view MacDonald expressed on many occasions that railroads would remain the primary mode of interstate transport. Early in the 1930s, trucks carried only a small percentage of all interstate freight - about 2 or 3 percent. By the end of the decade, the percentage had increased to 10 percent. Despite this growth, Interregional Highways stated:*

> *"[The] Committee does not suggest that there is need of special highway facilities for the accommodation or encouragement of long-distance trucking. All the evidence amassed by the highway-planning surveys points to the fact that the range of motortruck hauls is comparatively short. There is nothing to indicate the probability of an increasing range of such movements in the future.*

> *The length of truck hauls will be determined in the future as it has been in the past; by the competitive advantages at various distances of other modes of transportation. The probable early development of an efficient commercial air-freight service, together with the keener competition of a rejuvenated rail service, would seem to forecast a future shortening rather than a lengthening of average highway-freight hauls."*

The highway network proposed by Interregional Highways included 33,920 miles of superhighways that would connect regions through cities. It also included 4,470 miles of superhighways that would loop major cities. Ironically, given an assumption that rail would continue to dominate longer distance freight transportation, an increased role of trucking was not a priority in the vision:[39]

> *"Where manufacturing activity exists in greatest volume," Interregional Highways explained, "there it may be assumed are the points of origin and destination of the greatest volumes of motortruck traffic." With factories located mainly in large cities, the report used census data on values added by manufacturing industries to compare the recommended network to "the relative probability of intercity highway freight movement." On the assumption that trucks operated primarily at local and interregional distances, not long distances in interstate transportation, the report used this comparison to demonstrate that the length of the illustrative network was "the system of optimum extent from the standpoint of service to manufacturing industry," not to suggest the network would serve ever increasing truck volumes.*

---

[38] Ibid.

[39] Ibid.

Based on Interregional Highways, the Federal-Aid Highway Act of 1944 authorized designation of a 40,000-mile network "so located as to connect by routes, as direct as practicable, the principal metropolitan areas, cities, and industrial centers, to serve the national defense, and to connect at suitable border points with routes of continental importance in the Dominion of Canada and the Republic of Mexico." Under the 1944 Act, the network became the National System of Interstate Highways.

The Act was signed by President Roosevelt on December 20, 1944 but given the financial burden created by the War, there was no funding mechanism built in.

In spite of the fact that there were only relatively modest improvements to the highway network, overall vehicle traffic was expanding and motor carriers were making inroads into rail market share while rail passenger market share was also declining. Post war eliminations of fuel and tire rationing helped drive 1955 rail freight market share to below 50% for the first time while truck share nearly tripled since before the Great Depression. By 1958 rail share fell to 46 percent and truck share increased to 20%.[40]

Intercity Freight Market Share (Percent) by Mode

	1929	1944	1950	1955
Rail	75.0	67.8	56.2	49.4
Truck	3.3	5.3	16.3	17.7
Great Lakes/Rivers	17.5	13.7	15.4	17.0
Oil Pipelines	4.4	12.2	12.1	15.9

Source: Association of American Railroads

Between 1940 and 1955, truck miles across all United Stated roads and streets grew faster than passenger vehicle miles. While overall vehicle miles almost doubled, total truck miles increased 123% and the truck share of total vehicle miles grew 12%.

Estimated Trucks and Combination Miles of Travel on all Roads and Streets[41]

Year	All Vehicle-Miles (millions)	Truck Miles (millions)	Truck % of all vehicle-miles
1940	302.2	49.9	16.5%
1945	250.2	46.1	18.5%
1950	458.3	90.6	19.8%
1955	603.4	111.4	18.5%
1940-1955 % change	99.6%	123.2%	12.1%

The rail freight most targeted by motor carriers was the highest rated time-sensitive and shorter-haul less-than-carload business. Aiding motor carriers was the increased use of higher capacity tractor/trailer combination rigs. The segment of truck miles that grew the fastest over the most rail-vulnerable main rural roads was combination trucks. While total 1940-1955 main rural road truck miles grew 125%, combination truck miles grew almost 250% as the share of higher capacity combo truck miles increased from approximately 21% to 54%:

---

[40] Ibid. Derived from Highway Cost Allocation Report, 1961.

[41] The Highway Transport Research Branch, Bureau of Public Roads, *Public Roads: A Journal of Highway Research*, Volume 29, No. 5, Traffic and Travel Trends, 1955, p. 99, Accessed from: https://archive.org/details/publicroadsjourn29unse_3/page/n3/mode/2up, on February 24, 2023.

Estimated Combination Trucks Miles of Travel on Main Rural Roads[42]

Year	All Truck Vehicle-Miles (millions)	Combo Truck Miles (millions)	Combo Truck % of all truck-miles
1940	21.1	4.4	20.9%
1945	18.9	5.3	28.1%
1950	39.9	12.6	31.6%
1955	47.5	15.3	32.2%
1940-55 % change	125.1%	247.7%	54.0%

An expanded highway network did more than facilitate a growth in truck traffic. It also facilitated an increase in motor carrier productivity by allowing larger trailers and heavier loads. Between 1940 and 1955 the average weight carried per combination truck over the most rail competitive main rural roads increased 50% while ton-miles increased 396%:

Combination Truck Operating Efficiency over Main Rural Roads, 1940-1955[43]

Year	% Loaded	Avg. Weight per load	Ton-miles carried
1940	71.6%	7.4 tons	23.3 million
1945	69.2%	9.3 tons	34.2 million
1950	68.5%	10.6 tons	91.4 million
1955	68.2%	11.1 tons	115.6 million
1940-1955 % change	-4.7%	+50%	+396%

Heavy Gross Weight Truck Main Rural Road Loads per 1,000 total trucks, Pre-War-1955[44]

Year (summers)	30,000 lbs. or more	40,000 lbs. or more	50,000 lbs. or more
Pre-War	42	11	2
1945	143	58	22
1950	183	110	58
1955	202	128	76
Pre-war-1955 change	381%	1,064%	3,700%

Poor road quality inhibited heavy truck loads. A significant increase in paved roads enabled higher load weights. Before WW-II only 4% of main rural highway truck loads exceeded 30,000 pounds. By 1955 that proportion grew to 20%. Loads exceeding 50,000 pounds grew from less than 1% to almost 8%.

As a result of these trends, between 1936 and 1955 total combination tractor/trailer ton miles carried over main rural roads increased 729%:

Combination Truck Main Rural Road Ton-Miles Carried, 1936-1955[45]

Year	Rural Combo Truck Ton-Miles
1936	14 billion
1940	24 billion
1945	35 billion
1950	92 billion
1955	116 billion

---

[42] Ibid, p. 101.

[43] Ibid, p. 105.

[44] Ibid, p. 107

[45] Ibid, p, 104.

Although the Interregional Network of superhighways did not escape the launch pad in 1944 due to funding issues, the effort to create a superhighway effort did not die. President Dwight Eisenhower revived the plan in 1954. He challenged:[46]

> ... the Nation's Governors to work with a committee headed by General Lucius D. Clay (U.S. Army, retired) to find a way of financing a "grand plan" of highway improvement by every level of government. The Advisory Committee on a National Highway Program reported to the President in January 1955. In a chapter on "Use of Our Highways," the report explained that highway transportation consisted of "approximately 48 million passenger cars, 10 million trucks, and a quarter of a million buses, operating on 3,348,000 miles of roads and streets." Competition among the modes was acknowledged:
>
> "All forms of transportation are essential to the national economy, including waterways, railroads, airways, and pipelines, and their continued functioning as complementary services under equitable competitive conditions is important. Representatives of the railroads have pointed out to us the competitive threat represented by improved highway facilities and increasing truck haulage. However, this Committee was created to consider the highway network, and other media of transportation do not fall within its province."

Eisenhower transmitted the Clay Committee report to Congress on February 22. 1955. He prefaced it:[47]

> Our unity as a nation is sustained by free communication of thought and by easy transportation of people and goods. The ceaseless flow of information through the Republic is matched by individual and commercial movement over a vast system of interconnected highways crisscrossing the country and joining it at our national borders with friendly neighbors to the north and south.

The original proposal was to finance the 40,000 mile Interstate Highway plan with bonds that would permit its completion within 10 years:[48]

> Revenue from the existing 2-cent a gallon tax on gasoline and the tax on lubricating oils would be dedicated to retiring the bonds. Congress rejected this proposal almost immediately, in part because of the large amount of funds that would be needed to pay interest rather than build highways.
>
> Senator Albert Gore, Sr. (D-Tn.), Chairman of the Subcommittee on Roads, introduced a bill that proposed to continue the existing Federal-aid highway program, but with $500 million authorized for the Interstate System annually through Fiscal Year (FY) 1960. The bill did not contain a taxing method for raising the additional revenue for the Interstate System because under the Constitution, the U.S. House of Representatives must initiate tax legislation. Before leaving the Committee on Public Works, the bill was modified to increase Interstate funding to

---

[46] Weingroff, Richard F., Moving the Goods: As the Interstate Era Begins, U.S. Department of Transportation, Federal Highway Administration, updated September 8, 2017, Accessed from: https://www.fhwa.dot.gov/interstate/freight.cfm, on February 24, 2023.

[47] Ibid.

[48] Ibid.

$10 billion through FY 1961, with a Federal share of 75 percent. The Senate approved the bill on May 25, 1955.

Gore's House counterpart, Representative George H. Fallon (D-Md.), received permission from Speaker of the House Sam Rayburn (D-Tx.) to draft tax legislation that ordinarily would have originated in the Ways and Means Committee. His bill proposed graduated tax increases, including a penny hike in the 2-cent Federal gas tax (and another half-cent in 1970), as well as graduated tax increases on automobiles, trucks, and tires. With the increased revenue from these and other tax changes, Fallon believed the Interstate System could be built in 12 years on a pay-as-you-go-basis as funding came in.

The trucking industry objected strongly to the Fallon Bill. According to Transport Topics ("National Newspaper of the Motor Freight Carriers"), the American Trucking Association (ATA) calculated that the annual cost of the Fallon Bill to highway users would be $686 million. Heavy trucks and buses would pay about 45 percent of this added cost. The newspaper reported that John V. Lawrence, the managing director of ATA, advised members of the House Public Works and the Ways and Means Committees that the bill would increase taxes "to a confiscatory, ruinous and unjustified level." Further, Lawrence explained, "about half of the proposed dollar increase [would fall] upon less than 3 percent of the nation's motor vehicles." The present tax structure, he said, already resulted in an "enormously greater assessment against large vehicles than small vehicles." Singling out trucks in this way would "make indispensable truck service economically impossible and jeopardize the jobs of nearly seven million Americans."

When the Committee on Public Works held hearings on the Fallon Bill, the ATA's assistant general manager, William A. Bresnahan, testified that the trucking industry was one of the few groups willing to pay increased user taxes, but not if they fell disproportionately on truckers. The ATA favored tax increases "across the board" and would prefer no increase in the Federal highway program if the alternative was a program that imposed ruinous taxation on the industry.

The railroad industry operated over tracks they built and maintained themselves. Yet, motor carriers operated over a network of highways owned and operated by States and the Federal government with minimal user charges. Even without an aggressive national highway building program, primary road mileage increased from 217,000 miles to more than 500,000 miles in 1955.[49] Railroads realized that an interstate superhighway network would enable the trucking industry to rapidly increase the scope and pace of their incursion into rail market share.[50]

At the heart of the controversy was the longstanding rivalry between truckers and the railroads. As writer/historian Theodore H. White explained in Collier's magazine ("Where are Those New Roads?" in the issue of January 6, 1956):

"In modern America, truckmen and railway men have been as bitter and unforgiving enemies as sheepmen and cattlemen on the open range of Wyoming, 80 years ago. In the past 30 years the

---

[49] Kaufman, Lawrence H., *Leaders Count – The Story of the BNSF Railway*, Texas Monthly Custom Publications, Austin, TX, 2005, pp. 109
[50] Ibid.

trucking industry has grown to be a giant that grosses over $5 billion a year for freight haulage (against the railways' $8 billion).

If the great Interstate System goes through, with its near-level grades, its limited accesses, its numerous and heavy-paved lanes, the truckers - now engaged principally in short-run transport - will have a chance to gnaw away as successfully at the railways' long-haul freight business as the airlines have at the railways' long-haul passenger business, and the commuters' automobiles at their suburban passenger business."

Sensing a potential existential threat, the war between railroads and truckers was heating up:[51]

The truckers did not think the Fallon Bill placed what they saw as a disproportionate burden on their livelihood by chance, as White illustrated by quoting the ATA's Lawrence's comment on the railroad interests:

"They have intervened in the highway program, attempting to promote punitive taxes on big trucks which will cripple truck competition with their own freight operations... Congressmen have evidence of that on their desks in the form of a barrage of letters, wires and calls inspired by railroad interests, and often indeed sent to their offices in railroad envelopes. No such railroad lobby has descended on Washington in the history of the Republic as that which is now operating in support of the soak-the-truck proposals. It is this wrecking crew which is mainly responsible for throwing the highway situation out of perspective."

The privately owned railroad companies realized they could not stop the popular Interstate System, so they focused on reducing the competitive advantage they believed the Federal Government would be giving to their rivals. The railroad industry had made its views on highway user taxes known on many occasions. Industry officials, who believed that motor carriers were not being taxed at a level that equaled the public cost of providing highways for their use, had become experts in design and construction of highway pavements. Pavements, representatives of the railroads explained, had to have a stronger subbase and base and a thicker surface if they were to carry trucks instead of only passenger vehicles. Truckers ought to pay the difference. Earlier in the year, Burton N. Behling, an economist with the Association of American Railroads (AAR), had told the House Committee on Public Works that, "Unless properly graduated user charges are levied against these heavy vehicles, private automobiles and other light vehicles are made to bear highway costs on behalf of the heavy vehicles." Behling elaborated on his point that truckers were under-taxed:

"As the guiding principle, highways should be financed on the basis of adequate and properly scaled user-charges, so as not to disrupt the functioning of the Nation's entire system of transportation... A motor-fuel tax, standing alone and whether State or Federal, imposes a grossly inadequate charge upon heavy transportation vehicles which largely are the cause of the highway financial problem as it exists today. Every time a motorist buys a gallon of gasoline he is paying to have more heavy trucks disrupt his use of and pleasure from operating on our highways."

---

[51] Ibid.

By the time the Fallon Bill came up for consideration in the House, the ATA had mobilized to block approval. As the front page headline in Transport Topics put it: "INDUSTRY FIGHTS 'RUINOUS' ROAD TAXES."

The truckers led the battle, but rubber manufacturers, tire dealers, and farm groups were enlisted for the fight. A former member of the inactive Clay Committee, David Beck of the Teamsters Union, met with Speaker Rayburn to make clear the views of the union "whose resources," White explained, "are so important to Democrats in doubtful Congressional districts." In addition, Beck organized a campaign among the union's members. "Telegrams began to snow on Congress - an estimated 100,000 in all, 10,000 on Congressman Fallon's desk alone."

On July 27, 1955, as expected, the House rejected the Eisenhower proposal and the unpopular financing mechanism the Clay Committee had devised. However, in a shocking outcome, the House rejected the Fallon Bill by a wide margin, also largely because of the financing package in the bill. The New York Times reported that Speaker Rayburn blamed lobbyists for defeat of the Fallon Bill, which had been expected to pass easily:

"While he did not identify them, it is well known that representatives of the trucking industry, aided by gasoline and tire industry spokesmen, have been most active in buttonholing legislators and inspiring telegrams and letters against the proposed tax rises.

'The people who were going to have to pay for these roads put on a propaganda campaign that killed the bill,' the Speaker asserted.

Asked if he meant the trucking industry, he replied: "You can figure it out for yourself."

House Majority Leader John W. McCormack (D-Ma.) agreed. "Everyone wants a highway program but no one wants to pay for it. I have a sneaky idea that the truckers of the country played an important part in what happened."

The Congress adjourned without returning to the issue.

The battle for funding of the superhighway program continued with the motor carriers seeking minimal funding accountability while railroads sought to have motor carriers cover their fair share:[52]

In the months since the failure of the 1955 legislation, the trucking industry and others who had objected to the taxing mechanisms of the Fallon Bill realized they would have to compromise if they were to get the new roads they wanted. An opportunity to discuss a possible compromise arose in September 1955 when Secretary of Commerce Sinclair Weeks formed a Cabinet committee that included Secretary of the Treasury George Humphrey and the Secretaries of Defense, Agriculture, and Labor as well as a White House representative to find a way to rescue the highway program in 1956. Historian Mark H. Rose, in Interstate Express Highway Politics 1939-1989 (Revised Edition, The University of Tennessee Press, 1990), described how the truckers approached the Cabinet committee:

---

[52] Ibid.

"Truckers had made public, usually often, what they expected. At a series of conferences held during the last two weeks of October with members of the Cabinet Committee and their aides, heads of the trucking industry told their story again. Bonds and administration and anything else did not matter, just tax rates. Because the Fallon bill had imposed differential rates, especially on tires, they had opposed it. Truckers, a leader of the American Trucking Associations claimed, "were singled out in the Fallon Bill as the whipping boys." Tax equity, as they figured it out, amounted to uniform, one or two cent hikes on gasoline and tires. Without objection, moreover, they would pay another 2 percent excise on new trucks, provided proceeds went straight to highway construction."

Rose quoted the general manager of the Central Motor Freight Association, William Noorlag, Jr., to illustrate the conflicted view of the truckers:

"If it were not for the urgent need to get the big highway building program under way without further delay, every red-blooded trucker and his legion of allied industry and shipper friends would switch his position from vigorous support of the highway program to an out-right, last-ditch battle against the entire program."

Noorlag saw the industry's competitors in the railroad companies at the heart of the quandary facing the truckers:

"Unfortunately, that is what the railroads want the truckers to do so that the truckers would be blamed for killing the highway measure which the scheming railroads had set out to do by 'hook or crook.'"

A compromise for the $25 billion, 40,000 mile interstate superhighway project was reached in 1956:[53]

By early 1956, the truckers, oil industry, and others had agreed on a schedule of tax increases that included a 1-cent increase in the tax on gasoline and diesel, 3 more cents on a pound of rubber, and a 2-percent additional excise tax on new vehicles. With compromises in place, Representative Hale Boggs (D-La.) of the Ways and Means Committee developed legislation that would dedicate all highway user tax revenue to highway development by crediting the revenue to a new Highway Trust Fund. The fund was modeled on the Social Security Trust Fund, as suggested by Treasury Secretary Humphrey.

The revised Fallon-Boggs Bill passed the House by a vote of 388 to 19 and was sent to the Senate for consideration. As The New York Times pointed out in its article the following day, the one-sided vote "was attributed for the most part to the changed attitude of lobbies, mainly the trucking industry." The article explained:

"The truckers and others, including representatives of tire manufacturers, were said to have been won over by revision of the tax proposals to scale down their share of the increased burden."

The final bill was a combination of the Gore Bill and the Fallon-Boggs Bill, plus changes by the

---

[53] Ibid.

Conference Committee of the two Houses. It passed the House and Senate with little difficulty.
With President Eisenhower's signature on June 29, 1956, the Federal-Aid Highway Act of 1956
would launch the Interstate System that would have profound impacts on freight transportation
in the United States.

As a result, a Highway Trust Fund was created with the new taxes on fuel, rubber and new trucks to
finance the Interstate Highway System. It was to fund 90% of the costs with states covering the
remaining 10%. Highway funding immediately increased to $2.2 billion the year after passage
compared to $175 million the prior year. The goal was to complete the system (which was increased to
42,500 miles in 1968) by 1975.

The concern over who should pay for the new Interstate Highway System did not end with the passage
of the bill. In an effort to have a semblance of funding equity into the future, the bill included another
compromise. Section 210 of Title II of the Federal Highway Act of 1956 required that Congress be
provided information to help them determine, "what taxes should be imposed by the United States, and
in what amounts, in order to assure, insofar as practicable, an equitable distribution of the tax burden
among the various classes of persons using the Federal-aid highways or otherwise deriving benefits from
such highways."[54]

This requirement was the catalyst for the first "Highway Cost Allocation Report." The report, released
in 1961, included the following related to the impact of motor carrier competition with railroads:[55]

"Throughout the period 1929-58 the railroads have been the principal carriers of intercity freight.
Traffic transportation by rail in 1956 amounted to 655.9 billion ton-miles, a 44-percent increase
over the level of 1929. Although railroads have increased the volume of their traffic since 1929,
their relative position as carriers of intercity freight has deteriorated, both before and after
World War II. Since 1953, the railroads have carried less than 50 percent of total intercity freight
traffic - as opposed to 75 percent in 1929."

The report found that "in recent years competition among the various transport media has been
increasingly keen for various types of freight." The trend for "high-rated" merchandize was
illustrative of trends at the start of the Interstate era. The term "high-rated" referred to
commodities that commanded high haulage rates in relation to their weight because of their
high value, low density, fragility, or perishability. The report stated:

"The railroads have maintained their traffic in heavy-loading commodities, but high-rated, low-
density merchandise traveling on short hauls represents the railroads' initial and principal loss to
motor carriers. Much of the high-rated traffic for medium and long distances, including
transcontinental hauls, has also been diverted to trucks."

With the benefit of a rapidly improving operating infrastructure the motor carrier industry was
increasingly plucking off the railroad industry's highest margin commodities. The report added:[56]

---

[54] Ibid.
[55] Ibid.
[56] Ibid.

"Railroad freight traffic has declined in all general commodity classifications, but especially in less-than-carload lots, in animals and in manufactures and miscellaneous goods. These three represent the greatest losses in both the prewar and postwar periods.

These trends were reflected in a review of specific products, such as iron and steel products and transport of new motor vehicles, that had shifted from rail to road.

In short, a "persistent trend" was resulting in "highway carriers [taking] over increasing percentages of the movement of certain classes of products":

Not only were motor carriers picking off the highest rated railroad commodities, the report stated that they were also capitalizing on the new highway infrastructure to extend their competitive lengths-of-haul with no realistic end in sight:[57]

"Although their most advantageous field of activity is still the short-haul movement of high-rated cargoes, they are competing with the railroads in lengths of haul of 250 to 1,500 miles in the refrigerated hauling of fresh fruits and vegetables, in the hauling of canned fruits and vegetables, and in other cargo movements. Furthermore, they have shown marked progress in recent years in getting an increasing share of the business of moving commodities of lower rating, such as petroleum products, grain, and steel products."

"The progressive improvement of modern, high-speed, controlled-access highways, particularly on the Interstate System, should, by reducing time of travel, fuel consumption, and other operating expenses, improve the competitive position of the motor carriers of freight."

Market Backdrop

An ironic turn of events was that after World War II, the United States helped accelerate the decline of its manufacturing competitiveness and railroad industry. By the end of the War Japan and Europe, and especially Germany, were devastated countries. Major factors that led to WW II in Europe were the condition Germany was left in following World War I and the war reparations they were forced to pay. In order to promote future peace and stimulate markets for exported United States products, the United States government made a strategic decision to invest in Japan and Europe after WW II:[58]

From 1947 onward, the United States gave $13.3 billion in grants and loans to Germany and 15 other European countries, as well as $2.44 billion to Japan.

… from 1957 onward, Japan was able to normalize relations with all its former enemies, whether in Europe or East and Southeast Asia (except North Korea). Normalization with South Korea came in 1965 … Germany's re-integration into Europe took shape in the 1950s, by joining the European Economic Community and entry into NATO.

Supported by United States funding and trade incentives, these formerly devastated countries were able to rebuild their industrial infrastructure with the latest technologies. Meanwhile, the industrial

---

[57] Ibid.

[58] Stanzel, Volker, Germany and Japan: A Comeback Story, The Globalist, March 7, 2015, Accessed from: https://www.theglobalist.com/germany-and-japan-a-comeback-story/, on March 1, 2023.

infrastructure within the United States was aging over time and not keeping pace technologically with renewed foreign competition. This was a recipe for economic decline in the United States and the creation of the "Rust Belt:" [59]

> *The fall of the Rust Belt extends back to the 1950s, when Rust Belt firms such as General Motors and U.S. Steel dominated their industries and were among the biggest, most profitable businesses in the world. The Rust Belt was an economic giant at that time, accounting for more than half of all U.S. manufacturing jobs in 1950 and about 43 percent of all U.S. jobs. But after 1950, the Rust Belt began a long downturn.*
>
> *Powerful labor unions such as the United Auto Workers and the United Steel Workers ensured that there was also very limited labor competition. The unions negotiated higher wages through frequent and effective use of strikes and strike threats. Compared with other U.S. workers of similar education, experience and gender, we estimate, the average Rust Belt worker enjoyed about a 12 percent wage premium.*

The "Rust Belt" is typically defined as follows:[60]

> *The Rust Belt is a colloquial term used to describe the geographic region stretching from New York through the Midwest that was once dominated by the coal industry, steel production, and manufacturing. The Rust Belt became an industrial hub due to its proximity to the Great Lakes, canals, and rivers, which allowed companies to access raw materials and ship out finished products.*
>
> *Illinois, Indiana, Michigan, Missouri, New York, Ohio, Pennsylvania, West Virginia, and Wisconsin are considered to be the Rust Belt states. These states were the manufacturing center of the United States, employing a large part of the population in manufacturing jobs. As manufacturing jobs started moving to the South and overseas, the area witnessed large-scale unemployment, decay, and decreases in population as people left to find employment elsewhere.*

The growth of highly competitive water and highway-based competitors combined with the Rust Belt phenomena left railroads with excess capacity. If that was not enough, a third factor that harmed rail competitiveness was market regulation.

Regulatory Backdrop

Collusion by railroads prompted Congress to pass the Interstate Commerce Act and establish the Interstate Commerce Commission (ICC) in 1887. It was intended to assure the industry offered shippers "reasonable and just" rates but it did not empower the ICC to fix what railroads could charge. That changed in 1906 when the Hepburn Act empowered the ICC to set maximum rail rates. A Common Carrier obligation forced railroads to provide service and limited their ability to exit markets. It also inhibited railroads' ability to reduce rates to remain competitive with barges and trucks. By the 1950s,

---

[59] Ohanian, Lee E., *Competition and the Decline of the Rust Belt*, Federal Reserve Bank of Minneapolis, December 20, 2014, Accessed from: https://www.minneapolisfed.org/article/2014/competition-and-the-decline-of-the-rust-belt, on March 1, 2023.

[60] Chen, James, *Rust Belt: Definition, Why It's Called That, List of States*, Investopedia. November 29, 2022, Accessed from: https://www.investopedia.com/terms/r/rust-belt.asp, on March 1, 2023.

this increased the competitive pressure on coal and grain movements by barge over waterways improved by the government as well as other agricultural products and manufactured goods shipments over government-improved highways.

The Motor Carrier Act of 1935 amended the Interstate Commerce Act to give the ICC authority over trucking common carriers.[61] While all railroad business was regulated, only approximately 30% of motor carrier business was. ICC regulated truckers were restricted to certain routes and commodities. Agricultural commodities, a head-haul staple for rail transportation, were not regulated. A regulated trucker would carry regulated goods one way based on an ICC approved rate that assumed a 100% empty return. They could seek unregulated ag commodity backhauls at "backhaul" prices which undercut railroad's head haul business. ICC regulations inhibited the railroad's ability to offer a competitive price.

While the railroad industry faced stiff regulatory pricing restrictions, the Federal Highway Act of 1956 that authorized and funded the Interstate System also permitted increased truck weights and sizes:

> *That Act established weight limits to protect the Federal investment in the Interstate System from excessive damage caused by overweight commercial vehicles. The 1956 law included a maximum width limit of 96 inches, a single-axle weight limit of 18,000 pounds, a tandem-axle weight limit of 32,000 pounds, and a gross vehicle weight (GVW) limit of 73,280 pounds. These Interstate limits were established as a condition on the receipt of Federal-aid funds, and failure to implement or enforce the limits resulted in the withholding of Federal funds. It is important to note, however, that the 1956 Act also included a grandfather clause allowing States to retain any higher axle and GVW limits they had already enacted, as well as their authority to continue issuing overweight permits under the conditions in effect that year.* [62]

Although doing battle with a hand tied behind their back, railroads did not stand still in this competitive battle, especially with motor carriers. "Railroads' early attempts to develop intermodal service were thwarted by tight Interstate Commerce Commission (ICC) regulations governing rail rates vs. truckers' rates. But in 1954, the ICC allowed railroads to engage in trailer-on-flat-car (TOFC) service. By 1958, more than 32 railroads were offering TOFC, or "piggyback" service, compared with six in 1953."[63] On July 18, 1958, the New York Central Railroad inaugurated "Flexi-Van" service that carried highway trailers on flat cars to carry United States Mail, express, and other high priority shipments between Chicago and New York as well as between Chicago and Detroit, and between Boston and Chicago and St. Louis.[64]

---

[61] Interstate Commerce Act of 1887, Wikipedia, Accessed from: https://en.wikipedia.org/wiki/Interstate_Commerce_Act_of_1887, on February 24, 2023.

[62] Department of Transportation, Statement of Jeffrey F. Paniati before the U.S. House of Representatives Committee on Transportation and Infrastructure Subcommittee on Highways and Transit, July 9, 2008, accessed from: https://www.transportation.gov/testimony/truck-weights-and-lengths-assessing-impacts-existing-laws-and-regulations, on March 1, 2022.

[63] Weart, Walter, Intermodal: A top 20th Century transportation innovation, *Progressive Railroading*, June 2008, accessed on February 24, 2002 from: https://www.progressiverailroading.com/intermodal/article/Intermodal-A-top-20th-Century-transportation-innovation--17010

[64] NYC Passenger Service with Flexi Vans, *Model Railroader*, December 19, 2021, accessed from: https://cs.trains.com/mrr/f/13/p/290669/3379939.aspx, on March 1, 2023.

Chapter 2 - Piggyback on the Chicago, Burlington & Quincy and the Atchison, Topeka and Santa Fe

The BN predecessor road that had the longest "piggyback" history was the CB&Q (Q). "Piggyback began in an experimental way on the Burlington in 1939. Regular service started in 1940 between Chicago and Kansas City. Business was modest. In 1952 the road carried only 150 trailers system-wide. In 1954 over 800 were carried. From that point on, the business rose dramatically to nearly 16,000 trailers in 1957, 56,000 in 1960 and over 73,000 in 1965.[65]

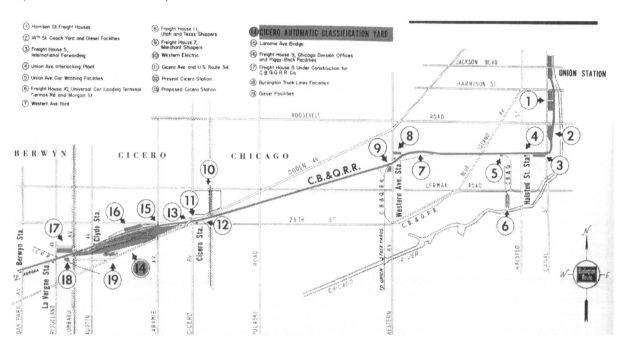

For that level of growth to occur the Q needed a piggyback facility in Chicago which is where Eastern railroads met Western railroads. The most logical place was the Cicero Yard. "With the growth of freight traffic through the Chicago terminal area, railroad management decided in 1955 that the yard in Cicero had to be revamped and mechanized to the greatest extent possible. A delegation of Burlington engineering and operating officials made several trips to visit hump yards in the East and South for pointers on what facilities to use at Cicero. The Q also drew on its own experiences during World War II in constructing hump retarder yards at Lincoln, Nebraska and Galesburg, Illinois. In effect, an entirely new yard was created at Cicero. Practically every track was moved, including the main lines which were moved north to allow for the new hump. Included in this project was the construction of seven new buildings, not including the Clyde diesel shop which had been built in the 1940s. The entire Cicero Automatic Classification Yard project was fully completed and put in service in 1958."[66]

It is important to understand the relation of the Cicero yard to downtown Chicago (9 miles east) as well as the Q's freight houses in the Western Avenue yard area as it relates to the future of BN's intermodal business. The above diagram shows their relative relationship.[67]

---

[65] Holck, Alfred J.J., *The Hub of Burlington Lines West*, South Platte Press, David City, Nebraska, 1991, p. 188.
[66] Spoor, Michael J., *Chicago, Burlington & Quincy In Color*, Volume I, Morning Sun Books, Edison, NJ, 1994, p.16.
[67] Ibid.

Important reference points that will figure prominently in Burlington Northern's intermodal history are point 14 which is the Cicero Hump Yard, point 16 which includes Freight House 9 and the Cicero Piggyback facilities and, approximately 2.5 miles east, point 7 (Western Ave. Yard), point 8 (Freight House 11 which housed Utah and Texas Shippers) and point 9 (Freight House 7 which housed Merchant Shippers). Freight was cross-docked at these freight houses between trucks and boxcars.

The CB&Q and the Chicago Tunnel Company

Point 1 on the map (above) represents another example of very early "intermodal" activity by the CB&Q. It was the Harrison Street Freight House. With its proximity to Downtown Chicago it was connected to the Chicago Tunnel Company's underground (40 feet below the street surface) railroad. Unable to keep up with growing motor carrier competition, the operation filed for bankruptcy in 1956 and was approved for abandonment in 1959:[68]

> *The gathering and distributing of package freight and the hauling of coal, cinders and excavated material are the particular services rendered by the Chicago tunnels which are owned and operated by the Chicago Tunnel Company and the Chicago Warehouse and Terminal Company. In their economic aspects, the tunnels are an integral part of Chicago's great scheme of trade and transportation and they are savers of time, labor and money. In their civic value they relieve street congestion, eliminate wear on the pavements and reduce the volume of noise and dirt. They offer sanitary advantages in the movement of foods and perishables, because the tunnels are clean and the air within them is pure and of even temperature. They are an influence in lowering the much-discussed cost of distribution.*

> *Twenty-four commercial houses have direct, individual connections with the tunnels through the facilities provided by the Chicago Warehouse and Terminal Company. These connections consist of tunnel approaches, switches, tracks, shafts and elevators for lifting cars to the level of the street floors; and are used only for the shipping and receiving of freight transported through the tunnels to and from railroad freight terminals. These connections have been in use for a long time. They are as much a part of the shipping facilities of these commercial houses as are packing and shipping rooms. Such dependence is placed on the tunnels that in many instances the buildings are not provided with the usual loading space for teams and trucks, and there is no possibility of securing such space without tearing out parts of the buildings. Tenants have been attracted to the warehouses by their desire for tunnel service. One of the large concerns with space in a warehouse near one of the "Universal Stations" is shipping an average of one hundred tons daily through the tunnels to various railroads.[69]*

Piggyback on the Chicago, Burlington & Quincy and the Atchison, Topeka and Santa Fe (continued)

---

[68] Tracy, Sherman W., President, Chicago Tunnel Company, Underground Transportation of Freight in Central Area, accessed from: https://chicagology.com/transportation/chicagotunnelco/, May 8, 2022.
[69] Ibid.

Following the completion of the total rebuild and creation of hump classification capability of the Cicero yard in 1958, piggyback trailer loading space was created on the north side of the yard south of Freight House 9 and southeast of the CECO Steel Products Co. Circus ramps were located on the east and west sides of the Inbound and Outbound House tracks and the concrete platform south of House 9. All of this was separated from the hump yard and yard receiving and departure tracks by the heavily utilized triple Main line tracks that carried all of the freight trains, plus passenger and commuter trains, as indicated in the diagram below.[70] Note how the overall facility was locked-in by residential streets and houses.

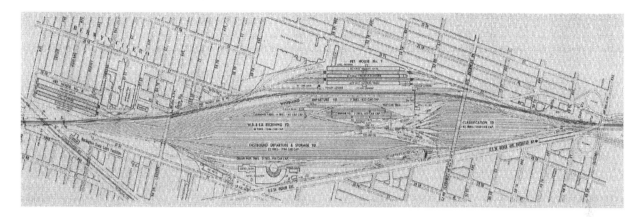

In July of 1960, *Trains* magazine included an article titled, "Piggyback Performance." The editors stated, "Piggyback has prompted the hottest freight-train performance in the history of American railroading. The carriers have undertaken to duplicate not only the trucker's container and tariff but also his door-to-door schedule."[71] It featured piggyback operations on three railroads including the Burlington because "of experience (Q has had TOFC since 1937) as well as unorthodoxy (TOFC is carried in first-class trains)." The Burlington section was titled "Burlington Nos. 61 and 14" and stated:

> *Piggyback has not added any train-miles on the Burlington; instead TOFC has been accommodated aboard existing hotshots, many of which are running significantly faster than they were prior to the piggyback boom. No. 61 is carded out of Chicago at 10:30 p.m. and into Denver at 2:30 a.m. the second morning, manages to cover 1000 miles in 29 hours by adding cars only at Galesburg, bypassing Omaha (Creston crews operate under an inter-division contract all the way to Lincoln via Pacific Junction), and pouring on the power – usually five units of FTs and F3s. No. 14, an overnight Omaha – Chicago mail train, accepts TOFC out of deference to the needs of meat packers, counts between 8 and 15 flats behind its pair of E8's in addition to the normal complement of mail cars. Speed is held to 60 mph because of piggyback's higher center of gravity. No. 14 is scheduled out of Council Bluffs (where piggyback is added) at 5:51 p.m., into Chicago at 5:35 a.m., a run of 493 miles.[72]*

[70] Spoor, p. 17.
[71] Piggyback Performance, *Trains*, Kalmbach Publishing Co., July, 1960, p. 46.
[72] Burlington Nos. 61 and 14 … Ridden by J.P. Lamb Jr., *Trains*, Kalmbach Publishing Co., July, 1960, p. 51.

In 1964 the Q commenced shipments of Burlington owned containers loaded with mail and general merchandise in conjunction with connecting railroads and Matson Shipping Lines to Hawaii. Pictured at left is such a container at the Matson dock in Hawaii. The containers were return-loaded with pineapple. Between 1964 and 1966 the rail-water program handled over 2,000 containers.[73]

In the summer of 1966 the Q completed construction of a two track Pacific Junction circus ramp at Pacific Junction, Iowa, "to accommodate increased meat and packing house shipments at Glenwood, Iowa, Phelps City, MO, and Omaha. We're also purchasing 200 refrigerated trailers to handle this added business, will lease them to Burlington Refrigerator Express."[74]

"The requirements for intermodal equipment at the Burlington had been laid down by Ken Schramm. The Burlington had been an early intermodal pioneer, but up until the mid-1950s had languished.

However, by the early 1960s Schramm had put the "Q" back on the fast track of intermodal growth. That meant terminal mechanization in the Burlington's burgeoning Cicero-Chicago terminal. Bids for the required crane closed in 1965. The crane (pictured left)[75] was a real humdinger, having a 68-foot span which could reach across five tracks and had a one and one-half minute cycle time, i.e. the time to complete the lift of one trailer. It was delivered January 5, 1966, and the invoice (including parts) was billed out at $89,000."[76] Schramm's title was Traffic Manager Merchandise-TOFC service and his operating counterpart, Operating Manager Merchandise-TOFC Service was M.L. Zadnichek. In 1966 the Q also opened new circus ramps in Brush, CO, Centralia, IL, Clinton and Glenwood, IA, Phelps, MO, and Minden, NE bringing the Q a total of 62 piggyback facilities.[77]

The overhead crane capability at Cicero made it easier to handle shipping containers which was highlighted in the CB&Q's 1967 Annual Report:

> One of the glamour categories of modern railroading, trailers on flatcar, or "piggyback", gained
> 13.7% to 87,169 units. Its growth has required the assignment, at Chicago's Cicero automatic
> yard, of two rubber-tired, electric-wheeled cranes, largest and most flexible in railroading. The

---

[73] Burlington Lines, *Burlington Bulletin*, May-June, 1966, p. 9, William *Greenwood Collection*, John W. Barriger III National Railroad Library at UMSL.

[74] Burlington Lines, *Burlington Bulletin*, May-June, 1966, p. 2, *Greenwood Collection*, Barriger Library at UMSL.

[75] Burlington Lines, *Burlington Bulletin*, May-June, 1966, p. 13, *Greenwood Collection*, Barriger Library at UMSL.

[76] DeBoer, David J., *Piggyback and Containers – A History of Rail Intermodal on America's Steel Highway*, Golden West Books, San Mateo, CA, 1992, p. 94.

[77] Burlington Lines, *Burlington Bulletin*, May-June, 1966, p. 13, *Greenwood Collection*, Barriger Library at UMSL.

trend to containerization promises to open new sources of traffic, and to regain some lost to other modes. Freight loaded into containers can be transferred from railcar to ship or truck with a minimum of handling cost, documentary red tape and pilferage. To a railroad, the containers provide a lower center of gravity when on a car, less weight than a truck trailer, lower clearances (important to some of Burlington's connecting railroads) and the flexibility of transfer to a truck chassis for door-to-door delivery or to an ocean-going vessel. In 1967 Burlington delivered the largest single containerized shipment ever to Chicago: 60 containers of Japanese electronic products.[78] (Pictured above)

The western railroad that was even more aggressive than the Burlington in developing intermodal business, capitalizing on the strength of its high speed Chicago-Los Angeles lane, was the Santa Fe. On January 17, 1968 it initiated service on the Super C charging $1,400 per trailer, making the run in 34 hours and 30 minutes. [79] This average speed of 63.5 mph over such a vast distance was almost as significant as the celebrated non-stop run of the new Burlington Zephyr from Denver to Chicago on May 26, 1934 to celebrate the reopening of the Century of Progress Exhibition in Chicago. It covered 1,015.4 miles in 785 minutes at an average speed of 77.61 mph while traversing a 215.7 mile segment of the trip at an average speed of more than 90 mph.[80]

In fact, that transit time only related to the maiden westbound run of the Super C which set a time record for any Chicago-Los Angeles train. The train's real schedule was always an incredibly fast 40 hours.[81] Based on 2,190 route miles this was an average speed, including enroute stops for refueling, crew changes and equipment inspections, of 54.75 mph.

In the revised edition of the book, *"History of the Atchison, Topeka and Santa Fe Railroad,"* authors Keith Bryant and Fred Frailey expanded on the Santa Fe's early pursuit of intermodal business:

> *In 1968, the Santa Fe "introduced its first all-piggyback train, named the Super C." That year, "the railroad handled only 137,000 units or 375 a day. This amounted to just 8 percent of ATSF business. But over the following decade the volume of intermodal traffic more than tripled, representing by 1978 fully 28 percent of Santa Fe carloadings. New mile-long all-piggyback trains popped up in the mid-1970s: Numbers 178 and 188 from Chicago to Los Angeles, and Numbers 189 and 199 from Chicago to Richmond (Oakland) started in 1976 to carry business for a new customer (UPS). Schedules were fifty hours from Chicago to Los Angeles and fifty-two hours from Chicago to Richmond (Oakland) or about ten hours faster than what had previously*

---

[78] Chicago, Burlington & Quincy Railroad Company, 1967 Annual Report, p. 5.
[79] Kaufman, Lawrence H., *Leaders Count – The Story of the BNSF Railway*, Texas Monthly Custom Publications, Austin, TX, 2005, pp. 159.
[80] Morgan, David P., *The Evolution of Power on the Burlington*, Chicago, Burlington & Quincy Railroad Company, 1963, p. 15.
[81] Fred Frailey email to Mark Cane, March 2, 2023.

existed. Each had an eastbound counterpart. Similar all-intermodal trains operated by 1976, Chicago-Denver and Chicago-Oklahoma City-Dallas."[82]

The advent of such a formidable motor carrier competitive schedule between Chicago and California was memorialized in popular lore. On January 1, 1967, Bakersfield, California native and Country Music Icon Red Simpson, who was best known for his trucking ballads, released a song on his album *"Truck Drivin' Fool"* entitled, *Piggyback Blues* with the following lyrics:[83]

"Piggyback Blues"
by Red Simpson

*I got the piggyback blues what's a feller to do
When the cab of a truck's been his home
I got the piggyback I gotta change my ways cause the long
old hauls're gone*

*Well the boss called us in about a month ago said fellow
the long hauls're through
Take your trailer to the railroad yard there's a flat car
waitin' for you
There's a flat car a waitin' for you*

*I'd like to see Mary in Abilene and Susie in Omaha
I'd like to see Jeannie in Albequerk' and Betty in
Wichita and Betty in Wichita
I got the piggyback blues...*

*Well these piggyback cars 're gonna change my life I'll
have to start to slippin' around
I'll have to get the kitch that I miss so much in the
places on the outskirts of town
Yeah the places on the outskirts of town
I got the piggyback blues...*

Bryant and Frailey add, however:

In company with other railroads, the Santa Fe's intermodal traffic came with a problem. To attract the traffic, the railroad had to offer fast, reliable service, which cost money. Yet it had to keep rates below those charged by trucking companies for all-highway handling, and those rates covered the costs barely or not at all. The railroad would need to find a way to lower costs or obtain higher rates. Super C was meant to do that – deliver premium service at a premium price. But most shippers turned their backs on the pricing. When the train's predominant shipper, the U.S. Post Office, awarded the Chicago-Los Angeles mail contract to Union Pacific, the train's

---

[82] Bryant Jr., Keith L., and Frailey, Fred W., *History of the Atchison, Topeka and Santa Fe Railway*, University of Nebraska Press, Lincoln, 2020, p. 335.

[83] Red Simpson, Piggyback Blues Lyrics, elyrics.net, Accessed from: https://www.elyrics.net/read/r/red-simpson-lyrics/piggyback-blues-lyrics.html, on March 4, 2022.

business shriveled to almost nothing, and it was discontinued in May 1976 – an experiment in differential pricing that failed.[84]

Red Simpson's 1967 eulogy for the long haul trucker in favor of piggyback would prove to be very premature, especially in light of railroad industry regulatory burdens and further regulatory relief and a highway network that would benefit the motor carrier industry.

---

[84] Bryant Jr., Keith L. and Frailey, Fred W., *History of the Atchison, Topeka and Santa Fe Railway*, University of Nebraska Press, Lincoln, 2020, p. 335.

Chapter 3 - The Advent of Burlington Northern Railroad's Coal Boom Conflicts with Resources Business Exploitation

The Genesis of BN's Coal Boom

The history of Burlington Northern Railroad's Intermodal business starting in the 1970s, and through 1995, can't be understood/appreciated unless one is aware of the context of what was happening within the company in the decade leading up to the establishment of the Intermodal Business Unit in 1981. The fallout from the internal battles related to BN's resources businesses would reverberate for more than a decade, through to the merger of BN and Santa Fe in 1995.

BN's Northern Pacific and Burlington Route predecessors served the Powder River Basin (PRB) of the Ft. Union Geologic Formation in Wyoming and Montana. The Northern Pacific's land grants included significant PRB coal deposits accessible through surface mining. Those coal deposits were formerly used to power steam locomotives. While the magnitude of the deposits was phenomenal, the coal had a low ash and sulfur content but also low BTU and relatively high (20-30%) water content. Its lower energy content made it less efficient to transport and burn than high sulfur/high BTU and low water content eastern coal mined from higher cost underground mining. It took three tons of typical; PRB coal to equal the BTU content of two tons of eastern coal that was also closer to Midwest utilities. That made it extremely difficult for PRB coal to be commercially competitive and it mostly remained in the ground. The growing smog problem coupled with increased environmental awareness brought about a change.

The United States Clean Air Act originated in 1970. Among other things, the law authorized the new Environmental Protection Agency to establish National Ambient Air Quality Standards (NAAQS) to regulate emissions of hazardous air pollutants. NAAQS were set for each state with the expectation that every state would meet theirs by 1975. The Act was amended in 1977 to set new goals for regions of the country that failed to meet their deadline.[85] A major target of the Act was sulfur dioxide emissions from coal-fired power plants. Burlington Northern was positioned to take advantage of these circumstances as electric utilities sought ways to comply with new air quality laws. In 1970 BN noted:

> *Unit train operations were greatly expanded in 1970 as increased numbers of such trains moved heavy tonnage over long distances. Low-sulphur coal, in large quantities, is being moved by unit train from deposits in Wyoming and Montana to electric generating stations in Midwestern and plains states.*[86]

> *In October, 1970, a new coal and ore department was established within the marketing department responsible for maximizing profits in this promising area.*[87]

In 1971 BN reported:

---

[85] United States Environmental Protection Agency, Summary of the Clean Air Act, September 12, 2022, Accessed from: https://www.epa.gov/laws-regulations/summary-clean-air-act, on March 7, 2023.

[86] Burlington Northern Inc., 1970 Annual Report, p. 7.

[87] Ibid, p. 9.

The demand for low-sulphur coal continued to grow as air pollution standards became increasingly widespread. At the close of 1971, the Company was operating more than 40 unit trains moving in excess of 300,000 tons of coal per week from western mines to destinations as far as 1,200 miles away. Plans are underway for the high volume movement of coal from a new mine at Decker, Montana to the Chicago area, and from another new mine at Gillette, Wyoming to Pueblo, Colorado.[88]

That Gillette area open-pit mine was owned by Amax and the Decker area mine was owned by Decker Coal. BN's didn't have sufficient cash flow to finance lines to the mines so they were financed by the coal companies and BN reimbursed them through reduced rates. The 15 mile line to the Amax Belle Ayr mine dropped south of the light density BN main approximately 10 miles east of Gillette.[89]

When the Amax-owned Belle Ayr mine opened in 1972, and commenced shipments to Pueblo, and the Decker mine commenced high volume operations, it signaled the beginning of the American coal industry's westward migration. Belle Ayr was the first ultra-efficient strip mine opened in the PRB.[90] Subbituminous PRB coal is found in deep (60-80 ft. thick seams) and broad deposits near just under the surface and it is the most prolific coal field in the world.[91] The cost to remove coal from strip mines was much lower than underground mines which lowered the break-even cost to mine, thereby offsetting some of its lower BTU-per-ton competitive disadvantage. The Clean-Air Act mandates clearly favored usage of low sulfur PRB coal.

The United States energy situation experienced another significant change in 1973 when the United States supported Israel in the Yom Kippur War. In retribution, the Organization of the Petroleum Exporting Countries (OPEC) approved an oil embargo on the United States triggering what came to be known as the 1973 Energy Crisis or the Oil Shock of 1973-74. This effectively shut off the exports of Arab crude oil to the U.S. followed by a series of steep production cuts. Before the embargo, oil traded for around $2.90 per barrel but it quadrupled to $11.65 by January 1974.[92] In addition to making life miserable for owners of cars and trucks, the subsequent rationing of fuel also created serious problems for electric utilities that fired their boilers with crude derived fuel oil. The spike in energy costs also triggered rampant inflation that had been building because of rampant US Government deficit spending to finance the Vietnam War, devaluations of the US dollar in 1971 and 1973, crop failures that triggered surges in world food prices in 1973-74 and a sharp deceleration in United States economic productivity.[93] Inflation as measured by average wholesale prices surged from an annual rate of 2

---

[88] Burlington Northern Inc., 1971 Annual Report, p. 7.

[89] Walters, Paul, Powder River Basin: Part One (BNSF), WaltersRail, January 7, 2023, Accessed from: http://www.waltersrail.com/2023/01/powder-river-basin-part-one-bnsf.html, on March 12, 2023.

[90] E&E News, Climatewire, The coal crisis just hit the Powder River Basin. Here's why., Accessed from: https://www.eenews.net/articles/the-coal-crisis-just-hit-powder-river-basin-heres-why/, on March 7, 2023.

[91] Wyoming State Geological Survey, Coal Production & Mining, Fourth Quarter, 2022, Accessed from: https://www.wsgs.wyo.gov/energy/coal-production-mining.aspx, on March 8, 2023.

[92] Investopedia, 1973 Energy Crisis, Accessed from: https://www.investopedia.com/1973-energy-crisis-definition-5222090, on March 7, 2023.

[93] Federal Reserve Archival System for Economic Research (FRASER), Federal Reserve Bank of St. Louis. "The Anguish of Central Banking," Page 688 (Page 2 of PDF), September, 1987, Accessed from: https://fraser.stlouisfed.org/files/docs/publications/FRB/pages/1985-1989/32252_1985-1989.pdf, on March 8, 2023.

percent from 1964 to 1968, to 4 percent from 1968 to 1972, and 10 percent from 1972 to 1978.[94] This also helped accelerate the competitive decline of the Rust Belt as it experienced a sharp downturn in industrial activity from the increased cost of domestic labor, competition from overseas, technology advancements replacing workers, and the capital intensive nature of manufacturing.[95] United States investments in Europe and Japan, to help them recover from the devastation of World War II, helped create powerful competitors utilizing the latest technologies in former stronghold United States capital intensive industries such as automobile, chemical and steel manufacturing. This, combined with improved global logistics capabilities and efforts of politically powerful United States labor unions to resist productivity improvement and labor cost control efforts, helped make the United States less competitive in global markets.

Burlington Northern was heavily dependent on a grain business subject to extreme seasonal fluctuations, forest products that were depressed by the effect of high interest rates on the home construction market and declining Rust Belt manufacturers. The railroad industry, including BN, was competing with a far more productive and expansive motor carrier industry enabled by the government maintained Interstate Highway network. It helped truckers pluck lucrative former rail-carried manufactured good shipments and unregulated agricultural products. Motor carriers fed a subsidized barge industry operating on rivers utilizing the government-developed and maintained lock and dam system.

These developments meant that coal represented a significant source of relatively secure future growth but BN was not equipped to handle it. Its self-constructed and self-maintained lines were built for lower volumes of lighter loads. The operation of heavy and long unit coal trains meant that the track infrastructure over the coal train network would have to be essentially rebuilt with relatively heavier rail, improved roadbed and increased track capacity. It also required the construction of an expanded infrastructure of locomotives, cars, signal and communication systems as well as equipment maintenance facilities. The pressure to aggressively build the rail infrastructure was coupled with pressure to develop Burlington Northern's resource businesses.

Railroad Investments Compete with Resource Business Opportunities

BN's predecessor Northern Pacific Railway was land and resource-rich due to the acreage and mineral rights it was awarded with its construction land-grants. It was chartered on July 2, 1864 to connect the Great Lakes with the Puget Sound and received 200 feet of right of way plus a land-grant award of 40 million acres. In return for the grant, non-military government shipments and U.S. Mail were carried at half rates until 1941. Troops and government property for military purposes were carried at half the prevailing rate until October, 1946 by which time it had been determined that land-grant railroads had paid back, through discounted rates, $10 for each dollar's worth of land they had been granted.[96] A major sticking point when the Burlington Northern merger was being negotiated was the stock exchange-rate between the component companies. Northern Pacific directors, led by Mr. Norton Simon, believed NP shareholders were entitled to a more favorable exchange rate because of its land and resource holdings. Of the 39.1 million acres of land the Northern Pacific had been granted, it still

---

[94] Ibid.

[95] Chen, James, Investopedia, Rust Belt: Definition, Why It's Called That, List of States, November 29, 2022, Accessed from: https://www.investopedia.com/terms/r/rust-belt.asp, on March 8, 2023.

[96] Yenne, Bill, The History of the Burlington Northern, Bonanza, New York, 1991, p. 42.

owned approximately 1.9 million acres and mineral rights to approximately 5.9 million acres as of December 31, 1970.[97] The scope of land and resources owned and controlled by the company is illustrated in the following map that was published in the 1976 Burlington Northern Inc. Annual Report:[98]

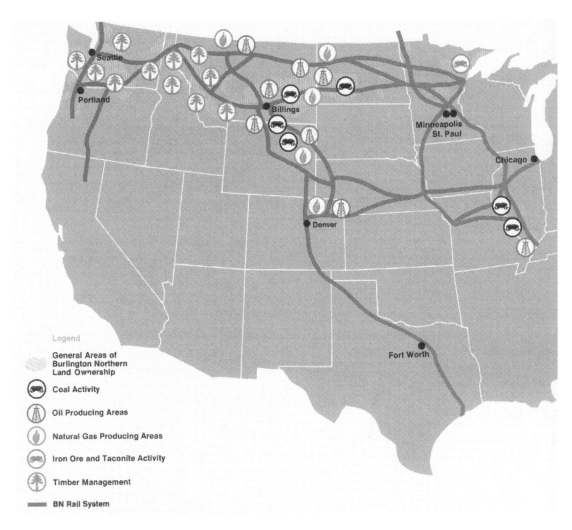

A major stumbling block that prevented full-scale land and resources exploitation was the fact that they were encumbered by covenants related to bonds issued to help the NP emerge from bankruptcy almost a century before. The NP was reorganized in 1886 with the help of New York financier J.P. Morgan.[99] Unfortunately, the company fell into receivership again in 1893. Financing associated with its emergence from receivership in 1896 included covenants attached to 100 and 150 year bonds to assure that the company did not develop resources in preference to investment in the railroad. The encumbrances affected "approximately 2,398 miles of the former Northern Pacific Railway Company's ("NP") main lines and 1,360 miles of NP's branch lines, together with substantially all of Railroad's natural resources properties."[100] "Under terms of these mortgages, Railroad is permitted to sell timber,

---

[97] Ibid, p. 40.
[98] Burlington Northern Inc., 1976 Annual Report, inside front cover.
[99] Kaufman, p. 26.
[100] Burlington Northern Inc, 1986 Annual Report Form 10-K, p. 11.

land and minerals and to lease mineral interests. However, the proceeds from such sales and leases, net of expenses and taxes, must be deposited with the trustees under such mortgages. Except for $500,000 of such proceeds annually, which must be applied to the purchase on the open market of bonds outstanding under such mortgages, such proceeds are available for withdrawal by Railroad upon certification to the mortgage trustees of additions and betterments to Railroad properties subject to those mortgages."[101]

Those bonds, due in 1996 and 2046, were not callable (bond holders could not be forced to sell the bonds to BN) so for all practical purposes they severely limited the ability to develop or sell land-grant properties. Because of this, NP shareholders were not able to realize what the land and resources would be worth on the open-market. Bitterness over that share-exchange ratio lingered post-merger, especially with Mr. Simon who was frustrated by the pace those properties were being developed and by his discomfort with the relative degree of BN's preferential investment in the railroad.

While Mr. Simon acquiesced at the time of the 1970 BN merger, he did not lose his resolve that the company become more aggressive in developing the resources on the lands it owned. He wanted it done in a way that made sense as an independent resource business and not just as a source of funding, as needed, for railroad projects. The BN had just consummated the merger and integration of the Great Northern, Northern Pacific, and Chicago, Burlington & Quincy Railroads at the same time as the Penn Central bankruptcy following the New York Central – Pennsylvania Railroads merger. The neighboring Milwaukee and Rock Island Railroads were also very sick. No relief from the heavy economic regulation the railroad industry was enduring was in sight. The Energy Crisis of 1973 was blazing with its accompanying shock to the global economy while the BN Railroad was just initiating what would be a massive capital investment push to carry Powder River Basin coal. The issue of where Burlington Northern should focus its investments came to a head at the BN's Fourth Annual Meeting of Stockholders in St. Paul, Minnesota on May 10, 1973. At that meeting, Mr. Simon made the following statement to shareholders:[102]

> First, I would like to speak briefly on the proposal which was approved to amend Article Four of the Certificate of Incorporation. This proposal is a direct result of my consistent efforts as Finance Chairman to develop a posture that will enhance the Company's cash position, which in turn could no doubt inure to the benefit of resource development. It will give the Company the flexibility to raise additional capital by issuance of a new class of Preferred Stock. In my opinion, this capital is one vital ingredient to broadening Burlington Northern's capability for proper development. I fought hard for this proposal and I consider the ultimate Board support, and the support by the Shareholders, as to be at least a vote indicating more confidence in the posture I have outlined.

> Today I voted against the proposed slate of directors. It had been suggested by some that to do so would be inconsistent, and a vote of "no confidence" in management – I don't think that is necessarily so, but if management judges it, that is their prerogative.

> For some time now I have been bothered by a feeling that there is a basic change in approach necessary for the betterment of operations of this company. I have been concerned about

---

[101] Ibid.
[102] Burlington Northern Inc., Report On Fourth Annual Meeting of Shareholders, May 10, 1973, *Mark S. Cane Collection*, John W. Barriger III National Railroad Library at UMSL.

various matters on an item by item basis. It was only when I recently received a letter from the Chairman that I really saw the necessity of giving additional overall consideration to my underlying concerns about this Company and my relationship to it. Needless to say, I am concerned, as all are, or should be, with the industry problems.

Many of you know that for more than twenty years I've pushed hard to make this Company more aware of the potential and responsibility it has in respect to its outside properties. There were some accomplishments. Much of the resistance I've met has been because our management team has grown-up in the railroad, is steeped in the traditions and practices of the railroad industry, and when it comes to important decisions, tends to put the railroad first. As a result, the priority, financial support and manpower applied to development of our natural resources has not progressed as it should. To this day, with more than eight million acres involved, I am advised we have only about 180 people, including all levels of employees, participating in the management of our vast natural resources.

For the last several years, getting the merger accomplished was considered to be a first consideration. During this period, progress on natural resources did not move forward at an appropriate pace. This last year, however, with merger problems getting well on their way, I expected things to accelerate. When management once again showed a pronounced and possibly an excessive tendency to "keep its eye down the track," however, I decided to strongly assert my responsibility as a Director. I made it a policy to ask questions at Board meetings; I urged management to use expert consultants in property development and the development of other resources; I requested resource maps and other information to keep myself properly informed between meetings; I provided what financial advice I could on policies that would foster development – and I succeeded in making my feelings well known. To me it is the Board's responsibility to thoroughly consider orders of priority in policy matters.

All of this effort has resulted in a moderate amount of progress, but it has also resulted in some disagreement on the Board. I don't regret this. I believe dissent and disagreement is healthy. I believe all the members of this Board should exercise a stronger role in guiding the broad direction of this corporation, and in overseeing results. I believe that management, and in particular, our Chairman, should strive to develop a more meaningful flow of information to Directors and should welcome their involvement in all significant policy matters. I believe we've heard too much about "management prerogatives" and had too little real policy participation on the part of the Board. The Board should not be involved in the day-to-day management of this Company; either we have a competent management team for that or not, but the Board should be participating in major decisions to a much greater extent than it has. It ought to be remembered – before somebody reminds us – that the ultimate responsibility to the stockholders and the public rests with the Board, not the officers they presumably elect.

Management responded to Mr. Simon's criticisms in the Annual Meeting Report with a list of resource business related accomplishments.[103] Shortly after that, because of continued pressure from the Board, although not having adopted a formal holding company structure, BN did create separate transportation and resource divisions. Both divisions had separate management teams, financial reporting, and budgets but the resource division still existed primarily to provide funds for the railroad's capital program. Robert Binger, a Minneapolis native from natural resource – oriented Boise Cascade

---

[103] ibid.

Company, was hired to manage BN's seven non-rail businesses that composed the resources division. Binger was appointed President, Resources Division, on July 1, 1973, less than two months after Norton Simon announced his dissent at the 1973 Shareholders' Meeting.[104] Less than a year later, on January 28, 1974, Mr. Simon resigned from the Board after 22 years of Board service to the Northern Pacific and Burlington Northern.[105]

Mark Cane recalled:[106]

> I attended that BN Annual Shareholders meeting but I didn't fully understand Norton Simon's issue. I was only a senior in high school and had no exposure to how businesses were, or should be, run. I was there to learn and remember the really heavy tension in the auditorium. I sure understood what the energy crisis was all about because gas prices had exploded making it a challenge to afford to fill up the gas tank of my used car. It wasn't uncommon to have lines at gas stations or have stations run out. Some states implemented gasoline rationing. Speed limits on highways were reduced to 55 MPH to save energy.

Concurrently, it was becoming clear that BN did not have the capacity it would need to handle the new coal business opportunity. BN had one route out of the PRB and it ran between Alliance, NE and Billings, MT, via Gillette. It had another line that ran from Billings towards Alliance and Denver through Casper and Guernsey, WY south of the prime PRB coal fields. Because it was becoming clear that the northern route would not provide sufficient capacity and would be a higher cost option for coal destined toward Texas and Colorado, it was determined that it would be beneficial to construct a line through the PRB to connect with the southern route. By this time the Belle Ayr line had been extended 11 more miles to Coal Creek Jct. to serve additional mines. BN filed an application with the ICC on October 19, 1972 to construct a new line that would extend Coal Creek Jct. to the southern line at Bridger Jct.[107] It would be the longest stretch of new railroad built in the United States since 1931 and would cut 155 route-miles for trains destined to Colorado and Texas.[108] Chicago & Northwestern Railroad recognized an opportunity to build into the PRB from a lightly used and under maintained "Lander Line" that extended 560 miles across northern Nebraska from Fremont to Casper, WY.[109] In May of 1973 C&NW filed their own application with the ICC to build into the Basin.[110] For competitive reasons the ICC suggested that BN and C&NW file a joint application. In 1975 BN and C&NW entered into a contract for the proposed joint ownership which was submitted to the ICC for approval.[111] On January 26, 1976 the ICC approved joint construction and joint ownership of a 112.5 mile line from Coal Creek Jct. to where C&NW's line connected with the proposed new line at Shawnee Jct. BN would further extend from Shawnee to

---

[104] Burlington Northern Inc., 1979 Form 10-K. p. 59, *Cane Collection*, Barriger Library at UMSL.

[105] Simon resigning post at Burlington Northern, *New York Times*, January 28, 1974, accessed from: https://www.nytimes.com/1974/01/28/archives/simon-resigning-post-at-burlington-northern.html, on February 9, 2022.

[106] Mark Cane's personal recollection, November 5, 2022.

[107] Frailey, Fred, Powder River Basin, *Trains Magazine*, November 1989, p. 45.

[108] Sermak, Robert M, *History of Alliance Division of the Burlington Northern, 1978-1982*, November, 1983, p. 11.

[109] Burns, Adam, Chicago and North Western Railway: "Route of the 400," American-rails.com, Accessed from: https://www.american-rails.com/C&NW.html, on March 16, 2023.

[110] ibid.

[111] Burlington Northern Inc., 1979 Annual Report, p. 21.

Bridger Jct.[112] C&NW could not come up with its share of the construction financing costs by its December 1, 1977 deadline so BN proceeded with construction by itself.

BN executives assumed that C&NW was no longer a competitive threat. Larry Kaufman quoted Richard Grayson saying:[113]

> *We thought we had the North Western out of the picture. Larry Provo (then C&NW chief executive) agreed with Lou (Menk) that they wouldn't have the money.*

That belief would prove to be premature following the untimely death of Provo of cancer at the age of 49 in October of 1976.[114]

Energy Transportation Systems, Inc. (ETSI)

That same year that Mr. Simon criticized BN management's coal focused "railroad first" prioritization of investments over resource business investment and development there was another group with its eye on the transportation of PRB coal. A group of companies created Energy Transportation Systems, Inc. (ETSI) with the intention of building a $3 billion pipeline to carry slurried PRB coal to utilities in Arkansas, Louisiana and Oklahoma.[115] It was jointly owned by the construction and engineering firm Bechtel, the Wall St. investment house Lehman Brothers Kuhn Loeb, Kansas-Nebraska Natural Gas Co., United Energy Resources and Atlantic Richfield.[116] Ironically, Frank Odasz, ETSI's chief representative and lobbyist in the Rocky Mountain region said BN was initially a minor investor and added:[117]

> *I think they did it just to spy on us.*

Coal would be pulverized at the mine and mixed with water to create slurry that would move through a pipeline at four miles per hour to the utility. There it would be separated from the water and dried before it was consumed in the utility's boiler. A much smaller and shorter 273 mile Black Mesa coal slurry pipeline had been in operation between the Southern Pacific owned Black Mesa Mine in Arizona to the Mohave power plant in Nevada since 1969. It moved 5 million tons of coal per year so the idea had precedent and a prior Railroad Industry connection.[118]

The plan had two primary hang-ups. The first was that water is a very scarce resource in the semi-arid west. The second is that the pipeline builders needed permission to cross railroad property. ETSI

---

[112] Walters, Paul, Powder River Basin: Part One (BNSF), WaltersRail, January 7, 2023, Accessed from: http://www.waltersrail.com/2023/01/powder-river-basin-part-one-bnsf.html, on March 12, 2023.

[113] Kaufman, Lawrence H., *Leaders Count – The Story of the BNSF Railway*, Texas Monthly Custom Publications, Austin, TX, 2005, p. 211.

[114] Larry S. Provo Dies; Was Railroad Chief, The New York Times, October, 21, 1976, Accessed from: https://www.nytimes.com/1976/10/21/archives/larry-s-provo-dies-was-railroad-chief-he-initiated-plan-for.html, on March 16, 2023.

[115] Shomon, Dan, UPI, An antitrust trial over whether Santa Fe Railroad conspired …, January 11, 1989, Accessed from: https://www.upi.com/Archives/1989/01/10/An-antitrust-trial-over-whether-Santa-Fe-Railroad-conspired/5484600411600/, on March 23, 2023.

[116] Whipple, Dan, Coal Slurry: an Idea that Came and Went, WyoHistory.org., November 14, 2014, Accessed from: https://www.wyohistory.org/encyclopedia/coal-slurry-idea-came-and-went, on March 10, 2023.

[117] Ibid.

[118] Ibid.

proposed to solve its water problem by drilling deep wells in Eastern Wyoming and removing 20,000 acre-feet per year of water from the Madison Formation Aquifer. This did not sit well with farmers, ranchers, and Native Americans. Crossing railroad property did not sit well with railroads. The pipeline would have to cross 65 rail lines to just reach Arkansas. Both factions worked to block construction of the pipeline which was intended to move 37.4 million tons per year from three Gillette area mines, more than seven times the volume of the Black Mesa pipeline.[119] Another issue that rankled railroads was that ETSI would not be regulated as a common carrier like railroads and, unlike regulated railroads, would be able to sign a "take or pay" contract for their carriage services. Its construction would be preceded by firm contractual commitments from coal companies and utilities. That would significantly reduce the financial risk of the pipeline operator while railroads could not contract for their services and assumed complete risk should their coal business fizzle. The playing field was not at all level.

The growing demand for low sulfur coal and the ETSI effort drew additional PRB coal slurry pipeline proposals. They included the Texas Eastern Pipeline from Decker, MT to Houston and the Gulf Interstate Pipeline from Gillette to the Columbia River in Oregon. The scope of proposed coal slurry pipelines is illustrated in this map:[120]

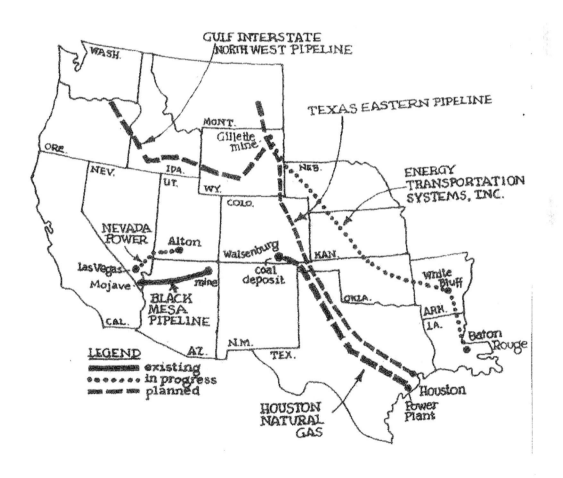

---

[119] Ibid.

[120] This map of coal slurry pipeline routes was drawn by Kathy Bogan and published in *High Country News* in 1979. It is used with gratitude, courtesy of Michael Leveton and *High Country News*.

The battle was on for ETSI to gain water rights and Eminent Domain rights to cross railroad property. BN had two major potential competitors in the PRB – the coal slurry pipelines and a dormant C&NW Railway.

The Energy Crisis and Clean Air Act Amendments Accelerate Coal Demand and BN Coal Transportation Investments

Amendments to the Clean Air Act of 1974 further increased demand for PRB coal.[121] BN aggressively ramped up its coal related investments. Bill Greenwood recalled:[122]

> *I was Director of Corporate Planning in St. Paul between 1975 and 1977. The bulk of my work was spent on planning for the coal build-up and how it would be integrated with BN's non-coal freight and oil, gas and lumber resource businesses. Justifying it financially was an incredible challenge. The required investments were overwhelming and we had no guarantees that the investments would pay off. The railroad wasn't generating enough cash to finance the program. Even when we added the cash generated from resources we were still way short of what was needed. Both Lou Menk and Bob Downing were absolute believers though. When we ran numbers and they fell short, Bob Downing would give us new assumptions to use. He would say, "I don't care what the numbers say, I want this project done." Ray Burton, who later was CEO of Trailer Train/TTX, was our Treasurer. He came up with absolute miracles with imaginative financing when interest rates were sky-high and we were cash starved. Somehow he did a lot of the financing off-balance sheet and helped us convince utilities to own coal cars to free up money for other things. The business was uncertain and between that and astronomical interest rates and without any viable secondary market it was nearly impossible to lease coal cars. What made our challenge especially tough was that we were regulated and could not sign contracts with the utilities. Our price levels were at the mercy of the Interstate Commerce Commission. The coal mine owners wouldn't build a new mine without long-term take-or-pay contracts with the utilities. They would get their money no matter what. The utilities were able to go to their Public Utilities Commissions and get their electricity rates adjusted to earn enough to recover their cost of capital. We were going it alone with absolutely no guarantees other than a lot of investments put into the ground that may not pay off. The board was especially hard on Menk and Downing because they were tired of poor rail returns compared to resources. I remember being on a general office elevator when Menk and Downing got on. We were all alone and they didn't acknowledge me. They had just gotten out of a board meeting where they had to ask for board authority for a lot more coal capital. I knew the justifications were shaky because of the assumptions Downing told us to use. I also knew financing sources were really shaky. I knew they had been beaten-up because they both looked totally worn out. Menk said, "Bob, this better work or we will both be looking for jobs."*

By 1976 coal became BN's largest source of transportation revenue. In 1977 BN served twelve PRB surface mines. Unfortunately, when BN initially worked with Texas, Arkansas, Missouri, Minnesota and Wisconsin electric utilities for the transportation of PRB coal it priced the business as if it were

---

[121] Wyoming State Geological Survey, Coal Production & Mining, Fourth Quarter, 2022, Accessed from: https://www.wsgs.wyo.gov/energy/coal-production-mining.aspx, on March 8, 2023.
[122] Bill Greenwood interview with Mark Cane, March 19, 2022.

incremental tonnage. The prices did not factor in the massive capital investments that would be required to build the infrastructure necessary to fully capitalize on the market potential. As a result, BN was generating marginal returns on its massive investments. In response to the marginal coal rates the 1977 Annual Report noted:[123]

> *The emphasis at BN was on increasing the profitability of a handful of movements in our unit train business that did not meet the company's test for rate of return on equity. These so-called missionary rates had been in effect, with only modest periodic escalations, since the beginning of the western coal boom in the late 1960s and early 1970s. The company has renegotiated some of these rates and is studying several others.*

In 1976 BN spent a record $586.7 million for maintenance of roadway and equipment that brought the seven-year total as of that time to $1.4 billion for roadway and $1.5 billion for equipment. In addition, $255.6 million was spent in 1976 on capital improvements bringing the seven year total to that time to $1.4 billion. Of that total, $933 million was for rail plant and fleet improvement and additions. Unfortunately, the return on equity generated from BN's capital investments, in an economy afflicted with inflation exceeding 10%, was only 2.3% in 1971, 3.2% in 1975 and 4.2% in 1976.[124] BN's 1976 Annual Report added:[125]

> *The 1977 capital plan calls for expenditures of approximately $328 million, of which $270 million has been allocated to the railroad. This is the largest capital program Burlington Northern has undertaken and is a part of the more than $2 billion we plan to spend on roadway and the car and locomotive fleets, 1977 through 1981.*

> *These very substantial outlays, past, present and planned, are required to increase the capacity of our rail plant and fleet to handle the escalating volume of coal traffic moving over out lines. The largest part of our future investments in roadway and equipment will be related to coal traffic.*

Continued Heavy Rail Capital Investments Trigger Shareholder Complaints

By the late 1970s, combined with barely compensatory rates that had been established when the business was starting out, heavy coal carrying capacity expenditures were exacerbating the company's cash crunch. Stockholders, who had traditionally looked at railroads as being in a similar investment class as utilities (and owned them primarily as a buy-and-hold investment for safe and steady dividend yields instead of an expectation of capital gains through stock price appreciation), were looking for growth in dividends. For example, the summary of questions and answers from the May 11, 1978, Annual Shareholders' meeting in St. Paul, Minnesota including the following: [126]

---

[123] Burlington Northern Inc., 1977 Annual Report, p. 9.

[124] Burlington Northern Inc., 1976 Annual Report, p. 4.

[125] Ibid.

[126] Burlington Northern Inc., Summary of the Annual Meeting of Stockholders and First Quarter Report 1978, p. 10, *Cane Collection*, Barriger Library at UMSL.

Mr. Harry Sova, a stockholder, asked that a more adequate dividend policy be instituted by slightly reducing capital expenditures being financed out of retained earnings. He introduced a resolution providing a formula for reduced capital expenditures to be acted upon by those present. Mr. Farrell (BN's Chief Legal Officer) pointed out that Article 7 of the company by-laws provided that directors elected by shareholders determine and fix the level of dividends to be paid by the corporation to the stockholders. Mr. Sova's resolution was determined to be asking stockholders to act directly on the capital budget. Mr. Sova stated that he was not attacking the board of directors or the company's management.

Mr. Menk said in the long range, it is in the best interests of stockholders to spend money to improve the property and be prepared for additional traffic.

Mr. Louis Sauer asked that the company give greater consideration to small stockholders in its dividend policy.

A stockholder expressed concern about the welfare of stockholders. He told Mr. Menk he would submit his remarks to him in writing.

On the other hand, another stockholder, who would begin a career with Burlington Northern two months later in June of 1978 as an Operating Department Management Trainee, offered a contrasting view: [127]

Mark Cane, a stockholder, expressed agreement with the dividend policy, saying he would rather see BN use a higher percentage of retained earnings to finance opportunities rather than issue more common stock, which would dilute the value of his shares, or to issue more debt, which would further hinder the company and subject his earnings to more fixed expenses."

Between 1969 and the 1978 shareholders' meeting, BN's massive coal carrying investments were not resulting in improved bottom-line performance.

BN Railroad 1969-1979 Financial Performance and Business Composition[128]

Year	Financial Performance				Revenue Composition			
	Revenue	Op. Inc.	Op. Ratio		Other	Coal	Ag	Piggyback
1969	$.907 B	$.056 B	93.8		-	-	-	-
1970	$.913 B	$.040 B	95.6		-	-	-	3.8%
1971	$1.029 B	$.055 B	94.7		-	-	-	4.0%
1972	$1.098 B	$.055 B	95.0		-	6.8%	-	4.2%
1973	$1.223 B	$.055 B	95.5		-	7.4%	-	4.5%
1974	$1.432 B	$.093 B	93.5		69.1%	10.0%	16.1%	4.8%
1975	$1.474 B	$.074 B	95.0		66.3%	14.3%	15.1%	4.3%
1976	$1.739 B	$.076 B	95.6		65.7%	15.8%	13.8%	4.7%
1977	$1.802 B	$.060 B	96.7		61.3%	20.7%	11.9%	6.1%
1978	$2.110 B	$.083 B	96.1		58.0%	23.6%	13.0%	5.4%
1979	$2.636 B	$.124 B	95.3		53.2%	27.5%	13.9%	5.4%

---

[127] Ibid, p. 11.
[128] Burlington Northern Inc., 1970-1979 Annual Reports.

As illustrated above, by the end of 1978 rail revenue had grown 133% but operating income had only grown 48%. Coal, as a percentage of total rail revenue increased from less than 7% to just less than 24%. BN's operating ratio deteriorated as coal investments increased. The company faced severe competitive pressures across all other BN business lines. Rampant cost inflation in fuel, material and labor costs was not being offset by adequate price increases. Even when the ICC permitted higher levels of rate increases, motor carriers were in a position to pluck off the most attractive business that shippers were more and more seeking to ship in smaller than carload shipment quantities given high inventory carrying costs. This, combined with remaining marginal legacy coal rates, all contributed to BN's dilemma.

Yet, shareholders were clamoring for higher dividends instead of further capital investments to support coal-carrying infrastructure. In response to this dividend policy dilemma, the company actually considered a "Tender Offer of New Issue Preferred Stock for Existing Common Stock of the Company." An internal document summarizing the proposal stated:

> *At the May 11, 1978 Annual Meeting of Stockholders, it was evident that certain shareholders were displeased with the common dividend payout remarking that it is less generous than payouts made in the period subsequent to merger or by a predecessor company. It was also apparent at the Meeting that other shareholders recognized that a low payout was in response to the requirements of a high capital expenditure program which hopefully will increase the return on shareholders' equity and subsequent appreciation in the value of the stock. This dichotomy in shareholder objectives gave rise to the supposition that perhaps those desirous of current return rather than speculation as to the future prospects of the company, could be offered preferred shares in exchange for existing common shares.*[129]

The tender-offer proposal was never adopted but it did sum up another pressure the cash-constrained company was under as it struggled to finance the build-up required for the coal carrying boom. Quarterly dividends per share would be increased from $.225 in 1978, to $.2625 in 1979, to $.3125 in 1980, and $.38 in 1981 plus an extra dividend of $.15 at the end of 1981.[130]

Cane recalled:[131]

> *By the time of this Shareholder meeting I had already earned an economics degree and was close to completing my MBA degree. Unlike the time of Norton Simon's 1973 speech, by early 1978 I understood income statements and balance sheets pretty well. I expected there would be appeals at the 1978 meeting to raise the dividend because it happened every year. I was nervous about saying anything but I really thought it was important that a shareholder voiced a contrary opinion about the need for BN to invest in a great growth opportunity. There was a lot of talk about the Powder River Basin being the equivalent for coal what Saudi Arabia was for crude oil and BN was the only practical way to get that low sulfur coal to market. It just seemed that short-term pain was tolerable for the promise of significant long-term financial gains. The railroad's profitability wasn't terrific and I knew enough to know that coal represented a unique*

---

[129] Internal Burlington Northern document, May, 1978, *William Greenwood Collection*, John W. Barriger III National Railroad Library at UMSL.
[130] Burlington Northern Inc., 1981 Annual Report, p. 18.
[131] Mark Cane's personal recollection, November 5, 2022.

opportunity for BN to significantly grow its income. I was the only shareholder that spoke in favor of continuing to direct cash into coal infrastructure instead of higher dividends.

BN Increases its All-in Commitment to Coal Transportation amid Renewed C&NW/UP Pressure While Seeking a Merger with the Frisco Railroad

In February of 1977, the Burlington Northern and St. Louis–San Francisco (Frisco) Railroads began a study to determine whether a merger would be in the best interests of stockholders. The study determined that a merger would improve the quality and efficiency of the rail service of both companies as well as annual financial benefits of $32.8 million before taxes (1976 dollars) as of the third year of a combination. The BN and Frisco then entered into an Agreement of Merger and Plan of Reorganization on November 15, 1977. A joint application for authority to consummate the merger was filed with the ICC on December 28, 1977. The merger would open the BN system to the Southeastern United States including the markets of Memphis, Birmingham, Dallas, Tulsa, and Mobile as well as the California – Southeast corridor with the Santa Fe over Avard, Oklahoma.[132] The shareholders approved the combination at the March 28, 1978 Stockholders Meeting. According to the 4R Act of 1976, the new regulatory timeline required the ICC to reach a decision on the merger application by April 21, 1980.[133]

The major emphasis was still on coal and the new Gillette-Orin Line was a big piece of the puzzle. With their inability to meet their deadline to fund their 50% share the C&NW Railway sought a "clarification" from the ICC. The Union Pacific stepped in and told the ICC that they would become an alternate competitive carrier for PRB coal.[134] In response, BN offered a "supplemental" agreement to give C&NW until December 1, 1979. C&NW then applied to the Federal Railroad Administration (FRA) for a $275 million loan guarantee under the provisions of the 4R Act. Of this total, $225 million would have been used to rebuild their "Lander Line" and $50 million would be applied to C&NW's 50% new-line share. It was an audacious proposal because it was 23 times as much as the FRA had OK'd to that point in total 4R Act loan guarantees.[135]

In a bitter irony, in 1977 UP CEO John Kenefick met with Atlantic Richfield Company (ARCO) executive Richard Bressler in New York. ARCO owned the PRB's Black Thunder and Coal Creek mines and was an original investor in the ETSI Pipeline. Kenefick said, "Dick was making the pitch we should put up money to help the North Western.[136] Assuming full commercial risk, BN commenced construction of the new line through the heart of the PRB in 1978 to serve new mines dependent on BN for coal delivery and to open a south end route. New coal oriented yards and maintenance and repair facilities were also constructed. Coal accounted for nearly half of total BN revenue-ton-miles and 30% of total company carloadings. Unit trains handled 87% of coal tonnage. Three new mines opened and nine new unit train movements were initiated to utilities in Arkansas, Iowa, Missouri, Nebraska, Texas and Wisconsin. In

---

[132] Burlington Northern Inc., Proxy Statement to Stockholders, March 28, 1978, *Cane Collection*, Barriger Library at UMSL.
[133] Burlington Northern Inc., 1979 Annual Report, p. 11.
[134] Frailey, Fred W., Powder River Country, *Trains Magazine*, November 1989, p. 53.
[135] C&NW: Going for a bundle from FRA, *Railway Age*, December 26, 1977, p. 12.
[136] Frailey, Fred W., Powder River Country, *Trains Magazine*, November 1989, p. 53.

1979, one new mine (bringing the total to 15) and eight additional utility destinations were added in Iowa, Kansas, Missouri, Texas, Wisconsin and Wyoming.[137]

The 1978 Annual Report added:[138]

> *In 1978, the company continued its program to raise depressed coal rates to compensatory levels. The Interstate Commerce Commission approved a 30 percent increase in coal rates to San Antonio, Texas, effective Dec. 1. BN also filed applications in 1978 to raise rates on coal moving to power plants in the Twin Cities and Becker, Minn. Other coal cases pending before the ICC involve moves to Redfield, and Flint Creek, Ark., Council Bluffs and Sergeant Bluff, Iowa. In the first quarter of 1979, additional rate increases ranging from 10 to 56 percent were requested on coal moving to Superior, Wis. and Cohasset, Minn. The ICC has permitted these increases to go into effect, subject to investigation and a possible refund should a lower rate be ordered later.*

The possibility of lower rates being ordered by the ICC later would be fateful. Chairman Lou Menk's and President and CEO Norm Lorentzsen's letter to shareholders in BN's 1979 Annual Report noted:[139]

> *The challenges we face with our railroad becomes more clear when we consider return on equity. In 1979, corporate return on equity was 8.7% but the railroad's return on average net investment was only 3.8 percent. This represents an improvement on the corporation's return of 6% and the railroad's return of 2.7 percent in 1978, but it is still substandard, reflecting the very narrow margin of profitability on rail operations.*
>
> *Of all our assets, the railroad offers the best opportunity for growth, but it also provides the greatest test of Burlington Northern's ability to succeed as a company. We cannot be content with allowing the strength of other activities to bolster weak earnings performance by the railroad. Nevertheless, rail earnings have improved and we are confident they will continue to do so as we move into the 1980s.*

These two career railroaders acknowledged that massive railroad investments were not returning anything close to an adequate return on investment in an environment plagued by rampant inflation. They acknowledged that BN's non-rail businesses were generating superior returns and earnings from those businesses were funding railroad investments. Yet, they restated their belief that the railroad represented BN's best future opportunity.

Specifically related to the coal transportation business, the 1979 Annual Report went on to state:

> *We are continuing our program to raise depressed coal rates to compensatory levels. During 1979 the ICC approved several coal rate increases for Burlington Northern and other railroads.*[140]
>
> *Coal transportation revenues rose 44% during the year providing 42% of the increase in total transportation revenues. Coal rates not subject to general freight rate increases rose an average of 7% during the year, contributing approximately 10% of the increase in coal transportation*

---

[137] Burlington Northern Inc., 1978 Annual Report, p. 5.
[138] Ibid.
[139] Burlington Northern Inc., 1979 Annual Report, p. 3.
[140] Ibid, p. 21.

revenues. Current coal rate decisions by the ICC have allowed railroads a return of only 10.6% on their capital, while our after tax cost of capital is in the range of 12 to 13 percent. Many of the coal rate increases are in various stages of hearings and appeals. Diesel fuel prices increased 108% to an average price paid of $.82 per gallon by year end ... due to inflation and fuel shortages.[141]

Those ICC coal rate decisions, subject to court appeal, were based on a provision in the new 4R Act involving "capital intensive" rates where more than $1 million in capital investment was required in order to provide new rail service.[142] Between 1971 and the end of 1979 BN had invested more than $1 billion in coal plant and equipment infrastructure. That included approximately $110 million for the new 116 mile Gillette-Orin coal line that began service on November 6, 1979.[143] With the coal business actually proving to be a significant growth opportunity in an overall stagnant industry, the C&NW did not give up. Union Pacific took advantage of an opportunity to capitalize on C&NW's weakness and get into the PRB. BN's 1980 Annual Report stated:

Coal transportation revenues for the year rose 31%, contributing 26% of the increase in total rail revenues. Coal rates not subject to general freight rate increases rose an average of 11% during 1980.

The Chicago and North Western Transportation Company and Union Pacific Railway Company are seeking entry to also serve the Powder River Basin coal mines and, to that extent, have filed an application with the Federal Railroad Administration seeking loan guarantees up to $300 million. This amount and $60 million provided by the Union Pacific would be used to pay North Western's share of the cost of the Gillette-Orin line completed by Burlington Northern in 1979. The loan guarantees would also be used by North Western to rehabilitate 45 miles of existing line and build 56 miles of new line for interchange with Union Pacific for delivery of this coal to destinations in the east and south. Burlington Northern opposes such guarantees as over $1 billion of Burlington Northern's funds have already been invested to develop the capacity to serve western coal fields.

The C&NW gave up on their original notion of rehabilitating their light density "Lander Line" and connecting to the new PRB line. In January, 1980, Union Pacific agreed to help C&NW finance their access into the PRB. With UP backing, C&NW obtained a $414 million line of credit from a bank consortium. They established a new subsidiary company called Western Rail Properties (WRPI) to finance the build-in with UP.[144] Now their goal was to utilize a short segment of that line to connect with the opportunistic Union Pacific who came to their rescue intent on capturing the most profitable long haul portions of shipments out of the PRB. Fred Frailey stated:[145]

BN, indignant, balked at reviving the joint-line accord, telling the ICC that it had risked its own money to build the Orin Line. North Western had agreed in writing to bow out if it couldn't hold up its end of the bargain by 1979... A private, anti-competitive deal between two railroads is no deal at all, the ICC replied. The commission hadn't set a deadline for C&NWs entry into the basin.

---

[141] Ibid, p. 28.

[142] ICC coal decisions: Santa Fe likes them, *Railway Age*, December 26, 1977, p. 12.

[143] Burlington Northern Inc., 1979 Annual Report, p. 7.

[144] Frailey, Fred W., Powder River Country, *Trains Magazine*, November 1989, p. 53.

[145] Ibid, p. 54.

Nor had it sanctioned any pay-up-or-drop-out pledge by the North Western. The ICC reaffirmed C&NWs right to enter the Basin in 1981. There followed some 18 months of protracted negotiation over what North Western owed Burlington Northern to become half-owner of the Orin Line. Finally losing patience, the ICC set the price at $76 million, a sum equal to half the original cost plus 14 percent interest and minus depreciation. The two railroads signed the documents in October 1983.

In 1980 BN was still fighting a heavily bolstered C&NW as well as ETSI for its coal transportation franchise. ETSI did not go away during the fight over the C&NW's access into the PRB. Bill Greenwood commented:[146]

The railroad industry's strategy in confronting the ETSI challenge was to refuse to grant pipeline rights-of-way across tracks. It wasn't a good one. The ETSI pipeline would have depended on an incredible amount of water to slurry the powdered coal in a very arid region. I was very active in the community when I was the Alliance Division Superintendent. We needed public support as we pursued our aggressive capacity expansion plan. I knew for a fact from my community interactions the pipeline people would not be able to secure the water they needed because the farmers and ranchers so strongly opposed it. They treasured that water. They had a lot of clout with their legislators and I am convinced they would have had any construction blocked. I tried to convince our people in St. Paul this was the case but they would not listen. I told them they should stay neutral and agree to let ETSI cross BN. I said they could use the ETSI pipeline in the arguments with the ICC that BN had substantial competition in the PRB so they didn't have to allow the C&NW to enter the Basin to maintain competition. That might have changed how the ICC dealt with the C&NW's access application. They wouldn't listen to me though.

Meanwhile, average coal train loadings per day on Greenwood's Alliance Division grew 176% over the two year period from 7.16 trains in January, 1979, to 19.55 in December, 1980.[147]

---

[146] Bill Greenwood interview with Mark Cane, November 7, 2022.
[147] Sermak, Robert M., History of Alliance Division of the Burlington Northern, 1978-1982, November, 1983, p. 14, *Greenwood Collection,* Barriger Library at UMSL.

Chapter 4 - Burlington Northern's Pre-Deregulation "Piggyback" Business Build-Up

Year to Year Piggyback Progress through 1979

As described earlier, Burlington Northern's predecessors and other railroads entered the "piggyback" business in the late 1950s – early 1960s. BN directed progressively more attention to its embryonic Piggyback business through the 1970s while the dominant focus was on capitalizing on its PRB coal opportunity. Based primarily on mentions of the business in Burlington Northern Annual Reports and Form 10-Ks, the following is a chronological account of the evolution of the piggyback business through 1979.

The powerful "Piggy-Packer" gently places a loaded marine container on a Great Northern flat car at Seattle. For rail and other "shore duty" this container is mounted on a chassis, which detaches when the container goes to sea.

In addition to what was described earlier about the CB&Q pre-1970, the Great Northern Railroad owned 190 "Flat cars, TOFC" in 1966 and 1967.[148] The GN's 1968 Annual Report reported, "Piggyback traffic had an outstanding year, with a 37% growth from 1967." [149] The same annual report stated that the company had purchased eleven 70-ton capacity dual-purpose flatcars capable of handling either trailers or marine containers at a cost of $21,200 each. It also included a picture of a P-70 Piggypacker lift device (right).[150]

BN's 1969 Annual Report (the first after the Northern Lines merger) stated, "A significant plus for Burlington Northern in 1969 was the continued rise of trailer-on-flat-car revenue, at an annual rate of approximately 18 percent, compared to the national average of approximately 5 percent. Burlington Northern marketing specialists are currently making an intensive analysis of this area to exploit every opportunity to capitalize on this potential." It included a picture of a GN marked P-70 Piggypacker in operation south of King Street Station as well as one of a Northern Pacific marked shipping container being lifted onto a ship.[151]

The 1970 BN Annual Report stated:

> *Burlington Northern greatly increased its volume of traffic moving in international trade. Tonnage was up 42% over 1969, primarily in trailer and container on flatcar movements. The company has container and trailer terminals at 192 locations and plans have been formulated to enlarge the capacity of those at several inland locations, as well as at port cities.[152]*

---

[148] Great Northern Railway Company, Seventy-Ninth Annual Report Statistical Supplement, 1967, p. 14, *Cane Collection*, Barriger Library at UMSL.
[149] Great Northern Railroad, 1968 Annual Report, p. 7
[150] Ibid, p. 9.
[151] Burlington Northern Inc., 1969 Annual Report.
[152] Burlington Northern Inc., Annual Report, 1970, p. 9.

The 1971 Annual Report reported, "An Intermodal Sales Division was established to coordinate planning and sales for such traffic as trailers and containers on flat cars, rail-to-barge, rail to Great Lakes boats and export-import traffic," that "Trailer on flatcar and container-on-flatcar revenues were up 18 percent over 1970," and that Piggypackers were operated at Chicago, Denver, Kansas City, Minneapolis, Pasco and Seattle.[153] James Nankivell was identified as the Vice President, Intermodal Sales.[154] The novel "Intermodal" label still had not displaced the "Piggyback" name for the TOFC/COFC business, however. BN introduced its first dedicated "piggyback" train, nicknamed the "Pacific Zip," shortly after Amtrak took over passenger service in late April or early May of 1971. Its running time between Chicago and Seattle was 50 hours (9 a.m. to 9:00 a.m. at Seattle) at a time when the next fastest freight to the Pacific Northwest on BN was 55 1/2 hours. Within three years the Pacific Zip became train number 3 and began carrying non-mail traffic and its schedule was slowed to around 56 hours.

The 1972 Report stated, "Operation of the Overland Mail between Chicago and Council Bluffs, Iowa, begun in July 1972, is a cooperative effort with Southern Pacific and Union Pacific to speed third class mail in both directions between Chicago and San Francisco. Transit time in each direction is 50 hours." In addition, "Trailer-on-flatcar and container-on flatcar revenues increased 12 percent over 1971. A full service trailer-on-flatcar rate was established on meat to Chicago and eastern markets. As a result, substantial tonnage formerly handled by motor carriers now moves by rail."[155] The "Overland Mail" was BN's Train #1 and its second dedicated piggyback train. Rob Leachman stated the following about it:[156]

> *In 1972, the United States Postal Service accepted a proposal from BN, UP, and SP for TOFC bulk mail movement from Chicago to Northern California, Idaho, Portland, and Denver. Burlington Northern's all-intermodal train No. 1 out of Chicago was interchanged to UP at Council Bluffs where it became UP's Overland Mail West (OMW) symbol freight. In addition to the bulk mail, BN added to the train its TOFC traffic destined to Los Angeles via UP and destined to Northern California via UP-SP.*

In 1974, "Piggyback, the industry's term for hauling containerized freight and highway trailers on flat cars, showed a 25 percent gain in revenues on top of the 19 percent increase achieved the previous year."[157]

In 1975, "Revenues from trailer-on-flatcar and container-on-flatcar traffic declined 9.2 percent to $63.1 million, although average length of haul rose 1.9 percent and average revenue per unit increased 10.4 percent."[158] The 1975 Annual Report added, "Results for 1975 indicate there has been no significant shift of freight from highway to rail in the wake of the 1973 energy crisis, although it had been widely expected by government and private industry. Government actions in raising truck axle-weight limitations and extending vehicle lengths appear to have placed the trucking industry in a stronger competitive position than it was before the Mideast oil embargo." Also contributing to the business was

---

[153] Burlington Northern Inc., 1971 Annual Report, p. 8.
[154] Ibid, p. 24.
[155] Burlington Northern Inc., 1972 Annual Report.
[156] Leachman, Rob, The Great Forwarder Fleet, *The Streamliner*, Union Pacific Historical Society, Volume 36, Number 3, Summer, 2022, p. 20.
[157] Burlington Northern Inc., 1974 Annual Report.
[158] Burlington Northern Inc., 1975 annual Report.

decline was that the Milwaukee Road won the Chicago-Spokane/Seattle USPS third class U.S. mail contract away from BN for the mail. In 1976 the UP won it from the Milwaukee Road.[159]

In 1976, "Revenues from trailer-on-flat-car and container-on-flat-car traffic rebounded 30 percent last year, climbing to $82.2 million from $63.1 million in recessionary 1975, surpassing even the $69.5 million achieved in the previous peak year of 1974. Profitability also improved. The average length of haul also continued to climb, increasing 13 percent to 977 miles from the 867 miles of 1975. The 1976 average also was 26 percent above the 777 miles-per-average-unit of 1971."[160] The Annual Report added, "More than 90 percent of BN's TOFC/COFC volume was carried on time-sensitive trains last year. This was credited with helping to raise the company's share of the mini-bridge market – the term for export or import freight that originates or terminates on the eastern seaboard, and moves by rail across the continent and by ship between the West Coast and the Far East. Land Bridge, on the other hand, is the terminology for rail freight service across country between two water movements. Mini-bridge and Land Bridge service eliminate the long haul through the Panama Canal."

With sun-drenched Mt. Rainier in the background, flat cars loaded with trailers and containers move out of BN's South Seattle Yard. Revenue from "piggyback" traffic in 1977 was $110.5 million, an increase of 34 percent over 1976.

BN's 1977 Annual Report used the name "Intermodal" for the "piggyback" or "TOFC/COFC" business for the first time. It reported James D. Nankivell as a Corporate Officer and Vice President, Market Development and Intermodal. In the most expansive account of "piggyback" activities reported to shareholders in the history of the company. In addition to containing the graphics[161] on the left and below, it stated:

Five years ago (1972) Burlington Northern's planners for intermodal traffic had some ideas that they believed would improve profitability over the long haul. That is exactly what is happening.

One of the two major segments of BN's intermodal traffic is the "piggyback" side of it – trailer-on-flatcar (TOFC) and container-on-flatcar (COFC) business. Revenue from this traffic in 1977 was $110.5 million, up 34 percent from1976. This gain continued a record of annual increases that has been unbroken since 1970, with the exception of recessionary 1975.

"Over the long haul" is a key phrase for trailer

---

[159] Western Railroad Discussion, Burlington Northern's Pacific Zip, Trainorders.com, January 15, 2020, Accessed from: https://www.trainorders.com/discussion/read.php?1,4939098,nodelay=1, on March 3, 2022.

[160] Burlington Northern Inc., 1976 Annual Report.

[161] Burlington Northern Inc., 1977 Annual Report, pp. 12-13.

and container business because profitability usually increases dramatically when utilization of equipment and facilities is improved and the loaded unit is moved over greater distances. Burlington Northern's success in increasing its length of piggyback haul has exceeded the goals

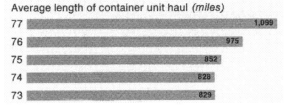

Average length of container unit haul *(miles)*

77	1,099
76	975
75	852
74	828
73	829

of the five-year plan. BN's average length of trailer and container unit haul for 1977 was 1,099 miles, compared with 985 miles the year before. The increase was an impressive 13 percent but what made it extraordinary was that the 1976 figure also had been 14 percent higher than the year before. In 1977 each move returned, on the average, $559 – up from $451 in 1976.

The 1,099-mile average trailer and container unit haul achieved by BN stands out against the railroad industry's estimated length of haul for all kinds of freight in 1976 – 535 miles. BN's own average length of haul for all freight in 1976 was 526 miles and 558 miles in 1977.

The five-year project to improve profitability of intermodal traffic was begun in 1973, after BN's Marketing Department completed a study of the traffic. The plan emphasized a total redirection of the sales effort toward markets for which BN's intermodal service was best suited and markets that had the maximum potential for profits. The goals set for each year were exceeded, culminating in the excellent results for 1977.

"Mini-bridge" cargo is import/export traffic between the East Coast or Gulf Coast and the Far East. This cargo previously was transported by ship via the Panama Canal. Now it goes by rail from or to the West Coast and ocean vessels beyond. This is a brand-new market for railroads and Burlington Northern has gained a sizable volume of the business, with good growth expected over the next five years.

"Micro-bridge" traffic encompasses import/export cargo flowing between interior points in the United States and Far East areas. This cargo is shipped under a single bill of lading. BN was the industry leader in development of a rate structure and through-transport system with the steamship industry.

To accommodate the increased traffic and the growth that is expected through 1982, BN has acquired more than 1,900 new trailers and new intermodal terminals have been put into operation in Chicago and Minneapolis/St. Paul. Terminals have been expanded in Seattle, Spokane, Denver, Kansas City and Vancouver, B.C. New lift devices for containers and trailers were installed at several primary intermodal terminals.

While some trailer and container traffic moves in trains with other freight, intermodal trains are run where the volume justifies it. There are two scheduled intermodal trains from Chicago to the Pacific Northwest, and one from the Northwest to Chicago. Two intermodal trains run from Chicago to the BN interchange with the Union Pacific at Grand Island, Neb.

A major problem has been the backhauling of empty trailers and containers, most of which are provided by the railroads. When a unit is unloaded and released to BN at destination, it is the railroad's responsibility to either return the empty to origin area or obtain a load in the opposite direction. Because manufactured products move westbound and field and forest products, which do not generally lend themselves to piggybacking eastward, BN once had to haul many empty trailers back to eastern terminals.

Steamship lines moving containerized freight inland had the same problem. Once a maritime container was loaded onto a BN flatcar and headed east, its owner may not have control of the unit for the same length of time. Under some rail rate structures, return of the empty container is the responsibility of the owner of the container.

Some BN trains were carrying loaded trailers and empty marine containers to west coast ports, while other trains were hauling loaded marine containers and empty trailers east to Chicago. This presented a problem as well as an opportunity to improve profitability. A partial solution was to encourage the transloading of ship's cargoes from containers to trailers on the West Coast, and at Chicago to encourage use of marine containers rather than trailers for westbound domestic traffic.

A development late in 1977 illustrates the part played by Burlington Northern's Marketing staff. A new carrier in Hawaii began moving canned pineapple in containers to Portland and Seattle for local consumption. Traffic destined for the Midwest had previously moved exclusively through California ports. BN immediately began working on a rate and service program. The carrier, Hawaiian Marine Lines, is now transloading canned pineapple from containers to trailers at Pacific Northwest ports for movement to points as far east as Chicago. A plan is now being worked out to extend this service to points east of Chicago.

BN is now avoiding thousands of profitless backhauls of empty trailers and containers every month. Results for 1977 show a 60 percent improvement over 1972 of hauls of empties.

Burlington Northern's efforts in intermodal traffic in 1977 – the end of the original five-year project – produced 6 percent of railroad revenues, and vastly improved profitability. The momentum developed to date is expected to carry through the next five years."[162]

In 1978 BN reported, "BN's trailer and container revenues have increased an average of 20 percent each year since 1975 with 1978 revenues rising to $112.6 million. This pattern of growth has been bolstered by a continuing program to increase piggyback handling facilities and to find return loads for trailers and containers that would otherwise travel empty. The company has piggyback facilities at 162 locations."[163] The Annual Report again recorded James Nankivell as Vice President Market Development and Intermodal. Nankivell is credited with arranging, "the Chicago-Denver service over the Burlington Northern" for UPS.[164] In addition, the October, 1978 issue of BN's employee magazine stated:[165]

Richard M. Gleason has been appointed to the position of assistant vice president, intermodal and international trade in St. Paul.

---

[162] Burlington Northern Inc., 1977 Annual Report, pp. 12-13.

[163] Burlington Northern Inc., 1978 Annual Report

[164] DeBoer, David J., *Piggyback and Containers – A History of Rail Intermodal on America's Steel Highway*, Golden West Books, San Marino, CA, 1992, p. 103.

[165] Gleason Appointed Asst. V.P. Intermodal, *Burlington Northern News*, Volume 9 No. 8, October 1978, p. 3, *Cane Collection*, Barriger Library at UMSL.

> *Formerly assistant general counsel, Gleason will direct and coordinate activities of the intermodal section of BN's marketing department. His responsibilities also extend to assisting other departments in meeting the demands of BN's trailer and container traffic.*

In 1979, "Intermodal traffic revenues increased 25 percent as more trailerloads were handled over longer distances. This year's revenue ton-miles for all commodities increased sixteen percent over 1978."[166] For the last time, the Annual Report recorded James Nankivell as Vice President Market Development and Intermodal. During this year an additional straddle-lift crane was acquired for Cicero along with 400 new 40' long "trailers for piggyback service."[167] The 1979 Report to Employees noted that the price of a "Piggyback Trailer" increased from $11,686 in 1978 to $12,300 in 1979.[168]

In 1980, container traffic "increased 78% to 148 million revenue ton miles."[169] BN also acquired 500 - 40' piggyback trailers.[170]

The table below illustrates the revenue Burlington Northern's "Piggyback" business generated compared to total gross freight revenue between 1970 and 1979. Piggyback revenue grew 302% from a very small base. Overwhelmed by coal growth, its share of total railroad revenue didn't appreciably increase in spite of its promise to be a motor carrier-competitive alternative.

BNRR Total vs. Piggyback Revenue, 1970-1979[171]

Year	BNRR Rev. ($ mm)	Piggyback Rev. ($mm)	% of Total BNRR Rev.
1970	$913	$35.0	3.8%
1971	1,029	41.3	4.0
1972	1,098	46.3	4.2
1973	1,223	55.1	4.5
1974	1,432	68.9	4.8
1975	1,474	63.1	4.3
1976	1,739	82.2	4.7
1977	1,802	110.5	6.1
1978	2,110	112.6	5.4
1979	2,636	140.8	5.4

What Inhibited Significant Piggyback Growth?

While motor carriers were forcing railroads to focus more on movement of bulk freight, the growth of piggyback and international land-bridge business helped railroads compete again for more time-sensitive business. Because of motor carrier competition, the business carried lower rates that would not typically allow recovery of fully allocated costs. Its carriage was justified to its critics by emphasizing

---

[166] Burlington Northern Inc., 1979 Annual Report, p. 28.

[167] Burlington Northern Inc., Burlington Northern News, Volume 10, No. 1, January 1979, p. 3.

[168] Burlington Northern Report to Employees For 1979, p. 13, *Greenwood Collection*, Barriger Library at UMSL.

[169] Burlington Northern Inc., 1980 Annual Report, p. 9.

[170] Burlington Northern Inc., 1980 Annual Report to Employees, p. 6.

[171] Burlington Northern Inc., 1970-1979 Annual Reports.

that it contributed to fixed costs that would otherwise be borne by other business. As a result, growth was inhibited by its marginal profitability as efforts continued to protect less time-sensitive and higher margin carload business.

A major inhibitor was service quality. Service-related piggyback criticism came from the outside and inside the railroads. Outside of premium service, and relatively high volume, lanes such as New York – Chicago, Chicago – Los Angeles and Chicago – Seattle, the bulk of piggyback service was provided by mixed freight trains whose service was not truck competitive. Piggyback cars carried on mixed-freight trains (those carrying a variety of car types) were subject to a significant amount of switching, including hump yard classification which led to the requirement of lading securement (blocking and bracing) that was significantly more than required for motor carrier service. In spite of the added time and expense invested in load securement, lading damage incidents were numerous which seriously impacted customer service, customer (dis)satisfaction, and the cost for the railroad to provide the service. Internal railroad criticism came from the knowledge that the business was barely, if at all, profitable due to discounted prices needed to attract the business from the highway, excessive loss and damage claims, employee injuries, and excessive terminal (ramp / deramp, switching and clerical) costs.

Dave Burns, a former BN Operations, Transportation and Intermodal executive said, "It was not that BN wasn't hauling some trailers around on flat cars. It was, but not efficiently, effectively or profitably. While we had decent facilities in Chicago and Seattle, most of the rest were "circus ramps", named for the method circuses employed to back their trailers up ramps and onto flat cars. In fact, Intermodal

 wasn't yet a meaningful term. We were in the Piggyback business, with the few flat cars originating at the 120 circus ramps, scattered throughout the system, merely attached to the rear of existing trains."[172] The image on the left is a Circus Train whose trailers were rolled on and off their cars at each circus stop.[173] Because freight cars utilized cushioned drawbars

Two 40-car trains of Royal American Shows carnival made special stop at Barstow, Ill., for cover photograph of "Amusement Business" magazine. Show reportedly is largest to move by rail.

between the cars to aid the engineer in train handling and starting a train from a stop on an incline, the end of the train experienced the most violent slack action as the train's slack would "run-in" on down-slopes and "run-out" on up-slopes.

Dave Howland served as a BN yardmaster at Galesburg, Illinois in the late 1970s/early 1980s and later led BN Intermodal's equipment group from 1990 thru the mid-1990s. He recalled:

> "A train 6,000 feet long would have approximately 240 feet of potential slack in it from the point of total compression of the cushioned drawbars for all cars on the train to total extension of the cushioned drawbars."[174]

---

[172] Burns, Dave, Transportation Department Days 1981-1982, *BN Expediter*, Volume 25, Number 4, 2017, p. 13.

[173] Burlington Lines, *Burlington Bulletin*, July-August-September, 1968, p. 9, *Greenwood Collection*, Barriger Library at UMSL.

[174] Dave Howland email to Mark Cane, February 20, 2022.

That cushioning "give" could amount to up to 240 feet of slack run-in or run-out if the locomotive engineer made no attempt to keep it bunched or extended as the train traversed over track undulations. In fact, BN engineers were encouraged to use their locomotive "dynamic brakes" to control their train speed instead of the air brakes on the cars of the train (which would help keep slack bunched or extended) in order to save fuel and brake shoe life. For a person in the end-of-train caboose or for lading toward the back of the train, the abrupt run-in or run-out of that slack was like violently hit a wall or riding a whip. Again, this was especially so near the end of the train where the full force of the slack action was experienced. It was not unusual for intra-train slack action to account for trailers with blown out doors or noses as the lading shifted due to slack action at the end of the train. The same effect was experienced at times when trailers on flatcars were classified in hump yards. Howland said:

> "Remember, 89' cars in mixed freight trains went over the hump. The suggested impact speed was 4 mph, however that was routinely exceeded. At Galesburg, we dumped more than one load on the ground, including a load of brass (that was to be minted into pennies) for the Denver mint. It came in on train #106 from the Southern Railroad and the rookie tower operator tried to drive down 3 loads of grain that were hung up with 2-89' loaded flats. Not good!"[175]

Howland also further explained below why, in their early days, piggyback terminal costs were so high, and service levels compared to motor carriers were so relatively poor, based on his prior Galesburg, Illinois yardmaster experience: [176]

> When domestic intermodal was young, it was done with 40' trailers and 85' or 89' flat cars that could carry 2 - 40' trailers, or 1 - 45' trailer. These cars were spotted at "circus ramps" after they had been switched out to ensure that all of the trailer stanchions, or hitches, were headed in the same direction. The stanchions were mounted on the end and middle of the cars, with all trailers headed the same direction on each track.
>
> After they were spotted, the bridge plates between the cars had to be put in place to allow the drivers to back the trailers down a string of cars, in many cases up to 900 feet long. These plates or "bridges" were mounted on the ends of the cars so that when all of the stanchions were headed in the same direction, there was one bridge plate on the left side on one car, and one on the right side of the next. When lowered into position, this allowed the cars and bridge plates to "bridge" the gap between the cars and act as a continuous drive lane extending from the circus ramp to the far end of the string of flatcars. All ramps had to keep extra "bridges," as they were sometimes missing on the inbound cars. More than one personal injury resulted from smashed or removed fingers or toes, and strained backs when raising and lowering these heavy steel plates.
>
> The clerks at each location had the responsibility of doing not only the paperwork involved with the billing of the cars, but also billing each trailer. They also were the ones doing the inbound equipment inspections of the highway assets, and handling the documentation of those inspections. Finally, at most locations, it was also a railroad clerk that handled the bridge plates and raising/lowering the trailer stanchions of the cars. Depending on the size of the ramp, this could consume one clerk for the day, one per shift, or multiple clerks per shift and in some cases, per duty per shift to keep up.

---

[175] Ibid.
[176] ibid.

Even at smaller ramps, all of the switching and hitch alignment could consume several hours of switching time to spot, and then again to pull the units after they were loaded. If multiple spots were required to handle the volume of traffic, each one required another switch from the 4-man switch crew, and then the cars had to be handled to the yard to be picked up, or switched into the train requiring even more valuable switch engine time. At larger ramps, like Chicago, this consumed several switch engine assignments per day.

Most ramps had an "east-end" and a "west-end" ramp to account for the direction the cars were turned, but some only had one, so the cars that were turned the wrong way had to go around the wye to turn them to correct direction, requiring additional switching time. Even if a ramp had two loading tracks for directional loading, it was common to have to pre-switch incoming cars so that all of them would be aligned the same way for loading and unloading.

It took a long time to load these cars as you could only load one trailer at a time on each track, and then the driver had to come off the cars to load the next trailer. After the driver pulled forward from the trailer, the trailer stanchion on the car had to be raised to lock the trailer's king pin in place to the 5th wheel on the stanchion. This was accomplished using a hand crank, or at larger facilities, a power crank from a truck, again, resulting in frequent personal injuries. More than one driver wound up backing the trailer off the side of the flat cars, resulting in more delays, damage and in some cases, injuries. Very few drivers had the skill, or the courage, to do this difficult work. Larger facilities had multiple tracks to handle up to 10 cars, or 20 trailers per spot requiring several drivers and "ground" clerks. This entire process had to be done in reverse when it came time to unload the cars, requiring all of the stanchions to be lowered for the driver to pull them off.

Related to skill needed to back trailers along a long string of flatcars, former IBU employee Tom Bauer recalled an experience from shortly after its formation:[177]

One summer we were doing strike training. I was encouraged to try backing a trailer onto a flat, and I came within a hairbreadth of putting the trailer wheels over the side of the car. I remember the Piggypacker was a piece of cake in comparison. I think I actually successfully loaded a couple of trailers.

Howland continued:[178]

If you had a bad trailer stanchion on a car, it had to be repaired before you could load the cars, or best case, you couldn't load that position and had to "blow a hitch". Also, you could only load 2-40' trailers on a car, and with the advent of 45' trailers, the cars could only carry 1 trailer due to the position of the stanchions.

Enter the "new" TTWX car designed to handle 2 - 45' trailers on the same car. This was fine, except the stanchions were on opposite ends of the car, and the trailers actually hung over the ends of the platform by about 9 inches on both ends. This required you to load one trailer on the east-end ramp, then move the car to the west-end ramp to load the other hitch. In addition, the

---

[177] Tom Bauer email to Mark Cane, March 13, 2022.
[178] Dave Howland email to Mark Cane, February 2, 2022.

car had to be the last to load on one end, and the first to load on the other end, and you could only load one on each spot of the track. The same handling was required at destination ramp for unloading. This car improved hitch utilization as the 45' trailers started to become the predominate asset, but greatly complicated and slowed down the loading and unloading process.

This car actually spelled the end of the circus ramp operations as we had known them for so many years. It became apparent that we had to move to a better method of loading cars with big side or overhead lift machines to keep operations going. The issue with this was that it took a lot of traffic to support these expensive machines, and the working area supporting their heavy footprint. That caused many smaller ramps to close due to small volumes, and the lack of the proper cars to supply them.

As you can imagine, as trains picked up trailers at each ramp along the route, they were going to multiple destinations, and they got mixed up depending on which direction the cars were turned at each ramp. An example would be, Denver, Sterling, McCook, Lincoln, Omaha, and Ottumwa originated loads brought to Galesburg to be switched to go to Chicago or Minneapolis and beyond. When they arrived at the hump yards, they were humped into the classification tracks to align with their destination, with no method to re-align the direction of the stanchions. That was done again when they reached their final destination with another set of switch engines. Humping required serious blocking and bracing rules and expense for the customers for intermodal movements to account for the impacts in the hump yard car classification bowls. All of this switching and handling resulted in serious transit delays that couldn't come close to highway transits. The result of the blocking expense and transit time led to a much smaller portion of the customers' business moving via rail, and at seriously discounted rates as compared to OTR trucking.

Former BN Intermodal executive Bill Berry added,

Another issue with the circus ramp operations is that they were mostly reclaimed freight yard tracks that were built for handling 40' cars. Track curvature could be severe with 40' cars able to traverse them without a problem but not 89' cars. As a result, it was common to have derailments as the 89' cars would crawl off the track. This did not endear the operating people to the piggyback business.[179]

Another major inhibiting factor was market responsiveness. The ICC controlled a railroad's ability to enter and exit markets as well as prices. Even though they were also regulated, motor carriers provided more responsive service and they tended to be more nimble. Regulatory relief was on the horizon by the end of the 1990s, however. Unfortunately, the motor carrier industry would also benefit from significant regulatory relief.

---

[179] Bill Berry interview with Mark Cane, March 19, 2022.

Chapter 5 - New Competitive Rail Industry Regulatory Challenges and Relief

As BN and the rest of the railroad industry were attempting to grow truck competitive piggyback services, the regulatory environment was working against them. The railroad industry suffered another competitive regulatory blow in 1975, and again in 1982, versus the motor carrier industry. The Federal-Aid Highway Amendments of 1974 (Public Law 93-643) became effective in 1975. It increased the Federal axle weight limits to the maximum allowed today. It, along with the gross weight limit of 80,000 pounds (36,000 kg). Current applications of the formula allow for up to 7 axles and 86 feet or more length between axle sets, and a maximum load of 105,500 lbs.[180] These Federal limits were maximums only, and several States chose to retain their lower, pre-1975 Interstate limits. The disruption to national uniformity created by these so-called "barrier States" prevented motor carriers from fully utilizing the new higher weight limits but this was a temporary reprieve for the railroad industry. [181]

> *The Surface Transportation Assistance Act of 1982 (Public Law 97-424) addressed this situation by making the 1975 maximum weights also the minimums States must allow on the Interstate System. This Act also expanded the Federal regulation of commercial vehicle size by requiring FHWA to designate a National Network of highways, including the Interstates, where States must allow commercial vehicles of certain dimensions and configurations to operate. This Act preempted the States from enforcing laws and regulations that would impose, on this National Network, trailer length limits of less than 48 feet for truck tractor-semitrailer combinations, or less than 28 feet for truck tractor semitrailer-trailer combinations (doubles), or imposing an overall length limitation of less than 45 feet for buses. States were prohibited from denying reasonable access for these vehicle combinations to terminals; facilities for food, fuel, repairs and rest; and points of loading and unloading for household goods carriers. The 1982 Act also established a maximum/minimum width limitation of 102 inches, grandfathered certain trailer dimensions in actual and lawful use in 1982, and authorized FHWA to adopt regulations to accommodate specialized equipment, such as automobile transporters. [182]*

Within a period of seven years, and not factoring in the productivity gains that accrued from a developed national network of Interstate Highways, motor carriers were able to increase their highway GVW limits (productivity) by 9.2%, trailer width by 6.3% from 96" to 102" and trailer length by 6.7% from 45' to 48'. In return for these productivity enhancements, size and weight changes in the 1982 Act were accompanied by changes in Federal truck taxes to better reflect the cost responsibility of heavy

---

[180] "Chapter 2: Truck Size and Weight Limits" (PDF). *Comprehensive Truck Size and Weight Study*. Federal Highway Administration. Retrieved from: https://www.fhwa.dot.gov/reports/tswstudy/Vol2-Chapter2.pdf, on February 5, 2022.

[181] Department of Transportation, Statement of Jeffrey F. Paniati before the U.S. House of Representatives Committee on Transportation and Infrastructure Subcommittee on Highways and Transit, July 9, 2008, accessed from: https://www.transportation.gov/testimony/truck-weights-and-lengths-assessing-impacts-existing-laws-and-regulations, on March 1, 2022.

[182] Ibid.

trucks. In addition to the tax on diesel fuel, there was a 12 percent excise tax on new truck and trailer sales, a tax on truck tires, and a heavy vehicle use tax that varies according to truck weight. [183]

Concurrent Efforts to Give the Railroad Industry Regulatory Relief

Competitive advances gained by motor and water carriers combined with structural economic changes that were contributing to the displacement of Northeastern and Midwestern manufacturing (creating the Rust Belt) resulted in significant financial harm to railroads. This was especially so in the Northeast and Midwest. The merger of the struggling Pennsylvania and New York Central Railroads into the Penn Central could not counter these fundamental market problems and they were on the verge of bankruptcy. This proved to be the needed catalyst to prompt Congress to deal with the railroad crisis through regulatory reform. It did so through four major acts.

National Railroad Passenger Service Act in 1970

The railroad industry had steadily suffered from losses associated with their mandated passenger train business. Government investments in the highway system and airports significantly increased the competitiveness of automobiles, airlines and interstate buses. This Act created the National Railroad Passenger Corporation (Amtrak) which took over intercity passenger train operations and removed a major source of freight railroad financial hemorrhaging.

Regional Railroad Reorganization (3R) Act

The second major source of railroad industry regulatory relief, passed in 1973, was the 3R Act. Effects related to the Rust Bowl phenomena as well as aggressive motor and water carrier competition contributed to financial straits for railroads in seventeen states in the Midwest and Northeast. There was simply too much legacy rail capacity chasing too little railroad-competitive freight and ICC regulations inhibited line abandonments. The most prominent financial failure was the massive Penn Central which was the product of the ill fated merger of the New York Central and Pennsylvania Railroads. Because railroads provided essential services it was a national emergency. Traditional bankruptcy liquidations or restructurings were not practical solutions.

Through the 3R Act, Congress created the U.S. Railway Association (USRA) and gave it a mandate to design a new rail network in the Northeast and Midwest. It was given authority to act independently and not be obstructed by legacy federal agencies and laws. This led to the rationalization of the Northeastern rail system. While this was a major feat it did not entirely solve the problem of excess rail capacity outside of the Northeast. The failure and liquidation of the Rock Island Railroad in 1975 and precarious state of the Milwaukee Road meant more regulatory relief was required.

Railroad Revitalization and Reform (4R) Act of 1976

The railroad industry was still competing with more nimble competitors because of rate and service regulation. Troubled railroads were not providing the levels of service required by customers who depended on the industry so it was becoming a national crisis. The 4R Act started the process of eliminating the most ominous elements of government regulation. It provided four important elements

---

[183] Ibid.

of relief. The first was in the ratemaking area. Where in the past railroads were bound to rigid ICC ratemaking constraints, the 4R Act gave railroads ICC regulated "zones of reasonableness" that they could set rates within without further ICC oversight. A second major element was the implementation of the USRA's recommendation for the restructuring of the Northeastern railroad network with the formation of Conrail. A third provided more flexibility for rail line abandonments. A fourth encouraged ICC approval of rail mergers that would tend to rationalize and improve the Nation's rail system. [184] While an improvement, it was still far from enough to give the railroad industry all of the tools it needed to revitalize itself.

Because economic malaise in the United States extended beyond the rail industry in the mid-1970s, the Administration of President Jimmy Carter took on deregulation as a major emphasis. It successfully worked with Congress to deregulate the airline industry in 1978. It also started to work in earnest on deregulation of the Motor Carrier and Railroad Industries but that would not happen until 1980.

---

[184] Kaufman, p. 189.

Chapter 6 - Frisco Merger, Bressler Arrival, and Momentum for the Holding Company Formation

By 1979 the railroad industry was still battling severe headwinds. While there were prospects for commercial regulatory relief, they still had not become law. Motor Carrier deregulation was also on the horizon and it posed significant threats to the railroads' market share of higher value, non-bulk commodities. Water carriers and pipelines also steadily increased their share of business formerly carried by railroads. ETSI was striving to utilize its planned pipeline to siphon off a significant portion of BN's new coal business. The economy was struggling, especially with persistent and significant double-digit inflation that the rail industry had trouble offsetting with price increases. Even if price increases were feasible they risked driving business to non-railroad competitors.

By 1980 the picture depicting the relative share of United States ton-miles carried by the main modes had changed significantly from 1955:

U.S. Ton-Miles of Freight, 1955-1980[185]
(% via mode)

	1955	1965	1970	1975	1980
Truck	17.7	19.4	18.7	19.9	18.6
Rail	49.4	37.6	34.7	33.0	30.7
Water	17.0	26.4	27.0	24.8	30.8
Pipeline	15.9	16.5	19.5	22.2	19.7

The share of relatively higher profit bulk commodities lost to U.S. Corps of Engineers-supported barges was especially significant. Again, in 1980, nimble motor carriers were on the verge of gaining significant regulatory relief in a high inflation market that favored smaller shipment lot-sizes compared to larger-lot sized rail carload transportation.

Lou Menk sought to merge with the Frisco because he understood that BN could increase its relevance and significance to current and potential customers by increasing its geographic scope and diversifying its business base that was heavily focused on coal and grain. The entire railroad landscape was changing as the weakest railroads either failed or were absorbed by stronger railroads.

Just as it was doing in the PRB, BN's arch-rival Union Pacific didn't sit still. On January 8, 1980 UP announced a merger agreement with the Missouri Pacific Corp. and its Missouri Pacific Railroad. It would combine UP's 9,700 mile route system with MP's 11,500 miles creating the third longest system in the country, connecting at Kansas City and Omaha. Its size would only trail the new BN-Frisco and

---

[185] Bureau of Transportation Statistics, Accessed from: https://www.bts.gov/archive/publications/national_transportation_statistics/2004/table_01_46, on March 1, 2023.

pending Chessie-Seaboard combination to form CSX Corporation.[186] Eyeing an entry into the PRB coal fields, UP chairman Daniel Evans said the merger would, "make a constructive contribution toward meeting the nation's energy needs by providing more efficient long-haul single-line coal transportation over the combined systems, as well as offering efficiencies arising out of coordinated operations."[187] In addition, UP purchased 87% of the stock of the Western Pacific and placed the shares in a voting trust pending ICC approval of a UP-WP combination. Post-approval, UP would acquire the remaining 13% of WP shares.[188] The combined railroad would give UP access to the lucrative Gulf of Mexico Chemical Coast and the ability to serve all four major West Coast port locations of Los Angeles/Long Beach, Oakland, Portland and Seattle/Tacoma.

The BN/Frisco merger was approved by the ICC on April 17, 1980, and consummated on November 21 at a cost of $137.6 million. It was financed with 5.06 million shares of BN common stock and 1.33 million shares of preferred stock.[189] It created the largest rail system in North America:

Burlington Northern Railroad Main Line Route Structure (Post Frisco Merger) [190]

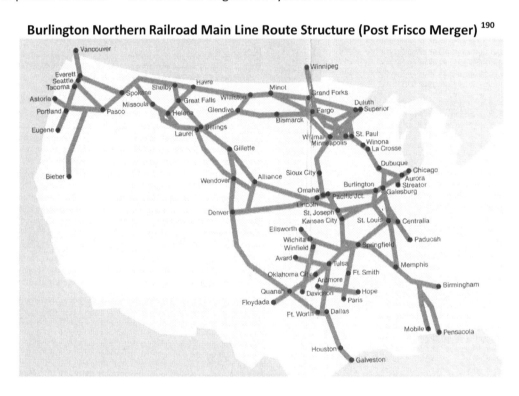

It wasn't clear who would run the combined operation. Menk had already served 43 years in the railroad industry and was approaching retirement age. The financial stress BN was under due to the massive coal investments combined with Menk's impending retirement provided the opportunity for BN's pro-resource board members to push for change. BN's board decided that with the expected

---

[186] Shifrin, Carole, Union Pacific, Missouri Pacific Plan Merger, The Washington Post, January 9, 1980, Accessed from: https://www.washingtonpost.com/archive/business/1980/01/09/union-pacific-missouri-pacific-plan-merger/fce5cacd-3e5a-4287-921c-1bb075f5d65b/, on March 14, 2023.

[187] Ibid.

[188] Holsendolph, Ernest, 3 Railroads Given Approval by I.C.C. to Merge in West, The New York Times, September 14, 1982, Accessed from: https://www.nytimes.com/1982/09/14/business/3-railroads-given-approval-by-icc-to-merge-in-west.html, on March 14, 2023.

[189] Burlington Northern Inc., 1980 Annual Report, pp. 11, 39.

[190] Burlington Northern Inc., 1980 Annual Report, pp. 24-25.

passage of the Staggers Act, the railroad needed a new type of leader in a deregulated environment. In addition, they believed BN's resources needed to be managed separately from the railroad.

Robert Wilson was the Chairman and CEO of Weyerhaeuser and BN Board member. Menk had appointed Norman Lorentzsen as his successor as CEO over the Transportation and Resource Divisions. Wilson wasn't comfortable and spoke with Menk about it. Larry Kaufman said Richard Bressler told him Lorentzsen wasn't working out. He said Menk agreed to find his successor from outside the company. Menk agreed to remain as chairman of the board until 1983 when he turned 65. The company would adopt a holding company structure. The new "outside" CEO would be charged with increasing BN's returns from its non-rail assets. [191]

Although the covenants in the encumbered Northern Pacific bonds tied income from land-grant properties to railroad investments, one can understand why Burlington Northern's Board, and especially the pro-resources faction, would have been frustrated with management's railroad-over-resources focus/bias through the year 1980. The following table illustrates the relative <u>returns-from</u> versus <u>investment-in</u> Burlington Northern's railroad and resource assets (resources = the businesses related to forest products, forest products manufacturing, oil & gas, coal & minerals and land & real estate):

Burlington Northern 1973-1980 Rail vs. Resources Performance ($ Millions)[192]

Year	Rail Revenue	Rail EBIT	Rail Cap. Inv	Rail Ops. ROI[193]		Resources Rev.	Resources EBIT	Resources Cap. Inv.
	BN Railroad Financials					BN Resources Financials		
1973	$1,223	$3.7	$141			$101	$54	$18
1974	1,432	36.9	128			107	57	15
1975	1,474	7.9	181	2.7%		111	52	15
1976	1,739	11.9	159	2.7%		148	58	24
1977	1,802	(10.7)	250	2.1%		169	78	20
1978	2,110	9.1	223	2.7%		213	99	22
1979	2,636	39.4	298	3.8%		306	112	33
1980	3,254	165.3	335	3.6%		366	123	40

While BN grew annual resources revenue and EBIT over this eight year period by 362% and 227% respectively, the amount of capital the company invested in the railroad exceeded that put into resource businesses by 920%. During that same time period the railroad's <u>cumulative</u> EBIT (earnings before income taxes) was only 37% of that generated by BN's resources businesses. In 1980, even after improved returns were being derived from the significant capital investments made to carry PRB coal, BN Railroad's pre-tax (EBIT) return that was generated against identifiable railroad assets was only 3.6% while the United States 1980 inflation and Fed Funds Interest Rates were 12.5% and 18.0% respectively.[194] Conversely, in 1980 the undermanaged resources businesses generated a pre-tax return on identifiable assets of 9.0%.

[191] Kaufman, pp. 208-209, 210.
[192] Burlington Northern Inc., 1973-1980 Annual Reports.
[193] Burlington Northern Inc., 1978 ,1979 and 1980 Forms 10K.
[194] Amadeo, Kimberly, The Balance, US Inflation Rate by Year From 1929 to 2023, March 31, 2023, accessed from https://www.thebalance.com/u-s-inflation-rate-history-by-year-and-forecast-3306093, on April 5, 2023.

BN's Board Hires Richard Bressler as Menk's Successor

The Board settled on Energy Industry executive Richard Bressler BN's new CEO. He had served as a vice president and treasurer of General Electric Company, senior vice president of American Airlines, senior vice president finance Atlantic Richfield Company (ARCO) (when he encouraged UP to enter the PRB) as and president of ARCO Chemical Company.[195] While employed by ARCO he served on the board of Minneapolis based General Mills, Inc. with Lou Menk. In addition, Paul L. Parker, General Mills' executive vice president and chief administrative officer, also served on BN's board of directors.[196] Therefore, both Menk and Parker already knew Bressler professionally before he was recruited to BN.

Bressler was hired on June 1, 1980.[197] Bill Greenwood, who was the Superintendent of BN's Alliance Division at the time, recalled:[198]

> We were spending a ton of money on the Alliance Division to build up our coal capacity and it was causing a real cash crunch. We were barely able to service our debt load. We had to load as many coal trains as possible every day while simultaneously building up our capacity. Bressler wanted to see what was going on for himself because it was such a focal point for the future of the company. I was told to give him a tour of the division on his first day with BN. I was really proud of what we were accomplishing. I even made sure to point out BN's 4,000 barrel per day oil refinery at Osage, WY when we drove by it in the hi-rail truck. BN refined oil from BN-owned oil wells and we got almost 10% of our diesel fuel from it. Bressler, the oil and refining man, scoffed at it saying it was a "shitty operation." He said it was so small that it would never make any money. Then he said to me, "I think the railroad business is shitty too."

Greenwood's comment about how financing the coal build-up was creating serious BN cash flow issues was not an exaggeration. The following table compares BN Railroad's income before income taxes to capital investments between 1975 and 1980:[199]

Burlington Northern Railroad Income Before Income Taxes vs. Capital Investments, 1975-1980 ($mm)

	1975	1976	1977	1978	1979	1980
IBIT	$7.9	$11.9	($10.7)	$8.8	$39.4	$165.3
Capital Expenditures	$181.4	$158.8	$249.8	$223.1	$297.8	$335.3

Note: Income before income taxes includes BN Railroad's share of Railroad-driven corporate interest expenses. Capital expenditures exclude operating leases.

Between 1975 and 1980, $1.45 billion (excluding operating leases) had been invested in the railroad but it generated cumulative pre-tax income of only $223 million. Of that, 74% was generated in 1980. Between 1976 and 1980 BN had invested $1.1 billion to increase coal hauling capacity alone.[200] As of December 31, 1979 BN Inc. had a deficit of $45.7 million of cash and short term investments on-hand.[201]

---

[195] Richard Main Bressler, Prabook, Accessed from: https://prabook.com/web/richard_main.bressler/1369935, on March 14, 2023.

[196] Burlington Northern Inc., 1980 annual Report, p. 49.

[197] Burlington Northern Inc., 1980 Form 10-K, p. 31, *Cane Collection*, Barriger Library at UMSL.

[198] Bill Greenwood interview with Mark Cane, January 9, 2023.

[199] 1975-1977 data sourced from Burlington Northern Inc., 1979 Annual Report, pp. 32-33; 1978-1980 data sourced from Burlington Northern Inc., 1980 Annual Report, pp. 32-33.

[200] Burlington Northern Inc., 1980 Annual Report, p. 5.

[201] Burlington Northern Inc., 1979 Annual Report, p. 37.

Bressler insisted that the railroad had to pay its own way and generate its own capital. He was not willing to have the railroad rely on resources to support its operational and capital needs. It was clear to him that this had been happening when he got involved in his first annual budget after he joined the company. According to an interview Larry Kaufman had with Bressler, he said:

> *"I got around to talking with Bob Binger (who was in charge of resources before the separate subsidiaries were established) one day. He was a very reticent fellow. I asked Frank Coyne (the BN's chief financial officer), "What goes on here? I just can't seem to understand what's going on in these resource businesses. I can't get anything out of Binger." "That's very difficult," Coyne told me. He said they gave Binger a budget of how much cash he had to produce. Of course, that was the secret to the thing."[202]*

Kaufman added that Binger knew he had to be tight with information he gave BN's finance people because it would lead to squeezing money from Binger's resources businesses. He said Bressler stated:[203]

> *He was absolutely right that everything he produced, if it turned up in cash, was taken away and something else was done with it. Binger's (impression) was that he just saw that money being poured into the railroad with no results. Of course, to a certain extent he was right.*

According to Kaufman, Bressler also stated:

> *I got the fellow who ran the real estate operation in one day. I was trying to figure out how these people ran these businesses ... We had all this property, jillions of acres. I asked him how he determined what was done. He said, 'Well, Mr. Coyne calls me up and tells me to sell some property because we need cash.' That was the way it was, too.[204]*

Looking back on the situation decades later makes it appear a bit comical in that BN land and resources income was funneled by railroaders to the railroad instead of resource related investments. For objectivity, it is helpful to remember that the vast majority of BN's non-rail real estate and natural resource assets were encumbered by the old 1893 NP bonds. As stated earlier, the encumbrances affected "approximately 2,398 miles of the former Northern Pacific Railway Company's ("NP") main lines and 1,360 miles of NP's branch lines, together with substantially all of Railroad's natural resources properties."[205]

> *Under terms of these mortgages, Railroad is permitted to sell timber, land and minerals and to lease mineral interests. However, the proceeds from such sales and leases, net of expenses and taxes, must be deposited with the trustees under such mortgages. Except for $500,000 of such proceeds annually, which must be applied to the purchase on the open market of bonds outstanding under such mortgages, such proceeds are available for withdrawal by Railroad upon*

---

[202] Kaufman, p. 223.
[203] Ibid.
[204] Ibid.
[205] Burlington Northern Inc, 1986 Annual Report Form 10-K, p. 11.

certification to the mortgage trustees of additions and betterments to Railroad properties subject to those mortgages.[206]

Therefore, the vast majority of the income from the land grant properties had to be invested in additions and betterments to specific former Northern Pacific rail property. There were many opportunities to do that to support new coal business flowing over the former NP from the Decker mines to the Midwest but not for former CB&Q routes or the new Gillette-Orin line which accounted for a much larger share of investment needs.

Those NP bond covenants, however, did not prevent BN from using income generated from unencumbered rail properties for business opportunities outside the railroad. The career railroaders who had run BN and its predecessors since their inception believed in a positive future for the railroad industry. Bressler, with his finance and energy industry background, did not share that bias.

Larry Kaufman reported that shortly after Bressler joined BN he told the board of directors:[207]

> *I don't see right now, if you forced me to tell you, whether we are going to make any money in this coal business. I see zero return on this enormous investment. We've got to figure out a way to turn this around. Either we have to cut back on this investment, or we've got to do something to improve the return.*

Bressler's belief about this business (he had recently encouraged Union Pacific to compete against BN and his employer had invested in ETSI) reinforced the bias of BN's resource-oriented board members that a better future depended on BN weaning railroad investments in preference to resources. It also increased the importance of improving rail margins. A leaner railroad could spin off cash to fund alternate higher return investments. Bressler determined that he needed a cost cutter to lead BN Railroad and the Frisco had a reputation for being a very lean operation. While the ICC approved the BN-Frisco merger on April 17, it was subject to court challenges and would not be consummated until November 21. Menk and Bressler appointed Frisco's Richard Grayson as BN's Vice Chairman and President Transportation Division effective December, 1980.[208]

In an interview with Larry Kaufman, Grayson commented:

> *Dick (Bressler) was not satisfied with what was going on at the railroad. He retired a few people. We were going to spend a tremendous amount of money to prepare for the coal business. When I got there, we had, I think, some 22 (actual or) potential lawsuits over the letters of intent (for coal transportation rates). They were all too low, and we couldn't make any money on them.*[209]

Norm Lorentzsen (who Bressler replaced as BN Inc. President and CEO) became Chairman of the Executive Committee of the Board and Transportation Division President Tom Lamphier retired. Grayson appointed his Frisco lieutenant William F. Thompson to head rail operations. Kaufman says Grayson said:

---

[206] Ibid.

[207] Kaufman, p. 215.

[208] Burlington Northern Inc., 1981 Form 10-K, p. 18.

[209] Kaufman, p. 211.

> *(The BN people) were a good bunch of railroad people, focused on maintenance. But they had never lived on hard times like the Frisco people. I had to shake out the management. Bill Thompson could get more out of a maintenance dollar in mechanical and engineering than anyone I've ever seen. There were a lot of things we saw that they could do without.* [210]

Bressler articulated his perspective on BN's future in an interview conducted for BN's 1980 Annual Report. He stated:[211]

> *In terms of absolute dollar growth over the next five years, the additional profit potential of our railroad is the best thing we've got going for us. Improved rail profits will come from two sources: one is revenue growth in coal and grain traffic; the other is our ability to control operating costs. During the past five years, our heavy rail investment program has put us near the top of the industry in terms of costs. In the future, we're going to take a much more aggressive approach on costs and we expect to measure results in terms of annual improvements in railroad return on assets.*

> *Greater percentage growth will come from our oil and gas business and our forest management operations during the next five years. Perhaps not during the next five years, but down the road those resources are going to be substantial businesses for us.*

He clearly believed coal and grain represented the best near term railroad growth opportunities. Intermodal business was understandably not on his radar. Related to coal rates he stated:[212]

> *I have met, so far, with 37 utility customers and I would say the visits have been good ones. We have talked candidly and, basically, the message is this: number one, Burlington Northern has not been getting rich off coal hauling and number two, we have invested well over $1 billion in that particular business. It is in the utilities' best interest as well as our own that our railroad make a reasonable return on its coal business. Otherwise we can't continue to invest in it and they can ill afford to have a rickety railroad deliver their fuel supply.*

> *I am aware of no instance in which a utility has been disadvantaged by buying Powder River Basin coal and shipping it by Burlington Northern's railroad. When you consider the cost of alternate fuel supplies, I think that their conversion to coal makes sense. I think we agree on that and I think we also agree that we've got to find ways to solve our differences on these rate questions outside the court system, which is lengthy and costly to both parties.*

Related to rail cost reduction opportunities he stated: [213]

> *It's going to be a while before we can get on top of our fuel costs. The diesel locomotive is a finely tuned machine that runs on premium liquid fuel. If we could make that machine run on bottom of the barrel oil, we could cut our costs almost in half.*

---

[210] Ibid, pp. 211-212.
[211] Burlington Northern Inc., 1980 Annual Report, p. 1.
[212] Ibid.
[213] Ibid.

> *One of my interests is in putting some money into quick payoff research and development efforts and also convincing manufacturers to get involved in projects to help us reduce fuel costs.*

Cost reductions were going to be critical to the prosperity of Burlington Northern Railroad and the rest of the Railroad Industry because the Motor Carrier Industry finally got the regulatory relief it had been seeking.

The Motor Carrier Act of 1980 Provides Truckers Massive Additional Regulatory Relief

The *Motor Carrier Act of 1980* further tipped the competitive balance away from the railroad industry. It created a massive deregulation of the trucking industry and was signed into law by President Carter on July 1, 1980. When he signed the bill he said:[214]

> *This is historic legislation. It will remove 45 years of excessive and inflationary Government restrictions and redtape. It will have a powerful anti-inflationary effect, reducing consumer costs by as much as $8 billion each year. And by ending wasteful practices, it will conserve annually hundreds of millions of gallons of precious fuel. All the citizens of our Nation will benefit from this legislation. Consumers will benefit, because almost every product we purchase has been shipped by truck, and outmoded regulations have inflated the prices that each one of us must pay. The shippers who use trucking will benefit as new service and price options appear. Labor will benefit from increased job opportunities. And the trucking industry itself will benefit from greater flexibility and new opportunities for innovation.*

A major overseer of the implementation of the Motor Carrier Act was Darius Gaskins who chaired the Interstate Commerce Commission following the Act's passage. While still bound to zones of price reasonableness, it freed formerly regulated motor carriers from interference by rate bureaus when setting their own rates. It also freed carriers to serve the markets they wanted to serve over the routes over which they chose to run. They could file independently for permission to quote prices outside of the zone of reasonableness. Carriers could also enter into contracts without regulatory review. The Act opened the truck market to transport brokers who could help carriers better match loads with available capacity.[215]

With new-found ability to compete in new markets and conduct business more efficiently it enabled a change in the motor carrier operating paradigm. It evolved from one that would just pass on price increases due to higher wages and operating costs to one where carriers had greater incentives to drive efficiency. Fortunately for the Railroad Industry, their regulatory relief finally came three and a half months later.

The Staggers Rail Act of 1980 Provides the Railroad Industry its Most Significant Regulatory Relief

---

[214] Motor Carrier Act of 1980, Wikipedia, Accessed from: https://en.wikipedia.org/wiki/Motor_Carrier_Act_of_1980, on February 8, 2022..
[215] Ibid.

That fourth major Act provided the most significant regulatory relief for the railroad industry. The Staggers Rail Act of 1980 was signed into law on October 14, 1980 as Public Law No. 96-448. Its stated goals were:[216]

> (1) to assist in rehabilitating the Nation's rail system to meet the demands of interstate commerce and national defense;
> (2) to reform Federal regulatory policy so as to preserve a safe and efficient rail system;
> (3) to assist the rail system to remain viable in the private sector of the economy;
> (4) to provide a regulatory process that balances the needs of carriers, shippers, and the public; and
> (5) to assist in the rehabilitation and financing of the rail system.

It brought about the most significant regulatory relief the railroad industry had ever experienced and replaced the regulatory structure that had existed since the Interstate Commerce Act of 1887: [217]

> *The major regulatory changes of the Staggers Act were as follows:*
> - *A rail carrier could establish any rate for a rail service unless the ICC were to determine that there was no effective competition for rail services.*
> - *Rail shippers and rail carriers would be allowed to establish contracts subject to no effective ICC review unless the Commission determined that the contract service would interfere with the rail carrier's ability to provide common carrier service (a finding rarely made that is not apparent in the history of the rail industry thereafter).*
> - *The scope of authority to control rates to prevent "discrimination" among shippers was substantially curtailed.*
> - *Across-the-board industry-wide rate increases were phased out.*
> - *The dismantling of the collective rate making machinery among railroads begun in 1976 was reaffirmed, with railroads not allowed to agree to rates they could perform on their own systems and were not allowed to participate in the determination of the rates on traffic in which they did not effectively participate.*
>
> *The Act also had provisions allowing the Commission to require access by one railroad to another railroad's facilities if one railroad had effective "bottleneck" control of traffic. The provisions dealt with "reciprocal switching" (handling of railroad cars between long-haul rail carriers and local customers) and trackage rights. However, the provisions did not have as much effect as the others mentioned.*

The passage of this Act did not eliminate rail regulation. Intermodal was basically deregulated but not carload business, such as coal and grain, where competition was limited.   In fact, in a slam against BN, the Staggers Act included a provision limiting "rate increases on a specified coal transportation line to San Antonio, Texas."[218]

---

[216] Congress.gov, S.1946 – Staggers Rail Act of 1980, Accessed from: https://www.congress.gov/bill/96th-congress/senate-bill/1946, on March 15, 2023.

[217] Wikipedia, Staggers Rail Act, accessed from https://en.wikipedia.org/wiki/Staggers_Rail_Act, on March 5, 2022.

[218] Congress.gov, S.1946 – Staggers Rail Act of 1980, Accessed from: https://www.congress.gov/bill/96th-congress/senate-bill/1946, on March 15, 2023.

Ironically, if that Staggers "carve out" hadn't occurred the Staggers Act might have never passed because of Burlington Northern. The City of San Antonio controlled its electric utility. In 1970 that utility generated 100% of its output from natural gas. By 1980 it was generating 25% from coal.[219] BN's PRB missionary coal rates stimulated that conversion from gas. When BN started to aggressively raise coal rates, with the approval of the ICC, San Antonio Mayor Lila Cockrell essentially declared war on BN and took her fight to Washington DC. Rush Loving commented:[220]

> *Well, early 1979 Congress was drafting a bill called the Staggers Act to give regular to railroad. I went to work in the White House for a year that summer and soon discovered that the draft of the bill that by then existed had a lot of new restrictions in it, a lot of new regulations that would have bankrupted the entire industry. Some of these regulations, and it was funny, I discovered later that the problem was Burlington Northern. The BN had gone into the coal business about 10 years earlier, and Lou Menk who was its chairman had set extremely low rates for hauling the coal. The rates were so low they were not making money on the moves. Rates didn't cover the deterioration of the track and all of that. …. Well finally, Menk's marketing people convinced him that they were indeed losing money, and indeed they needed to raise their rates and raise them pretty steeply. Well, when they jacked up those rates, the utilities all over the Midwest and the southwest, who were buying BN coal went into a – well raised Hell is what they did. These people were led by a little lady in San Antonio who was the mayor down there named Lila Cockrell. Ms. Cockrell was short and rotund and very grandmotherly with big glasses. Well, she did not know anything about the ICC but she knew a lot about the politics and about the Congress. And so she proceeded to go to the halls of Congress and start twisting arms and she got other utilities who were affected to do the same thing. And pretty soon, they were rewriting the Staggers bill. And they were putting these amendments on that were going to choke the railroads. I worked for Jimmy Carter in the White House and I liked him but I never thought he was very decisive. But this time he and his legislative staff really came through. Came through big time. They went to Congress, worked with the leaders of Congress, they got the bill redrafted and in early 1980, Carter signed the Staggers Act freeing the railroads.*

As head of the ICC at the time, Darius Gaskins was in the middle of deregulation battle. He had this to say about Rush Loving's account:[221]

> *He was basically right. Lila Cockrell got heavily involved and she got her carve-out. Senator Lloyd Bentsen was also from Texas. He was the Senate Majority Leader and had a lot of sway with the legislation. He deserves a lot of credit for actually getting the bill through.*

Fortunately for the future of the rail industry, and especially its Intermodal business, the Staggers Act survived. Combined with the prior 4R Act's greater flexibility to abandon or sell money-losing branch lines and redundant main lines, it finally gave the railroad industry the ability to control more of its

---

[219] CPS Energy, Powering Our Community's Future, Power Generation Diversification 1970-2021, Accessed from: https://www.cpsenergy.com/en/about-us/powering-our-communitys-future.html?linkvar=sidenavigation, on April 30, 2023.

[220] Loving Jr., Rush, Rise and Fall of the Railroad Industry, Speech to the Virginia Historical Society, Richmond, Virginia, September 8, 2016, CSPAN3, American History TV, accessed from: https://www.c-span.org/video/?414914-1/rise-fall-railroad-industry, on April 26, 2023.

[221] Darius Gaskins interview with Mark Cane, May 1, 2023.

economic destiny. It gave railroads the ability to manage their enterprises like businesses with differential pricing and confidential contracts while choosing the markets it would compete in.

The Staggers Act also brought a unique challenge - adapting to life in a much more deregulated environment. The rail industry was used to collective rate-making and attempts to pass on cost increases while market share drifted away. All of a sudden railroad employees became subject to antitrust laws when the Act became effective. Railroads were used to collectively setting prices with competitors in Rate Bureau meetings and jointly defending those prices in ICC hearings. That was now illegal. True marketing was a foreign concept because the industry had so little historical control over two of the prime elements of marketing – the product/service and how it is priced. The industry historically did less "selling" of its services and more "solicitation" because prices were essentially non-negotiable. "Marketing Departments did not exist – what came closest to "marketing" occurred in Traffic Departments.

In addition to learning how to truly market and sell, learning how to operate in a deregulated environment against an aggressive, nimble and newly deregulated motor carrier industry competitor would also be a significant challenge. This increased the necessity to aggressively reduce costs.

The United States was falling into a severe recession in 1981. The greatest opportunity for near-term expense reduction would come from labor costs and that was the primary emphasis within BN under the leadership of Richard Grayson and William F. Thompson. "Top line" help was essential too. With the benefit of the Staggers Act, railroads gained limited relief from Common Carrier obligations providing greater flexibility to enter and exit businesses. It would also allow the railroad to differentiate prices and package services without regulatory oversight. Success in that revolutionary environment required a "marketing" rather than "traffic" orientation as well as an orientation focused on customers and return-on-assets. Bressler and his board wanted to form a holding company to eliminate the dominance of BN Railroad over the resources businesses and oversee and develop the company's lines of business. Bressler sought outside help to gain insights as to how a holding company could best be structured and operated. He also wanted ideas for how the BN Railroad could be best structured to take advantage of deregulation.

The 1980-1981 Booz, Allen & Hamilton Study

In late August, 1980, two months after the arrival of Bressler, two months before the implementation of the Staggers Act, and three months before the arrival of Grayson, Bressler retained the management consulting firm Booz Allen Hamilton (BAH) to undertake an analysis of BN and the companies it owned. It was conducted by six BAH consultants (from their general management and transportation practices, lead by Gary Silverman) and during the process of the study more than 150 internal interviews were conducted with stakeholders inside and outside the company. They visited all BN regions and operations and provided study progress updates to, among others, the Personnel Committee of BN's Board of Directors, Dick Bressler and Dick Grayson. BAH's Silverman presented the findings of their study to Burlington Northern's full Board of Directors on January 26, 1981.

The following is a summary of major points taken from the actual board presentation. [222]

- Based on 1979 results, BN is a $3.2 billion enterprise earning in excess of $175 million, pre-tax with approximately 81% of revenue coming from the railroad but only 23% of pre-tax profits
- BN revenue and growth rates were strong during the 1975-1979 period and among peers exceeded only by Union Pacific
- Returns, however, were lower than these peers with the BN generating profit margins, return on assets (ROA) and return on equity (ROE) of 4.6%, 2.8% and 5.4% respectively compared to the peer group that generated 10.9%, 6.7% and 11.9% respectively
- BN was highly leveraged and had limited ability to cover its debt service. Its total 1979 leverage of assets/net worth was 2.15 but its ratio of times interest earned was only around 2. This compared to industry averages of 2.15 and 6.53 and Union Pacific at 2 and 10. [223]
- BN's rail asset intensity was higher than its peers
- Among BN peers, companies with greater asset diversity experienced better performance

1979 Railroad	Profit Margin	ROA	ROE
Burlington Northern	1.6%	1.1%	1.9%
Union Pacific	11.7%	6.7%	9.5%
Southern Pacific	3.2%	1.9%	3.5%
Santa Fe	6.8%	4.6%	5.8%
Soo Line	14.9%	9.0%	12.5%
Missouri Pacific	9.5%	6.9%	10.9%
Industry Average	9.2%	5.8%	8.8%

1979 BN Subsidiary	Asset Turnover	Profit Margin	ROA	ROE
BN Railroad	0.7	1.6%	1.2%	1.9%
BN Transport	2.2	(.03)%	(6.0)%	(9.2)%
BN Air Freight	6.4	8.1%	51.7%	46.9%
BN Forest Products	1.7	32.2%	55.1%	53.3%
BN Oil & Gas	2.6	25.8%	67.1%	59.0%
BN Coal	2.8	80.2%	224.6%	205.5%
BN Land	*	72.6%	*	*

- BN's rail performance in terms of profit margins, ROA and ROE (below) was well below its peers in 1979 coming in at 1.6%, 1.1% and 1.9% respectively compared to the peer group's average of 9.2%, 5.8% and 8.8% (left). [224]
- BN's investments in fixed assets have produced above average revenue growth suggesting that sub-par returns reflect pricing and/or productivity
- BN's non-railroad businesses (except trucking) have performed significantly better than the railroad (left)[225]
- BN's business mix provides a solid foundation for future profitable growth with a railroad that has the largest network, a trucking business with a strong regional reputation, an air freight forwarder with strong domestic and international bases of operation, an energy business with vast coal and oil/gas properties and lease holdings, a forest products business with rich timber lands and diversified manufacturing, and real estate holdings with significant industrial and commercial properties
- The strengths of BN's organization at the time were a dedicated and experienced top management team, diversified products, services, markets and geography, a dominant position in a number of markets, an impressive asset base on which to build and technical and functional management depth

---

[222] Original Presentation by Gary Silverman to Burlington Northern's Board of Directors, of Booz Allen Hamilton's study of Burlington Northern entitled, "The Recommended Organization," St. Paul, MN, January 21, 1981, *Greenwood Collection*, Barriger Library at UMSL.

[223] Ibid, p. 7.

[224] Ibid, p. 10.

[225] Ibid, p. 12.

- The BN also had a number of weaknesses with its organization at the time including, a combined corporate and railroad staff that has weakened performance, inadequate strategic planning capabilities throughout the organization, the lack of the development of broad-gauged general managers within the railroad, a functional organization within the railroad that diluted its product/market focus and regions not provided the freedom to act as cost centers

BAH provided BN organization structure recommendations to yield:
- The framework to divide the business into stand-alone operating units corresponding to distinct product/market segments
- Improved ability to take a pragmatic and balanced approach to existing capital and people limitations
- Increased focus on the long-range strategic well-being of the enterprise
- Aggressive profit improvement and operating performance orientation within the railroad
- Increased attention on major profit and growth opportunities in the non-railroad businesses
- Clear and measurable objectives to reward management for superior results

Based on these factors, BAH recommended one organizational approach that they believed was superior to all other options. It called for the adoption of a holding company structure for these reasons:
- An objective appraisal of competing investment alternatives can only be made at the summit
- The nature of each business, and requirements for success, is substantially different one from another
- There is a need for single executive leadership for each of the major businesses
- The need for coordination within business units is significant to successfully bring together the requisite resources to allow each business to grow to its fullest potential
- The need for coordination across business units is minimal with the possible exception of land resources
- Each of the business units is large enough to justify some functional duplication with respect to financial, personnel, legal and public activities

Under this structure the holding company would focus their efforts on charting the future direction of the company and allocating resources. The responsibility for successful business operations would be in the hands of a CEO of each line of business. The relationship of the CEO's to corporate management would principally be in the areas of planning, obtaining financial resources and reporting financial results. Each line of business would be organized into business units as appropriate and have a full complement of staff resources to carry out its mission.

Using this concept as a model, BAH took the additional step and proposed an organization structure to the Board for the holding company, the railroad , and non-railroad BN businesses to address the strengths, weaknesses, opportunities and threats it was facing.

For BN Railroad, BAH noted that it was faced with two distinct challenges that would significantly impact future performance:
- Improving profitability and return on investment in each commodity market it served
- Reducing costs and increasing operating efficiency

For the Railroad, BAH recommended:[226]

---

[226] Ibid, p. 33.

- The creation of a two-person CEO/COO team to focus additional management expertise on improvement opportunities and allow for sharing of responsibility to ensure that adequate top management direction was given to revitalizing the organization and creating an entrepreneurial, profit-making environment. The COO and support staff would report to the CEO. Operations, Coal and Taconite, Marketing & Pricing and Sales & Service would report to the COO.[227] Specific areas of focus for the COO would be detailed plans with demanding operating and profit targets, a firmer grip on costs and improved efficiency to enhance the railroad's overall profit outlook, timely and responsive customer service consistent with marketplace requirements and sound management succession.
- A full scale staff capability including a chief planning and administrative officer leading strategic planning, management services, personnel, accounting/controls and labor relations
- A full scale headquarters operations staff responsibility for managing specific system-wide functions, planning, and monitoring performance, and supporting field operations in specialized disciplines
- Six operating regions (Chicago, Springfield, Twin Cities, Denver, Billings, Seattle/Portland) organized and managed as cost centers with increased control and authority over day-to-day operations
- The establishment of the Coal/Taconite business as a separate profit center
- Profit responsible business units corresponding to commodity based market segments – intermodal, grain, forest products, food and manufactured products
- A public affairs department handling public affairs, advertising and community relations
- A law department organized to support the business with pricing services, litigation and claims, tax and general counsel
- A materials function reporting to the CEO to manage inventory control, fleet and purchasing
- The C&S and FW&D railroads would remain as separate profit centers reporting to the rail CEO

Their recommendations dove deeper into the structure within each major organizational element. BAH stated that a new Marketing and Pricing approach was called for that entailed:
- Commodity based Business Units with profit responsibility reflecting the distinct and different needs of the railroad's various products/market
- Based on an analysis of BN's products, markets, customers, service requirements, train movement and other operational requirements the establishment of five commodity based business units focused on Grain, Forest Products, Food and Manufactured Products and Intermodal as well as a Pricing Services and Industrial Development groups.[228]
- The designation of strong general managers who would be strong advocates for their assigned product/market and provide the basis for an enhanced profit orientation throughout the railroad
- Responsibilities within each business unit for planning, economic analysis, market research and service planning
- In addition to marketing and pricing, expanded functional authority within each business unit for equipment and service planning that would interface with the operating department on issues impacting their products/market
- Product managers to focus on segments within the business unit, serving as an extension of the business unit general manager and as an advocate for his or her assigned commodity

---

[227] Ibid, p. 34.
[228] Ibid, p. 37.

- In recognition of its importance, having the Coal and Taconite business report directly to the COO and be organized similar to the other business units but with responsibilities for hopper car management.
- A Sales and Service group, maintaining its regional structure, that would support all business units and report to the COO

The Board accepted the general recommendations presented to them by BAH. Several weeks later Richard Bressler held a staff conference in Palm Springs, California that was attended by 45+ of BN's senior leaders and their spouses. At that meeting, Bressler told the attendees about the BAH study and about its presentation to the Board on January 26, 1981. This was three months after the passage of the Staggers Act and six months after the passage of the Motor Carrier Act. He said the Board accepted its recommendations and that the Board decided to present the establishment of Holding Company and company restructuring to BN's shareholders at the May, 1981 Annual Shareholders' Meeting. He added that it was "terribly important" that everyone understood the objectives, roles, players and how the organization would work in practice. He said it would not happen overnight and that some fine tuning would likely be required.[229]

Bressler then introduced BAH's Gary Silverman and he gave the Palm Springs group the same presentation he had given the BN Board. Following his presentation there was a question/answer session regarding details of the restructuring. The organizational restructuring of the railroad progressed immediately as it did not require shareholder approval.

Shareholders approved the formation of the holding company in May of 1981 and Bressler located BN's corporate headquarters in Seattle. The holding company operated along the lines recommended by BAH when it came to budgeting and capital resource allocation across operating divisions.

Louis Menk and Norman Lorentzsen Leave BN

When Richard Bressler was hired the plan was for Lou Menk to remain as board chairman until he turned 65 in 1984. Menk didn't wait that long. After Bressler left BN's board with the impression that the investments BN made in its coal business was likely to be Menk's Folly, he resigned from BN's board in December of 1981. Bressler assumed his position with no legacy oversight. The last remaining coal/railroad advocate, Norman Lorentzsen, also left BN's board. In May, 1982, Menk joined troubled International Harvester Company as its chairman and chief executive officer. He had served on the IH board since 1974. Menk replaced IH CEO and fellow BN board member Warren Hayford.[230] Hayford had served on BN's board since 1979.[231] Menk is credited with helping to rescue the faltering industrial giant over a 20 month period when it was on the brink of bankruptcy.[232]

---

[229] Transcript of R. M. Bressler's and Gary Silverman's comments related to the Booz Allen Hamilton Presentation at Burlington Northern's 1981 Staff Conference in Palm Springs, California, *Greenwood Collection*, Barriger Library at UMSL.

[230] Management Lineup at Harvester, Louis Menk, *The New York Times*, May 4, 1982, Accessed from: https://www.nytimes.com/1982/05/04/business/management-lineup-at-harvester-louis-menk.html, on March 17, 2023.

[231] Burlington Northern Inc., 1979 Annual Report, p. 3.

[232] Railroad Executive Louis W. Menk, 81, Chicago Tribune, November 28, 1999, Accessed from: https://www.chicagotribune.com/news/ct-xpm-1999-11-28-9911280216-story.html, on March 17, 2023.

Continued Rust Belt Decline

The transition of Louis Menk from BN to International Harvester was ironic. He shifted from one industry that had been significantly impacted by the decline of the Rust Belt to another one. IH had been one of the corporations contributing to the United States global manufacturing and agricultural dominance post WW-II. It would have been unthinkable to associate IH with bankruptcy decades earlier. Ohanian pointed out two key factors that brought such a transition about. These same factors impacted the railroad industry post WW-II: [233]

> First, recent theories of industry growth argue that lack of competitive pressure leads to low levels of industry innovation, productivity growth and industry growth. This follows from the idea that industries not faced with vigorous competition can maintain their market leadership without needing to pursue costly innovations, leading to stagnation in production.
> The second reason is that competitive pressure in Rust Belt product and labor markets was indeed very low between 1950 and 1980 ... Moreover, recent research suggests that Rust Belt industries were in fact able to limit competition by successfully lobbying for government protection from competition for much of this period.

He added:[234]

> Prior to 1980, market shares for Rust Belt auto, steel and rubber producers were as high as 90 percent. Price markups were also high. There is considerable evidence of oligopolistic behavior as Rust Belt industries successfully lobbied Congress for protection against both competitors and antitrust prosecution. The Rust Belt's ability to block competition and create monopolies within these industries allowed it to succeed without having to spend on innovation and improved practices. The region's auto, steel and tire producers did not adopt the latest technologies, and labor productivity growth averaged only about 2 percent per year prior to 1980, compared with nearly 3 percent per year in the rest of the United States.

His earlier cited comment also impacted the railroad industry:[235]

> Powerful labor unions such as the United Auto Workers and the United Steel Workers ensured that there was also very limited labor competition. The unions negotiated higher wages through frequent and effective use of strikes and strike threats.

Prime industrial railroad customers were progressively losing their competitive edge against global competitors, especially those from Germany and Japan whose industries were rebuilt with the latest technologies following WW-II. Pressures to open the United States to more international trade opened the door to aggressive competition. In a similar way, the deregulation of the Motor Carrier Industry and the subsequent growth on non-union truckload carriers increased the competitive pressure on the heavily unionized Railroad Industry.

---

[233] Ohanian, Lee E., Competition and the Decline of the Rust Belt, Federal Reserve Bank of Minneapolis, December 20, 2014, Accessed from: https://www.minneapolisfed.org/article/2014/competition-and-the-decline-of-the-rust-belt, on March 1, 2023.
[234] Ibid.
[235] Ibid.

United States heavy industry had to rebuild but ominous labor agreements and non-competitive labor costs drove the transition of manufacturing supported by the latest higher-quality and lower-cost technologies to the non-union south and offshore. Even regulations such as import quotas for automobiles that limited foreign competition for finished vehicles did not tend to hinder intermodal shipments of automobile parts. Unlike manufacturers, railroads could not "relocate" away from non-competitive labor agreements. While the manufacturing relocation transition was not beneficial, in general, for Burlington Northern and the railroad industry, it was good for the Intermodal business which also provided the most effective means to participate in the globalization of trade and to compete against a revitalized Motor Carrier Industry.

BN's establishment of an Intermodal Business Unit gave it the potential to capitalize on the new marketplace opportunities but actually being able to capitalize on them would prove to be incredibly challenging.

Chapter 7 – 1981 and the Birth of Burlington Northern's Intermodal Business Unit (IBU)

The Staggers Act, which essentially deregulated railroads, provided the opportunity for railroads' "Piggyback" business to be managed like a real business. Prior to deregulation, railroads were primarily locked to their rail network and had little to no service and pricing flexibility. Deregulation offered railroads the opportunity to aggressively pursue markets off of their rail network without the regulatory restrictions that inhibited innovation and responsiveness. In addition, truckers were historically viewed by railroaders as the hated enemy because of the magnitude of profitable rail market share they had "stolen" over the previous decades. Deregulation of the railroad and motor carrier industries provided unprecedented opportunities for railroads to work with truckers. "The idea that truckers and railroaders might cooperate to serve common customers was heresy within major railroads. Yet that was the theory behind the intermodal opportunity."[236] Intermodal was also the Railroad Industry's best method of taking advantage of international trade growth.

Bill Greenwood was the Superintendent of BN Railroad's high-profile Alliance Division at the time of the Booz Allen study. He had been there since being promoted in 1979 from his position as Terminal Superintendent of BN's Minneapolis/St. Paul terminal. It included the showcase Northtown hump yard which had been built at a cost of $44 million in 1976.[237]

Greenwood's rail industry experience dated back to 1956 when he was hired by the CB&Q to work as an agent-operator on its Aurora Division during summers through his college years. He worked in the banking industry following his 1960 graduation from Marquette University. He rejoined the Q in April of 1963 as a demurrage supervisor and then served in a number of operating department capacities including traveling car agent, assistant trainmaster, regional manager freight equipment, trainmaster, asst. superintendent of the Cicero terminal and staff asst. to the AVP operations. From that position he moved out of operations to become BN Railroad's Director of Corporate Planning.[238] His prior finance industry experience coupled with his ground-up CB&Q/BN operating and planning positions gave him an impressive resume of experiences (as well as exposure/visibility). He was on a fast-track preparing him for broader general management responsibilities.

The greatest challenge he faced on the Alliance Division was the need to effectively manage the massive construction efforts underway to dramatically increase BN coal carrying capacity while simultaneously keeping trains running to assure that cash was generated to finance the cash-starved railroad. As previously mentioned, in this capacity he had escorted Richard Bressler for a tour of the Division not long after his BN arrival in 1980. He had also hosted a pre-Bressler special train for BN's Board of Directors, on May 9 & 10, 1980. It gave directors first-hand exposure to what the Alliance Division coal capacity build-up entailed and was actually accomplishing.[239] Experiences such as these also provided more exposure to Greenwood.

---

[236] Katzenbach, Jon R., and Smith, Douglas K., *The Wisdom of Teams – Creating the High-Performance Organization*, Harvard Business School Press, Boston, 1993, p. 29.

[237] Burlington Northern: Super Railroad, *Corporate Report Magazine*, November 1980, p. 163.

[238] Katzenbach and Smith. p. 29.

[239] Mark Cane's personal calendar.

On a long list, one of the greatest individual challenges Greenwood faced in Alliance was employee alcohol abuse: [240]

> *I had a major, major problem on the division - alcohol abuse. They were so short of people, they were hiring anybody that could breathe, practically, and most of them were kids -- 19 years old, 20 years old. And my predecessor held his meetings with the union guys at the American Legion Club in the evening. So, you know what our team did? We fired 160 people for alcohol abuse in the first, probably 90 days I was there. It was awful.*

Fran Coyne (BN Human Resources) called Greenwood in Alliance and asked if he would be interested in heading the new "piggyback" business unit. They wanted someone with operating experience. Greenwood expressed interest and was brought in to interview in St. Paul with former commerce lawyer, and Intermodal Marketing leader, Dick Gleason who was BN's Marketing VP. The interview went well. After he returned to Alliance he called sixteen friends/former co-workers to get their opinion about this potential opportunity. According to Greenwood, fifteen of the sixteen said, "There is no way in Hell you should take this job because at best it was a high-risk dead-end venture. They said I would never be able to get back into operations and most likely I would just get fired. The person who suggested I take the job said if I only did a good job I would probably get fired anyway but if I did a great job I might survive. That person was Fran Coyne."[241] He was called with an offer from Gleason to lead the new Intermodal Business Unit (IBU) as its Senior Asst. Vice President, effective March 1, 1981, the official date of the implementation of the BAH organization recommendations in Marketing and Sales. In spite of the prevailing opinions: [242]

> *"Greenwood accepted because he believed deregulation promised an opportunity to move intermodal from obscurity to prominence. Deregulation, he knew, meant competition; competition meant newfound power for customers; and customers, he sensed, would demand far more innovative and responsive products, services and prices. In Greenwood's mind, the coming changes would shift business away from boxcars to the more flexible and effective containers and trailers offered by intermodal. He believed Burlington Northern intermodal could lead the way, so he quickly set about putting together a team to make it happen. He vastly underestimated, however, the range and difficulty of the obstacles that would crop up along the way."*

Greenwood said he accepted the job for two more reasons:

> *The first is that I did not like the Frisco culture and what it brought to the Operations Department. I didn't think I could survive in that environment anyway. Others had told me the new Executive VP Operations Bill Thompson would ask me how I would deal with an employee who was not doing what he was instructed to do. I said I would coach them and if they still did not perform I would take disciplinary action. I was told Thompson would tell me, "Wrong answer. You should take them behind a boxcar and kick the shit out of them." I could not work in that sort of culture so I wanted to get away from that. The second and more important reason*

---

[240] National Railroad Hall of Fame, William E. Greenwood, Chief Operating Officer (retired) Burlington Northern Railroad, Interview Transcript, July 30, 2020: Accessed from: https://www.nrrhof.org/greenwood-transcript, Accessed on May 7, 2022.

[241] Bill Greenwood interview with Mark Cane, May 1, 2022.

[242] Katzenbach and Smith, p. 29.

was that I perceived the intermodal opportunity as a "green field site" where I could really have an impact on the business for our customers, employees and shareholders in a way that could have a seismic impact – way beyond anything that I could do in Operations. I sensed that I would not be limited by boundaries that I couldn't overcome. I would be able to do things I couldn't do anyplace else – to shape the job the way I wanted it to be. [243]

Greenwood was asked why Gleason picked him for the job: [244]

I think there were four reasons. The first is that HR had me on a fast track list so if he hired me it would make him look good in the eyes of HR. Second, Gleason was a former CB&Q attorney and I was a former Q employee so he thought we could get along better in an era where former railroad affiliations were important. Third, I believe Gleason thought operating people were ignorant so he could control me. Fourth, intermodal involved a lot of operations so having an operating person on the job would help.

Greenwood also mentioned a fifth reason: [245]

And you want to make sure that this piggyback stuff wouldn't take business out of boxcars and put it in piggyback, because he wanted it to stay in boxcars. I didn't know that until much later.

Katzenbach and Smith accurately summed up BN's "piggyback" situation in early 1981: [246]

Burlington Northern typified railroading's reluctant approach to intermodal. At best it grudgingly considered it a necessary evil, not a real business opportunity. In the words of one observer, the railroad's intermodal infrastructure was pitiful. Burlington Northern had more than 160 truck-to-train connecting ramps spread around the country in a patchwork that bore no relation to customer needs or operational effectiveness. Each of these ramps received stepchild treatment from the boxcar-oriented, trucker-resistant railyard managers who operated them. In addition, Burlington's intermodal equipment was old, poorly maintained, and poorly operated. Most people associated with intermodal responsibilities tended to be undistinguished performers in dead-end careers. The company's intermodal results mirrored these efforts, and in 1981 Burlington Northern ranked at the bottom of the industry.

Bill DeWitt (about whom more will be discussed later) was working for the BNI Holding Company at the time as the Transportation Analyst covering BN Railroad, BN Airfreight and BN Transport. He said BNI had no interest in the railroad's intermodal business. Their big concerns were growing the resources portfolio, rail capital expenditures for coal, and extracting cash from the railroad to fund resources growth. [247]

---

[243] Bill Greenwood interview with Mark Cane, May 2, 2022.

[244] Ibid.

[245] National Railroad Hall of Fame, William E. Greenwood, Chief Operating Officer (retired) Burlington Northern Railroad, Interview Transcript, July 30, 2020: Accessed from: https://www.nrrhof.org/greenwood-transcript, Accessed on May 7, 2022.

[246] Katzenbach and Smith, p. 30.

[247] Email from Bill DeWitt to Mark Cane, February 24, 2022.

At that time there was no overall railroad responsibility for intermodal ramp operations as responsibility for them was dispersed across the operating regions and divisions, except for ramps on the former Frisco. The diffusion of responsibility for ramp management meant that there were no standard operating practices or performance standards. Some of the "piggyback" service offerings included motor carrier service included in the truck-rail-truck price that was provided through BN. There was no point of accountability for such highway service. Railroad information systems to support operations, service measurement and pricing were all set up for railcars that never left the tracks so they were essentially incompatible with the intermodal business model. Legacy costing systems were designed to support the railroad's carload business and utilized ICC-based regulatory formulas. Most of the costs attributed to a move were based on averages from across the enterprise instead of activity-based costs at the individual movement level based on that individual move's actual operating characteristics. As a result it was basically impossible to know for sure whether any individual piece of intermodal business was profitable or not. Intermodal just did not "fit" and was therefore looked at, more than not, as an illegitimate step-child. Those dedicated people whose job was to market and sell the business had no real champions within the business to act as Sponsors/Guardian Angels for them when it came to resource allocation, support systems development and service expansion and improvement.

In addition, among the major United States railroads, Burlington Northern had what was fundamentally the worst intermodal "franchise" in the industry. BN had great coal, grain and lumber franchises but the coal, grain and lumber tends to be mined and harvested where people don't live. The best intermodal markets are where there is the most industrial production, international trade (ports) and population. Even after the Frisco merger, BN had only one service lane with superior intermodal potential and that was between Chicago and the Pacific Northwest. The rest of the network consisted of relatively low-population markets that, for the most part, were too close to one another to make intermodal economically viable. Once Tom Finkbiner, who at the time was the leader of Norfolk Southern Railroad's intermodal business, said to Mark Cane, who at the time was the leader of BN's intermodal business, "I thought our intermodal franchise was bad but yours really doesn't go anywhere intermodal customers want to go."[248] While that was a bit of an exaggeration, it wasn't far off the mark compared to the Santa Fe's, Union Pacific's, Southern Pacific's who all served the vast California market as well as Conrail's intermodal franchise which covered key Atlantic ports and the population-dense U.S. Northeast. Therefore, BN's intermodal situation presented a monumental market challenge as well as a significant performance challenge. Yet, Greenwood and those he recruited to join him were not daunted. The first "outside" person Greenwood recruited to join him for this new challenge was with him in Alliance:

> Greenwood knew that few people, including his new boss (Dick Gleason VP-Marketing) shared his optimism or enthusiasm. Yet he could not build intermodal by himself. Not only were existing resources insufficient but, in an attitude critical to a potential team leader, he knew he did not have all the answers. He needed help and began by recruiting Mark Cane, a young, financially astute manager, to come with him from operations.[249]

Cane is the BN shareholder mentioned before who had supported the retention of BN earnings for investment into the coal franchise at the 1978 shareholders' meeting.

Cane recalled:[250]

---

[248] Tom Finkbiner comment to Mark Cane at Paine Webber's Intermodal Conference, March 9, 1993.
[249] Katzenbach and Smith, p. 31.
[250] Mark Cane's personal recollection.

My father worked as a cook on the dining cars of the Great Northern Railroad's passenger trains. He snuck me on the trains during several 1960s summers on the run between Chicago and Seattle so I could help him in the dining car's kitchen. That gave me some first-hand knowledge of a prime part of the GN/BN rail (and especially intermodal) franchise. Given my interest in, and experience on, the Great Northern, I bought one share of GN stock when I was 11 years old in 1966. It converted to a share of BN stock at merger time. That gave me access to quarterly and annual reports and the right to attend shareholder meetings and spurred my interest in business. I would get out of school on shareholder meeting days through high school, college and graduate school to attend the meetings. For three summers I worked as a cook, waiter or porter on Amtrak's Empire Builder passenger train between Chicago and Seattle to pay for my college education. This gave me even more knowledge about rail operations and this key BN corridor. A year before my college graduation I approached Robert Binger after a shareholder meeting ended and said I was interested in BN's management training program. Binger introduced me to Dave Ylkanen who was BN's VP Human Resources. Ylkanen said BN wouldn't have training program openings for the year of my college graduation due to the recession. He encouraged me to continue my education and get my MBA. I did that and before my MBA graduation I signed up for BN's on-campus interview. I think I was one of maybe two who signed up for BN interviews which showed how "popular" the idea of working for a railroad was at the time. BN's HR recruiter was Dick Hall who was a GN passenger train Dining Car Department "refugee" who knew my Dad really well. He remembered when my Dad had bootlegged "his kid" onto the trains and had him unofficially working on the dining cars in the 1960s.

Dick Hall and I spent most of the on-campus interview time reminiscing about the GN passenger train days. Dick set up second interviews with both the Corporate Planning (Ken Sanders and Ken Hoepner) and Operations Departments (Joe Galassi) at BN's Headquarters. Both Operations and Corporate Planning said they wanted to hire me and I was offered a position in the Corporate Management Training Program. I was given a choice of starting my career in Corporate Planning or field operations following the training program. I chose field operations in order to learn the business from the ground level. When I told my fellow graduate school classmates I accepted a job with Burlington Northern rather than other job opportunities I had they were shocked, saying things like, "railroads are dead." I told them all I saw with BN was opportunity.

Cane previously worked with Greenwood when he was BN's Minneapolis/St. Paul Terminal Superintendent. At the time Cane was an operations department trainee on the Twin Cities Region to prepare him for an Asst. Trainmaster position (comparable to an Asst. Plant Manager in the manufacturing world). Cane said:[251]

I was assigned to work in Greenwood's Northtown terminal for one week of my nine month training program. Instead of mostly riding switch engines and observing train humping operations I asked Greenwood if he had any special projects he wished he could pursue but he couldn't because he did not have the time or help. Greenwood said he had a lot of things he wished he could investigate including a study of lading damage being done during "hump" classification operations, an analysis of switchmen personal injuries, as well as an analysis of switch engine productivity within the terminal complex. I said I would be happy to help and because the list of opportunities was so long, and time to pursue them was so short, I asked

---

[251] Ibid.

Greenwood if he could arrange to have my training schedule modified. I said I was supposed to spend six weeks with area engineering which would include work such as copying property maps for prospective property/track leases and conducting grade crossing studies (counting cars that crossed the tracks per hour at specific grade crossings). I told Greenwood I thought I could get a good idea of what area engineering did within two weeks making four weeks possibly available for projects that would have a greater potential impact on BN service levels, productivity and shareholder return. Bill liked the idea and said he would see what he could do.

Greenwood called Fran Coyne (who had been supportive of Greenwood during his career) and asked about changing Cane's trainee schedule. Greenwood recalled: [252]

Fran reluctantly agreed to it but cautioned that it could get Cane into trouble if word got out that he requested a schedule change. Coyne said he would say I was the one who initiated the idea and then added, "Greenwood, if this doesn't work you might get fired." So, with more difficulty than one would expect, I arranged the time swap. Just before Cane moved to Galesburg, IL at the end of his training program I told him I would like to work with him in the future.

A year later, he was an Asst. Trainmaster in Galesburg. I had been transferred to run the Alliance Division and we needed a ton of help. I said I had a Trainmaster position for him that would focus on increasing the number of coal trains loaded per day, reducing the time it took to get trains across the division, increasing the productivity of the maintenance/engineering work force and assuring that the coal trains were run with their maximum car count. I asked if he would like to take it and he said yes. That's why he was in Alliance when I accepted the Intermodal job. I had a hint in January that I was going to get the Intermodal job and told Cane about it before it was public knowledge. I said I would try to get him on my team there too. From that time on we did preliminary work on possible intermodal strategies, especially related to hub centers and dedicated intermodal trains, before we moved to St. Paul.

Cane added:[253]

I was transferred effective March 1, 1981 but was not released from Alliance until March 15. Bill gave me the opportunity to help build-up BN's capability to participate in BN's potentially huge coal opportunity. Railroads still had a reputation of being a dying industry and coal could help reverse the decline and create growth. As unlikely as it seemed at the time, both Bill and I truly saw an equal or greater rail industry and BN opportunity with intermodal. In addition, both of us saw it as being a reliable source of business that wouldn't be as seasonal as the grain business BN was so reliant on. We believed it could help BN be even more of a growth story. We started to formulate preliminary intermodal ideas at his Alliance house.

When Greenwood first got to St. Paul he sized up his new employees: [254]

---

[252] Bill Greenwood interview with Mark Cane, March 18, 2022.

[253] Mark Cane's personal recollection.

[254] National Railroad Hall of Fame, William E. Greenwood, Chief Operating Officer (retired) Burlington Northern Railroad, Interview Transcript, July 30, 2020: Accessed from: https://www.nrrhof.org/greenwood-transcript, Accessed on May 7, 2022.

Well now I've been transferred in St. Paul. It was one of those deals, I had one week to get there. So, I take my team of marketing people out to lunch. And they all ordered martinis. I just got through firing people for two years for that. It was so uncomfortable. And then, some of them ordered two martinis. And some decided not to go back to the office with me because they wanted another drink! Oh, here we go again. So, I called a couple of them in. I said, "You need to go through treatment. You stop. You can't do it. I'll help you through treatment, and you won't lose your job. But if you don't do it, you'll lose your job, especially if you keep drinking on the job." So, a couple people took me up on it and went through treatment. It worked good.

So, everybody's talking a language I don't understand. They're talking about TCF territory in this territory, and that pricing thing and this pricing meeting. It's all pre-deregulation stuff, where the government controlled everything. I couldn't participate in discussions because I didn't know what they were talking about. And anyway, I started reading up on this new thing called 'deregulation.' I thought, "Oh, my gosh," you know, "We aren't ready for this." And I called the guys in, "What's this mean?" And they said, "Well, it doesn't mean hardly anything." "Well it's gotta mean something!"

Deregulation did mean something and he did find help among the employees he inherited.

Greenwood discovered another enthusiast in Emmett Brady, who had been in intermodal for many years. Unlike some of his lackluster colleagues, Brady immediately caught on to Greenwood's vision and demonstrated his readiness and energy to help in any way possible.[255]

As Dave Burns (another future IBU team member) put it, Brady was "an old-head from the now defunct Passenger Department, but who had the fire for one more charge, and also an extensive network with which to help turn adversaries into at least some cooperation."[256] Many of the "Passenger Department" refugees who had guaranteed Burlington Northern employment due to merger labor protection guarantees and were not "slotted" elsewhere were assigned to intermodal. Before Greenwood's arrival Brady had been responsible for intermodal forecasting and planning and he continued in that role within the IBU. "Emmett was worth his weight in gold as we would run into the many areas where we needed help from other departments."[257]

Quite by accident, Greenwood hired a third man, Ken Hoepner, from outside the company. Shortly after taking his new job, Greenwood received a call from Hoepner, an old friend with both BN operations and strategic planning experience, who wanted to use Greenwood as a job reference. But Greenwood had other ideas.

"I was telling Bill about the new job I wanted," recalls Hoepner, "when there was this big silence at the other end of the phone. I thought, 'Jeez, he's hung up.' So I said, 'Bill, are you still there?'"

"He said, 'Yeah, I'm here.' Then he went on. 'Listen, forget about that new job. Let me tell you about this intermodal opportunity. We want to do something that has never been done before.

---

[255] Ibid, p. 31.

[256] Burns, Dave, Intermodal Days 1982-1992, *The BN Expediter*, Volume 26, Number 4, Friends of the Burlington Northern Railroad, October 2018, p. 10.

[257] Ibid, p. 12.

I don't know a lot about this – we're going to have to define it from day one. But we're putting together a team and I'd like you to join us.'"

Sensing a rare opportunity as well as the chance to join his old friend, Hoepner said okay. He joined Greenwood, Brady and Cane, he remembers with a chuckle, on April Fools' Day, 1981.[258]

Hoepner earned his Master's Degree in Industrial Management at the University of Wisconsin–Stout and following graduation was hired directly into BN's Corporate Planning Department. He worked on Bill Greenwood's BN Corporate Planning team and succeeded him as Director after Greenwood got transferred to his Terminal Superintendent position. Hoepner had interviewed Mark Cane for a possible Corporate Planning position when he was being recruited by BN so they knew one another when Greenwood brought them together. For career development, Hoepner had been transferred from Corporate Planning to a position as BN's Minnesota Division Asst. Superintendent – Transportation where he was responsible for train and yard operations across the division. Hoepner was highly regarded and there was a desire to better prepare him for broader general management responsibility. In the BN culture he needed operating experience which is why he left his staff career-track and took a line position. While he was on that job he was recruited by the Drott Division of J.I. Case to be their Manager-Business Planning in Racine, Wisconsin.[259] He had called Greenwood while he was on that position that which resulted in Hoepner's 1981 April Fools' Day experience.

Greenwood, Cane, Brady and Hoepner had first-hand knowledge of "Piggyback's" poor reputation within the BN for low profitability and a concern that if its capabilities were built-up it would poach carload business already carried by BN at higher profitability levels. They all intimately knew Piggyback business was also a hassle for the operating department to deal with because it utilized specialized and inconvenient operating ramps and did not work well within the flow of the other non unit-train businesses. As Dave Burns said of his former operating department experience, "I did not care so much for what was on the train, nor even how much, as I did about running it on time. Truth be told, I liked light trains. It made meeting our train and performance goals easier to meet."[260] The "messiness" of the piggyback business complicated operating department goal performance achievement.

Internal support was essential for the business to actually become a true business and get the resources it needed to not only defend newly vulnerable BN market share - as a result of motor carrier deregulation – but to also have an infrastructure capable of going on offense in a deregulated market to gain market share. Greenwood, Brady, Hoepner and Cane all knew that it was imperative that the BN intermodal product be driven by what was marketable and not just what the railroad produced. That was counter to railroad culture which was of the mentality that one had to sell what one produced as opposed to producing what one could profitably sell. They embraced the Booz Allen Hamilton vision that BN had to become a market driven organization and that it was up to the new Strategic Business Units to lead that effort.

By this time they had settled on three major intermodal strategies – hub centers, dedicated trains with new technology equipment and "marketing packages." In addition, the team also settled on an overall

---

[258] Katzenbach and Smith, p. 31.

[259] Kenneth R. Hoepner Resume, 1995.

[260] Burns, Dave, Transportation Department Days 1981-1982, *BN Expediter*, Volume 25, Number 4, Friends of the Burlington Northern Railroad, 2017, p. 13.

vision / objective that would be accomplished through the successful implementation of the three basic strategies:

> *By 1986 become the recognized intermodal leader in terms of customer service, innovation, market share and profitability.*

Between 1974 and 1979 BN's non-coal, non-grain and carload (non-intermodal) merchandise business had grown revenue as follows compared to intermodal:

BN Carload Merchandise vs. Intermodal Revenue Performance (current $millions)[261]

	1974	1975	1976	1977	1978	1979
Intermodal	68.9	63.1	82.2	110.5	112.6	140.8
Non-IM Merchandise	914.1	890.9	1031.8	1079.5	1199.4	1383.2
Rate Increases	18%	11%	4%	9%	7%	8.3%

Every year while regulated, one of the most important things BN management, and the management of other railroads, reported to shareholders and Wall Street in annual reports was the level of rate increases allowed by the ICC. Not all of the permitted rate increases were realized due to competitive conditions. BN's 1979 Annual Report stated that during the 1975–1979 period the ICC allowed rate increases of 54%, for BN's merchandise business but the "effective yield" of what was actually realized was 40%. During this same period BN's current dollar merchandise revenue grew from $890.9 million to $1,383.2 million or 55% so in constant (non-inflated) dollars merchandise revenue grew only 15% or an average of 3% a year. Along this line, in BN's 1981 Form 10-K the company stated, "During the 1979-1981 period, Railroad was authorized to place into effect a number of general freight rate increases. These aggregated approximately 41% on an annualized basis. However, the effective compounded yield of the increases placed into effect by Railroad amounted to approximately 33%, as it was necessary to impose certain hold-downs and limitations from authorized increases."[262] Immediately before Motor Carrier industry deregulation the carload merchandise business was barely maintaining share.

Meanwhile, economic, demographic and logistics trends (with the increased competitiveness of trucks utilizing a completed and comprehensive Interstate Highway System) were driving the relocation of manufacturing, warehousing and distribution centers away from rail-served sites. The movement towards off-shore manufacturing to take advantage of lower labor costs was blossoming. Industry rail sidings were being paved-over to create truck loading/unloading docks. Sustained soaring inflation was driving customers' attention to management of not just transportation rates but total distribution costs, including inventory carrying costs and safety stocks. That was resulting in the desire for more frequent shipments of smaller (less than railcar load) lot sizes with a premium placed on consistent, reliable service that railroads had difficulty providing. In addition to gaining deregulation of prices and routes, motor carriers were on the verge of gaining productivity-enhancing increases in trailer lengths, weights and widths that made them an even more formidable competitor for rail merchandise shipments. As previously mentioned, the Surface Transportation Assistance Act of 1982 was about to allow motor carriers to increase their highway Gross Vehicle Weight (GVW) limits (productivity) by 9.2%, trailer width by 6.3% from 96" to 102" and trailer length by 6.7% from 45' to 48' across the United States and with an additional uniform increase in trailer lengths to 53' on the horizon.

---

[261] Burlington Northern Inc., 1974-1979 Annual Reports and Forms 10-K.
[262] Burlington Northern Inc., 1981 Form 10-K. p. 7.

BN simply did not have an intermodal offering from the standpoints of quality or capacity that was capable of protecting its merchandise business from more aggressive motor carrier competition that was better suited to compete in the rapidly changing competitive environment. This is the major threat BN's new intermodal team had to convince BN's leadership was real and imminent. It wouldn't be enough to convince the rail CEO that the threat was real and grave. The leaders of every functional group of the railroad had to be convinced of the reality and imminence of the existential threat if intermodal would ever get the resources and support it needed to combat it.

Greenwood arrived in St. Paul from Alliance on March 1, 1981. Hoepner arrived from Racine, Wisconsin on April 1. Cane arrived from Alliance on March 17. They joined Brady who was already there and:

> *"… immediately turned their attention to a number of priorities. They set out to transform their business unit from a dumping ground of low performers to a more proactive, talented group of people – hardly an easy task. In addition, they methodically sought and used internal and external speaking engagements to counter intermodal's poor image. Finally, they set up an intermodal task force with representatives from across the railroad to study the intermodal opportunity and develop a truly cross-functional strategy for seizing it."[263]*

Greenwood added:

> *We met every morning at eight o'clock. And we had about a 10-15-minute meeting; discuss the day's activities, how we were going to go. We developed strategic plans.[264]*

In addition to countering intermodal's poor image, the speaking opportunities were also used to explain to railroad employees what was going on in the competitive world – how customers were changing their logistics patterns out of necessity, what motor carriers were doing with their freedoms gained through deregulation and what competing railroads were doing. A big focus was on trying to get BN employees to see the customer as a cherished asset instead of a hassle – the reason for the BN's existence. Reflecting this challenge is an experience Bill Greenwood had while talking with management employees of an operating division where a roadmaster (someone responsible for maintaining a designated geographic area of BN trackage) said to him: [265]

> *"If we didn't have all these damned trains I could get my track up to standard and keep it that way." This guy meant well but he thought his job was to have perfect track without regard to what the track was for. He was totally focused on his track and he had no concern for the customer. We struggled with that sentiment across the railroad. There was simply little to no focus on the customer.*

On April 6 and 7, 1981, Greenwood led an Intermodal Business Unit (IBU) staff meeting off-site in St. Paul. It was an opportunity for him to share his vision for the business as well as frankly discuss the obstacles that the fledgling unit faced. It gave the new team the opportunity to share their views and for the new team to bond. This was followed by similar sessions with people involved in intermodal

---

[263] Katzenbach and Smith, p. 32.

[264] National Railroad Hall of Fame, William E. Greenwood, Chief Operating Officer (retired) Burlington Northern Railroad, Interview Transcript, July 30, 2020: Accessed from: https://www.nrrhof.org/greenwood-transcript, Accessed on May 7, 2022.

[265] Bill Greenwood interview with Mark Cane, March 18, 2022.

field ramp operations, field intermodal equipment distribution and intermodal field sales in Chicago on June 23-24, Memphis on June 30, Denver on July 14-15 and Seattle on July 28-29. The vast majority of these people were not a part of the formal IBU organization and yet they were essential team members.

The team was already starting to investigate new equipment that could revolutionize the way intermodal business was handled. On May 29 the brash and visionary Robert Reebie, the founder of the RoadRailer technology (highway trailers equipped with retractable rail wheels that hooked together to form a train without cars under the trailers) and custodian of an operating set of RoadRailer trailers, came to St. Paul to brief the new IBU team on his views of the future of intermodal and the role his technology should play in it.

Greenwood also reached outside the company for help in figuring out how to take advantage of deregulation to tackle the new intermodal challenge: [266]

> *Then I called our biggest piggyback shipper, guy by the name of R.C. Matney. I said, "RC, have you been reading up on deregulation and what it means for you?" "Yeah," he says, "I have." I said, "I think it's a huge opportunity for us." I said, "Let's get together." So, we got together, he said, "I tell you what. If you will write me a one-page contract, I will guarantee you ten new trailer loads of business a day from Chicago to Seattle and back, and here's the price I have to have it at." Now at that time, our price was something like $3,000 for a load coming east, and it was like $100...no, it was $3,000 coming east. I think it was almost $6,000 round trip, is what I recall. Well he wanted a price of, I think, $3,000 round trip, something like that. Well, I went through the math and thought, "Well hell, we don't have any business now at the prices we have, so what difference does it make what the price is? He had a third-party logistics company called National Piggyback. And so, anyway, we wrote the elements of the contract that we thought we had to have in it on my back porch in my home near Minneapolis, and I took it to our law department. And they said, you know, there's no such thing as one-page contract in our business. I said, "Well let's try." And a guy by the name of Doug Babb who was like the number two lawyer -- good guy -- he worked with me on it. He gave us a one-page contract. And, so we got that approved. Within a month we're handling 100 National Piggyback trailers a week of business between Chicago and Seattle, round trip. A hundred!*

On June 15, a Marketing strategy session was held with BNRR president and CEO Grayson. By this day BN's stock price had fallen to $53 per share, 18.5% lower than what it was on the day the new IBU was created, as the negative effects of deregulation and a weakening economy were beginning to be felt. It was a high risk experience for Greenwood because he had only been on the job for such a short period of time. The IBU's outline of BN's market and competitive threats were presented to Grayson along with the vision of what a thoroughly redesigned BN intermodal business would look like. Grayson was very concerned about intermodal profitability but equally concerned about the competitive impact of deregulation on BN's carload businesses. That gave Greenwood the opportunity to plant the seeds with him for the desired Intermodal Task Force.

Following that meeting Greenwood took opportunities to speak with Grayson and Sr. VP Marketing and Sales Ivan Ethington about BN's perceived risks in more detail. This did not endear him to Dick Gleason

---

[266] National Railroad Hall of Fame, William E. Greenwood, Chief Operating Officer (retired) Burlington Northern Railroad, Interview Transcript, July 30, 2020: Accessed from: https://www.nrrhof.org/greenwood-transcript, Accessed on May 7, 2022.

or particularly to Ethington who had a close relationship with Gleason (who even handled Ethington's personal income tax preparation).[267] Greenwood found a receptive ear with Grayson however. He presented the idea of a task force to Grayson and he gave it a green light. He asked Greenwood to come up with a task force plan.

A letter was prepared by Ken Hoepner with the assistance of Greenwood, Brady and Cane, from Grayson to Ethington (and copied to Garland (VP and Treasurer), Engle (VP Law) and McGee (CEO BN Transport) on July 17. It stated: [268]

> *As a follow-up to the strategic plan presentations made to me by the business units of the Marketing Department and as a follow-up to the questions generated at that meeting, I ask that an Intermodal Task Force be formed immediately to identify, analyze and review the following:*
>
> - *Any vulnerable portions of our railcar business that could be diverted to the highway during the next few years.*
> - *The steps that would be needed to accelerate BN's intermodal program and therefore protect any business from being diverted to the highway.*
> - *An estimate of the savings to BN that could be achieved if a more aggressive intermodal effort is adopted by BN.*
>
> *It would be appropriate for W.E. Greenwood to organize the Intermodal Task Force and be its project leader. A report should be provided by October 1 followed by a presentation before November 1, 1981. The Task Force should submit its findings and a set of recommendations for BN railroad management to consider.*
>
> *Mr. Greenwood will be following up soon with you and those getting a copy regarding proposed participants to work as Task Force members from the several departments of the railroad.*

The fact that Greenwood was able to get this accomplished with Grayson without going through the normal chain of command didn't endear him to his new boss Dick Gleason. Greenwood was car-pooling to/from work with Gerald Davies, the leader of the new Food and Manufactured Products Business Unit. Davies and Greenwood would share ideas for how to work with Gleason. Davies said he would just do what Gleason wanted to avoid getting fired. Greenwood said he would do what he thought was right for the customers and shareholders. Davies said Greenwood was an idealist and would tell him Gleason did not like him and he would probably get fired.[269]

Meanwhile, while BN was positioning itself to possibly emphasize and build its "piggyback" business, the Union Pacific was taking the opposite tack:[270]

> *With deregulation phasing in during the 1980s, intermodal was de-emphasized by Union Pacific. Marketing, pricing, and managing the door-to-door service was outsourced to shippers' agents and intermodal marketing companies.*

[267] Bill Greenwood interview with Mark Cane, March 18, 2022.
[268] R.C. Grayson letter to I.C. Ethington, July 17, 1981, *Greenwood Collection*, Barriger Library at UMSL.
[269] Bill Greenwood interview with Mark Cane, May 2, 2022.
[270] Leachman, Rob, The Great Forwarder Fleet, *The Streamliner*, Union Pacific Historical Society, Volume 36, Number 3, Summer, 2022, p. 35.

Chapter 8 - The 1981 Intermodal Task Force

The July 17, 1981 Grayson letter officially launched the Intermodal Task Force effort.[271] A key restriction put on Greenwood was that only a defensive plan could be formulated by the task force – an offensive plan to grow intermodal share was forbidden. Grayson and Ethington also gave the OK for the desired composition of the task force's 15 member executive "Review Group" who would be expected to literally sign the final task force report - to signify their endorsement of its analysis and recommendations. The task force was actually formed on July 22, 1981.

The intermodal team had already formulated a set of strategies and desired next steps. Given the indifference of some company leaders, and outright animosity of others towards intermodal, it was believed it was essential that these ideas had to appear to come from others. Leaders in the company outside of intermodal had to buy-in to the risks the company faced and the opportunity intermodal represented. To gain corporate buy-in/sponsorship the task force Review Group consisted of top executives of Information Systems, Operations Services, Strategic Planning, Sales & Service, Labor Relations, Marketing & Pricing, Transportation, Engineering, Treasury, Government Affairs, Law, Mechanical and Costs and Statistics with Greenwood being the project manager. The first Review Group meeting was held on July 31. They held subsequent meetings on August 18, September 1, September 15, October 1, October 15 and October 22.

A description of how deregulation of the motor carrier industry was impacting the market was given to the Task Force team on August 18. In it, Larry Schwarz, BN Transport's Sr. Vice President Marketing, stated that since deregulation of routes and rates had become effective, motor carriers had been using rate cutting as a "marketing" tool. He said there was no real innovative rate making to-date and that the industry had an over-capacity and underutilization situation. Recall that the new Motor Carrier Act eliminated the control of the ICC over markets carriers operated in. Schwarz added that "Over 3,000 new carriers had entered the market since July 1, 1980 compared to an average of 500 per-year prior to that" and that there were, "Now over 30 Nationwide Motor Carriers versus a 'handful' prior to Act."[272]

As recommended by the new IBU team of four, and engineered by Greenwood, the responsibility for the study of competitive threats, the assessment of the intermodal opportunity and the cross-functional strategy for seizing the opportunity was "owned" by fifteen cross-functional executives.

> *"I was assigned as the transportation function's representative to the task force," says Dave Burns, who joined Greenwood's team from the task force in early 1982. "The intermodal guys had this smart idea that if what they thought was going to happen to the railroad was stuff coming out of boxcars and going to trailers, they'd be much better off if they could get the rest of*

---

[271] All of the details related to the Intermodal Task Force findings and recommendations, including recommended next steps come from two original documents: "Burlington Northern Intermodal Task Force Report," and "The Intermodal Task Force, A Presentation of the Results, November, 1981," *Greenwood Collection*, Barriger Library at UMSL.

[272] Larry J. Schwarz, BNT's Role in Stepped-Up BN Intermodal Program Planning Meeting 8/18/81, *Greenwood Collection*, Barriger Library at UMSL.

Burlington Northern to say it rather than the intermodal business unit sounding like prophets of doom."[273]

In addition to Burns, more than forty people from every function and business unit participated at a working level on the task force.[274] It had three specific objectives:

1. To identify the vulnerable portions of BN Railroad's volume.
2. To define an intermodal system that could protect the vulnerable portion of the business.
3. To assess potential savings of a stepped-up intermodal program on:
   - Classification yard use and construction
   - Locomotive design, sizing, and fleet size
   - Freight car fleet size
   - Mechanical car maintenance needs for shops and yards
   - Track structure and maintenance needs
   - Train crew consists
   - Clerical and administrative requirements

Regarding objective #1, $425.0 million of Food and Manufactured Products, and $65.7 million of Forest Products revenue ($490.7 million in total) was identified as "worst case" estimate of BN carload business threatened by diversion to motor carrier by 1985.[275]

Grand Total Divertible BNRR Business (1981 Base)

Forecast Group	Divertible Tons (mm)	Divertible RTMS (B)	Divertible Cars	Divertible Revenue ($MM)
Food & Mfg.	13.853 mm	10.515 B	344,545	$425.017 mm
Forest Prod.	2.132 mm	1.964 B	49,400	$65.732 mm
Grand Total	15.985 mm	12.479 B	393,945	$490.749 mm

This amounted to 28% of BN's non-coal, non-grain and non-intermodal revenue using a 1981 baseline and $164.2 million of estimated profit margin contribution (see Appendix 1). Mark Cane recalled:[276]

> *I was the IBU's planning manager at the time. One of my task force responsibilities was to work with Dick Lewis and his team and the planning managers of the other business units on the divertibility study. Dick was the AVP Marketing Services and his team coordinated business forecasting. Dick did a great job of making the exercise a serious one because Dick Gleason, Gerald Davies' Food and Manufactured Products and Gary Schlaeger's Forest Products business units didn't believe in the exercise and didn't support it. Gleason insisted that the Task Force report stress that the estimated $491 million of divertible revenue and $164 million of divertible margin was based on an assumption that the F&MP and FP BUs did nothing to prevent diversion. He seemed to be more concerned about protecting those business units than the business itself. They were basically calling us ignorant "operating people" and "Chicken Little" shouting that the "sky is falling." We in the IBU were alarmed. We saw fundamental shifts in shipping practices occurring rapidly that just took rail car shipments out of the picture. We witnessed shippers*

---

[273] Katzenbach and Smith, p. 32.

[274] Ibid.

[275] Burlington Northern Intermodal Task Force Report, November, 1981, p. 3. See Appendix 1 for a detailed report of estimated "worst case" divertible business, *Greenwood Collection*, Barriger Library at UMSL.

[276] Mark Cane's personal recollection supported by Task Force documents.

paving over their railcar loading docks and reducing the size of shipments because astronomical interest rates caused soaring inventory carrying costs. When we mentioned this we were told we were too new to Marketing to know better and "this too shall pass," while we clearly saw long term structural supply chain management changes taking place. We knew BN Railroad's total pre-tax income in 1980 was $165 million and the estimated $164 million divertible business margin would more than wipe that out because the cash contribution associated with the divertible business significantly exceeded its reported margin. Diverted business would not immediately eliminate train starts because trainloads of business wouldn't be lost. Trains running shorter meant there would be substantial operating costs that the study didn't allocate to divertible business. That would reduce the profitability of the remaining business and we couldn't estimate the impact of that. Having the study's integrity discounted was very frustrating.

Regarding Task Force objective #2:

- BN's 140+ intermodal ramp network be consolidated into a network of 34 key Hub Centers over a five year period. Inefficient ramps would be closed and high potential facilities would be developed that would serve as the hub for business within a 150 mile radius that would be drayed to and from that hub. The IBU wanted each hub to be run by a sales and operating oriented individual from the motor carrier industry to facilitate entrepreneurial thinking and a spirit of blending the best of rail and truck service. Each hub would also have a profit and loss statement to measure performance and provide a tool to help facilitate profit improvements. Each hub would be mechanized with lift on/off equipment and "circus" style operations would cease. Capital for two Chicago overhead cranes and seven side-lift devices would be needed for 1982.
- New intermodal equipment was tested by task force members and the task force decided that because of the density of the divertible traffic, RoadRailers (a concept where the highway trailer also moved directly on the rails as a "car" within a trailer train) would not be recommended because it was more suited to low density loads such as parcels. The task force recommended the acquisition and deployment of ten-platform light-weight articulated intermodal cars (Ten-Pack/Itel Impack). These cars had been heavily tested by Santa Fe and they had used them successfully for several years.
- The task force identified a network of twelve key market corridors that should be served by dedicated intermodal trains that would eliminate "humping" of intermodal cars as well as unnecessary switching and most intra-train slack action.
- The task force identified how important service would be in a stepped-up intermodal program. That would require the fine-tuning of schedules focused more on consistent and reliable performance of a shipment from origin Hub cut-off to destination Hub availability than only on-time train performance. The Staggers Act did not deregulate railroad costs so it was assumed that trains would be manned by four-man crews. No favorable agreements allowing a crew size reduction were envisioned. Cabooses were mandatory due to labor agreements so they were also factored into the plan.

A five year equipment and facilities capital plan was also recommended. It included:
- $16.6 million for 38 Hub Center lift devices (3 overhead cranes and 35 side-lifts)
- $271 million for new trailers (if purchased) or $63 million per year (by 1986) of annual trailer rental fees if a purchase option was not pursued.

- Leasing of Ten-Pak/Impack cars at a rate of $94.80 per day per 10 platform car which would cost $40.6 million per year by 1986.
- $86.4 million for the development of Hub Centers through 1986 starting with $15.7 million in 1982.
- $10 million for six minicomputers and the development of a networked Intermodal Hub Management information system.

1986 Annual Divertible Railcar and Intermodal Cost Comparison (1981$)

Cost Element	Railcar Option	Intermodal Option	Rail to IML Change
Line Haul	$183.0 mm	$177.3 mm	$-5.7 mm
Car Ownership	$91.8 mm	$114.3 mm	$+22.5 mm
Switching	$36.3 mm	$7.3 mm	$-29.0 mm
Station Clerical	$7.0 mm	$6.9 mm	$-.1 mm
Loss and Damage	$5.3 mm	$1.1 mm	$-4.2 mm
General Overhead	$1.6 mm	$2.2 mm	$+.6 mm
Special Services	$1.4 mm	$7.6 mm	$+6.2 mm
Pick-up & Delivery	0	$13.7 mm	$+13.7 mm
Ramp & Deramp	0	$15.5 mm	$+15.5 mm
Total Cost	$326.6 mm	$345.9 mm	$+19.5 mm

The task force estimated that it would actually be more profitable for BN to handle the vulnerable business via dedicated intermodal trains rather than via mixed freight trains. 1986 costs associated with the intermodal option for line haul, car ownership, switching, station clerical, loss & damage, general overhead, special services, intermodal drayage, and hub ramp / deramp were projected to be $345.9 million for the intermodal option versus $326.6 million for the carload option, an annual increase of $19.5 million.[277]

On the revenue side, however, the business was assumed to be priced at motor carriers' full cost levels. That resulted in projected annual revenue from divertible business of $588.5 million for the intermodal option versus $490.7 million for the carload option, resulting in an annual divertible business revenue gain of $97.8 million. Thus, the vulnerable business' 1986 projected intermodal option annual margin was $78.3 million higher than the projected the 1986 carload option.[278]

1986 Contribution Margin As Stated in Annual 1981 Dollars (Millions)

	Railcar Option	Intermodal Option	Railcar to Intermodal Change
Contribution Margin (Revenue less Expense)	$164.3 mm	$242.6 mm	$+78.3 mm

There were other associated financial impacts from the plan.

- By 1986 the plan would result in a surplus of 14,100 freight cars that could be sold for $21.2 million.
- By 1986 there would be a savings of 10 locomotives countered by the need for 22 more cabooses for a net capital savings of $7.5 million+.
- In addition, the ideal locomotive identified for intermodal trains was the four-axle GP-39-2 which cost 9.5% less than the standard six-axle SD-40-2. It would be more fuel efficient and also have lower operating/maintenance costs.

---

[277] Burlington Northern Intermodal Task Force Report, November, 1981, p. 13, *Greenwood Collection*, Barriger Library at UMSL.
[278] Ibid, p. 15.

- The maintenance cost for a 10-platform Ten-Pak car was 40% less than the per-platform equivalent standard two-platform car.
- Because intermodal freight bills were paid faster than conventional freight bills it was estimated that BN would take advantage of 30 days faster payment on $490 million of revenue. During the task force time of explosive inflation it was estimated that faster bill collection would be worth a recurring $6.0 million a year (assuming a 15% simple interest rate).

The key conclusions of the interdepartmental task force were that:
- BN was subject to a substantial loss of business, that the business units had plans in place to counter the risks (which was subject to debate but was also a politically "untouchable" topic) and those plans needed time to be implemented
- Intermodal was a profitable alternative, that new equipment could reduce intermodal costs
- Numerous items needed further research, that intermodal still had to pass ROI tests
- It was imperative that BN prepare for a transition.

These were the task force's recommendations and proposed next steps:
- Establish a system to identify and monitor when, where, and why changes occur to the vulnerable business.
- Identify which parts of the vulnerable business were profitable, including the refinement of a costing system for intermodal business by the Costs and Statistics Department.
- Lower the costs of BN's Intermodal operation.
- Have the IBU, Transportation, Mechanical, Engineering and Industrial Engineering staffs work together to thoroughly test equipment proposed for use in intermodal service such as the Ten-Pac concept car, the Budd LoPac double stack car, the Trailer Train 4-Runner car and GP39-2 locomotives.
- Have the Operating Dept., Labor Relations and the IBU work together to identify appropriate agencies to consolidate in accordance with the "Hub Concept Plan" and prepare a time-phased plan to do so.
- Have Mechanical and Transportation continue to use the new intermodal equipment so as to become more effective in using and maintaining the equipment.
- Have the IBU work with the Operating Dept., Industrial Engineering, Engineering, and Station Services staffs to prepare an effective year-by-year, detailed plan for the investment in intermodal terminal facilities and terminal equipment to lower BN's operating costs.
- Coordinate BN's acquisition plan for new railcars, intermodal equipment, and trailers with BN's equipment retirement plans.
- Have the Marketing & Pricing Dept. accelerate development of its equipment planning system for fitting equipment demand with proper fleet size.
- Have the Marketing & Pricing Department work with the Operating Dept. on a potential program for the acceleration of surplus railcar retirements.
- Have BN departments work with Trailer Train on an accelerated basis for the testing and acceptance of new intermodal car concepts.
- Prepare a total marketing package for the vulnerable business.
- Have the Business Units work with Transportation on a Service Planning system that is oriented to meeting BN Customers' demand.
- Have Sales & Service Department work with the Business Units to identify the most vulnerable, profitable business and then prepare a marketing package tailored to having BN retain the business and market share.

- Have Business Units work with Public Affairs Department on an appropriate advertising campaign to handle the transition to Intermodal.
- Have the Sales & Service Department and the Business Units jointly develop a system to measure the effectiveness of the individual marketing packages that are implemented.
- Build the commitment of BN's employees for the total marketing package for the vulnerable business.
- Have W. E. Greenwood work with the Operating Dept. and Labor Relations Department to prepare a formal presentation for use with union leaders and the union members.
- Have departments work with Human Resources Department on development of training programs for supervisors to effectively communicate the role each employee has in making the railroad successful in any transition.

The Intermodal Task Force:

Mr. G. R. Clinkenbeard
Mr. B. C. Davidson
Mr. M. M. Donahue
Mr. W. H. Egan
Mr. A. E. Egbers
Mr. R. M. Gleason
Mr. T. C. Whitacre
Mr. R. G. Brohaugh
Mr. H. P. Burton
Mr. A. M. Fitzwater
Mr. W. R. Power
Mr. W. D. Smith
Mr. R. E. Taylor
Mr. L. L. Van Zinderen
Mr. W. E. Greenwood, Project Manager

The fifteen members of the Intermodal Task Force (left) signed the findings and broad recommendations of the Final Intermodal Task Force Report on October 30, 1981.[279]

On October 20, 1981 Ivan Ethington (Executive VP Marketing and Sales) sent a letter to W.F. Thompson (Executive VP Operations), R.F. Garland (Sr. VP Administration and Planning), R. M. Gleason (VP Marketing and Greenwood's boss) and W. H. Egan (VP Sales and Service). In it he told them that the Intermodal Task Force Final Report would be delivered by Bill Greenwood to Dick Grayson and himself on November 18. He asked that they all attend and they did. In spite of the serious findings of the task force, and the fact that senior leaders in all of their organizations had signed off on its findings and recommendations, it landed with a thud. While there was concern about the implications of the findings for BN, there was even more doubt about their validity. There was an overriding concern about the profitability of the piggyback business with a focus on the rearview mirror instead of the future and what the task force said had to be done to essentially re-make "piggyback" into a vibrant "intermodal" business. No authority was given to proceed with the Hub Center strategy and tepid approval was given to pursue the car-only equipment strategy (with no pursuit of lower cost locomotives beneficial for Intermodal service or dedicated trains). Of the group, only Grayson seemed to take the study seriously. Only he seemed even modestly sympathetic to the intermodal cause.

Life During and After the Intermodal Task Force Effort

The new BN Intermodal Business Unit team had to do more than facilitate the production and completion of the Task Force study and recommendations. Among other things, they needed to familiarize themselves with, and run, an existing undermanaged business through a recession in post-deregulation confusion. They had to bring the rest of the inherited intermodal organization up to speed with what the task force recommended, recruit new members, familiarize themselves with BN Intermodal's market, competition and customers, understand what was working and what wasn't, triage

---

[279] Ibid, p. c.

opportunities, secure triage capital, identify a detailed organization structure that would be best suited to attack the opportunity, get authority for positions that would be necessary to move successfully ahead (in a company-wide cost-cutting environment), and pursue the task force recommendations.

An important task was to assess BN intermodal pricing strategy and tactics. Pricing practices were largely driven by what was done in a regulated environment. For example, because a standard intermodal flatcar carried two trailers there was a natural desire to fill the car with two trailers. Therefore, there was a legacy industry practice of pricing domestic intermodal shipments with two-trailer rates. If a shipper's agent (most domestic business was handled through "third parties" such as Shipper's Agents and Shipper's Associations because it was very complex to arrange intermodal shipments) could not come up with a second trailer from origin A to destination B at the same time, the shipment would probably go to a motor carrier who dealt in single trailer lots. There was a lot of discussion back and forth about whether BN should break from the standard industry practice and offer single-trailer rates. BN did it first and the industry followed. It was an early attempt to be easier to do business with. In addition, contracts were not allowed under regulation. BN took advantage of the ability to enter into contracts with Intermodal shippers in order to drive partnerships with "third parties" and secure a more reliable stream of business (recall National Piggyback example above).

During regular hours, relatively large legacy customers like United Parcel Service (UPS) and Sea-Land had to be courted by the new team and assured that BN treasured their business while the new IBU explored how to gain a higher share of their business. A formal presentation was made to UPS on November 13 in an effort to accomplish this.

Connecting railroads also had to be courted and familiarized with the BN's new people and plans. Such a meeting was held in Philadelphia on October 2 with Malcolm Sanders (who was the leader of Conrail's intermodal marketing). Similar meetings were held with intermodal executives of other connecting/partner railroads (while carefully avoiding new antitrust risks that came with deregulation because in some instances partners could also be competitors). These meetings opened the door to information sharing about things such as information system support, new equipment evaluations and intermodal terminal operating techniques.

Greenwood continued his outside speaking engagements too: [280]

> *You couldn't write contracts until deregulation. Deregulation allowed us to write contracts, and before that you had to go to the government to get approval for the price changes. Twenty railroads would meet, a hundred people would meet at the Union League (Club) in Chicago to debate what the price is that we could charge from Chicago to Seattle.*
>
> *I gave a talk, after only being on the job about six months, to the National Association of Commerce Attorneys -- and that was their title, 'commerce attorney'. That's all they did was handle issues for railroads and shippers at these meetings that would take place all the time about what the price ought to be. And again, I'm kind of ignorant, so I'm giving this talk, and oh, the first question a guy asked, "You know what you just said? You just told us we're all out of a*

---

[280] National Railroad Hall of Fame, William E. Greenwood, Chief Operating Officer (retired) Burlington Northern Railroad, Interview Transcript, July 30, 2020: Accessed from: https://www.nrrhof.org/greenwood-transcript, on May 7, 2022.

job." You want to know something? There were 10,000 in Minneapolis for their convention. Five years later there were zero commerce attorneys left.

He also spoke before meetings of Piggyback Industry associations: [281]

I gave a lot of talks. I was asked. I'd kind of been getting known for shaking things up in the marketplace. And so, I was getting a lot of invitations to talk about it, but I'm still ignorant. I don't know much about this stuff. I had a talk at the Union League Club in Chicago. I gave a talk there about all the things we're gonna look at doing and what the future is of this thing called piggyback on the Burlington Northern. And a guy came up to me. He was the founder of (Hub City Terminals), and uh, I forgot his name for the moment (Phil Yeager). Anyway, he came up to me afterwards. And he said, "You know, I didn't like anything you had to say. You basically told me you don't need me." And I told him, "Well, no, I need you." I don't know why, but you know... (Laughter) Anyway, so I got to develop a relationship with him, you know, over why he felt what I was saying was going to happen to him, so. These were channels of distribution issues. How we were going to channel ourselves and our place in the marketplace. And I was talking about us having our own channel. We managed ourselves all the way to the customer. Piggyback was totally third-party people. We sold to third party people, and they brokered. They were our brokers.

In addition, the reorganized make-up of the new IBU also included responsibility for BN's domestic and import motor vehicle hauling business. The commercial needs of that business had to be investigated and addressed (which would be accomplished between January and October of 1982) because the Union Pacific, Milwaukee Road and Soo Line were also becoming especially aggressive in utilizing their newly obtained deregulation flexibility to attack this market. BN's business in this segment had to be protected while the intermodal strategy was being formulated and implemented and the same could be done for the motor vehicle business segment. In addition, in the aftermath of the Frisco merger the new IBU inherited responsibility for the operation of motor vehicle handling facilities on the former Frisco as well as the former Frisco piggyback ramps. Having BN intermodal terminals (and intermodal equipment management) report to the new IBU had been envisioned in the Booz Allen study but hadn't yet been implemented outside of former Frisco territory.

It was vitally important to spread the task force information within the company and obtain formal approval to start implementation of its recommendations. Greenwood, Hoepner and Cane conducted marathon task force related meetings on weekends and evenings at the general office and Greenwood's home to hone the intermodal message and strategize execution.

A meeting was held with Richard Grayson on November 24 to review intermodal profitability and again obtain his support for the task force recommendations. Because he wanted to discuss capital needed to initiate the Hub Center plan Greenwood brought Axel Holland with him. As former BN intermodal executive Dennis Gustin recalled:

1981 finds me working for Ron Aase in the Transportation Department in Minneapolis at the Galaxy Building doing reports, train logs and programming. This is where I met Axel Holland, who was then the TC Region Intermodal Manager. During lunch hours, I would sit with him and he would outline this grandiose plan: to expand the then current intermodal network through a

---

[281] Ibid.

truck supported hub and spoke design. I always found Axel entertaining and dedicated to this new idea, all the while puffing on his pipe. His idea sounded logical; however, I recall thinking at the time the boys in GOB would never accept it. My GN/BN years in GOB Transportation (beginning in 1967) never gave me the impression I was in a forward-thinking company, but that's a whole other story.[282]

After formation of the IBU Greenwood appointed Holland (who he had known from his Minneapolis/St. Paul Terminal Superintendent experience) Director of Hub Operations which at the time meant he only had the Springfield Region ramps officially reporting to him. The transfer of responsibility to the IBU for all non-Frisco BN ramps, and the transfer of responsibility for all intermodal equipment acquisition and distribution, still had not been approved in spite of the BAH recommendations. As Dennis Gustin indicated, Holland had been responsible for ramp operations on the Twin Cities Region. He was appointed Manager TCF in 1974, well before the formation of the IBU and he joined the IBU as Director Terminal Operations on June 1, 1981.[283] Holland was very knowledgeable and capable and a tough negotiator who believed in the IBU vision. An immigrant from Germany, he spoke with a thick German accent. He was a patriotic Major in the Minnesota National Guard and worked as a group leader for military intelligence specializing in interrogations of prisoners. Grayson wanted to understand the vision for Hub design at the November 24 meeting. Holland took a blueprint for the Denver Hub for which expansion capital was needed. Another important point of reference related to Grayson is that while his former Frisco Railroad had been active in the intermodal business, none of their facilities were mechanized – all were circus ramps. While the industry had begun an extremely slow conversion to mechanization, Frisco had not participated. In 1965 the U.S. railroad industry had 2,100 intermodal facilities but only 63 (3%) were mechanized. By 1975 the industry had reduced the number of facilities to 1,500 but only 110 (7%) were mechanized. Even four years later, by 1985, when the industry's count of intermodal facilities declined to 420, only 150 (36%) will have been mechanized.[284]

Grayson looked at Holland's blueprint which contained a layout for loading tracks, trailer parking paving and fifth wheel pads. He said to Holland, "I have a lot of experience with piggyback ramps. You don't need this much land and paving for your trailers. Your cost estimates are way too high." Holland was puzzled and asked what he meant. Grayson said, "You don't need that much space to turn the trailers." Holland took a deep puff on his ever-present pipe, looked again at the blueprint, ran some quick calculations and said with his thick "R-rolling" German accent, "Mr. Grayson Sir, you have made a very serious error Mr. Grayson." Grayson was shocked because no one in the Frisco culture ever questioned or talked to him like that. Greenwood's heart stopped and he had to struggle to resume breathing while Holland took another deep pipe-puff and repeated what he had just said. Grayson asked Holland why he questioned him. Rolling his "Rs", Holland replied, "Mr. Grayson, trailers are no longer 35 feet long, Mr. Grayson. Mr. Grayson, trailers are now 45 feet long. You need enough space to turn trailers that are at least 45 feet long Mr. Grayson because before long trailers will be 48 feet long. Mr. Grayson, we need to build facilities that will handle trailers of today and tomorrow, not trailers of more than a decade ago that are 35 feet long." Holland went on to say, "Mr. Grayson, another part of your very serious error is that trailers don't just magically lift themselves and turn themselves. You need enough space for a lift device to pick the trailer up, pull it out and turn it before setting it down." Instead of being the then-current standard, as indicated in the table below, 35' long trailers were the standard more than two decades prior to this meeting date which reflected Grayson's total lack of knowledge

---

[282] Email from Dennis Gustin to Mark Cane, February 10, 2022.
[283] Axel Holland, Burlington Northern Internal Resume and Personal Data Inventory, last updated 7/16/1992.
[284] DeBoer, p. 84.

about piggyback terminal "lift" operations and even how long it had been since Grayson had fully focused on piggyback circus operations. Grayson was startled and said, "I guess you are right."[285] That exchange gained credibility for the IBU but the authority to proceed with the Task Force plan, including capital for a Denver Hub Center, was still withheld.

Legal United States Highway Trailer Lengths Over the Years[286]

Years	Trailer Length
1930-1950	30 ft.
1950-1958	35 ft.
1959-1982	40 ft.
1980-1989	45 ft.
1982-1989[a]	48 ft.
1989 – present	53 ft.

[a]: Surface Transportation Act of 1982

---

[285] Bill Greenwood interview with Mark Cane, March 18, 2022.

[286] Panza, James D., Dawson, Richard W., Sellberg, Ronald P., *The TTX Story, Volume 1*, The Pennsylvania Railroad Technical & Historical Society, Allentown, Pennsylvania, 2018, p. 198.

Chapter 9 - Attempts to Implement Intermodal Task Force Recommendations in 1982

A presentation of task force findings was delivered to St. Paul BN general office employees in the main floor auditorium on January 8, 1982. This was followed by another IBU staff conference on January 11, a task force follow-up service planning meeting with Transportation on January 13 and an equipment planning model meeting with Marketing Services and Transportation on January 25. In addition, because of the importance of establishing a public identity and new brand image for the new BN Intermodal, work was initiated with BN's Public Affairs Group to develop a promotion plan. Plans for a new BN Intermodal brochure were developed with Public Affairs on January 26, 1982.

To make up for the relative inattention that had been placed on the Motor Vehicle business since the formation of the IBU, in March, 1982 a Motor Vehicle Action Group was formed. The intent was to basically clone the intermodal task force approach and, on a much smaller scale, apply it to BN's Motor Vehicle business. A MV market development meeting was held on January 26 and Action Group meetings were held on March 2 and March 30, 1982.

The full task force recommendations still had to be presented to Grayson, Ethington, and the other BN Railroad Executives that were not a part of the signatory Review Group. A meeting with this group was finally arranged for February 26, 1982. As Dave Burns stated, "Senior Management was impressed and concerned but not yet entirely ready to commit to the costs, focus and actions required to bring on-line an entirely new, untried business model, most of it revolutionary for a railroad. Plus, there were just so many other issues going on at that time."[287] It was a major let-down for the team. The economy had been hit hard by a continuing recession that was triggered to get inflation under control. The Holding Company was restless about railroad profitability and the dominant BNRR focus was cost reduction.

The 1982 recession was whacking BN Railroad's carload businesses and the export grain business was soft. It was clear by the end of the first quarter that it would not be a good year for the railroad and the businesses that were getting whacked the hardest were those that the Intermodal Task Force said would be the most vulnerable. In spite of recession-related pressures to cut costs, and although BN Intermodal's planned "what" had been largely determined, the "how" was still going to be challenging. Bill Greenwood continued to build his high performance team. As Jim Collins stated in his book *Good to Great: Why Some Companies Make the Leap … and Others Don't*:[288]

> We expected that good-to-great leaders would begin by setting a new vision and strategy. We found instead that they first got the right people on the bus, the wrong people off the bus, and the right people in the right seats—and then they figured out where to drive it. The old adage "People are your most important asset" turns out to be wrong. People are not your most important asset. The right people are.

---

[287] Dave Burns, "Transportation Department Days 1981-1982, *The BN Expediter*, Volume 25, Number 4, Friends of the Burlington Northern Railroad, 2017, p. 13.
[288] Goodreads, Good to Great quotes, Accessed from: https://www.goodreads.com/work/quotes/1094028-good-to-great-why-some-companies-make-the-leap-and-others-don-t, January 26, 2023.

Burns, DeWitt, Trafton and Berry join the Intermodal Leadership Team

In March, 1982 the intermodal team worked with BN's Transportation and Mechanical departments, among others, to test the RoadRailer technology. Loads were solicited to make it possible to run an entire RoadRailer trailer train between Chicago and Seattle measuring fuel consumption, load handling characteristics and everything else imaginable to compare it to conventional and other new technologies. As a test to measure RoadRailer ride quality someone put a glass filled with water inside the rear of the last trailer in the train. At destination the glass was upright, in the same spot it was originally placed and still full of water[289] – the RoadRailer's ride quality claims were verified.

As a representative of Transportation on the Task Force, Dave Burns accompanied Bill Greenwood on the Seattle to Chicago leg of the trip. Greenwood had a vacancy for a new position, General Manager Hub Design and Construction (which would later be re-titled GM Hub Operations). Greenwood had consulted with members of the IBU leadership team about who might be a good candidate for the job and Burns' name consistently came up. The team's rationale, among other things, was that Burns had a solid track record of success through a string of progressive operating assignments and leading BN operating divisions. He had started on the Great Northern as a management trainee, worked in the Bridge and Building Department, as a Trainmaster, worked in Labor Relations, served as a Terminal Superintendent, handled four Division Superintendent assignments, plus Region operations and ultimately (capping off 20 pre- IBU years of service) General Superintendent Transportation. On top of that vast experience base he had impeccable moral values and credibility, a tireless work ethic, and based on his task force contributions a real belief in selfless teamwork and a growing belief in the IBU's message and potential. He could also help reduce the organizational barriers between Intermodal, Transportation, Mechanical, Engineering and Field Operations. Greenwood totally agreed. He offered the GM position to Burns on the train's first night out of Seattle. As Burns related: [290]

> *I knew enough about the general IBU plan to sense the great potential it possessed. My head told me I didn't know anything about Hub design and construction, let alone operations. But my heart told me maybe this was why I had come to St. Paul less than a year ago. Here was my opportunity to be in on the ground floor of something special, significant, and valuable to BN. If you will, one of those opportunities to grow something entirely new while growing myself. I think Bill said something about sleeping on it but I instead accepted on the spot. The actual appointment came through Monday, March 29. April 1, 1982 was my first official day as a member of the Intermodal Team. On that first day, as would be the custom for many years to come, I met with the core leadership team in Bill's office at 8 am.*

Bill Greenwood recalled:

> *Dave had everything to lose when he accepted the job. He was basically terminating his operating department career. He became our cheerleader because he passionately believed so much in what we were doing. He was willing to take risks. He used to remind us of what he called the Jesuit Principle of Management – "It is better to seek forgiveness than to ask for*

---

[289] Tom Bauer email to Mark Cane, April 21, 2022.
[290] Burns, Dave, Transportation Department Days 1981-1982, *BN Expediter*, Volume 25, Number 4, Friends of the Burlington Northern Railroad, 2017, p.14

permission." We had to do that to survive. In retrospect, I am convinced we could not have accomplished what we did without Dave Burns.[291]

Bill DeWitt had been an Intermodal Task Force observer.[292] At the time he was the Transportation Analyst for the BN Holding Company with the responsibility to keep an eye on the railroad, BN's trucking company BN Transport (BNT) and BN Airfreight (BNAFI). While in college he worked summers for the Chicago, South Shore and South Bend Railroad repairing railcars as a carman's helper and later as a Brakeman / Collector on the South Shore's Chicago commuter operation. He worked for eight hours and then would work an additional eight on a freight switch crew. He also got an internship as an Industrial Engineer on a boxcar renovation project at Conrail's Beech Grove shop. He joined the Navy and left active duty after two years with the rank of Lieutenant and continued his service in the Navy Reserves. After discharge from active duty he earned his MBA degree at the University of Tennessee from which he was hired into BN's Management Training program. After working in field operations on the Pacific Division, as an Assistant Trainmaster in Burlington, Iowa and a Hannibal Division Trainmaster out of Galesburg, Illinois he was appointed Asst. Superintendent Administration on the Lincoln (Nebraska) Division. He was then transferred to St. Paul into Corporate Planning after Ken Hoepner moved into Operations. While he was Director–Corporate Planning, Walter Drexel (who joined BNI as VP Strategic Planning from Atlantic Richfield's Anaconda Copper subsidiary in February of 1981) asked him to join the Holding Company's Strategic Planning Group as the Transportation Analyst. Bressler had no interest in BNAFI after they told Bressler they wanted to buy their own aircraft so he sold them to Pittston on March 19, 1982. DeWitt was told he was no longer needed and he could go back to the railroad or take a severance. He chose to stay with BN Railroad and was informed that the new IBU had an open marketing position and was referred to Greenwood. Bill Greenwood offered the job to DeWitt and he officially joined the IBU in April of 1982 as a Manager-Intermodal Marketing in the Pricing section. DeWitt was familiar with what had transpired with the Task Force in his observer role. He had also extended some of his Task Force trips from Seattle over some weekends. He knew the core team was working weekends on unofficial offensive strategies and tactics (to complement official defensive strategies). He was invited to join-in so he had been interacting with the core team for several months before his official hire-date. His operating background coupled with his financial and planning skills, tireless work ethic and belief in the intermodal opportunity made him a perfect fit and he immediately assumed a position on the core leadership team. He also brought a knack for classical market research and promotion that the rest of the team lacked, addressing another critical void.

Gordon Trafton was a graduate of the University of Colorado.[293] He worked for BN as a track sectionman and track department truck driver during summers to finance his education. He joined BN as a management trainee in January of 1978, slotted for a position in Operations. He was assigned to Lincoln, Nebraska as an Asst. Trainmaster after his training program on the Seattle Region. Given the pressing need for supervision on the rapidly growing Alliance Division he was offered an extraordinarily challenging job by Bill Greenwood as night Trainmaster in Edgemont, South Dakota. Trafton accepted it effective January of 1980. The joke on the Division was that, "Edgemont wasn't the end of the world, but you could see it from there." Trafton reported to the day trainmaster who told him he really needed to live in Edgemont, as opposed to Hot Springs (25 miles away) or Custer (42 miles away) where there was a bit of privacy, decent housing and more civilization. He said there was an overwhelming

---

[291] Bill Greenwood interview with Mark Cane, May 3, 2022.

[292] Information in this section based on Bill DeWitt's resume and Bill DeWitt's email to Mark Cane, February 23, 2022.

[293] Information in this section based on Gordon Trafton's resume and email to Mark Cane, March 4, 2022.

need for close train crew supervision. Former BN executive Jake Greeling worked out of Edgemont before Trafton and said:[294]

> *I drove 42 mountain miles to Edgemont every time I got called for work. The reason we lived in Custer was because Edgemont was not a very desirable location. It still had a lot of dirt streets and there were bad water issues.*

Among the "bad water issues" in Edgemont was radiation contamination. Living in a very small town like Edgemont for a railroad supervisor was like living in a fishbowl, especially for a young single man. Everyone knew what everyone else was doing, including those rail employees who he was supervising. Trafton had endured six months of a "killer" schedule, working with an unreasonable supervising co-worker and extraordinarily young and border-line militant train-service employees. Wanting to move on to other challenges, Trafton called Jack Thies who worked in Freight Car Management in St. Paul. Trafton had known him from his prior experience and told him about his dilemma. Thies said they had a position open in his department. He told him he was well qualified but getting from Edgemont to there would be a challenge. Trafton then called BN's Director of Human Resources Fran Coyne and told him his dilemma. He said if BN had nothing for him he would move on but that his preference was to stay with BN. He also said he knew a position was open in Freight Car Management. Coyne said it was an unusual situation but he would see what he could do. Coyne then called Greenwood and told him what had transpired. What Trafton did broke all company protocols so he then asked if Trafton should be fired. Greenwood said he would investigate more and then call Coyne back. Greenwood then went down the hall and talked to Mark Cane and told him the situation. He asked what he thought of Trafton because Coyne asked if he should be fired. Cane said all of his experiences with Trafton had been really good and that BN had invested a lot in him. Cane said he thought he was definitely worth saving. Greenwood thanked him and checked to see where Trafton was. It turned out he was in Alliance for an investigation and staff meeting. Greenwood learned he was in the staff meeting and entered the room. There was a chair open by Trafton and Greenwood sat in it.

> *I leaned over and asked Gordon what he was doing for lunch. He said he didn't have plans so I invited him to have lunch in my house. There I asked what was going on and he told me. I thanked him for his hard work and honesty, told him how much I would hate to lose him on the Division. I asked him to hold on a bit and not do anything hastily without talking with me first. Then I took him back to the meeting. Following our lunch I called Fran Coyne and said Gordon had done a superb job in Edgemont and that I would be very sorry to lose him. I also said BN had invested a lot in him and because he was such a good employee he would have no trouble getting a good job elsewhere. I asked Coyne to do what had to be done, including running interference for me within the HQ Operations and Transportation staffs, to accommodate Gordon. Just like Fran had done when I called on him for help in the past, he said he would do what he could but added, "Greenwood, if this doesn't work you might get fired."*[295]

Within a few days Bill Reilly, the Alliance Division Asst. Superintendent Transportation, called Trafton and said there was an opportunity for him in St. Paul in the Freight Car Management Department and he thought Trafton should take it. On the strength of Greenwood's endorsement, Trafton was offered the position in St. Paul effective July 1, 1980. A year and a half later, after the formation of the IBU,

---

[294] Poplowski, Dave, 23 Years on the BN/BNSF, Jake Greeling: Oral History (Part 1) – Alliance Division, *The BN Expediter*, Volume 28, Number 3, July, 2020, p. 12
[295] Bill Greenwood interview with Mark Cane, March 18, 2022.

Hoepner (Director Equipment and Service) had a position open for a liaison with Transportation to work on TOFC/COFC train service and schedules and he asked if anyone knew of someone with a customer oriented operations background who could be a good fit. Mark Cane said he thought Trafton would be an ideal fit and that he was working in the same building. Greenwood fully agreed. Hoepner interviewed Trafton and immediately knew he was the right person and offered him the job. Trafton joined the IBU on January 1, 1982.

Bill Berry started working for the Frisco Railroad out of high school while he was going to college at Southwest Missouri State University in Springfield, MO. He attended classes during the day and worked as a Diesel Shop Laborer at night and also a night watchman in the Car Repair Shop. He earned his Bachelor's degree in Agriculture Economics and Finance and then entered the Army. He served 1 ½ years of active duty, including time served in Korea. Following release from the Army he entered graduate school at Missouri State for a MS in Business Administration. While back in school he resumed work with the Frisco as a Mechanical Department laborer. By December of 1976 he had completed enough credits to complete his MBA degree but he lacked his dissertation. His supervisor told him with his education and capability he shouldn't be working there. He was told to go to the Frisco Headquarters building and meet with Mr. Bud Thomas. Berry said he couldn't go then because he was covered with dirt and grease. His supervisor said Thomas was waiting for him and he needed to go right away so he did. Thomas was responsible for all of the Frisco piggyback ramp operations and, in spite of the grease and dirt, he offered Berry a job as a ramp manager in Memphis. Berry accepted that job effective in December, 1976. He worked on the piggyback circus ramp at Memphis until June of 1981. That was the same time that the IBU was formed. He was offered the position of Assistant Manager TCF on the Twin Cities Region, based in Minneapolis, and he accepted. With Axel Holland's transfer from the Twin Cities Region to the IBU in St. Paul, Berry was then promoted to Manager – TCF reporting to Ron Aase of the Twin Cities Region. He served on that job for one and a half years with a lot of his work focused on making the Midway Hub start successful and closing circus ramps within the Midway Hub's territory. In September, 1983 he was offered Ken Hoepner's former job as the IBU Director of Intermodal Equipment after Hoepner was promoted to AVP Intermodal Marketing.[296]

A variety of strengths characterized the expanded core team. [297]

> *Each of the men brought with him a reputation as a renegade within the railroad; each believed strongly in Greenwood. Interestingly, none of them had ever had marketing experience while all of them had operating experience. But Greenwood had not insisted on a proven marketing track record; instinctively he picked people with the potential to develop the skills needed to meet the team's performance challenges – and they did.*
>
> *'We were coming into a marketing group," says Mark Cane, "but none of us had ever been in marketing before. I think that worked to our advantage because we brought fresh perspective and didn't carry any baggage. Moreover, it was clear to all of us that we had to restructure the way the business operated in order to make it marketable.'*
>
> *Each of the men did assume individual roles. DeWitt emerged as the primary marketer, Burns, and Berry focused on intermodal hub and equipment operations, Greenwood on sales, and Hoepner, Brady and Cane on strategy, finance and planning. Trafton was the primary train*

---

[296] William K. Berry Resume, December 21, 1993, and interview with Mark Cane, March 19, 2022.
[297] Katzenbach and Smith, pp. 38-39.

service liaison/voice of Intermodal with the Transportation department and field rail operations. He also developed a close relationship with the critical customer, UPS. Yet given their common operating backgrounds and recent introduction to marketing, the team also developed interchangeable skills in these critical disciplines – all of which reinforced their mutual confidence and capability and gave them greater flexibility than they otherwise would have had.

Leadership was also shared across the entire team. Greenwood characterizes his own role as fostering a creative environment within the team while focusing primarily on selling Intermodal to the rest of the company and its customers. Much of the team's intellectual leadership came from DeWitt, Cane and Hoepner. Burns emerged as the critical social leader who provided constant positive feedback and reinforcement.

'I never worked for Bill Greenwood," comments Ken Hoepner. 'I worked with Bill Greenwood.'

Another critical role Greenwood played internally was to patrol the political boundaries so that the team could focus on the business with a bubble of protection. Externally he worked hard to promote the new BN Intermodal vision and "brand."

Walter Drexel Takes the BN Railroad Helm

On April 1, 1982 Walter Drexel was appointed President and COO of BN Railroad reporting to Richard Grayson, although word of his appointment had leaked out earlier. Grayson moved up to Chairman and CEO–Burlington Northern Transportation Group. Drexel came to the BN Holding Company (BNI) with zero railroad experience from Atlantic Richfield where he had worked with Richard Bressler. Between 1975 and 1977 Drexel had been ARCO's general tax officer. He was ARCO treasurer from July 1977-October 1978. In October 1978 he was transferred to ARCO's Anaconda Copper Company subsidiary as a vice president. As mentioned earlier, in February, 1981 Bressler hired him to be BNI's VP strategic planning and then Sr. VP strategic planning in May, 1981.

The impact of the recession was reflected in BN's stock price. It had fallen from $65 per share on March 1, 1981 when the BAH reorganization recommendations were implemented and the IBU and other strategic business units were officially formed, to $53 per share on June 15, 1981 when Grayson approved the formation of the Intermodal Task Force. It fell further to $46 per share on the day Drexel took over leadership of the railroad from Grayson – a drop of more than 29% in just over a year.

Drexel's appointment changed the dynamics for the IBU because a new person had to be convinced about the wisdom of the intermodal plan. Instead of convincing a traditional operations-steeped railroad executive (Grayson) about the merits of the Task Force based IBU plan, a new judge would be a non-railroad finance-oriented executive.

In an interview with Larry Kaufman, Drexel described what he encountered when he arrived in St. Paul:

I found out that the culture was much worse than I had anticipated – how locked in everybody was … When I first got there, I talked to them some about customers, and they just looked at me with a blank look like "What in the world is a customer? We run trains. That's what we do. We run trains." The asset that BN had was a tremendous base. I don't think there's any question about that. They had great territory, "great franchise," as the railroad people like to call it. They had a great asset base and probably had more assets – as we found out – than they needed if it was run efficiently.[298]

Drexel's actual view of railroad people and the railroad business was not news to the IBU team. As mentioned already, before joining the intermodal team, Bill DeWitt worked for Drexel at the Holding Company in Seattle as the Transportation Planning Analyst focused on the railroad. He made the IBU team aware of how the railroad was perceived in Seattle – it was a cow to be milked. He explained what to expect, and how to best tailor the intermodal message to Drexel.

Unfortunately, Greenwood's boss Dick Gleason tried to turn Drexel against Greenwood and the Intermodal team. Greenwood said: [299]

> *And Drexel didn't like me. In fact, my boss didn't like me, who was Dick Gleason. He hired me for one reason; he didn't expect me to get aggressive. And it winded up I was making my business unit more significant and important than all of the other business units that were under him. Well, I was under him too, but I didn't get any support from him. He tried to actually get me fired. And he got with Mr. Drexel. He got a partner to help him. Drexel thought I should be fired, too.*

Not being liked didn't deter Greenwood and the team. Greenwood got on Drexel's calendar to present the intermodal plan to him on April 6, 1982 and it lasted from 9 am to 4 pm. Drexel wanted the plan fine-tuned and for it to contain stronger Hub location rationalizations. Many IBU team meetings were conducted to make that happen and another presentation was made to Drexel on May 17. That still didn't satisfy him so it was back to the drawing board. Another meeting was set up for July 19 with Drexel and Grayson with the hope that the IBU would finally obtain a Task Force green light – eight months after the Task Force had completed its recommendations. Greenwood recalls, "My intention was to get approval for the establishment of the entire hub center plan according to the schedule we had developed."[300] The whole IBU headquarters staff was aware of it. It was supposed to be a one hour meeting. Dave Burns stated: [301]

> *"Our proposal for the first two hub starts were Chicago and Denver."*[302] *Chicago and Denver were already mechanized and could accommodate the new generation rail cars. They also had decent mixed-freight service between them with UPS serving as a customer that drew other customers. "The traffic potential was huge, affording quick growth to permit unit (dedicated intermodal) train operation between the two on an overnight schedule competitive with over-the-road truck. Bill Greenwood took what we thought was a compelling case to senior management on Monday, July 19, 1982. The meeting was supposed to go for one hour, and the rest of us waited anxiously."*

[298] Kaufman, p. 230.

[299] National Railroad Hall of Fame, William E. Greenwood, Chief Operating Officer (retired) Burlington Northern Railroad, Interview Transcript, July 30, 2020: Accessed from: https://www.nrrhof.org/greenwood-transcript, Accessed on May 7, 2022.

[300] Bill Greenwood interview with Mark Cane, March 18, 2022.

[301] Ibid.

[302] Dave Burns, Intermodal Days 1982-1992, *BN Expediter* Volume 26, Number 4, Friends of the Burlington Northern Railroad, October 2018, p. 12.

As Katzenbach and Smith documented: [303]

> *The actual meeting was even worse than Greenwood had expected. Instead of an hour it lasted almost four. One of the senior executives clearly opposed the hubs from the beginning, and no amount of fact or emotion would budge him. Luckily, the other executive who had done some intermodal work earlier in his career was nervously supportive. But he did not want to take any big risks.*
>
> *For hours, they went back and forth on the merits and risks of the proposal, with Greenwood doing his best to counter objections, ameliorate fears, collect on old favors, and promise them anything to get the go-ahead. His best efforts failed.*
>
> *In the end,' says Greenwood, 'the two men said they would not approve the proposal until intermodal proved it could do what it said. They wanted us to pilot the concept. And, they picked the two worst possible locations to let us try.'*
>
> *One guy didn't believe we could hold onto all of our existing business while closing ramps and constructing new hubs. So he picked Midway in Minnesota, which involved closing the greatest number of outlying circus ramps. The other did not think we could build the business like we projected. So he picked Portland, where we faced the strongest railroad competition.*
>
> *It was a test, Greenwood believes, "to see us fail."*

Bill Greenwood vividly remembered decades later that the guy who chose Portland was Drexel:

> *Dick Gleason got to Drexel and at the time he didn't care for us or our business at all. Gleason and many in the other business units perceived us as a threat to the BN carload business. Drexel acted as if he really wanted us to fail and he clearly doubted that we could compete with the Union Pacific. The guy who chose Midway was Grayson. He liked the spunk of our group and acted to counteract Drexel's disdain. If he hadn't been in that meeting I don't think we would have gotten a green light to proceed. All through the meeting Drexel would try to shoot down just about everything I said but Grayson would diplomatically throw me a life-line to help me out. Being one focused on cost cutting, he liked the idea of shutting down inefficient facilities like all of the circus ramps in the Midway market area. He had a sense that we could do it and in his role as Vice Chairman and boss of Drexel he saved the day for us. If not for Dick Grayson I don't know what would have come of BN's intermodal business.[304]*
>
> *When the meeting finished, Greenwood was exhausted and discouraged. It was not what he had hoped for, and certainly not what the team or the business unit were expecting. Still, he knew it was better than nothing. That evening, when Bill returned, the anxious group packed the only space that would hold them all. The anticipation on their faces made it even more difficult for Bill to break the news. "It's not what we hoped," he said, "but we do have the okay on two hubs. I think we should give it a shot.[305]*

---

[303] Katzenbach and Smith, p. 36.
[304] Bill Greenwood interview with Mark Cane, March 19, 2022.
[305] Katzenbach and Smith, p. 36.

In some ways, Bill had underestimated the heart in his group. Sure they were disappointed and there was a momentary silence. Everyone instantly recognized the difficulties associated with the two chosen hubs. In addition to the number of ramps to be closed in association with the Midway, Minnesota Hub, and the competition in Portland, Oregon, the hubs were scheduled to open in the winter of 1982-1983, when construction would be stalled by cold weather and business slowed by the country's deep recession. A less committed and self-sufficient group might have given up in discouragement, frustration, or a pending sense of failure. Not the Intermodal Team. They had a green light; not the one they hoped for, but still a green light. So within seconds of Bill's announcement, the room began to buzz with statements of support, resolve, excitement and determination.[306]

We had this coiled energy," remarks Bill DeWitt. "I had never participated in anything where we had so thoroughly thought out all the interrelated issues needed to get things done. We already knew how we were going to handle the ramp closings, where we would get the new equipment from, and how we were going to run it. To us, this was the go-ahead to finally do something.[307]

A few days before the Midway Hub was to open, Bill Berry came to the St. Paul GOB for a meeting. He saw Bill Greenwood at the building entrance. They quickly chatted about how the Midway project would be a big challenge for Berry. With a more serious expression than Berry had ever seen on Greenwood's face, Greenwood said, "Bill, this has to work." Berry responded, "It will."[308]

What Might Have Been – a 1982 BN/Santa Fe Merger?

In his book, *Leaders Count*, Larry Kaufman said he was told by Richard Bressler that he had approached John Reed, the CEO of Santa Fe Industries about a proposal to merge BN and Santa Fe in 1982. He quoted Bressler:[309]

I went to call on John Reed because it was fairly apparent that a merger of those two properties – plus the fact that they had all those resources at that same time – it was a good fit. John was always in the operations room. That's where he spent his time. Then they'd have to call him. He'd have to come up, and I could tell that I was boring him because he kept looking at his watch as if he had to get back.

Our proposal made him very, very uncomfortable. When I first proposed it, I recognized he was uncomfortable with me talking about that. So I took Grayson with me on another visit because he knew Dick, and Dick was kind of old-shoe. They would chat a little bit about one thing or another. But Dick recognized that would have been a good merger if we could have pulled it off. So we talked and talked. John would listen, but he would never say very much.

Kaufman said Reed did not reply to Bressler's proposal and Bressler added: [310]

---

[306] Katzenbach and Smith, pp. 36-37.

[307] Ibid, p. 37.

[308] Bill Berry interview with Mark Cane, March 19, 2022.

[309] Kaufman, pp 231-232.

[310] Ibid, p. 232.

So we went down to see him again. Again it was the same sort of pattern – a little byplay. Finally I said, "Well, John, we're here because we thought by now you'd have some response to us on our proposal." With that, he reaches into his pocket. He pulls out his billfold. Then there's this slip of paper, obviously written by his general counsel. He reads from the paper: "The Santa Fe has no interest in a merger with the BN at this time." He folds up the slip of paper and puts it back in his pocket.

Reed had attempted to merge with the Southern Pacific as announced on May 15, 1980. Then ICC Chairman Darius Guskins was quoted as immediately saying the merger, "raises in my mind questions about possible anti-competitive consequences." On September 12, 1980 they called the proposed merger off. [311] Reed was retired by his Board on December 1, 1982.[312] The desire to merge Santa Fe with the SP did not go away though. Reed's successor announced another merger attempt with the SP on December 23, 1983.[313]

BN's Intermodal Business story would have dramatically changed if a merger between BN and Santa Fe would have occurred at that time. BN would have been the purchaser and it will never be known what intermodal philosophies/strategies would have prevailed. What is certain is that BN's intermodal franchise, which was the weakest in the West, would have immediately become the strongest. In addition to having the best single-line route between Chicago and Seattle, Chicago and Denver and between the Southeast and the Pacific Northwest, BN would have also had the best single-line intermodal routes between Chicago and California, between California and Texas and the Southeast, plus one of the best routes between the Midwest and Texas.

Bill DeWitt, who at the time of the Bressler–Reed inquiry was the BNI Holding Company Transportation Analyst, was unaware of this proposal. He said, "I did not know this was going on. Bressler was very secretive and he really wanted to put cash into the natural resources companies, which he did. Railroad or transportation was not his interest as indicated by his sale of BNAFI to Pittston and BNT to Schlumberger."[314]

Barbarians Still at the Gates

It was July of 1982, just over a year after the formation of the IBU, and the IBU finally had the authority to proceed with a portion of the Task Force hub recommendations. The approval of the Portland Hub included authority for a lift device plus $700,000 for facility expansion which would ultimately be completed in December.[315] Work had been progressing for a year on testing new equipment types and developing new marketing approaches. The IBU only had lift-on/lift-off capability at six (Chicago, Seattle, Spokane, Midway (Minneapolis/St. Paul), Denver and Kansas City) of what in actuality was 139 BN intermodal ramps. This lift-on/lift-off capability was a holdover from the late 1960s and mid 1970s. BN had the same number of dedicated intermodal trains in operation (five – all between Chicago and

---

[311] Bryant and Frailey, p. 341.

[312] Ibid, p. 345.

[313] Ibid p. 346.

[314] Bill DeWitt email to Mark Cane, February 23, 2022.

[315] BN: Big Switch at Cicero, *Railway Age Magazine*, January, 1983.

Seattle) as it had in 1981.[316] In spite of that, growth of business at Cicero (Chicago) had that facility bursting at the seams so badly that it was not uncommon for 100 trucks to be lined up outside the Cicero check-in gate (and releasing diesel exhaust) on Cicero's city streets (drawing the ire of the citizens and elected officials). The Memphis facility was hitting its capacity as a circus ramp which also inhibited its ability to receive international container business. The lack of lift devices, in general, severely limited the ability to use new equipment technologies with their associated improved locomotive and fuel efficiency, lower rental and maintenance costs and their associated improved ride qualities, not to mention the inability to handle chassis-less containerized international business.

In addition, while other railroads were on the watch for what BN intermodal would do next,[317] the BN organization seemed to be going out of its way to hinder intermodal development.   One of the most controversial aspects of the Hub strategy was the plan: [318]

> *"to hire truckers to operate each of the hubs and to bring them in at a job grade high enough to merit bonuses:*
>
> *'People were still in the mind-set of regulation,' says Bill DeWitt, 'where truckers are the absolute worst enemy you could possibly think of. And here we want to go hire truckers to run operations right in the heart of the railroad!'"*

In addition, DeWitt was leading the charge for an aggressive promotion and advertising effort that would highlight BN Intermodal's connectivity with the Interstate Highway System with images of trucks and not trains. As Dave Burns recalled, "I always thought our advertising efforts were part of our growing recognition and increasing business. Railroads, and certainly BN at that time, didn't advertise much, but we did. We utilized trade journals read not just by shippers but by motor carriers. To me, these ads were eye appealing, catchy and compelling. They were also a source of pride for the unit and especially the hub teams."[319]

This attitude went to the top of the organization as illustrated by the struggle to get the first two hubs approved. [320]

> *"What had been mostly organizational indifference to intermodal prior to 1981 had turned into active hostility by 1982. The increasingly outspoken and aggressive Intermodal Team challenged others at Burlington Northern by recommending that capital dollars, customers, freight, people and resources be shifted from boxcars to flatcars. The team made no secret of their desire to build a new kind of cross functional organization that would knock down the traditional barriers between marketing, operations, accounting, information systems, and so on. And they aggressively pursued ways of cooperating with truckers. Such possibilities distressed those comfortable with "business as usual"; the team became a real threat to the status quo.*

---

[316] Gordon Trafton, Burlington Northern Intermodal Train Implementation Outline, March 25, 1986, *Greenwood Collection*, Barriger Library at UMSL.

[317] BN: Big Switch at Cicero, *Railway Age Magazine*, January, 1983.

[318] Katzenbach and Smith, p. 35.

[319] Burns, Dave, Intermodal Days 1982-1992, *BN Expediter* Volume 26, Number 4, Friends of the Burlington Northern Railroad, October 2018, p. 13.

[320] Katzenbach and Smith, p. 33-34.

> *"There was this terrible dichotomy between the external world and the internal world," says Greenwood. "The external world knew we were onto something. Inside, however, there was this terrible misunderstanding and resistance. Even my own boss was out to get us and was virtually drumming up support from the rest of his marketing organization to bury us."*

> *Many people in addition to Greenwood's boss were antagonized by the maverick personalities and brash dreams of the Intermodal Team. Whenever possible, these naysayers loudly criticized intermodal, and they made it tough to get resources, information, people, and permissions. At times the hostility verged on sabotage. According to the team, for example, one executive rigged an equipment bid to prevent intermodal from working with a preferred vendor on a critical new generation of flatcar. All of which made the Intermodal Team into a tighter, more self-sufficient unit.*

> *"Every time you walked into the building," remembers Ken Hoepner, "you looked around and saw howitzers aimed at you. To us it meant only one thing: "Guys, we're in this together.""*

What especially frustrated the IBU team was that due to deregulation and the recession, the most vulnerable parts of BN's business were continuing to hemorrhage market share and after more than a year in existence, Intermodal was still not positioned to do much of anything about it.

Yet, Richard Bressler's attitude about the railroad was changing a bit. The August, 1982 issue of *Trains Magazine* included an op-ed article penned by him. In it he said, "The golden age of railroading is yet to come." In the article he confined the rail opportunities to coal and grain transportation. Intermodal was still not on his radar.[321]

Barbarians Within the Gates – The 1982 Organization Study

The ink was hardly dry on the BAH organization study that had created the Operating Regions and Strategic Business Units (including the IBU). Drexel's response was to expand the cost cutting drive that Grayson's William F. Thompson had been executing within the Operating Department. On June 16, 1982 (one month prior to the approval of the two "pilot" hubs) he announced that "separate but coordinated studies would be made of each department of the railroad for the purpose of examining its existing <u>organization structure</u> and <u>location(s)</u>." (Emphasis in original)[322]

The effort was led by the overall Study Team leader and AVP Strategic Planning, Lyle Reed. The Marketing and Pricing segment of the study was led by the Operating Department's Bill Allen, Director Operations Analysis. Assisting Allen were Curt Kehr who worked in Cost Control and Budgets for the Mechanical Department, Gerald Davies who was the Sr. AVP of the Food and Manufactured Products SBU and Intermodal's Ken Hoepner. Reed, Allen and Kehr were known for their lack of support of (and even perceived animosity toward) the IBU and Davies' business unit had the most business subject to

---

[321] Bressler, Richard M., Operating trains, after all, is a business, *Trains Magazine*, Trains Turntable ... a page of opinion, August, 1982.
[322] BN 1982 Organization Study – This and all subsequent information quoted from this study comes from the original final report document for the "Marketing and Pricing Department's portion of the study, *Greenwood Collection*, Barriger Library at UMSL.

diversion as identified by the recently completed Intermodal Task Force. The deck was stacked against the IBU.

The Team Leader (Allen) would be responsible for preparing and submitting a final report based on the position reached as a result of the study, including observations, interviews, and analysis of the various data collected during the study. The study was to document:

- The Mission of the department
- Functions / activities of the department
- Staffing of the department
- Management principles and techniques
- Control / measurement devices / systems used by the department
- Overall results / benefits to the company and, to bear in mind that the corporate objective was to "do more with less".

An important BN intermodal-related issue that the new study would address is who should have responsibility for equipment acquisition and distribution. The BAH study had recommended that this should go to the Strategic Business Unit where it made sense such as with coal, intermodal and perhaps grain. This hadn't set well with the functional departments and as a result hadn't been implemented.

On June 15, 1982, BN Controller Robert Garland put out a letter[323] to William F. Thompson (Sr. VP Operations), John Tierney (VP Purchasing and Material) and Richard Gleason (VP Marketing) in which he said:

> *"For your files, I am attaching a signed copy of our policy memorandum on the functions of the Equipment Steering Committee, of which I am to serve as Chairman and Mr. Donahue as secretary.*
>
> *This committee will guide the Working Car Committee, of which Mr. Galassi is chairman."*

Donahue was the VP Strategic Planning and Galassi led Operations Support. The Equipment Steering Committee decree stated that they controlled revenue freight cars, trailers, locomotives, cabooses, and company service cars. Marketing and Pricing and Sales would be responsible for revenue freight equipment economics and market strategy. Per Garland's letter, Operations would be responsible for equipment distribution, technical performance and maintenance, Purchasing and Material would be responsible for equipment acquisition, Strategic Planning would be responsible for economic review and strategic fit and Accounting and BNI Finance would be responsible for financing, including leasing.

Instead of pushing more responsibility and P&L accountability for activities and decisions to the place in the organization (the SBU) where things came together as Booz Allen Hamilton had suggested, and which had been approved, the functional organizations retrenched. Garland's letter went on to say the Working Equipment Committee would be responsible for providing the Steering Committee with economic and strategic justification for making acquisition decisions including pertinent information as to demand characteristics, utilization, condition and fleet size.

---

[323]R.F. Garland letter to W.F. Thompson, J. Tierney, and R.M. Gleason, June 15, 1982, All quotes from the original document, *Greenwood Collection*, Barriger Library at UMSL .

Equipment modification and rebuild programs would be referred to the Steering Committee except for minor programs for which a minimum budget would be established for use at the discretion of the Working Equipment Committee (WEC). The WEC was to submit recommendations of budgeted amounts for such minor modifications.

Normal short term demand situations involving locomotives, cabooses and certain car situations would continue to be handled by the Operations Department. It was also made clear that the Purchasing and Material Department had the primary company responsibility for contacts, relationships, and negotiations with vendors and that P&M would keep other departments informed of vendor contacts relevant to equipment planning activities.

This letter was an important element of the Allen study. As it related to the IBU the Allen study stated,

> *"In accordance with the Booz-Allen and Hamilton proposal, this unit is structured in the same manner as the other three units with one additional section included in it – Terminal Operations.*
>
> *According to the (BAH) consultant's report, the intermodal terminal operations should be controlled by the IBU to respond to the unique service requirements of its customers. Included responsibilities would be:*
> > *Opening , closing or improving of ramp facilities,*
> > *Scheduling for truck pickup and delivery in coordination with rail operations,*
> > *Maintaining relationships with truckers and agents, and,*
> > *The overall management of the intermodal terminals."*

Responding to (and contradicting) the BAH recommendation the Organization Study report stated,

> *The concept of separable industries is exemplified in the Business Unit approach and embodies the notion that it will be Marketing in charge after the separation is completed. This view is incompatible with railroad operation for the following reasons:*
>
> *Two of the elements that make railroads competitive, service and equipment, are operating elements. The third, price, is clearly an element of marketing. Marketing has a critical role in making Operations responsive to market forces but the industry remains an operating industry. The railroad industry is not separable. Those assets which can clearly be assigned to any one Business Unit are only a small portion of the total asset base. Similarly, with the possible exception of coal and to a lesser extent Intermodal, those portions of operating cost which can clearly be assigned to one Business Unit are only a small portion of total operating cost. The existence of costing systems which purport to make this separation only confuses the issue. These systems provide an economic guideline separation of costs, not the type of accurate accounting costs that operating decisions can be based on.*
>
> *For these reasons it is felt that Marketing's role should be to perform market research, define products, determine prices, and communicate with customers regarding Burlington Northern's products. Marketing should define service and equipment concepts and provide revenue justification for proposed programs, but the Marketing Department should not be responsible for operating decisions.*

<u>The Hub Center Concept</u>

It was projected that each hub center would operate as a profit center under the control of a profit-driven manager. The success or failure of the center would be reflected through the use of a comprehensive P&L reporting and accounting system.

In order to design, develop, program and implement the necessary computerized reporting and control systems envisioned by the Intermodal Unit, it was projected that it would require the services of about 10% (16 employees) of the development staff of the Management Services Department. Additionally, specific projects for other departments related to a stepped-up intermodal program would have to be identified and progressed with the assistance of Management Services personnel. Further, it was estimated that six minicomputers would be required for the development of an Intermodal Ramp Management Network System.

As of the time this current study started in mid-June, it was our understanding that preliminary plans had been formulated for starting pilot hub center operations at two points – Twin Cities (Midway) and Portland, Oregon. During the course of the study, we have been informed that authority has been granted for starting these pilot operations with a limited staff at each location on or about October 1, 1982.

Our position is that the hub center concept is theoretically sound and should be given a chance to prove itself in actual operation. However, we have rather strong reservations about the existing capabilities within the company to produce accurate, complete and meaningful measurement reports on a current and consistent basis which would tell Management whether or not such an operation was truly profitable. For this reason we think Management has made a prudent decision in approaching the implementation of this concept on a pilot basis. Such a limited operation can be closely monitored with information and reports produced manually if necessary. As the concept proves to be effective, it should be implemented at additional select locations on the railroad.

<u>Intermodal Operations in General</u>

It was also our understanding when this study commenced that the Intermodal Business Unit had authority and control over the distribution of multi-level (autos) and TOFC (flatcars) rail equipment, both loaded and empty, as well as trailers/vans while off-rail. Apparently this authority and control over rail equipment has been transferred to the Transportation Section of the Operations Department as per Mr. R.F. Garland's letter of June 15, 1982. The Vice President-Transportation, Mr. T. C. Whitacre, informed us on August 26, 1982 that his department was preparing to perform this distribution process effective October 1, 1982. As a result, certain activities presently being performed in the Marketing and Pricing Department (specifically by the Equipment / Service section of the Intermodal Business Unit) should be eliminated there concurrently with the transfer of those activities to the Transportation Section of the Operations Department.

Although the responsibility for intermodal terminal operations has been assigned to the Intermodal Business Unit, they are exercising control over such operations on only one region of the railroad – Springfield. It is felt that they should exercise this vested authority over these specified operations at all locations on the railroad. Varying intermodal terminal operation practices, methods and procedures exist at different points. Effective and consistent controls are not apparent at some points at the present time. The Intermodal Business Unit could serve the railroad well during the next 2-3 years by establishing standardization and uniformity in the policies, practices and procedures related to intermodal terminal operations. Such an improved base of operations would, in turn, enhance the success of the hub center concept.

The project team went on to recommend that the name of the department change from Marketing and Pricing to Market Development and Pricing, that SBU leaders' position titles be downgraded from Sr. AVP to AVP, and that the responsibility for business forecasting be transferred from the SBUs to a central forecasting group reporting to the VP Marketing and Pricing.

The team leader (Allen) included, within the report recommendations, his belief that the re-staffing plan (including the elimination of 55 positions across Marketing and Pricing) *"did not go nearly far enough in terms of eliminating what he considers to be non-essential activities and functions."* He added, "The Team Leader feels that the philosophy of permissive management exists in this department to an excessive degree. As a result, non-essential activities and functions are permitted on an on-going basis. The role and functions of this department need to be more precisely defined, after which the staffing levels can again be adjusted for proper execution of the functions supporting that precisely defined role." (Emphasis in the original.)

The study's general conclusion, dated September 23, 1982, stated,

> *"We find no fault with the basic concept of the Business Unit approach to pricing as implemented on the BN Railroad. Specialization along commodity lines for pricing purposes creates the organizational structure in which a more precise and definitive effort can be pursued in the related and supporting functions of market research and development and business, service, and equipment planning. (Emphasis in the original)*
>
> *The implementation of the approach is incomplete. As it currently stands, the department seems to be overstaffed. This is partially the result of incomplete changes which have contributed to less than desirable structuring in some sections. It is also the result of the over-specialization of the functions of some employees **and an over-extension of the perceived role of the Marketing and Pricing Department"**.* (Emphasis added)

The statement by the "team leader" that the basic concept of the business units was to specialize along commodity lines for pricing purposes reflected a total misunderstanding of the importance the endorsed and partially implemented BAH study placed on having points of authority and accountability for major subsets of the business that would exploit the new operational and commercial freedoms that deregulation enabled. Those major subsets of the business were expected to act like businesses within the business and have prudent entrepreneurial energy released. While the recommendation to keep Hub Operations in Intermodal was a win, the loss of equipment authority and management was a significant setback because the second of the three main Intermodal strategies was focused on it. The loss of forecasting responsibility to a central group made no sense because it was counter to the whole philosophy that justified strategic business units – focused responsibility and accountability for performance within a business unit. The lack of the designation of added position authorities to the IBU for Hub management meant the recommendation that the IBU run the ramps wasn't actionable except on the Springfield Region. Fortunately for the IBU, Ken Hoepner was on the Marketing and Pricing organization assessment team which was a credit to Bill Greenwood's ability to effectively patrol boundaries and influence outcomes. The "we have never done it that way" outcome was not great but without Hoepner's influence it would have been a lot worse.

The final shot in the general conclusions about "an over-extension of the perceived role of the Marketing and Pricing Department," was a succinct way to characterize the internal environment Intermodal had to navigate while external motor carrier and railroad deregulation and economy-related competitive challenges were intensifying. Functional BN departments had not yet come to understand that they had internal customers and the Strategic Business Units were important ones. They did not understand that it was BN's customers who mattered most and the Strategic Business Units, including Intermodal, were the face of that customer to the organization. Serving the Business Units well was the best way to satisfy the ultimate customers and shareholders. They also had trouble coming to grips with the fact that the business of BN was not to run trains – it was to satisfy BN's current and prospective customers with a competitive, customer responsive and cost competitive service.

Roger Simon, who would later handle equipment management for the IBU, accurately summed-up the environment within the above-referenced Equipment Working Committee:

> I got the Car Committee job and that required me to coordinate with the business units to get their projects approved by the Car Committee. This was a new world as the business units expected the members of the Car Committee to rubber stamp Marketing projects. Nothing could be further from the truth. The majority of the Car Committee included Frisco people that had a different perspective on equipment and didn't pay much attention to Marketing recommendations and were determined to reduce the size of the merged company's fleet. The Mechanical Department was spending money on pet equipment types that had no future in the company.[324]

Hockey great Wayne Gretzky's father is reputed to have said, "Go to where the puck is going, not where it has been."[325] Unlike Booz Allen Hamilton, the leaders of the Organization Study did not consider where the railroad should be going and then design around that. They were focused on what had been before deregulation and recommended an organization to preserve it.

Northwestern University and "Marketing Myopia"

Related to directing the railroad toward where it should be going, a significant event related to Bill DeWitt and Northwestern University occurred in 1982. Mark Cane recalled[326]

> When the Intermodal Business Unit was first created in 1981 our initial leadership team recognized that what BN was selling with a significant part of its rail portfolio wasn't synchronized with where the market was heading. We tried to warn the company that a significant portion of the carload business was vulnerable and we didn't have a service offering to effectively protect it. We also didn't have a service offering that would help us grow and we didn't believe the company could shrink its way to prosperity. We knew what we believed conceptually but didn't have an effective way to label it.

---

[324] Roger Simon email to Mark Cane, March 1, 2022.

[325] Christensen, Derek, Skate to Where the Puck is Going, accessed from: https://www.derekchristensen.com/skate-to-where-the-puck-is-going/, February 24, 2022.

[326] Mark Cane's personal recollection.

That changed after Bill DeWitt went to Northwestern University in 1982 for an executive program on Industrial Marketing Strategy. Our leadership team was mostly composed of "operating" people. The only exposure any of us had to marketing was what we got from our college courses. That Northwestern course was a revelation to Bill and what he brought back made it a revelation for the rest of us. With DeWitt's encouragement, Bill Greenwood, Ken Hoepner and I went through the same program at separate times afterwards. One of the professors was Phil Kotler,[327] who was considered one of the foremost marketing experts of the time. Kotler had the class read a Harvard Business Review article that was written in 1960 by Theodore Levitt[328] called "Marketing Myopia." In it, Levitt (who also popularized the term "globalization") talked about how dominant companies or industries eventually succumbed. One of the primary reasons was that they were myopic – short sighted. They would focus on their short term needs and focus their strategies around short term objectives. Worse, they would focus on trying to continue selling what they made rather than adapt with the market and make what would profitably sell. Kotler stressed Levitt's point and said either you listen to your customers and adapt or you will fail because markets are generally efficient. Competitors are always trying to take what you have and if they listen to customers better than you do, and fill that need, customers will not need you. Kotler singled out the railroad industry as a contemporary example of Marketing Myopia. He stressed that their short-sighted behavior showed they thought they were in the "railroad" business instead of the logistics business and it was why the industry was suffering. We got the message and knew it especially applied to BN and the railroad/logistics industry that was going through a major, deregulation and globalization driven, metamorphosis. Kotler gave us a label for why we felt such an urgency to develop the intermodal business on BN. It drove us to be innovative so that we would be making what the market wanted, and even more importantly , what customers were telling us they would be wanting well into the future. This drove Bill Greenwood. It earned the IBU the support of Darius Gaskins and is why he was such a staunch BN Intermodal supporter after he joined BN. We continued to get push-back by the railroad organization that was comfortable continuing to make and sell what had always been made. They didn't want to go through the hassle of adaptation and making what would best meet the needs of customers.

There were two other professors from that Industrial Marketing Strategy course who would be instrumental for us as our team of Operating Department refugees was learning how to become effective industrial marketers. One was Louis Stern who was an expert in the management of marketing channels.[329] He helped us understand issues related to selling through third parties and the importance of not losing your market identity because of a choice to market through intermediaries. The other was Dan Nimer who was a value-based pricing expert.[330] He helped us understand the importance of pricing for capturing value and the incredible financial positive leverage from price increases and negative leverage from price reductions. He would even sell his business card to anyone who asked for it to illustrate his maxim that anything of value is

[327] Wikipedia, Philip Kotler, Accessed from: https://en.wikipedia.org/wiki/Philip_Kotler, on August 18, 2022.
[328] Wikipedia, Theodore Levitt, Accessed from: https://en.wikipedia.org/wiki/Theodore_Levitt, on August 18, 2022.
[329] Northwestern / Kellogg Faculty Directory, Louis Stern, Accessed from: https://www.kellogg.northwestern.edu/faculty/directory/stern_louis.aspx, on November 12, 2022.
[330] Linked-In, Dan Nimer, Accessed from: https://www.linkedin.com/in/dan-nimer-370b6420/ ,Accessed on November 12, 2022.

worth paying for. He taught us a special formula that we would consider when developing our product, creating an advertisement, or putting a value on our service:

SW^2C = So What, Who Cares?

His point was that it was critical that everything you did had to create value or it was not worth doing. If anything you planned couldn't pass the "SW^2C" test you shouldn't do it.

Bill Greenwood recalled:[331]

> *Kotler reinforced our conviction that we couldn't be comfortable as a traditional railroad. We had to innovate and think out of the box. He really gave us confidence that the approach our new Intermodal team was taking was right. Stern stressed how imperative it was to control your selling channels. Nimer really hammered home the value of differentiating your product or service and being able to increase your price by even just $1. He would ask how much business we would lose if we raised price by $1. The people in the room would say, "probably none of it." He would then ask why we didn't raise prices by a dollar. He stressed that if you didn't lose business that dollar fell right to the bottom line. On the other hand he also stressed how devastating price cuts are in low margin businesses.*

Mark Cane added:[332]

> *Another very important point Dan Nimer stressed was the importance of knowing true marginal costs in order to understand how much business one could afford to lose and keep profitability flat with a price increase. One also needed to know true marginal costs to understand how much business one would have to gain to keep profits flat after a price increase. We learned that BN's costing systems were based on ICC formulas that used a lot of system average costs that didn't relate to true activity-based marginal costs.*
>
> *As finance people took over the railroad there also was an increase in pressure to evaluate businesses based on fully-allocated costs. There was pressure to arbitrarily allocate fixed-costs. Intermodal was among the lowest margin businesses in the railroad portfolio. We knew that in a high fixed-cost and high fixed-asset business like a railroad, even lower margin businesses were important for covering fixed-costs and improving total return on assets.*

As it related to Richard Bressler's emphasis, Larry Kaufman stated:[333]

> *As capital-intensive network businesses, railroads traditionally had considered volume growth the most important criterion for success. It was a proxy for revenue. If a piece of business contributed one cent above its direct operating expense toward covering fixed cost, it was worth having, even if ultimately the railroad lost money on a fully allocated basis. Bressler challenged the revenue focus of the railroad managers almost from his first day in St. Paul. He pointed out that revenue was meaningless unless there were profits and the only measurement that counted for stockholders and investment bankers was returns on equity or return on investment.*

---

[331] Bill Greenwood interview with Mark Cane, November 7, 2022.
[332] Mark Cane's personal recollection.
[333] Kaufman, p. 221.

The financial accounting based fixed-cost orientation differed from the IBU's managerial accounting based view of how to improve overall profitability and return on assets.

Darius Gaskins Arrives Just in Time

Darius Gaskins was, "A West Point graduate who earned an advanced engineering degree at the University of Michigan," and who "had been in the Air Force space program. When the military lost its manned space flight program to the civilian National Aeronautics and Space Administration, he resigned his commission in 1967 and went back to school, earning a doctorate in economics at Michigan."[334]

From there he joined the faculty of the University of California – Berkeley and taught economics, moved on to the Department of the Interior in Washington to work on resource policy, to the Federal Trade Commission as director of its Bureau of economics, to the Civil Aeronautics Board, then to the Department of Energy. From there, President Jimmy Carter appointed him to the Interstate Commerce Commission in 1979. Gaskins served as ICC chairman during the period when deregulation was being debated and enacted. He was also the ICC chair when the BN-Frisco merger was approved, the Rock Island Railroad was shut down and liquidated, and the Milwaukee Railroad was sold to the Soo Line.[335]

While at the ICC he met Richard Bressler:[336]

> *I first met Dick Bressler when I was the Chairman of the Commission in 1980, late '80. I believe it was after the passage of the Staggers Act. He was a pretty conscientious CEO because he realized that a lot of the issues that the railroad had had to do with the regulators. So, he decided it made sense as the new CEO to come see the regulators. So, he came to my office, and not too many CEOs came to my office, I mean, it wasn't a common thing. In those days, anyway. And we had a nice chat and I asked him a series of, I guess, provocative questions. I said, You have a wonderful property there. You've got railroads that run all over the country and you've got this emerging coal franchise. How come you don't make any money?*
>
> *And he hmphed and hmphed, but he was well aware of the substandard economic performance. But we talked about political issues in general and the railroad business in general and then he left. Well, the election comes along, Reagan's elected, he informs me that I'm not going to be the Chairman, he's going to appoint Reese Taylor as Chairman. I still had a spot on the Commission, but I didn't want to sit there in a chair and have somebody else run the place, so I said, Nah, I'll resign. So, here it is January, I've got to decide what I'm going to do. Bressler had invited me to a policy conference of the railroad, and I went out and met all the railroad executives–*
>
> *It was in February. They said, Would you be interested in joining us? We probably can find room for you in this organization. I said, Well, I don't think that would be smart for either one of us because I just finished approving your merger, and you don't need to have a lot of questions about that process, and I don't want to have my integrity impugned by what appears to be a*

---

[334] Railrunner, Directors, Darius Gaskins, Accessed from: https://railrunner.com/vision/directors/, on March 17, 2023.

[335] Ibid.

[336] National Railroad Hall of Fame, Darius W. Gaskins Interview Transcript, November 5, 2020. Accessed from: https://www.nrrhof.org/darius-w-gaskins-jr, on March 20, 2023.

little short-term gain based on that, so let's just say we had a nice conversation and that's the end of it. I had a friend, same friend that got me the job at Interior, who was working for Natomas Oil and Gas Company. He was the President of it in Houston, Texas. He offered me a job.

Gaskins took a job with Natomas but after a year decided he didn't want to stay:[337]

So, I got on the phone. I called the only people I could think to call -- because I didn't want to be an academic at this point. The only people I thought to call were two railroads that had talked to me about potentially joining them. One was the Santa Fe, and one was the Burlington Northern. I called the Santa Fe. I think I got Larry Cena. I think that's who I talked to. He says, Well, I'll ask, I'll ask around, Darius. We'll see what we can do. He didn't get back to me. About two months later, I ran into him somewhere, and he said, I asked around. We didn't have any real spot for you, so we didn't want to pursue it. But I called Bressler, and a week later, I get this call from Dick Grayson, who was the Chairman of the railroad for him, to meet him in Fort Worth. And Walter Drexel, the current President of the railroad and I met there, and they offered me a job as the Head of Marketing. It was kind of a new position. They had marketing people, but they didn't have an overall Head of Marketing. They didn't give me everything, they didn't give me the coal department, but they gave me all the other marketing departments: intermodal, grain, chemicals, so forth. That's how I got the job.

Gaskins joined the BN in St. Paul on August 1, 1982 as Senior Vice President Marketing and Sales, reporting to Drexel. Reporting to Gaskins were Dick Gleason and Bill Egan (Vice President Sales and Service). All of the SBUs reported to Dick Gleason and, as mentioned previously, he was especially hard on Greenwood and the Intermodal team. As Greenwood was quoted earlier, "Even my own boss was out to get us and was virtually drumming up support from the rest of his marketing organization to bury us."[338]

Gaskins sensed this from his first day on the job. His style was unusual except for within the Intermodal Unit where performance, and not titles, mattered. He truly "managed by walking around." From his first day on the job one would see Gaskins walking around Marketing's seventh floor of the St. Paul General Office Building. He would poke his head into anyone's office and just sit down and start a dialogue. He wanted to get to know people. He would ask what projects were being worked on and why. He wanted to know details and probed with a blitz of rapid-fire penetrating questions. He wanted to know the revenue forecast and how performance was tracking versus plan. He would ask if anything was getting in the way of progressing things that resonated with him. He probed and judged the capabilities and integrity of individuals. After pretty much every Gaskins "patrol" through the IBU, the people visited would draw up a memo for Greenwood and the core leadership team so that all knew what was talked about and what, if anything, Gaskins had instructed as a follow-up. While Greenwood was delighted by the interest and frankness Gaskins was displaying with the Intermodal team and for the Intermodal business, Gleason was not. He wanted to know what was said and why. He instructed people to not talk to Gaskins, or if they were forced to talk with him to not reveal more than a minimum of information. Gleason also continued to undermine Greenwood and the IBU with Drexel who took a liking to Gleason.[339]

---

[337] Ibid.

[338] Katzenbach and Smith, p. 33.

[339] Bill Greenwood interview with Mark Cane, March 20, 2022.

Greenwood added this about Gleason, Gaskins and Gerald Davies:

> *I remember one time, Gleason called all of us business unit leaders into his office. He says "Guys, we got this new guy here, Gaskins. We all got to stick together." He says, "He's dangerous. This guy is going to be hard to deal with." A guy that I used to ride to work with, Gerald Davies, head of another business unit, he says, "Greenwood, Gleason is gonna fire you because you're not being cooperative on fending off Gaskins." I said, "Hey, if there's gonna be a battle there, I know whose side I want to be on!"* [340]

> *Davies used to tease me saying, "All you Intermodal guys are like robots. You press a button on your chests and you all say, "We have three Intermodal strategies, Hub Centers, new technology equipment in dedicated trains and marketing packages." I thought that was great but he wasn't an Intermodal fan and thought it was funny. What is ironic is that shortly before we were going to move to Ft. Worth in 1984 I was riding home with him and out of the blue he said, "A crazy thing happened to me today." I didn't think much of it because crazy things were happening every day. I asked him what it was and he said, "You were right about Gaskins. I got fired." That ended our carpooling and he took a job with the CSX Railroad. Gaskins' arrival didn't work out well for Davies but it happened just in time for BN and especially our Intermodal business.* [341]

The obstruction of information flow that Gleason was causing was not at all lost on Gaskins. He stated:[342]

> *I knew there was some tension there and I had other people– the Head of Operations came to me and said, You know, that guy Gleason, he's peeing on your leg, you realize that? And I knew what that meant, and I said, Nah, that's okay, we can handle that. It's not the end of the world. So, he stayed in that position and I worked around him, and I got to know [Bill] Greenwood real well because he had a lot on his plate, and I thought intermodal has a lot of possibilities.*

The overall issues went beyond Gleason though. Gaskins told Larry Kaufman: [343]

> *I really did think the only way this railroad was going to really get where it needed to be was that we had to change the culture for everybody. We couldn't just have a select group that knew what the answer was, because you could already see the Frisco guys running into trouble. They knew how to run a railroad, at least a railroad in the southeastern part of the United States – a small railroad – and they were used to yelling at people and bossing them around. But it wasn't clear they knew what they were doing with the big Rocky Mountain railroad.*

Gaskins was intrigued by the intermodal opportunity because it was the best example within the company of a way to rapidly exploit the freedoms that deregulation (which he had a unique vested

---

[340] National Railroad Hall of Fame, William E. Greenwood, Chief Operating Officer (retired) Burlington Northern Railroad, Interview Transcript, July 30, 2020: Accessed from: https://www.nrrhof.org/greenwood-transcript, Accessed on May 7, 2022.

[341] Bill Greenwood interview with Mark Cane, May 3, 2022.

[342] National Railroad Hall of Fame, Darius W. Gaskins Interview Transcript, November 5, 2020. Accessed from: https://www.nrrhof.org/darius-w-gaskins-jr, on March 20, 2023.

[343] Kaufman, p. 252.

interest in) had enabled. He quickly sensed the frustrations the IBU team was working through. He had a series of meetings with Greenwood and others on the team to better understand what the Task Force had concluded and what progress was being made on the recommendations . He wanted to understand more about the customer base and the profitability of the business. He wanted to know how plans were progressing toward the establishment of the "pilot" Midway and Portland hubs that had been approved just before his arrival. He was intrigued and encouraged by the decision the IBU made to hire hub managers from the motor carrier industry and make them responsible for sales too. He wanted to know, in intimate detail, all about the new equipment technologies that were being tested. He wanted to know what the schedule of Hub conversions should be after Midway and Portland, what terminal facilities needed capital help before they could be converted to Hubs, and how market research and financial analysis was supporting the effort. He also wanted to know from Hoepner what was really happening within the Marketing reorganization study.

Gaskins attended the September 23 presentation of the Organization Study findings and recommendations to Drexel. After that meeting Greenwood and Hoepner explained to Gaskins how important it was that intermodal had responsibility for equipment acquisition and management and how important it was to provide position authorities (that the study did not recommend) to support Dave Burns and Axel Holland with the Hub rollout. On September 30, 1982 the entire department was called to the auditorium for a presentation of the findings and results. On October 15, however, study team leader Bill Allen put out a letter, dated October 15, 1982, stating the following;[344]

> *An oral presentation of this report was made to Mr. Drexel on Thursday, September 23, 1982, at 1300 hours. In addition to Mr. Drexel, the following were in attendance:*
>
> > *Mr. D.W. Gaskins*
> > *Mr. R. M. Gleason*
> > *Mr. L. D. Reed*
> > *Mr. G. K. Davies*
> > *Mr. B. C. Allen – Study Team Leader*
>
> *The Team Leader has now been officially informed by Mr. Reed that subsequent to that presentation, the following specific decisions have been made by Management:*
>
> *The restructuring/restaffing of the department will be implemented over time generally as recommended with a few exceptions.*
> *The forecasting function will be performed by one assigned employee in each business unit together with two assigned employees in the support section.*
> *All TOFC ramp operations / functions on the railroad will be under the jurisdiction of the Intermodal Business Unit. In order to accomplish this, authority was granted to establish three additional District Manager positions in the field.*
> *Responsibility for the distribution of TOFC rail equipment will reside in the Intermodal Business Unit.*
> *Responsibility for distribution of multi-level (auto) rail equipment will reside in the Transportation Section of the Operations Department.*
> > > > > > > > *B. C. Allen*

---

[344] Allen, B. C., Study Team Leader, Marketing and Pricing Department Organization Study Supplemental Statement, October 15, 1982, *Greenwood Collection*, Barriger Library at UMSL.

In support of the IBU, Gaskins exercised the authority of his new position to restore what the Booz Allen study had envisioned and facilitated. It provided a real shot in the arm for IBU morale because it was clear that if they could continuously earn it, Gaskins would support them.

Bill Greenwood recalled how much Gaskins worked to have the back of his team: [345]

> *Just before the conclusion of the "1982 Organization Study Task Force," the project leader and one of his top associates went to Gaskins' office and told him they had information about something one of the business units was doing wrong. Gaskins got up from his chair, grabbed the two by the backs of their necks and physically threw them out of his office screaming, "If you ever come back here again telling me what the business units are doing wrong I will fire you." The two secretaries who witnessed this were startled when they saw Gaskins screaming at these guys while threatening their jobs but it really increased their respect for him because they knew that was typical of how staff groups worked within the company. For them it was actually refreshing to see.*

Greenwood added: [346]

> *So, we all had to make a presentation to Gaskins. I remember my first presentation to him. I went in there, and I had an agenda for him, and I had a slideshow. This was back when we had slides. He said, "Okay, I got this agenda. Only talk to me about the last two items and forget those slides." It was bang, bang, bang, question, question, question. I walked out of there, 'Whoo!' I had an hour meeting with him in ten minutes, but I said, "I like this guy." So Gaskins and I never talked directly much because he was busy getting himself established and everything. He's why I never lost my job. It's because now Dick Gleason reported to him.*

Gaskins also helped clear the way for the IBU to secure badly needed capital authority to expand the Cicero (Chicago) facility and enable Memphis to handle international container business: [347]

> *The team tightened its belt and worked virtually around the clock to launch the Midway hub in October 1982 and the Portland hub in November. Talk about bad timing! The winter was even colder than normal, the country was in recession, and the freight business did slow after Christmas as it always does.*

Concurrently, the IBU was deliberately attempting to reposition the image of the business and change its identity from "piggyback" or "TOFC/COFC" (with all of the negative connotations) to "Intermodal." The theme, *"Innovative Intermodal Service"* (service mark on the left) was chosen to build the new brand/image to also stress the underlying principle of "service." It was deliberately designed to appear like a "BN green" Interstate

---

[345] Bill Greenwood interview with Mark Cane, May 3, 2022.

[346] National Railroad Hall of Fame, William E. Greenwood, Chief Operating Officer (retired) Burlington Northern Railroad, Interview Transcript, July 30, 2020: Accessed from: https://www.nrrhof.org/greenwood-transcript, Accessed on May 7, 2022.

[347] Katzenbach and Smith, p. 37.

Highway sign to build on the image of BN Intermodal's association with the Interstate Highway System. The new theme and design were first used on January 1, 1983. The application for their Trademark was filed on April 18, 1983 and the Trademark was registered on June 12, 1984.[348] This new brand and image repositioning effort would build momentum with the establishment of the Hubs. Each Hub roll-out would be accompanied by targeted print advertising and associated collateral support material such as brochures featuring the new brand ID.

Work had to be done to prepare Midway and Portland for operation as a hub and promote them before their conversion. Dave Burns worked with Human Resources to recruit motor carrier experienced candidates, preferably from the local Hub market area. Bill Greenwood said, "We developed a profile of the average trucking person we would hire. Ideally, the person would be between 33 and 38 years old, have a college degree, have experience in both sales/marketing and operations, be entrepreneurial and have a strong local-customer focus."[349] Burns and Axel Holland worked on facilities modifications that would be required and a template for the process of competitively bidding out hub administrative and ground operations functions. While Midway already had the benefit of lift devices, Portland had to be converted from circus to lift-on, lift-off operation which required the acquisition of a lift device and preparation of the ground to handle such a heavy piece of equipment. Bill DeWitt developed market promotion plans and spearheaded their execution.

Doug Rodel, with 12 years of motor carrier experience, was hired from St. Paul based Murphy Motor Freight[350] effective October 16[351] as BN's first hub manager for Midway and Dave Johnson was hired for Portland. Immediately after their start dates, both were brought to the St. Paul General Office for intermodal orientations with the IBU staff. It was important that they understood the strategy, had a chance to meet new team mates they would be interacting with. They got a better understanding for how intermodal worked, including pricing and equipment distribution. This orientation process was fine-tuned over time for subsequent Hub Manager new-hires based on feedback from the new Hub managers so that there was a sound template. A "living" working template for the necessary steps to accomplish the ramp-to-hub conversion was modified based on the Midway and Portland experiences, with added tweaks as further experience was accumulated. It would get a real work-out over the next 3 years as the ramp-to-hub conversion process progressed and IBU market research and promotion/advertising techniques and skills were honed.

Dave Johnson's (who's Hub was in the process of being expanded) St. Paul orientation trip in November was also unique in that the new Western Regional Intermodal Operations Manager, Julian Woolford, a railroad operations veteran, also joined him. Woolford's position had been created after the previously discussed Organization Study results were "tweaked" with the help of Darius Gaskins. That gave Woolford and Johnson an even greater opportunity to get to know each other and learn together.

---

[348] United States Patent and Trademark Office, Burlington Northern Railroad Company, BN *Innovative Intermodal Service* Trademark Application Details, accessed from: https://uspto.report/TM/73421962, on June 20, 2022. (BNSF Railroad relinquished their rights to it on March 19, 2005 and it is un-revivable.)
[349] Deregulation Plus Market Research Steer BN Deeper into Trucking, *Fleet Owner Magazine*, February, 1986.
[350] Oslund, John J., *Minneapolis Tribune*, BN, Union to Discuss Road-rail Program, April 31, 1983.
[351] M.H Haskin letter to Mr. Douglas J. Rodel, September 29, 1982, furnished by Doug Rodel, April 26, 2022.

A New and Important Transportation Department Advocate

Another major development that would pay longer term dividends was the development of an Intermodal advocate in the Transportation Department. The philosophy of the Transportation Department was, "when you generate enough business we may give you a dedicated train." Given the effects of the 1981-82 recession that was whacking the economy there was tremendous pressure within the company to consolidate trains and minimize train-miles. This put the IBU in an extremely tough spot because the company mentality was to sell what you make instead of making what you can sell. Outside of intermodal it was difficult to find a risk-taking mentality. How do you have a service available that will defensively protect BN's vulnerable market share if those within the company refuse to establish it? How do you offensively compete for motor carrier market share if those within the company refuse to establish motor carrier competitive service offerings?

This challenge was also felt when it came to protecting the IBU's existing intermodal share. As mentioned earlier, United Parcel Service (UPS) was one of the IBU's largest domestic customers. UPS business was carried over BN's best service routes: Chicago and Midway – Seattle and Chicago – Denver. The Chicago-Denver lane was the first one in which UPS utilized BN's service.[352] UPS was a heavily unionized company with Teamsters driving their trucks. UPS could only utilize intermodal in place of Teamster driven trailers if they were initiating service to new geographies, if they had significantly imbalanced business within a lane, or if they obtained a special dispensation from labor. Once those routes became "intermodal routes" UPS was totally dependent on the railroad to perform up to their standards. For them a late trailer was not just a single service failure. If that trailer missed a scheduled sort at the UPS sort center it typically lost a day's worth of service for as many packages as were contained in that trailer. It would not be uncommon for each UPS trailer to contain several hundred packages so a late train incident would result in up to 20+ late UPS trailers. Therefore, late trains would easily cause more than a thousand UPS service failures for its customers in addition to the negative impacts to UPS' network and costs (such as when they were forced to perform an entire re-sort). UPS employees' compensation was correlated with service performance which heightened awareness and scrutiny of railroad performance even more.

After Gordon Trafton joined the IBU in early 1982 to focus on train schedules and service, he was also designated to be the primary IBU liaison with UPS. Trafton's operating background, diligence and character really appealed to the IBU's UPS interfaces. After his IBU assignment he visited with UPS contacts in Denver. To better understand their operation and needs he requested, and was permitted, to dress up in a brown UPS delivery driver's uniform and accompany the driver on his route and deliver packages for a full day. In early 1982, BN's service from Chicago to Denver was terrible due to weather and operating performance problems. UPS management was furious and Trafton was taking the brunt of their fury. Trafton submitted a proposal to the Transportation Department to modify the schedule of the prime Chicago-Denver UPS carrying mixed-freight train (Train 63). He believed it would improve its on-time performance which would help to significantly reduce, if not eliminate, UPS service failures. He didn't get a reply to his proposal even after multiple inquiries. Trafton had been attending the daily morning Transportation staff meetings in which train performance issues were reviewed. Having had a field operating background gave Trafton some credibility with the operating group but his association with Marketing, and worse than that with "that pain-in-the-a** loser" Intermodal, didn't make him overly welcomed. At about the same time a new Assistant Vice President Transportation began attending the meetings. His name was Hunter Harrison and he came from the Frisco. He had a

---

[352] DeBoer, p. 103.

reputation for tolerating no "bull" and, as they say, "taking no prisoners." He was passionate about running a precision operation because of the improved customer service, asset utilization and cost control benefits that resulted. At one of the meetings he attended, Trafton mentioned the problems with Train 63's performance and how BN was gambling with the loss of all of the UPS business between Chicago and Denver. One day after one of Harrison's first meetings, Trafton had just gotten back to his desk when his phone rang. Harrison was on the other end and asked him to come to his office right away. When Trafton arrived, Harrison asked him to sit down. He began to drill him about the issues related to the UPS service failures related to Train 63. He asked Trafton why nothing had been done to address them. Trafton described recent service failures and explained to Harrison that 63's schedule provided no recovery ability, particularly during the winter. He went on to say that he had submitted a proposal to Transportation for a schedule modification which he believed would fix the problems with the current schedule. Ironically, his new proposed schedule was 30 minutes longer than the current schedule with trailer availability 15 minutes later. That longer schedule would allow for more consistent on-time train arrivals and trailer availability and still meet the needs of UPS. Trafton had learned through his work with UPS that train arrival and especially trailer-availability consistency were what UPS valued most. They had to allow UPS to deliver their trailers to the sort center by the scheduled sort time. Harrison asked what response he had gotten and Trafton said he was told it was being evaluated. Harrison then asked when Trafton's proposal had been submitted and he said, "two weeks ago," (in reality it had been nearly three weeks). Harrison became furious and asked who Trafton had dealt with (which he was reluctant to reveal because it was already difficult to get changes made to improve intermodal schedules and he didn't want it to become even more difficult). Little did he know how things were about to change. Trafton shared the names of his Transportation contacts, Harrison said he would take care of it, and Trafton left. Within five minutes of returning to his desk, Trafton was visited by one of those Transportation contacts who had just gotten off the phone with Harrison. The individual asked what Trafton's proposal was for Train 63, and he said he would print it out and deliver it to him. The contact said he needed it quickly and he would wait for it. After producing the proposed schedule, Trafton asked whether the schedule would be implemented anytime soon and the Transportation contact responded that it would be effective by the end of the day, or he and others would be looking for new jobs.[353]

Once the new schedule was implemented the performance of Train 63 and trailer availability at the Denver Hub improved significantly. UPS was delighted and their business was saved and would grow as a result. The incident gained significant credibility for BN Intermodal and Trafton in the eyes of UPS, Hunter Harrison and among the participants of Transportation's morning meeting. It was unheard of for anyone from Marketing to ask for time to be added to a train schedule, but it was an example of the broad business-based approach and focus the IBU had. Harrison would become a staunch supporter of Intermodal, always aggressively questioning things. Once Harrison was convinced, the IBU couldn't have asked for a better ally. He would become critical for the introduction of new intermodal trains, the reduction of intermodal train operating costs and the improvement of intermodal train performance.

That support was put to the test shortly after Train 63's performance issues were resolved. One assumption that had been made in association with the opening of the Portland Hub was that it would benefit from dedicated train service between Portland and Chicago. As mentioned earlier, Union Pacific had better service than BN in this corridor. In fact, UP carried the UPS business between these points and that tended to draw business from other customers. The market was aware that if UPS utilized an intermodal service, that service had to be good. The IBU utilized a novel volume-based train costing

---

[353] Email from Gordon Trafton to Mark Cane, March 4, 2022.

model that was developed with the assistance of BN's Costs and Statistics Department to develop pro-forma train P&Ls based on the volume forecasts the IBU had developed in coordination with the new Hub staff and even the Operating Department through Harrison. Trafton worked up competitive and do-able schedules with his Transportation counterparts. In addition, a market-oriented promotion plan for the train was developed. With all of this information a meeting was scheduled with Harrison to introduce him to the model, explain how it worked, explain the promotion plan for the trains, and what the pro-forma projected eastbound and westbound train P&Ls looked like on a month- by-month basis following the initiation of new train service. Further, the model showed on a train-by-train basis how a train would lose money for several months as a level of service performance was established but that it would become solidly profitable within six to nine months. The concept of whether the IBU could get Harrison's support for making what you can profitably sell was put to the test. Harrison wasn't wild about the BN having to endure a period of loss as a reputation for solid service performance was established. This was especially so during the 1982 recession when the operating department's focus was on consolidating trains and reducing train starts.

Largely due to the trust which had been generated with Intermodal in the eyes of Harrison, he agreed to go along with the establishment of Train #24 which initiated service during the last week of June. The July 1 Press Release associated with the new train stated: [354]

> *Burlington Northern Railroad has added a new intermodal train to Chicago for customers in the Portland, Ore., area.*
>
> *Train 24, which began service last week, trims more than 10 hours from the previous Portland – Chicago schedule. The train departs BN's Portland hub center at 12:30 a.m. Tuesday through Saturday, with third-morning trailer availability for Minneapolis - St. Paul and early third-afternoon trailer availability for Chicago. Customers can drop off trailers and containers at Portland as late as 11:00 p.m. Monday through Friday.*
>
> *The train's 11 p.m. cutoff is just as important to BN customers as is the faster schedule. The previous cutoff time of 6:30 p.m. made it especially difficult for customers located outside the Portland metropolitan area to deliver a trailer to the hub in time for an evening train departure.*
>
> *BN is completing a paving project at its Portland hub and is adding a second lift device to speed trailer and container handling.*

After inauguration of the train, manual records from the actual train consists were utilized to create daily P&Ls and shared with Harrison. It was challenging early on because the volume was slower to ramp up than expected and the operation of short intermodal trains across BN's network created second guessing that became heated at times. However, the growth and financial performance of the trains worked out as the IBU had projected which was a critical component of the success of the Portland and Midway Hubs and solidified Harrison's support.

The impact Harrison had on Intermodal was greatly misunderstood by most, particularly in the Operating Department. What few understood was the fact that Harrison was aligned with the views of members of the IBU leadership team, all of whom had prior operating experience, about what had to be

---

[354] Burlington Northern Railroad, Press Release, BN Railroad Adds Intermodal Train Between Portland and Chicago, July 1, 1982, *Greenwood Collection*, Barriger Library at UMSL.

done to profitably grow the intermodal business. A prime example of this is another significant Harrison intervention that helped the IBU - the amount of locomotive power assigned to Intermodal trains. It was not uncommon for Train 3 between Chicago and Seattle to be assigned a ratio of 6+ horsepower-per-training-ton (HPT). At times more than the typical four high-horsepower locomotives were required. A primary factor behind such HPT assignment reasoning at the time was in-service failures in the SD40-2 locomotive fleet, particularly in the winter. It was not uncommon during winter for two of the four locomotives powering Train 3 to fail enroute. This would create a need to add unplanned locomotives enroute which then disrupted other train service, compounding the network cost and service impact. Trains would arrive in Seattle with five or more locomotives and half of them were out of service. Operating trains with 6+ HPT was excessive and costly and the IBU opposed it. Yet there was concern that the cost of excess horsepower insurance was less than the cost of business lost due to service failures. One day Harrison challenged Trafton and asked him to justify the reasonableness of assigning such high HPT ratios to intermodal trains. Trafton said the IBU opposed such high ratios for cost reasons but given the mean-time-between-failures (MTBF) for the SD40-2 fleet, there wasn't a reasonable choice given the impact of locomotive failure related customer service failures. Harrison then asked why nothing had been done about it up to that point. Trafton responded that Intermodal didn't assign the locomotives to the train or dictate HPT standards. He said the IBU felt helpless to effect any change and was paying for 6 HPT but in many cases, especially during winter, getting only 3 HPT of service. Harrison was unhappy with his response but understood that for Intermodal's (and BN's) service quality to be improved and costs to be reduced, something had to change with BN's SD40-2 locomotive fleet reliability performance. He immediately went to work to change the willingness of BN's Operating culture to accept a common belief that any train's locomotive consist couldn't operate to destination without enroute failures. He challenged the Mechanical Department to identify the root causes of failures and attack the quality issue. He instituted new locomotive service reliability metrics and benchmarks and made locomotive-failure-caused train delays very visible to the organization. The HPT was reduced in half for most intermodal trains which made failures even more visible. The pressure was on and the Mechanical Department leadership didn't want to have to explain why locomotive failures were the root-cause of late intermodal trains, particularly in the Morning Meeting. Locomotive reliability metrics improved. This was another example of Harrison's unconventional, controversial and yet effective method of effecting changes in a culture that was not used to confrontation and on-the-point accountability. It was also an early sign of what arguably would become one of the main components of his operating philosophy that lives on today in the railroad industry through its adoption of Precision Scheduled Railroading – asset utilization/velocity.

Six other significant developments occurred for the IBU in 1982. One that may not seem significant given how information technology has evolved since then, but was an example of the drive and ingenuity of the Unit, was the acquisition of two of the first personal computers in the company. The work performed for the Task Force and hub market plans required an incredible amount of analysis. The planning section of the team researched PCs and in late 1981 actually bought one of the first portable IBM PCs that was carried like a suitcase with a fold-out CRT screen. That PC quickly became relatively obsolete because of its lack of storage and slow processing speed. Next, in early 1982 an IBM PC-XT with a "massive" 10 MB hard drive was purchased at the Dayton's Department Store in downtown St. Paul. The desire for a good spreadsheet program was expressed and the salesperson said "Lotus 1,2,3" was the best one he was aware of so that program, along with a printer, was purchased too. Several IBU employees undertook a crash self-taught, under-fire course on how to run Lotus. The PC became the main tool used for IBU forecasting, budgeting and financial simulations. As indicated above, in 1982 and 1983 it would become the tool used to measure intermodal train load factors, estimate train P&Ls and simulate new train break-even points and profit and loss scenarios such as with the new Portland train.

To make the train financial simulation tool possible the Costs and Statistics Department was asked to prepare a matrix showing what the cost would be to run a single locomotive with a full train crew between planned hub center origin and destination pairs. Then they were asked to provide a matrix across the future hub network pairs for what the cost would be to run an additional locomotive on a train - again with no cars. Then they were asked to provide a series of matrices for what it would cost to add a car loaded with one loaded trailer, then a car with two loaded trailers on it, then another car with the same characteristics and so on with similar information if containers were carried. Trailing tonnage charts indicated how many cars a locomotive could haul on any route before a second locomotive was required. With this information, for which significant political capital was spent to obtain, the PC was utilized as a tool to measure a train's true marginal P&L (although it was an extremely time intensive manual effort to get the data entered). The acquisition infuriated the Management Services (IT) Department because they wanted control over such expenditures. It was a perfect example of putting into practice that phrase Dave Burns brought the team – his "Jesuit principle" of management: "It is much easier to ask for forgiveness than for permission."[355] The IBU continued to wear that principle out.

A **Second** was a troubling discovery regarding BN Railroad's billing and revenue accounting systems. The reports that Marketing got related to revenue generation were based on a "revenue estimator." The system did not capture actual revenue generated through the use of actual rate files crossed against actual shipment data. When the IBU would examine data related to intermodal shipments the revenue at a movement level between origin and destination pairs frequently looked out of whack. For example, a shipment between Chicago and Seattle might show revenue of $1000 when another shipment between these points might show revenue of $4,260 while the price for each should have been $1,555. An inordinate amount of time had to be spent with revenue accounting to fix the revenue estimator files which raised questions about the reliability of the data overall, especially as this data fed the costing system which made the IBU question the reliability of the profit accounting system. What was more alarming is that while visiting with Intermodal Marketing Companies and motor carrier customers such as UPS and Roadway Express, it was learned that railroads tended to not bill for up to 10% of the shipments that they tendered to railroads. They said BN was better than the average (billed for more than 90% of shipments) but it was alarming none-the-less. At one meeting Bert Dopp, who was the coordinator of intermodal line-haul substitution for Roadway Express, was asked about business

opportunities in other traffic lanes. He reached over and grabbed a stack of sheets of paper and said something to the effect of, "We can talk about other lanes but, first, when are you going to finally bill me for these shipments because my accounting people are driving me nuts about it." This information was shared with the IBU terminal operations team, freight accounting and the information systems department so that BN's billing processes would be reassessed and patches created to fix root causes of the problem related to accounting and information systems. It pointed out the need for substantial help on the information technology front. Dealing with the deep recession and the onslaught of deregulation was bad enough but not even billing for the service you provide was insanity. As a result, another thing this information drove was an immediate multi-department effort to "Close the Cracks (CTC)" so that BN captured the revenue it was due. Tom Bauer was assigned to this effort from Intermodal. He had been

---

[355] Katzenbach and Smith, p. 39.

recently hired as an IBU planning analyst and aside from being the wizard on the new IBM PC, he had been working to fix the issues with the "revenue estimator." The CTC effort was lead by Dave Hull from the Customer Accounting group. The inter-departmental team was even issued hats (above).[356]

Another means to assist with this effort to tighten up billing control was to mandate that all billing information for a shipment must be received before, or at the time, a shipment arrives at the origin Hub gate. Prior to this, third parties would frequently direct drayage companies to deliver a trailer to BN and park it at the facility where it sat until shipping instructions arrived. When this happened the shipment would be at risk of not being shipped because it was not known where to ship it to. This prevented track-side trailer placement upon trailer arrival, clogged up the ramp's parking space and raised intra-facility trailer hostling costs. For market research and pricing control purposes the IBU requested information on who the beneficial shipper and receiver of the shipment was. The IBU wanted this information to better understand who the real customers were and to help it avoid competing with itself for business it was already carrying. It was not uncommon for a third party to request a special rate for business that only later would the IBU discover that it was already handling that business through a different third party at a higher rate. Unfortunately, other railroads were not mandating this information so for competitive reasons it was not yet mandated. The image on the left (*Greenwood Collection*, Barriger Library at UMSL) is the notice of the new

WE WILL . . .

☞ Provide expedited trailer movement

☞ Spot your shipment to trackside

☞ Minimize your drivers' time at the ramp

BUT WE NEED YOUR HELP

We need to have the information on the back of this page provided on all TOFC/COFC shipments, hazardous and non-hazardous alike, prior to or upon arrival at gate. This will provide information for expedited trailer movement and billing and will enable our crews to direct your shipment to trackside for immediate loading instead of to a holding area to await forwarding instructions.

policy change. After it was instituted there were a number of shipments that were refused at the gate for lack of information. It was a rocky transition but in relatively short order the kinks were worked out.

The **third** major 1982 development was the ICC's approval of the combination of the Union Pacific, Missouri Pacific and Western Pacific Railroads on October 20 and executed in December. The Union Pacific was already a formidable competitor with routes from Chicago (via the Chicago & Northwestern Railroad) to both Seattle/Portland and Los Angeles while BN only had a Chicago - Pacific Northwest route. Among other significant BN intermodal implications, this now gave the UP a single line route (via the C&NW) between the California Bay Area and the Midwest and the best intermodal route between the Midwest and Texas in addition to their pre-existing routes to Los Angeles and Seattle/Portland.

The **fourth** was the indication in December from Sea-Land, BN's largest international intermodal customer, that effective in January, 1983 they would be shifting their PNW-Chicago business to the Union Pacific in conjunction with a total West Coast service package that the UP would now be able to offer them (post-merger). Another major factor was that the Port of Seattle's Terminal 5, where Sea-Land loaded and unloaded their container ships, was about six miles closer to the Union Pacific Argo intermodal yard than BN's South Seattle facility.

---

[356] Tom Bauer email to Mark Cane, including CTC hat picture, March 14, 2022.

The last factor was price. One of the primary Sea-Land decision makers was Bob Ingram who would later become an even bigger part of the BN Intermodal story. Sea-Land had been a customer of the GN and then BN railroads since the 1960s but they demanded a price the IBU was unwilling to match. Gaskins and Gleason were briefed on the decision on December 17 and Drexel was briefed on January 25, 1983. The IBU committed to Drexel to more than make-up for the Sea-Land revenue loss in 1983 by gaining share with multiple smaller steamship lines (at higher prices than Sea-Land demanded) that were already calling on Seattle, or were in the process of adding Seattle to their Transpacific service.

The loss of Sea-Land's business was a significant blow to the new BN IBU. The GN and NP railroads had a longstanding relationship with the Port of Seattle but Seattle's "intermodal" service had been primarily roll-on, roll-off (RORO) service of trailers driven onto barges for transportation to and from Alaska. In the late 1950s Malcom McLean changed that with his innovative pursuit of containerization of what was formerly break-bulk cargo. [357]

> *It was Malcom McLean, the owner of a trucking company, who eventually made the first investment in movable boxes in a size similar to a truck trailer and shipped them from Newark to Houston in April, 1956. He eventually expanded his concept to other U.S. routes: the West Coast to Hawaii, Miami to Puerto Rico.*
>
> *McLean's greatest challenges were with the unions of the ports in which he set up his operations; while West Coast ports' unions embraced the system, the East Coast unions were more difficult to convince. He also had difficulties convincing port authorities to invest in cranes and docks; in particular the Port of New York was unwilling to invest in docks that were wide enough to allow trucks to come alongside ships.*

The advent of containerization of maritime cargo blossomed on the East Coast of the United States and spread to California, drawn by its huge population base. Seattle was in a tough spot because it did not offer a large local, or even extended, population base. As a result, in spite of being a full shipping-day closer to Japan due to the "Great Circle" route, Seattle's port stagnated in the post-war 1950s because the Los Angeles basin alone offered local population almost 5 times larger than Seattle.[358]

The Port of Seattle decided to adopt a "build it and they will come" strategy and, [359]

> *"made a bold decision to develop container-handling facilities before any shipping companies had announced their intention to locate container-ship operations on Seattle's Elliot Bay on the Puget Sound. In 1962, the Port unveiled a $30 million terminal-building plan. The plan involved installing specialized cranes that could reach out over ships to load and unload containers, clearing acres for container storage, installing electrical lines and outlets for powering refrigerated containers, and building facilities for customs agents, shipping company personnel and longshore workers."*

---

[357] David, Pierre A. & Stewart, Richard D., *International Logistics – The Management of International Trade Operations*, Cengage Learning, Mason, OH, 2010, p. 321.

[358] Ott, Jennfer, Container Shipping in Seattle: Origins and Early Years, November 5, 2014, obtained through: https://www.historylink.org/File/10924, accessed February 28, 2022.

[359] Ibid.

In anticipation of success in attracting containerization based shipping companies the Port negotiated with the Pacific Coast longshoremen to adopt the "Mechanization and Modernization Agreement," an agreement vigorously fought by longshore labor on the U.S. East Coast. In 1964, McLean's Sea-Land Service was attracted to Seattle and leased the newly container-capable Terminal 5. Sea-Land then made Seattle the headquarters of its West coast operations[360] and the relationship with the Great Northern Railroad was established. After 18 years of working together to grow the Seattle intermodal business, the Sea-Land/GN-BN relationship was reduced from BN having basically all of Sea-Land's Seattle originated containerized cargo for inland destinations to primarily Minneapolis/St. Paul business that the UP could not effectively reach.

Concurrent with Sea-Land's decision, driven by Bob Ingram, to shift their Seattle business to Union Pacific was their announcement that they would not be renewing their Terminal 5 lease with the Port. "Instead, Sea-Land entered a 30-year contract with the Port of Tacoma. Jack Helton, the Vice President of Sea-Land's Alaska Division, explained that the business decision to move from Seattle to Tacoma was based on:

> *Room to grow, labor productivity, and economics …. We will save a million dollars a year in operating costs. Tacoma's new rail yard will greatly reduce costs of moving containers.*[361]

It would take the Port of Tacoma three years to build this new terminal for Sea-Land and its on-dock intermodal operation on the Sitcum Waterway at a cost of $44 million.[362] This facility would be jointly served by BN and the Union Pacific but the relocation would give the IBU an opportunity to regain Sea-Land's business.

The **fifth** was approval to expand the Cicero (Chicago) intermodal facility and equip Memphis with a lift device. BN's Chicago carload classification yard and primary intermodal ramp operation was in Cicero (a much smaller secondary facility was at Western Avenue). The intermodal portion of the Cicero operation was bursting at the seams and a combination of the downturn in carload business plus a transfer of Cicero carload business classification work to the Eola and Galesburg, Illinois yards freed up more space for intermodal operations. With the help of Gaskins, the IBU obtained $2.5 million of capital authority to turn the north side of the Cicero yard complex into primarily a container handling operation with two side loading lift devices to support the rapidly growing international business. It also permitted the conversion and expansion of the south side of the yard so it could be primarily a trailer handling operation with four overhead cranes. For Memphis, $550,000 was approved for a "shoestring" modification of the facility and to equip it with the first lift device on the former Frisco Railroad.[363]

A **sixth** was the decision to relocate the railroad's headquarters Operating Department functions from St. Paul to Overland Park. "Grayson had announced in 1982 that the railroad was considering relocating its headquarters. At the time, Minnesota's economic and tax policies were viewed broadly as unfriendly to business. The first study was thorough and run by the railroad's head of strategic planning. (W)hen the study was completed, the railroad decided to stay in St. Paul."[364] There was no secret about how the

---

[360] Ibid.

[361] Oldham, Kit, Sea-Land begins shipping operations at Port of Tacoma on May 13, 1985, History Link.org, posted January 16, 2008, accessed from: https://www.historylink.org/File/8463, on March 11, 2022.

[362] Ibid.

[363] BN: Big Switch at Cicero, *Railway Age Magazine*, January, 1983.

[364] Kaufman, p. 229.

former Frisco executives disliked the Minnesota weather and high tax climate. The harsher than normal winter of 1981-82 only fed that sentiment. Grayson gave his Executive VP Operations Bill Thompson authority to find a different headquarters for Operations and he chose Overland Park, Kansas. That relocation occurred by the end of 1982. The separation of headquarters Transportation, Mechanical and Engineering staffs from the Marketing Department, and especially the cross functional IBU that was so reliant on the Operations Department for the execution of its strategies, harmed the interaction between the groups. It was no longer possible to conveniently meet face-to-face and casual interactions, such as over lunch in the cafeteria, now became impossible.

1982 Intermodal Business Unit (IBU) Performance

In spite of the deep recession, the IBU finished 1982 with an intermodal revenue growth over 1981 of $6.2 million (+2.3%) on flat overall volume. The IBU's prime Chicago–PNW and Chicago–Denver corridors' volume was up 6-8% with the help of the new Portland–Chicago dedicated train. Growth was tempered because the IBU deliberately decided to not participate in some of the rate-cutting (such as that encountered with Sea-Land) that had been taking place.[365]

In 1982, 77% of Intermodal revenue was domestic and 23% was international. Of the domestic business, 56% came from third parties, 26% came from motor carriers (primarily UPS) and 18% came from beneficial freight owners (direct retail). Of the international business, 60% came from steamship companies, 20% came from third parties, 13% came from ports and 7% was from beneficial shippers. Six scheduled dedicated intermodal trains carried 35% of BN's intermodal business.

Unfortunately, total railroad performance was awful. The 1982 BN Annual Report summarized the result of the full year carnage:

> *Revenues were $3.8 billion, down 8 percent; operating income was $245 million, down 31 percent. In statistics for the year, rail traffic volume as measured in revenue ton miles declined 10 percent to 158 billion. The forest products commodity group traffic was down 23%; food and manufactured products commodity group traffic was down 26% from 1981 levels. However, there were bright spots with important implications for the railroad's future. For example, deregulation provides greater flexibility in meeting customer needs, and our marketing efforts have been reorganized to take advantage of the new opportunities.*[366]

The Intermodal Task Force suggested that 28% of BN's Food and Manufactured Products and Forest Products business was vulnerable to motor carriers by 1986. <u>Their respective 23% and 26% drops meant that the worst case scenario was almost fully realized in less than one year.</u> <u>Because of internal BN obstruction, no Intermodal alternative was available to protect it.</u> What made the situation worse was that grain was also having a down year with volume down 17% vs. 1981 while grain revenue fell 11%. Fortunately, coal revenue increased 12%.[367]

Bill Greenwood commented:[368]

---

[365] BN: Big Switch at Cicero, *Railway Age Magazine*, January, 1983.
[366] Burlington Northern Inc., 1982 Annual Report, p. 6.
[367] Ibid.
[368] Bill Greenwood interview with Mark Cane, January 24, 2023.

Our Intermodal Task Force predicted that we were likely to bleed carload market share. It was incredibly frustrating that it was happening and we had no effective defense. I was told that we were really on to something when I talked to people outside the company about what we were trying to build with BN Intermodal. Yet, we couldn't convince our own company. Our biggest obstacles were within our own company and that would not change for a long time.

Chapter 10 - Pursuing the Three Intermodal Strategies in 1983

The pursuit of the three strategies survived the Intermodal Task Force and the 1982 reorganization study that attempted to turn the IBU back into what would have been primarily a marketing and pricing organization. The first strategy focused on Hubs was gaining traction but the second strategy focused on new technology equipment in dedicated trains and the third focused on marketing packages were lagging. The IBU's AVP Pricing who was inherited when the unit was formed had difficulty operating in a deregulated environment. Bill Greenwood recalled:

> He was a wonderful man but couldn't adapt to the deregulated pricing world. Among a group of aggressive risk takers pushing the envelope of innovation, he was not comfortable with change. When we talked about changes he would say, "I don't necessarily disagree with that but this is why it won't work." We had to be willing to take measured risks or we wouldn't succeed. [369]

Ken Hoepner, who had been Director Equipment and Service since IBU formation, was stretched too thin because his hands were in too many baskets. Bill DeWitt was being inhibited from exploring more "cutting edge" marketing efforts. To address this, Bill Greenwood demoted the AVP Pricing and promoted Ken Hoepner to AVP Intermodal Marketing and Pricing with Ralph Muellner in charge of International Marketing, Bill DeWitt in charge of Domestic Marketing focused on motor carriers and the IMC segment, and Cliff Kath as Director Domestic Marketing focused on direct, non-motor carrier customer opportunities. Pricing authority was vested with these directors for their segment, eliminating a separate "pricing" section. In addition, in late 1983 Bill Berry was brought in as Director Equipment and Service, from District Manager Intermodal Facility Operations on the Twin Cities Region, to fill Hoepner's former position. In August, before formally moving on to his new Marketing position, Hopener hired Roger Simon to be Manager TOFC/COFC Equipment Utilization from the Marketing Services Group after Simon's predecessor was promoted to Bill Berry's former position. This equipped the group to execute its strategies more effectively.

Strategy #1: Convert a Vast Network of Ramps to a Lean Network of Hubs

As of January 1, 1983, BN had lift devices at its intermodal facilities at Chicago, Denver, Kansas City, Lincoln, Midway, Mobile (restricted to 60,000 lbs. Gross weight for containers), Portland, South Seattle, Spokane, Tacoma and Wichita (also containers limited to 60k GW).[370] The two "pilot" hubs, Midway and Portland, were established in October and November of 1982. Marketing brochures were developed for both Hubs, as indicated by Midway's (outside and inside of the tri-fold) shown below (*Greenwood Collection*, Barriger Library at UMSL) but that was the relatively easy work. The start-up processes were challenging for both locations commercially because of the poor economy and operationally because there was no prior experience for doing what had to be done to establish such a totally new business paradigm. In addition, as previously mentioned, the normally harsh Minnesota winter weather was

---

[369] Bill Greenwood interview with Mark Cane, March 18, 2022.
[370] Burlington Northern Railroad 1983 Appointment Calendar, *Greenwood Collection*, Barriger Library at UMSL.

worse than usual for cold and snow making the effort even more difficult. On the operating side there were a number of other challenges.

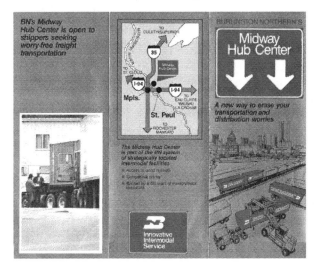

Primarily because of the amount of international business from and to Seattle, the Minneapolis/ St. Paul ramp had been equipped with a lift device since before 1970. One of the first things done after Doug Rodel got his feet on the ground at Midway was to put the contracted ramp operations work out for bid in an attempt to gain better service at a lower cost. The majority of the operations had been contracted to BNI subsidiary BN Transport (BNT). BNT employees operated the lift devices, performed check-in equipment inspection, secured trailers and containers onto rail cars, and performed trailer and container hostling within the facility. They also handled drayage. The only intermodal related operating task performed by BN employees, represented by the Brotherhood of Railway and Airline Clerks (BRAC), was computer reporting to generate movement and revenue data. BNT employees were represented by the Teamsters Union. Due to union rules, the IBU could not seek an alternative to the BRAC represented railroad clerks but the IBU was not bound to a union-represented contractor for the balance of the work.

BNT attempted to retain the work but was not the successful bidder. That created a political problem because BNT was a sister company that also reported to Richard Grayson. In the discussion about the performance of the BNI operating units in 1982, the BNI Annual Report section on BNT said,

> *BNT (and Frisco Transportation Co.) reported a 6% revenue reduction due to the recession and an operating loss of $3 million vs. an income of $.55 mm in 1981. BNT plans to increase its sales and geographic coverage during the coming year and to expand its intermodal volume in cooperation with BN railroad.* [371]

In the spirit of holding each subsidiary independently accountable, the IBU was ultimately not forced to retain them at a higher cost than the open market offered. BNT's replacement created an operational problem because the winning bidder's employees had to be trained for the work. Intermodal lift device operators and ground-workers were anything but common in those days. One didn't just recruit them off the street. Dennis Gustin recalled:

---

[371] Burlington Northern Inc., 1982 Annual Report, p. 9.

> *The change-out of ramp contractor was a disaster. These folks came out of Chicago, expanding on their operators experience as lift operators. Kirchhoff (a contracted service provider) and I spend two days testing their personnel. They had zero intermodal experience. They advised quietly to us they were all fork lift operators. Needless to say things did not go well nor did anybody want to hear our negative opinions prior to change. This was a real sore spot; a re-bid fixed this issue. There were days the trailer damage caused by the unqualified and poorly supervised lift device operators appeared to have been caused by an aerial attack.[372]*

The ramp/deramp service was re-bid and won by a contractor from Detroit. They proved to be a successful contractor but there was much more to do.

 The process of shutting down ramps in the Midway Hub service area was put into gear. The ability to quickly shut these operations down was facilitated by the new flexibility provided by deregulation which meant that ICC approval was not necessary. Existing customers served by remote ramps intended for closure (Minnesota points: Brainerd, Cloquet, Duluth, International Falls, Roseau, St. Cloud, Willmar, and Winona as well as Wisconsin points (La Crosse and Superior) plus Sioux Falls, SD had to be worked with to establish new service via truck to/from Midway. It took approximately six months to complete the task for Midway.

Bill Greenwood recalled:

> *Midway was the hub Grayson chose. He liked the idea of cost reduction related to ramp closures but he really doubted that we could retain the business from ramps that were closed. He asked for detailed reports of business volume at each of these locations before and after closure. The reports showed that we actually grew our business as we promised we would and I never heard anything more from him about it.[373]*

As previously mentioned, the conversion from ramp to hub at Portland had similar but also different challenges. Portland was not equipped with a lift device – it was only a circus ramp. The approval authority for Portland as the second pilot hub included capital for a lift device and facility preparation and paving to accommodate lift-on/lift-off operations.

In spite of their start-up challenges, by mid-January 1983 it was clear that the Midway and Portland hubs were both performing much better than the forecasts that had been committed to support their approval. As a result, a meeting was held with Gaskins and Drexel on February 15 to seek approval for the balance of the first Task Force hub development and ramp closure plan. The meeting was successful and an aggressive schedule of Hub starts was developed starting with Seattle in April, Memphis in May, St. Louis in July, Denver in August, Spokane in September, Birmingham in October, and Kansas City in November of 1983. The meeting also brought authority to spend $16 million for expanded Hub track infrastructure, added parking spaces in Chicago, Seattle and Birmingham along with lift devices for Memphis and St. Louis.[374] Hub conversions were also scheduled for 1984 with Galesburg, Illinois in February, Dallas in March, Houston and Fargo in May, Springfield, Missouri in July, Mobile in August, and

---

[372] Dennis Gustin email to Mark Cane, February 10, 2022.
[373] Mark Cane interview with Bill Greenwood, May 3, 2022.
[374] Burlington Northern Railroad, Innovative Intermodal Service – A Progress Report from Burlington Northern, December 1983, *Greenwood Collection*, Barriger Library at UMSL.

Omaha in September. The final two hub conversions, Chicago and Billings, were scheduled for January of 1985.

While approval to proceed was received it didn't mean there was smooth sailing ahead to complete the hub conversion process. As Dave Burns related, starting in 1983:

> "Each hub proposal had to be justified by the rigorous BN Authority for Expenditure (AFE) process, with well crafted cost-value benefit analysis. You didn't just walk in and ask for $100 million (which doesn't sound like much now, but 35 years ago it was a staggering amount, especially for a company still struggling with the huge costs of the ramp-up necessitated by the explosion in low sulphur coal). Here again we were able to create coalitions with activist individuals in Engineering, Mechanical, Revenue and Cost Accounting, Property Acquisition, and numerous other groups to prepare 21 AFEs in a phased, sequential order over 5 years. But with the compelling cost-benefit analysis prepared so carefully and thoroughly, and at the phased rate and successes we were generating, the funding did get the approval as we needed it."[375]

The investment in intermodal facilities was featured in a nationwide ad (left, *Greenwood Collection*, Barriger Library at UMSL). It appeared in transportation magazines targeting beneficial shippers to establish a strong demand-pull brand identity for BN Intermodal.

Meanwhile, work was completed at Cicero and Memphis. Forecasts were updated to help determine when other facilities would hit capacity limits. Work was also conducted to determine an ideal Hub configuration. The location of intermodal facilities was mostly a matter of default – wherever space was available in locations where good highway access and train service was available. That meant encroaching on freight car yard space for intermodal operations.

Strategies were also honed for how to best handle relationships with current and potential future Hub contractors. On May 18, 1983 a meeting was held with one of the Intermodal Industry's Founding Fathers, Peter Novas, about the possibility of a total turnkey relationship for the future Birmingham hub. Novas was considered an industry innovator from his days leading Illinois Central Railroad's intermodal business. The IBU chose to ultimately manage the operation using the template it had already developed but the pursuit of new ideas did not stop. New Hub managers hired from the motor carrier industry brought new ideas as to how best handle the motor carrier extension of the IBU's services including the establishment of highway satellite Hubs. These satellites allowed BN's IBU to take advantage of the new regulatory freedoms to capitalize on the best of what rail and motor carrier operations could deliver for the customer. The following maps show the pre and post 1982-83 construction layout of the combined Cicero rail-carload facility.[376]

---

[375] Burns, Dave, Intermodal Days 1982-1992, *The BN Expediter*, Volume 26, Number 4, Friends of the Burlington Northern Railroad, October 2018, p. 12.
[376] BN: Big Switch at Cicero, *Railway Age Magazine*, January, 1983

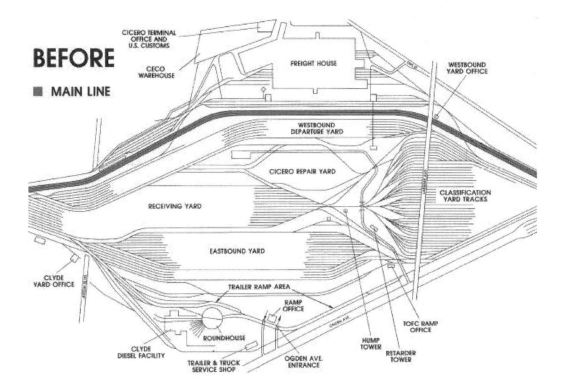

The North and South sides capacity expansion at Cicero was completed in February and it came just in time. Cicero's 1982 peak monthly volume was 18,000 loads in October and 1983 volume was expected to average 20,500 a month. This was the result:[377]

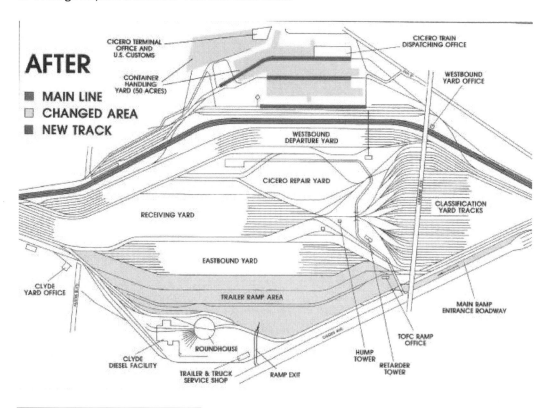

---

[377] Ibid

Strategy #2: Utilize New Technology Equipment in Dedicated Intermodal Trains

As mentioned previously, Robert Reebie's Bi-Modal Corporation's RoadRailer technology had been tested in BN revenue service in 1982. Bi-Modal was funded by North American Railcar Co. Reebie needed a new home for his equipment because the Illinois Central let their lease on the equipment expire. On September 27, 1982 the IC announced that they were discontinuing their RoadRailer service. Harry Bruce, IC's senior vice president of marketing said:[378]

> *The service operated at break-even for 2-3 weeks, but demand fell off quickly; and the company lost some $500,000 on the service in the first year. It just frittered off. It would be 60-70 loads per week and we needed 100-110 to break even. It was just the economy.*

The IBU was very interested in this technology because of what it offered especially in the areas of economy and ride quality. It had been successfully tested at the Association of American Railroads' R&D test track at speeds up to 105 miles per hour. Because it eliminated the railcar it offered a significantly reduced train weight compared to conventional piggyback train. The lack of a car also reduced the height helping to reduce aerodynamic drag. The trailers were only 12 inches apart when assembled in a train which reduced drag and limited how widely a door could be opened. This significantly reduced the possibility of cargo theft. In 1978, Bi-Modal put out a brochure that touted its positive attributes. The cutting edge alternate TOFC technology at the time was the Santa Fe Railroad's articulated, skeleton platform "10-Pack Fuel Foiler." Labeled "articulated TOFC," the brochure compared it to the RoadRailer technology:

Comparison versus Conventional TOFC[379]

Factor	Articulated TOFC	RoadRailer
Equipment investment	-16%	-42%
Line-haul tare weight	-24%	-64%
Fuel consumption	-12%	-44%
Terminal land	Same	-25%

It also had disadvantages. The Mark IV technology (pictured below)[380] was the state-of-the-art at the time of the BN test. It had rail wheels permanently attached to the highway trailer which increased the tare weight of the trailer by 4,500 pounds. That created a 4,500 pound competitive disadvantage versus motor carriers for heavier loads that would weigh-out (meet maximum legal total vehicle and lading highway weights) before they cubed-out (totally filled the trailer with lading). In addition, it was a technology that was not easily compatible with conventional intermodal train operations. A RoadRailer transition car was developed that would allow a string of RoadRailer trailers to be connected to a train of conventional intermodal cars but the RoadRailers could only be handled at the rear of the train making for very complex train and terminal logistics and end-of-train slack -action-related cargo damage

---

[378] Rail Discontinues RoadRailer Service, Journal of Commerce, September 27, 1982.

[379] Panza, James D., Dawson, Richard W., Sellberg, Ronald P., *The TTX Story*, Volume 1, the Pennsylvania Railroad Technical & Historical Society, 2018, p. 120.

[380] Ibid, used with permission.

Mark IV RoadRailer with the railroad wheelset an integral part of the 48-ft. trailer.
(Jim Panza photo)

risk. Studies showed that RoadRailers were an attractive option for haul lengths shorter than what was economically viable for conventional equipment but it would have to be as part of a dedicated RoadRailer network. A network operation was needed to be able to provide broad geographic coverage and increase the opportunity to find return-loads into the network to cut competitiveness-killing empty drayage miles. Unfortunately, as mentioned earlier, the BN had the worst "intermodal franchise" among the major railroads. At the time, connecting rail carriers east of BN expressed no interest in jointly developing the potentially rich "black hole" intermodal zone within 300-400 miles east and west of Chicago and the Mississippi River. It was accepted that conventional intermodal could not be economically viable for hauls lengths of less than 600-700 miles. That meant hauls like Kansas City or Minneapolis/St. Paul to Chicago were uneconomical but markets such as Kansas City–Detroit, or Minneapolis/St. Paul–Columbus, Ohio would conceivably work with single-rail-line operations. Due to poor connecting service, the vast majority of domestic intermodal shipments interchanged between western and eastern railroads at Chicago were highway (rubber) interchanged instead of rail (steel) interchanged. That added significant lift and drayage costs. In spite of a very high level of interest, the RoadRailer technology did not yet find a home on BN.

That was not the case for technologies such as light-weight articulated flatcars and double stack cars which stacked two containers in one car well. The Ten-Pack concept car, the Budd LoPac double stack car, and the Trailer Train 4 Runner car were all tested by BN in the 1981-1983 time period.

The Intermodal Task Force had recommended the use of light-weight articulated flatcars made possible by the switch to all mechanized (lift on/off) hub centers. These would enable improved customer service (less slack action related damage) and improved line-haul economics which would be a boost for domestic business. They were not well suited for international (ISO) shipping containers that would preferably move flush on a car deck (without a chassis). The rapid changes in legal trailer sizes complicated the problem because an effective trailer-life could run 7-9 years while it was not uncommon to get 35-40 years of life from a well-maintained flatcar. Rapid changes in legal trailer lengths created a significant car obsolescence risk.

The development of the articulated "Fuel Foiler" car began on the Santa Fe in 1977 as a "Six-Pack" that would carry six 45' long trailers. By 1979 the car went into production as a "10-Pack" (pictured at right)[381] with ten articulated trailer-carrying units. The patent rights for this car were sold to Itel Corporation and they partnered with FMC Marine and Rail Division during late 1981-1982 to produce them under the brand name "IMPACK." BN tested them in a 10-unit configuration primarily between

---

[381] Panza, Dawson, Sellberg, p. 192, used with permission.

Chicago and Seattle. At the same time Trailer Train Company (later known as TTX), the rail industry's jointly owned car supply company, began development with ACF Industries of a four platform light-weight intermodal car that they would name the "4-Runner." The Union Pacific Railroad would order 101 of these cars from Trailer Train in 1981. Like the 10-Pack, they were designed to handle trailers up to 45' long. Unlike the 10-Pack, this car passed the AAR's "squeeze test" which made it fully interchangeable with other railroads. The 10-Pack was only interchangeable with railroads willing to

accept it. By late 1982 through early 1983 car builders Thrall, Whitehead and Kales, FMC, and Pullman also came up with concept cars. At the same time demand for more container carrying capacity was growing and trailers up to 48' long and 8'6" wide were approved. With a nose-mounted refrigeration unit the car had to provide space for what in essence was a 50' refrigerated trailer. To accommodate a container or up to 50' of total trailer length Trailer Train introduced the light weight Front Runner car with trailer mounting hitches that were cushioned to help absorb train slack action forces. By the end on 1983 Trailer Train ordered 500 Front runner cars manufactured by Trinity Industries, Thrall Car (formerly Whitehead and Kales), United-American Car, Portec, BSC and Pacific Car and Foundry.[382] They also ordered 20 Thrall ARC-5 and 20 Itel IMPACK cars (pictured on left, courtesy of Bill Greenwood) in mid 1983. Berwick Forge also developed a container-only spine car. BN was heavily involved in the testing of all of these "spine type" cars, requisitioning them from Trailer Train, and then deploying them in revenue service.

Concurrently with development activity for lightweight articulated spine type cars, double stack cars were also being developed:

> *An early and growing intermodal customer for the Southern Pacific was Sea-Land. They had developed a large flow of Mini-bridge containers between the West Coast and the Gulf (i.e., the movement of containers between ports by rail rather than by ship). In the process of developing Minibridge, Sea-Land had reached into the rail industry and hired a tall, brash young man named Bob Ingram. Ingram had spent short stints with the New York Central, Norfolk and Western, and Central Railroad of New Jersey. Ingram was interested in everything intermodal, and viewed all things that were inefficient with sharp disdain. Ingram had earlier been intrigued with the old General Motors / A.T. Kearney depressed center flatcar for stacking containers.[383]*

Ingram asked the SP to investigate this concept and they commenced work on it with American Car and Foundry (ACF) to develop a prototype car. [384]

> *Well-hole cars had been part of the heavy-duty flatcar fleet for many years and were used to carry very high loads. A container placed in a well was easily held in place. What was different about the SP car was that it nested a second container on top of the one in the well. The*

[382] Ibid, p. 202, used with permission.
[383] DeBoer, p. 139.
[384] Ibid.

container supports at the corners of the well were 14in. above the top of the rail, so the top of two 8ft., 6in. high containers was 18ft., 2in. above the top of the rail. The tops of taller containers were higher yet. This would not be acceptable on many intermodal routes at the time, perhaps not on most of them, but that was not a problem on SP's route to Houston. [385]

The cars utilized bulkheads on each end to secure the containers but they were limited to carrying containers 35 or 40 ft. long. By 1981 this technology had developed to the point that it could be put into regular operation. SP placed an order for 42 articulated three-well car sets (like those operating on the BN pictured above)[386] with ACF Industries.[387] Notice the bulkheads on the ends of each container well.

ACF wasn't alone in pursuing double stack technology. Before SP's production order with ACF was completed in 1981, "both Budd Company and Youngstown Steel Door (YSD) developed articulated well cars that were intended to carry both trailers and containers. Budd, which had previously built only passenger cars, developed the LoPac 2000 and YSD designed the Backpacker. Neither car was built in production quantities by the company that designed it. Budd licensed its well car design to Thrall Car Manufacturing shortly thereafter, and Trinity Industries built the YSD Backpacker several years later. Neither car incorporated bulkheads at the ends of the wells to secure an upper container like the SP/ACF cars.[388] The Budd car utilized maritime "interbox connectors" (IBCs) to affix the top container to the bottom container in the well, just as containers are affixed to one another on a container ship.

Sea-Land competitor American President Lines (APL) started land-bridge container operations between Los Angeles and New York on conventional COFC cars routed Union Pacific–Chicago & Northwestern (C&NW)–Conrail in 1978. In 1980 they leased their own COFC cars from Itel and created their proprietary dedicated "Liner Train" service over this route. The railroads only performed a haulage service for APL who provided all trailing equipment (except the caboose). By the end of 1983 APL placed an order with Thrall to replace conventional COFC cars with their container-only double stack cars.[389]

As indicated earlier, on the trailer front the legally allowable length and width was a moving target. That made it hard to handle capacity planning because as with cars, trailers were at risk of becoming commercially obsolete before they wore out. The legal trailer length was increased to 45 feet in 1982 and the majority of BN's fleet was only 40 feet long. Leasing companies were starting to fill the void by supplying 45' trailers but the new legal width-limit was expected to increase from 96" to 102". In 1982 the IBU got authority to acquire 500 new trailers. It was important that the IBU have a proprietary supply of trailers to provide leverage in lease negotiations with lessors that typically supplied trailers with daily rates and the opportunity to return them to the lessor when not needed (per diem relief). Betting on-the-come, an IBU order was placed in 1982 to build all of them 102" wide even though they were not yet legal. The Surface Transportation Assistance Act of 1982 that permitted 102" wide trailers

---

[385]Panza, Dawson, Sellberg, p. 235-236.

[386] Ibid, p. 193, used with permission.

[387] Ibid, p. 236.

[388] Ibid, p. 237.

[389] Ibid, pp. 237-238.

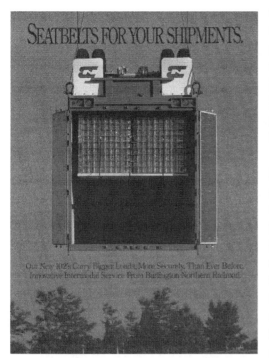

SEATBELTS FOR YOUR SHIPMENTS.

Our New 102's Carry Bigger Loads, More Securely, Than Ever Before.
Innovative Intermodal Service From Burlington Northern Railroad.

was signed on January 6, 1983 so the trailers under construction were able to be put into service in 1983. In another move that increased the competitiveness of trucks versus rail, the Act also preempted states from trailer length limits of less than 48' across the federally supported National Highway Network and assured truckers reasonable access to terminals, food, lodging, etc.[390] Truck trailer size limits increased from 45'X96" to 48'X102".

BN's new trailers were novel on several fronts. First, almost all trailers in intermodal service were painted white without graphics aside from what was needed by law and for trailer identification. The IBU had them painted brilliant Cascade Green, the official color of BN Railroad and the same color as BN's locomotives. The intent was for them to stand out and scream "BN Intermodal" and they did. In addition, given that the IBU was deliberately attempting to reposition the business and change its identity from "piggyback" (with all of its negative connotations) to "intermodal," the theme, "*Innovative Intermodal Service*" was plastered on the sides of the trailers in bold white letters with white streamers behind the label to symbolize forward progress. In addition, in an attempt to address the lading damage problem, which was one of the biggest problems associated with intermodal, the trailers were designed with floor tracks so a load could be secured to the trailer's floor. An advertising campaign for transportation and logistics magazines (those read by decision-making beneficial customers) was built around the trailers. The theme was, "Seatbelts for Your Shipments" and the ad featured a picture of a trailer being held upside-down with a suspended load of canned beverages viewed through the open rear doors (pictured left, *Greenwood Collection*, Barriger Library at UMSL). This was an example of integration of the equipment and marketing strategies.

The 500 new BN green trailers did not provide enough trailer capacity to handle the growth of the business. The IBU needed more trailer capacity but trailers that could be sourced on the daily lease market carried a significant cost premium because of per diem relief privileges. Addressing this problem through longer-term financial arrangements was difficult because BN's Equipment Steering Committee wasn't willing to approve longer-term trailer leases. Bill Greenwood's Delegation of Authority <u>did</u> allow him to enter into leases of less than a year without oversight. Starting in the third quarter of 1983, Bill Berry and Roger Simon began to enter into 364 day trailer leases. They barely fit into Greenwood's authority but it was enough to get the job done. Leasing companies were well aware of the fact that the IBU had distinguished BN as the innovative leader in the industry which was being borne out by how fast BN's business was growing. The leases would typically come with a six month notification to terminate to give the leasing company some security. Attracting trailer supply under the 364 day agreement (which came to be known within the leasing industry as the "BN Lease") helped to reduce BN's equipment costs while generating needed capacity. By doing this in a way that worked around the

---

[390] U.S Department of Transportation, Hearing on Truck Weights and Lengths: Assessing the Impacts of Existing Laws and Regulations, July 9, 2008, Accessed from: https://www.transportation.gov/testimony/truck-weights-and-lengths-assessing-impacts-existing-laws-and-regulations, on March 17, 2023.

corporate bureaucracy, the IBU also impacted the daily trailer lease market because it pressured leasing companies to offer BN better cost and more favorable repair and trailer-return terms.

Bill Greenwood recalled:

> I was at the head table of a Chicago Traffic Club dinner and there were probably a thousand people in attendance. I didn't know the guy sitting next to me, who happened to be a finance industry guy from New York. He turned my name placard to find out who I was with. He saw BN and said, "You sons-of-bitches at BN are ruining the trailer leasing market.[391]

Mark Cane recalled an interesting story related to the "Seatbelts for your Shipments" upside-down trailer advertisement:[392]

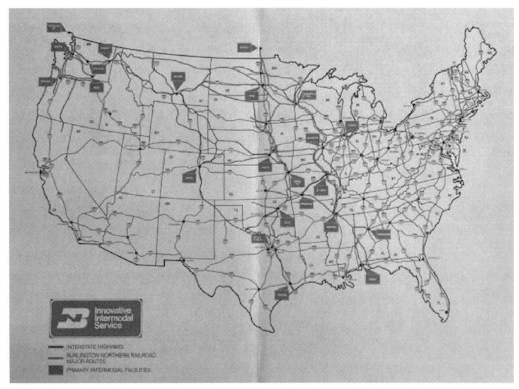

> Shortly after that ad started to run in the logistics trade media, Ken Hoepner attended Northwestern University's Industrial Marketing Strategy course. We were all really proud of that ad because it was such an attention grabber. Dan Nimer was stressing SW^2C and its use in advertising in his class. Ken said Nimer asked if any of the class participants had examples of their ads so that they could be evaluated against SW^2C and Ken held up the trailer ad. Ken said Nimer took a look and commented on how innovative it was. Ken said he was feeling really proud about it and then Nimer dug deeper. Nimer asked what the ad's value point was and Ken said it was intermodal shipment damage reduction because of the floor securement system that was built into the trailer. Nimer then asked if damage was an issue in intermodal and Ken said it was a significant issue. Nimer then looked at him and asked why BN Intermodal would run an ad that stressed a major service deficiency. Nimer then said we could create more value if we eliminated what caused the damage. We learned a lot from that lesson. It reinforced our drive to eliminate the causes of shipment damage and changed our advertising approach.

---

[391] Bill Greenwood interview with Mark Cane, May 3, 2022.

[392] Mark Cane's personal recollection, November 13, 2022.

Strategy #3 - Customer Oriented Marketing Packages

The IBU's third major strategy, in addition to developing a network of lean strategically located Hub Centers run by motor carriers, and the operation of a network of dedicated intermodal trains utilizing new technology equipment, was to develop marketing packages that would appeal to current and prospective customers. This included shedding the "piggyback" reputation and brand ID and repositioning BN's intermodal product and image. The goal was to be in a position to not only protect BN's vulnerable market share but also take share from over-the-road truckers by either cooperating or competing with them.

A big part of the "brand identification" modification effort was to firmly establish BN Intermodal's connection of its green "*Innovative Intermodal Service*" service mark with similar green Interstate Highway signs and the extension of its service through cooperation with motor carriers.   This was counter to Burlington Northern's culture on several fronts.

> *Burlington Northern had a long-standing practice of maintaining a low profile in the press; Intermodal advertised heavily. To appeal to truckers, they consciously, and to the rest of the railroad heretically, excluded trains from their ads.*[393]

Brochures, ads and maps (including the January, 1983 version shown above, *Greenwood Collection*, Barriger Library at UMSL) continued to picture the "*Innovative Intermodal Service*" brand label within a green box that looked like an Interstate Highway sign. As opposed to appearing in traditional "rail industry" publications, ads were run in publications that IBU market research showed would hit the eyes of transportation decision makers. Maps included the BN route across the United States plus the

Interstate Highway network, not other railroads. When BN's Corporate Secretary learned that Bill DeWitt had arranged for this he threatened to have him fired.[394]

Examples of Intermodal ads, all of which featured qualities intended to

distinguish BN's service are shown above and below (*Greenwood Collection*, Barriger Library at UMSL). Appendix 2 contains a progression of full page BN *Innovative Intermodal Service* themed ads.

---

[393] Katzenbach and Smith, p. 39.
[394] Bill DeWitt interview with Mark Cane, February 23, 2022.

The IBU also worked hard to reposition its relationship with its domestic marketing channels. Hassles associated with regulation and railroad industry practices such as two-trailer rates, lack of accountability for freight claims, and confusing "TOFC Service Plans," made it difficult for a beneficial shipper to utilize piggyback directly from a railroad so they overwhelmingly shied away from it. To fill a transportation market void, an "industry" of intermodal middle-men developed. These intermediaries between railroads and beneficial customers, many of whom were started-up by former railroad salespeople, re- sold the rail intermodal services as part of a package including such things as drayage, equipment supply, billing, shipment tracking and freight claims administration. These intermediaries were shippers agents like Hub City, National Piggyback and Alliance Shippers, freight forwarders such as Clipper EXXPRESS and shippers associations such as ITOFCA and the Pacific Northwest Perishable Shippers Association. These intermediaries were very independent with little to no allegiance to any particular railroad. It was the goal of the IBU to make them agents of the IBU as much or more than agents of the beneficial shipper. The IBU wanted its services presented to the market with professionalism by agents who represented BN. This was extremely important because BN's relatively poor intermodal "franchise" precluded it from being able to effectively sell its services exclusively with its own proprietary sales force. BN's geographic coverage capability was vastly inferior to that of an unregulated motor carrier while beneficial shippers attempted to minimize the number of transportation companies they would work with in order to improve the fluidity and effectiveness of their internal logistics operations.

The IBU developed "product and services" guides to educate these intermediaries about the depth and breadth of BN's intermodal services and provide extensive contact information. This intermediary industry assumed the name "third parties," over time. That name carried relatively poor connotations similar to the "piggyback" label. The IBU would only refer to them, directly and in its promotion and advertising material, as "Intermodal Marketing Companies (IMCs)" to improve their image.

In addition, as hub centers were progressively established the IBU's motor carrier-industry-experienced Hub Managers developed closer relationships with "qualified" drayage companies, especially as they developed "satellite hubs." To expand BN's geographic coverage, satellite hubs were established in markets within a hub's extended area. They were intended to help retain business subject to loss when ramps were shut down as well as to gain share in the territory of other railroads that BN could not reach via rail. Prices and service standards were established with the physical connection to the "parent" hub managed through drayage companies under the supervision of the parent hub. From the standpoint of the customer, the off-line hubs operated as if they were on-line hubs.

The IBU developed special incentives for the IMCs that would rebate a small share of the revenue they generated back to them as promotion credits. If the IMC advertised its services and included BN Intermodal (in a way pre-approved by the IBU) in the promotion piece they could apply to the IBU for recovery of some or all of their cost by redeeming their promotion credits. Intermodal contracts with IMCs also included conditions that called for freight bill payments to BN to drawn by BN via "Sight Drafts." BN got the authority to "draft" the IMC's bank account monthly for shipments that were tendered to BN by that IMC. This reduced the bad-debt risk BN assumed in doing business with IMCs who, aside from the largest, tended to be marginally capitalized. It also significantly reduced accounts receivable which was especially important in the early 1980s high interest rate environment.

In 1983 the International side of the business was also evolving at light-speed due to a significant growth in international trade and the explosive growth of containerization. Steamship companies such as Sea-Land and APL were delivering well more than a full trainload of containers when their ships arrived at Seattle. They were also developing their own inland logistics networks to make themselves easier to do business with for their customers and help differentiate themselves from other steamship lines.

Capitalizing on an Integrated IBU Focus on Equipment Productivity

As mentioned earlier, Bill Berry assumed responsibility for intermodal equipment management in mid-1983 after Ken Hoepner was promoted. Roger Simon joined the IBU at approximately the same time. In addition to testing every new equipment technology that hit the market there was a need to more effectively operate a rapidly growing business. Simon recalled some of his early experiences with the IBU related to an increased focus on comprehensive operating effectiveness and efficiencies:[395]

> I was not on the first team when the Intermodal Business Unit was established. I was drafted by Ken Hoepner and came on board in August of 1983. I was given Dennis Larson's title as Manager of TOFC/COFC Equipment. Dennis was not a detail guy.
>
> The job of managing the equipment was a mess. When I came on board, one of the two women that did the detail work quit and the other was overwhelmed. We were printing off train consists and counting the Intermodal cars and trailers on the trains. Many things fell through the cracks. A couple things stood out in my mind. When the business unit was established, nothing changed in a couple regions of the Operating Department. The Seattle Region Operating Department continued to distribute Intermodal cars and trailers and paid no attention to our directives. We looked at a train arriving at Spokane and blocked it so equipment would be distributed between the Seattle and Portland Hubs. When the train left Spokane, the entire train was blocked by the Operating Department for Seattle. On the other end of the railroad, the Frisco Railroad still had its distribution people in the Operating Department and they took care of their customers. We had no control over the situation.

---

[395] Roger Simon email to Mark Cane, January 27, 2022.

In addition, there were departments, especially the Accounting Department in St. Paul, who saw the establishment of the business unit as an answer to all their problems. All of the disputes over Intermodal equipment per diem were sent to the business unit. They didn't have the people or the knowledge to research claims and resolve the issues. When they got to the business unit, Dennis Larson would mark the files "Beth, pls handle" and she had a credenza full of these notes that she didn't have the time or knowledge to investigate. In addition, "Beth" wanted to get back to Seattle where she had family and she got a job in Seattle shortly after I came on board.

The first major priority was to get a handle on the Trailer Train situation. Fortunately, Car Distribution people like Jim Pratt and Bernie Armstrong were creating new computer reports to support their equipment needs. They opened the door for me to join them and include Intermodal equipment as part of their field reporting and computer reports. We put together the first Intermodal car reports and could actually count the number of Trailer Train or other ownership cars on our system. We didn't get a chance to verify some of the numbers and we had to work other "bugs" out of the reports but we were headed in the right direction. I remember that we had short daily morning meetings with Bill Greenwood and for the first time told him we had "X" number of Intermodal cars on line. He started asking questions right away for which I had no answers...yet. I told him no questions please and he must have thought I was some kind of nut.

As far as per diem relief on Trailer Train cars, Trailer Train's rules were that you had to give them car numbers and the location of the cars five days before you could put them on relief. After you gave them this information, they would contact other railroads to see if they wanted the equipment. We had to deliver the cars to the requesting railroad. This required that we had knowledge of what other railroads were doing as far as business levels or could we cut a deal with them to not ask for the cars. This got to be an educated guessing game that we got very good at playing. We gambled a lot but won most of the time and saved lots of money. We finally got a handle on the car situation.

As far as trailer distribution, Ken Krismer on the Seattle Region was easy to work with. We had a couple meetings in Seattle to understand his concerns with Marketing people blocking trains and distributing equipment. I'm not sure I'm so persuasive or he was under the gun to cut jobs, but we took control of distribution. The Frisco Region was a different story where we "invited them" to cease and desist.

We made progress slowly. One of the things that I enjoyed was working with, or should I say on, is the trailer leasing companies. I loved per diem incentives. We offered increased utilization for lower per diem rates to all of the leasing companies. Only Transamerica followed-up and we negotiated a package that produced a $600,000 rebate to BN Intermodal for one year's utilization numbers. A Win-Win for both companies. Another program we had was to generate enough off-line per diem revenue to offset on-line per diem costs. We came close several times but only accomplished it once.

American President Lines (APL) Prepares to Disrupt the Industry

Next to Sea-Land, American President Lines was the most aggressive early adopters of cargo containerization technology. Between 1969 and 1971 the share of its business that moved by containers grew from 29% to 58%.[396] In 1977 it transitioned from the provision of world-wide freight service to an exclusive focus on the trans-Pacific trade. That same year they hired Don Orris from the DRGW Railroad to develop an inland logistics network.[397] "In 1978 the company began work on the concept of seamless integrated intermodal service in the U.S. market: the idea of moving containerized goods via ship, train and truck under one company identity. By 1979, APL started the "Liner Train," a direct rail land-bridge service transporting containers from Los Angeles to New York using its own rail cars, leading to the most reliable delivery of containers of the time."[398] The Linertrain was routed over the Union Pacific between LA/Long Beach and Fremont, NE, C&NW between Fremont and Chicago and Conrail between Chicago and the New York / New Jersey ports.[399] BN's IBU staff was aware that APL had investigated the use of articulated spine-type cars as well as double-stack technology.

"By the end of 1983, APL had placed an order with Thrall for double-stack well cars built under license from Budd. The initial order for 65 cars, …, was soon followed by an order for an additional 188 cars. These were delivered between March, 1984 and October 1985."[400] The APL cars had five articulated

units each with hydraulic end-of-car cushioning to lessen slack-action and since APL was only interested in shipping containers, they had no trailer handling capability. Another important feature of the cars was that they were a well-only stack car. As shown (left), they did not have bulkheads to secure the top container and instead relied on ISO (seagoing) interbox connectors (IBCs). The bottom of the car wells were restricted to 40' containers but a longer container (such as a 45' container shown in the picture left) could be handled in the first and fifth wells. [401]

In 1983 APL was still moving the vast majority of its containers across the western U.S. via the Union Pacific. That did not prevent them from talking with BN in 1983 about BN's interest in handling the line-haul for APL's Linertrain service between Seattle and Chicago, especially after the Union Pacific had taken BN's Sea-Land business and the business of both of these fierce rivals was handled by the same underlying carrier.

The IBU conducted a two day strategy session on September 19 and 20, 1983 to settle on a decision about APL's business. The biggest positive about pursuing APL's business was that BN had locomotive and line-haul capacity available to handle the business. A second was that APL would provide the vast majority of the cars the service needed (reducing BN's capital cost) because provision of their own cars was part of their plan. A third was that it would be a quick way to replace volume after the loss of Sea-

---

[396] American President Lines, Wikipedia, accessed from: https://en.wikipedia.org/wiki/American_President_Lines, March 6, 2022.
[397] Wall St. Transcript, Don Orris, accessed from: https://www.twst.com/bio/donald-c-orris/ , on November 17, 2022.
[398] Ibid.
[399] Panza, Dawson and Sellberg, p. 237.
[400] Ibid, p. 238.
[401] Ibid p. 238, image used with permission.

Land's business. There were also several negatives. The first was that APL wanted a lower price than what Sea-Land demanded and which the IBU had refused to match. The second was that the IBU was capacity constrained in Seattle. The third was that APL wanted authority to fill their westbound containers with domestic cargo marketed by them at what would be deeply discounted rates. During this era, the head-haul for international business was eastbound and the back-haul was westbound. The volume of containerized imports versus exports was in the 8 to 1 range. That meant 7 of every 8 containers would typically move westbound empty on the Linertrain. On the other hand the head-haul for domestic cargo was westbound by a ratio of about 4 to 1. As a result, about 75% of the domestic trailers carried from the PNW back to Chicago moved empty. APL's eastbound prices more than made up for the structural westbound empty container return cost. BN's westbound trailer prices more than made up for the structural eastbound empty return cost. The IBU was keenly aware that APL was transitioning to double stack technology because they factored that into their price demands. BN had the best service in the Chicago–Seattle corridor which was attractive to APL but they didn't want to pay a higher price for it.

APL's business would crowd-out other more profitable shippers at capacity constrained Seattle. It was clear that if BN gave in to APL's demands it would not only contribute to a price war for eastbound international business (on the cusp of the expected introduction of disruptive double stack technology that essentially doubled the productivity of a train), it would also, in all probability, contribute to a westbound domestic cargo price war. APL would have an incentive to backhaul-price head-haul westbound domestic business in their containers with the help of third parties who had no rail carrier allegiance. The two most valuable assets in-play in the situation were APL's customers and BN's superior line haul capability. BN could not control APL's customers but it could defend the value of its franchise. The IBU team chose to not match APL's price demand and its demand to utilize BN's franchise to add another domestic competitor in the best -service Chicago–Seattle corridor.

Knowing of APL's talks with BN, UP didn't want to lose APL's business:

> "Orris proceeded to negotiate a completely "bare bones" rate contract for movement of APL stack trains with Union Pacific's Don Shum. The contract called for APL to furnish the cars, containers and chassis. The Union Pacific was to supply terminal services and "hook and haul" road service. With control over pricing, equipment and service, combined with the bulk of the savings from double-stack equipment, Don Orris was in business. Shortly after, in exchange for more volume from American President Lines and a major main line siding extension investment by UP, Shum and Orris extended the initial UP contract to a ten year period."[402]

The experiences with Sea-Land and APL caused quite a bit of IBU soul searching. The significant growth of international trade was shifting the dynamics of the intermodal market. As a result the IBU seriously studied whether or not it should purchase Sea-Land or APL. Doing so could give BN the ability to flex the same market power on other railroads they were flexing with BN while giving BN an avenue to extend its intermodal franchise off of the BN network. Sea-Land and APL were building national networks fueled by the international cargo they controlled. In the end it was decided that it would not be the best use of BN resources and it was too difficult to develop a sound business case for a holding company that wanted to milk the railroad and favored energy industry investments. The Steamship business, already at this time, had a reputation for being cutthroat over the water (one of the big reasons APL wanted to differentiate itself inland). It was a great business to be in during good economic times and a horrible

---

[402] DeBoer, pp. 153-154.

business to be in during bad economic times. The cumulative losses that came during the business cycle troughs tended to exceed the profits that came during peaks. In addition, unlike the railroad business where the barriers to entry were extraordinarily high (for example, another railroad between Chicago and Seattle will never be built), the barriers to entry to the Steamship business were relatively low (ships were not that difficult to get and the Pacific Ocean could accommodate many more ships.) This drove BN's international intermodal strategy to pursue double stack technology, increase its focus on the many smaller steamship companies, and do what it could to provide them services that helped them level the competitive playing field against the Sea-Lands and APLs. This drove BN's breakthrough strategy, spearheaded by Ralph Muellner, to offer these steamship lines a "Common User" double stack train option. This was one element of what BN had to do to continue to improve its service for the rest of the international marketplace players.

The Need for International Terminal Capacity in Seattle

As indicated in the APL analysis, by mid-1983 it was clear that BN's terminal capacity situation in Seattle would be soon overwhelmed. With the acceleration of the relocation of US Manufacturing capacity to the Far East, the significant growth in Trans-Pacific containerized international trade was only projected to accelerate. Seattle had no on-dock intermodal facilities and the UP's Argo facility was less than 2 miles away from the docks. BN had an intermodal facility about 10 miles south of Seattle in Tukwilla. International containers had to be drayed those 10 miles from-and-to the port's docks. BN needed a near-dock facility. Fortunately it had a yard called Stacy Street within a few blocks of the port. Efforts intensified during the fourth quarter to seek the conversion of the Stacy Street yard into the near-dock facility BN needed. The Seattle Hub Center had been established in April of 1983 so Seattle's new Hub Manager, Roger Stiles, was on-board to assist the effort.

Should BN Purchase a Third Party Intermodal Marketing Company?

One of the biggest frustrations the IBU experienced with its domestic segment was the separation BN had from the ultimate (beneficial) customers. The overwhelming face of intermodal service was the Intermodal Marketing Company (aka Third Party). By default, BN's customer was the IMC instead of the beneficial cargo owner. As indicated earlier, the IMC did not tend to have any sort of allegiance to rail carriers. Because the barriers to entry into the IMC business were so low, they tended to compete primarily on the basis of price. Again, railroads were mostly insulated from the beneficial customer. That is what drove the IBU to focus on BN-differentiating demand-pull advertising targeting them. The IMC handled the drayage and relationship with the underlying railroad. The freight bill the customer received came from the IMC without any sort of identification as to what railroad was the backbone of the service. In fact, the IMC "owned" the customer. It was not readily apparent to the railroad whose freight was actually in a trailer. That separation/isolation from the end customer was troubling for the IBU. There was great frustration that BN didn't control its destiny.

In its 1984 Strategic Plan submitted on June 3, 1983 the IBU's first two original Intermodal Task Force strategies related to Hubs and dedicated trains were restated. The third strategy related to marketing packages was enahnced as follows:

> *Draw upon the Hub Center/dedicated train capabilities to offer new retail-level service to shippers who are not now rail customers and who choose not to arrange their transportation through third parties.*[403]

One way to address this would be to buy an IMC. It would immediately gain the IBU an experienced and entrepreneurial intermodal sales force. It would immediately gain systems support for the management of door-to-door intermodal service. It would immediately gain drayage management capability. During 1983 serious discussions and studies were conducted about the pros and cons of the acquisition of one or more IMCs. The leading candidate studied was National Piggyback which was the largest IMC, owned and operated by R.C. Matney. Matney was an intermodal industry pioneer and was highly respected both within and outside the IBU. In a nutshell, however, the IBU did not pursue an IMC acquisition. IMC executives and salespeople tended to be extraordinarily entrepreneurial with a willingness to tolerate high risk. Next to their customer, the most important IMC asset was the salespeople. If their IMC were acquired by a major corporation it was believed that the risk of losing those people was high – BN would pay a lot for something and assume a high risk of losing what it intended to buy. In addition, if BN bought one IMC it would likely alienate other IMCs and give them an incentive to steer their business away from BN. Recalling that BN had the worst major railroad intermodal franchise, the "BN IMC" would have to rely on service from other underlying railroads to be able to present a package of intermodal transportation offerings that made it geographically competitive. This was especially important given the trend by beneficial shippers to reduce the number of carriers they did business with. It was deemed at that time that other railroads would be resistant to giving a "BN IMC" competitive pricing authority over their networks. To make a long story short, the perceived risks of purchasing an IMC outweighed the perceived benefits. This exercise proved to emphasize even more the importance of BN working even harder on improving and differentiating its intermodal service, promoting its brand to beneficial customers and improving BN's geographic intermodal franchise. The team wanted to make it hard for quality IMCs to not represent BN's services.

RoadRailer Southwest Express

The IBU had a high level of interest in the RoadRailer technology and yet lacked a network ideally suited for its implementation. The 1981 Task Force conclusion had been to focus domestic trailer business on lightweight articulated cars. The Illinois Central-Gulf (ICG) had initiated what they called *"Supermode"* service on the 370 mile corridor between Louisville, KY and Memphis on September 28, 1981. The RoadRailer equipment test on BN in 1982 was conducted while this operation was underway. The ICG was unable to get a reduced train crew agreement but decided to pursue the effort anyway. Unfortunately, operation with a four-man crew and caboose made it uneconomical and it was shut down after a year of operation.[404]

Reebie then turned to Conrail about their interest in utilizing RoadRailers on the 400+ mile corridor between New York City and Buffalo. Conrail said it was not interested in acquiring or operating the RoadRailer equipment but they "said that it would not object to Reebie running RoadRailer equipment on Conrail through Bi-Modal."[405] Reebie initiated operation of the *Empire State Express* on November 2,

---

[403] Burlington Northern Railroad, 1984-1998 Strategic Plan, June 3, 1983, *Greenwood Collection*, Barriger Library at UMSL.
[404] DeBoer, p 129-130.
[405] Ibid p. 130.

1982 with the benefit of 3 man-crews that Conrail was able to negotiate with labor. Unfortunately, in spite of being in a market with substantial truck traffic the route competed with truckers able to run "turnpike doubles" which are two large twin-trailers pulled by a single truck tractor and driver.[406] Bi-Modal owner "North American Car was running into financial problems completely unrelated to Bi-Modal. Early in 1984 North American informed Reebie that he would have to make it on his own with both RoadRailer and the Empire State Xpress operations. With an operating deficit running more than a million dollars a year, Bi-Modal closed down the Empire State Xpress in July of that year.[407]

With the knowledge that the Empire State Express was going to struggle to survive, Reebie continued his discussions with the IBU. RoadRailer needed to operate in longer-haul markets with more than a single metropolitan area on the route structure. Because BN was competitively disadvantaged in the Chicago – Texas corridor, Reebie was offered that market as a possible destination for his assets. Reebie was interested and the BN 1984-1998 Strategic Plan, completed on June 3, 1983, stated:

> *The proposed hauling of RoadRailer trains on BNRR has also been agreed to in principle, subject to finalizing an operating contract. It is a pooling agreement, without fall-back trackage rights which would allow RoadRailer to operate independently over BNRR lines. In this proposal, RoadRailer would solicit business in its own account over the Chicago–Kansas City–Dallas–Houston corridor in its own specialized highway/rail trailers to be handled by BN over BN trackage.[408]*

This service was to be called the *Southwest Express*. Again, what made it attractive for the IBU is that it was competitively disadvantaged in that lane. Its cost structure prevented it from pursuing short-haul business and the ramps at Dallas (Irving) and Houston had looming capacity and location issues and were not yet mechanized. RoadRailers needed less land to operate in a terminal than conventional equipment and did not require lift devices so it represented an opportunity to increase BN's return on an underutilized service lane and underutilized facilities with little capital exposure. While negotiations continued with labor on a reduced crew operating agreement, BN conducted another RoadRailer test train run on August 14-15, 1983. On August 23, Walter Drexel (who by this time had become somewhat more supportive of IBU initiatives) signed the pooling agreement contract with Bi-Modal. On October 6, Reebie formally proposed a BN equity infusion into Bi-Modal but that was refused.[409] That killed the project.

Dallas Smith Trailers

Motor Vehicles were transported by rail in multi-level cars. Over time they evolved from having open sides to eventually becoming fully enclosed to minimize vehicle damage in transit. Aside from hobos liking to ride in cars (with sheltered heat and a radio) as they rode freight trains, autos in open multi-level cars (as pictured below)[410] were a magnet for kids throwing rocks as trains passed by. In addition, a

---

[406] Ibid

[407] Ibid.

[408] Burlington Northern Railroad, 1984-1998 Strategic Plan, Future Applications of Trackage Rights and Pooling Agreements, June 3, 1983, p.4, *Greenwood Collection*, Barriger Library at UMSL.

[409] Bill Greenwood's 1983 Personal Calendar.

[410] Burlington Lines, *Burlington Bulletin*, January/February, 1966, p. 8, *Greenwood Collection*, Barriger Library at UMSL.

railroad had to provide an unloading facility for the motor vehicle manufacturer at end points. The

manufacturers wanted exclusive facilities for their cars and once a railroad built a facility for a manufacturer it created a high barrier to entry for a competing railroad. In an effort to disrupt this historic way business was done, the IBU expressed interest in technology that would offer the transportation of cars in fully enclosed trailers using robotics to

At Claycomo plant near Kansas City, new autos and farm trac- who do not need a full carload of either cars or tractors by reduc-tors share some rack car. Arrangement benefits those Ford dealers ing amount of funds invested in inventory.

load and unload the automobiles. They would utilize a Hub center at origin and destination and allow the possibility of dealer-direct delivery with the trailer that carried the vehicles from the manufacturing plant. This would eliminate the exclusive unloading facility barrier to entry and permit a better integration of automotive line-haul service into high priority intermodal trains. A possible answer to this was the Dallas Smith trailer.

Self-loading robotic van trailer, which will be used by BN to haul automobiles from manufacturing plants to dealers, is expected to reduce damage problems.

Developed by Dallas Smith Property Brokers, Phoenix, and manufactured by Transportation Mfg. Corp., Roswell, N.M., the robotic trailer uses hydraulically operated arms built into the trailer to load and unload automobiles, each of which is cradled in a pair of steel bars (see photo above). Each trailer holds eight cars, which, in the words of a Ford Motor Co. official, "will arrive at our dealerships without damage from road debris, vandals, or the elements."[411]

The IBU was first introduced to Dallas Smith in June, 1982 and first investigated the Dallas Smith technology in early 1983. The first experimental run of it in BN intermodal service was on March 13, 1983 and the ceremonial first loading was on March 25 at Ford Motor Company's Wayne Michigan plant.[412] The trip went well and a more elaborate loading ceremony was held with Ford on April 26. The BN automotive marketing person focused on this opportunity was Jerry Taylor.

> *The Dallas Smith trailer coincides perfectly with our hub-center concept,' says Taylor. 'We'll use motor-carrier contractors to haul Dallas Smith trailers from the plant to our rail hub.*
>
> *The trailers then move by rail to a hub center near the auto dealer. Once grounded there, other contract motor carriers will take them directly to the dealer.[413]*

Darius Gaskins supported the Dallas Smith venture. It fit with what the IBU came to call his "Plant a thousand flowers" philosophy. He supported experimenting with potentially disruptive ventures (that

---

[411] Jacobus, William W., Intermodal – BN Relies on Truckers to Run Hub Centers, *Fleet Owner*, February 1986.

[412] Bill Greenwood's personal calendars, accessed on March 28, 2022.

[413] Jacobus, William W., Intermodal – BN Relies on Truckers to Run Hub Centers, *Fleet Owner*, February 1986.

wouldn't require a "bet the bank" wager) with the expectation that most may fail but if only one or two of the "thousand flowers" planted actually blooms it will have been well worth it.

Stampede Pass Route Mothballed

As predicted by the 1981 Intermodal Task Force, BN's carload business was diminishing. A lack of corporate faith in an intermodal option meant that there was not an adequate intermodal infrastructure to retain it or aggressively capture motor carrier market share. With BN's aggressive cost reduction push, all excess/underutilized assets were scrutinized in an effort to reduce maintenance and operating costs, eliminate redundant capacity and repurpose redundant assets. Among the assets evaluated was BN's choice of routes between Spokane and the Puget Sound.

Three of the greatest sappers of railroad operating efficiency are mileage, grade and curvature. The optimal route minimizes them all. BN had the 328 mile long former Great Northern's Stevens Pass route between Spokane and Seattle via Wenatchee and Everett, including the 7.8 mile Cascade Tunnel.[414] It had an advantage of less overall curvature but had the largest grade deficiency. Its eastbound grade is 2.2% for 11 miles between Skykomish and Scenic, WA. Its westbound grade ranges from 1.6% to 2.2% for 33 miles between Peshastin and Berne, WA.[415]

The route between Spokane and Seattle via Wishram and Vancouver, WA had reasonable curvature and much more attractive grades because so much of the route paralleled the Columbia River. Its 542 mile route length was its big disadvantage.[416] The added 214 miles is a time and expense sapper and totally eliminated BN's 265 route mile (and three train crew district) advantage between Chicago and Seattle versus the Union Pacific.[417] Because this route also served Portland there was no question that it would remain open but perhaps it could effectively handle even more business.

BN's 1983 Washington Routes

BN also had the former Northern Pacific Stampede Pass route between Spokane and Seattle via Pasco, WA (bold dotted line on left). At 395 miles it is 67 miles longer than the former Great Northern's route. It has a more favorable grade with only 6 miles of 2.2% westbound grade and 10.25 miles of 2.2% eastbound grade between Easton and Lester, WA.[418]

Primarily because of its 67 mile route advantage, a decision was made that the former Great Northern's Stevens Pass/Cascade Tunnel route would remain open. The section of the route over the Stampede Pass was mothballed on August 20.[419]

[414] BNSF 6003 Rail Miles Inquiry, Accessed from: https://bnsf.com/bnsf.was6/RailMiles/RMCentralController, on February 4, 2023.
[415] Hidy, Hidy, & Scott with Hofsommer, Great Northern Railway Ruling Grades on Main Freight Routes, p. 328.
[416] Ibid.
[417] BN Intermodal Task Force, Finance Subteam – Competitive Rail Analysis, October, 1992, p. 6, *Greenwood Collection*, Barriger Library at UMSL .
[418] Hidy, Hidy, & Scott with Hofsommer, Northern Pacific Railway Ruling Grades on Minneapolis-Seattle, p. 328.
[419] David Sprau email to Mark Cane, February 5, 2023.

Other Significant 1983 Events

In February, Walter Drexel was promoted to Chairman, President and Chief Executive Officer of BN Railroad. In July, Robert Garland (Sr. VP Administration and Planning) was dismissed and replaced by Don Wood. Wood was another veteran of ARCO that had been recruited to the BNI Holding Company in Seattle. In April of 1981 he replaced Drexel as BNI's Senior VP Strategic Planning and then in April of 1982 was appointed BNI's Sr. VP Finance and Planning.[420] Wood also had no railroad experience.

On September 1, 1983, Hunter Harrison was promoted to Vice President Transportation.[421] This was especially significant for the IBU because of the role Harrison had been playing in the improvement of BN's intermodal train service and his relationship with the IBU's key customer UPS. In addition, as part of the 1981 Intermodal Task Force effort a corporate policy had been established that said, "Dedicated Trains–Operate as authorized by VP Operations, based on profitability justification by Marketing Department."[422] While the IBU had been working under this policy already, the promotion of Harrison to VP Transportation facilitated the IBU's ability to get things done with Harrison related to trains.

On October 1, 1983 the Midway Hub celebrated its first birthday. "The Hub ... has had a very good first year, according to District Manager Bill Berry. Volume during the first half of 1983, compared to the same period last year (before the hub opened), is up 42 percent, he said."[423]

The final major event of 1983 was the announcement that BN was moving the railroad's headquarters. A year earlier Grayson told the State of Minnesota that BN railroad would remain in St. Paul. But Larry Kaufman stated:

> *after Grayson retired, Drexel told a staff meeting that the railroad was moving, adding, "And this time there will be no study." He instructed Michael Donahue, the railroad's vice president of strategic planning to "put them in a building where nobody will know it was the railroad," recalled Thomas J Matthews, who had been brought in as senior vice president of administration and human resources. "Those were his specific instructions, as well as find a place where (a lot of executives) would not go."[424]*

Bill Greenwood added: [425]

> *I'm in Drexel's office in St. Paul, and he says, "Look at it out this window. Look at it." Well, you know, in Minnesota in April, the ice is still on the lakes, the snow was dirty, and the sky's cloudy. It's not very pretty. "Who wants to live in this hellhole?"*

---

[420] Burlington Northern Inc.,1983 Annual Report, p. 17.

[421] Burlington Northern Railroad, *BN News*, October 1983, p. 4, *Greenwood Collection*, Barriger Library at UMSL.

[422] Transportation Division Report, Intermodal Task Force Meeting, August 18, 1981, *Greenwood Collection*, Barriger Library at UMSL.

[423] Burlington Northern Railroad, *BN News*, October 1983, p. 5, *Greenwood Collection*, Barriger Library at UMSL.

[424] Kaufman, p. 229.

[425] National Railroad Hall of Fame, William E. Greenwood, Chief Operating Officer (retired) Burlington Northern Railroad, Interview Transcript, July 30, 2020: Accessed from: https://www.nrrhof.org/greenwood-transcript, Accessed on May 7, 2022.

So, he called his boss, Dick Bressler in Seattle and said, "I don't like it here. You mind if I move the headquarters?" And Bressler said, "Well, I don't like the politics in Minnesota, either. Go ahead and move it."

So, in '84, out of all the locations the search team came up with, they came up with a file of four or five: Denver; Seattle; Chicago; Lincoln, Nebraska. And that was it. Drexel looks at the list, and he said, "I don't see Texas on here." "Well, no, sir. We have a secondary line in Texas. Our main line doesn't go there." "I want Texas on this list!" (Laughs.) So, Dallas-Fort Worth got put on the list. We wound up in his fraternity brother's office building in downtown Fort Worth.

Unfortunately for the IBU, Ken Hoepner did not want to move. He was recruited by the Soo Line Railroad to become their Vice President Marketing and he left the IBU in early 1984. Emmett Brady chose to take an early retirement buy-out package which left two big IBU voids to be filled in 1984.

First Non-Trucker BN Hub Manager Selected for Spokane

Enabled by the successful implementation of the Hub Center concept at Midway and Portland in late 1982, by the end of 1983 Hubs had been established at Seattle in April, Memphis in May, St. Louis in July, Denver in August, Spokane in September, Birmingham in October, and Kansas City in November. Among these, all but Spokane was established with a Hub Manager from the motor carrier industry with experience in that extended local market area. Spokane was the exception because of the lack of candidates who met the IBU's high standards. That dilemma was fixed as related by Dennis Gustin who had been working with Doug Rodel as the operations manager at the Midway Hub since its inception:

> *In the summer of 83', my wife and I traveled Amtrak to Spokane and loved the area. That summer at a Midway staff meeting, Doug (Rodel), Axel (Holland), Dave (Burns), Bill (Greenwood), Paul Bergeland (BN Human Resources and the primary Hub Manager recruiter), and others discussed that there were no available candidates for the Spokane Hub manager position. Bill G. suggests "we may have to go inside." I throw my hat in the ring. Two months later, I was on Northwest Air to the Lilac City, where I will spend the next 16 years.*[426]

The promotion of an internal candidate when that internal candidate was the best available option proved that the IBU would exercise prudent flexibility, do the right thing, and not just hold to a principle if the principle resulted in a sub-optimal outcome.

1983 Performance Wrap-up

Climbing out of the deep 1981-82 recession, the IBU finished 1983 with an intermodal revenue growth over 1982 of $62.3 million (+22.8%) on a 16.5% volume growth.[427] As promised, the IBU more than made up for the lost Sea-Land business. Total railroad performance also improved:

---

[426] Dennis Gustin email to Mark Cane, February 10, 2022.
[427] Internal BN Document, *Greenwood Collection*, Barriger Library at UMSL.

In 1983 rail traffic was up 9 percent, with grain, forest products, intermodal and coal all showing satisfactory gains. Coal shipments, which accounted for 57 percent of total revenue ton miles, reflected an increase in average revenue per ton mile of 6 percent.

The Railroad's efforts to accomplish its long-term objective of being the low cost producer of quality transportation service brought continued gains in productivity. During 1983, the railroad operating ratio was reduced to 82.3 percent which is now one of the best in the industry.[428]

The following chart illustrates BN Intermodal revenue performance from the inception of the IBU in 1981 through 1983 compared to the non-coal, grain and intermodal (F&M) businesses and the total financial performance of the railroad.

Burlington Northern Railroad 1981-1983 Financial Performance ($ millions) [429]

	IML Rev.	F&M Rev.	BNRR Rev.	BNRR Op. Inc.	BNRR OR	BNI LT Debt	Pref. Stock	Int. Exp.	Div. Exp.	Debt/ Cap.
1981	$267	$1,598	$4,088	$527	87.1%	$1,330	$105	$140	$58	29%
1982	273	1,261	3,773	457	87.9%	1,333	105	136	71	27%
1983	335	1,218	4,058	734	81.9%	2,930	709	142	87	41%

The Intermodal Task Force had suggested that "worst-case," 28% of BN's 1981 Food and Manufactured Products and Forest Products ("F&M") revenue was vulnerable to motor carriers by 1986. Their total revenue decline increased from 21.1% by the end of 1982 to 23.8% by the end of 1983. Coal (+13%) and grain (+12%) had strong years in 1983.

---

[428] Burlington Northern Inc., 1983 Annual Report, p. 1.
[429] Internal BN Document (*Greenwood Collection*, Barriger Library at UMSL) and Burlington Northern Inc., 1981-1983 Annual Reports.

Chapter 11 – BN Intermodal's Positive Momentum Builds in 1984

BN's St. Paul based employees who decided to stay with the company and move to Ft. Worth had to prepare to sell existing homes, buy new homes in Texas, uproot families and make the move. It was disruptive for all as the year started. The IBU was asked by BN's Human Resources Department to determine whether or not it would be in BN's best interest to move employees' household goods via BN intermodal from Midway to Dallas. The local agent for Bekins Van Lines won the relocation contract and worked with the IBU to see if a competitive cost and service package could be worked out. The answer proved to be no primarily because BN had no dedicated intermodal train service between Minnesota and Texas and the cost and service quality available from mixed-train service wasn't competitive. In addition, the BN Irving (Dallas) intermodal facility had no lift device. It was still a circus ramp operation.

The 1984 "White Paper"

The 1984 progression of Hub start-ups would proceed according to the original plan of Galesburg, Illinois in February, Irving (Dallas) in March, Houston and Fargo (Dilworth, MN) in May, Springfield, MO in July, Mobile in August and Omaha in September. Unfortunately, both equipment and hub capacity were under tremendous pressure and the business was about to hit a wall. The IBU was delivering as it had promised but continued concerns, especially from Drexel, the new Executive VP-Finance Don Wood, and the Strategic Planning Department, about the profitability of BN's intermodal business were hindering approval of the capital needed to fully implement the intermodal plan. In February, Darius Gaskins met with the IBU leadership team and said he wanted a fully-allocated-cost based Intermodal ROI model developed to again quantify the intermodal strategic plan as part of an Intermodal "White Paper." Mark Cane recalled:[430]

> *Darius said he wanted a "white paper" and we asked him what a "white paper" was. He wanted something to summarize the competitive intermodal environment, BN Intermodal's strategies, what has happened since the 1981 IBU formation, what BN's Intermodal business was worth to BN, what BN's Intermodal plan was worth to BN and what was needed to progress the plan. Bill Greenwood turned to me and said, "Well Mark, you heard him. Write a White Paper." I swallowed hard, said OK and got to work on it. Darius said to limit it to five pages.*

It was accomplished with 5½ pages as follows:[431]

---

[430] Mark Cane's personal recollection, March 17, 2023.
[431] Burlington Northern Railroad's Intermodal Program, (the "White Paper"), submitted May 2, 1984, *Greenwood Collection*, Barriger Library at UMSL.

Burlington Northern Railroad's Intermodal Program
Background

On a sustained basis, railroads have been providing intermodal service (trailer and container on flat car, or TOFC/COFC) since about 1960. Until early 1981, the business had been heavily regulated by the Interstate Commerce Act. In this regulated environment, prices were set jointly by competing carriers and services offered were fairly uniform. Deregulation arrived with railroads trying to sell a generic product.

Since price is the prime differentiating feature among generic products, the first reaction after deregulation by some in the rail industry was to utilize new pricing freedoms to buy market share. Partial deregulation of the motor carrier industry in early 1982, which removed market entry and exit barriers, further heightened competition for the transportation of loaded trailers and containers. It quickly became clear that to succeed in this new, continually changing environment, Burlington Northern Railroad had to lower its intermodal cost structure, streamline its physical plant and devise ways to differentiate its intermodal product from that of its competitors.

While transportation has been adapting to deregulation, the shipping public has been transitioning from a traffic and rate orientation to sophisticated physical distribution management.

Evolution from Regulation to Market Driven: The Three Strategies

When your product is generic and the only significant marketing variable is price, your degree of success is controlled by that single variable with resulting limited control over your destiny. In order to establish some control in the marketplace, BN Railroad initiated three major Intermodal Strategies regarding Hub Centers, dedicated trains utilizing new technology equipment, and development of customer-needs-oriented service packages.

The Hub Center Strategy focuses on reducing costs and improving customer service through the consolidation of about 140 ramps that were in operation in early 1981 into a network of 20-25 Hub Centers by the end of 1985. Hubs are managed by individuals with trucking expertise under a profit center structure. Implementation of the Hub Strategy is achieving success in lowering ramp/deramp costs and drayage costs. Also, ramps within the Hub's service radius that were formerly served by local rail service are now served through lower cost contract motor carriage. As a result, service time is reduced, customer service levels and equipment utilization are increased, and the effective market area has been expanded beyond BN's existing rail system.

The second strategy focuses on the development of a system of dedicated intermodal trains operating between Hub Centers on reliable and predictable schedules utilizing new technology equipment. Dedicated train operation helps improve equipment utilization and reduces equipment and lading damage.

The potential for damage reduction is a key benefit of the new technology equipment. The combination of dedicated trains and articulated equipment is expected to eliminate customer expenses for securing loads as well as the negative perception of intermodal as a damage prone transportation mode. Both of these factors are negligible for a pure truck movement.

A second important potential benefit of the new technology equipment is the ability to reduce line haul train costs. Utilization of some versions of the new technology equipment will allow train weight reductions of up to 20% compared to conventional equipment operation. Through weight reduction and aerodynamic effects, the goal is to achieve a 20% reduction in locomotive power and fuel expense.

The third strategy focuses on the development of customer-needs-oriented intermodal service packages. In order for BN to break from the generic intermodal product mold, it is imperative to continue defining what has value to the customer, so that a differentiated product package can be offered. This is crucial because the more competitors are alike, the more competition they face.

Customer oriented service packages mean more than offering, for example, a 60 hour schedule from Chicago to Seattle. Our competitors may offer the same or better. Customer oriented packages concentrate on offering what the customer values. These could include such options as:

- *Predictable, reliable service*
- *Guaranteed arrival time with a rebate for non-performance*
- *Lading insurance dependent on commodity value*
- *Ability to provide specific equipment types*
- *Varied payment plans*
- *Electronic data interchange*
- *Quick and courteous response to inquiries*

The customer oriented strategy provides the focus for the first two strategies since customer's values need to be reflected in how intermodal physical capabilities and systems are implemented. Through implementation of this customer responsive strategy, BN's intermodal product is evolving from one that was regulated to one that is market driven.

Where Does The Intermodal Program Stand?

By the end of 1984 the Hub Center concept will have been implemented at 17 locations. Dedicated trains will be in operation between Chicago and Denver, Chicago and the Pacific Northwest, Memphis and Avard, and Birmingham and the Pacific Northwest. Due to the rebounding economy and successful initiation of the three strategies by the entire railroad organization, BN Intermodal volume will have grown 41% and revenue will have increased 60% over 1982. The Burlington Northern Railroad has established itself as the innovative leader in the Intermodal transportation industry.

Capacity, however, has been reached at several key hubs. Shortages of trailers and flat cars are occurring and the capacity of support information systems to assist in managing the hubs, distribute equipment and provide timely market intelligence has been exceeded. Thus, the intermodal business is at a crossroads. In order to position BN's intermodal business to handle projected business volume at customer service levels deemed necessary, capital investment of almost $300 million between 1984 and 1987 will be required. An overriding concern is the profitability of BN's intermodal business and its ability to generate an adequate return on such a significant investment.

The Profitability Study

To address this issue, BN's Intermodal (TOFC/COFC) business has been analyzed in a special project as a hypothetical stand alone profit center. Direct intermodal costs and assets, as well as a proportion of BN Railroad fixed costs and assets, were arbitrarily and hypothetically allocated to the business to generate a pro forma, after full tax (6% state, 46% Federal), income statement and return on assets. The proportion of intermodal revenue to total BN Railroad revenue proved to be the most conservative, arbitrary fixed cost and overhead asset allocation method. By this method, BN's intermodal business performed as follows in 1982 and 1983:

	Revenue (MM)	After Tax Net Income (MM)	After Tax Profit Margin	After Tax Return on Assets(*)
1982	$271.7	$13.3	4.9%	8.2%
1983	$331.5	$20.1	6.1%	8.5%

* Asset base included direct intermodal assets (Hub land, lift devices, trailers) at their estimated market value plus arbitrarily allocated overhead BNRR assets at their book value.

Return on assets grew slower than profit margin in 1983 because the direct intermodal asset base grew and the allocation of overhead assets was larger in 1983 than in 1982. (Intermodal revenue grew faster than the revenue for the railroad as a whole.)

Successful continued implementation of the three strategies, supported by the proposed investment program is expected to result in the following:

	Revenue (MM)*	After Tax Net Income (MM)*	After Tax Profit Margin	After Tax Return on Assets(*)
1984	$436.0	$37.4	8.6%	10.4%
1985	$466.7	$43.9	9.4%	9.3%
1986	$523.6	$57.2	10.9%	9.6%
1987	$583.8	$74.9	12.8%	10.2%

* Constant 1984 dollars

Projected revenue growth between 1984 and 1985 reflects the effects of the SP/ATSF Merger. Return on assets are not expected to grow as fast as profit margin. Since intermodal investments were assumed to be purchases rather than leases, the direct BN intermodal asset base is expected to grow rapidly. Despite this, the main reason return on assets growth does not mirror profit margin growth is due to an increased share of BNRR assets being arbitrarily allocated to the Intermodal business.

Based on this hypothetical analysis, the incremental benefits expected to accrue to BNRR as a result of the Intermodal investment program through 1987 would have an after tax internal rate of return of 46.6% and an after tax net present value of $263 million (6% discount rate).

Key Factors For The Success Of The Intermodal Program

The Intermodal plan is driven by a major overriding assumption; that the Burlington Northern Railroad will be successful in developing superior quality, motor-carrier-alternative product that will be reflected in higher charges and increased market share, maximizing the rate of return on the business to BNI's stockholders. There are five key factors that will determine the degree of the program's success. Effectively addressing these factors will give BN Railroad the capability to be the driving force in the intermodal market.

Customer

Traditionally, the railroad industry under regulation has tended not to consider customer's needs but rather dealt with customer groups in adversarial I.C.C. proceedings. Adversarial attitudes cannot be sustained when doing business in today's competitive transportation environment. For BN's intermodal program to succeed, the customer's needs and perceptions must be identified and effectively dealt with in constructing customer oriented packages. This customer and marketplace orientation will be a major element in developing a superior quality intermodal product.

Competition

Although BNRR has become an acknowledged leader in the intermodal marketplace, a sustainable competitive edge must be developed. In addition to addressing customer needs, an awareness of what current competitive and potential substitution is doing and is capable of doing must be maintained.

Costs

To be profitably competitive, BN must continue to manage Intermodal costs. BN's existing Intermodal cost structure effectively limits BN's potential market to shipments greater than 700 miles for dense commodities and 850 miles for light commodities. Reductions in the elements of Intermodal's cost structure (labor, fuel, equipment, Hubs, empty miles) can increase the effective competitive range both on and off BN's rail system.

Capacity

The BN Intermodal system will require capacity expansion in Hubs, equipment and information systems to respond to the marketplace and achieve the business projections. Information systems are needed to assist in better utilizing existing and planned resources. In addition, electronic information systems are becoming a requirement for transportation carriers to be utilized in customers' physical distribution systems. Decisions regarding whether to lease or buy additional capacity needs in these areas will be driven by rate of return considerations.

Commitment

To be successful, the Intermodal program must earn the commitment of the entire Burlington Northern organization. Reflecting the needs and values of the customer, there must be a commitment to quality, innovation and responsiveness.

Observations

In the continually changing transportation environment, success will be measured not only by effective cost management, but by creating a sustainable competitive edge through flexible and customer responsive packages'. BN's intermodal program addresses these issues and lays the foundation for continued profitable growth.

"White Paper" Outcome

The "White Paper" ROI model results were presented to the Senior Equipment Steering Committee on March 13. The model results were presented to Lou Dell'Osso who was Wood's replacement as Sr. VP Planning for the BNI Holding Company. The full paper was submitted to Gaskins in its final form on May 2, 1984.[432] Overall, it received a mixed response. Gaskins drilled into the methodology and was pleased with it and the analysis that supported it. Other significant decision makers had difficulty believing that BN's Intermodal business was really profitable, especially on a "fully allocated cost" basis. Intermodal had one of the lowest "revenue-to-long-range-incremental-cost (LRIC)" ratios in the BNRR portfolio which made it look much less attractive than the coal or merchandise businesses that had higher revenue/LRIC ratios. Although the numbers used in the Intermodal White Paper financial analysis came from BN's official financial performance measurement systems, the finance and planning people did not trust them. That made it extremely difficult for the IBU because it was at the mercy of historic biases and negative sentiment toward the business.

The first part of the problem was referred to earlier. The Finance and Planning people (and even the vast majority of the Operating Department executives) had a financial accounting mindset with a bias focused on arbitrary fixed cost allocations. The White Paper ROI model had arbitrarily used Intermodal's percent of railroad revenue as its fixed cost allocation basis which was a harsher method (on Intermodal) than revenue-ton-miles or tonnage. A second part of the problem was that they had trouble with the managerial accounting mindset that drove the IBU. By definition, true fixed costs existed in a high fixed-cost and extremely long-term asset intensive business like Burlington Northern whether the Intermodal business existed or not. If BN's Intermodal business went away, the railroad's fixed costs and the vast majority of the long-life assets would not disappear. They would still have to be covered by the other business lines. With its development of the previously mentioned train P&L system, the IBU was striving to develop a true activity-based costing system that would be the foundation of a true managerial accounting system. Unfortunately, due to Intermodal's inability to get the support it needed for its full information system needs, that tool did not yet exist.

Another part of the problem was that, for the most part, outside of the IBU (Hunter Harrison being an exception) there was a vast under-appreciation of the power of asset velocity. While BN's Intermodal business did have lower margins than that of other business lines like coal, food and manufactured products and forest products, Intermodal had the highest asset velocity ratios in the portfolio. The loads generated per year by Intermodal cars and trailers ran up to 4X the velocity of that of carload business equipment. The velocity of loads processed per dollar of facility value or per square feet of facility in the IBU's Hub Centers blew away the comparable ratios for carload freight classification yards. In addition, BN's intermodal trains did not use the vast network of branch lines and yards and only used a small fraction of the BN's main-line capacity outside of the PNW-Chicago Corridor. Asset velocity drives return

---

[432] Mark Cane's personal calendar and personal recollections.

on assets and even low margin businesses can be attractive from the standpoint of return on assets with good asset velocity. If this were not so, grocery supermarkets or superstores could not financially survive given their relatively low margin percentages. This asset velocity philosophy drove the IBU.

Outside of the IBU it was a dilemma that couldn't be shaken but fortunately Darius Gaskins and Harrison bought into it. Gaskins understood it easily because of his strong academic economics as well as applied economics background. Harrison did not have the academic background but he understood it instinctively and it would later drive his pursuit of Precision Scheduled Railroading. Because of Gaskins' backing and the inability of the financial people to totally disregard the White Paper's analysis and result, more of the IBU's capital needs were funded. The finance and planning people were asked to propose alternate measures of IBU performance but declined and chose to continue sniping about intermodal profitability and obstructing aggressive intermodal development instead.

Relocation Impacts and Organizational Emphasis Changes[433]

The relocation to Ft. Worth of those who chose to stay with BN was to have been completed by July, 1984. The process of selling houses, buying new houses, relocating, uprooting and resettling families was a big employee distraction. By April it was clear who among IBU staff would be leaving the company and who would be staying. With the loss of Hoepner and the impending loss of Brady, Greenwood held an organization planning meeting with Burns, Berry, DeWitt and Cane who, all were in the process of relocating, to explore opportunities to restructure the organization in a way that would address responsibility and accountability gaps that were becoming apparent. The group agreed that it was time to strengthen the organization's marketing focus on customer segments, service segments and information systems support.

Reporting to Greenwood, Bill DeWitt was still in charge of Domestic Intermodal Marketing and he split organizational emphasis across the segments of IMCs, Motor Carriers (including UPS, LTL carriers and truckload carriers) and interline (business done in coordination with connecting rail carriers). He recruited Bruce Herndon, the St. Louis Hub Manager (and trucking industry alum), to focus on the motor carrier segment. Cane was placed in charge of intermodal train service development and oversight, information systems support and IBU planning. Cliff Kath was shifted to domestic motor vehicle marketing from a focus on domestic marketing for direct sales to non-motor carrier customers (which was shifted to telemarketing in the BN Sales Department). Bill Berry continued to oversee intermodal equipment. Dave Burns continued to oversee Hubs.

Hub Start-ups Continue[434]

The relocation-related disruptions couldn't be allowed to impact the schedule of new Hub starts. All of the work associated with Hub Manager recruiting, facility preparation, lift device acquisition, train and switching service adjustments and efforts associated with market research, customer focus groups, Hub promotions material had to converge on-time. They did in support of Galesburg, Illinois in February, Irving (Dallas) in March, Houston in May, Dilworth (Fargo) in May, Springfield (Missouri) in July, Mobile and Chicago (Cicero) in August (advanced from the original plan of 1985), and Omaha/Lincoln in

---

[433] Ibid.
[434] Ibid.

September. Yet, by year-end, lift capability was still lacking at Amarillo, Billings, Pasco, Dilworth (Fargo), Springfield, Tulsa and Vancouver, BC, meaning that these facilities were restricted to conventional cars and circus loading and unloading (which also meant international shipments in containers had to be on a chassis). The year ended with 17 hubs in operation with 4 left for 1985.

The Birmingham Hub, with its new lift capability, was expanded to more than double its former capacity. It was also the pioneer for the development of highway satellite hubs with the establishment of one off of BN's system in Atlanta. From the standpoint of the customer, the Atlanta satellite facility was a BN location as pricing was set up from that point to/from other hubs on the BN network. An IMC would arrange for a load to be tendered to BN's Atlanta "drop lot" and the Birmingham Hub arranged for it to be trucked to Birmingham where it would be loaded for train service. The Omaha/Lincoln Hub established a similar facility off of BN's line in Des Moines.

With the presence of Hubs at Seattle, Portland, Spokane, Kansas City, Springfield, Memphis and Birmingham, and with the assistance of Hunter Harrison, dedicated intermodal train service was added between the PNW and Birmingham.

Sales and Service Reorganization

Effective August 1, 1984 Joe Galassi was promoted from Transportation to lead BN's Sales and Property Management Department.[435] This displaced Bill Egan who had headed sales. A new position, VP International Marketing and Sales, was created for him and he assumed responsibility for international intermodal marketing and pricing including international motor vehicle marketing from the IBU, and sales from Galassi. The transfer of international intermodal marketing out of the IBU was unfortunate as it didn't facilitate the working relationship with the intermodal hubs, equipment, systems, train service and planning efforts. Ralph Muellner, the Director International Marketing, and his team within the IBU switched their reporting relationship. Muellner was extremely effective, well liked by customers, and protective of the international business he was accountable for. Unfortunately, he perceived that the IBU had a domestic orientation and a bias against international business. He demonstrated a lack of trust in other members of the IBU leadership team and as a result he tended to not share information. This organizational division only made that working relationship more challenging.

The Sales and Service reorganization exacerbated a feature that had been creating sub-optimal results for the IBU. Jack Round was appointed AVP Intermodal Sales and Telemarketing Sales, reporting to Galassi. Dave Johnson was promoted from his Portland Hub Manager position to Director Intermodal Sales and Don Buchholtz, Jim Cully and Kevin Wager were appointed Regional Sales Managers reporting to Johnson. Telemarketing included an Intermodal Sales subgroup. Meanwhile, as part of the Hub concept, a Hub Center Account Manager was assigned to each Hub as it was established. The Hub Sales Manager reported directly to the Sales organization's Regional Sales Manager with a dotted-line reporting relationship to the Hub Manager. In addition to Hub operations responsibility and accountability, the Hub Manager was also expected to be responsible and accountable for the Hub's P&L and Intermodal sales in his or her geographic area. This relationship worked well for most Hub Managers who were fortunate to have industrious Hub Account Managers assigned to their Hub. Unfortunately, several were assigned more "traditional" rail sales people who lacked the knowledge,

---

[435] Internal COMPASS message from E. W. Ritter, Sr. Assistant Vice-President, General Manager Sales, to BN's entire sales force, July 13, 1984, *Greenwood Collection*, Barriger Library at UMSL.

selling skills, and motivation that aggressive motor carrier experienced Hub Managers were accustomed to. This reorganization did not repair this deficiency.

Not only did the IBU have to struggle with lack of control over their primary domestic sales channel (IMCs) but it also had no control over its internal international marketing and sales and internal domestic sales efforts.

BN Information Systems Deficiencies[436]

The IBU had been able to get a little help from the information systems department to assist with revenue billing and the operation of Hub Centers but it was woefully inadequate compared to what was needed. A big problem was that the technology of the business was far outstripping the ability of legacy systems to support it. The legacy operations support system was built to support carload shipments that never left the rail. If cars left BN property it was to a connecting railroad. This was a symptom of a company information systems sickness that went back to before the 1970 BN merger.

While Bill Greenwood was a traveling car agent in the late 1960s he was assigned to the GN-NP-CB&Q merger committee:

> One of the things that I did was get on a merger committee. And there were three of us, and our job was to see, go around and see and analyze every railroad in the industry's data system so that we could come back with a recommendation about where the best data system was; benchmarking, basically. And I did that. That's why I got the advantage of seeing every railroad headquarters in the United States, the major railroads; get to know some of the people and see what their data system was. [437]

And whose was the best?

> Well, in my view, in our view, it was the Southern Railroad. And the worst was the Southern Pacific Railroad. So, we came back with a recommendation. Guess what? We went with the Southern Pacific system! I learned we were merely window dressing to come up with something, come up with the right answer. We came up with the wrong answer. Because our vice president of finance at the time was from the Southern Pacific. He wanted us to use their system. Terrible system. I mean, it was labor intensive and capital intensive. And we paid the price for 10 years of... And indeed, what you're interested in is data accuracy. They had the worst data accuracy of any system, and the Southern had the best. [438]

BN's unwillingness to follow the recommendation of Greenwood and his associates would come to haunt BN Railroad and its intermodal business for years to come and the IBU was suffering from it two decades later.

---

[436] Mark Cane's personal calendar and personal recollections.
[437] National Railroad Hall of Fame, William E. Greenwood, Chief Operating Officer (retired) Burlington Northern Railroad, Interview Transcript, July 30, 2020: Accessed from: https://www.nrrhof.org/greenwood-transcript, on May 7, 2022.
[438] Ibid.

Intermodal's trailers left railroad tracks and railroad property. The system was set up to support a single rail-bound carload as the level of activity. A Ten-Pack car would have up to ten trailers on it. Systems had been modified to handle two trailers on a car but ten was unthinkable. A five well double stack car could handle up to 15 containers if two twenty foot containers were loaded in the bottoms of the wells and single forty foot containers were loaded on top of them in each well. RoadRailer trailers could leave the property at any grade crossing, not just at Hub Centers. In addition, Hub managers were acting as entrepreneurs and opening satellite highway hubs off of BN's system that were designed to appear from a service standpoint no different than an on-line hub. Prices were set up for moves such as from Birmingham's offline highway satellite hub in Atlanta to the satellite hub in Des Moines. Revenue and cost accounting systems built for traditional railroad operations and set up to handle moves restricted to BN's physical property couldn't relate to Intermodal's physical reality. This is just the tip of the proverbial iceberg as it relates to how intermodal operations didn't fit the systems. It was also challenging on the revenue and cost accounting side where trailers and containers were the unit of revenue and not the car. The systems needs were many but getting the help needed was a matter of triage. The place of greatest need was Hubs. Starting in April a series of meetings were held with ISS to initiate work on a Hub Management System.

In July, Bill DeWitt was returning home from visits with customers and he struck up a conversation with the woman sitting next to him on the plane. They shared information about their respective jobs and DeWitt found out that she was a senior consultant for an information systems consulting firm – Nolan, Norton and Company (NNC). She said her firm helped clients do ground-up work scoping out their information systems needs and putting together a business case for systems development. DeWitt explained a bit of Intermodal's systems dilemma and it sounded to DeWitt like NNC could really help the IBU. After returning to Ft. Worth he told Mark Cane about the encounter and gave him the woman's card. Cane called her and set up a meeting on August 1 in Ft. Worth for NNC to introduce IBU leadership to their approach for assisting a corporation in the development of a long-range plan for information systems. That led to several subsequent meetings to scope out how a consulting engagement with NNC would work, what resources would be required, and what it would cost. NNC delivered a project proposal on September 24 for an 8-9 week project for a cost of $60,000 plus out-of-pocket expenses. An engagement with NNC proved to be unworkable at that time given all of the other fires that were burning. The Information Systems Department was able to provide some stop-gap systems help for the Hubs but not nearly enough. The long-range information systems plan issue would be revisited in 1985.

APL Competitive Concerns Realized

As anticipated, Don Orris leveraged stack technology to aggressively increase APL's competitiveness:[439]

> *In 1984 the American President Lines brought double-stack technology into the public spotlight with the onset of full page color advertising. That same year a service with three trains per week was initiated between Union Pacific's Los Angeles Intermodal facility and Chicago & Northwestern's venerable Wood Street facility in Chicago. APL instantly began to funnel its eastbound import containers to the new double-stack service. Refilling the majority of the boxes that did not return with export freight became an immediate priority. While stack car economics had kept the costs of empty container returns under control, real profit leverage existed in operating loads in both directions – and that meant domestic freight.*

---

[439] DeBoer, pp. 155-156.

For an old line steamship company like American President Lines this was a major departure from its core business. But Don Orris had already initiated Liner Train service, using standard 89-foot cars, and APL itself was being run by someone who definitely was not a "webfoot." APL, through its acquisition by, and later spinoff from Natomas, acquired a tall, quiet, extremely competent Chief Executive Officer in the person of Bruce Seaton. He saw the leverage and the potential of turning his "steamship company" into a true intermodal company.

Reloading was accomplished by offering cut rates to third parties for westbound domestic freight on the days the Liner Trains operated. Limited day of the week operations led to customer coordination problems with pickup of boxes, loading and scheduling for train departures. Railroads who operated daily services had a distinct advantage.

(Orris) still required a massive jump in traffic in order to build up to daily train frequency. To accomplish this he pursued two goals. First, he began to move "beyond Chicago" traffic in blocks on his existing trains. While this helped to build his eastbound volume, it merely added to the empty westbound woes. However, in 1984 he played his trump card. In order to build both bidirectional volume and fill his Chicago westbound empties, APL bought the largest existing third party, National Piggyback. This was a company built by R.C. Matney, a self-effacing, extremely bright man.

At the time when the purchase price of $65 million was announced, many observers thought that someone at American President Lines' Oakland headquarters had "slipped a cog." All that money for assets consisting of "telephones, desks and folks who went home at night." Strategically, however, it balanced up the existing APL trains, allowing them to move to daily departures, and it gave them a critical mass that would allow APL to survive if things became highly competitive.

Not only did APL set itself up for entry into the domestic intermodal market. As part of their effort to attract Steamship Lines to call on Seattle, the Port of Seattle expanded their effort to act as an agent of small lines for their United States inland transportation services. They had been concentrating on servicing eastbound imports and westbound exports. Given the evolution of APL and Sea-Land into more fully integrated physical distribution companies, they decided to expand their efforts to support smaller lines that did not have the wherewithal to manage more extensive inland operations. They hired Tom Shurstad, a former BN operating department employee as part of that effort. On September 10, 1984 Shurstad met with Bill Greenwood to request a westbound domestic contract from BN.[440] He requested a "sweetheart deal" but was offered one at standard prices.

Other Significant Intermodal Initiatives

The railroad industry was competing on the revenue side in a deregulated marketplace but its labor costs for train operations were stuck in the regulated era. Historic labor agreements required trains to be staffed with an engineer, a conductor, and two to three brakemen, in addition to an occasional locomotive fireman. For the train crew, a day's pay was earned for every 100 miles the train operated which had been established decades earlier. In addition, cabooses were required even though new technology for monitoring train operations made them functionally obsolete for line haul operations.

---

[440] Bill Greenwood's personal calendar.

This cost structure was a major factor in making intermodal service uncompetitive versus motor carrier for hauls shorter than 700-800 miles. Meanwhile, the majority of the motor carrier business took place in lanes shorter than 800 miles. Such markets were enticing but unattainable for BN Intermodal. Starting in May, a series of meetings were held with Labor Relations to put together a strategy for working with the train operating labor organizations to see if special agreements could be reached for reduced crews for short-haul corridor intermodal service. The timing was not deemed to be right, but the stage was set to further pursue this initiative.

In addition, BN had been testing double stack technology and APL and Sea-Land were initiating service utilizing double stack cars. On top of information system related issues, several projects were initiated to determine what BN would have to do to physically accommodate broad-based double stack service. For example, lift devices would have to be modified to do top-picking of containers because "piggypacker" grab arms used to lift trailers on and off flatcars would be physically unable to reach into the double stack car wells. In addition, double stacked containers would run into clearance issues at various locations across the railroad so implementation of that technology would require plant modifications. Modifications would even range to trackside platforms such as from past passenger operations that limited horizontal ("AAR Plate C") clearance close to track level.

On the international intermodal front, the IBU made a decision to discontinue payment of per-diem charges to steamship companies and leasing companies for marine containers. In addition to eliminating a "substantial amount of clerical activity focused on monitoring, billing and collection by water carriers, and validation and payment by the railroad," BN also "eliminated an annual pay-out of approximately $750,000 a year in per diem charges."[441] BN also eliminated the practice of the free return of empty containers from the east to PNW ports to secure an added source of revenue and encourage the development of export business in those containers. In addition, in 1984 the Japanese-Six water carrier lines consortium decided to shift their large container ships from California to the PNW. "Two large carrier lines now have assured us they will commence operations in the PNW the last half of this year. Together they project handling more than 18,000 containers annually via PNW ports," Egan says.[442] The decision by the Japanese carriers to do this was stimulated by BN's commitment to carry their containers on double stack cars on BN's common user stack train to Chicago. APL and Sea-Land had been touting the improved ride quality stack trains provided compared to the slack-action prone conventional cars to customers and other lines needed that capability to stay service-competitive. In addition, BN was able to share some of the economies double stack cars generated with them to help them stay economically viable. As an aid to Steamship companies who now had to pay for the westbound return of empties, and to stimulate the shipment of loaded export containers, BN also instituted a "750-mile free-repositioning" program for containers. BN would move the container up to 750 miles for free if it was utilized to generate an export load to PNW ports over the BN.

Two innovations came from the new Hub teams:[443]

---

[441] Burlington Northern Railroad, *BN News*, August-September, 1984, p. 7-8, *Greenwood Collection*, Barriger Library at UMSL.

[442] Ibid, p. 8.

[443] William E. Greenwood, Transportation Research Board, Transportation Research Record 1029, Burlington Northern Railroad's View of Intermodal Hub Centers and Their Impact on Productivity and Customer Service, 1985, accessed from: https://onlinepubs.trb.org/Onlinepubs/trr/1985/1029/1029-008.pdf, on June 20, 2022.

> *- Hub center personnel invented lift shoe adapters that permit older lift devices to handle wider trailers plus enable all BN lift equipment to safely handle privately owned trailers that do not have lift pads*

> *- Hub center personnel adapted weight scales from the logging industry to intermodal use, so that each unit is weighed as it is lifted*

The lift shoe adapters gave older lift devices the ability to cost effectively handle the new green 102" wide trailers, of which BN had 1,500 in its fleet by the end of 1994,[444] as well as trailers owned by motor carriers and private fleets that were not built with intermodal lift plates. The addition of scale capability to lift devices gave BN the ability to determine actual trailer weights to help conformance with highway weight laws as well as eliminate overweight trailers to allow for safer train loading practices.

Bill Greenwood is Promoted

While the White Paper helped ease some of Intermodal's obstacles, it didn't fix the lack of support Dick Gleason was providing the IBU. Gaskins was very aware of this and took action. Effective August 7, 1984 he promoted Bill Greenwood to a full vice president title (VP Intermodal) with a reporting relationship directly to him as opposed to through Gleason. The press release for the promotion announcement contained the following quotes from Gaskins: [445]

> *Our intermodal business unit has enjoyed excellent growth over the past few years under Bill's leadership. The unit has full responsibility for marketing and pricing, equipment, service levels and all Hub Centers and other intermodal facilities. This change reflects the growing importance of this segment of our business and BN's commitment to meeting our customers' needs.*

Garland Resigns, Wood Arrives, Donahue and Reed Promoted, Wackstein Hired

On May 1, 1984 Robert Garland, Senior Vice President Finance, resigned "to pursue other business interests." Effective that date, Accounting, Information Resources and property tax all reported directly to ARCO alum Donald Wood, Senior Vice President Administration and Planning.[446] Effective July 1, former VP Strategic Planning Mike Donahue was promoted to VP Market and Service Planning—Coal and Lyle Reed, former Sr. AVP Staff, was promoted to VP Strategic Planning, reporting to Wood.[447] In addition, George Clinkenbeard retired as VP Management Information Resource on June 1 and was replaced at the end of the year by Eli Wackstein who had been VP Management Information Systems

---

[444] Ibid.

[445] Burlington Northern Railroad, Burlington Northern Railroad Promotes Greenwood to Vice President, Intermodal, August 7, 1984, *Greenwood Collection*, Barriger Library at UMSL.

[446] Burlington Northern Railroad, *BN News*, June 1984, p. 3.

[447] Ibid, p. 4.

with BNRR's sister company, El Paso Natural Gas Co.[448] Taking Wood's place as BNI's VP Finance and Planning was Lou Dell'Osso who had been El Paso Natural Gas's VP Planning and Economics.[449]

BN's PRB Coal Monopoly is Lost, and More

Between 1974 and 1984 BN's Intermodal revenue grew 414%. That growth was dwarfed by coal which grew 1,166% from a base twice as large. It wouldn't have happened without the massive Louis Menk-led capital investments made in the Powder River Basin (PRB) and throughout other parts of the system for extensive track additions and upgrades, new bridges, the installation of state of the art train dispatching and signaling systems and car and locomotive repair facilities. As stated earlier, the key to unlocking the Powder River Basin's potential was the new line BN opened in 1979. It gave BN a monopoly on the business but it was short-lived.

BN and the C&NW/Union Pacific joint venture Western Rail Properties (WRPI) reached an agreement in October of 1983 for WRPI to purchase a share of the Gillette-Orin Line. That enabled WRPI to begin construction and it alowed the first C&NW-UP coal train being loaded from the PRB on August 15, 1984.

UP's cost to underwrite C&NW's Connector Line into the PRB exceeded $325 million.[450] The WRPI deal included a provision that any coal headed to the Midwest would be interchanged by UP to the C&NW at Council Bluffs, IA:

> *The C&NW started carrying PRB coal in mid-1984. They, in conjunction with the Union Pacific and the Missouri Pacific, immediately entered into long term contracts to take what had been BN's coal business to utility plants serving Arkansas, Louisiana and Wisconsin for Arkansas Power and Light, Central Louisiana Electric Company and Wisconsin Power and Light starting in January, 1995,.[451]*

> *Railroad has approximately two-thirds of its unit train and coal traffic under contract and is actively pursuing negotiations with several utilities for long-term contracts. If successful, some of these contracts will settle outstanding litigation before the courts or the ICC.[452]*

The loss of BN's PRB coal monopoly resulted in the loss of a significant amount of coal business as well as margin compression on coal business to UP-competitive customers BN was able to retain. Resulting BN profit pressure that this triggered lessened the size of BN Railroad's free-cash-flow pool that could be utilized to support BN's growing Intermodal capital needs.

The C&NW-UP incursion into the PRB did not stop there either. Frailey noted:[453]

---

[448] Burlington Northern Railroad, *BN News*, January-February, 1985, p. 2, *Greenwood Collection*, Barriger Library at UMSL.

[449] Burlington Northern Inc., 1984 Annual Report Form 10-K.

[450] Union Pacific Railroad, Connector Line Opens in Wyoming, August 16, 1984, Accessed from: https://www.up.com/timeline/index.cfm/connector-line, on March 24, 2023.

[451] Burlington Northern Inc., 1984 Annual Report, Form 10-K, p. 6.

[452] Ibid.

[453] Frailey, Fred W., Powder River Country, *Trains Magazine*, November, 1989, p. 54.

North Western no sooner entered the Orin Line than it went back to the ICC, seeking to extend its reach. Joint track was never envisioned all the way to Donkey Creek. Indeed, Provo had forsworn any right to go north of Coal Creek Junction (Milepost 26.2) in the joint-line accord of 1975 a provision the ICC had disallowed at the time as anti-competitive. Mines north of Coal Creek were upset at the lack of two railroad access, and with half its $414 million line of credit still unused, North Western was happy now to oblige them. (In the meantime, Sun Company had simply built its own 1.5-mile extension from the Cordero Mine lead to Coal Creek Junction to give C&NW entry.)

Again the Interstate Commerce Commission went against BN. In late 1985 it gave C&NW permission to build north 10.8 miles from Coal Creek Junction to East Caballo Junction to reach the four mines on the Orin Line still served exclusively by Burlington Northern. North Western had surveyed a route and was about to let contracts when BN in late 1986 agreed to extend half-ownership to East Caballo Junction, for $27 million.

That essentially opened the entire PRB to C&NW-UP competition. It was not the end of the trouble. Through the entire BN-C&NW-UP battle over PRB access, ETSI was lurking in the background but stifled because it could not obtain eminent domain rights to cross rail lines. The access of the C&NW-UP into the basin spelled the end of ETSI. Recall what BN had stated in 1984:

The C&NW started carrying PRB coal in mid-1984. They, in conjunction with the Union Pacific and the Missouri Pacific, immediately entered into long term contracts to take what had been BN's coal business to utility plants serving Arkansas, Louisiana …

The ETSI line was intended to carry coal to Oklahoma, Arkansas and Louisiana.[454]

ETSI was beaten out by Chicago & Northwestern Railroad for a major coal supply contract with Arkansas Power & Light, which may have contributed to its demise. In 1983, Texas Eastern became the project manager for ETSI. Then, in August 1984, the Wall Street Journal reported that Texas Eastern was abandoning its plans for a slurry line.

Aside from far-from-resolved water supply challenges, the long term loss of the Arkansas Power & Light opportunity combined with the decline in rates that accompanied C&NW-UP competition eliminated the pipeline's economic feasibility. That did not stop ETSI's backers from continuing their fight against BN and other western railroads which would also create longer term collateral intermodal consequences:[455]

Railroad was served in 1984 with a subpoena in connection with a United States Department of Justice grand jury investigation to determine whether certain rail carriers may have violated Sections One and Two of the Sherman Antitrust Act in connection with proposed coal slurry pipelines.

The Company, Railroad, Union Pacific Corporation, Missouri Pacific Corporation, Kansas City Southern Industries, Inc., Kansas City Southern Railroad Company and C&NW are defendants in a private action filed by Energy Transportation Systems Inc. ("ETSI"), in the Federal District Court

---

[454] Whipple, Dan, Coal Slurry: an Idea that Came and Went, WyoHistory.org., Accessed from: https://www.wyohistory.org/encyclopedia/coal-slurry-idea-came-and-went, on March 20, 2023.
[455] Burlington Northern Inc., 1985 Annual Report Form 10-K, p. 12.

for the Eastern District of Texas at Beaumont. The suit seeks unspecified damages in excess of $940 million from the defendants and injunctive relief. The complaint alleges that the railroad defendants violated antitrust laws by conspiring to restrain trade, monopolizing and attempting to monopolize the transportation of Powder River Basin coal to destinations in Kansas, Texas, Louisiana, Arkansas and Oklahoma. During 1985, ETSI petitioned the Court to amend its complaint to include the Santa Fe as a defendant. Also, Arkansas Power and Light filed a motion to intervene as a plaintiff.

The total damages ETSI backers would attempt to recover from the railroad industry exceeded $940 million in addition to injunctive relief.[456]

More Bad 1984 Coal News

In 1984, before the entry of the C&NW-UP into the PRB, BN was loading as many as 35 unit coal trains a day out of the PRB.[457] As if the C&NW-UP entry wasn't bad enough, by the start of 1984 BN found that the coal carrying track infrastructure it had invested so much in wasn't lasting as long as it was supposed to. Trackage outside of the Gillette-Orin line that was handling the most coal tonnage was rapidly deteriorating. On the Alliance Division's Alliance-Ravenna Subdivision:[458]

> *BN finished laying new welded rail across this 238-mile stretch in 1979. "But the track wasn't maintained the way, in retrospect, it was supposed to be," says Ron Bacon, the Alliance-based assistant superintendent for maintenance. "We took out 112-pound rail that had seen more than 1 billion gross ton-miles, and thought we had solved the problem. We hadn't." Dolomite, a limestone-like rock used as ballast, was dissolving from effects of water and the weight of traffic. In 1984 the track was down in the mud again everywhere. The process of restoring this one subdivision to higher standards would last five years, into 1989. To a greater or lesser extent, most of the old Alliance Division ... was in similar straits.*

Operating costs were skyrocketing because trains had to be slowed down due to deteriorated track conditions and track had to be temporarily taken out of service for maintenance. The railroad pipeline that had been working so efficiently was getting clogged because velocity fell. Train crews were unable to complete their runs before they exceeded the legal hours of service they could operate. Labor costs skyrocketed. Because demand for coal was not falling, the utilities were not getting the amount of coal they needed to operate. As a result, they demanded that more sets of coal trains be put into service. Coal sets in service skyrocketed to 250 in August, 1984 and BN coal train cycle-times were up to 180 percent of schedule.[459] At the 100% of cycle-time plan, only 139 sets should have been required. At an average of four locomotives per set, this triggered a demand for more than 400 additional locomotives to carry the same amount of coal. Because that many locomotives were not available, trains were run with less than ideal power which further compounded the congestion problem. In addition to a ballooning operating cost dilemma, the failure of the investments to last as long as their initially planned life also caused increased and unplanned capital investments. This reduction in coal cost efficiency coupled with added demand for capital meant that BN's IBU had another impediment put in its path as

---

[456] Burlington Northern Inc., 1986 Annual Report Form 10-K, p. 13.

[457] Frailey, Fred W., Powder River Country, *Trains Magazine*, November, 1989, p. 50.

[458] Ibid, p. 55-56.

[459] Ibid, pp. 56-57.

it sought capital to grow and locomotives for new dedicated trains. A problem nearly identical to this would afflict BN's Intermodal business a decade later. Its impact would be even worse.

Intermodal's Internal Profile Rises

The growth of BN's Intermodal business and the capital and operating support needed to capitalize on the potential of the business, plus the fact that it might be a key to help unlock the stalemate with labor over train crew sizes was gaining it much more visibility within the corporation. More frequent meetings were held with people like Tom Matthews who was the leader of the Human Resources and Labor Relations Department, Don Wood who was the Sr. VP Finance and Lou Dell'Osso the head of planning for the Holding Company. Finally, on November 13, Bill Greenwood made a presentation to Richard Bressler (who had previously shown little to no interest in the Intermodal business) about the state of the competitive business environment, how the business was progressing with the three strategies, the returns BN's Intermodal business was generating and was projected to generate. He also explained what was needed to keep the plan progressing, especially in light of the fact that UP's entry into the PRB coal franchise meant that source of railroad revenue growth (coal) had peaked and was starting to deteriorate.[460]

1984 Performance Wrap-Up

By 1984 the massive bet-the-company coal business wager made a decade earlier by Lou Menk and Bob Downing was paying off just as the C&NW-UP crashed the party. From a position in 1979 of being nearly unable to cover its debt service and having the poorest railroad industry profit performance, as pointed out in the 1981 Booz Allen presentation, the railroad had achieved a stunning turnaround by 1984. The railroad had been essentially remade economically as illustrated in the following chart of railroad revenue, operating income and business composition:[461]

	1974-84 BNRR Financial Performance			1974-84 BNRR Revenue Composition			
	Freight Revenue	Operating Income	Operating Ratio	Coal	Ag	Other	IML
1974	$1.432 B	$.093 B	93.5%	10.0%	16.1%	69.1%	4.8%
1975	1.474 B	.074 B	95.0%	14.3%	15.1%	66.3%	4.3%
1976	1.739 B	.076 B	95.6%	15.8	13.8	65.7	4.7%
1977	1.802 B	.060 B	96.7%	20.7	11.9	61.3	6.1%
1978	2.110 B	.083 B	96.1%	23.6	13.0	58.0	5.4%
1979	2.636 B	.124 B	95.3%	27.5	13.9	53.2	5.4%
1980	3.254 B	.278 B	91.5%	29.0	16.3	-	-
1981	4.088 B	.527 B	87.1%	25.9	14.4	53.2	6.5%
1982	3.773 B	.457 B	87.9%	31.4	13.9	47.5	7.2%
1983	4.058 B	.734 B	81.9%	38.9	14.0	38.8	8.3%
1984	4.490 B	.980 B	78.2%	41.4	14.2	34.5	9.9%

---

[460] Bill Greenwood's personal calendar.
[461] Burlington Northern Inc., 1974-1984 Annual Reports and Forms 10-K.

While coal generated only 10% of BN's railroad revenue in 1974, its proportion quadrupled to 41.4% in 1984. The Intermodal proportion of BN Railroad's revenue doubled while carload food, manufactured, industrial and forest products revenue collapsed 50% in spite of the addition of the coal-free and intermodal-light Frisco Railroad's business. During the same time period, railroad revenue and operating income increased 207% and 954% respectively. On the strength of the lucrative coal business boom, BN Railroad set a second consecutive record for profitability, generating operating income just under $1 billion and an operating ratio below 80 for the first time in company history.

BN's 1984 intermodal revenue grew a phenomenal $108 million (+32.2%) over 1983 on a 23% volume increase.[462] Intermodal volume at Chicago increased 30%. In spite of this incredible performance, Intermodal was not mentioned in BN Inc's 1984 Annual Report–Form 10K. Since formation of the IBU in 1981 the business unit had generated volume growth of 43.1% and revenue growth of 66.2% with the assistance of a doubling of daily dedicated trains from five to ten (including the 1984 conversion of Chicago-Denver Train #63 and the designation of ten additional mixed-freight trains as "Intermodal").[463] During the same time period BN's most vulnerable non-coal, non-grain, non-intermodal businesses experienced a unit volume loss of 34.9% and a revenue loss of 20.8%. During the same period, overall railroad volume, including coal, grain, and intermodal, fell 1.7% but revenue grew 13.3%.

The following table illustrates BN Intermodal revenue performance since the inception of the IBU in 1981 through 1984 compared to BNRR's most motor-carrier vulnerable carload food, lumber and manufactured products (F&M) businesses and the total railroad[464] in addition to BNRR operating income and BNI long term debt ($millions).

Burlington Northern Railroad 1981-1984 Financial Performance ($ millions) [465]

	IML Rev.	F&M Rev.	BNRR Rev.	BNRR Op. Inc.	BNRR OR	BNI LT Debt	Pref. Stock	Int. Exp.	Div. Exp.	Debt/ Cap.
1981	$267	$1,598	$4,088	$527	87.1%	$1,330	$105	$140	$58	29%
1982	273	1,261	3,773	457	87.9%	1,333	105	136	71	27%
1983	335	1,218	4,058	734	81.9%	2,930	709	142	87	41%
1984	443	1,265	4,490	980	78.2%	2,454	697	310	130	35%

Such lofty operating income and low operating ratio levels, and such a lofty proportion of coal revenue, would not be achieved again until 1995.[466] While these records were the product of Lou Menk's vision for the remaking of BN Railroad, Richard Bressler was remaking BN Inc. with the cash-flow that was generated by the railroad business he said was "shitty" just 5 years before.[467] The growth in BNI's long-term debt load between 1982 and 1983 was driven primarily by his acquisition of a controlling interest

---

[462] Internal BN Document, *Greenwood Collection*, Barriger Library at UMSL.

[463] Trafton, Gordon, Burlington Northern Intermodal Train Implementation Outline, March 25, 1986, *Greenwood Collection*, Barriger Library at UMSL.

[464] Internal BN Document, *Greenwood Collection*, Barriger Library at UMSL.

[465] Burlington Northern Inc., 1981-1984 Annual Reports and Forms 10-K

[466] Note: Earl Currie pointed out that BN's reported financial performance between 1982 and 1983 also benefited from changes in operating and maintenance financial reporting methodology. "In the second quarter of 1983 accounting for railroad track structure was changed from the "retirement-replacement-betterment" method to the ratable depreciation method. This change increased BN's 1983 net income by $86.564 million." See Currie's, *BN-Frisco, A Tough Merger*, p. 14.

[467] Bill Greenwood interview with Mark Cane, January 9, 2023.

of The El Paso Company and its natural gas pipeline, gas and oil exploration and production properties and chemical manufacturing capabilities.

By the first quarter of 1983, $617 million had been expended for El Paso which was financed through $367 million of cash (some sourced from the sale of BNAFI for $177 million) and $250 million of revolving credit debt. [468] The complete El Paso acquisition was accomplished in 1983, partially financed through the issuance of $338 million of preferred stock. The biggest reason for the increase in total BNI long term debt and the debt to capitalization ratio in 1983 was the financing of the El Paso purchase plus the assumption of El Paso's long term debt. This was paid down by almost $500 million in 1984 due to BNI's strong $630 million increase in cash from operations, powered by the significant coal-business-fueled cash flow increase produced by BN Railroad. Interest expense jumped to $310 million from $142 million, however.

In February, 1984 BNI entered into a $200 million Interest Rate Swap agreement @ 12.35%, plus convertible notes with a 13% coupon, due in 1992. [469] That helps put into perspective the interest rate environment at the time for a company with a sterling credit rating, and how much of a strain BN's debt created. Such high interest rates kept the internal investment hurdle rate high which added to the difficulty of getting intermodal capital projects approved.

Another valuable perspective is how significantly BN Railroad's productivity improved. The following table illustrates BN's employment levels and locomotive fleet size versus revenue ton miles between 1978 and 1984:

BN Railroad Employee and Locomotive Productivity, 1978-1984[470]

	RTMs (B)	Avg. Employees	RTMs per Employee (mm)	Freight Locomotives	RTMs per Frt. Loco. (mm)
1978	116.3	46,684	2.491	1,860	62.5
1979	135.0	49,559	2.724	2,039	66.2
1980	170.6	58,965	2.893	2,856	59.7
1981	174.9	55,347	3.160	2,606	67.1
1982	157.9	46,015	3.431	2,200	71.8
1983	172.3	40,914	4.211	2,088	82.5
1984	200.6	39,791	5.041	2,310	86.8

From the time of the 1980 BN-Frisco merger and 1984, BN Railroad reduced its employee count by 32.5% and increased its revenue –ton-miles per employee by 74%. One important measure of asset productivity, RTMs per freight locomotive, improved 45% during the same period. Such productivity improvements were critical to the achievement of BN Railroad's record 1984 income in the post-Staggers Act world.

---

[468] Burlington Northern Inc., 1982 Form 10-K.
[469] Burlington Northern Inc., 1984 Annual Report Form 10-K
[470] Burlington Northern Inc., 1979-1984 Railway Financial and Operating Statistics, CS 14.1 Reports, *Greenwood Collection*, Barriger Library at UMSL.

Chapter 12 - A Year of Disruptive 1985 Transitions

By the end of 1984 it was becoming clear to the IBU that double stack cars would be the car of the future for international business. Containership holds were built to handle 40' and 20' long containers and the vast majority of the business was done in forty foot containers. A few water carriers handled 45' containers but they were the minor exception. This made the stack car especially well-suited for international container transport because the box sizes were quite stable, unlike the domestic trailer transportation market that had increased lengths from 40' to 45' to 48' within a five year period. In addition, the trucking industry was exerting pressure to allow a maximum length of 53'. For a long-lived asset like a rail car, especially one in which a fixed-length container well was involved, international containers had a minimal market obsolescence risk making stack car ownership even more attractive. Surging trans-Pacific trade was driving significant increases in containership sizes that were resulting in the off-loading of much more than one double stack train load of containers with each port call.

The results of BN's double stack car tests had gone well and Sea-Land was gradually increasing their use of stack cars since their initial tests with the Southern Pacific in 1978-79. As mentioned previously, APL was also gradually acquiring double stack cars (since 1983) for their Linertrain. The economics and market were driving the IBU toward stack car acquisition to better service its customers, especially in association with BN's new Seattle International Gateway intermodal terminal that was under construction at the Stacy Street Yard site.

On February 4, 1985 Bill Greenwood and IBU leadership team members met with Walter Drexel and Darius Gaskins to explain the evolving international business market dynamics, the results of double stack car tests on BN.[471] They explained the compelling business case for BN to acquire stack cars, which were as yet unavailable from Trailer Train. BN's pursuit of Sea-Land's business out of the pending new Port of Tacoma on-dock facility was also discussed, including how that business would be utilizing stack cars. In late 1984 Sea-Land leased 19 "Twin-Stack" cars from Gunderson and shortly thereafter ordered another 83 of these cars for delivery in the spring of 1985.[472] Bill Greenwood, who was on Trailer Train's Board, and Bill Berry, who was now in charge of intermodal equipment, worked with Trailer Train to encourage them to enter the double stack car supply market.

The IBU was given authorization to tack-on to Sea-Land's container-only stack car order (which the SP Railroad also did). Unlike APL's stack cars, these cars had bulkheads. Both BN and the SP had concerns about the safety of using inter-box connectors (IBCs) to connect stacked (top tier) containers on the car and for safety's sake it was believed that the use of bulkheads to secure the top container was more prudent. In addition, the use of IBCs to secure containers was more labor intensive in the terminal as a ground person had to install the IBCs. There was also a concern about the theft/loss of IBCs.

In many respects it seemed as if the IBU didn't have bad luck it would have no luck at all. During the same time Greenwood and team were seeking capital dollars for projects necessary for the IBU to deliver on the financial forecasts in the White Paper ROI model, including the stack cars, the effect of the UP's entry into the PRB was being felt in BN's revenue production. In addition, signs were that it would be a bad year for the up and down (in many ways feast-or-famine) grain business and the food and manufactured products business wasn't keeping up with their 1984 revenue levels. For the year,

---

[471] Mark Cane's personal calendar.
[472] Panza, Dawson, Sellberg, pp. 238-239.

grain revenue would end up being down $200 million (29%) and coal revenue would be down more than 13% ($221 million) compared to 1984. This produced another across-the-board cost reduction edict and the growing IBU was not spared. A series of compulsory cost reduction meetings and initiatives made it even harder for the stretched IBU staff to handle a long list of strategic initiatives.

Continued Internal Promotion of Intermodal

In early 1985 a special train trip was conducted in an attempt to educate BN executives about market trends, BN's motor carrier competition, and what it would take for BN's Intermodal product to be successful. Tom Doty was hired to run BN's Hub is Springfield, Missouri and was on that trip. He said:[473]

> I was recruited to BN from American Freightways when the Springfield Hub was opened in July, 1984. In the second quarter of 1985 all Hubs put together inventories of their market opportunities, service requirements and business forecasts. Around that time I got a call from my boss telling me there was going to be a special business car trip for some BN execs from Ft. Worth to Memphis. He said they wanted new Hub managers on each leg of the trip. I thought it sounded fun – take a train ride on fancy business cars and eat good food. He sent an email with the train schedule and who would be on board. It said I was supposed to ride from Tulsa to Springfield. My operations manager Ed Miller, who had been a BN and Frisco employee for 25 years, looked at it and his eyes got big. Then he looked at me and said, "You don't know who these people are, do you?" I told him I honestly didn't. I said I recognized Darius Gaskins who was EVP Marketing and Bill Greenwood who led Intermodal but no one beyond that. He said, "These are the top dozen executives in the company and I have never seen anything like this." It even had former CEO Mr. Louis Menk on it.

> One of the reasons for the trip was to introduce the executives to BN's new Hub managers from the trucking industry. A bigger reason was to help convince the big brass to pump more money into the intermodal business to compete with over the road trucking which was a big opportunity for the railroad.

> I talked with the Hub managers who rode from Dallas to Tulsa before I got on the train. I asked how it went and what to expect. They said it was a great trip – that it was a cake walk. They said after they were introduced they went to the dome car and ate peanuts. That's not how it went for me. As we were leaving Tulsa, Gaskins and Greenwood summoned me to sit with the big group and for the next several hours they grilled me about the trucking business. They wanted to use me, as a former trucker, to explain how big the market opportunity was but also how tough the challenge would be to convert it to Intermodal. We were working on trying to get labor agreements to start Expediter trains so we talked about that too. Gaskins and Greenwood saw it but the other execs didn't understand the market or the competition and they were not Intermodal fans. They really didn't believe in the business. I didn't realize how big our battle inside the company was going to be.

> When we got to Springfield I thought I would be able to go home but Greenwood invited me to dinner on the business car so we could talk more. Then he invited me to ride to Memphis the

---

[473] Tom Doty email to Mark Cane, May 4, 2023.

*next day to continue our discussions. I am not sure if I convinced anyone but things got better
for us when we got Expediter trains. We didn't have a lot to sell before that.*

Genesis of BN's Expediter Trains

In a backhanded way there was one "benefit" from the significant 1985 business downturn in BN's
"core" businesses and it related to new excess capacity. The company found itself with excess
locomotives, track capacity and train service employees. Greenwood and the IBU leadership team
thought the IBU could help the company's situation by reevaluating its pursuit of shorter haul
intermodal markets. Intermodal had difficulty making money in markets of less than 700-800 miles,
driven by high origin and destination point costs, especially drayage expense. If a motor carrier's costs
were the typical $1/mile in load-balanced lanes, their total cost for a 500-mile haul would be $500.
Whereas a motor carrier would typically pick up a load at origin and then drive directly to the
destination point, an intermodal move required a dray plus a Hub lift-on at origin and a Hub lift-off and
dray to the ultimate customer at destination. In addition, it was not unusual to see a $50 per load fee for
the Intermodal Marketing Company (IMC) factored into the intermodal shipment equation. It would be
common for those costs to add up to $250-$300 dollars even if the origin and destination customers
were within the Hub's local commercial zone. Furthermore, the intermodal move typically required
$25-50 of load securement expenses that weren't required for the move via truck. For an intermodal
move, $275 to $350 would be expended before the move traversed any appreciable distance between
the origin and destination customers. On a 500 mile shipment, those costs amounted to $.55 to $.70
per mile before the intermodal shipment moved out of the origin Hub center. The inability to spread
those costs over the number of miles needed to allow intermodal's lower line-haul costs per mile to
swing the cost equation into intermodal's favor is what kept intermodal out of short-haul service lanes.
Intermodal was cost effective for longer hauls because those "terminal costs" would be spread over
many miles.

Piggyback service in short-haul lanes had been tried in the past. The Illinois Central-Gulf (ICG) Railroad
ran three round-trip per day *Slingshot* trains limited to 15 cars with two-man crews and no cabooses
between Chicago and St. Louis in 1975, but it quickly failed financially. At the same time the Federal
Railroad Administration (FRA) obtained $6 million of Congressional authority to subsidize the initiation
of a demonstration short haul (400-800-mile lane) piggyback service with reduced crew sizes. The
Slingshot did not qualify because it was too short of a lane. It resulted in the Milwaukee Road *Sprint*
demonstration between Chicago and Minneapolis/St. Paul. The BN was not considered for this
operation because, according to Dave DeBoer, "We visited the Burlington Northern, but between a new
terminal and the normal shakedown bugs in Chicago and an under-construction terminal in a muddy
cornfield in the Twin Cities area, the Burlington Northern had its hands full."[474]

The Milwaukee Road *Sprint* operation featured 3-man crews and commenced service on June 5, 1978. It
was an operational success with 95% on-time trailer availability performance. With the FRA financial
subsidy and initial business commitments from the U.S. Postal Service and UPS, the Sprint service was
financially viable and after a successful application with the FRA for an extension of the demonstration,
frequency was increased to six pairs of trains per day. The 1979 recession severely impacted business
volume, and after the FRA subsidy expired the service experienced a steady decline.[475]

---

[474] DeBoer, David J., *Piggyback and Containers – A History of Rail Intermodal on America's Steel Highway*, Golden
West Books, San Mateo, CA, 1992, p. 125.
[475] DeBoer, pp. 123-127.

In early 1985 the IBU leadership team mentioned that perhaps intermodal could utilize excess BN capacity to Darius Gaskins. The idea was to pursue shorter haul lanes and, in the process, be a source of cash for the company. Even though such business would not cover its fully allocated costs, anything that contributed to the railroad's fixed cost coverage could be beneficial for the BN. In addition, the BN was dealing with a longstanding adversarial labor relationship and such a venture could potentially help improve that and even demonstrate that operating trains without historic crew sizes and cabooses could be conducted safely.

With the support of Gaskins, Bill Greenwood prepared to run the idea by BN executives. The IBU called it the *"BN 600"* project. On February 28, 1985, IBU leadership first met with BN's Strategic Planning group and then leaders in Operations, Labor Relations and Finance, giving them the *BN 600* presentation. In it the IBU explained the competitive situation versus motor carriers and that even with new technology "spine cars" it was basically impossible for intermodal to make money in lanes shorter than 600 miles with BN's train and engine crew labor costs. The typical train was staffed by an engineer, a conductor, and two brakemen. On occasion this four-person crew actually grew to six if a local labor agreement required a fireman and third brakeman. Whereas on a 600 mile haul the labor cost for a motor carrier would be a full day's wage for one truck driver, the labor cost for a train operation would be four to six times six because for a 600-mile trip each train operating employee was paid a day's wage for each 100 miles traveled. For a 600-mile trip the train labor costs would be 24-36 man-days of pay (not including "arbitrary" payments). In addition, the average "daily" wage for a truck driver was 25-40% less than that for a conductor, engineer, or brakeman. This, plus the rest of the economic picture of truck versus intermodal costs, was included in the presentation.

The IBU explained, however, that the business downturn had resulted in idle locomotives that were being paid for whether they were used or not, idle (laid off) train and engine employees, and excess track capacity. Other railroads had experimented with short corridor intermodal trains for which they negotiated special labor agreements to operate with three-person crews, but they were primarily restricted to limited market pairs and not a full network. What if BN could negotiate a special labor agreement with the operating crafts in select geographic locations for operation of two-person crews without a caboose for special intermodal trains? Those trains would be designed to serve shorter haul markets BN was not competing in - which meant new business. Such a condition would be necessary as a foundation for a new labor agreement. In addition, BN would agree to limit the size of such new business trains to 30 conventional intermodal car lengths (up to 60 trailers) in order to lessen the need for additional locomotive power, and if for some reason, more than 30 cars of business were generated on a specific day, an added crew person would be called to serve on that trip. In the effort to put people back to work and gain service reliability credibility in the market (and in the eyes of BN employees) to generate new BN business, BN would commit to run the scheduled trains even if no business had been generated to build a better reputation for service reliability.

Before this initiative began, the IBU had used the *"BN 600"* theme, but it was in advertisements stressing the notion of Truck/Rail partnership in an effort to entice shippers to utilize BN Intermodal for hauls lengths of greater than 600 miles long (see ad above, *Greenwood Collection*, Barriger Library at UMSL). This new effort used that theme to help intermodal break into markets shorter than 600 miles.

Again, there were three primary objectives related to the BN 600 initiative. First, attempt to get a breakthrough labor agreement with train operating crews of an engineer and conductor and no caboose. If BN management could earn credibility in the eyes of labor, the BN 600 initiative could possibly facilitate similar negotiations across the railroad. Second, establish a service that would be a breakthrough from the market's standpoint and raise visibility, improving the reputation of intermodal service in general and BN Intermodal specifically. Third, to generate cash contribution for BN on a plant that had significant excess capacity with the foreknowledge that the service would be low margin and not nearly cover fully-allocated costs. There was no talk about what would happen when capacity filled up and retention of the business would require new capital expenditures. The thought was that if the BN 600 initiative refilled the plant with business contributing positively to BN's cash flow and caused capacity issues, it would be a good problem that could be addressed later.

The consensus was that it was worth a try, so Labor Relations set up a meeting with General Chairmen from the train and operating unions in Ft. Worth on March 15, 1985.[476] During this meeting Greenwood and Cane explained the competitive situation BN faced in the intermodal market. Greenwood explained the competitive situation with customers and truck competitors. Cane explained the rail cost structure for a typical shorter-haul intermodal move with the current train operating labor agreements. This was in an effort to help them understand what BN was competing against versus trucks in short-haul corridors, and why help would be needed for the company to compete in them, and serve new customers, while creating new jobs. Greenwood and the head of Labor Relations said if they would authorize a two person crew agreement with the crews running through traditional crew change points to the next hub center, the company would be willing to give new services a try. The response was non-committal, but at least there was dialogue.

Another influential event for the short-haul train initiative was the IBU's hiring of Ned Treat in late February, 1985. Mark Cane had been a proponent of beefing up the IBU's operations research analytical capability, and he put together a business case to justify it. Bill Greenwood was able to secure a position authority and Cane initiated a search that yielded Treat. Following logistics-related service as an Army officer in Vietnam, Treat earned his MBA specializing in management science, a DBA in transportation and logistics, plus a MS in engineering science and mechanics from the University of Tennessee. He had worked as a research scientist for The Institute for Energy Analysis at Oak Ridge, Tennessee, for nine years and had authored numerous logistics related research reports.[477] He filled the IBU's advanced analytical firepower gap. One of the first projects he was assigned was to take a rudimentary manual build-a-train costing model, update the cost factors with the Costs and Statistics Department based on a reduced crew agreement, and create a dynamic train network cost simulation model on an IBU personal computer. His simulation model reduced the time it took to assess the financial results of changes to train networks from four hours to five minutes. It was an essential tool for the development and fine-tuning of what would become the Expediter Train Network.

---

[476] Mark Cane's personal calendar.
[477] Ned L. Treat Resume, 1995.

The Springfield Operating Region had the most surplus track and labor capacity. In addition, in the March meeting with General Chairmen, Bill Greenwood had a positive interaction with John Reynolds, a General Chairman on that Region, who seemed willing to give such a venture a try. This was contrary to the reaction from a Northern BN territory General Chairman, Mel Winter, who said to Greenwood:

> *"...'I will never agree to a change in work rules that we have worked 100 years to get. I don't care a hoot about creating jobs for these younger guys,' as he pointed to a young General Chairman who was standing nearby."*[478]

From the IBU's standpoint the Springfield Region (former Frisco Railroad) also presented the best opportunity to establish a mini-network of dedicated intermodal trains between the promising truck-dominant markets of Kansas City, Memphis, Birmingham, St. Louis, Springfield, Tulsa and Dallas. The Springfield Region's VP Bob Howery, Operations AVP Andy Thompson, and Labor Relations Director Lyle Burk were all extremely supportive of the idea and it was again presented to the General Chairmen who represented Springfield Region train and engine crews. Greenwood was part of that meeting, and he presented the idea of this proposed network with trains running six days-a-week which would keep train crews balanced, minimizing employees' time away from home. It was stressed that if this proposal were adopted that the trains would run with the highest priority which would make the jobs running these trains highly sought-after. In addition, the importance that the best engineers operate the locomotives on these trains was stressed because in order to reduce competitive costs, customers would be told to not secure their loads any different than they did for a movement over the highway. The trains had to be expertly operated so that intra-train slack-action would not damage the cargo. If the IBU did not have to discount the price of the service to offset additional lading securement costs, it made the service that much more financially viable.

The General Chairmen said they would take the proposed labor agreement to their Union locals for an employee vote, which was the key to unlocking the opportunity. Ahead of the vote, Greenwood met with employees across the Springfield Region in town-hall settings and shared the same market, competitive, and proposed service network information with all of them. The employees were encouraged to ask as many questions as they wanted. One of the biggest concerns was the integrity of management and their willingness to actually run the trains as promised. Greenwood said as much as they were concerned about this issue, prospective customers would be even more concerned. He stressed that if BN were to put on the services, customers would not just automatically abandon their current carriers and switch their shipments from truck to BN. They had to gain confidence that BN would be there to consistently serve them. Greenwood said it would take time to convince the market so once a decision was reached to initiate the service, BN had to make a commitment to run the trains even if no trailers were tendered by customers. BN had to be willing to incur start-up losses on the service to establish market credibility.

While this was happening, the IBU's Don Meyer was appointed as the Manager-Expediter Project, reporting to Bill Greenwood. "Expediter" was the name the IBU thought best fit the spirit of the proposed new services. Meyer immediately started to put together a set of possible train schedules and Hub cutoff and availability times with the IBU's Gordon Trafton, his Lane Management team, and the Hub Managers on the Springfield Region. Meyer, with the assistance of Jim Klemett, IBU Senior Analyst Research and Promotion (who IBU Marketing Director Bill DeWitt had recruited to his Marketing team) led the effort to put together a competitive pricing matrix and promotion and advertising material

---

[478] Bill Greenwood interview with Mark Cane, May 4, 2022.

BN innovations make intermodal work for you.

NEW BN EXPEDITER CUTS YOUR COSTS ON SHORT-HAUL SHIPMENTS.

(example on left and below, *Greenwood Collection*, Barriger Library at UMSL) that would be critical to raise market awareness of new Expediter services if the labor agreement were approved. Ned Treat was asked to incorporate the pricing matrices into his train simulation model. With the assistance of the Hub Managers, Meyer created volume forecasts which were also fed into Treat's model so that a full-blown activity–based simulation of Expediter train and Expediter network financial performance could be generated.

The Springfield train and engine Union employees voted in favor of the novel two-person crew agreement as proposed. They asked for a commitment on the part of the company, and BN agreed to run the network for six months, reevaluating after that.

With the approval of the new labor agreement Meyer and Trafton (and his team) worked with Transportation, the Springfield Region, and the Hub Managers to establish the train schedules, Hub cutoffs, and availability times. Meyer worked with the IBU's Bill Berry and his Intermodal Equipment team to assure adequate flatcar and trailer availability. He worked with BN's Sales Department to set up meetings with the affected Hub sales people and Telemarketing sales to explain what the Expediter operation would offer customers and to review the pricing structure. He arranged meetings with major IMCs to raise their awareness of the new services that were about to be introduced. He stressed to both BN's salespeople and the IMCs that BN would not expect shipments to be secured (blocked and braced) any differently than if the shipments were to move via motor carrier. He had to work with BN's Freight Claims Department to be sure that claims for Expediter shipment lading damage were not denied if standard motor carrier equivalent load securement levels had been employed by the customer.

BN innovations make intermodal work for you.

It was a massive effort that culminated in the commencement of the new service on September 8, 1985. The entire process was all reviewed in a meeting with BNRR Chief Executive Walter Drexel and Darius Gaskins on September 17, 1985. During the meeting Greenwood, Meyer and Cane presented the Expediter implementation plan, the forecasts and expected economics, and stressed that the operation would contribute positive cash flow by utilizing excess capacity but that the operation would not cover fully allocated costs. Meyer also reviewed the promotion material that would be associated with Expediter rollout. Drexel was reminded that during start-up, trains would likely be run with little or no business, but that it was imperative for Labor to generate trust in BN management and for customers to believe in the integrity of the service. The partnership with organized labor and the opportunity to utilize this venture to reposition the image of Intermodal's reputation in the marketplace were stressed as well as the belief that success of the venture with the reduced crew agreement on the Springfield Region might provide the seeds for similar cooperative Labor/Management efforts on other BN Regions. Related to starting Expediter business from scratch and incurring losses during start-up, Darius Gaskins commented:[479]

> *We already knew our customers pretty well. I mean, you know, by this time, we were negotiating with the Hub Group and all, but we knew the intermodal customer fairly well so we thought we could get the boxes. It's a risk, I mean, there's risks in everything, but I always thought that was manageable. Because I knew the market was there, you could just look at the data, you know. There's a lot of trucks going back and forth over that same distance, and all you need to do is put a competitive service in and you'll get your fair share. But that's what investment's all about! I mean, how do you run a business if you're not willing to invest money in it?*

In its February, 1986 issue *Fleet Owner* Magazine published an extensive story about BN's Intermodal business. Fleet Owner's primary audience were motor carriers and operators of private fleets such as Wal-Mart and Kimberly-Clark who handled a portion of their over the road logistics in-house with their own private trucking operation. This segment was a major target market for BN Intermodal. That *Fleet Owner* article had the following to say about the initiation of BN's Expediters: [480]

> *An important part of BN's customer-oriented approach to the marketplace was a lot of nationwide market research that, among other things, revealed that BN could not compete against motor carriers in certain corridors with hauls under 600 miles. With that in mind, each hub center was asked to survey the industrial base in its area by looking at the number of 45 ft. trailer loads moving in and out of the area and where those trailers were going.*

> *"There were some tremendous volumes uncovered," says Cochran (BN Birmingham Hub Manager). For example, between his market area (the Southeast from Birmingham to the Atlantic Ocean) and the Dallas-Ft. Worth area, there were 50,000 trailer loads a year moving in the lanes. "Because BN's rates and costs were so high, we were missing all that freight," says Cochran.*

> *Greenwood, vice president of intermodal at that time, took those marketing data to the railroad's operating unions and, according to Cochran, said, "Here is all this business that we could get, but we can't do it with a 4-man crew riding the train." He told them that the railroad was willing to cut rates drastically to get some of that business, but they (the unions) would have to make some concessions, too. Greenwood asked them to meet him halfway.*

> *Cochran said it took almost a year, but agreement finally was reached and the Expediter trains began to operate with 2-man crews early in September 1985. The contract calls for the railroad to run the dedicated trains every day, six days a week for six months. At the end of the six months, the self-renewing contract will be reviewed, and the railroad will have the right to eliminate some trains or alter the schedules.*

> *BN's Expediter is operating among intermodal hub centers in Dallas, St. Louis, Birmingham, Kansas City, Springfield, Mo., Memphis and Tulsa. Cochran describes the initial network as a big*

---

[479] National Railroad Hall of Fame, Darius W. Gaskins, Jr. Interview Transcript, November 5, 2020, Accessed from: https://www.nrrhof.org/darius-w-gaskins-jr, on March 23, 2023.
[480] Jacobus, William W., Intermodal – BN Relies on Truckers to Run Hub Centers, *Fleet Owner*, February 1986.

"X" with Springfield in the center. St. Louis is at the end of the northeast leg, Kansas City the northwest, with Tulsa and Memphis completing the four points. Dallas and Birmingham hang off the southern legs like "tails" (see map below). Dedicated trains provide daily service among those points. BN also includes satellite hubs in that Expediter service network.

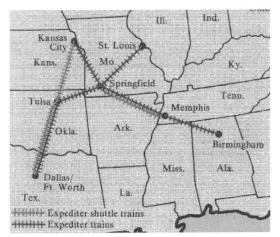

For example, the railroad publishes tariffs on the Expediter route between Atlanta and Dallas, or any of the other six hubs in the network. That means that a load going Expediter becomes top priority the minute it arrives at the Atlanta satellite. If it arrives by 2 pm, it is guaranteed to be aboard that night's Expediter out of Birmingham, which will arrive, say, in Dallas at 10 am the second day.

The train leaving Birmingham conceivably could have a block of trailers on flatcars (TOFCs) for all or any of the six hub centers. At Memphis, it could drop off the blocks of cars for that hub, pick up outbound blocks from there, and head for Springfield, the axis of the system. At Springfield, blocks of cars could be switched in various directions. There are Expediter trains running in each direction on both legs of the "X" every day, so at Springfield, the Birmingham to Kansas City train switches out blocks northbound to St. Louis and southbound to Tulsa and Dallas. It picks up blocks from those hubs headed for Kansas City. Its counterpart going to Birmingham does the same, and so forth."

The article went on to explain how the network was modified post start-up in response to marketplace demands:[481]

As the system evolved, BN found that in some lanes where the distance between hub centers was less than 500 miles, for example Kansas City – Tulsa, truckers offered overnight service. To be competitive, BN Expediters, make shuttle runs between those hubs. Currently, those so-called short trains run between Kansas City and Tulsa, Tulsa and Dallas, and between Memphis and Springfield.

"We put those trains on because of competitive reasons on the highways," says Cochran.

Initially, the Expediter trains to Birmingham created an overload on Monday, traditionally the heaviest day of the week for motor carriers. "We came in one Monday and we had 100 loads to go to the satellite hubs, mainly Atlanta, and we didn't have 100 tractors out there to run them with," says Cochran.

What we did to alleviate that problem, and to bring joy to the carriers, was to have Winn Express, the operator of the Atlanta satellite, stay open from 2 to 11 pm on Sunday to receive trailers.

The article added that through January, 1986, "... the new dedicated Expediter service claims 98% on-time delivery for all loads, and a 99.9% damage-free record."[482]

---

[481] Ibid.

The April, 1986 issue of *The Private Carrier* magazine also carried an article authored by Don Meyer about the Expediter service. This magazine's target market was also private fleet owners and operators. In it Meyer complemented, and added to information provided in the *Fleet Owner* article that is meaningful in the context of the history of BN's Intermodal business: [483]

> *From that first day, traffic has built steadily and we have delivered what we promised our customers: Consistent on-time performance and infinitesimal freight damage. To all who remember the old days of rail "piggyback" service, the Expediter exemplifies changes that have brought an entirely new look to the intermodal industry, particularly on BN. As Dave Munsey, assistant vice president of National Piggyback in St. Louis, told us: "I feel the BN Expediter is the most revolutionary thing I've seen a major railroad carrier do."*
>
> *Like many business stories, the Expediter project began with a simple question: how to attract more business to short rail corridors? Preceding that question, however – in fact, enabling us to even realistically ask it – was the whole redesign of BN's intermodal strategy in 1981.*
>
> *We came up with approaches totally different from those of pre-deregulation days. For one thing, our entire focus changed from inward to outward. Our driving force, we decided, would be the desires and needs of the customer, nothing else; providing the customer with the appropriate service and equipment, as well as price, would determine our survival.*
>
> *For another thing, we changed our vocabulary (and are trying to change that of others) by eliminating the word "piggyback" to denote intermodal transportation and using instead the word, "partnership."*
>
> *We raised a (green and) white BN flag of truce to the trucking industry. Fighting with truckers over business had won us the dubious distinction of getting a very small slice of the intermodal transportation pie. So we told motor carriers; please consider us a reliable and consistent alternative means of transportation. Let's work together.*
>
> *Aside from our "customer foremost" strategy, we developed two others:*
> - *Run dedicated intermodal trains with new generation equipment, which would minimize damage from switching cars and maximize our capabilities and performance.*
> - *Establish a system of hub centers to originate and receive these dedicated trains, with trucks picking up and delivering freight at the hubs from a radius of several hundred miles.*
>
> *By early 1985 we had 20 hub centers in operation, along with "satellite" hubs that now number 27. For example, Atlanta is a highway satellite of the Birmingham hub center and Nashville is a highway satellite of Memphis. We also have steadily increased the number of intermodal trains until we now are running 33 – at last count.*

---

[482] Ibid.

[483] Meyer, Don, BN's New Step – How Burlington Northern broke through the traditional wisdom to provide short haul intermodal serviced over distances of less than 750 miles, *The Private Carrier*, April, 1986, pp. 29-30, 44.

Through all of this our intermodal business unit and the entire railroad affected every efficiency, and cost control , we could think of while at the same time providing service improvements.

It was against that background that we looked at market studies which showed a vast business potential over distances of less than 750 miles. Could we come up with a program to give customers in such corridors good alternative service to highway?

BN's Springfield Region offered an excellent laboratory in which to test the concept. On the north were St. Louis and Kansas City; to the south, Memphis and Dallas / Ft. Worth; to the southeast Birmingham; and nestled in between, Tulsa and Springfield. There was a hub center in each of those cities so our structure for a program was already in place. Distances between the hubs were perfectly suited to the plan. Finally, the region's track network was underutilized so there would be no particular difficulties from an operating standpoint in adding trains.

But there was one big question: How could we possibly offer such a program and be competitive given our costs? The greatest portion of those costs went for labor: running a train 100 miles meant paying four or even six crew members a day's wages. In addition, the traditional 100-mile day required frequent crew changes en route, which meant, in sum, that BN would have a tough time offering reliable intermodal train service at competitive rates over those corridors.

As we faced that discouraging reality, many of our train crew members faced their own dismay, being laid off due to declining business.

So while the business was out there, we couldn't go after it under the existing rules of the game. The only answer was to change the rules.

Bill Greenwood, vice president for intermodal, explained our situation to leaders of the United Transportation Union (UTU) and Brotherhood of Locomotive Engineers (BLE). One study showed just how critical rail labor cost was in an era of ever-intensifying competition from trucks: In 1972, average annual compensation for truckers was $11,000 and for railroad workers $14,000. By 1984 the spread had grown a bit more dramatic, to almost $45,000 on the rail side against less than $30,000 on the truck side.

Mr. Greenwood also pointed out that under standard labor rules, the 700 mile run between Kansas City and Birmingham – a planned Expediter corridor – would require up to 21 train crew man days to operate one train between those cities. In contrast, a two-man (run through" crew working over the same route would mean four days wages.

Therefore, he said, BN could get in on the potential business opportunities of the proposed Expediter network only with a two-man crew and "run through" agreement (crew taking a train through consolidated crew districts). For BN's part, Greenwood promised, we would offer the most attractive rates we could. Was it a deal?

The union leaders listened and then took the proposal to their memberships. In early summer, they voted for ratification of the agreement, the first of its kind in the railroad industry.

On July 2, BN announced creation of the Expediter program: Seven-day-a-week non-stop service between intermodal hub centers on these corridors: Birmingham – Kansas City, Kansas City –

Dallas, St. Louis – Dallas, and St. Louis – Birmingham, also covering Memphis, Tulsa and Springfield, MO.

Citing BN's "innovative intermodal service" motto, Mr. Greenwood says of the Expediters:

"The intense competition in transportation today demands innovative approaches if we are to give customers better service and competitive prices. This is one of those approaches."

Top officers of the unions called the agreement an opportunity for new business that would mean about 100 new jobs and callbacks for laid-off workers.

The agreement was viewed "as a cooperative effort to give BN a new tool to aggressively compete for business, which will serve our mutual interests," says J.W. Reynolds, UTU General Chairman. "Both parties recognized a need to do something and that it would take the cooperation of both labor and management."

"Not only does the agreement create more jobs for engineers, it demonstrates labor's willingness to keep pace with the changing economic and competitive climate," says W.C. Walpert, BLE General Chairman.

Through the summer, a special task force worked with hub center managers and sales people in gathering information needed to make final decisions. People in the field provided guidelines on everything – pricing, sales, operations, even the type of advertising that would be done, particularly in their area. They fanned out over the territories to explain the new program, many utilizing expertise gained in years in the trucking industry and all fighting head-on on the negative intermodal image built in the past on frequently delayed and/or damaged shipments.

There were more than a few surprised, and pleased, looks on customers' faces when they were told that Expediter loads would require no more blocking and bracing than for a highway move and that their shipments would leave and arrive on schedule, and they could "take that to the bank" in more ways than one.

As head of the task force, my primary goal was to make sure we got everyone totally involved and that we all communicated. What it amounted to was a network of people, as well as hubs, all geared to making this thing go.

Actually, there was nowhere to go but up – we had moved fewer than 1,800 loads in those Expediter corridors in all of 1984.

Our first day of Expediter operation, a Sunday, we handled a grand total of 16 loads; on Friday of that first week we were up to 136 and the trend has been steadily, if not dramatically, upward. But we exceeded that entire 1984 volume by the end of Expediter's first three weeks.

As with any project, there were a few rough spots. But our teamwork concept paid off in many ways, from the mechanical department's servicing of equipment to train operations to labor's steadfast support and the outstanding performance of Expediter train crews.

The Expediter agreement allowed us to operate trains with up to 60 platforms (30 cars) and no caboose. On Sept. 18, we ran our first 30-car train.

Before the end of September we exceeded the 800-units a week figure and before year's end passed the 1,000 mark. Since then, volume has continued to increase. By the end of February, we had moved more than 21,000 loads.

Just as important, the number of third parties and motor carriers using Expediter also showed a steady rise.

Most importantly, our customer acceptance has been very good. Some were initially skeptical, such as Bill Rollins, assistant vice president, Tri-State Consolidators, Dallas.

"Whenever a carrier says they're establishing a new service between this point and another, I wait a month or two to see if they're still doing what they said they'd do." Rollins told us, "The BN Expediter has been consistent from the very beginning ... it's been excellent."

Shippers agent Bob Jensen, president of Hub City, St. Louis, observes, "When you take the time to dispatch to time of arrival, we can accommodate the customer on any day of the week he wants and we can get the freight there in a reasonable amount of time ... in a lot of cases it's faster than the truckers can get it there."

Certainly, we appreciate such comments. We also appreciate the faith of those shippers and others in this venture and the support and hard work of our people, which made those comments possible. As an example of Expediter's performance, a look at one day's schedule recently showed a big E, for early, on every Expediter train entry. Put another way, the report was all A's, for availability of loads to shippers.

After moving more than 21,000 loads, we have recorded a damage to lading rate that is almost invisible, affecting a total of seven loads; damage was minor and three of those loads were damaged in a single derailment.

As for service, we have had two "bad order" locomotives out of all those runs, as of this writing.

Expediter has reopened markets for some shippers, like the one Bob Scott, our Tulsa manager, knows who "got out of shipping down to north Texas because of transportation costs; Expediter got him back in there."

And it has stimulated business, too, adds Bill Nessler, Tulsa account manager. "When you interest a customer in an Expediter rate, often he will then ask, "Well, what do you have for Denver, or Houston?'"

Labor has gone an extra mile in its support. In January, representatives of the UTU and BLE accompanied Nessler on an Expediter-promotion visit to third parties and customers in Ft. Smith, Ark., a very competitive area.

"It was a good orientation for all of us," he says. "I learned more about their work and they learned about sales. The first thing that surprised them was how competitive the situation is."

Overall, we feel a lot of pride in the way Expediter has gone from an idea to a viable transportation program servicing a large segment of this nation. But I think its greatest significance lies in what Expediter can portend for the future of intermodal transportation, indeed, for transportation and other industries in general. That is, a willingness by labor and management to look at a situation, recognize the challenges and opportunities, and together act to create a means of meeting those challenges and seizing those opportunities. It is a spirit that says, it makes no difference what the fashion was yesterday, we can do what is necessary to respond to the needs of today's situation, today's customers.

Expediter is one way BN is responding. We have other strategies and technologies working or waiting in the wings, including possible new Expediter routes. Whatever the customer wants, we will try to do. We believe that's one credo that should never change.

The Expediters were becoming a success from the standpoints of BN cash-flow, BN Intermodal business awareness and BN Intermodal reputation-building. In addition, one of the most significant things Expediters accomplished was to bring "management" and "labor" together on a high profile initiative. Employees were getting a first-hand education about the competitive nature of the business and were being rewarded with new premium jobs for flexibility in labor agreements. Although this arrangement would not cure the caustic labor-company relations, it did help.

Extensive Market Analyses

The "*nationwide market research*" that Don Meyer and Birmingham Hub Manager Earle Cochran referred to was part of a multi-pronged effort. While the 1981 Intermodal Task Force focused on divertible BN carload business, the IBU supplemented this information with competitive railroad market research as well as estimated truck flow data through sources including the Association of American Railroad's 1% waybill samples and motor carrier freight flow estimates from data bases such as Reebie Associates' *Transearch* and Paul Roberts' *Transmode* databases. The information gained from this research helped improve the effectiveness of the Hub rollout planning and implementation effort. This information was supplemented at the Hub level (prior to the opening of a specific Hub) by telephone surveys of current and potential customer traffic managers within a Hub's market area plus Hub market area Focus Groups conducted by market research firm Elrick and Lavidge.

A major second phase of this effort was an initiative that was undertaken in early 1985. Each Hub Manager and his or her associated Hub Sales Manager was charged with developing a 'Hub Inventory." That inventory was to include an assessment of the total over-the-road market volume between their Hub market area and the market areas of other BN Hubs (assisted by Bill DeWitt's Marketing team), a review of the Hub's current capacity, a forecast of business that they expected to generate, and a projection of how the forecast would impact capacity utilization. These "Inventories" were presented to the IBU leadership in Ft. Worth starting with the Fargo-Dilworth and Spokane Hub teams on April 30, 1985 and finishing with the Tulsa Hub team on May 28. Not only did these analyses factor into the Expediter plans but they also fed into other train service planning, equipment planning and hub capital planning plus the establishment of performance goals.

Seattle International Gateway (SIG)

By July 1, 1985 BN had begun operation of its new Seattle near-dock international intermodal facility named Seattle International Gateway (SIG). It was located within one mile of the Seattle container docks and two miles closer to the port container terminals than Union Pacific's Argo intermodal facility. Closer proximity to the Port was a major competitive advantage because it enabled reduced drayage time and costs. Since it was a new operation, no labor organization had "rights" to the work. It gave the IBU an opportunity to do a clean-sheet start. The IBU worked with John Gray to help figure out the best clean-sheet approach to take. Gray had run the Intermodal business of the Western Pacific Railroad until the WP was acquired along with the Missouri Pacific by the Union Pacific Railroad in September of 1982. He then decided to get into the business of being a contract operator of intermodal facilities. The IBU decided to have the facility operated by a turnkey contractor and Gray's Pacific Rail Services (PRS) was selected to perform the turnkey work. Representation of the facilities' workers was desired by the Longshoremen, Teamsters and the Brotherhood of Railway and Airline Clerks (BRAC). The IBU was not opposed to organized labor but it was essential that the operation's costs were market-competitive and high levels of safety and service performance would be maintained. It was important that the operation not be bogged down by rigid and disruptive work rules and labor strife. PRS worked with the BRAC organization to craft a new agreement that would give furloughed BN railroad clerks preferential employment treatment. It was market-competitive and excluded onerous work rules. PRS performed all clerical and operating functions. It was a win-win for the IBU, PRS and BRAC represented employees. The BN/PRS and then BNSF/PRS partnership at SIG would last almost 30 years.[484]

There was one special aspect of the SIG facility that would make it relatively unique among BN's Hub centers. In addition to its prime location, of which BN had relatively few, SIG gave the IBU its best opportunity to build a facility essentially from scratch in a way that would allow for significant car, container and train handling efficiencies. Given the "illegitimate child" status that BN Intermodal continually fought up to the time of the 1995 ATSF merger, BN's Hub capacity needs were overwhelmingly met in a non-strategic manner – build as you can get funding approved in a crisis mode. The IBU was essentially forced to utilize space it could wrangle within yards around rail-car operations. Capacity expansion projects were shoe-horned in as yard space was deemed unnecessary and could be freed-up and for the most part "done on the cheap." BN's unwillingness to support the adoption of a long-term strategic development plan for Intermodal contrasted immeasurably compared to what was done to position the company to capitalize on its coal opportunity. With coal, a strategic long term investment plan was developed and was executed in a disciplined, methodical, manner through up and down economic and company performance cycles. Examples of strategic coal infrastructure investments included the new Gillette – Orin line, locomotives, second and third main lines, centralized traffic control, new dispatch centers, extended sidings, concrete ties, new car and locomotive maintenance and repair shops, high capacity aluminum coal hoppers and massive bridge replacements.

Because the IBU was not allowed to methodically pursue a comparable, well thought out, strategic plan with optimal Hub designs, BN would suffer from a significant long-term disadvantage in Hub efficiency. Compared to its competitors' terminal facilities, most BN Hubs would end up with less efficient inspection gates, fewer and sub-optimally located trailer and container parking spaces per acre, fewer spots for railcars per acre, and short and inefficient car loading tracks that hindered overhead crane and lift device and train make-up productivity. This inflicted an ongoing per-lift "tax" on BN's Intermodal profitability. This would become especially apparent in 1992 as will be explained later.

---

[484] John Gray email to Mark Cane, March 11, 2022.

BN Recaptures Sea-Land's Business

In early 1985 BN and Sea-Land entered into negotiations for BN to provide service for them in and out of the new Port of Tacoma on-dock terminal via double stack cars. The fact that the business would come out of Tacoma meant that Sea-Land would not have to be served through BN's new SIG terminal. SIG capacity would be available to serve other steamship lines calling on Seattle. As stated earlier, BN had lost Sea-Land's business to the UP in 1982 but Sea-Land was unhappy with the UP's service levels. Sea-Land was also unhappy that the UP also carried APL's business under a "most favored nation" contract. In the process, BN won their PNW business back from the UP. On May 13, 1985 the Port of Tacoma inaugurated service of a new on-dock facility it had constructed in order to compete with the Port of Seattle. As mentioned previously, it was constructed for Sea-Land under a 30-year contract. The first Sea-Land ship to call on Tacoma was the *Endurance*.

> *"The Endurance, carrying 481 containers from Yokohama, Japan, was the first Sea-Land ship to unload at the new terminal. Work began at 7:00 a.m. on May 13, 1985, as four gangs of longshoremen began discharging the containers. Eight workers aboard the ship unlashed the 40-foot-long containers, which the Hitachi cranes lifted from the ship onto tractor truck chassis. After four longshore workers secured a container, the trucks moved it the short distance to the intermodal yard …. Within six hours all 481 containers had been transferred from the Endurance to the train cars, which would haul them to Chicago and New York."*[485]

Sea-Land's Chicago business was handled in the BN's Chicago Western Avenue facility.

At Tacoma, Teamster drivers drayed the containers 100, or so, yards to the intermodal operation for loading onto double stack cars. That facility was also operated by John Gray's PRS, in partnership with Stevedoring Services of America (SSA). Gray won the terminal contract from the Port of Tacoma and he negotiated a special off-dock agreement with the Tacoma ILWU local that was facilitated through Jimmy Herman, the head of the ILWU.[486] By this time Sea-Land had gained its independence. Sea-Land founder Macolm McLean had sold the company to R.J. Reynolds (RJR) in May of 1969 in order to have a source of funding to acquire large and fast container ships. Sea-Land remained a part of RJR until June of 1984 when it was spun-off to shareholders as an independent publicly traded company. That year it generated its highest revenue and earnings in its 28 year history.[487]

The new Sea-Land contract resulted in the addition of dedicated BN contact trains 7, 8, 9, and 10 between Tacoma and Chicago.

---

[485] Oldham, Kit, Sea-Land begins shipping operations at Port of Tacoma on May 13, 1985, History Link.org, posted January 16, 2008, accessed from: https://www.historylink.org/File/8463, on March 11, 2022.
[486] John Gray email to Mark Cane, March 10, 2022.
[487] Wikipedia, Malcom McLean, Accessed from: https://en.wikipedia.org/wiki/Malcom_McLean, on March 11, 2022.

Trailer Train Buys Stack Cars but BN Objects to Conditions

APL was purchasing stack cars without bulkheads for their Liner-Train while Sea-Land, BN and SP were purchasing stack cars with bulkheads due to a lingering concern about the safely of securing the top containers with ISO Interbox Connectors. At Trailer-Train's November 29, 1984 Board Meeting:

> *Bill Thompson, V.P – Fleet Management, told the Board that the company was considering furnishing well cars of existing design to pool participating railroads for assignment to maritime shippers. TTX would provide the cars only if a participating railroad issued a Car Order Form TD-100 (the means by which a member requested TTX to provide specific cars for its use) and if the shipper provided an adequate indemnity for a substantial portion of the debt service for the cars. The Board authorized the acquisition of up to 48 five unit articulated well cars at an estimated cost of $7.5 million, subject to receipt of an indemnity for their debt service. Representatives of BN, FEC, NS, Seaboard System, and ATSF (12 out of the 36 members of the Board of directors) opposed the motion, but it passed by a majority vote.*

> *The market for intermodal cars was changing rapidly and by the time of the March 21, 1985 meeting of the Board of Directors, TTX management asked that the resolutions approved only four months previously be modified. The company was receiving requests for significantly more double-stack cars and not all of those requests were related to specific shippers or steamship companies. Instead of requiring indemnities of the railcar debt, the Company proposed providing well cars to participants, subject to an initial three-year turn-back period, followed by a six-month notification of turn-back thereafter. Thus, TTX would have the confidence that, for at least three years, the railroads would commit to using – and paying for the use of – the cars. The Board authorized the acquisition of 1,000 wells (200 five-unit cars) under the revised turn-back provisions. Appropriate supplements were added to the Form A Car Contract. The authorization was approved by 28 of the 37 members of the Board, with some representatives of BN, C&NW, NS and UP objecting.*[488]

BN objected to the first resolution because it was clearly an attempt to subsidize APL's expansion of the use of stack car technology without having to expend the capital themselves. It was not unlike how the ICC gave the C&NW (and the UP) the benefit of entering the Powder River Basin coal fields without compensating BN for the risk it took to actually build what became the joint-line. The IBU did not believe that should be the role of Trailer Train. The same logic applied to BN's objection to the second resolution that eliminated a debt indemnity in return for a 3-year car commitment which essentially turned Trailer Train into a leasing company. That was not what it was chartered for.

Some of the railroads interested in obtaining well cars from TTX, like SP and BN, were not yet willing to rely on IBCs to secure upper containers and preferred a bulkhead-style well car. Consequently, TTX ordered 100 five-unit bulkhead style well cars … from Gunderson … delivered from July to September of 1985.[489]

---

[488] Panza, Dawson, Sellberg, p. 239.
[489] Ibid, p. 240.

BN's Common-User Stack Train

The two equipment technologies that were proving to have the greatest near term potential for cost and service improvement were articulated spine-cars utilized primarily for domestic trailer business and articulated double stack cars. Articulation was proving to generate significant ride quality improvements resulting in reduced lading loss and damage and both technologies offered fuel savings potential.

Ralph Muellner had been an aggressive proponent of double stack technology. Aside from articulation facilitated ride-quality benefits it offered the potential for significant economic advantages by essentially cutting the per-container line-haul train movement cost by up to half. It fit perfectly with the international business that moved in large quantities between select high-density origination-destination pairs. Operating stack equipment in less dense lanes would result in less than optimal car-well utilization but lanes such as Seattle / Tacoma–Chicago were ideal applications. The rapid growth of Far East–United States containerized trade combined with the transition toward larger and larger container ships only magnified the stack technology advantage in dense lanes.

A lot of work had to be accomplished to enable BN to handle double stack technology. This included changes with the operations, accounting and the information systems departments so that BN's operating and accounting systems could handle (and account for) business done on stack cars. A meeting was held with Walter Drexel and Darius Gaskins on February 4 to brief them on how stack cars were changing the competitive landscape with special emphasis on APL, Sea-Land and Maersk. They were briefed on stack train economics and how the SIG facility would improve BN's competitive position as well as the implications for Chicago facilities. Their support was sought for outright stack car purchases as well as longer than one-year commitments to Trailer Train to secure cars through them. Ralph Muellner explained his desire to offer a common-user train service.

A regularly scheduled dedicated common-user double stack train service (with BN secured cars) was created to make it easier for smaller steamship lines to compete with the larger lines that could contract for their own unit train service. This helped make it possible for (then) smaller lines such as Hyundai, Hanjin, COSCO, Evergreen, MOL, NOL, OOCL, and NYK to be competitive inland until they grew their own business to the point where they could contract for full trains. It also allowed smaller lines such as Westwood, who would never generate trainload quantities, to benefit from double stack ride quality and economics. This was consistent with the IBU philosophy that it was in the business of helping its customers be competitive in their own markets.

Beneficial customers also took note of the service improvements stack technology offered:

> *The Japanese had set up auto assembly plants in America's heartland. Nissan and Honda already had plant locations and were early users of rail containers. The movement of containers on standard 89-foot flatcars produced a certain amount of unavoidable product damage due to slack action, the crack-the-whip impacts inherent to trains made up of individual cars.*
>
> *Dick Frick, an early Southern Pacific intermodalist, left the company to join Honda, but he still kept his intermodal hand in from the container side. Through the use of an add-on to a consultant's study at Honda, Frick promoted a test of stack cars destined for its plant in Marysville, Ohio, using motorcycles and auto parts. The ride quality of the tests were outstanding, and as a result containerized parts movements began to shift to stack cars. In Asia*

word quickly spread. Many Asian shippers began to insist that their freight also be moved by stack cars rather than TOFC or COFC on 89-footers.[490]

Dick Frick's stack car test was arranged by Ralph Muellner and Phil Carroll who had BN responsibility for the Honda business. Wanting to work directly with the railroad, Frick had no interest in working with intermediary steamship-line stack train operators. The containerized Honda parts business became a regular user of the Common User train service. Honda's reports of the high quality of BN's service only drove more business to the Common User service.

BN Works to Save RoadRailer from Bankruptcy

BN conducted a successful RoadRailer test in 1982 but had not found a market to deploy the technology in. The Southwest Express project had failed to launch. As mentioned before, BN's underlying franchise wasn't well suited to a network operation of RoadRailer trains and the IBU struggled to get capital funding for less risky and more fundamental projects such as double stack cars, hub expansions and information systems. Some specific RoadRailer applications had promise though. Unfortunately, the RoadRailer technology and assets were owned by North American Car (NAC), a subsidiary of Air Cargo operator Flying Tiger Line. North American declared Chapter 11 bankruptcy in December, 1984 and that put the RoadRailer assets and technology in jeopardy.

The IBU still believed in the technology, especially with modifications that had been made to it to remove the rail wheel from the trailer (to eliminate much of the disparity between the tare (light) weight of the trailer compared to a competitive highway trailer) and utilize a rail truck that was shared by coupled RoadRailer trailers in the rail mode. Bill DeWitt led the BN RoadRailer rescue initiative which ultimately led to BN working with Craig Duchossois, of Duchossois Industries who owned Thrall Car Manufacturing Company (also a manufacturer of double stack cars) and General Motors. Duchossois agreed to purchase the trailers out of bankruptcy. BN Intermodal agreed to lease the RoadRailer equipment from Duchossois Industries/Thrall and BN and GM agreed to a contract for BN to haul GM parts from Michigan over the road to BN's Cicero (Chicago) Hub to GM's St. Louis manufacturing plant with RoadRailers. This followed a test for GM on July 10-11 of parts from Michigan over the Cicero Hub to Kansas City. Bill DeWitt added, "Bill Greenwood, Doug Babb and I were at the hearing in California when RoadRailer was purchased by Craig D... "[491] DeWitt was referring to a bankruptcy court hearing in Los Angeles on March 26 where NAC's assets were liquidated. Babb was from BN's Law Department. While the service performed extremely well it was not financially viable for BN. Larry Gross, who worked for Bi-Modal Corporation (which was North American Car's RoadRailer division) said, "BN's commitment was to lease the existing equipment and start the service between Chicago and St. Louis. After a time, the lease was assumed by NS and the train extended to Detroit, which was the birth of Triple Crown."[492] Thus, as will be elaborated on later, BN's IBU saved RoadRailer and facilitated the start of NS Triple Crown service.

On September 30 Bill Greenwood met with Labor Relations leader Jim Dagnon, Charlie Bryan and Roy Buchanan who were the joint leaders of the Operations Department and Don Baker who was the Chicago Region VP. The subject was to develop a strategy for dealing with George Hitz who was the

---

[490] DeBoer, pp. 158-159.
[491] Email from Bill DeWitt to Mark Cane, March 15, 2022.
[492] Email from Larry Gross to Mark Cane, March 14, 2022.

General Chairman of the UTU on the former CB&Q lines. The desire was to gain an Expediter-type agreement through him to operate the RoadRailer train, referred to above, for General Motors. That was followed with a meeting with Hitz and his lieutenants in Chicago on October 7.[493] An agreement was ratified which opened the door to the service.

Another Crack at a Strategic Intermodal Information Systems Plan

On April 10, Eli Wackstein, the relatively new head of the Information Systems Department, came to Ft. Worth from St. Paul (where Information Systems was based) to meet with the IBU. Following an orientation to BN's Intermodal business, the competitive environment and the three Intermodal strategies, each member of the IBU leadership team presented him with a summary of the systems tools their area of concentration utilized, their quality, and what information systems gaps existed.[494]

The points stressed were that BN's systems were designed for railcars and not intermodal, that operating systems support was dearly lacking on the rail between hubs, within the hub complex and over the highway, that equipment support systems did not give the IBU the ability to manage, measure and control equipment close to the level that was necessary, that revenue systems related to price storage and retrieval and billing were inadequate, that costing systems did not allow activity-based measurement and management and that management information was inaccurate and untimely. It was explained to him that beyond the operating level, systems support was lacking to facilitate market planning, financial planning, facilities planning, equipment planning, and human resources planning.

It was an overwhelming experience for Wackstein because it was so clear that the gap between what was, and what was needed, was so stark. It provided the opportunity for the IBU to plant the seed for the need for a comprehensive Intermodal systems overview and the development of an Intermodal systems plan. He was informed about the exploratory work that had been done with Nolan, Norton & Co. and the desire to follow up on that opportunity because the skill did not exist in-house to get the job done. He said he would be open to receiving a proposal.

Wackstein asked what the next step would be. At the time Mark Cane was the point person for IBU systems. He asked that Wackstein appoint a point person who would work with him to visit with NNC to develop an Intermodal Systems Plan proposal. Wackstein asked if Cane had anyone in mind and he answered Jim Zachau. Cane had first worked with Zachau during a strike when he was a management trainee in the Northtown yard. They both worked in the yard office making sure the proper paperwork and computer data entry work was done to support train operations by management crews. Bill Greenwood knew Zachau because of his work at Northtown on the Yard Management System while he was Superintendent there. Greenwood gave Zachau his highest recommendation because he knew he was apolitical, customer oriented, and he got things done. Zachau had also worked on trying to provide Intermodal support with a rudimentary Hub Management System so he was at least somewhat familiar with intermodal terminal operations.

Within a month Wackstein gave the OK and Cane set up a meeting with NNC in Boston for June 5-6. Wackstein informed Zachau that he would be assigned to a special Intermodal project and that Cane would be his liaison. Zachau was told to accompany Cane to meet with NNC in Boston. Cane set up a

---

[493] Bill Greenwood's personal calendar.

[494] This entire section is supported by Mark Cane's personal calendars and personal recollections.

meeting with Zachau for May 29 to orient him to what had been presented to Wackstein on April 10 and to discuss the approach that would be taken. The meeting in Boston was especially enlightening for Zachau because he said it was the first time he had been exposed to such a comprehensive and systematic information technology approach. Both Cane and Zachau believed it was essential to develop a project proposal and present it to BN leadership. Back to St. Paul, Zachau briefed Wackstein on what he learned and offered his recommendation to proceed. Cane did the same with IBU leadership when he returned to Ft. Worth. Still lacking was approval to proceed from Darius Gaskins.

On June 18-20 the IBU held a staff conference in Houston. Gaskins was invited to participate and make an address to the group. During a break between sessions Gaskins, Greenwood, DeWitt, Berry, Burns and Cane were chatting in the common area outside of the ballroom the conference was being conducted in. Greenwood said to Cane, "Why don't you tell Darius about Nolan Norton?" Gaskins said, "About what?" Cane went on to tell him how badly Intermodal needed a total assessment of comprehensive intermodal information systems support quality, system support needs, and a plan to fill the gap. Gaskins asked about NNC and as Cane told him about them he stopped Cane, pointed his finger in his chest and vehemently said, "I don't trust 'Gucci guys!' Are you telling me you want to hire 'Gucci guys?'" Cane said yes and Gaskins asked why. Cane said the IBU would not be able to meet the market or financial plan laid out in the White Paper without comprehensive information systems support. He added that continued reliance on systems designed for a carload business with patches on it for Intermodal would not work. Gaskins said, "If it were your money would you spend it on this?" Cane said yes and Greenwood and the rest of the leadership team piped-in with their support. Gaskins told Cane to have NNC give him a presentation on what they would do and what it would cost. NNC came to Ft. Worth and presented to Gaskins, Wackstein and the IBU staff. NNC had one of their senior executives, Bob Hanson (who would become a bigger BN factor in a few years) make the presentation. In July, Gaskins and Wackstein gave their approval to proceed with NNC.

That triggered a massive effort starting in August that included extensive IBU field and HQ staff involvement (across all functions) plus involvement from associated departments. Multiple workshops were conducted across BN's network to identify what systems and hardware were being used to support the IBU's and Intermodal support departments' efforts, assess the functional and technical quality of the IBU's systems, identify gaps in system support and attempt to quantify the value that appropriate systems support would generate. These sessions ran through December with a great deal of work put into developing and ranking information systems proposals. On January 28, 1986 a preliminary meeting was held with Bill Greenwood and Eli Wackstein and a final presentation was given to Gaskins, Wackstein and Greenwood on January 30. The presentation was well received and it stimulated a flurry of strategic information systems support activity starting in 1986.

Where to Locate the Dallas/Ft. Worth Hub and What to Do About Chicago?

BN's DFW Hub was located in the Dallas suburb, Irving (not far from the Dallas Cowboy's stadium). From a market standpoint it was in a terrific location, right off of the Airport Freeway, but it was in a horrible location from a rail operations standpoint. It was a stub-end facility which meant trains could not efficiently run through it and cars had to be wyed and shoved into it onto stub tracks. It was very difficult to modify it for lift operations and it had inadequate car and trailer parking capacity. As was usual, Intermodal operations were conducted there because that was the location of the legacy circus ramp. The May 28 DFW Hub Inventory prepared by the Hub staff screamed that the current facility would not be adequate intermediate-term much less long-term. Multiple meetings were held into July evaluating alternate sites and their associated financial justifications. The Industrial Development Department salivated over the Irving Hub property because it had an estimated market value of $4 million. By June, two other potential DFW Hub locations were settled on - in the Dallas suburb Lancaster and the North Ft. Worth Yard. The Lancaster location had good highway access but as Dave Burns recalls, "It had a 1% grade and was in a growing residential location. North Ft. Worth was too small, had poor truck access, and no expansion potential."[495] Both Lancaster and North Ft. Worth options came with very high, and difficult to justify, price tags. Unfortunately, BN's intermodal franchise was relatively weak in Texas and the profitability of Texas operations was on the low end of the portfolio. By July it was clear that a combination of these factors meant that a solution to the Irving problem would keep getting pushed into the future and band-aids would continue to be applied to make the Irving location workable. Given the lack of other acceptable solutions the decision was made to invest $2.5 million in the Irving facility to buy at least several years of needed capacity and efficiency improvements.

The Chicago situation was the opposite. The expansion of the Cicero facility into the north side of the yard in 1983 was only a patch fix and by August and September of 1985 efforts were initiated to attempt to take over more of the Cicero rail car yard for Intermodal operations. The satellite terminal at the former freight house complex at Western Avenue was already utilized to regain Sea-Land's business. On October 1 a meeting was held to determine whether BN would like to participate in the construction of a terminal for Sea-Land at the Clearing Yard in Chicago which would have freed Western Avenue for other steamship customers. It was decided that BN would decline that invitation which jeopardized the retention of that business. Bob Ingram and Mike Collins of Sea-Land were informed of BN's decision on November 26.[496] The IBU was betting that the overall quality of BN's service would compel Sea-Land to stay with BN and Sea-Land did.

BN's Chicago Neutral Chassis Pool

The capacity challenge in Chicago, especially on the CECO (north) side of the Hub, was exacerbated by the need to have chassis available for containers served by the Common User train. BN was servicing multiple customers who were expected to provide their own chassis for movement outside of the Hub. As a result the facility was flooded with chassis whose use was restricted to a particular customer. This was complicating internal facility logistics as drivers had to hunt and peck to find their chassis, having them married to a container with a roving lift device, and it was also tying up valuable parking spaces. It also meant that drayage firm drivers could not use one chassis they may have delivered for XYZ Shipping Line for an outbound load for ABC Line, thereby adding costs and inefficiencies to the supply chains of BN's customers in addition to reducing the effective CECO facility capacity.

To address this challenge the IBU worked with Transamerica to design and implement another innovation - the rail industry's first "neutral chassis pool." Chassis from this pool could be used by all BN customers. The IBU required the use of these chassis which upset some customers but those concerns were worked out and over time this innovation would become even more important to the IBU. Neutral chassis pools were eventually adopted by the entire industry.

---

[495] Dave Burns email to Mark Cane, April 12, 2020.
[496] Bill Greenwood's personal calendar.

BN Automotive Business Leadership

Since the formation of strategic business units following the BAH study in 1981, BN's Automotive business had been part of the IBU. Given all that was going on in both the intermodal and automotive businesses it was decided that Automotive should be spun out of the IBU to provide better focus. The first of two final candidates to run the new business unit was the person who managed the plant-to-dealer motor vehicle transportation for a major motor vehicle manufacturer. Aside from being a good business person he would bring a unique customer perspective to the job. The other was Dan Flood, an executive of a major Haul-Away Motor Carrier, who had an especially good relationship with General Motors (who BN had little market share with). Haul-Away carriers handled transportation between motor vehicle manufacturing plants and rail-heads, between rail-heads and motor vehicle dealers and between plants and motor vehicle dealers when no rail transportation was involved. They were very influential with the MV manufacturers. The hiring of trucking executives to manage Hub centers had worked well for the IBU. Dan Flood was offered and accepted the job in August of 1985.[497]

Dallas Smith Trailers

Similar to its intermodal franchise, BN's motor vehicle transportation franchise was relatively weak. BN carried almost all of the import motor vehicle business from the Pacific Northwest except for Toyota which UP carried out of Portland. While BN carried Ford vehicles in BN-competitive markets, UP carried almost all of the General Motors and Chrysler business to BN-served markets. The fact that the vehicle manufacturer required the railroad to build them independent unloading facilities in all markets meant it was extremely difficult to capture new market share. Since the Smith trailer would allow vehicles to utilize intermodal trains and hub centers and avoid motor vehicle terminals, that barrier to new market entry would conceivably be eliminated. This made the technology especially attractive to BN.

On March 4, 1985, Dallas Smith and Ford announced a three-year contract between Smith and Ford for the use of 50 Dallas Smith Trailers for shipment over BN points. Initial test results of the Dallas Smith trailer technology for the damage-free, dealer-direct transportation of motor vehicles were very positive. They were so successful that on August 23, 1985 Burlington Northern Inc. purchased $4 million worth of Dallas Smith Engineering Corp. (DSE) stock. The purchase agreement included options to purchase more stock at specified dates within 30 months of the initial purchase closing-date at the initial per share price. If exercised, these purchases would increase BNI's ownership percentage of DSE to approximately 35% of the company.[498]

As of October 15, 1985, Ford Motor Company had accepted the first 50 trailers produced by DSE and put them in service to BN points. They also indicated that they would like to utilize 300 trailers. Chrysler accepted 4 trailers. General Motors agreed to accept 6-12. American Motors said they would like to try them. On the import vehicle side, Toyota, Honda, Nissan and Hyundai said they would utilize them on a continuous movement basis (reloading eastbound what was shipped west with domestic vehicles). Isuzu

---

[497] Bill Greenwood's personal notes, *Greenwood Collection*, Barriger Library at UMSL.
[498] Burlington Northern Inc., Dallas Smith Stock Purchase Agreement, August 23, 1985, *Greenwood Collection*, Barriger Library at UMSL.

expressed an interest and a proposal from Mazda was being prepared. In addition, Alaska Hydro-Train wanted to test the trailer for its rail-barge to Alaska.[499]

Critical to the effort was an assumption that each trailer would generate a minimum of three round trips per month and would carry 7 automobiles. It was also expected that the technology would be adapted to handle mid-sized vehicles and small trucks.

On December 17, 1985, Ford's Chuck Wilkins sent a letter to Dan Flood, BN's VP Automotive, with a summary of modifications made to the Smith program. He mentioned that when Dallas Smith was acting as a shipper's agent, Ford had signed a "lengthy contract with him to test 50 of his robotic trailers over a period of three years. With his decision to lease the trailers and to turn responsibility for conducting trailer testing over to the Burlington Northern, that contract is now void."[500] Wilkins asked for a brief letter of agreement with BN.

Burlington Northern Inc.'s Motor Carrier Industry Presence

As discussed earlier, BNI owned BN Transport (BNT) and inherited Frisco Transportation (FT) with the Frisco Railroad merger. FT was then incorporated into BNT. The IBU had a relationship with BNT that predated the formation of the business unit. As indicated earlier, BNT had participated in the 1981 Intermodal Task Force at the request of Richard Grayson to whom both BN Railroad and BNT reported at the time. The 1982 BNI Annual Report stated:

> *BN Transport Inc. (BNT) and the smaller Frisco Transportation Company reported combined 1982 revenues of $76 million, down 6 percent from 1981. As a result of lower revenues, the trucking operation posted an operating loss of $3 million in 1982 compared with operating income of $553,000 in 1981. The year-to-date decline was the result of the economic recession and of the increased rate competition that developed in the deregulated environment. BNT plans to increase its sales and geographical coverage during the coming year and to expand its intermodal volume in cooperation with BN Railroad.[501]*

Unfortunately, BNT continued to lose competitive bids for services at IBU Hubs and was losing competitive over-the-road trucking battles in the deregulated market environment. Their core business model was the classic truckload carrier model – run a single driver from origin dock to destination dock in longer-haul markets. They had no interest in utilizing intermodal as a substitute service for their core line-haul operations. They had no interest in changing that model to one focused on drayage. They did obtain a BN Intermodal contract, however, and acted as a broker/third party for some intermodal shipments. That did not reverse a performance decline that resulted in a reverse from $.55 million operating income in 1981 to an operating loss of $4 million in 1983. The 1983 BN Annual Report Form 10-K stated the following and included the accompanying statistics:

---

[499] Burlington Northern Marketing Update on Dallas Smith Robotic Trailer and Hub Concepts, October 15, 1985, *Greenwood Collection*, Barriger Library at UMSL.

[500] C.F. Wilkins, Ford Motor Company, letter to T.D. Flood of Burlington Northern. December 17, 1985, *Greenwood Collection*, Barriger Library at UMSL.

[501] Burlington Northern Inc., 1982 Annual Report, p. 9.

During 1983 BN Transport Inc. furnished common carrier freight service, under authorities granted by the ICC, in the 48 contiguous states. Trucking revenues declined 14% in 1983 and 1982 declined 6% from 1981, due to competition and the effects of deregulation.[502]

BN Transport Performance Statistics[503]
($millions)

	1983	1982	1981
Revenues	65.352	75.840	80.269
Costs and Expenses	69.322	78.765	79.716
Operating Income (Loss)	(3.970)	(2.925)	.553
Assets	16.003	18.026	22.150

BNI hired Mike Lawrence in May, 1984 to address the BNT situation. Lawrence had been an executive with Schneider National Inc., one of the largest truckload carriers in the United States. He had served as Schneider's Vice President Marketing from July 1980 to April 1981, Senior Vice President, Marketing and Corporate Development from April 1981 to November 1981 and President, Independent Contractor Group from November 1981 to May 1984.[504] He was highly regarded in the transportation industry. Shortly after his arrival, in September, 1984 he sold BN's BN Transport business to The Santa Fe Trail Transportation Company (SFT).[505]

SFT-BNT continued to provide some services to the IBU and they held a BN intermodal services contract. By April of 1985 their business had declined to such a degree that they were required by BN's accounting department to pay up-front for intermodal transportation services purchased from BN (put on a cash basis). IBU customers were notified that BN would not move SFT-BNT trailers until up-front payment was received. Concurrent with that they had to fund a Letter of Credit to their insurance carrier which decimated their working capital. They were unable to meet their payroll and had to cease operations.[506] New contractors had to be secured to handle the little remaining work SFT-BNT had been doing at the hubs.

Meanwhile, Lawrence started to build a new motor carrier business. BNI's 1985 Annual Report Form-10K noted the following:

Burlington Northern Motor Carriers Inc. ("BNMC"), formed in 1985, has acquired several independent trucking companies with operations east of the Rocky Mountains. BNMC serves primarily the truckload-only dry van market.[507]

News of this development did not faze the IBU's less-than-truckload motor carrier customers but it was unsettling for the IBU's third parties. They were not threatened by BNT but Mike Lawrence was a different matter. There was a concern that a BN IBU – BNMC partnership would enable BN to deal

---

[502] Ibid, pp. 7 & 21.

[503] Burlington Northern Inc., 1983 Annual Report From 10-K, pp. 22-23

[504] Burlington Northern Inc., 1985 Annual Report Form 10-K, p. 16.

[505] Letter from Avery Z. Eliscu, Chairman and Chief Executive Officer, and Leonard J. Lewensohn, President, Santa Fe Trail Transportation Company, to William E. Greenwood, Vice President Intermodal, Burlington Northern Railroad, April 30, 1985, *Greenwood Collection*, Barriger Library at UMSL.

[506] Ibid.

[507] Burlington Northern Inc., 1985 Annual Report Form 10-K, p. 10.

directly with shippers and displace them. On May 3, 1984 Norfolk Southern Corporation purchased North American Van Lines (who operated a highly regarded truckload operation) from PepsiCo[508] which increased paranoia in the third party community. The IBU had to assure them that BNMC was an independent subsidiary of BNI and they would be treated as any other client of the IBU would be treated.

Solicitation of Schneider National

As indicated above, Schneider National was one of the leading US truckload motor carriers. It was founded by Don Schneider and he ran a profitable first-class operation utilizing company drivers (not owner-operators for quality control reasons) supported by cutting-edge information systems support. Continuous attempts had been made to interest Schneider National into using BN Intermodal as a substitute line-haul service provider for them in a partnership that would capitalize on the best of what both rail and truck modes had to offer. Finally, Don Schneider agreed to meet with Bill Greenwood and Bill DeWitt. Because Schneider was based in Green Bay, WI, it was suggested that the meeting take place at the Cicero Hub so Schneider could see BN's intermodal operation in-action. That meeting took place on July 30, 1985.[509] According to DeWitt, "It was a beautiful, sunny July day and the Hub was handling a lot of trailers and containers. We gave Schneider a tour and explained to him what was going on. When we sat down at the end of the tour he said we had a really nice operation but he couldn't get over the poor reputation intermodal had in the marketplace for damage and inconsistent service. DeWitt added, "When we pointed out that UPS utilized us it didn't faze him." He told Greenwood and DeWitt, "I don't think there will ever be a Schneider shipment going over railroads." DeWitt said it was a cordial meeting and Schneider flew back to Green Bay.[510]

Bill Greenwood added:

> There was a tremendous amount of activity going on at the Hub that day. Don Schneider was taking it all in as we toured the operation. He asked a lot of questions. Finally he said, "With all of this equipment handling I can't see how you can make any money. This intermodal stuff isn't for me. Then he said a Schneider trailer would never ride a train.[511]

Walter Drexel Promotes BN Intermodal

As stated earlier, in the 1982–1983 era BN Railroad CEO Walter Drexel was not remotely close to being an IBU advocate. That started to change as the IBU continued to push the innovation envelope, with the support of Darius Gaskins, and meet or exceed its aggressive business plan. He accompanied Bill Greenwood on trips to call on customers in the Far East. In June of 1985 Drexel even agreed to serve as the Keynote Speaker at the International Intermodal Expo in Atlanta. The Expo was the biggest event of the year in the intermodal business so securing this speaking engagement for BN was a coup made possible by BN's aggressiveness in the marketplace. The speech the IBU prepared for him was very well

---

[508] Wikipedia, Norfolk Southern, accessed from: https://en.wikipedia.org/wiki/North_American_Van_Lines, on March 30, 2022.
[509] Bill Greenwood personal calendar, Year 1985.
[510] Bill DeWitt interview with Mark Cane, April 3, 2022.
[511] Bill Greenwood interview with Mark Cane, May 4, 2022.

received. On June 18, 1985 he was sent the following letter[512] from James A. Ryder, Chairman of JARAX International (a James A. Ryder Company). He was the founder of the Ryder organization:

> *Mr. Drexel:*
>
> *I very much enjoyed your remarks during the recent 1985 International Intermodal Expo in Atlanta. As a large and fast growing customer of your company, your comments regarding the "Hub" concept you are establishing, and your stated intention of making allies of truckers rather than adversaries, were especially refreshing.*
>
> *As a leading Shipper's Agent and Trucking company, we welcome the opportunity to participate in any aspects of your program that could be mutually beneficial.*
>
> *Again, my congratulations on your fine address and any comments and further information related to your current plans would be most welcome.*
>
> *Regards,*
> *(s) James A Ryder*
> *Chairman*
> *JARAX International*

Darius Gaskins is Promoted

On July 17, 1985 Darius Gaskins was promoted to president and COO of BN Railroad with Drexel remaining CEO and Chairman. A July 7, 1985 BNRR press release stated: [513]

> *Reporting to Gaskins will be Executive Vice President Don Wood; John Hertog, Coal and Taconite; Lyle Reed, Vice President, Planning and Evaluation; and the Marketing and Sales Department.*
>
> *Gaskins, along with Donald Engle, Senior Vice President Law and Government Affairs; and Lee Sundby, Senior Vice President, Administration; will report to Drexel.*

To make him a Drexel succession candidate, Don Wood had been previously transferred from running BNRR's finance and accounting functions to leading the Operations Department. Effective in December Gaskins would be promoted to president and CEO of BNRR with Drexel becoming Vice Chairman of BNI.[514] When Drexel was appointed Vice Chairman of BNI in December, Richard Grayson retired. Drexel was not a fan of Darius Gaskins and did not support his elevation to the CEO position of BN Railroad. Gaskins said:[515]

[512] James A. Ryder letter to Mr. W. A. Drexel, June 18, 1985, *Greenwood Collection*, Barriger Library at UMSL.
[513] BNRR Corporate Communications Department, Management Change Announced, July 18, 1985, *Greenwood Collection*, Barriger Library at UMSL.
[514] Burlington Northern Inc., 1986 Annual Report Form 10-K, pp. 16-17.
[515] National Railroad Hall of Fame, Darius W. Gaskins, Jr., Interview Transcript, November 5, 2020, Accessed from: https://www.nrrhof.org/darius-w-gaskins-jr, on March 20, 2023.

Bressler decided, long story short, that I'm the guy to be the President. Drexel's going to retire; he didn't like the railroad business much, and he's going to retire. He was a treasurer at ARCO with Dick Bressler. He brought him in as a numbers guy. That's what his primary function was. He never got into the marketing details, and he certainly didn't get into the operating details because he recognized that he didn't know much about that. And he didn't like the railroad.

Bill Greenwood adds a little more color as to how BN's Drexel era at BN ended:

Tom Matthews told me Drexel shared his plan with him to get more control over the railroad. After he got his 1985 bonus check from Bressler he planned to fly to Seattle and thank him and then suggest that he was considering retirement. He expected Bressler to encourage him to stay and then Drexel would say he would only stay on the condition that he could run the railroad unencumbered and fire Darius Gaskins. It turns out that Drexel did what he said he would do but instead of asking him to stay, Bressler walked him into the area outside his office and announced to everyone that he had good news to share - that Drexel had decided to retire.[516]

Bill Greenwood is Promoted Again

Bill Greenwood describes how he found out Darius Gaskins selected to him to succeed him after Bressler promoted Gaskins to run BN Railroad:

One day, Darius Gaskins called me into his office. He said, "I've been watching you. I like the way you work," and he said, "I just got promoted. I've been promoted to president of the company, and I want to make you senior vice president of marketing over all the business units." [517]

On November 11, 1985 BNRR announced that Gaskins' former position had been filled[518]:

Burlington Northern Railroad today announced the appointment of William E. Greenwood as Senior Vice President, Marketing and Sales. He has been Vice President for Intermodal Operations since August 1, 1984.

The appointment is effective immediately, said Darius Gaskins, Jr., President and Chief Operating Officer. Gaskins was Greenwood's predecessor in the senior marketing post.

The Intermodal Department will continue to report to Greenwood, along with Don W. Scott, Vice President Sales and Property Management, Murry W. Watson, Vice President International Marketing and Sales, Richard M. Gleason, Vice President Marketing and Pricing, and Daniel Flood, Vice President Automotive Marketing.

Several significant things were pointed out in this announcement. Aside from announcing the well-earned promotion for Greenwood it mentioned the Intermodal Department would continue to report to

---

[516] Bill Greenwood interview with Mark Cane, May 4, 2022.

[517] National Railroad Hall of Fame, William E. Greenwood, Chief Operating Officer (retired) Burlington Northern Railroad, Interview Transcript, July 30, 2020: Accessed from: https://www.nrrhof.org/greenwood-transcript, Accessed on May 7, 2022.

[518] Harmening, T.E., AVP Corporate Communications, Notice to all employees, November 6, 1985, *Greenwood Collection*, Barriger Library at UMSL.

him. All of his former Intermodal direct-reports continued to be his direct-reports until his replacement was selected. Second, it mentioned that Murry Watson was VP International. In 1984 Dick Gleason hired the flamboyant Watson to succeed Gerald Davies as Sr. AVP of Food and Consumer Products as it was split from Industrial Products. Before Greenwood's promotion, Gaskins promoted Watson to replace Bill Egan as the leader of International Marketing and Sales efforts. Egan was demoted to Sr. AVP Sales with responsibility for only telemarketing. Third, Don Scott was identified as VP of Sales and Property Management. Scott came from the Operating Department for cross fertilization/career development and replaced Joe Galassi who had served as VP Sales after also coming from the Operating Department for cross fertilization/career development. Galassi returned to the Operating Department as VP Transportation under Don Wood. Fourth, the same Dick Gleason who had made Greenwood's life so difficult was now going to be Greenwood's direct report. When Gaskins offered Greenwood the job they talked about Gleason. This is Gaskins' recollection of the situation:[519]

> *Gleason– it was not working out real well with him. Personally, I was going to fire Gleason anyway because once I'd picked Greenwood, I mean, it was a kick in the face. Not only that, but I didn't think it was working well. The two of us were at warheads, at loggerheads. So, I was going to get rid of him, but I said, Well, let's give Bill a chance. So, I called him in my office, I said, Bill, I'm promoting you, and that's a congratulations, but now you have a decision to make. What do you want to do about Dick Gleason? Greenwood thought for a minute, and he said, I want to fire him. I said, Fine, I'll do it. So, I fired him. That's another huge story, but it turns out that Drexel, who was my boss, who hated railroads, liked Gleason. They were pals, right? So, I go in to tell Drexel out of courtesy that I'm firing this guy, I'm going to fire him today, and he said, Do me a favor. Let me get out of the building before you do it. [laughs.] And I'll never forget that, I mean, c'mon. You gotta fire somebody, you might as well tell him, right? What are you doing, "get out of the building"? [laughs.]*

Bill Greenwood's recollection was similar: [520]

> *So, he said, "Okay, here's a quick question for you. What are you gonna do about Dick Gleason?" I thought, "Oh my gosh. This is a test." "I'll be honest," I said, "I'm going to fire him." He said, "Right answer." He said, "I'll do it for you." And so, that began, you know, just a massive and wonderful change that took place in marketing that I was able to do.*

Gaskins' appointment to President also helped to temporarily remove some of the internal obstacles the IBU had been continually encountering. Recall the following from the earlier days of the IBU:[521]

> *Many people in addition to Greenwood's boss were antagonized by the maverick personalities and brash dreams of the Intermodal Team. Whenever possible, these naysayers loudly criticized intermodal, and they made it tough to get resources, information, people, and permissions. At times the hostility verged on sabotage. According to the team, for example, one executive rigged*

---

[519] National Railroad Hall of Fame, Darius W. Gaskins Interview Transcript, Accessed from: https://www.nrrhof.org/darius-w-gaskins-jr, on March 20, 2023.

[520] National Railroad Hall of Fame, William E. Greenwood, Chief Operating Officer (retired) Burlington Northern Railroad, Interview Transcript, July 30, 2020: Accessed from: https://www.nrrhof.org/greenwood-transcript, Accessed on May 7, 2022.

[521] Katzenbach and Smith, p. 34.

an equipment bid to prevent intermodal from working with a preferred vendor on a critical new generation of flatcar.

That executive who rigged the bid to undermine the IBU was the VP of Purchasing and Materials. Gaskins was very aware of the incident and he didn't forget it. In addition to dealing with Gleason he said, "I fired my purchasing guy when I was CEO. "[522]

BN Intermodal Network as of August, 1985

In August, 1985 the IBU published and distributed, "The Burlington Northern Innovative Intermodal Handbook," for use by its salespeople and agents. Aside from changing the brand of its service from "Piggyback" with all of its negative connotations to "Intermodal," there was a need to remove the "mystique" around the service and explain it to break down barriers to get potential beneficial

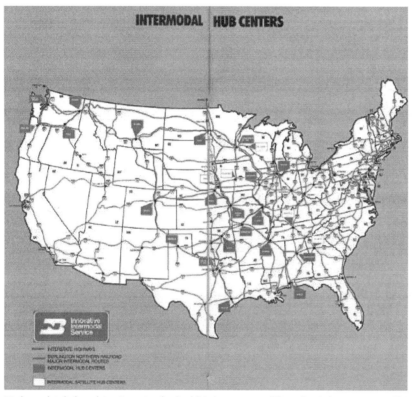

customers and motor carriers to use it. The brochure included an extensive Table of Contents covering the gamut of issues/subjects related to transacting intermodal service.[523] This was in-fact missionary work being done for the entire Intermodal industry. Although BN and the IBU bore the brunt of the effort and expense to do this, it was critical for the IBU to overcome its "worst geographic franchise in the industry" weakness and move BN from being in the last place position among railroads to achieving its original 1981 Intermodal Task Force objective of becoming the rail industry's leader. Included in this brochure was a map (left) of BN Hubs which by this time included highway satellites in Atlanta, Eau Claire (WI), Des Moines and Omaha. Omaha was a satellite of a rail Hub at Lincoln because it hadn't yet been relocated to Omaha.[524]

---

[522] National Railroad Hall of Fame, Darius W. Gaskins Interview Transcript, Accessed from: https://www.nrrhof.org/darius-w-gaskins-jr, on March 20, 2023.

[523] The Burlington Northern Innovative Intermodal Handbook, August, 1985, pp.4-5, *Greenwood Collection*, Barriger Library at UMSL.

[524] Ibid, pp. 24-25.

BN Intermodal Train Service Growth Through 1985

By the end of 1985 the IBU and its customers had the benefit of 37 trains that carried a higher profile "Intermodal" designation, of which 26 were dedicated. [525] In addition to the ten dedicated Expediter network trains, dedicated intermodal trains were in service between: Chicago and Portland (EB and WB), Chicago and Seattle, Chicago and Tacoma, Birmingham and Seattle/Portland, and Chicago and Denver. Non-dedicated Intermodal trains operated between Chicago and Billings, Chicago and Dallas/Houston, Chicago and Kansas City connecting with the SP Railroad, Chicago and Denver including one running through with the DRGW Railroad (Salt Lake City & CA Bay Area), Houston and the PNW, and Avard Gateway service with the Santa Fe Railway connecting California with St. Louis and Memphis (and Birmingham via connecting train service).

More Expediters?

Given the success the Springfield Region Expediters were generating, the IBU was working with Labor Relations and the Operating Regions to lay groundwork for the expansion of the Expediter network. Again, this was done as part of a corporate initiative to work with the operating labor organizations to expand the use of two person crews, improve BN's labor/management relations, and generate new positive cash-flow business over an underutilized fixed-asset base. Meetings were held with Denver Region General Chairmen on September 18, 1985 and Chicago Region General Chairmen on October 7. [526]

New BN Intermodal 800 Number

Effective September, 18, 1985 all BN Intermodal Hub Centers and Sales Offices could be called through a single phone number: 800-858-2626. The 2626 ending corresponded with "BNBN" on the phone dial pad. This was done in conjunction with Strategy #3 so BN would be easier to do business with.[527] This innovation, which may seem incredibly insignificant in the 2020s, was instituted at a time when toll-free numbers were relatively rare as a marketing tool to make BN Intermodal easier to do business with.

Highway Satellite Hub Growth

As has already been stated, BN's Intermodal franchise, in terms of the geography it covered, was the worst among the largest railroads in the United States. As a result, one of the major tactics associated with the Strategy #1 development of Hub Centers was to extend the reach of BN to potential customers via the highway. The establishment of satellite highway hubs was progressing by the end of 1985. The Hub that had the largest highway satellite opportunity was Birmingham and its progress was documented in the previously cited *Fleet Owner* Magazine article: [528]

---

[525] Gordon Trafton, Burlington Northern Intermodal Train Implementation Outline, March 25, 1986, *Greenwood Collection*, Barriger Library at UMSL.
[526] Bill Greenwood's personal calendars.
[527] New Short-Haul Intermodal Service from Burlington Northern – BN Expediter Brochure, August, 1985, *Greenwood Collection*, Barriger Library at UMSL.
[528] Jacobus, William W., *Fleet Owner*, Intermodal – BN Relies on Truckers to Run Hub Centers, February 1986.

Behind BN's management is a railroad system that is developing a rapidly expanding partnership with motor carriers. Truckers, in fact, are approaching the railroad for business because they like the way that system works.

The operation of a typical hub center defines the concept best. The Dixie Hub Center in Birmingham, for example, has seven satellite hubs that feed and receive revenue loads to and from the rail hub.

Earle Cochran, Birmingham hub manager, currently uses 28 regional contract motor carriers to serve his network. The carriers, which are contracted to move loads over the road, often have several power units dedicated to the railroad, with others available if needed. Cochran's satellites are in Augusta, Atlanta, Columbia and Savannah, GA, Charlotte and Greensboro, NC, and Greenville, SC.

"We publish rates to and from our satellites as though they were rail-served facilities," says Cochran. "For example, a trailer that's coming from a customer in Seattle to Atlanta will move by train from Seattle to the Birmingham hub. It is then grounded at Birmingham, processed by an intermodal clerk, and passed to a highway dispatcher who selects the motor carrier to deliver it. He notifies the carrier that the load is at the hub center and enters it into his computer as dispatched to the carrier.

Loads are dispatched as early as 4:30 am to a number of carriers working out of each hub. Most of the waiting carriers that delivered loads during the night from satellite hubs get the first loads in the morning. "We've developed such a volume that dispatchers no longer have to give formal notification to carriers that a given load is in," says Cochran.

"Because Expediter trains have a service schedule that shows cutoff and availability times at all our hub centers and satellite hubs, the carriers can come and wait for loads they know are on those trains," says Cochran.

"For example, our availability time at Atlanta is 10 am local time. The inbound train is unloaded in Birmingham and we are dispatching trailers by 5:30 am Atlanta time," he says. "It is three hours running time to Atlanta, so to have those trailers available there by 10 am, we have to have drivers waiting in Birmingham at 4:30 am because of the time change."

Birmingham highway dispatcher Billy McMurray knows the night before what carriers he is going to have on hand the next morning, because he has been notified by the carriers and his counterparts at the satellites. He also knows what is coming in on the Expediters, so he is able to assign loads in advance to those early-morning arrivals.

McMurray's first priority is to assign the satellite loads out in the morning. He matches loads with the early carriers so they get automatic backhauls. His second priority is leftover loads from the day before, if there are any. Then he starts calling other contract carriers and assigning loads to them.

Meanwhile, non-Expediter loads moving in and out of the hubs are handled by local carriers that work directly for the shippers. In the case of the Atlanta satellite, some of that freight is handled by Win Express Co. Inc., a regional carrier that actually operates the satellite for Burlington Northern.

According to Cochran, the carriers that shuttle both Expediter and regular loads between the hub center and the satellites like the arrangement. "It's a clean run," he says. "Instead of delivering to customers, which might involve all kinds of waiting time, this is just a drop-and-pull.

"That's the main reason we set it up that way, to keep the linehaul operation completely pure. I'm getting my freight hauled, basically, at backhaul rates of about $1.05 / mi. and paying for it in one direction," says Cochran.

"Conventional intermodal thinking is round-trip rates. We pay for 1-way moves. That was the only way we could reach out so far from our hub center and still be competitive with over-the-road truckers. For example, if you were to pay the guy for Birmingham to Atlanta and back, you're looking at $300. That shoots you out of the water price-wise. You've got $300 drayage before it even gets on the train."

Loads that arrive at a BN hub are covered by the railroad's liability insurance. "We have liability for what happens to that load from then on. We've had incidents where loads were wrecked en route from Atlanta to Birmingham. When that happens, we pay the claim."

Whenever there is a mishap, or other special circumstance, BN has to be flexible, says Cochran. A load destined to meet a ship in Seattle, for example, went off the highway between Charlotte and the Birmingham hub. Cochran sent another trailer to off-load the wrecked unit and take it to Birmingham, but a day was lost doing that. If the load had gone by train, it would have missed the ship, so BN dispatched a driver team to truck it straight to Seattle.

"I also arranged with my counterpart in Seattle to take a load that would have come by rail and give it to that team to bring back to Birmingham," says Cochran. The cost difference between shipping the load by highway and intermodal – about $3,000 – became part of a claim, including $6,000 damage to the original trailer, which was charged to the carrier that had the accident.

The Birmingham hub center handled a total of 5,537 revenue loads last November (1985). Out of that total, 1,085 loads, roughly 20%, either originated or terminated at one of the seven satellite hubs. Not surprisingly, Earle Cochran is currently negotiating with carriers in three other cities to have them establish BN satellites and bring the total in the Southeast to 10.

McMurray's Birmingham records also reflect the rapid growth of BN's revenue loads running through the satellites. During January, 1985, he handled 343 loads. By July, it was 540, and he tallied 1,085 in November.

The rest originated or terminated at Birmingham as far as the railroad is concerned. But, actually, those loads came from or went to Tennessee, Alabama, South Georgia, and Mississippi.

The expansion of the highway satellite network was a great example of the Hub strategy in action. The expansion of BN's market presence into the satellite market areas could have been possible if connecting railroads offered service to connect with BN. Unfortunately, their haul lengths made them unattractive to them so without the highway extensions those markets would have been lost to BN.

In spite of continued internal and external obstacles, as 1985 was coming to an end the success of highway satellites, along with so many of the other IBU initiatives implemented during its four years of life, were bearing fruit. It was resulting in the outcome that the IBU strove to achieve when it initially established its brash 1981 overarching and strategy driving goal:

> By 1986 become the recognized intermodal leader in terms of customer service, innovation, market share and profitability.

Stampede Pass Route Briefly Reopened and Quickly Shut Down Again

Former Burlington Northern dispatcher David Sprau recalled a brief 1985 Intermodal incident related to the mothballed Stampede Pass route between Spokane and Seattle:[529]

> On August 20, 1985, an eastbound intermodal train derailed on the Columbia River Bridge at Rock Island, ten miles east of Wenatchee, WA on the former Great Northern route. A fire ensued and it was determined the bridge would be out of service approximately ten days. Detours began immediately over the ex-Spokane, Portland & Seattle line through Wishram WA, but a subsequent accident closed that line for what was expected to be about one week.

> Consequently, at the urging of Seattle Superintendent Jerry K. Vaden, BN reluctantly re-opened the former Northern Pacific Stampede pass line, to keep traffic moving. Extra board Train Order Operators re-opened several boarded-up stations along the route, and detour operation began over trackage idled two years previously.

> Double-stack intermodal cars traditionally had been prohibited on this route, but published clearances appeared close enough to safely try an experiment. Vaden placed a carload of empty double-stack containers behind the engine of an eastbound train and instructed Road Foreman of Engines Gerald L. Neswick to ride and watch actual clearances with a floodlight. So this train passed through Stampede Tunnel at about 5 MPH and Neswick later reported the containers cleared the tunnel ceiling by 3 to 5 inches the whole distance. While this was insufficient for operation at normal operating speed, Vaden believed a little ballast, tie and track work might improve clearances to an acceptable six or eight inches or more, resulting in the probability of getting double stack and other trains between Seattle and Pasco over that line in seven hours instead of the current ten or more via Vancouver WA and Wishram. Upon reporting these findings, advising he had kept the line open pending a decision, he was curtly told to close the route immediately. "I got my hand slapped for keeping it open," he stated afterward.
> During that time, Gerry Neswick came into the dispatchers' office to share his findings with me because we both had been NP employees before the merger and he thought I'd enjoy the discussion. He mentioned how difficult it had been to focus the floodlight with water dripping on his head and related other trivia he'd observed.

> Those detours lasted approximately one week and were the only revenue trains moved over the ex-NP Stampede Pass between the time the line was shut down on August 20, 1983 and when it was reopened on December 7, 1996.

---

[529] Daid Sprau email to Mark Cane, February 5, 2023.

BN's volume of stack train business was rapidly growing because of the initiation of BN's Common User Stack Train service as well as the recapture of Sea-Land's business. Only 8'6" high international ISO containers were in use at the time. The Cascade tunnel on the Stevens Pass route could accommodate an 8'6" and 9'6" container stacked on top of one another. As David Sprau indicated, the Stampede Tunnel could handle two 8'6" containers but the 3-5" of clearance Road Foreman Neswick observed would not allow containers higher than that. That, plus a continued downturn in divertible carload business, compounded by the UP's entry into the Powder River Basin, led to the decision to return the line to mothball status. The line would prove to be valuable in the future, however. The way Jerry Vaden's initiative, that minimized the impact of more than a week's worth of service failures, was "rewarded" was a symptom of the "command and control" nature of BN's militaristic culture at the time. While the inclusive and innovation-promoting climate within the IBU was a relative oasis, that general company culture served to increase the challenges the IBU confronted as it attempted to get the resources it needed to aggressively grow the business and pursue innovations.

BNI Buys Southland Royalty Company to Expand Oil and Gas Assets

Before the creation of the IBU, Lou Menk was rightly accused of utilizing BN Inc. resource business income to support the railroad. It enabled the development of BN's coal business. Since the formation of the IBU, BN Inc. could be rightly accused of utilizing the railroad to fund resource business investments. That trend continued at the end of 1985. Southland Royalty Company and its oil and gas operations were acquired by BNI on December 13, 1985 for $730 million. The acquisition increased BNI's oil and gas reserve position by 32%.[530] It was financed with new debt and drove BNI's total long-term debt to $3.118 billion and the debt to capitalization ratio to 41%.[531] It helped drive BNI's annual interest expense to $312 million in 1985 million compared to $142 million in 1983.

1985 Performance Wrap-up

The following table illustrates BN Intermodal revenue performance from the inception of the IBU in 1981 through 1985 compared to the food, lumber and manufactured products (F&M) businesses in addition to BNRR operating income and BNI long term debt. The 1981 Task Force had identified a "worst case" risk of $490.7 million of food and manufactured and forest products business that was vulnerable to diversion by 1985. In 1985 food and manufactured and forest products revenue was $393 million less than 1981. While Intermodal revenue grew $218 million (81.6%) during the same time period, the majority of the growth came from UPS, International and LTL customers plus a small contribution from the new Springfield Region Expediter services. None of these sources were factors in the 1981 Intermodal Task Force divertible share projections.

---

[530] Richard M. Bressler Letter to Shareholders, Burlington Northern Inc. 1985 Annual Report Form 10-K.
[531] Burlington Northern Inc., 1986 Annual Report Form 10-K, p. 19-20.

Burlington Northern Railroad 1981-1985 Financial Performance ($ Millions) [532]

	IML Rev.	F&M Rev.	BNRR Rev.	BNRR Op. Inc.	BNRR OR	BNI LT Debt	Pref. Stock	Int. Exp.	Div. Exp.	Debt/ Cap.
1981	$267	$1,598	$4,088	$527	87.1%	$1,330	$105	$140	$58	29%
1982	273	1,261	3,773	457	87.9%	1,333	105	136	71	27%
1983	335	1,218	4,058	734	81.9%	2,930	709	142	87	41%
1984	443	1,265	4,490	980	78.2%	2,454	697	310	130	35%
1985	485	1,205	4,098	822	79.9%	3,118	519	312	184	41%

In addition, as mentioned earlier, 1985 grain revenue fell $200 million (29%) due to crop yield issues and coal revenue fell more than 13% ($221 million) compared to 1984 due to C&NW/UP PRB access-related business losses and competitive rate cuts. The total revenue loss from these backbone businesses combined with the continued deterioration of the Food & Manufactured Products and Forest Products businesses totaled $481 million. The profit situation was helped by a $67 million reduction in fuel and labor costs between 1984 and 1985.[533] This illustrated the importance of having a more balanced business portfolio that Intermodal helped provide. It also emphasized the importance of profitability improvements the new IBU was generating on its baseline business which had a greater impact on corporate profitability than it was given credit for.

Despite BN Railroad's income decline, BNI reported an increase in net income and earnings per share. Revenue fell from 1984's $9.156 billion to $8.651 billion and operating income fell from $1.449 billion to $1.365 billion. Resources operating income increased from $469 million to $543 million. BNI net income grew from $608 million to $658 million and earnings per share grew from $7.15 to $8.03.[534] With the fall-off in railroad performance, Bressler's strategy to invest in BN's resource businesses in preference to BN Railroad was paying off.

---

[532] Burlington Northern Inc., 1981-1985 Annual Reports/Forms 10-K.
[533] Burlington Northern Inc., 1985 Annual Report Form 10-K, p. 19.
[534] Inside cover, Burlington Northern Inc., 1985 Annual Report Form 10-K.

Chapter 13 – Intermodal Advances in 1986 While Coal and Resource Business Challenges Persist

Because of the C&NW-UP entry into the Powder River Basin, 1986 would be another year of significant BNRR coal revenue loss due to lost contracts and lower prices for new and renewed contracts. Unfortunately, as the year was unfolding the grain business was not expected to rebound from depressed 1985 levels which would put added pressure on rail income. This renewed cost reduction pressures as well as a renewed emphasis on being aggressive in the retention of existing business and the securement of new business over a rail operating plant that had even more excess capacity than 1985. In addition, reductions in oil and gas prices were pressuring valuations of BNI's oil and gas properties.

While celebrated, the promotion of Greenwood brought about a strange feeling in the IBU because his full-time presence and direct leadership were lost after four years. The IBU leadership team still reported to him but he was not nearly as accessible as in the past. Regardless, given the competitive challenges the company was faced, the emphasis was to continue prudently growing the business while exercising prudent cost control.

1986 IBU Goals

Specific 1986 IBU goals[535] included:

-   Achieve gross revenue of $346.5 MM, Margin of $95.4 MM, and Margin ROA (Hub) of 70%.
-   Expand implementation of Expediter type train service to at least one additional corridor by July 1, in addition to RoadRailer.
-   Coordinate RoadRailer development with other business units to secure at least one new major commitment for an ongoing movement for Mark IV or Mark V technology.
-   Establish customer service/quality control capability for hub centers by October 1
-   Develop and implement a contracted composite labor force for at least one hub by December 31.
-   Increase Intermodal non-equipment productivity by at least 7% by lowering non-equipment RESBU expense per revenue unit handled to $66 from $70.40 in 1985.
-   Increase Intermodal equipment productivity by at least 5% by lowering non-auto equipment RESBU expense per revenue unit handled to $109 from $115 in 1985.
-   Increase the attractiveness of using BN intermodal by implementing a one-page transportation contract by February 1, a direct payment option by June 1, and by providing an insurance option by Sept. 1.
-   Broaden Intermodal's customer base by signing the following to transportation contracts to move an average of the following number of revenue units per month, each:
    -   75 TBCA Brokers … Average 20 units per month each
    -   20 AISA members … average 10 units per month each
    -   30 Class I General Commodity Motor Carriers (Top 100) … 20 units
    -   100 other Class I Carriers … Average 20 units per month each

---

[535] Internal BN Document, Burlington Northern Intermodal Department 1986 Goals, *Greenwood Collection*, Barriger Library at UMSL.

15 Private Fleet operators
- Complete Intermodal's strategic information systems plan by February 15 in conjunction with the Nolan, Norton & Co. project and initiate design and implementation of Intermodal information systems plan priority and schedule.

The IBU revenue goal only applied to domestic business because Murry Watson had accountability for international business. RESBU was the name for BN's internal responsibility budgeting system. The TBCA is the Transportation Brokers Conference of America which represented mostly truck brokers – the goal was to expose them to BN's intermodal capabilities and solicit their business. The AISA is the American Institute for Shippers Associations – the goal was to directly call on members who were not BN clients.

Information Systems Initiative – Next Steps

The IBU goals accompanied a 1986 list of things BN Intermodal must do well that were developed as part of the comprehensive information systems project with NNC. The whole purpose of the information systems initiative was to focus efforts so that systems were designed around the needs of the business and BN Intermodal's customers. This was more effective than having systems that the business had to build its processes around as had been done previously. These "Must Do Wells"[536] included:

- *We must provide consistent, reliable, damage-free service.*
- *We must consistently provide products that are superior to those of our competitors. Customers must be assured that their freight will arrive damage-free and on schedule.*
- *We must identify and meet the needs of our current and target markets.*
- *We must effectively segment our markets and develop a thorough understanding of the needs of target segments. Our products must be tailored to those needs. Information must be communicated to the sales force on a timely basis to respond to our customers. Overall, we must be easy to do business with.*
- *We must cost effectively control our equipment on and off rail.*
- *We must maintain a balance of equipment between hubs and effectively match train cars and trailers. Trailer performance must be monitored and controlled. Equipment flexibility (e.g. lift capability) must be provided at hubs.*
- *We must improve responsiveness to customer inquiries.*
- *We must have accurate information on our customers and on the freight we carry. Communications with customers must use the most effective means – phone, paper or electronic.*
- *We must innovate and differentiate in products, service and equipment.*
- *We must differentiate our products according to market needs to provide our customers with viable service options. We must develop new ways of handling freight and equipment at hubs. Overall we must develop and maintain a culture and infrastructure which supports innovation; we must be receptive to new technology.*
- *We must accurately measure and control volume, revenue and costs.*
- *We must accurately measure volume, revenue and costs by corridor, train and hub. Freight movement must be balanced over time to avoid periods of over-demand or movement of empty cars. Pricing is one method by which we can affect timing and routing of freight.*

---

[536] Internal BN Intermodal document, *Greenwood Collection*, Barriger Library at UMSL.

- *We must accurately forecast volume, revenue and costs.*
- *We must understand the dynamics of our markets and be able to develop models and forecasts of volume, revenue and costs by corridor, train and hub. New facilities and equipment must be available to meet market demand. Capital investments must be justified to assure adequate return to shareholders.*
- *We must develop and apply quantitative success measures for Intermodal.*
- *We must determine the proper indicators and measurements of success for business activities and facilities (e.g. hubs, satellites). Management should be decentralized to provide sufficient authority to those responsible for meeting success targets.*

Every item on the "Must Do Wells" list started with the customer and revolved around accurate and timely information. The IBU had taken the initiative to drive the process of consistently getting it for customers, itself, and support organizations, who participated directly in the process.

The final presentation of the results of the strategic systems project was delivered to Gaskins, Greenwood, the IBU leadership team, the leaders of the Information Systems Department (ISSD) and the Finance and Accounting Department on January 30, 1986 (prior to the February 15 goal). Although it presented a daunting challenge, it was received well and a joint IBU/ISSD systems development effort was approved.

Meetings to review the IBU's 1986 strategic direction were held with the broader organization in Ft. Worth on February 3, Atlanta on February 4, Chicago on February 5 and Seattle on February 6. Systems architecture and development meetings with ISSD were held throughout the first quarter. Arthur Anderson was brought in to assist in the design and development of the Intermodal Business Information System (IBIS) that would include the service and activity-based financial measurement systems included in the systems architecture. An orientation presentation was conducted for ISSD staff in St. Paul to better familiarize them with BN's intermodal customers, their needs, the competition and the nature of the intermodal business.[537]

In January the Internal Audit Department was asked to audit the Expediter operation to verify that it was in actuality generating positive BN cash flow. That audit started in March.[538]

Greenwood Attempts to Hire John Gray[539]

There was still a major BN organization void. Since Bill Greenwood's promotion in mid-November of 1985 a search had been underway for his replacement. Greenwood's preferred choice to replace him was John Gray who had run Western Pacific Railroad's intermodal business and was the person the IBU turned to for help with the innovative Seattle International Gateway operating arrangement. He was considered one of the best minds in the intermodal business and he got the right things done the right way. Gray shared the IBU vision of what had to be done to develop and run the intermodal business in a way that was best for customers and shareholders. Unfortunately (for BN), there were two primary factors that made it unworkable for him. The first is that he owned and ran successful intermodal terminal operations and consulting businesses he did not want to relinquish. In addition, working for BN

---

[537] Mark Cane's personal calendar.
[538] Ibid.
[539] John Gray interview with Mark Cane, April 21, 2022.

would have entailed a significant pay cut if he had to discard his other ventures. Yet, he really got along well with Greenwood and was still intrigued by the opportunity to help a railroad optimize their intermodal business. The second was that even though the job appealed to him, and given his entrepreneurial drive, he was concerned that railroad bureaucracy and traditional thinking would prevent the IBU from achieving its potential. Greenwood told him he could put his businesses in a blind trust to get over the first hurdle.[540] Gray could not come to grips with how to totally disengage physically or, from the standpoint of an image, of him having a conflict of interest even with a blind trust so he withdrew himself from consideration. BN's Intermodal history would have been much different if it had worked out between BN and John Gray in 1986.

Steve Nieman Hired to Lead the IBU

In April, Steve Nieman was recruited from Consolidated Freightways (CF) to lead the IBU. CF was one of the largest Less than Truckload (LTL) motor carriers in the United States. The CF LTL operation utilized Teamster labor and, as much as possible, utilized intermodal (including BN) for line-haul substitution. The Teamster's National Master Freight labor agreement restricted unionized carriers to a maximum intermodal substitution of 6% of their total shipment miles. CF also operated non-union regional truckload services (Conway) and a freight brokerage (CF Forwarding) that was a third party customer of BN Intermodal. Given the IBU's pursuit of motor carrier industry customers, the bet was that Nieman would aid the endeavor. In addition, the operation of an LTL network was similar to the hub and spoke system BN had established. As with BN's hubs, LTL terminals operated with a local sales and operating focus with the terminal team evaluated with a local P&L. Those similarities added to the rationale for his hiring. When asked why he hired Nieman, Bill Greenwood said:

> *Aside from a background I was looking for he had a good track record on his resume and his references checked out. He was personable and I thought he had a personality that would mesh with the personality of the IBU. He seemed to embrace the intermodal vision in a way that would continue its advancement. I wasn't totally comfortable with him and because it was such an important position to fill I would have liked to have taken more time to interview more candidates. Darius was impatient. He was comfortable with him and kept pressuring me to act quickly – he said just do it so, without being totally comfortable, I did.*[541]

Nieman had a steep learning curve to conquer and the members of the IBU leadership team did their best to get him up-to-speed quickly. It was clear that the RoadRailer service for GM between Chicago and St. Louis would not be viable financially. The Cicero Hub needed an expansion. Additional BN double stack car capacity was needed. APL was expanding its double stack train service that was being fed domestic business through its acquisition of National Piggyback. On April 26, the Board of Sea-Land approved its acquisition by CSX Corporation for $28 per share, subject to ICC approval. Sea-Land had been under pressure from activist investor Harold Simmons and CSX acted as Sea-Land's "white knight" with its $742 million acquisition.[542] While the Springfield Region Expediter service was being audited, negotiations were underway to expand Expediter services to other Operating Regions. The Intermodal Information Systems effort was moving rapidly. Hubs were expanding the use of Highway Satellites.

---

[540] Bill Greenwood interview with Mark Cane, March 22, 2022.

[541] Ibid.

[542] *New York Times*, Sea-Land, CSX, April 26, 1986, accessed from: https://www.nytimes.com/1986/04/26/business/sea-land-csx.html, on May 14, 2022.

Discussions were underway with connecting railroads about the possibility of expansion into their networks. The IBU had "taken over marketing of the Dallas Smith trailers and will soon begin intermodal movement of Ford automobiles from the Chicago area to the Pacific Northwest, according to Jerry Taylor, a spokesman for BN's automotive marketing unit."[543]

Dick Lewis, who had been AVP Marketing Services, was promoted to Sr. AVP Strategic Planning after Lyle Reed was transferred, by Darius Gaskins, to the Seattle Region as General Manager under Bill Francis. To fill Lewis' spot, Bill Greenwood tapped Bill DeWitt and he left the IBU in April, leaving his Director Intermodal Marketing position vacant. While the pace of developments was typical for the IBU, it was a lot for Nieman to digest, especially given that he was new to the railroad industry, new to BN, and new to the intermodal business.

IBU Organization Issues

As mentioned earlier, the sales function for BN's Intermodal services was very fractured and dysfunctional. In January, with Bill Greenwood's blessing,[544] Bill DeWitt contracted with Dave Craven to conduct an analysis of the sales organization as it related to Intermodal. Craven, who was highly regarded in logistics circles, was a marketing professor at Texas Christian University in Ft. Worth.

In addition, Mark Cane had been responsible for the small Intermodal team led by Gordon Trafton that interfaced with marketing, sales and operations for issues related to existing and potential train service. The team was overwhelmed because BN's Intermodal train network had grown from seven dedicated and two non-dedicated trains by the end of 1983 to 29 dedicated (with the early 1986 addition of RoadRailer service for General Motors between Chicago and St. Louis) and 13 non-dedicated trains by March 25, 1986.

Cane had been an advocate for the adoption of a "product management" framework within Intermodal that would expand the service quality and P&L focus that existed in the Hubs with the Hub Managers to something similar for Intermodal service within BN's corridors. The appointment of Don Meyer to lead the Springfield Region Expediter Project was a trial utilization of that organizational philosophy. Given the continued need for even more dedicated Intermodal trains and the likelihood of an expansion of Expediter services off of the Springfield Region, he believed the IBU needed advocates for corridor services that would act like product managers in a company such as Procter and Gamble for products such as *Tide* detergent, or General Mills for *Wheaties* cereal. The product or brand managers for those products "owned" them and advocated for them. Their success was measured against the success of their product or brand. He was advocating for a point of "ownership" and accountability for the service levels and P&Ls of BN's Intermodal trains. Given the advances that were being made with the information systems initiative, at least rudimentary tools needed to have the service quality and financial performance measurements to enable such an organizational emphasis was within reach. Among others, Cane had a lengthy meeting with Steve Nieman on April 28 to lay out the rationale for such an organizational emphasis as well as how the IBU could be organizationally restructured to address this as well as the other organizational needs that had come about due to how the business was growing and evolving.[545]

---

[543] Jacobus, William W., *Fleet Owner*, Intermodal – BN Relies on Truckers to Run Hub Centers, February 1986.
[544] Bill Greenwood personal calendar, January 3, 1986.
[545] Mark Cane personal calendar.

In addition, in the IBU's equipment group there was no control over trailer repair and maintenance. This work was controlled by the Mechanical Department who also controlled freight car and locomotive repair and maintenance. In July of 1985, Bill Berry proposed to the Mechanical group that responsibility for trailers should belong to Intermodal because trailers were solely an IBU asset.[546] Mechanical said no to his request because "their job" was repair and maintenance.[547] Berry's point was that maintenance of trailers was fractured from the IBU's accountability for the overall management of BN's trailer assets. His point was that a similar argument was thrown in the path of the IBU's desire to have equipment distribution included in the IBU. The Transportation Department at the time said it was their job to manage equipment distribution. Yet, when the function was transferred to the IBU and a holistic business process (rather than strictly functional) orientation was employed, the integrated IBU focus brought about significantly improved equipment availability/order-fill rates while at the same time generating an annualized $3 million in equipment cost reductions per year. With the promotion of Greenwood, this subject was pursued again on February 12.[548]

Finally, Cane was also responsible for the IBU's information systems efforts. The Nolan Norton initiative had been extremely time-consuming. With the completion of that effort, and the authority to pursue the resulting prioritized systems development efforts, the work load was growing exponentially. There was an urgent need for full-time and sole-focused leadership of that effort.

By April the dedicated information systems leadership void was filled with the transfer of Jack Round from Sales to Director Intermodal Systems. He was a physically imposing and boisterous, chain-smoking man with an incredible sense of urgency which made him perfect for the job. By May, ten months after Bill Berry had initiated his effort, and with the "coercion" of Bill Greenwood, Duane Reckinger was transferred from Mechanical to Berry's team in the IBU as Manager TOFC/COFC Equipment Maintenance. He was also perfect for the job and in the ideal organizational location to thrive. Round's availability was made possible by Bill Greenwood's elimination of a separate Sales function in April and the incorporation of Sales into each business unit. In April, Bill DeWitt (before moving to Marketing Resources) brought in the highly regarded and experienced Marv Dowell to serve as Market Manager Field Marketing and the Hub Account Managers finally started to report solely to Hub Managers. The lane management challenges were yet to be dealt with.[549]

RoadRailer Venture Transferred to Norfolk Southern

The Chicago Region and IBU were successful in getting a reduced operating crew size agreement and, as previously mentioned, it was utilized to put the RoadRailer trailers the BN had rescued from the NAC bankruptcy to work. In January, RoadRailer service was initiated for General Motors to move parts from the Detroit area to GM's Wentzville plant outside of Louis. The intent was for it to be a joint operation with the GTW Railroad but they declined to participate. Because of the high drayage costs between Chicago and Detroit, combined with the relatively short rail length of haul, the service was not financially viable. The IBU worked with General Motors and Norfolk Southern who had a direct GM

---

[546] Letter from Bill Berry to R. L. Coulter, July 15, 1985, *Greenwood Collection*, Barriger Library at UMSL.

[547] Letter from R.E. Taylor to W.E. Greenwood, August 19, 1985, *Greenwood Collection*, Barriger Library at UMSL.

[548] W. K. Berry letter to Mr. W. E. Greenwood, February 12, 1986, *Greenwood Collection*, Barriger Library at UMSL.

[549] Mark Cane's personal calendars and 1996 IBU organization charts, *Greenwood Collection*, Barriger Library at UMSL.

plant to GM plant rail route between Detroit and St. Louis, to see if NS would be interested in taking over the operation.

> *Ed Kreyling, Norfolk Southern's Vice President of Marketing, took up the case for RoadRailer and sold the corporation on establishing the operation. NS took over the BN operation in July of 1986 and subleased the 220 RoadRailer units under a short term lease.*[550]

As Larry Gross mentioned earlier, this was the genesis for Norfolk Southern's "Triple Crown" service which grew into a significant Conrail/Norfolk Southern subsidiary operating a RoadRailer network primarily east of the Mississippi River. Unlike BN, the NS had a franchise much better suited to RoadRailer operation with its larger population and industrial activity centers. Therefore, while an eye was open for other RoadRailer opportunities, active development efforts were put on the back-burner in favor of other initiatives.

The RoadRailer saga again pointed out one of the biggest, if not THE biggest, strategic weakness that BN's Intermodal business faced. Its underlying franchise was the weakest among the major United States railroads. The RoadRailer technology was good but it did not fit well within the territory where BN trackage was located.

Chicago Hub Situation

A meeting was held on August 11, 1986 at the Cicero Hub with members of the IBU and local and regional Operations Department staff members to review the Chicago Intermodal terminal capacity situation and outlook. In an August 13 memo[551], Dave Burns noted that the Western Avenue operation that housed Sea-Land was handling an annual rate of 60,000 lifts compared to its theoretical capacity of 72,000. The combined Ogden (south side) and CECO (north side) operation would have a theoretical capacity of 380,000 annual lifts after the completion of the 1986 capital expenditure project. At the time the forecast was for Ogden/CECO to have demand for 336,000 lifts in 1986, 370,000 in 1987 and 407,000 in 1988. As of this time forecasts had not yet been adjusted for the likely possibility of added Expediter services such as between Chicago and Midway.

There were several action items that came out of the meeting including an analysis of expansion into the Clyde Roundhouse area, added expansion into the rail yard, local property acquisition and the substitution of "steel" interchange with eastern railroads in place of "rubber interchange." Because the Chicago rail terminal complex was so congested it was extremely difficult to accomplish time and cost effective interchanges between western and eastern railroads in Chicago. Therefore a majority of the less-than-trainload business between carriers was grounded and trucked between terminals in order to meet customer service requirements. This substitute trucking was referred to as "rubber interchange" as opposed to steel -wheel interchange.

---

[550] DeBoer, pp 131, 133.
[551] D. H. Burns, Memorandum, Chicago Hub Center, August 13, 1986, *Greenwood Collection*, Barriger Library at UMSL.

IBU Organization Restructuring

On July 23, 1986 Steve Nieman issued letters to all IBU employees as well as to the leaders of BN's other business units announcing a major IBU organization change. With minor tweaks, the organization had remained relatively stable since 1982 while the three major strategies related to Hubs, new equipment technologies and dedicated trains, and marketing packages were implemented. By 1986 the business had grown and evolved to the point that a major organization redesign was warranted. Nieman's letter read: [552]

> *The following is a summary of Intermodal organization changes that will be effective by August 1.*
>
> *As of August 1, the District Manager layer is being eliminated. The Chicago, Seattle, Denver, Portland, Memphis, Irving and Birmingham Hubs and Axel Holland will report directly to Dave Burns. The remaining fifteen Hubs will report directly to Axel. At the time the District Manager positions were created it was intended they exist to facilitate the development of the Hub network and integrate newly hired Hub Managers into the railroad organization. Dennis Larson, Ray Robinson and Julian Woolford have done an excellent job of accomplishing what we set out to do. Dennis will remain in St. Paul as Manager – Hub Development, reporting to Axel Holland, to provide system-wide support on activities such as Hub relocations, construction projects and coordination of operations with connecting railroads. Julian will assume responsibility for the Pasco Hub for Gay Minnich who along with Ray Robinson is transferring to Ft. Worth.*
>
> *As of July 16, Bill Berry's responsibilities have been expanded to include Planning. Gary Agnew now reports to Bill and is responsible for all forecasting and budgeting for the department. Ned Treat now heads an Operations Research / Industrial Engineering section reporting to Bill which will include an Industrial Engineer and an individual responsible for data control. Also, Lee Springer and Bob Atwell now report to Bill. (note – Springer had been responsible for Hub lift equipment maintenance and Atwell had been responsible for Hub contract administration and budgeting, both reporting to Burns.)*
>
> *Marv Dowell now reports directly to me as Director – Field Marketing.*
>
> *Mark Cane is now responsible for all facets of Marketing except Field Marketing as Bill DeWitt's former position has been eliminated. Bruce Herndon retains responsibility for marketing to carriers but his scope of responsibility has been increased to cover rail and water carriers (domestic business) in addition to motor carriers. Don Buchholz has transferred from John Hall's group to Intermodal and will concentrate on rail carrier marketing, under Bruce. Norm Brehm retains responsibility for marketing to Agents, Brokers and Associations. In addition, Norm assumes responsibility for administration of contracts, price quotes, the rules memorandum, etc.*
>
> *As of August 1, we will begin full scale "product management" thanks to the success of Don Meyer and his team with this management approach with the Expediter. Don will assume responsibility for our Northern Lanes which basically is between the Midwest and Pacific Northwest. Ray Robinson will assume responsibility for the Central Lanes, that is the Mississippi*

---

[552] Steve Nieman, Letter to All Intermodal Employees, July 23, 1986, *Greenwood Collection*, Barriger Library at UMSL.

> *River territory (including the existing Expediters) and the Pacific Northwest – Southeast territory. Gay Minnich will be responsible for the Western Lanes, including Pacific Northwest – Texas and Chicago – Denver. Their responsibilities will include overall service and profitability within their assigned service areas.*
>
> *These changes … have been made to better address our challenges and opportunities in the marketplace. Although organization charts show solid functional lines I want to stress that Intermodal will continue to behave more as a flexible matrix organization with human resources targeted to opportunities. That is, there have been and will continue to be many dotted lines.*
>
> *You may notice there are a few more positions now than before. Despite the pressure for "count" reductions, Bill Greenwood agreed to the above changes and net position increase given that the overall Intermodal salary expense would not increase. This was accomplished through trade of authorized, vacant higher grade positions for several lower grade positions. Unlike reorganizations in other parts of the railroad, this one was accomplished without loss (in fact a slight gain) of Intermodal jobs. This is a credit to your efforts to make Intermodal a success and indicates top management's confidence in our ability to continue generating profitable Intermodal growth.*

Nieman's letter referred to "pressure for 'count' reductions." Given the continued loss of BN coal business to the C&NW-UP and another poor grain year the company was under significant cost reduction pressure. Intermodal was essentially the only business segment in the company that was growing and Gaskins and Greenwood supported the rationale provided by the IBU for not starving it. Mark Cane added, "We teased Bill DeWitt that we traded him for two analysts."

Three more significant features of the reorganization were not mentioned in Nieman's letter. First, Jack Round was given increased direct support for the Intermodal information systems effort with three small teams to focus on operating support systems, marketing support systems and revenue management/pricing support systems in coordination with the Information Systems Department. Second is the "loss" of Gordon Trafton to the Transportation Department. Hunter Harrison had been transferred from VP Transportation to VP Chicago Region and Joe Galassi assumed Harrison's position. Trafton was recruited to report to Galassi in Overland Park, earning a well deserved promotion to Director of Operations Service Planning. While the IBU "lost" Trafton, he was now in an even better position to help the new IBU Lane Market Managers. The third was the repair of the fracture between the Hub Managers and the Hub sales effort. The original Hub design called for Hub sales people to report to the Hub Manager and, as previously mentioned, after four years of parochial organizational opposition it was finally accomplished through Bill Greenwood.

Initiation of Lane Management

On August 4 Robinson and Minnich began their service as Lane Market Managers, joining Don Meyer who actually started his service for the Northern Corridor in conjunction with Expediter service planning between Chicago and Midway. Cane and Meyer held service awareness meetings with Seattle Region field staff in Portland on July 8, Pasco on July 9 and Seattle on July 10 during which the Lane Management concept was described and a review of BN's intermodal business was given. It was stressed that Meyer and his team had broad commercial responsibility for BN's Northern Corridor Intermodal train service and that his team would also be handling IBU related train schedule issues that used to be handled by Gordon Trafton and his team. Similar meetings were held between the appropriate Lane Market Manager and the Transportation staff in Overland Park on September 2 and with staffs of the Chicago Region on September 4, Springfield Region on September 12, Twin Cities Region on September 13, and Denver Region on September 22 (timed to coincide with a Denver Hub open-house related to completion of its capacity expansion). Another Lane Market Management meeting occurred with the International Intermodal staff in Seattle on September 24.[553]

With the exception of the supportive Chicago Region, at all of the meetings the tenor was civil but there was an underlying (and unfortunately expected) tone of the need for the IBU to "stay in its lane." This echoed the reaction Bill Greenwood had received when he wanted responsibility and accountability for terminal and equipment management when the IBU was formed, the reaction Gordon Trafton had received from Transportation in the pre-Hunter Harrison days and the response Bill Berry received from System Mechanical when he logically sought responsibility and accountability for trailer repair.

New Expediters and the Prospect of a Detroit Expediter and IBU Hub

In June, Expediter service started between Chicago and Memphis and in early September it started between Chicago and Midway.[554] The Chicago–Midway Expediter had two vocal proponents. One was UPS who had witnessed the incredible on-time performance (98-99% on-time from cut-off to availability) of the original Expediter network and were interested in rail substitution between Chicago and the Twin Cities. The other was Hunter Harrison who was also gung-ho for the Chicago–Memphis leg. After he became VP of the Chicago Region, he and the IBU discussed potential Expediter opportunities on his region after the original network had proven itself. Recalling that the Expediter initiative was as much a labor relations effort as an effort to generate free cash flow on an underutilized physical plant, the following quotes from Harrison add more context: [555]

> In the case of the Chicago-Twin Cities Expediter trains, Harrison recalls, "the labor leaders said they understood, but there was no way they could sell it to their people. So we went to various locations and had mass meetings with them. We told them what we wanted, let them vent their emotions, told them what we saw happening, tried to be honest with them. We went back several times and were finally successful."

> He believes operating people ought to know more about the marketing side of the business, but to do that "you don't have to go into the Marketing department; just talk to the customers." Recently the Chicago Region held a three-day open house for customers to help promote the Chicago – Memphis and Chicago – Twin Cities Expediter services. "We had all our people – mechanical, engineering, operating, human resources and all – out there with the customers. It was amazing the opportunities we found, the dialog we created, just sitting down with customers and finding out what's going on."

---

[553] Mark Cane's personal calendar.

[554] Burlington Northern Railroad, *BN News*, September-October, 1986, pp. 4-5, *Greenwood Collection*, Barriger Library at UMSL.

[555] Shedd, Tom, *Modern Railroads*, Burlington Northern: Aggressive, Innovative – and Thoroughly Non-Traditional, November, 1986, p. 36.

Negotiations were also underway to obtain Expediter labor agreements elsewhere on the Chicago Region, on the Seattle Region between Seattle and Portland and on the former Colorado & Southern (C&S) between Denver and Irving and the Fort Worth and Denver (FW&D) between Irving and Houston. In addition to the Chicago – Midway segment, the Denver–Irving segment was especially desired by UPS. The IBU had meetings with UPS as early as February 18[556] about the possibility of serving them. It would take work on their part with the Teamsters union and on the IBU's part to secure a labor agreement but, unlike other corridor segments, Denver-Irving did not have significant excess capacity due to a high volume of coal trains. C&NW-UP access into the PRB primarily cut into BN coal market share into the Midwest but not Texas. This created added challenges for developing a schedule that could meet UPS needs for consistency and reliability around their DFW and Denver facility sort schedules while at the same time not increasing BN's costs to operate coal trains.

One additional potential Expediter prospect was totally unconventional. Its background revolved around a business development between Ford Motor Company and Mazda. Ford had opened the Michigan Casting Center in the Detroit suburb of Flat Rock in 1972. Ford had established a strategic manufacturing alliance with Mazda (as GM had done with Toyota and Chrysler had done with Mitsubishi), and in 1985 they started construction of a new plant on that site that would manufacture Mazda MX-6 and Ford Probe coupes starting in September of 1987.[557] Ralph Muellner (BN's Director International Marketing) had been working with Mazda on the possibility of utilizing BN's Common-User double stack train service to handle their import parts destined for that plant for production of both Ford and Mazda vehicles. Ideally such a move would run all the way to Detroit over rail, but such a short haul between Chicago and Detroit didn't interest the GTW, Conrail or NS railroads except at a revenue-division level that would make it unattractive for BN. In addition, regular railroad-to-railroad steel-wheel interchange service through Chicago was not just bad – it was also terribly inconsistent. The cost to run the containers over the highway from Chicago to Detroit was also unattractive so Muellner asked the IBU service team if they could help. Mark Cane recalled:[558]

> *Our Expediters were creating quite a stir in the rail industry in 1986. Building on that, I initiated discussions with Andy Kalabus (who was in charge of intermodal marketing on the Grand Trunk Western Railroad) to see if the GTW might be interested in a novel business arrangement to win Mazda's business plus other business between Detroit and points west. The first meeting was held in Detroit on June 10. I explained to Kalabus what BN's Expediter service was all about. I carried him through the steps the IBU had gone through to justify the service, how the labor negotiation strategy worked, and how the financial performance of the business was measured with the IBU's new activity-based costing system. Mazda's business was discussed as well as other intermodal market opportunities between Detroit and points on the BN network. I planted the seeds with Kalabus about the possibility of the GTW negotiating a Detroit–Chicago Expediter-type labor agreement, the possibility of BN establishing a GTW operated BN Expediter into Detroit, and the establishment of a physical BN presence in GTW's Detroit intermodal facility (with a BN Hub Manager). In addition, I proposed a novel financial arrangement where revenue would not be divided according to the traditional division of movement route miles, but instead on a mileage division related to activity-based long-range train margins after coverage of activity-based operating costs were calculated on a like-basis. This was a lot to digest. I*

---

[556] Mark Cane personal calendar

[557] Wikipedia, Flat Rock Assembly Plant, accessed from:
https://en.wikipedia.org/wiki/Flat_Rock_Assembly_Plant#cite_note-5, on April 8, 2022.

[558] Mark Cane's recollection supplemented with meeting notes and personal calendar information.

explained how the IBU's new costing system worked, how such a new operation and means of doing business could work and asked Kalabus to think about it and "take the temperature" of GTW senior management to see how they might receive it. I closed by saying that the rail industry had, since its inception, operated its interline relationships on a "zero-sum-game" basis where "the more I can get out of you the better it is for me." I said the IBU was interested in the possibility of a relationship where the GTW was actually operating, and being rewarded, as an extension of BN's intermodal network in a true win-win way where both carriers thought and acted as one while maintaining their independence.

IBU Service Performance Measurement

The railroad industry had decades of experience measuring passenger and freight service through the benchmark of on-time train performance. As indicated above, the IBU promoted its Expediter service performance with a cutoff-availability measure. It didn't matter whether the origin or destination point for measurement was a rail hub or highway satellite hub, for the IBU's customers. What was important was whether the trailer or container was available for pick-up or tendered for delivery within the IBU's published service parameters. While train performance was important, it didn't matter if a train was on-time but trailers and containers were unavailable.

BN's service measurement systems were built around train performance so one of the major information systems initiatives was to have the ability to capture data for trailer and container performance both on and off rail. With the Lane Management teams there was a focal point for the establishment of Hub service profiles that showed "negotiated" cutoff-availability performance standards between each hub. These standards were then utilized by the new Service Performance Measurement System (SPMS). The system surfaced significant problems with data integrity that resulted in much more work to be accomplished for the IBU to have the competitive information tools it needed.

Meanwhile, "negotiated" was the operative word. Not only did the System, Regional, Division and Terminal Operating groups have to commit to train service standards between Hubs. The Hubs had to commit to gate cutoff-times for arriving loads that gave them enough time to "ramp" a trainload of trailers and containers on the specific cars, on the specific tracks as they pre-blocked cars to minimize Operating Department switching. They had to commit to times they would "release" tracks of loaded cars to the Mechanical crews for inspection and Operating Department crews for train assembly and departure. The Hubs also had to work through their highway satellite Hubs to establish cutoff and availability criteria for operations between the satellites and their "Mother" Hub. The Hub had to make similar commitments related to grounding an entire train's trailers and containers for availability commitments for inbound shipments and drayage when delivery to a highway satellite was involved.

By July of 1986 the Lane Teams had accomplished this for all IBU rail and highway Hubs except for the satellite hubs at Missoula, Shelby, Wenatchee and Klamath Falls.[559] This information was published for the IBU sales team and customers. This actual measurement and management of shipments rather than just trains was later adopted by BN in its "Service by Design" (SBD) effort which will be mentioned later. SBD on the BN was the precursor for what became known as Precision Scheduled Railroading.

---

[559] Mark Cane letter to Steve Nieman, Mid-year 1986 goal accomplishment, July 3, 1986, *Greenwood Collection*, Barriger Library at UMSL.

Original Expediter Continuation? End Haul-Length Restrictions?

As the original Springfield Region Expediters approached their one-year anniversary, a decision had to be made whether to continue them. From the IBU's standpoint they had accomplished what they were intended to do as it related to bringing on new business and improving the image of intermodal in general and that of BN and BN's Intermodal business in particular. The Expediters had filled excess capacity, generated positive BN cash flow, and survived an internal audit. However, from the standpoint of the Springfield Region operating unions, an extension of the labor agreement still had to be approved for the service to continue.

One new thing the IBU desired was an elimination of the 700-mile length-of-haul restriction for business handled in Expediter service that was a part of the original Springfield Region agreement. The IBU was working on Expediter agreements without haul-length restrictions that could link Houston, Chicago, Galesburg, Minneapolis/St. Paul and Lincoln/Omaha to the network and the IBU had very little market share between these and the original Expediter markets.

On August 25, 1986, meetings were held with members of the operating unions in Tulsa and Kansas City, on August 26 in Memphis and on August 27 in Springfield.[560] At each session, Regional VP Bob Howery or Asst. VP Andy Thompson, assisted by Labor Relations Director Lyle Burk, reviewed the operating results for the services and the number of jobs they had created. They also stressed the superior quality of the new jobs. Mark Cane, who represented the IBU, added:[561]

> *I explained the competitive environment and how motor carriers were capitalizing on the ability to run 48' trailers. I told the employees that truckers were on the verge of becoming even more competitive with the authority to run longer (53') trailers. I compared the relative cost of truck versus rail operations with standard rail labor agreements versus the Expediter agreement. I explained how the IBU had penetrated markets off of BN's rail network through our satellites as part of an explanation of the impact the services created in the marketplace. I also shared a frank financial assessment of the financial performance of the services. I had to stress that the services did not meet their fully-allocated costs and that, while they had proven beneficial for BN's employees, they were also beneficial for BN's customers and shareholders as long as significant investments were not required to retain or grow the business. I expressed our desire to eliminate the haul-length restriction (but not the maximum train car count restriction), illustrating market potential if the network were extended to permit business into and out of the markets we wanted to extend to. I showed that BN had little to no traffic in these lanes for competitive cost and service reasons.*

> *Many questions were asked, and I gave honest answers. What especially impressed the employees is that BN management kept its word and continued to run the trains through the difficult start-up period when there were days when a train would be run with little to no business. Fortunately, the organizations in all locations voted to extend the labor agreements and remove the haul-length restrictions.*

---

[560] Mark Cane's personal calendar.
[561] Mark Cane's personal recollection.

While the original Springfield Region Expediter agreement was being modified and extended an effort was underway to sell BN's lines east of Memphis which would include the Birmingham and Mobile Hubs and the Memphis–Birmingham Expediter leg. These lines were generating very marginal returns from all BN business which made reinvestment in them challenging. Their sale was encumbered by a lien in the "Frisco First Mortgage." [562] This impediment contributed to the decision to retain the lines.

Hub Capital Investments

The Denver Hub was essentially rebuilt at a cost of $5.9 million. Additional investments included $4.7 million for Kansas City, $2.5 million for Irving (as previously mentioned) due to the inability to locate and justify an alternate site, and $1.2 million for Tulsa. [563] The investments at Kansas City, Irving and Tulsa were not dependent on Expediter business for their financial justifications but the investments did help reduce operating costs at these Hubs which improved Expediter business cash-flow.

BN Double Stack Service Capability

During 1986 K Line initiated its own double stack train service[564] over UP. This brought the total to four lines (APL, Sea-Land, Maersk, and K-Line) having their "own" trains operated with their own cars. In addition, the SP opened a 150 acre International Container Transfer Facility (ICTF) adjacent to the Los Angeles/Long Beach port complex which significantly increased their competitive power.[565]

By November, 1986 the IBU had "ownership" of 280 bulkhead-type double stack cars in its car fleet through both direct acquisition and extended Trailer Train commitments plus 30 more bulkhead-type cars were on order from Gunderson.[566] By the end of the year the industry would have 13,000 stack wells in service[567] and the BN IBU would have almost 24% of them, not including those utilized by Sea-Land.

This stack car capacity controlled by the IBU gave it the ability to offer Ralph Muellner's Common User train to more steamship line customers. The Common User train was a boon to Hanjin Container Lines who opened its first exclusive container terminal in Seattle in 1986[568] because it gave them the ability to experience double stack car service quality without having to manage it. This was important to them because that same year they resigned from the Asia North America Eastbound Rate Agreement (ANERA) meaning that it had to operate independently with their own ships (not share space on ships with other Conference members. Hanjin was unable to participate in subsidies offered by the South Korean

---

[562] Art Zaegle note to Bill Greenwood, August 27, 1986, attached to letter to Mr. R. L. Lewis from Arthur R. Zaegel. August 26, 1986, *Greenwood Collection*, Barriger Library at UMSL.

[563] Burlington Northern Railroad, *BN News*, September-October, 1986, pp. 4-5.

[564] Kawaskai Kisen Kaisha, Ltd., accessed from: https://www.company-histories.com/Kawasaki-Kisen-Kaisha-Ltd-Company-History.html , on April 7, 2022.

[565] DeBoer, p. 177.

[566] Shedd, Tom, *Modern Railroads*, Burlington Northern: Aggressive, Innovative – and Thoroughly Non-Traditional, November, 1986, p. 23.

[567] DeBoer, p. 160.

[568] Hanjin Shipping Co., Ltd., accessed from: https://www.company-histories.com/Hanjin-Shipping-Co-Ltd-Company-History.html, on April 7, 2022.

government because Sea-Land owned a minority position in them.[569] Not having to own and operate stack car services allowed them to target their capital to their core business. As of 1986, NYK and BN's predecessor GN had a working relationship for almost 100 years. Because their shipping service transactions were denominated in Dollars, NYK was experiencing a financial shock due to the doubling of the value of the Yen versus the U.S. Dollar between 1985 and 1987.[570] Not having to purchase their own stack car capacity was also extremely important to them. Hyundai established full container service between the Far East and Seattle at the same time so they also benefited.[571] Weyerhaeuser's Westwood Shipping Lines subsidiary launched a joint sailing agreement with Gearbulk Container Services in 1986 which allowed them to upgrade their eastbound Transpacific service to a weekly frequency[572] so the Common User train service was perfect for them too.

Jim Kelly Rejoins BN

Jim Kelly had joined BN as a management trainee following active duty service in the US Navy. Following his training program he served on the Chicago Region as an Asst. Trainmaster in Cicero (while Bill Greenwood was the Asst. Terminal Superintendent), Asst. TOFC/ COFC manager at the Cicero ramp and then Trainmaster in the Cicero terminal. He was then recruited to Trailer Train where he worked in a number of capacities including Manager of Industry Relations and Manager of Market Development. From these capacities he interacted with intermodal groups on all major railroads and other intermodal industry players, creating a treasure of connections.[573]

Kelly commented:[574]

> After I left BN I worked for Trailer Train for eight years. During that time I had a chance to get to know all of the railroads and their intermodal people and products. At practically every visit I made, my contacts would ask me, "What is BN's Intermodal group doing now?" I was really impressed with how the BN people were so customer focused and so trusted by their customer base. They were by far the most innovative of all the railroads and if I were to work for any railroad again I wanted it to be BN. Additionally, BN employees were allowed, and encouraged, to be creative to push for improvements for their company and customers. No other railroad trusted their people to exercise that privilege. On top of everything else their people had a high level of integrity – they were tough but fair. When they told you something you could trust that it was true. If they promised to do something you could trust that they would follow through.

In 1986 he was recruited by Ralph Muellner to bring his prior operating and Trailer Train experience and rejoin BN as International Marketing Manager in Chicago. One of the first things he encountered was that BN was running the Sea-Land and Common User Stack trains extremely well over the continent but interchanges with Eastern railroads in Chicago were a disaster. A second was that BN's relationship

---

[569] Ibid.

[570] Nippon Yusen Kabushiki Kaisha (NYK), accessed from: https://www.company-histories.com/Nippon-Yusen-Kabushiki-Kaisha-NYK-Company-History.html, on April 7, 2022.

[571] Wikipedia, HMM, accessed from: https://en.wikipedia.org/wiki/HMM_(company), on April 7, 2022.

[572] Westwood Shipping Lines, Subsidiary of Weyerhaeuser, accessed from: https://www.wsl.com/About/History, on April 7, 2022.

[573] Jim Kelly and Bill Greenwood Resumes.

[574] Jim Kelly interview with Mark Cane, September 22, 2022.

with the U. S. Customs Service, housed at Freight House 9, was rocky, at best, and it was reflected in the slow Customs clearances provided to IBU customers. While BN Intermodal was providing excellent transportation service the paperwork was causing service failures that jeopardized business.

Related to the second issue first, he arranged for a meeting between the Hub staff, the Customs Service and contacts he had made with the Midwest Foreign Commerce Agency. In Jim's words, "We fixed the problems in short order and the BN housed Customs Service became the best railroad Customs Facility in Chicago. It became a competitive advantage for us."[575]

Related to the first issue of horrible Chicago railroad interchanges, getting a fix for this problem was critical because the Cicero Hub did not have capacity to handle all of the business that had to be interchanged with Eastern railroads. Neither BN nor BN's customers could afford the cost associated with highway (rubber) interchanges. Kelly arranged a meeting with Chicago Region VP Hunter Harrison and the Chicago Region Service Manager John Carnahan. With his prior knowledge of general Chicago railroad operations Kelly explained to Harrison that if BN reestablished a physical connection with the Indiana Harbor Belt (IHB) Railroad at Congress Park, and if an interchange agreement were negotiated with them, BN double stack cars for interchange could be set out by BN at Congress Park and immediately be met by an IHB crew for delivery to Conrail. Harrison asked Carnahan if that made sense and Carnahan said it did. Harrison asked what it would cost to reestablish the physical connection and Kelly said he had gotten an estimate of $6,000 from Harrison's engineering staff. Harrison asked if Kelly could come up with the money and he said yes. Harrison said, "This is a no-brainer, let's get it done." Kelly got the money through the IBU, Harrison restored the interchange track, and Carnahan arranged for the IHB interchange agreement. Kelly then worked with Chicago Terminal Superintendent Dave Starling to improve the sets of cars to the Hub and delivery of cars to Western Avenue for Sea-Land, to the Pacella Western Electric facility and for connections to the Norfolk Southern and CSX.[576]

In addition, in 1985 Maersk established a dedicated stack train service between Tacoma and their Croxton, NJ facility.[577] Seeking a way to get BN participation in this business, Kelly utilized some of his former Trailer Train-related contacts. After the physical IHB connection was restored in 1986 he asked Maersk's Tom Cook what BN would have to do to gain some of this business. Kelly recalled:

> *Tom Cook said he was not happy with the UP/C&NW service and he would be willing to do a direct test of BN vs. UP service. If BN could beat UP he would award BN some of the business. He told me he would give the UP 20 loaded stack cars and BN 20 loaded stack cars at Tacoma for a head-to-head race to New Jersey and, "let's see who wins." John Carnahan and I called Conrails's VP of Operations who I got to know well while I was at Trailer Train. We told him about the Maersk opportunity and asked if he would be willing to arrange to have a crew to meet a trainload of Maersk business at the newly restored Congress Park connection. He said Conrail was having difficulty with their connection with the C&NW-UP and that he would be happy to do it because it would be much easier for Conrail. The test was arranged and Maersk released a trainload to the UP while the cars for BN were still being loaded. Despite the head-start advantage given to the UP, and facilitated by the clean IHB Conrail connection, the BN train*

---

[575] Jim Kelly letter to Mark Cane, April 11, 2022.
[576] Ibid.
[577] Maersk's one hundred years in the USA, 09 July 2019, accessed from: https://www.maersk.com/news/articles/2019/07/10/maersk-one-hundred-years-usa, on April 11, 2022.

was already being unloaded at the Croxton facility by the time the UP train arrived in the Croxton rail yard. As a result, BN won Croxton destined Maersk stack train business out of Tacoma.[578]

Domestic Containerization?

The IBU leadership team held a domestic containerization strategy session all morning on September 25. The railroad industry had a significant sunk cost in the domestic trailer infrastructure and domestic containerization would require a replacement of that infrastructure. That infrastructure would not just go away if domestic containerization were pursued.

APL was making waves in transcontinental lanes by working to fill their empty westbound 40' containers with domestic cargo through their acquisition of National Piggyback. In 1986 they were also experimenting with containers intended exclusively for domestic usage. They displayed the first 48' X 102" wide container at the Atlanta Intermodal Expo. At 12,000 pounds it was heavy and it had small 103" high doors compared to 110" high doors in highway (including intermodal) trailers. It also had large interior "knee braces" for the top pick castings.[579] All of these features hurt their competitiveness versus motor carriers. Such containers would not fit in the bulkhead-equipped stack cars operated by BN, the SP and Sea-Land but APL's cars lacked bulkheads and utilized ISO interbox connectors (IBCs) to connect containers in the top well position. While APL could accommodate larger containers in the top well of their stack cars, their container had what was deemed to be significant competitive weaknesses.

With the benefit of significant experience with various equipment technologies, in April of 1986 the IBU's planning team had completed an assessment of "the relative operating costs associated with various equipment technologies as a function of haul-length and business volume."[580] This analysis showed significant potential double stack benefits for BN's domestic business but that the "best" equipment was very situational. There were other factors that were discussed such as:

- Significant pressure was being exerted by the motor carrier industry to extend national legal trailer lengths to 53' so what length of domestic container, and double stack car well, should be planned for?
- Another major competitive threat was the risk that motor carriers would get authority to haul twin-48' trailers across the entire western Interstate Highway system. They already had authority in some states to handle Longer Combination Vehicles (LCVs) in configurations including twin-48' trailer "Turnpike Doubles" and in some western states "Rocky Mountain Doubles consisting of a trailer up to 48' long combined with a 28' trailer.[581] The American Trucking Association was promoting the idea of making their use comprehensive in the USA.
- While evidence was mounting through APL's experience that ISO IBCs would safely secure a top container in a stack car well, BN was still not convinced of its safety. While the IBU had done a lot to improve chassis management with its Chicago neutral pool, chassis and containers were still management intensive and space consuming compared to trailers.

---

[578] Jim Kelly letter to Mark Cane, April 11, 2022.
[579] DeBoer, pp. 167, 169.
[580] Mark Cane letter to Steve Nieman, Mid-year 1986 goal accomplishment, July 3, 1986, *Greenwood Collection*, Barriger Library at UMSL.
[581] James Gleick, *New York Times*, Accident Study Cites Double-Trailer Trucks, May 3, 1988.

- While a trailer required a one-and-done lift, a container required a lift to a chassis and in many cases lifts off a chassis to an on-site stacked container storage area and then more lifts to retrieve containers from storage. What would this mean for intra-Hub logistics and lift devices?
- To be competitive with motor carriers a domestic container would have to be 9'6" high and BN had clearance issues if two of those containers were stacked on top of one another in a stack car, including through the 7.8 mile long Cascade Tunnel between Seattle and Spokane and the bridge over the Mississippi River at Burlington, Iowa on the Chicago-Denver route.

The Santa Fe Railway's president Larry Cena had been a pioneer in the development of spine cars for the haulage of trailers and it was common knowledge that he, and therefore the Santa Fe, was essentially "married" to trailers. As Frailey pointed out:

> *Cena believed that double-stack transportation wasn't as cost effective as the Santa Fe's fleet of low-weight, low-slung, fuel-efficient but single level Fuel Foiler cars. As a result the Santa Fe all but boycotted double stack cars ...*[582]

Cena had a reputation as an industry leader and his views couldn't be totally ignored. In addition, among other things (as has been mentioned repeatedly), BN had a relatively poor domestic intermodal franchise outside of the Northern Corridor. Double Stack technology was beneficial in dense markets where there was enough volume to permit stacking to essentially allow two trainloads of business to be carried in the length of one train. There were few Hub market-pairs where volume made that possible.

As a result of these and other factors it was deemed that domestic containerization was both an opportunity and risk. It was a market phenomenon requiring close monitoring and continual reevaluation but, at that time, it was deemed not something for BN to dive into.

Dallas Smith Trailer

The BN had been actively testing the Dallas Smith trailer for the shipment of motor vehicles and utilizing them in revenue service since 1985. BNI had even purchased stock and further purchase options in the Dallas Smith Corporation in October, 1985. On July 18, 1986 BNI and Dallas Smith modified BNI's 1985 agreement to extend the schedule of dates for it to purchase additional Dallas Smith stock. This was done to allow additional time for testing of the trailers in revenue service.[583] By August 26, 1986 there were 184 trailers in service over BN serving nine automotive customers. BN was even going to sublease 50 trailers to the Union Pacific and Conrail for Chrysler.[584] On December 1, 1986, Chuck Wilkins of Ford Motor Company sent a letter to BN's Dan Flood expressing concerns.[585] He said, "early loss and damage statistics, while indicating a favorable downward trend, have not yet reached what we believe to be an acceptable level for this type of equipment." Wilkins also expressed other concerns:

---

[582] Bryant and Frailey, p. 367.

[583] Luino Dell'Osso, Jr. letter to Mr. Earl Dallas Smith, July 18, 1986, *Greenwood Collection*, Barriger Library at UMSL.

[584] Dallas Smith, Status Report of Customer Utilization of the Dallas Smith Trailer as of August 20, 1986, *Greenwood Collection*, Barriger Library at UMSL.

[585] C.F. Wilkins letter to Mr. T.D. Flood, December 1, 1986, *Greenwood Collection*, Barriger Library at UMSL.

- That a commitment by Dallas Smith to be able to accommodate large vehicles, like the Crown Victoria, would not meet its November 4 deadline and that a second generation trailer would be required.
- That the trailers still had not been modified, as promised, to allow shipment of 8 small vehicles.
- That the loading time per trailer has not met the promised 30 minute standard
- That Ford was unwilling to continue to pay a rate per vehicle shipped equivalent to the rate when utilizing conventional tri-level rail cars

On December 16, 1986 Dan Flood sent a letter to Wilkins informing him that, as of December 15, 1986, BN had suspended the Ford/BN test between Chicago and Seattle until, "Dallas Smith Engineering cured the deficient performance of the trailers and address the areas of concern stated in your letter."[586]

A Strained Relationship Builds Between BN and Trailer Train

Trailer Train Company was originally formed in 1955 by the Pennsylvania and Norfolk & Western Railroads and Rail-Trailer Company to be in the business of providing piggyback cars to its owning railroads and promote the use of rail piggyback. Among Burlington Northern predecessors, the Frisco purchased 500 shares of Trailer Train on May 4, 1956, and the CB&Q, NP and GN Railroads bought-in on October 26, 1956, April 28, 1960, and June 8, 1960 respectively, each owning 500 shares. By 1964 there would be one freight forwarder and 40 different railroad owners. Given the decline in the industry and subsequent bankruptcies and mergers, by July 6, 1987 there were only 17 separate railroad owners and BN owned 2,000 shares, slightly less than 10% of the company.[587] After its formation, BN's IBU developed what became, in many respects, a love-hate relationship with Trailer Train. The IBU was the only railroad managing its intermodal business through an integrated profit-accountable business unit. In addition, BN's IBU was the most innovative and aggressive in the industry when it came to running its business. Trailer Train gave the impression to IBU leaders that it was in a position to dictate how the intermodal business would be run.

For the first 30 years of its existence, "TTX had never paid out a cash dividend to its owners. It instead decreased its car hire rates for use of its equipment in order to operate on a "break even" basis, plus retained earnings in order to keep a solid credit rating."[588] Although Trailer Train promoted the belief that the pooling agreement they operated under resulted in the cheapest intermodal car expenses that railroads could obtain, the IBU found it compelling to acquire its own cars and it did so, to the chagrin of Trailer Train. As previously stated, BN also opposed Trailer Trains' subsidization of BN competitor APL and other non-owners of Trailer Train, unless they were an open-market leasing company. Bill Berry and Roger Simon of the IBU equipment team pushed the envelope, to the great discomfort of Trailer Train, for a reduction in Trailer Train's car hire and mileage rates for cars as well and everything else from maintenance costs to liberalizing per diem relief terms. As indicated in the following table, Trailer Train was not operating at a "break even" level through the adjustment of their car hire rates through 1986:

---

[586] T.D. Flood letter to Mr. C.F. Wilkins, December 16, 1986, *Greenwood Collection*, Barriger Library at UMSL.
[587] Panza, Dawson, Sellberg, pp. 53-65.
[588] Ibid, pp. 65-66.

Trailer Train Financial Metrics, 1981-1986 ($millions) [589]

	1981	1982	1983	1984	1985	1986
Revenue	492.4	445.0	433.4	481.5	450.0	463.0
Net Income	21.7	1.6	8.8	44.7	38.8	34.4
Long-term Debt	687.3	609.2	555.0	521.6	505.3	523.8
Retained Income	399.3	400.9	409.7	450.1	488.9	320.8

Bouncing back from the recession years of 1981-1983, Trailer Train generated net income of $44.7 million in 1984 and $38.8 million in 1985. BNRR did not have the ability to generate a true P&L for the IBU but Trailer Train, in all probability, generated significantly more after-tax net income on a fully-allocated cost basis than the IBU did. From BN's standpoint it made no sense for Trailer Train to retain all of those earnings and, if reductions in car hire rates were not agreed to, a dividend was encouraged. On March 14, 1986 the Trailer Train Board approved a $1,000 per share dividend to all shareholders ($19 million total) that was paid on April 1. This was worth approximately $1.9 million to BN. The company had $149 million of actual cash on hand after the dividend was paid. [590]

> Through the mid-1980s there were three heavily intertwined major issues confronting TTX senior management.
> 1. Overtures from parties outside the railroad industry, referred to as third-party investors, to purchase shares of TTX stock from its owner railroads.
> 2. Pressure from certain owner railroads to issue cash dividends to the shareowners.
> 3. A large disparity between the heaviest users of TTX equipment as compared to those members who owned the most stock due to the mergers and acquisitions.
>
> The goal of the-third party investors would be to sell out at a profit following an increase in the value of TTX's stock. They had no long-term interest in the company for the reasons for its existence. BN first offered to sell its 2,000 shares of Trailer Train stock back to the company on May 22, 1986. This offer was rejected, but it opened the door for more discussions regarding the prospect of selling the Company to outside investors. It was even suggested that Trailer Train make an initial public offering (IPO) of its stock. There were member railroads who wanted to take the cash; other member railroads were against any such sale. Two major allies of TTX (who did not want the company to be sold to non-railroad interests) were Stanley Crane of Conrail and Dick Davidson of UP. [591]

BN was still not satisfied with the April dividend. With no reductions in car hire rates forthcoming, BN pressed for a more substantial dividend payment at the end of 1986. At the December 4, 1986 Board meeting a dividend of $180 million was authorized for payment effective December 15, 1986. The Board authorized Trailer Train to fund the payment with the help of $80 million of revolving credit. [592] This dividend was worth approximately $18 million more to BN, bringing total 1986 BN dividend payments to approximately $20 million. It also made Trailer Train less attractive to outside investors.

---

[589] Ibid, p. 295.
[590] Ibid, p. 66.
[591] Ibid, p. 65.
[592] Ibid, p. 66.

Although the IBU highly-respected Trailer Train employees and valued the services Trailer Train provided, the 1986 dividends and BN's offer to sell its Trailer Train shares did not repair the testy relationship between the two companies.

ICC Rejects Proposed SF-SP Merger

"On July 24, a conclusive 4-1 vote of the Interstate Commerce Commission ordered the Santa Fe Southern Pacific Corp. to divest itself of either the Santa Fe or Southern Pacific Railroad. The two lines had been running separately pending the ICC vote, since the holding companies' merger three years ago. The company will challenge the decision blocking the planned railroad merger."[593] If the merger had been approved it would have ended the IBU's joint BN-ATSF service between the Southeast and California over Avard, OK, as well as a joint BN-SP Chicago–Southern California Intermodal service interlined over the Kansas City gateway.

Given that SFSP intended to challenge the ICC decision, BN worked up a Memorandum of Intent with SPSF that would have called for the following had the merger been subsequently approved:[594]

- BN to receive bridge trackage rights between Houston, Texas, and Colton, California, via the SP line running through El Paso and Phoenix. BN to have right to interchange traffic for through rail service with any carrier at Colton, El Paso and Houston
- BN entitled to locate an intermodal facility(ies) adjacent to SPSF trackage in Los Angeles. BN to receive trackage rights to operate COFC/TOFC trains between Colton and those Los Angeles intermodal facilities.
- BN entitled to utilize SPSF Intermodal Container Transfer Facility ("ICTF") serving the Los Angeles and Long Beach ports. BN to receive trackage rights to operate COFC trains between ICTF and Colton.
- In lieu of trackage rights, SPSF will handle BN traffic, as agent of BN, over the trackage rights lines described above.
- BN has option to exercise trackage rights for intermodal trains only, and simultaneously utilize the haulage and rate making authority for other types of traffic.
- BN to grant SFSP trackage rights between: Tulsa and Avard, Oklahoma; Oklahoma City and Tulsa, Oklahoma; Amarillo and Fort Worth, Texas; Fort Madison, Iowa and St. Louis, Missouri.

If BN had gained the trackage rights to Houston, Ralph Muellner was confident that given the strength of BN's relationship with Sea-Land, BN would be able to win $20-25 million of Sea-Land business as well as "all sorts of positive arrangements with CSX east of the Mississippi," for international business.[595]

---

[593] Burlington Northern Railroad, *BN News*, September-October, 1986, p. 3, *Greenwood Collection*, Barriger Library at UMSL.

[594] SFSP Merger Letter from Douglas J. Babb to D.W. Gaskins, Jr., W.E. Greenwood, A.M. Fitzwater, D.W. Scott, November 4, 1986, *Greenwood Collection*, Barriger Library at UMSL.

[595] Negotiations with SFSP, letter from Ralph Muellner to WEG (Bill Greenwood), November 11, 1986, *Greenwood Collection*, Barriger Library at UMSL.

Union Pacific Buys Overnite Transportation Company

On September 18, 1986, Union Pacific announced that it was buying Overnite Transportation Company for $43.25 per share ($1.2 billion in cash), a 39.5% premium to its pre-announcement valuation. A Los Angeles Times article said, "The combination will significantly strengthen Union Pacific's freight moving operations and provide the New York – based company with the framework to expand its intermodal – sea, rail, and truck – delivery system across the United States." UP's chairman, president and chief executive William Cook was quoted, "Overnite will be a natural fit with our railroad subsidiaries. There are substantial opportunities to utilize our existing rail system and customer base to support Overnite market growth and development in the West and Southwest." The article mentioned that Overnite operated four terminals in California – Fresno, Los Angeles, Oakland and Sacramento. Overnite chairman Harwood Cochrane was quoted, "With this new combination of rail and truck service, we'll certainly add terminals in California." The article added, "Wall Street analysts said Union Pacific's offer represents a diversification step that made sense for the company because of growing problems in the U.S. railroad industry. Railroads have been hurt by overcapacity and loss of revenue from troubled steel, grain and automotive sectors, which traditionally account for the bulk of rail freight. They are also under increasing competitive pressure to serve all of the customers in their delivery systems by relying on other modes of transportation such as trucking and shipping."[596]

The underlying competitive railroad industry conditions that the article quoted were essentially the same ones that the IBU had been preaching to BN, to mixed effect, since the 1981 Intermodal Task Force. The IBU team was asked what sense the acquisition made and what the competitive ramifications would be for BN. The reply was that Overnite was in the less-than-truckload business but concentrated in the eastern United States. It had not yet extended operations to the Pacific Northwest or Denver. Overnite was highly regarded and was a non-union carrier. BN had customers in the LTL business including Roadway, Consolidated Freightways (Steve Nieman's former employer) and Yellow Freight and they were heavily unionized. As mentioned previously, the Teamsters Master Freight Agreement restricted the proportion of business they and UPS could run via rail intermodal in substitute line-haul service but Overnite did not have that restriction. The overall belief was that the acquisition could make sense but it was a very expensive way to acquire a sales force. There was a risk that the lower cost and non-union Overnite could take share from the unionized carriers utilizing BN, but chances were greater that it would alienate UP from the other LTL carriers in that segment that BN was pursuing. The belief was also strong that Overnite would continue to be subject to unionization pressure so from the IBU's standpoint there were better uses of money. [597]

Competitive Situation Increases the Focus on Labor Costs

The 1986 *Modern Railroads* article focusing on BNRR included the following interchange with Darius Gaskins related to BN's situation with labor which the IBU was in the midst of: [598]

[596] *Los Angeles Times*, Nancy Yoshihara, Union Pacific Will Acquire Overnite for $1.2 Billion, September 19, 1986.
[597] Mark Cane's personal recollection, August 12, 2022.
[598] Shedd, Tom, *Modern Railroads*, Burlington Northern: Aggressive, Innovative – and Thoroughly Non-Traditional, November, 1986, pp. 21-22, *Greenwood Collection*, Barriger Library at UMSL.

Commenting on the environment in which BN finds itself, Gaskins notes that the "smokestack" economy, the world of many BN customers, has not done well in the last five years. "Basically there's a lot less rail freight out there than we had hoped there would be.

"At the same time competitive pressures are the strongest they've ever been and they won't let up. The trucking industry will continue to run mean and lean; it will get more competitive from new, lower-cost companies in the truckload segment. Railroads are getting into the swing of what they can do under Staggers, so we're getting more competition from other railroads. The result has been a steady downward pressure on rates for the past two years, and it will continue."

To stay viable BN (and for that matter all railroads) must cut costs; and to cut costs it must look at labor, since that constitutes about 50 percent of total costs. So far BN, like other railroads, has substituted capital for labor or has gotten rid of individuals it didn't need. But that's getting harder now.

Gaskins says, "Almost everybody we have has a job to do under the work agreements we have now. It's a question of whether we can organize in a different way to do the job more effectively, or find someone else who can do it at less cost."

"I am a little frustrated about this," he adds. "In several situations our people have shown a lot of teamwork and innovation in bringing down costs, yet the labor organizations and managements have to sit down together and try to do more."

Looking more generally at the problem of labor costs, Gaskins observes, "If you look at autos and steel, you see examples of wage structures that are high compared with the average. When that happens you will have a problem remaining viable in the competitive world.

"The railroads face that kind of problem – our wage levels are too high and our work rules are too restrictive. It took us a long time to get here, and we won't get out of this overnight; but I'm hopeful that we can freeze wages where they are, eliminate wasteful work rules, and share increased profits with our employees. I ultimately want all of our employees to have a direct stake in the profitability of the BN."

Current employment at BN totals about 35,000, down from 59,000 in 1980. "If we were to start from scratch, with no union contracts and no restrictions," says Gaskins, "we could operate the property with substantially fewer people. There's a lot of room to take costs out."

BN has announced that it will probably withdraw from national labor negotiations for the next round in 1988. It believes its needs are different from those of railroads in other parts of the country. It expects 1988 negotiations to be tough; and it wants the flexibility of calling its own shots.

In the same article, Hunter Harrison said:[599]

---

[599] Ibid.

> *"I'm not sure even system negotiations on BN property are appropriate in every situation. What might be appropriate in Birmingham might not be right in Seattle. You have different markets, different work forces. It's important that we localize some issues."*

The IBU's Expediter trains were proving that trains could be safely run with two-person crews; the Seattle International Gateway facility was efficiently working with its novel, lower cost and higher service levels producing labor agreement, other Hubs were effectively utilizing contract labor and Bill Berry's team was effectively utilizing contract labor for the repair of trailers, lift devices and railcars. There was still a lot more work to do on the competitive labor front, however.

VCAs, Line Sales and the "Black Hole"

BN Railroad continued to have excess track capacity through many parts of its network combined with the excessive train operating labor cost situation. A significant focus was placed on working more intently with connecting railroads to improve service and drive more volume but also possible line sales to either other class I railroads or to short-line operators who would not be encumbered with BN's labor contracts.

On October 13 one of the first "short line" sales was effective. The 152 mile portion of the former Northern Pacific route east of the Cascade Mountain range between Pasco and Cle Elum, WA was sold to Nick Temple who formed the Washington Central Railroad (WCRC).[600] Temple was able to operate with fewer crew members per train which allowed him to be more flexible in serving customers on the line as it interchanged business with Burlington Northern at Pasco. The line west of Cle Elum over the Stampede Pass to Auburn and Seattle/Tacoma continued to be owned by Burlington Northern but remained in mothball status.

An interesting fact related to this line sale is the degree to which it revealed the "market rate" for train and engine crew labor. On September 23, Pasco-based United Transportation Union local chairman A.J. Sanderson sent a letter to UTU general chairman Fred Hardin. In it he explained what he knew about Nick Temple and the sale prospects. He also mentioned that Temple was advertising for employees. He said some unemployed UTU members had contacted Temple and were told he was thinking of paying a flat $81 per day for a work shift of up to 12 hours with no work-rule restrictions or arbitrary payments. He then said:[601]

> *After going public and advertising for employees, Mr. Temple now offers a daily rate of $64.00 regardless of the number of hours worked. This reduction was no doubt the result of receiving in excess of 2000 applications before refusing applications. He but advertised to fill less than 20 jobs. Mr. Temple warns these prospective employees that if employed by the Washington Central and then at a later date they choose to accept union representation, that he will let the railroad line revert back to the Burlington Northern and they will lose their job.*

---

[600] Trainweb.org, Washington Central Railroad – WCRC, Accessed from: http://trainweb.org/rosters/WCRC.html, on February 6, 2023.

[601] A.J. Sanderson letter to Mr. Fred A. Hardin, International President, United Transportation Union, September 23, 1986, pp. 2-3, *Greenwood Collection*, Barriger Library at UMSL.

This illustrated the degree to which a "free market" could impact the cost of railroad train operations. BN, and especially the Intermodal business, was deregulated commercially but up to this time its union-represented labor costs were not. The fact that there were more 100 job applications for each fixed-daily-rate and work-rule-free job at costs more than 21% below what Temple had originally considered illustrated the degree to which BN's short line program could revitalize the financial and service competitiveness of rail service in short line markets. It also showed how BN's primary line labor costs exceeded the open market.

As of December BN had prepared a list of 1,236 miles of additional "short line" sale candidates plus 2,300 miles of main lines that were under consideration for sale.[602] Included in this later list were the lines between Laurel, MT and Sandpoint, ID (part of BN's second east-west main line through MT), the line between Laurel, MT and Casper, WY (part of a second east-west main line through Wyoming) and (as previously mentioned) the main lines east of Memphis. The IBU's Pacific Northwest–Southeast train utilized the line through Wyoming and Montana. The IBU also utilized the lines east of Memphis to serve the Hubs at Birmingham and Mobile.

BN also signed a Voluntary Cooperation Agreement (VCA) with the CSX railroad for carload business on November 20. VCAs were intended to help eliminate marketing and operating barriers between cooperating railroads so that they could present a more seamless offering to customers. The CSX VCA provided for the origin carrier to select shipment routes and prices for both carriers. It provided long haul routes for BN, access to new markets in the Southeast, reduced empty car miles and improved responsiveness to customers.[603]

The IBU had been attempting to create closer working relationships for potential "through service" business with Conrail, CSX, NS, SP, Santa Fe and the GTW, among others but for the most part the effects were ineffective because of the "zero sum game" or, in other words, "I win – You lose," nature of interline service. The dominant philosophy was, "The more I can make on my division of revenue the better off I am so I will squeeze everything I can get out of you, my connecting carrier." That sentiment came from an environment where carriers were more focused on protecting what they had, or their share of the pie, instead of one focused on getting new pies to share or sharing a much bigger pie. It was not a productive way to do business but that is the way it was.

The IBU especially wanted to open up markets in what it called the "black hole" area which was approximately 400 miles east and west of the Mississippi River which was pretty much the place where eastern railroads met western railroads. The vast majority of truck business flowed in markets less than 800 miles in length such as Columbus – Kansas City, Minneapolis – Cleveland, Pittsburg – Dallas and Atlanta – Kansas City.

Railroads looked at their portion of such intermodal hauls as being unattractive because they were too short when from the standpoint of the market they would be attractive for intermodal if they were operated by a single rail carrier. If two connecting railroads could find a way to act like one, these market pairs would be prime intermodal candidates from the standpoints of mileage and business density. This is the message the IBU communicated but it was a tough battle to change historic biases.

---

[602] Bill Greenwood, Senior Staff Meeting Marketing Comments, December, 1986, *Greenwood Collection*, Barriger Library at UMSL.
[603] Ibid.

Power by the Hour Locomotives

Recall that Darius Gaskins said the following in a *Modern Railroads* magazine interview that reflected the dilemma the railroad industry faced at the time and spurred the short line/line sale initiative:[604]

> *"If you look at autos and steel, you see examples of wage structures that are high compared with the average. When that happens you will have a problem remaining viable in the competitive world.*
>
> *"The railroads face that kind of problem – our wage levels are too high and our work rules are too restrictive. It took us a long time to get here, and we won't get out of this overnight; but I'm hopeful that we can freeze wages where they are, eliminate wasteful work rules, and share increased profits with our employees. I ultimately want all of our employees to have a direct stake in the profitability of the BN."*

With a keen understanding that BN's uncompetitive labor cost and work rule structure in a deregulated environment was an existential threat to the company, Gaskins left no stone unturned in an effort to make BN more competitive. In addition, BN no longer had a Powder River Basin coal handling monopoly which threatened the profitability of that core business that so much of BN's future had been staked on.

In addition to initiatives such as line sales, Gaskins pushed the innovation envelope by proposing to locomotive manufacturers that BN purchase the product locomotives provided instead of the locomotives themselves. He wanted the locomotive supplier to also provide the locomotive maintenance unencumbered by BN's labor costs and work rules.

BN's 1986 Annual Report Form 10-K included the following:[605]

> *In October 1986, Railroad entered into an electrical power purchase agreement under which payment is based on the number of megawatt hours of energy consumed, subject to specified take-or-pay minimum. The agreement requires a number of locomotives sufficient to provide necessary megawatt hours to Railroad.*

It made no sense to pay for locomotives while they were out of service. As Paul Withers stated:[606]

> *In an industry first, Burlington Northern began purchasing "power by the hour" from a group of 100 SD60s owned by EMD and leased to Oakway, Inc., a subsidiary of Cornnell Rice & Sugar, a New Jersey corporation. Instead of leasing locomotives from a bank or equipment leasing company, BN purchases only the electrical energy exerted by the locomotive.*
>
> *Most locomotive leases are made on a daily, weekly, or monthly basis, regardless of whether the unit is moving freight or idling at a servicing facility. The Oakways, on the other hand, are leased to Burlington Northern on a kilowatt-hour basis. This means that BN pays for only the time the*

---

[604] Shedd, Tom, *Modern Railroads*, Burlington Northern: Aggressive, Innovative – and Thoroughly Non-Traditional, November, 1986, pp. 21-22, *Greenwood Collection*, Barriger Library at UMSL.
[605] Burlington Northern Inc., 1986 Annual Report Form 10-K, p. 40.
[606] Withers, Paul, Electro-Motive EMD SD-60, sourced from http://oakway.qstation.org/, on October 5, 2022.

locomotive is in operation or service - although it costs the carrier more to operate the locomotive at Run 8 than when it is idling between runs.

Probably the most interesting thing about the Oakways is the maintenance and repair of the units. Rather than the locomotive lessor being responsible for service, the Oakways are maintained at an off-site location by EMD personnel. Initially, the work was done at a Colorado & Wyoming shop at Trinidad, Colo.

At 3,800 horsepower, they were almost 27% more powerful and more fuel-efficient than the standard 3,000 HP units predominantly used in coal service. In addition to reducing maintenance costs, the agreement increased the incentive the manufacturer had to improve locomotive operating reliability because they only were paid for when they were mechanically out of service. The Chicago Tribune stated:[607]

When the power-by-the-hour agreements were first drawn, railroad officials were hoping to achieve an average of 65 to 70 days between mechanical failures, compared to the dismal 25 to 35 days …

According to former BN Chief Mechanical Officer Ed Bauer:[608]

We had a goal of increasing our mean-time-between-failures to 90 days because that coincided with the mandatory 90 Day Federal Railroad Administration inspection. If we could get locomotives to that level of reliability it would eliminate even more out-of-service time.

The first locomotives replaced by PBTY power were the old GE U-25s and U-28s whose MTBF was in the 25-30 day range. EMD had a real incentive to build reliability into the locomotives and maintain them properly because they didn't get paid for idle power. When our unions won the right in court to maintain the locomotives we still had EMD supervise the maintenance. The work was shifted from Colorado to the BN shop in Kansas City. Although we wanted to have a composite work force, the unions did agree to a reduction in crafts to only machinists, electricians and laborers, eliminating the pipefitters and carpenter crafts. It was a very successful initiative and helped us improve our productivity and quality across the rest of our shops.

This arrangement was so successful that the PBTH purchase agreement would be increased from 100 to 200 locomotives:[609]

In December 1987, Railroad entered into another locomotive electrical power purchase agreement for a ten-year term.

BN's locomotive fleet's mean-time-between-failure performance improved to 55.2 days in 1988, 62.6 days in 1989 and 69.5 days in 1990.[610] This was very beneficial for BN's Intermodal service.

---

[607] *Chicago Tribune*, Power-By-the-Hour - A Rail Success Story, April 15, 1989.
[608] Ed Bauer interview with Mark Cane, October 5, 2022.
[609] Burlington Northern Inc., 1987 Annual Report Form 10-K, p. 40.
[610] Burlington Northern Inc., 1988, 1989 and 1990 Annual Reports Forms 10-K.

BN – Santa Fe Avard Gateway

For decades the Santa Fe and Frisco railroads had interchanged business between the U.S. Southeast and California at a junction in Oklahoma called Avard. Each railroad would interchange complete trains with each other. In the days of the Frisco Railroad it was a major element of their business because the Frisco depended on a great deal of "overhead" business for its survival. It was the primary bridge between southeastern railroads and the Santa Fe.

As carload business continued to be lost to motor carriers and US manufacturing was shifting off-shore the importance of the Avard Gateway faded but business opportunities over it did not vanish. What had vanished, for the most part, was market competitive service over the gateway. For BN it was a relatively short haul and business that was handled over it was very imbalanced making it marginally profitable. Santa Fe's prime focus was on their Chicago–California lane so the Avard Gateway got little attention.

The lack of effectiveness of this corridor contributed heavily to a poor return on BN's route between Birmingham and St. Louis and Avard. The BN segment with the worst return over this route was between Memphis and Birmingham. Meanwhile there was a large and growing truck and international container market between California and the Southeast that BN and Santa Fe were not effectively competing for.

Horrible business imbalance, and Santa Fe's lack of emphasis on the corridor, contributed significantly to its lack of profitability. Within the BN Intermodal portfolio, business over Avard with the Santa Fe was among the least profitable. The following table shows intermodal volume between 1982 and 1986. The counts only include revenue-shipments and do not account for a significant volume of unprofitable empty trailers Santa Fe sent eastbound to the BN. Because it was a "blind" steel-wheel interchange (meaning the trains were not inspected at Avard), Santa Fe would also send their "bad order" trailers to BN and BN then had to "eat" the cost to repair those trailers.

BN-Santa Fe Avard Gateway Intermodal Volume, 1981-1986 [611]

	1982	1983	1984	1985	1986[1]
To CA / AZ					
Trailers	13,000	20,000	16,000	15,000	14,500
Containers	1,500	3,600	6,000	5,500	4,000
From CA / AZ					
Trailers	6,000	8,000	9,000	8,200	6,200
Containers	1,700	2,000	2,300	2,300	10,200

[1] 5 months actual, 7 months projected

On August 1 Bill Greenwood proposed a VCA between BN and Santa Fe over this gateway, specifically between Birmingham/Memphis and the West Coast, in an attempt to address inferior service and profitability. For Intermodal business it would have called for dedicated intermodal trains with run-through power (locomotives) on a coordinated train schedule. It would have included business to and from all BN Hubs in Missouri, Tennessee and Alabama, Santa Fe terminals in Arizona and California, plus interchange business to and from eastern railroads. Each railroad would appoint one person to oversee

---

[611] ATSF/BN Intermodal VCA talking points, August 27, 1986, *Greenwood Collection*, Barriger Library at UMSL.

the VCA. BN would have pricing authority for westbound shipments and Santa Fe would have pricing authority for eastbound shipments plus westbound shipments interchanged from eastern railroads.[612]

On August 11, Tom Fitzgerald, Santa Fe's Vice President – Traffic told Greenwood, "We are very much interested in promoting this VCA arrangement between the southeast and California."[613] Unfortunately, neither railroad could get over its parochial differences so the VCA proposal did not progress.

Chicago – Kansas City Expediter

On December 1, Expediter Service was started between Chicago and Kansas City. It provided another link to the original Springfield Region Expediter network that was no longer encumbered with a length of haul restriction. It was also supported by a new three year contract with General Motors for the handling of automotive parts to GM's Kansas City manufacturing plant that was expected to generate $8 million per year of revenue for the IBU.[614]

Gerald Grinstein Begins BNRR Involvement

Gerald Grinstein had been Chief of Staff for Washington State Senator Warren Magnuson and was prominent in Democratic Party circles. In April, 1983, while working as a partner in the law firm Preston, Thorgrimson, Ellis & Holman, he joined the Board of Western Airlines as its Chairman. In January, 1984 he was elected by the Board to be Western's President and Chief Operating Officer. In January, 1985 he was promoted to Chief Executive Officer.[615] In 1985 he joined the Board of Burlington Northern Inc.

In 1986 Grinstein was appointed to a newly formed committee of BNI's Board called the Railroad Review Board along with Walter Drexel, Richard Grayson, Mary Garst (Cattle Manager of the Garst Company), and Arnold Weber (President Northwestern University).[616]

On September 9, 1986 Western Airlines and Delta Airlines announced a merger agreement providing for Delta's acquisition of Western for $860 million. Looking ahead, Western would become a wholly owned subsidiary of Delta on April 1, 1987.[617] That same month Grinstein would resign his position of Chairman and Chief Executive Officer of Western and become Vice Chairman of the Board of BNI.[618]

---

[612] Ibid.

[613] T.J. Fitzgerald letter to Mr. William E. Greenwood, April 11, 1986, *Greenwood Collection*, Barriger Library at UMSL.

[614] Bill Greenwood, Senior Staff Meeting Marketing Comments, December, 1986, *Greenwood Collection*, Barriger Library at UMSL.

[615] Burlington Northern Inc., Notice of Annual Meeting of Stockholders and Proxy Statement, February 26, 1986, *Cane Collection*, Barriger Library at UMSL.

[616] Burlington Northern Inc., 1986 Annual Report Form 10-K, p. 51.

[617] Delta Flight Museum, Western Historical Timeline, accessed from: https://www.deltamuseum.org/exhibits/delta-history/family-tree/western-airlines/decades/1980s, on April 5, 2022.

[618] Burlington Northern Inc., 1987 Annual Report Form 10-K, p. 16.

BNI Takes a Massive Asset and Accounting Charge Write-off

As mentioned earlier, it was known that 1986 would be a bad year financially for the railroad. In addition, low 1986 energy prices were devaluing oil and natural gas assets. The average sales price per barrel of Meridian (BNI's oil and gas subsidiary) crude oil fell 51% from $28.63 in 1984 to $14.06 in 1986 and between those years the price of Meridian natural gas fell 39%.[619] El Paso Natural Gas pipeline throughput fell 18% and their gas sales fell 60% in 1986 versus 1985. As a result, BNI decided it would be prudent to clear the decks and take the financial hit in 1986.

Modern Railroads Magazine reported:

> *"In July BNI announced a major pretax, non-cash charge of $1.9 billion. Of this a little more than $1 billion was against the railroad, including $686 million to reflect a change from composite to the unit depreciation method; and a $352 million for a write-off of surplus, obsolete or otherwise unproductive railroad assets. The balance of the big cash charge was against oil and gas operations reflecting the depressed petroleum industry.*

> *"The $352 million charge is associated with assets we no longer have, or that had lost their value," Gaskins explains. "Our old accounting method didn't explicitly take away an asset that had been lost or destroyed. We went to a method that puts assets into classes of equal economic life, and writes them down immediately whenever there is a loss."[620]*

As stated in the BNI 1986 Annual Report - Form 10-K, the company also set aside "$122 million for coal rate litigation reserves, including interest"[621] related to cases with the City Public Service Board of San Antonio, Texas and Iowa Public Service Company, in addition to $1.1 billion in non-cash charges. BNI reported the following:

> *The non-cash pretax Special Charge of $957 million includes a writedown of the Company's oil and gas properties and a writeoff of surplus railroad assets. The after tax impact of this Special Charge increased 1986 Net Loss by $802 million, $10.83 per share.*

> *At June 30, 1986 the company's unamortized oil and gas capitalized costs exceeded the present value of future net revenues based on the newly adopted successful efforts method of accounting for oil and gas properties. As a result, the Company recorded a $605 million pretax charge to reflect the substantial decline in oil and gas prices.*

> *Also in the second quarter of 1986, the Company conducted a review of its railroad physical properties. The Special Charge includes a $352 million provision for surplus, obsolete or otherwise unproductive assets including locomotives, rolling stock and abandoned track.[622]*

---

[619] Burlington Northern Inc., 1986 Annual Report From 10-K, p. 6.

[620] Shedd, Tom, *Modern Railroads*, Burlington Northern: Aggressive, Innovative – and Thoroughly Non-Traditional, November, 1986, p. 23, *Greenwood Collection*, Barriger Library at UMSL.

[621] Burlington Northern Inc., 1986 Annual Report From 10-K, p. 28.

[622] Ibid, p. 31-32.

In addition BNI's change in the method of accounting for its oil and gas properties from the full cost method to the successful efforts method reduced reported income for years 1985 and before by $133 million.[623] The Railroad's method of depreciation was also changed:

> *Also in the second quarter of 1986, the Company adopted a method of depreciation for the majority of its railroad transportation properties that closely approximates a unit method rather than the composite method of depreciation previously used. This method was adopted to more accurately reflect physical use of assets in the current deregulated transportation environment. The new method has been applied to prior years property acquisitions resulting in a $336 million after tax charge to the first quarter 1986. The new method is also effective for the full year1986 which had the effect of increasing net loss for 1986 by $41 million, or $.55 per share.[624]*

As indicated in the Annual Report From 10-K comment, the BNRR's method of depreciation was switched to the unit method *"to more accurately reflect physical use of assets in the current deregulated transportation environment."* From a practical standpoint, because depreciation is a non-cash cost this change did not directly impact the actual pre-tax cash generated from rail operations but it significantly changed reported income by accelerating the rate of reported depreciation. As stated above, it reduced BNRR's reported income from years prior to 1986 by $336 million (after-tax) and reduced reported income for 1986 by $41 million ($.55 per share). It made the railroad's operating ratio look worse but created a large tax-loss carry-forward which served to reduce BNI's income taxes which improved BNI's cash flow.

As a result of the write-offs, "Standard and Poor's Corp. lowered the credit rating from A to A-minus on BNI's long term debts … However, the company's short-term loan ratings remained at A1 because of strong cash flow generated by BNI's railroad and gas pipeline businesses."[625]

The price of BNI stock closed at a pre-write-off/special-charge high of $82.37 per share on March 14, 1986. Post-announcement, by August 4 it had fallen 42% to a closing price of $47.88.[626] This did anything but please shareholders or the "Street." With echoes from 1978 when shareholders were clamoring for higher dividends, BNI's Board announced a 25% dividend increase to $2.00 per share as a sign of confidence in the company's future cash generation capability.

1986 BNI, BNRR and BN Intermodal Performance Recap

Whereas Richard Bressler's strategy to invest in resources in preference to the railroad looked to be paying off with a "Midas touch" at the end of 1985, the picture looked very different at the end of 1986. Again, the average sales price per barrel of Meridian (BNI's oil and gas subsidiary) crude oil fell 51% from $28.63 in 1984 to $14.06 in 1986 and between those years the price of Meridian natural gas fell 39%[627] In addition, El Paso Natural Gas sales of natural gas fell 60% in 1986 versus 1985. It appeared as if BNI

---

[623] Ibid, p. 31.

[624] Ibid, p. 31.

[625] Burlington Northern Railroad, *BN News*, September – October, 1986, p. 2, *Greenwood Collection*, Barriger Library at UMSL.

[626] Burlington Northern Santa Fe, LLC, Burlington Northern Inc. ("BNI") stock prices from 1/2/1980 to 9/21/1995, accessed from: http://www.bnsf.com, on April 9, 2022.

[627] Burlington Northern Inc., 1986 Annual Report Form 10-K, p. 6.

was using a significant amount of BNRR cash flow and BNRR debt service capability to support BNI's long-term debt financing to "buy high" and "sell low" which resulted in a major charge/write-off:

BN Inc. 1986 Asset Write-Off and Accounting Change Impact ($ millions unless specified) [628]

	1986	1985 Restated	1985	1984
Revenue	6,941	8,651	8,651	9,156
Operating Income	(129)	1,246	1,365	1,449
Net Income	(860)	596	658	608
Earnings per share ($)	(12.07)	7.19	8.03	7.15
Total Assets	10,651	12,256	12,512	11,424
Long-term Debt	3,394	3,118	3,118	2,454
Preferred Stock	62	519	519	697
Common Stockholder's Equity	3,534	4,512	4,645	4,171
Book Value per Common Share ($)	47.90	61.32	63.13	56.98

BNI took a $605 million special charge to restate the value of oil and gas business that nearly wiped out the $730 million that had just been spent to acquire Southland's oil and gas reserves and business at the end of 1985. Yet the debt to finance that acquisition did not disappear as long-term debt swelled to $3.4 billion from $3.1 billion at the end of 1985. As indicated above, shareholder's equity fell 24% from the pre-charge 1985 level.

In 1986, IBU revenue grew $37.6 million (+7.8%) to $522.7 million, topping a half-billion dollars for the first time. At the same time coal revenue fell another $361.5 million (-22.2%) due to the effects of the C&NW-UP entry into the PRB. Grain revenue fell $36.2 million (-6.3%) and the rest of the rail portfolio's revenue fell another $6.5 million ($399 million less than its pre- Intermodal Task Force level). Reported BNRR Operating Income was $152.8 million (including the Trailer Train dividends). Unadjusted for the special non-cash charges related to assets and the depreciation method change, operating income was $506 million after accounting for the $122 million cash reserve for coal rate litigation. BNI's long-term debt increase to $3.4 billion drove interest expense to $389 million and it, combined with the effects of the asset write-offs, drove BN's debt to capitalization ratio to an all-time high of 49%. The following table reflects the performance of the IBU relative to BNRR overall:

Burlington Northern Railroad 1981-1986 Financial Performance ($ millions) [629]

	IML Rev.	BNRR Rev.	BNRR OI	BNRR OR	BNI LT Debt	Pref. Stock	Int. Exp.	Div. Exp.	Debt/ Cap.
1981	$267	$4,088	$527	87.1%	$1,330	$105	$140	$58	29%
1982	273	3,773	457	87.9%	1,333	105	136	71	27%
1983	335	4,058	734	81.9%	2,930	709	142	87	41%
1984	443	4,490	980	78.2%	2,454	697	310	130	35%
1985	485	4,098	822	79.9%	3,118	519	312	184	41%
1986	523	3,801	506[a]	86.7%	3,394	62	389	123	49%

---

[628] Burlington Northern Inc., 1986 and 1987 Annual Reports Forms 10-K
[629] Burlington Northern Inc., 1981-1986 Annual Reports and Forms 10-K.

^a Reported Operating Income was $152.8 mm, including approximately $20 million (pre-tax) of IBU driven Trailer Train dividends. It would have been a rounded $506 mm including a $122 million coal rate litigation reserve but excluding the special non-cash charge of $352 mm.

As has been repeatedly implied, and stated outright, the IBU continually fought an ongoing and ingrained bias against it based on the assumption that it was not profitable. There was a continuous sentiment that BNRR would be better off without Intermodal. A comparative view of BNRR performance in 1986 compared to the first year of the IBU's existence challenges this IBU millstone. The following chart shows the comparative revenue of BNRR's major business components along with BNRR's operating income with 1986 adjusted for the write-offs related to the 1986 change in depreciation method and the coal case litigations referenced above:

Comparative BNRR Performance 1981 vs. 1986 ($millions, current dollars)[630]

	1981	1986	$ Change	% Change
Coal Revenue	1,213	1,269	56	+4.6
Ag Revenue	649	536	(113)	-17.4
Non-Coal/Ag/IML (Other) Revenue	1,598	1,199	(399)	-25.0
Intermodal Revenue	267	523	256	+95.9
BNRR Non-Intermodal Revenue	3,825	3,242	(583)	-15.2
BNRR Total Revenue	4,092	3,765	(327)	-8.0
BNRR Operating Income	527	628[a]	101	+19.2

^a Operating income adjusted for the non-cash charges and the coal litigation reserve but includes approximately $20 million in IBU driven Trailer Train dividends.

There is no question that a significant portion of the improvement in BNRR profitability, despite the 8% drop in BNRR revenue, came from relentless cost cutting efforts. That said, coal prices in 1981 did not reflect the competitive effect of C&NW-UP entry into the PRB. The 4.6% 1981-1986 growth in coal revenue was generated on revenue-ton-miles growth of only 3.2%.[631] Revenue from the supposedly more profitable Ag and "Other" carload businesses fell 17.4% and 25% respectively and total BNRR Non-Intermodal revenue fell 15.2%. Yet, comparative BN operating income rose 19.2% and the operating ratio dropped .4 points. It will never be known for sure but it stretches objective reason to believe that BNRR's 1986 operating income and operating ratio would have been better than what it was in 1981, or that they wouldn't have been significantly worse, without the $256 million (95.9%) growth in Intermodal revenue given BNRR's highly leveraged business structure.

---

[630] Burlington Northern Inc., 1981 and 1986 Annual Reports and Forms 10-K.
[631] Burlington Northern Annual Reports, 10-Ks.

Chapter 14 – 1987 is a Year of Continued Intermodal Growth but also Major Transitions

In late January Bill Greenwood elevated Steve Nieman's position to Group VP Intermodal and brought International Marketing and Sales, under Murry Watson, and Automotive, under Dan Flood, back under the IBU organizational umbrella. The fracture of International Intermodal from the IBU was hurting the overall effectiveness of the business and this was done to help repair that. In addition, the Automotive business was focusing heavily on the Dallas Smith trailer technology which depended on IBU support.

BN's IBU achieved the overall objective it had set for itself in 1981 – "become the recognized intermodal leader in terms of customer service, innovation, market share and profitability by 1986." Claimed achievement of this objective was backed up with fact. During this era *Progressive Railroading Magazine* ran a monthly column called *Intermodalism … Just My Opinion* by an author with the pseudonym of Paul V. Carr. After his December 1986 column had crowned BN Intermodal the top performer in the industry, the January 1987 issue of his column carried the title, "People Make it Happen." It stated: [632]

> The column last month talked about a major shift in relative ranking among three carriers – Burlington Northern, Santa Fe, and Southern Pacific. This month we turn to the intermodal organizations of these companies in an attempt to understand their past and current performance.
>
> Let us now turn to a comparison of the organizational structure of the carriers that have shown the largest shifts in relative position in intermodal loadings. First, let's look at the big winner over the past five years – BN.
>
> Five years ago, BN Intermodal was structured like most railroads (i.e. intermodal operations reported to a centralized intermodal officer who also directed a centralized marketing and pricing effort).
>
> BN, under Bill Greenwood, dramatically restructured this effort. They kept a centralized planning, equipment, and operations group where efficiencies and discipline could be designed into the system.
>
> More importantly, however, they pressed for a decentralized commercial system. Small ramps were closed to consolidate and concentrate both scarce capital and scare management talent into a hub system. Most railroads have taken this physical step. BN moved a large step beyond that by giving the hub managers both operating and commercial responsibility. The sales function and local pricing authority rests with the hub manager.
>
> Coverage of major accounts (both domestic and international) still rests in the marketing functions in Ft. Worth, Texas. BN thus has the best of both worlds – it has a local sales force that understands the product (since there is no operating / sales split) and a knowledgeable headquarters group to deal with major customers.
>
> Like democracy, it isn't perfect, but it does appear to be highly effective.
>
> My predictions? Watch for BN to continue to press ahead aggressively.

---

[632] Paul V. Carr, *Modern Railroads*, Intermodalism – People Make it Happen, January, 1987, *Greenwood Collection*, Barriger Library at UMSL.

The IBU Presses Ahead Aggressively but also Reassesses

In December of 1986 Mark Cane, who had responsibility for domestic marketing and intermodal train service management, sent a letter to his direct reports concerning 1987 goals. It reflected a change in tone for the business that reflected "Paul Carr's" expectation for continued aggressiveness but with a bit of tempering. It stated:

> *This coming year will be challenging for us in many ways. We have evolved from an underlying growth strategy to one that focuses on improving return on assets. We have worked hard on developing systems support to help us measure return to make the above possible. We have claimed a high level of service sensitivity and the same systems will help us measure and improve our service performance. We have identified interline railroads as a significant market opportunity and are on the threshold of innovative joint venture arrangements. We have identified the need to mature our relationship with third parties through channel management. We have identified the need to become door-to-door providers of transportation service to better manage our destiny. We must respond to the domestic double stack challenge / opportunity. Clearly, 1987 will be a pivotal year with regard to the future degree of success of BN Intermodal.*[633]

The letter went on to specify a partial list of 1997 goals across marketing functions including:[634]

Segment
- *Establishment of a BN Agreement Holder statement of policy.*
- *Refinement of BN transportation agreement qualifications*
- *Development of a customer seminar*
- *Timely capture of billing information*

Segment (Interline)
- *Establishment of offline BN rail hubs*
- *Establishment of through interline service*
- *Establishment of bi-directional joint line prices*
- *Establishment of online joint hubs*

Lanes
- *Establishment of service quality measurement / control systems*
- *Establishment of additional Expediters*
- *Hub service profile updates*
- *Determination of Intermodal product profitability*

Joint Segment and Corridor

---

[633] Mark Cane letter to N.D. Brehm, B.D. Herndon, D.D. Meyer, G. B. Minnich, R. R. Robinson, Subject: 1987 Goals, December 12, 1986, *Greenwood Collection*, Barriger Library at UMSL.
[634] Ibid.

- *Reevaluation of our charge levels and establishment of a pricing strategy for individual product lines including seasonal pricing*
- *Establishment of an implementation plan for door-to-door service*
- *Development of BN Intermodal product manuals and product knowledge seminars*
- *Development of a service failure notification system*

Despite all of the internal and external obstacles it faced, the BN had somewhat miraculously gone from the laggard among the major railroads to the industry leader. It was a shock to the industry because the underlying relative weakness of BN's intermodal franchise was well known. Unfortunately information system support to truly manage the business more effectively was under development but still unavailable. What was clear was that while the IBU had significantly grown the business, the truly big winners profit- wise were those providing services connected with the rail service provided by BN and other railroads. As indicated previously, Trailer Train was generating handsome profits. Railcar and trailer makers and equipment lessors were profiting nicely. Contract terminal ramp/deramp operators were doing well. Intermodal third parties (IMCs) were profiting nicely as evidenced by APL's $65 million acquisition of National Piggyback (for basically an extraordinarily asset-light sales, customer relationship, service and billing interface) in 1984. Steamship operators were doing well with their businesses as evidenced by the $800 million CSX purchase of Sea-Land. The best drayage company owners were hardly starving. Yet, the industry players that controlled the most essential intermodal value chain component with the highest barriers to competitive entry, BN and its rail industry counterparts, were challenged to generate adequate returns on the business.

A point that cannot be stressed enough is that the business was extremely fragmented. That fragmentation was beneficial for the players that were accessories to the core line-haul intermodal business but it was hurting railroads that were unwilling or unable to vertically integrate their intermodal service. The railroad with the greatest competitive network coverage advantage, and thereby the railroad with the best opportunity to vertically integrate (Union Pacific), was not capitalizing on it. Another railroad would never be built while equipment manufacturers, lessors, third parties, and drayage companies were replaceable/interchangeable. Only APL, to their credit, was putting the package together with the benefit of a broad geographic footprint but they did not control the most valuable element of the service from the standpoint of barrier to competitive entry. Continued BNRR profit pressure and a reduction of excess capacity required a reset of emphasis.

Instead of focusing on expanding the number of firms selling BN's intermodal service (one of the 1986 goals) it was deemed more appropriate at this stage of the IBU's development to focus on quality of representation over quantity.

The goal areas identified for 1987 were intended to accelerate progress against these challenges.

Domestic Marketing Organization Adjustment

In order to have the domestic marketing organization better aligned with the IBU goals, Norm Brehm, who had been Market Manager responsible for marketing and pricing through the IMC segment was reassigned to focus on marketing and pricing for the interline rail segment. Tom Doty, Hub Manager in Springfield, was recruited to focus on the IMC segment in January. His prior motor carrier experience was expected to be heavily utilized as the IBU's approach with the IMC channel was reassessed and efforts were made to explore expansion of domestic container and door-to-door services. In

September, Kirk Williams, who had been Superintendent-Highway Operations in Chicago, and was a former LTL motor carrier executive, was promoted to Market Manager Carriers in place of Bruce Herndon who was assigned Market Manager–Central Lanes. His insights into expansion of domestic container and door-to-door services were also to be counted on.

Aggressive Expediter Service Expansion

A total of 24 new Expediter trains were added in 1987. New Expediter service was established between Minneapolis/St. Paul and St. Louis on February 24 that allowed improved service between St. Louis and the Pacific Northwest, Denver, and California points via interchange with the SP or Santa Fe railroads. In addition it connected the Twin Cities with the original Expediter markets. Omaha (which had been relocated from Lincoln) was also added to the network to and from Chicago and Kansas City. On March 2, Expediter service started between Dallas and Houston and Chicago–Dallas service started on March 30. Expediter service between Seattle and Portland was also started which allowed improved service between Seattle and California and Arizona markets in cooperation with the SP Railroad. Expediter service between Dallas and Denver (primarily to serve UPS) now linked Denver to Houston. The elimination of length of haul limits allowed the IBU to grow the business while selectively replacing lower margin business with higher margin business on the Expediter trains.

Santa Fe Adopts BN's Expediter Strategy

The Santa Fe followed BN's Expediter strategy:

> *Following a pattern pursued by other railroads, the Santa Fe in 1986 had launched its Quality Service Network to compete for intermodal business in untraditional, shorter-haul markets bound roughly by Kansas City, Denver, El Paso, Houston and, later, Oklahoma City. The eight train pairs were called Q trains. In 1987, the first full year of operation, Q trains handled fifty-five thousand units (all new business) and the annual report implied that they were a great success. But were they? Even though the unions had agreed to reduced crew sizes over extended districts, rates were kept low to attract customers, and train Q-DVOK operated circuitously to eastern Kansas before heading south, whereas competitor Burlington Northern could serve Denver-Dallas and Denver- Houston over what amounted to a straight line.*[635]

As much as BN suffered from a relatively poor intermodal "franchise" except for the Chicago–PNW and Chicago–Denver lanes, the stand-alone ATSF markets outside of the Chicago–California and Dallas-California lanes were worse. The Q network markets were less attractive than BN's Expediter markets. The only BN "competitive" markets in the ATSF's Q network were between Denver and Texas and Kansas City and Texas but Q service acted more as a possible price-spoiler than a competitive threat to BN. In addition to the ATSF having to deal with significantly more route miles between Denver and Texas than BN, as cited above, the ATSF ramp that served Denver "was 40 miles south of downtown and its routings were not competitive with those of BN."[636] For service between Kansas City and Texas, the elimination of haul-length restrictions on BN allowed the IBU to connect Texas with more relatively attractive markets such as Chicago, St. Louis and Minneapolis/St. Paul in its Expediter Network over that

---

[635] Bryant and Frailey, pp. 363-364.
[636] Ibid, p. 368.

route. Yielding poorly priced Kansas City–Texas business to the Santa Fe was not that serious for the IBU. As Nieman used to say, "There is no such thing as bad freight but there are bad rates…"

BN Establishes a Detroit Hub

The first meeting with Andy Kalabus of the GTW regarding the possibility of BN establishing rail Hub presence in Detroit, and Expediter type Chicago-Detroit dedicated BN train service, was on June 10, 1986. The GTW was successful in negotiating an Expediter type labor agreement and in May, 1987 dedicated BN train service between Detroit and Chicago was initiated. Jim Crighton, BN's Superintendent Hub Operations in Seattle accepted an offer to be BN's first off-line rail Hub manager at the GTW's Detroit intermodal facility. Crighton says:[637]

> *I had reported to Gary Ailts who was the Seattle Hub Manager. He left BN and I put in my name to replace him. Instead, the Portland Hub Manager, Doc Wallner was moved to Seattle. Doc knew of my interest in the job and he told me, "Congratulations – You are being promoted to Hub Manager and he told me to report to the new Hub in Detroit. It was a real culture shock working through another railroad but it turned into a great experience for me and my family. It would not have been successful without the help of the GTW's Andy Kalabus. We started the first off-line Hub from scratch so everything was a new experience. One of the biggest challenges was to get our connecting train through the rail maze of Chicago. Eventually the Santa Fe copied us and put in a representative of their own in the Detroit Hub too.*

The train service, and BN's first off-line rail hub, were in operation prior to the September, 1987

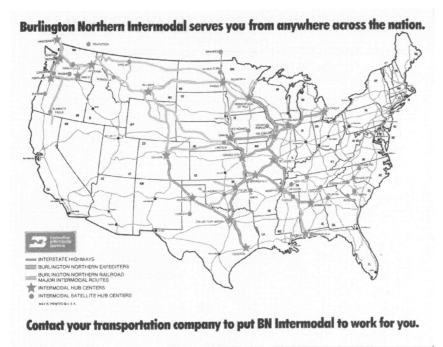

Mazda/Ford Flat Rock assembly plant opening. The Detroit Expediter trains ran into issues navigating through the Chicago mess between railroads so the service required significant oversight but it was worth the effort.

With the completion of the Chicago–Detroit Expediter leg, the map of BN's intermodal services, including Expediter routes indicated in bold-gray, rail Hubs and highway satellite hubs as of May, 1987 is shown on this map and in Appendix 3.[638]

---

[637] Jim Crighton interview with Mark Cane, August 8, 2022.
[638] BN Intermodal Map, including Expediter routes, May, 1987, *Greenwood Collection*, Barriger Library at UMSL .

Domestic Channel Management

The IBU hadn't been shy about its desire to address the issue of intermodal industry fragmentation and its effect on customer service and profitability but it wasn't the only one to share that concern. After Norfolk Southern took over the lease of the RoadRailer trailers BN had rescued from North American Car's bankruptcy, they established the Triple Crown subsidiary to develop and manage a business built on the use of RoadRailers between major cities on the NS. With the leadership of management they acquired in the North American Van Lines acquisition they chose to manage the entire network door-to-door and sell it with their own sales force, cutting out the third party channel. The UP established an in-house third party and the CSX pending consolidation with Sea-Land threatened the same. This created a concern about BN's intent.

To address this head-on, in March, the IBU distributed its first BN Intermodal News newsletter.[639] In addition to commenting on BN's intermodal volume growth of 33% above 1985 and a growth rate of 18% through March of 1987, it gave an update on Expediter train initiations and addressed the wholesale vs. retail issue directly:

> *Burlington Northern's dynamic growth in 1986 occurred largely because of our partnership with wholesalers, and we're holding to the win-win approach that brought us this far. Instead of creating an in-house third party as several railroads have, we continue to look to our partners to add value to the beneficial owner's transportation package.*
>
> *BN is committed to marketing domestic intermodal business primarily through third parties and motor carriers because we recognize wholesalers can provide quality geographic market coverage and customer service.*
>
> *There are, though, beneficial freight owners who will use our services only if they can work directly with the railroad. Many of them aren't aware of the value of the wholesaler's service, so we always try to "sell" this value to support the wholesale channel and still obtain the business. However, if the customer insists on excluding the wholesaler, we then attempt to satisfy his transportation needs.*
>
> *We also communicate directly with these customers about our superior innovative intermodal service to make certain it's on track and meeting their needs. And as long as we and our partners sell this service as well as price, routing decisions that swing on $5 to $25 price differentials stand a good chance of swinging BN's way.*

In addition, an Intermodal Product Manual[640] was developed and distributed to BN's IMC channel participants that included a policy statement intended to articulate what BN expected from an agent and what an agent had a right to expect from BN. It stated:

---

[639] *BN Intermodal News*, Vol. 1, No. 1, March, 1987, p. 1, *Greenwood Collection*, Barriger Library at UMSL.
[640] BN Intermodal Product Manual, Section 1, 1987, *Greenwood Collection*, Barriger Library at UMSL.

Burlington Northern's Innovative Intermodal Partnership

Burlington Northern has elected to sell its intermodal transportation services primarily through transportation companies because we recognize wholesalers can provide quality geographic market coverage and customer service. We communicate directly with our customers to make sure their needs are being met. In return, we expect our customers to sell BN's services and communicate with us about how we can better meet our ultimate customers' needs.

Burlington Northern's Responsibilities

- *Provide consistent, reliable train service and drayage to and from the Hub Centers at a value-competitive price.*
- *Provide modern equipment in good repair.*
- *Provide qualified sales leads to our customers.*
- *Provide educational materials and promotional support to our customers.*
- *Provide current, accurate billings and honor legitimate damage claims.*

Transportation Partners' Responsibilities

- *Maintain an excellent reputation as a recognized company with multistate transportation services and the ability to produce bidirectional freight shipments.*
- *Employ a qualified sales force that is knowledgeable about BN's services and willing to promote features and qualities that distinguish these services from those of our competitors.*
- *Keep BN informed about current and future market trends so BN can remain customer-responsive.*
- *Comply with industry standards and maintain financial responsibility with BN.*
- *Act as a liaison between BN and customers by handling billing, filing claims and resolving disputes.*

Several significant changes related to channel management were made in 1987. They included changes in the incentive programs for volume due to the increase in slim-margin Expediter services, reductions in incentives for quick payment of bills due to lower interest rates and a reduction in BN's liability limits related to lading damage.

Refinement of BN Transportation Agreement Qualifications

Another channel management initiative was a refinement of the qualifications for IMCs/Transportation Brokers to hold a domestic contract with BN. They were tightened and, in the process, almost 100 agreements were cancelled by BN. The 1986 initiative to aggressively expand the contract holder base proved that more was not necessarily better.[641]

---

[641] Mark Cane letter to S.C. Nieman re: 1987 marketing accomplishments vs. goals, December 22, 1987, *Greenwood Collection*, Barriger Library at UMSL.

Bill Greenwood Promoted Again and Don Wood "Leaves" BNRR

In January, 1987 Bill Greenwood was promoted to Executive Vice President Marketing and Sales from Senior VP.[642] In February, Joe Galassi replaced Don Wood as BNRR's Executive Vice President – Operations.[643] Wood had been brought in from the Holding Company by Walter Drexel and following Drexel's departure he left BN altogether. Larry Kaufman stated:

> When it became obvious to Drexel and the board that Woods was not the right choice, he was succeeded by Joe Galassi, a longtime BN executive who had begun his career before the 1970 Northern Lines merger. Galassi had an operating background and also had spent a couple of years in charge of the railroad's real estate and industrial department during the ascendency of Frisco executives.[644]

Although Kaufman credited Drexel with the departure of Wood, it actually happened a year after Drexel left BN, when Darius Gaskins was the President and CEO of BN Railroad. Gaskins said:

> Don was the head of the Operations Department and I gave him a fair job evaluation. Wood thought he deserved a better review and was really upset about it. He got into the company jet and flew to Seattle. He complained to Bressler about me and basically told him it was going to be him or me. Bressler told Wood he stood by me and then told me what Wood had done. He said it was fine with him if I fired him and I did.[645]

Information Systems Progress[646]

On April 9 John Tierney, who was in charge of BN's Information Systems Department, sent Bill Greenwood a letter[647] including the following:

> The ISS organization is rapidly reaching the limit of current headcount authority which has us about 23 positions short of the number that will be required to meet delivery schedules which have been furnished to your people for Intermodal and other Marketing systems development projects. Overall, we are short 52 positions to meet all of the department's current commitments.

Tierney went on to say that he thought he would be able to get the position authorities and that he would let Greenwood know if he ran into trouble. Within two weeks, this letter was followed up with a letter from Joe Galassi (Operations) to those reporting to him stating that, due to BNRR income running $103 million below the BNRR 1987 income budget of $578 million, he had agreed to a 3% under-run of the Operating Departments budgeted expense per revenue-ton-mile for the balance of the year. He

---

[642] Burlington Northern Inc. 1989 Form 10-K, p. 11.

[643] Ibid.

[644] Kaufman, p. 271-272.

[645] Darius Gaskins interview with Mark Cane, May 26, 2022.

[646] Mark Cane letter to S.C. Nieman re: 1987 marketing accomplishments vs. goals, December 22, 1987, *Greenwood Collection*, Barriger Library at UMSL.

[647] Letter from John Tierney to Bill Greenwood, April 9, 1987, *Greenwood Collection*, Barriger Library at UMSL.

also said, "It goes without saying that we don't want to lose sight of our other goals, such as enhanced service quality. As is often the case, we must simultaneously deal with competing goals."[648]

One of the information system goals was to establish service quality measurement/control systems support. Going into 1987, all the IBU had to measure service performance was COMPASS system reports on train on-time performance and MCSM which had been developed to measure cars. This still did not suit the intermodal business which required cutoff-to-availability and dock-to-dock shipment performance. In March, the Lane groups were able to get the assistance of a consultant brought in to help Jack Round and his team who was able to deliver to them what came to be known as the Intermodal Service Performance Measurement System (SPMS). Unfortunately it pointed out more serious data integrity issues but it gave the team the ability to attack the root cause of the data issues with Dave Burns' Hub team. The teams furthered their work on the development of service standards that allowed for the system-supplied identification of service failures and control metrics. This proved to be essential for the United States Postal Service Contract that came up for bid in the middle of the year. That contract called for what the new system delivered as it relates to service performance measurement and exception reporting.

Related to this was the development of a service failure notification system. A system was initiated whereby Overland Park Transportation would notify a contact person for each Lane team when there was a service failure related to such things as derailments, washouts and bad order car set-outs. The IBU had purchased its own voice-mail system (the first in BN) that was used to notify those with customer contact responsibilities. The service standards and notify-parties were already established which were later used to provide electronic notification of service failures directly to customers.

The IBU was still struggling with accurate activity based financial performance measurement. Throughout the year the Marketing team worked with Jack Round's team and the Costs and Statistics Department to improve the integrity of the new Intermodal P&L System. With every improvement step taken in the development effort, data integrity became a bigger issue. In addition, the Information Systems and Costs and Statistics Department had still not totally fixed the system so that it would handle "platform equivalents" to account for new generation equipment such as articulated stack and skeleton cars. The next quantum level of P&L system improvement was scheduled for January of 1988.

Establishment of IBU Product Line Based Pricing Strategies

In 1987 the domestic marketing team significantly changed pricing philosophy, switching from pricing to drive volume (to fill excess capacity) to pricing to drive margin.[649] The theme of "Volume is Vanity and Margin is Sanity," was adopted. While this effort started before he arrived, Steve Nieman offered a way to look at prices that was helpful in support of this initiative. As mentioned previously, he reminded the team that, "There is no such thing as bad freight but there is such a thing as a bad rate. What is a good rate for you may be a bad rate for someone else and what may be a bad rate for you may be a good rate for someone else." What may seem to be an irrational price to one might be perfectly rational for another given different market and operating circumstances.

---

[648] Joseph R. Galassi letter to DE Baker, WW Francis, EH Harrison, RS Howery, TR Hackney, WA Hatton, DE Henderson, April 20, 1987, *Greenwood Collection*, Barriger Library at UMSL.
[649] Mark Cane letter to S.C. Nieman re: 1987 marketing accomplishments vs. goals, December 22, 1987, *Greenwood Collection*, Barriger Library at UMSL.

While the lack of good decision support tools hindered the effort, the Carrier team was able to establish differential (marginally higher) contract prices for their segment, including UPS and LTL carriers, who demanded the highest service levels. A commitment to delegate more pricing authority to the field sales people was fulfilled and, with the benefit of improved systems, the process was monitored and managed so that a cascading of prices, that some feared, did not materialize. More prices were raised in 1987 than in any year since the formation of the IBU in 1981, one of the most significant being for perishable business from the Pacific Northwest. What made it especially significant is that it was the first attempt at seasonal pricing – timed with the PNW apple harvest. Fred Tolan, who ran the Pacific Northwest Perishable Shippers Association, was upset but Nieman supported the Marketing team.

One of the things that helped the pricing effort was the work the Lane teams had done to compile competitive service profiles providing better-than-ever information about BN's relative service. Better knowledge of BN's competitive profile helped when a price increase was being fought or a price reduction was requested.

In addition, on May 9 Mark Cane sent a letter to all Hub Managers, National Marketing Executives and Hub Market Managers that included information the Ft. Worth Marketing teams were already aware of. It stated: [650]

> *All Hub Managers*
> *All National Marketing Executives*
> *All Hub Market Managers*
>
> *I am sending this to you because it gives some insights related to our transition from a growth driven business strategy where we have judged success primarily through revenue unit and lift count increases. As discussed at the staff conference last January, our focus in 1987 is on margin growth.*
>
> *Because we are a relatively high fixed cost business, volume growth is generally compatible with margin growth. (The more you move, the lower your unit costs.) However, what we are in the process of attempting to do better is focus growth where we can best take advantage of fixed cost leverage such as on under capacity trains, especially on individual moves where the ratio of true variable cost to price is low. We are also attempting to become more aggressive with selective price increases. In many cases this will result in lost volume. There are cases where we will be better off for this. These are lose/win cases we are searching for.*
>
> *We have established a leadership position in this business in which all railroads complain about a lack of profitability. There are many lanes where prices are now driven by other railroads, not motor carrier competition. Perhaps there are opportunities in these lanes for us to establish a position of price leadership such as we did with our recent increase on 102s out of the PNW. We won't know unless we try, so we'll try.*
>
> *Meanwhile, our reliance on agents to sell the bulk of our service does put us in a difficult position in achieving price increases. Unlike us, they have historically made their gravy on the buy (the*

---

[650] Mark Cane letter to All Hub Managers, All National Marketing Executives, All Hub Market Managers, May 9, 1987, *Greenwood Collection*, Barriger Library at UMSL.

less we charge the more they can make), not the sell. Therefore we need to show them how to make it on the sell by differentiating themselves through value added services. We are in the process of helping ourselves in this regard by tightening contract qualifications. After all, if our distributors aren't providing value added customer support functions we don't need them.

This leads to another related transition we are going through with is more differential pricing. Our differential pricing now and in the past had been basically volume driven. For example, if you buy a lot you get a bigger refund. The fact is that you don't have to charge the same to all who purchase the same volume. Rather, price differentials should be dependent on the value we get from the agent (e.g. things such as promotion of lane balance) and, again, by the functions they perform. Meanwhile, the more they do for the beneficial owner and the better they do it, the more likely it is they will get us new market share that hopefully never was intermodal before. Agents who are in the business of just shifting intermodal share from other agents or to the lowest prevailing rail price provide us little or no long term value. The key to differential pricing is a uniform set (and application) of criteria which we are in the process of developing.

Finally, another key to our ability to obtain and retain higher prices is real and perceived differentiation of BN's Intermodal service. In addition to requests for guidance on the above, you will be increasingly asked to help us determine how our service stacks up compared to our competition. We consistently are told that we are the best in the business. This has worth and perhaps we are not capitalizing on it as best we could. Our advertising and promotion is now more product benefit focused than it has ever been but we must have opportunities to be even more aggressive in promoting how much better BN is (and taking advantage of it).

Don't be discouraged if lift count drops due to price increases and we are better off for it. Dave, Marv and Axel are committed to what we are trying to do.

Borrowing from what was learned three years before from Dan Nimer at the Northwestern Industrial Marketing Strategy seminar, attached to the letter were tables that showed the relationship between price, volume, variable costs and profitability. It gave guidance on a break-even percent decrease in sales with a given price increase and a break-even percent increase in unit sales with a given price reduction. It illustrated how, for example, in a 60% variable cost business (not unlike a lot of BN's intermodal business) a price reduction of 5% had to drive a 14% increase in volume to break-even and how a 5% price increase would permit a loss of 11% of business to still break-even.[651] Everything hinged on having good information.

Change in the IBU Promotion and Advertising Strategy

As alluded to in the above letter, between 1981 and 1986 BN's Intermodal promotion and advertising strategy was to educate customers and potential customers about what intermodal was, establish BN's brand identity, promote new services and promote the cost savings intermodal could provide a customer.

---

[651] Ibid.

As Mark Cane related to Steve Nieman, "We significantly changed our advertising approach in 1987 to one that stresses value, differentiates BN, is directed at beneficial owners for demand-pull, and does not call our service "CHEAP."[652]

Strengthening BN Intermodal's Media Image

In August, Steve Nieman and Mark Cane visited with the editors of two of the most prominent publications among the media for the intermodal business. On August 10 they met with *Journal of Commerce* editors in New York followed by a meeting on August 11 with the editors of the *Intermodal Reporter* in Washington, DC.[653] Both meetings resulted in open and frank dialogue about a number of the initiatives that BN had undertaken to establish an industry leading position. The fact that the meetings were initiated by BN and that Neiman and Cane were so forthcoming with answers proved to pay handsome dividends and positioned BN's Intermodal business well.

The Unrelenting Competitive Environment

On April 9, Bill Greenwood sent a confidential letter to Jim Dagnon (Labor Relations) with copies to Joe Galassi (Operations) and Tom Matthews (Administration) summarizing whet he learned after a visit with cereal maker Kellogg's. The letter[654] said,

> *I have attached a letter from them which outlines the information they shared with us about the transition that has taken place from rail to truck in their business because of demands for better service from their customers. The point they are at now is to decide whether or not to finish converting the balance of their business to truck or take steps that would stem any further market share shifts. I thought this information may be useful in future discussions with Labor about the seriousness of our need for lower costs and changes in work rules.*

The accompanying table summarized outbound modal shares for each of the five Kellogg's plants between 1983 and 1986. The following summarizes the combined total across all plants:

Kellogg Company Outbound Transportation Modal Share Shift, 1983-1986

Mode	1983	1984	1985	1986
Rail	80.4%	49.0%	31.2%	24.5%
Truck	13.8%	37.0%	51.7%	55.3%
Customer Pick-up	5.8%	14.0%	17.1%	20.2%

Kellogg customer pick-up shipments also moved via truck so, fulfilling what the 1981 Intermodal Task Force had warned, in three years outbound rail share had fallen almost 70% reflecting the unrelenting competitive environment and the need for competitive rail service and economics. It is not known how much, if any, of the truck business utilized substitute line-haul intermodal service.

---

[652] Mark Cane letter to S. C. Nieman re: 1987 marketing accomplishments vs. goals, December 22, 1987, *Greenwood Collection*, Barriger Library at UMSL.

[653] Mark Cane's personal calendar.

[654] William E. Greenwood letter to Jim Dagnon, Subject: The Kellogg Company, April 9, 1987, *Greenwood Collection*, Barriger Library at UMSL.

The Kellogg situation bore out exactly what the IBU had been preaching would happen in the competitive battle between rail and truck in the deregulated environment. The competitive balance had swung even more in the favor of motor carriers with increased legal trailer sizes and weights.

CSX-Sea-Land Intermodal, Inc. (CSXI) is Born

On October 28, 1987[655] CSX/Sea-Land Intermodal was established as a Delaware Corporation following the ICC's approval of CSX Corporation's 1986 purchase of Sea-Land Corporation for $800 million. The integration of CSX's intermodal business with Sea-Land "gave Sea-Land access to the new modern CSX Bedford Park facility at Chicago and ended the need for a separate Sea-Land terminal in that city."[656] Alex Mandel was appointed Chairman and McNeil Porter from Sea-Land the original CEO of CSXI. Ron Sorrow, a trucking industry executive, became COO. "CSX/Sea-Land Intermodal continued to develop and integrate into a full service carrier." Leveraging their Sea-Land business, "CSX/Sea-Land Intermodal Company also operated over other rail carriers. As a result it was able, like American President Lines, to price its service directly to customers and third parties on a nationwide basis."[657]

The movement of Sea-Land's business to Bedford Park freed up Western Avenue and the IBU moved Hanjin's business there.

Gerald Grinstein's Presence and BN Railroad Role Solidified

In April, following completion of the sale of Western Airlines to Delta Airlines, Grinstein was elected Vice Chairman of BNI.[658] He had already been participating on the BN Railroad Committee of BNI's Board. Darius Gaskins recalled:[659]

> When [Gerald] Grinstein, my successor on the railroad, came in, he came in as a Chairman. We had split the railroad off and he's the Chairman. He immediately took over labor negotiations. That was his bailiwick. That was why he was brought in because he was going to solve the labor problem.

Bill Greenwood added:[660]

> Bressler made Jerry Grinstein the Vice Chairman of BNI and located him in Ft. Worth to oversee BN Railroad. We were going through challenging labor relations issues and Grinstein had a reputation of for being able to fix labor relations problems. After his involvement in the sale of Western to Delta he was supposedly a deal maker too. Both of those things appealed to

---

[655] Delaware Secretary of State Business Registration, CSX/Sea-Land Intermodal, Inc., accessed from: https://www.bizapedia.com/de/csxsea-land-intermodal-inc.html, on April 12, 2022.

[656] DeBoer, p. 157.

[657] Ibid, p. 157-158.

[658] Burlington Northern Inc., 1987 Annual Report From 10-K

[659] National Railroad Hall of Fame, Darius W. Gaskins Interview Transcript, Accessed from: https://www.nrrhof.org/darius-w-gaskins-jr, on March 20, 2023.

[660] Bill Greenwood interview with Mark Cane, May 31, 2022.

Bressler. With that appointment, Darius Gaskins reported to Grinstein instead of Bressler. It would prove to be a dark day for BN.

Interline Development Efforts

Multiple meetings were held throughout the year with Conrail, Norfolk Southern, CSX, ATSF, DRGW and SP about enhancing interline services and the possibility of the establishment of Detroit-like offline BN rail hubs. Unfortunately, none bore much fruit. The DRGW would not agree to an off-line BN Hub in Salt Lake City, the Eastern roads were uninterested in BN Hubs in Atlanta, Columbus or elsewhere and the Santa Fe was non-committal about Avard Gateway service improvements. Partnership discussions about joint Chicago facilities were also unproductive. Meetings late in the year with CSXI were different because by then they had taken responsibility for handling Sea-Land's land-based transportation services. They were acting more like a customer than a connecting carrier.

While the Santa Fe VCA discussions were dormant, they did inquire about trackage rights between Avard and Tulsa on May 5 and mentioned that Steve Nieman did not object to it.[661] Later in the year Gerald Grinstein sent a letter[662] to Santa Fe / Southern Pacific President and Chief Executive Officer Robert Krebs to confirm a phone discussion they had. In the letter Grinstein confirmed a proposal in which BN would grant to the Santa Fe "marketing and bridge-operating rights over Avard to Memphis including Memphis as an origin/destination" as well as "marketing and bridge operating rights over Avard to St. Louis including St. Louis as an origin/destination." The rights would last 25 years and not be assignable. BN would handle Santa Fe intermodal business at its St. Louis and Memphis Hubs.

After give and take, on December 17, Santa Fe sent a counter proposal to BN[663] and the project went back into Limbo.

Dallas Smith Lawsuit

On January 10, 1987 there was a Dallas Smith Board meeting with BN represented.[664] On January 15, 1987 Dan Flood sent the following notification to the 11 BN automotive customers who were utilizing the Dallas Smith Trailer for motor vehicle shipments:[665]

As information, Burlington Northern Railroad Company filed suit against the Dallas Smith Engineering Corporation on January 15, 1987. The suit alleges that Dallas Smith Engineering breached certain contractual commitments to Burlington Northern. The suit was filed after Burlington Northern encountered problems with the Dallas Smith trailers that were not being resolved to our satisfaction.

---

[661] T. J. Fitzgerald letter to Mr. W.E. Greenwood, May 5, 1987, Greenwood *Collection*, Barriger Library at UMSL.

[662] Gerald Grinstein letter to Mr. Robert D. Krebs, September 2, 1987, Greenwood *Collection*, Barriger Library at UMSL.

[663] A.J. Lawson letter to Mr. Richard L. Lewis, December 17, 1987, Greenwood *Collection*, Barriger Library at UMSL.

[664] Bill Greenwood personal calendar.

[665] T.D. Flood letter regarding Dallas Smith Engineering Corporation to the transportation executives of 11 BN automotive customers, January 15, 1987, Greenwood *Collection*, Barriger Library at UMSL.

The suit was instituted to preserve certain contractual rights and remedies for Burlington Northern. Burlington Northern has proposed that the parties seek to resolve their differences out of court, and has offered to meet with Dallas Smith Engineering Corporation to work out a solution to the problems.

The BN ended up with an out of court settlement that voided its Dallas Smith Engineering agreement in return for twelve monthly $100,000 payments by BN to DSE.[666] The venture turned into an expensive flower that did not bloom. Ken Hoepner used to have a saying, "When you are on the cutting edge you are going to take a few nicks." Not all innovations pursued by BN Intermodal worked out. Darius Gaskins commented:[667]

We spent a lot of money – I don't know, three, four, five million dollars – in developing this thing, and it didn't work! We got to the point where – and I should have known this, I was an engineer after all – it didn't work because it was what you call an open-loop system. You'd tell a computer where to put the car, but then if there are any error messages that build up, they would accumulate. So, over time, it would make more and more mistakes and then pretty soon, it would make a catastrophic mistake and drop one of these cars on the ground or something [laughs]. So, we tried it a little bit and we said, Uh-uh, this is faulty. And we stopped doing it, at which point we had a big fight with the, quote, "inventor"–he was really a promoter, but he was an inventor–and we got out of it. I suspected Bressler would give me a real dressing down. No problem, Darius, just keep doing it. This one didn't work, don't let that inhibit you. So, he was a risk taker by definition, I give him credit for that.

Trailer Train Saga Continues

In spite of the payment of the special $180 million December, 1986 dividend, on March 5, 1987 Trailer Train CEO Ray Burton received an offer from The Prospect Group to acquire it for an all-cash offer in excess of its book value of $330 million, subject to due diligence that would last no longer than ten days. This offer placed the pre-tax value of BN's share of Trailer Train at approximately $33 million. The Prospect Group was a venture capital firm that also owned the Mid-South Railroad, among other holdings.[668]

This was quite appealing to BN and especially the owners who used little or none of Trailer Train's services but Trailer Train's Board rejected the offer. Ray Burton came to Ft. Worth on April 2 and met with Gaskins, Greenwood and Nieman to talk about BN's position regarding Trailer Train.

Trailer Train *"owners with higher utilization than owned stock felt that their payments to TTX were just going to another railroad's bottom line, including that of their competitors. In response to this inequity, Ray Burton prepared a plan that required certain members to purchase 50% of the stock of those members that wished to sell. The buyers put up $95 million to acquire*

---

[666] Frank L. Nageotte, Chairman Dallas Smith Engineering Corporation, letter to Mr. W.E. Greenwood, June 27, 1988, *Greenwood Collection*, Barriger Library at UMSL.

[667] National Railroad Hall of Fame, Darius W. Gaskins, Jr., Interview Transcript, November 5, 2020, Accessed from: https://www.nrrhof.org/darius-w-gaskins-jr, on March 20, 2023.

[668] Letter from W. Wallace McDowell, Jr., Chairman Prospect Group, to Raymond C. Burton, Jr., President and Chief Executive Officer, Trailer Train Company, March 5, 1987, *Greenwood Collection*, Barriger Library at UMSL.

additional shares. At the same time, TTX agreed to put up $42 million to purchase a portion of the stock of smaller railroads on a basis that would equate ownership and usage for those lines. The Board approved the original proposal, called the Stock Transfer Plan, on July 7, 1987, with only Guilford's B&M objecting. The buying railroads insisted that an application be made to the ICC to extend the company's pooling authority for 15 years, and that all parties would enter into a Restrictive Stock Transfer Agreement, the purpose of which restricted the ability of any shareholder to again attempt to sell the company. TTX expected the ICC to grant the 15 year extension without delay, but encountered an unexpected turn of events in that proceeding.

TTX operated under the authority originally granted by the ICC in 1974 in an order that covered both the flatcar and boxcar pools after an unremarkable proceeding. In late 1987 Greenbrier Companies, the parent company of Gunderson, Inc., filed in opposition of the pooling authority. Greenbrier's complaint was that TTX had enough purchasing power to control the price of the equipment it was purchasing claiming TTX was a "monopsony." Greenbrier was also able to get the attention of the Department of Justice (DOJ) *in its attempt to block TTX's application and DOJ entered as a party in opposition, which is a rarity."[669]*

"Despite the support of several TTX suppliers, ICC ruled in a 4-1 vote to grant anti-trust immunity but limited to a five-year period beginning in October, 1989. The ICC upheld the right of TTX to continue to purchase and own equipment for its pool of equipment. However, the ICC rescinded the right of the Company to assign specific cars to specific railroads as of October 1989, believing that the assignment was too much like a lease. It also ended TTX's practice of allocation where TTX would guarantee a certain amount of capacity to a carrier. Cars that were currently assigned were permitted to complete the terms of their assignments before becoming part of the free-running fleet."[670]

Roger Simon, the IBU's Manager Equipment Utilization at the time, has a contrasting recollection, which was shared by others in the industry, of what was transpiring in 1987 as Trailer Train sought its Pooling Authority renewal: [671]

BN had outstanding relationships with Gunderson for Intermodal cars and Stoughton Trailer for trailers and containers. Both companies recognized the direction that the Intermodal Industry was going and worked very hard to innovate and satisfy the demand. These relationships were built and tested over time to the benefit of the industry.

Trailer Train was the major supplier of Intermodal Cars to the industry and most of the railroads, including ATSF, accepted their programs. However, BN was not satisfied with the slow pace that Trailer Train was moving toward double stack equipment or innovation. Trailer Train's "know it all" attitude coupled with their attempts to incorporate out of date equipment into the Intermodal industry was sickening. Many wanted to know what BN was doing. Trailer Train requested a meeting in Ft. Worth in 1987 to discuss our plans and about half way through the meeting they got up and walked out to tell their executives in Chicago our plans to work with Gunderson to innovate and supply as much double stack equipment as possible to handle our business.

---

[669] Panza, Dawson, Sellberg, p. 67.
[670] Ibid, p. 68.
[671] Email from Roger Simon to Mark Cane, January 22, 2022.

> *Trailer Train immediately put pressure on Gunderson to stop working with BN. However, Gunderson told Trailer Train that they would do whatever BN wanted the same as if Trailer Train made the request. The relationship between Gunderson and Trailer Train was on thin ice for a long time. Gunderson questioned Trailer Train's anti-trust immunity before the ICC. At the same time Trailer Train was not giving Gunderson any car orders. Although both sides deny it had anything to do with it, new car orders started for Gunderson after the immunity issue was dropped by Gunderson. Gunderson had a balancing act in this situation but could always count on BN to lease and use the new innovative cars that were produced.*

While the elimination of Trailer Train's ability to guarantee a certain amount of capacity to a carrier could have hurt BN, the superior ability of IBU's equipment team to control equipment minimized any possible negative impact. The IBU was vindicated in its belief that Trailer Train's assignment of equipment to specific railroads, as it was doing for APL through the Union Pacific, was improper.

R.C. Matney and RoadRailer

On July 8, 1986 R.C. Matney called Bill Greenwood to propose a "project to make RoadRailer an instant success."[672] It had been two years since Matney had sold National Piggyback to APL and his non-compete agreement was coming to an end. In addition, the RoadRailer equipment BN subleased to the NS to inaugurate their Triple Crown service consisted of Mark IV trailers that had attached rail wheels which resulted in a weight penalty with regard to the amount of lading that could be carried over highways. Triple Crown had been purchasing Mark V technology equipment that allowed trailers to ride on detachable rail trucks as indicated above.[673] Discussions related to Matney's idea did not progress in 1986 but they were re-ignited in 1987. He was forming a new IMC called Mark VII and was interested in possibly venturing with BN to utilize RoadRailer equipment. Multiple meetings were held with him, including one on September 10 with Gaskins, Greenwood and Nieman.[674] The Domestic Marketing team spent December 16 reviewing the cost structure of the Mark V RoadRailer technology.[675]

Santa Fe Avard Gateway Proposal

The untapped intermodal market opportunity between the Southeast and California continued to be a frustration for the IBU. Because the BN physical plant between eastern gateways of St. Louis and Memphis and the Santa Fe interchange point at Avard, Oklahoma continued to be vastly underutilized, it was a frustration for the BN's carload businesses and the entire company at a time there was a wholesale reassessment of which rail segments to retain, sell or abandon.

---

[672] Bill Greenwood's personal calendar.

[673] Deregulation Plus Market Research Steer BN Deeper into Trucking, *Fleet Owner*, February, 1986, p. 7, *Greenwood Collection*, Barriger Library at UMSL.

[674] Ibid.

[675] Mark Cane's personal calendar.

BURLINGTON NORTHERN INC.

GERALD GRINSTEIN
Vice Chairman

777 Main Street
Ft. Worth, Texas 76102
(817) 878-2272

September 2, 1987

Mr. Robert D. Krebs
President & Chief Executive Officer
Santa Fe/Southern Pacific Corporation
224 South Michigan Avenue
Chicago, IL 60604

Dear Rob:

As we discussed on the telephone, the attached document outlines a concept we've developed to improve both Santa Fe and Burlington Northern profits in two key corridors. The concept provides ATSF access to St. Louis and Memphis in exchange for shared profits over the jointly-operated lines. We are proposing that ATSF assume all marketing, pricing and operating responsibilities for its account over the Avard-to-Memphis and Avard-to-St. Louis corridors. Investment expenses in the corridors would be shared and profits split.

The proposal is attractive to both companies for the following reasons:

- The ability to attract substantial amounts of new business by serving new markets.

- The ability for both roads to provide better service to our customers.

- A means to improve asset utilization.

- A means to reduce unit costs.

We believe this concept is based on sound economic and marketing underpinnings. We further believe that the traffic-generating potential of combined incremental BN and ATSF traffic is so large (in excess of 100,000 carloads annually) as to create a very profitable joint relationship for both parties. Clearly, the proposal carries risks for <u>both</u> entities as well, for without substantial increases in traffic, BN and ATSF would share in a rather small pool of profits. Our proposal rests on the notion of risk and return for both parties with an incentive for both to grow and prosper.

This concept will certainly require discussion and refinement. I ask that you review the proposal, keeping in mind that this is an initial concept only. We are flexible and open to other suggestions you may have.

After you've had a chance to review this with your people, I would welcome the opportunity to talk further.

Sincerely,

Gerald Grinstein

Enclosures

bcc: GASKINS
     HILLY

Recall the success of the novel profit-sharing approach the IBU had employed in getting the cooperation of the GTW for a BN Hub in Detroit. That, combined with the success the IBU had in getting a reduced crew agreement without a mileage restriction on the Springfield Region, stimulated a novel BN proposal. On September 2, 1987, Jerry Grinstein called Santa Fe/Southern Pacific Corporation's president and CEO Robert Krebs to propose that BN grant Santa Fe gain-sharing-based marketing and bridge operating rights over BN to run this corridor. He followed it up with a letter and an initial draft of a conceptual offer (left).[676] Grinstein blind-copied the letter to Darius Gaskins and his former Western Airlines labor relations associate Joe Hilly who he had recruited to BN. Attached to the letter was a more detailed explanation of the proposal (below).

Krebs forwarded the letter to Santa Fe Railway president John Swartz who responded to Grinstein by letter on September 16. In it he complimented BN's approach stating:[677]

Your proposed approach shows considerable originality, and I believe that some variation on this general theme might provide the basis for a mutually advantageous arrangement. I have asked my Traffic and Operations people to give the matter a thorough analysis, and I will be in touch the week of September 21 to set a time and place for discussions on the matter.

---

[676] Gerald Grinstein letter to Mr. Robert D. Krebs, September 2, 1987, *Greenwood Collection*, Barriger Library at UMSL.

[677] W. John Swartz letter to Mr. Gerald Grinstein, September 16, 1987, *Greenwood Collection*, Barriger Library at UMSL.

PROPOSED ATSF/BN AGREEMENT

CORRIDORS AND TERMINALS

- BN would grant to ATSF marketing and bridge operating rights over Avard to Memphis including Memphis as an origin/destination.
- BN would grant to ATSF marketing and bridge operating rights over Avard to St. Louis including St. Louis as an origin/destination.

OPERATING AND MARKETING

- ATSF may move their trains and traffic for interchange to carriers other than BN.

  On bridge traffic, ATSF will be free to set their own prices for services performed.

- Traffic interlined between ATSF and BN which originates or terminates on the corridors would be interchanged at Avard and move on BN trains at agreed rates and visions.

- BN would guarantee track standards and timetable specs over corridors.

PROFITS

- ATSF will establish and identify the revenues (FREIGHT REVENUES) it receives for the transportation services it provided over the lines of the ATSF and the BN corridors.

- The FREIGHT REVENUES shall be allocated to the CORRIDOR by the percentage the CORRIDOR distance is to the combined distance of the ATSF and corridor haul (mileage prorate formula). The result is defined as CORRIDOR REVENUE.

- CORRIDOR EXPENSES will be established as:

  a. Full variable costs per car mile (adjusted periodically for inflation), plus

  b. Terminal/interchange charges to BN, plus

  c. Terminal/interchange charges to third parties to effect interchange, plus

  d. ATSF payment for return on road and property investment in corridors.

- The difference between CORRIDOR REVENUES and CORRIDOR EXPENSES will be split:

  a. ATSF   50%
  b. BN   50%

TERMS

- Operating/Marketing rights are non-assignable by ATSF to anyone including future purchaser of ATSF without BN agreement.

- Terms for each corridor would be for 25 years; renewable upon renegotiation.

- ATSF would pay BN a one-time fee equal to the revenue BN earned on traffic which moved as "bridge traffic" in the preceding year.

He added that he regretted being unable to progress the proposal more rapidly but, "we have a number of high priority projects in progress at the present time."

On September 30, Grinstein replied:[678]

Thanks for your letter of September 16 which arrived while I was out of the country.

I know your plate is awfully full right now and therefore I thought that maybe we could make some progress by having Bill Greenwood, our Senior Vice President of Markeintg (sic), talk to his counterpart in your shop.

On October 5, Swartz responded to Grinstein stating he had run the BN proposal by his marketing and operating personnel and added:[679]

Although we are quite receptive to the idea of working with Burlington Northern to find ways to channel more traffic across these lines under a mutually beneficial arrangement, they found your specific proposal to be adverse to Santa Fe's best interest.

He went on to suggest three possible different approaches in reverse order of complexity – a lease of the lines to the Santa Fe, a normal trackage rights arrangement, and a "partnership" arrangement with "an equitable division of expenses and contribution above expenses." He added, "This would be more the type of arrangement suggested in your earlier letter, but it would require the most complex agreement." A summary of concerns was attached and the proposed 50-50 split of margin was the Santa Fe's biggest obstacle to the proposal. The bottom line was that the "specific terms offered by BN would be far less attractive to Santa Fe than our current divisions and interchange arrangement via Avard."

The proposal continued to be negotiated with Dick Lewis' Planning and Evaluation group taking the lead for BN. On December 17, Dick Lewis received a counter response from A. J. Lawson, Santa Fe's Assistant to the President with a proposal that BN grant the Santa Fe an exclusive lease of the line from Avard to

---

[678] Gerald Grinstein letter to Mr. W. John Swartz, September 30, 1987, *Greenwood Collection*, Barriger Library at UMSL .

[679] W. John Swartz letter to Mr. Gerald Grinstein, October 5, 1987, *Greenwood Collection*, Barriger Library at UMSL.

Tulsa and then turn over marketing (sales, promotion and pricing) rights to Santa Fe for business between Memphis and Tulsa and St. Louis and Tulsa. BN's gain-sharing opportunity would come from a revenue division premium for volumes in excess of the 1987 business level base. The proposal was that if this arrangement were implemented, and it worked out, a broader gain-sharing agreement could be considered later.[680]

The negotiations faded but the market opportunity did not go away. The exercise was another example of the difficulty the railroad industry had in effectively capturing interline synergies when operating under separate profit and loss statements in the zero-sum-game (I win when I can get you to lose) world.

Murry Watson and BN Worldwide (BNWW)

On July 7, Mike Karl (BNRR's Senior AVP & Managing Director – Coal Export) sent a letter to Bill Greenwood suggesting that, "a small group be authorized and formed in Marketing and be charged with developing new business for the railroad that is controlled abroad. This group will identify opportunities, develop and initiate action plans and act as consultants to the business units who will take over the feasible projects and carry them to fruition. The off-shore business development group must have direct access to the technical skills of the Business Units. This concept would fail at the outset without the development of a teamwork atmosphere within the total marketing effort. The new group would not become involved in service level, equipment use or acquisition, nor price level negotiations, unless directed by the involved business unit."[681]

Greenwood shared the letter with all of his direct reports including Murry Watson. Watson, VP International Marketing and Sales, was a consummate salesman, long on ideas but short on details. He already had a somewhat similar view as that described by Karl and believed that BN Railroad could leverage its reputation in the global logistics marketplace through an asset-light integrated international intermodal network presence. On July 20 Watson gave up his International Marketing and Sales responsibility and was charged with developing his idea, still reporting to Nieman. [682] Ralph Muellner was promoted to Vice President International Marketing and Sales, reporting to Nieman. On August 13 Watson arranged a lunch followed by an afternoon meeting with Darius Gaskins, Bill Greenwood and Steve Nieman to propose a new project consistent with his vision that was less passive than Karl's. [683] He was asked to put together a more detailed plan. He continued to provide updates to his plan throughout the balance of the year and effective January 1, 1988 Watson was appointed President of a new venture called BN Worldwide reporting to Steve Nieman.[684] While reporting to Nieman, it was going to be independent of the Railroad with oversight by a Board comprised of BN Railroad executives. The desire was to free the venture from the Railroad bureaucracy that had been hindering BN's IBU.

---

[680] A. J. Lawson letter to Mr. Richard L. Lewis, December 17, 1987, *Greenwood Collection*, Barriger Library at UMSL.

[681] Michael H. Karl letter to Mr. W.E. Greenwood, July 7, 1987, *Greenwood Collection*, Barriger Library at UMSL.

[682] BN Marketing Organization Chart, July 20, 1987, *Greenwood Collection*, Barriger Library at UMSL.

[683] Bill Greenwood personal calendar.

[684] BN Marketing Organization Chart, January 1, 1988, *Greenwood Collection*, Barriger Library at UMSL.

The Rebirth of the Winona Bridge Railway Company (WBRC)

As mentioned previously, the Expediter strategy had several main objectives – to generate positive cash flow from an underutilized asset base, improve the image of BN Intermodal in the marketplace, improve the image of BN Railroad in the marketplace, and generate improved relations with organized labor. Any good-will that had been generated with BN's operating crafts did not extend to the former Great Northern and Northern Pacific territories, including the IBU's prime route between Minneapolis / St. Paul and Seattle and the trains between Birmingham and the PNW and between the PNW and Texas and service for the Fargo and Billings Hubs. With a clear understanding of the competitive situation BNRR was facing, as exemplified by the information from Kellogg's, on September 2, Jim Dagnon sent a letter to M.M. Winter and D.E. Wegler who were United Transportation Union General Chairman for operating employees on these territories. In it he said: [685]

> As you know, local Carrier officers have been approaching your Local Chairmen asking them to enter into local agreements, as provided in Article 12 of the 12/5/80 Crew Consist Agreement, raising car and train length limits for reduced crew operations to 121 cars and 6,840 feet.

He asked them to encourage Local Chairmen to enter into local agreements to extend the limits. He reminded them that when the 1980 agreement had been entered into, BN had agreed to provide personal leave days to Crew Consist protected employees in return for the assurance that the agreement would be quickly ratified. He said they had been receiving those benefits for 8 years with nothing in return for BN and that if agreements were not forthcoming those benefits would be eliminated. In addition, Crew Consist protected employees would be eligible for "productivity fund" payments of up to one-third of their income for working on a reduced crew and employees were forgoing that income opportunity. He reminded the General Chairmen that those employees were foregoing significant income.

The Kellogg's experience was only the tip of the proverbial iceberg when it came to the impact motor carrier competition was having on the railroad industry. In addition, even business segments such as BN's grain business were impacted by global competition by improvements in agricultural technology and where a great crop year in Ukraine, Argentina and Brazil could knock US grain in BN served areas out of the global export market due to transportation costs. Within the intermodal business, by the mid-late 1980s, companies were looking to shift more and more of their off-shore production to Southeast Asian countries. The BN had a competitive advantage in the PNW compared to California ports for import business from Japan and South Korea. It is one sailing day shorter but that advantage shifts to California for sailings from Singapore.

The risk of universal motor carrier use of the previously mentioned Turnpike Doubles and Rocky Mountain Doubles was also taken seriously. Comparative costs for a hypothetical 1,000 Mile Haul using 45' or 48' Boxes on a 6,000 Foot Train were previously cited in the discussion of comparative double-stack economics. Where line-haul motor carrier costs were placed at approximately $.75 per mile for a 48' trailer, Turnpike Double 48s would reduce that to as low as $.375 per mile. Not only would that bring about significant price competition and drive lower rail prices for all truck competitive rail commodities, it would also nearly eliminate any cost advantage for 48' rail intermodal shipments at a

[685] James B. Dagnon letter to M.W. Winter and D.E. Wegler, September 2, 1987, *Greenwood Collection*, Barriger Library at UMSL.

hypothetical line-haul cost of $.43 per mile for a RoadRailer trailer, $.413 for a trailer on a spine car or $.312 for a container in a stack car in an unlikely perfectly full and fully load-balanced train.

People including Darius Gaskins, Bill Greenwood, BN's AG Commodities and Strategic Planning teams, and the IBU leadership team recognized an existential threat to BN if BN's unnecessarily high labor costs were not addressed.   As mentioned previously when the IBU formulated its Expediter strategy, there was no logical reason why a train crew should require four to six crew members. Gaskins said:[686]

> *... you had to have four or five people on a train, and had to have a caboose, and had to have all these things. That was part of the labor agreement, and so you had to renegotiate your labor agreements, fight your way through it, but eventually the railroads got down to a crew consist of two people, consistently. They're relatively highly paid, but it's a big difference paying two people to run a train than paying five.*
>
> *I think the statistic when I went and joined the BN, we had an average of 5.2 people on a train, because some places we had to have six because of a local codicil or something in the labor agreement.*

Advances in communications and operating technology made excess crew members redundant but the rail industry was burdened with decades old labor agreements that were a legacy of a different era. The Expediter experience showed that trains could operate safely with two person crews and no caboose. In addition to being required to operate with redundant labor, train operating agreements included complicated work rules associated with arbitrary payments for things such as initial and final terminal delay, held-away-from-home payments and runarounds that added to the challenge. Mechanical craft agreements restricted the ability of the railroad to utilize a composite employee who could work as jack-of-all-trades within shops. Railroads negotiated with up to 14 different labor crafts.

Having been one of the architects of deregulation, Gaskins was especially sensitive to the vulnerability a carrier had when the commercial side of their business was deregulated but the cost side wasn't. As made clear by BN's coal experience and the imposing influence the ICC was having on BN as it related to rate caps, negating contracts and forced market entry, the Staggers Act did not deregulate that commercial side of that business. It was clear that there was an existential threat if BN and the railroad industry could not get crew size and work rule relief in a market where deregulated motor carriers were becoming an ever greater threat. Unions had to be convinced of the reality of this and that labor relief would make railroads more competitive and create the opportunity for new jobs.

Attempts to convince the Labor Organizations that these threats were real were proving to be futile. The Organizations were focused on "today" and a sense of invincibility. Something had to change to convince the labor organizations to change their position when it came to what, in essence, had become ingrained featherbedding. Darius Gaskins, Bill Greenwood and Jim Dagnon convinced Jerry Grinstein that some drastic measures were required. Another player was brought into the picture. At Western Airlines, Grinstein had the previously-mentioned Joe Hilly as his Vice President - Employee Relations and he handled labor negotiations. He stayed with Delta after their takeover of Western but Grinstein brought him to BN in July, 1987 as VP Labor Relations Planning.[687] Grinstein also brought in his friend

---

[686] National Railroad Hall of Fame, Darius W. Gaskins, Jr., Interview Transcript, November 5, 2020, Accessed from: https://www.nrrhof.org/darius-w-gaskins-jr, on March 20, 2023.
[687] Burlington Northern Inc., 1991 Form 10-K, p. 9.

Wayne Horvitz as a labor consultant. Horvitz had been appointed by President Jimmy Carter as the director of the Federal Mediation and Conciliation Service in 1977.[688] His involvement in labor mediation included leading roles in:[689]

- Averting a national strike between AT&T and the Communication Workers of America and International Brotherhood of Electrical Workers in 1977
- Restructuring the leadership of the United Mine Workers in 1978 that helped end a 110 day strike of the United Mine Workers
- Aversion of a national strike of the United States Postal workers
- The negotiation of a new master freight agreement and end of a ten day nationwide strike by the Teamsters in 1979

As tough as negotiating with pilots unions may have been, bargaining with rail operating crafts would prove to Grinstein, Horvitz and Hilly to be significantly more difficult. There were already indications that Grinstein, who would talk a tough talk, would lack the resolve to follow through with tough and decisive action. Larry Kaufman commented on how Tom Matthews, who was brought in from the airline industry before Grinstein to run BN's labor relations, knew this first-hand:

> *Grinstein ... had a politician's need to be "loved," and that affected the way he continued the drive to change the culture. As Matthews put it, Bressler didn't care what labor thought of him. It just didn't bother him at all. Grinstein, on the other hand, "would have a heart attack" if union leaders called him what they called Bressler.*[690]

The 1987 Annual Report Form 10-K included these comments:

> *Labor negotiations with all the unions will be conducted during 1988, and the Railroad has indicated its intention to bargain with the railroad labor organizations independently of other railroads. Railroad is unable to predict the results of such negotiations.*[691]

In advance of these negotiations there were two measures involving the IBU that were intended to shake-up the status quo. The first was:

> *In November 1987, Railroad granted its wholly owned subsidiary, Winona Bridge Railway Company ("WBRC") trackage rights over 1,860 miles of Railroad's lines from Seattle to Winona Junction (Wisconsin). WBRC may serve shippers only at Railroad's intermodal hub centers at St. Paul, Seattle and Spokane. WBRC will target new intermodal traffic moving in the Seattle-St. Paul corridor.*[692]

Gaskins led the development of the idea of using the WBRC corporate structure as a way to break through the unwillingness of BN's most intransigent unions – the United Transportation Union and Brotherhood of Locomotive Engineers on the former Great Northern and Northern Pacific lines – to negotiate competitive labor agreements. WBRC owned BN's bridge that crossed the Mississippi River at

---

[688] Wikipedia, Wayne L. Horvitz, Accessed from: www.en.m.Wikipedia.org, on November 5, 2022.
[689] Ibid.
[690] Kaufman, p. 269.
[691] Burlington Northern Inc., 1987 Annual Report Form 10-K, p. 12.
[692] Burlington Northern Inc., 1987 Annual Report Form 10-K, p. 4.

Winona, MN. The idea was for WBRC to be granted trackage rights to operate over BN between St. Paul and Seattle. WBRC would be non-union but employees would have the right to unionize. Trains would operate with two crew members, be focused on Intermodal business, and lease their own locomotives and intermodal cars, trailers and containers.

Gaskins added:[693]

> *Interestingly enough, we did Winona Bridge because we had already had success at the southern part of the railroad with our Expediter trains. These were trains where we got agreement to run two-man crews under the normal labor agreement, but just two people on them. They were for short distances, intermodal movements of about 500 miles. They were profitable and we were growing it pretty aggressively, but we couldn't crack the Northern Tier because the people in the north were most secure, they were the least sensitive to truck competition or anything else. They just had these jobs for life, and they didn't see it the way we did. They didn't see that we had an opportunity to make things better for everybody. They thought it [was] just, You're going to take our jobs away from us through the guise of these Expediter trains.*

Bill Greenwood had been talking with Mike Donahue, BN's retired former VP Strategic Planning and leader of its Coal Business Unit, about the concept behind WBRC in mid-1987. On September 28 Donahue sent Greenwood a letter stating:

> *Along the lines of our recent conversations I concur it is timely we set up a joint meeting with Labor Relations and the Law Departments to agree on marketing concepts necessary to initiate the possible Northern Lines New Business Project.*
>
> *As you are aware, to begin with we are looking for a new market niche which would be clear cut and distinguishable from BN's current business. We could seek new and incremental opportunities that should be competitively available. I'm assuming origins, routes, schedules, service levels, rates, and contracts of this new incremental business should be solicited so there is minimum erotion (sic) of your existing base business?*
>
> *During our joint meeting, preferably early in the week of November 5, we can discuss and agree with you and/or your representatives on the above as well as the specific market definitions as to how the subsidiary can be completely autonomous and independent.*[694]

That same letter included a draft project plan with timelines for issues related to things including crews, new business, operating plan, legal, public relations, accounting / administration and labor direction.

The legal formation of WBRC occurred on November 16. On November 18, news of WBRC's formation was announced. A "backgrounder" stated information including the following:[695]

---

[693] National Railroad Hall of Fame, Darius W. Gaskins, Jr., Interview Transcript, November 5, 2020, Accessed from: https://www.nrrhof.org/darius-w-gaskins-jr, on March 20, 2023.

[694] Michael M. Donahue letter to William E. Greenwood, September 28, 1987, *Greenwood Collection*, Barriger Library at UMSL.

[695] Burlington Northern Railroad, Background Information for Your Use, November 18, 1987, *Greenwood Collection*, Barriger Library at UMSL.

On Nov. 16 BNRR and the Winona Bridge Railway Co., a wholly owned subsidiary of BNRR, signed an agreement under which Winona will operate trains using trackage rights on BN between Winona Junction, Wis., and Seattle, a distance of 1,860 miles. Winona Junction is 110 track miles southeast of St. Paul.

Today (Nov. 18) Winona filed with the ICC a notice of exemption, which will be effective Nov. 25.

Winona Bridge Railway is expected to start train operations by January at the earliest.

The trackage-rights route is BN's northern line (Twin Cities, Fargo, Minot, Havre, Sandpoint, Spokane, Everett and Seattle.) Winona cannot serve and switch industries along the BN trackage. Winona can pick up and set out traffic at the BN's intermodal hub centers in St. Paul, Spokane and Seattle.

Winona's objective is to gain new intermodal business (trainload only) and operate Expediter-style with short crews (usually 2 persons).

This is from the notice of exemption "The parties envision that initially BN will provide the equipment, financing, and support services necessary for Winona to operate. The transaction is designed to enable Winona to operate as a low-cost carrier handling traffic under contract in the Winona-St. Paul-Seattle corridor. Winona intends to develop new business currently moving on carriers other than BN and via other modes, and for which BN is not currently price-competitive."

Winona anticipates negotiating transportation contracts for exempt traffic (primarily TOFC/COFC business), for movements which are not time-sensitive.

The exemption notice states: "The transaction will have the ancillary benefit of increasing utilization of BN's rail plant during off-peak times through Winona's use of these trackage rights. Because Winona will target only new business opportunities for its transportation contract movements, and not existing BN traffic, it is not anticipated that any current BN employees will be adversely impacted by this transaction. Winona and BN are nonetheless agreeable to the imposition of the standard labor protective conditions. This would be protection of current earnings of up to six years.

Mike Donahue is president of Winona and Tom Whitacre is vice president.

The IBU was directly in the middle of this initiative. Tom Whitacre, identified as WBRC's vice president, was BN's retired former vice president transportation. Like BN Worldwide, WBRC was to be under the BN umbrella with a Board composed of BN executives but it was to be independent of the stifling BN Railroad bureaucracy.

Montana Rail Link (MRL) is Born

The second major initiative related to shaking up the Northern Lines labor status quo situation that directly impacted the IBU was the deal that created Montana Rail Link (MRL). As mentioned earlier, as of December, 1986 BN had prepared a list of 1,236 miles of "short line" sale candidates plus 2,300 miles of main lines that were under consideration for sale.[696] Included in this later list was the line between Laurel, Montana and Sandpoint, Idaho which was part of BN's second east-west main line through Montana. Given continued competitive market pressures, excess capacity, the need to ration capital, and cost reduction pressure, Darius Gaskins said:[697]

> *We had a big problem in the Northern Tier of our railroad, and that was the state of Montana. Because there used to be three railroads in Montana, right? In 1970, the (GN), Burlington & Quincy and the Northern Pacific merged and then we put the Milwaukee Railroad out of business, effectively, through competition. So, it went from three to one, and it was a lot of bad feelings in the state of Montana. They were angry with us, and then we were trying to abandon facilities and lay off people and everything, and everything we did upset those folks.*

> *It was really annoying, I mean, they were yelling at us and they were taking punitive actions where they could. We also had in the state of Montana, we had some environmental problems. We had a place where we used to treat ties, and you put nasty stuff on ties so that they don't rot, and nasty stuff, when it gets into the river or the aquifer or something, it's not good. So, we had a serious problem in Livingston, I think it was, with the residue of a tie plant. So, I'm looking at this whole picture saying, This Montana, this is bad. I'm not getting any headway with the politics of this. I can't schmooze these guys because they're mad at us and every time I try to do something to raise our profitability, reduce our plant size, they're killing me. So, I was with my short line sales guy, we were flying across Montana, and I said – his name is John – I said, John, can you think of a big chunk of the railroad that we could sell to somebody out here in Montana, so we can sell it to them and they can deal with the political problems, the environmental problems, with the this and the that. I explained my concept, and he thought about it and he says, I think we should sell them the old NP line. That was the basis of Montana Rail Link.*

The John who Gaskins referred to was John Hall. Gaskins continued:

> *We got some investment bankers. They went out and tracked down people. They found Denny Washington, who was a famous entrepreneur in Montana who had a trucking business and at that time was a billionaire, I think, or close to it. Very well connected with the state people. He had given a million dollars to the University of Montana for their football stadium. Everybody knew him. His wife had been … Miss Montana, that kind of thing, yeah, when she graduated. So, he was a very prominent guy and a pretty good businessman. So, we went to him and we struck a deal. And the deal was, we'd give him traffic in the eastern part of the state, and he would haul it over to Sandpoint, Idaho, across the state, and he'd give it back to us. If he took any traffic on the line for his own account, he got to keep that, but he hauled ours for a fee, a negotiated fee, which had a complicated escalator in it and so forth and so on. That part of the deal was relatively straightforward. What was not so straightforward was what happened to the liabilities for the environmental thing and for the labor contract. Because the first thing Denny Washington does, he says, Okay, I got this property. We had some lawsuits and, you know, a little acrimony. But he says, I have this property, so he sits down with the two unions, the UTU and the BLE, Brotherhood of Locomotive Engineers, and he says, I've got a deal here. I got this*

---

[696] Bill Greenwood, Senior Staff Meeting Marketing Comments, December, 1986, *Greenwood Collection*, Barriger Library at UMSL.

[697] National Railroad Hall of Fame, Darius W. Gaskins, Jr., Interview Transcript, November 5, 2020, Accessed from: https://www.nrrhof.org/darius-w-gaskins-jr, on March 20, 2023.

railroad and I need a contract. I want to use you and your people, I love unions, but I'm not sure I need both of you. Does either one of you want to take – all the jobs? And then there's a cooker: we can only use two people on each train because we're starting up, we need to have our costs [low]. Well, BLE put their hand up, We'll do it! We'll do it. UTU said, ABSOLUTELY NOT. We want that caboose on there, we will only take our jobs, we don't want the BLE– So Denny said, Fine. BLE it is! And he cut a deal with BLE. Well, what that did is, the UTU, they were our toughest opposition on jobs, and they had won up until that point. They had blocked us with Winona Bridge, they had blocked us with abandonments. They were very successful in holding the traditional consist agreement and keeping the little caboose on the end of the train. That was their dream. But this one broke the dam because at that point, we had a railroad operating in our account, for us, across the state of Montana with two people on it and no caboose! On top of that, Denny Washington offered profit sharing to these guys, so if they met certain targets, they got bigger bonuses, and they didn't even want it. He forced them to take it because he believed in it.

The line was transferred to Dennis Washington and his Montana Rail Link on October 31, 1987. MRL was guaranteed a minimum amount of business that they would handle for BN as a bridge carrier across their railroad between Laurel, MT and Sandpoint, ID. This included intermodal trains operating between the PNW and Texas and Birmingham. BN, effectively, got the first two-person train crew agreement in the industry for one of the most labor-intransigent parts of its system. Although the deal was a 60 year lease and not a sale, it was a signal to BN's organized labor that things had to, and would, change. This was especially so in combination with Winona Bridge.

BN Domestic Containerization Groundwork

Much higher on the priority list than RoadRailers was the direction BN should take with domestic containerization. As previously discussed, the IBU had kept the domestic containerization issue on the stove top but it was on the back burner through 1986 even as APL introduced the first domestic containers for use on their Liner-Trains. Their containers were too heavy and had door heights of only 103" compared to 110" for BN's intermodal trailers. In his book Dave DeBoer commented:

> *Having gained a well-earned reputation for intermodal innovations under Bill Greenwood, the Burlington Northern had been very active in the adoption of international stack technology. Ralph Muellner had made the BN a major force in handling international containers. But as Greenwood was promoted to the top marketing job, the BN had languished on the application of Third-Generation technology to domestic traffic.*[698]

DeBoer was unaware of what was really going on. Mark Cane had stated to the Domestic Marketing team leaders in December of 1986, as 1987 goals were being finalized, "We must respond to the domestic double stack challenge/opportunity."[699] On February 9 and 10, 1987, all-day domestic containerization brainstorming meetings were held with the team. The desire was to not just come up with a reaction to the domestic containerization challenge. The vision was to capitalize on what was perceived to be an opportunity to attack the domestic containerization opportunity in a way that addressed the previously mentioned fragmentation, dock-to-dock service and channel management

---

[698] DeBoer, p. 167.
[699] Mark Cane letter, Subject: 1987 Goals, December 12, 1986, *Greenwood Collection*, Barriger Library at UMSL.

shortcomings in the intermodal business that were keeping intermodal from achieving its competitive and profit potential.

Hypothetical Costs For 1,000 Mile Haul – 45' or 48' Boxes, 6,000 Foot Train[700]

Car Type	Linehaul Cost	Car Capital/ Maintenance	Box Capital	Total Ramp To Ramp	Boxes per Train	Cost per Box
89' car/trailer	$46,800	$4,050	$2,830	$53,680	130	$413
89' car/cont.	$46,200	$4,050	$1,910	$52,160	130	$401
Spine/trailer	$38,600	$4,420	$2,390	$45,410	110	$413
Spine/cont.	$38,000	$4,420	$1,620	$44,040	110	$400
Stack/cont.	$51,000	$5,400	$2,790	$59,190	190	$312
RoadRailer	$24,700	$2,400	$4,130	$32,230	75	$430

Bill Berry's Equipment and Planning team worked in conjunction with the marketing team to reassess the relative economics of the various technologies. The results of that study were similar to what DeBoer published above.

Since the 1981 Intermodal Task Force had recommended the utilization of skeleton type cars to carry trailers, the legal trailer length limit had increased to 48' versus 45'. A spine car was similar to the skeleton car but could handle either a trailer or container. The above table doesn't give an equivalent view of conventional car versus other technologies because an 89' car could not handle two 48' trailers or containers. While the cost per box for conventional 89' cars looked to be comparable to Spines, it also assumed the use of 45' trailers or containers which would not be motor carrier competitive long-term. A competitive domestic trailer or container would have to be at least 48' long and this length was assumed in the above analysis for Spines, Stacks and RoadRailer. The limitation of 75 RoadRailers in a train was due to regulations that restricted RoadRailer train lengths due to the strength limits of the trailers needed to pull trailing trailers in a train and also the risk of train string-lining around curves on ascending grades.

Every one of the technologies analyzed above produced a significantly lower line-haul cost than the total line-haul cost for a well-run motor carrier, at the time, of approximately 75 cents per mile.[701] When terminal and chassis costs were factored into the analysis it reduced the competitiveness of domestic containerization with spine cars and improved the relative performance of RoadRailers and Spines with 48' trailers but not by enough to overcome the relative 25% improvement in line-haul productivity.

A major hurdle for BN was that, for safety reasons, the company policy had been to utilize stack cars with bulkheads. A domestic containerization network would have to utilize containers of multiple lengths. The cars with bulkheads worked well for a static international system using 20' and 40' containers in 40' wells but it would not work when 45', 48' and even 53' containers were utilized. The BN bulkhead cars could handle a 45' container in the top position of the three middle wells of the five-well car through the use of "flippers" but that was not a competitive long-term solution.[702] In addition, ISO containers were 8' wide while the domestic trailer standard was 8'6' wide. Therefore the domestic container standard would have to be same and the stack cars BN had acquired (for containers up to 40' long and 8' wide) would not work effectively. Due to the safety record that had been accumulated by

---

[700] DeBoer, pp. 172-173, used with permission granted on May 14, 2022.
[701] Ibid, p. 173.
[702] Panza, Dawson, Sellberg, p. 240.

stack cars without bulkheads, BN reassessed its position. Supported by the counsel provided by industry expert Alan Zarembski, and his ZETA-TECH Associates (whom the IBU met with on June 24),[703] and Ron Newman of BN's Research and Development Department, in anticipation of domestic containerization, BN changed its policy. As a result, by the end of 1987 the only railroads who were only utilizing stack cars with bulkheads were the SP and CSX.[704]

Additional meetings were held to refine a Domestic Containerization plan throughout the year and in September Mark Cane and Bill Berry assigned Kirk Williams (former Superintendent Highway Operations in Chicago and then Market Manager- Carriers) and Planning Analyst David Proctor to team up to prepare a dock-to-dock domestic containerization service plan.

Unfortunately, Steve Nieman was verbally supportive of the effort but when it came to making hard decisions he dragged his feet. As the year progressed it became clearer and clearer to Mark Cane and Bill Berry that the IBU had to act decisively, sooner rather than later, on the domestic containerization effort. An update of the progress the team had made was given to Nieman on October 12[705] and a green light to aggressively proceed was anticipated. It did not come. The competitive clock was ticking and both Berry and Cane knew the future of the IBU was jeopardized by inaction. They met on November 2[706] to strategize how to keep momentum going without Nieman's unqualified support. They decided that the risk of working around Nieman had to be taken. Mark Cane agreed to schedule a meeting with Bill Greenwood to brief him on the dilemma. At that meeting Cane explained the dilemma and Greenwood asked what he could do to help. Given the experience the IBU had with John Gray on the blank-sheet development of the SIG facility in Seattle he asked for permission to schedule a meeting with Gray in which Berry and Cane would lay out the vision for a clean-sheet BN domestic containerization business. The plan the IBU had envisioned included a restructured channel approach with agents whereby they would be selectively chosen as carrier agents. The venture would provide for door-to-door service and specially designed motor carrier competitive 48' BN containers. The venture would also be utilized to manage domestic reloads of westbound international containers to assist Common User Stack Train customers and help them stay out of the US domestic market. Key elements of that effort would be a remote Customer Service Center free of union people-selection and work-rule restrictions that would handle container booking and work with the Hubs on drayage scheduling. The service center would oversee door-to-door service performance. It was believed it could also be utilized to help international shippers with their inland logistics. The critical need of a central point for booking and door-to-door oversight had been brought to the surface with the 1987 U.S. Postal Service contract. It called for door-to-door service by the railroad and for the lanes BN won, the IBU struggled with comprehensive door-to-door service. Not all Hubs were equally positioned to manage significant drayage service. In his report on 1987 goal performance Mark Cane told Steve Nieman, "The Post Office experience has taught us that we won't be effective door-to-door with our current structure."[707] Given the continued lack of BN systems to support such a venture the plan also envisioned that the contractor would assist in the provision of such systems support. Greenwood gave his approval and said he would brief Darius Gaskins. Based on this, and other issues including a lack of responsiveness

---

[703] Mark Cane's calendar.
[704] Panza, Dawson, Sellberg, p. 244.
[705] Mark Cane's personal calendar.
[706] Ibid.
[707] Mark Cane letter to S.C. Nieman, 1987 marketing accomplishments vs. goals, December 22, 1987, *Greenwood Collection*, Barriger Library at UMSL.

related to the RoadRailer initiative with R.C. Matney, Greenwood also initiated efforts to find a replacement for Nieman.[708]

On November 12, Berry and Cane met with Gray at the Stevedoring Services of America office in Long Beach and laid out the very general domestic containerization plan.[709] Gray had also been frustrated with the fragmented nature of the intermodal business. He said he bought-in to the vision, provided valuable insight about how the plan could be improved, and said he was all-in regarding his willingness to help. Meanwhile, Bill Greenwood's personal calendar shows a phone call with Bob Ingram on November 19.[710]

Another meeting was held with Nieman on November 17 to review progress with the domestic containerization plan.[711] The support that John Gray indicated he would work to provide was included as part of the plan and Nieman was pleased with it. Planning with Gray proceeded and Bill Greenwood was briefed about further progress on November 30.[712] On December 22 in that same letter to Nieman, Cane stated:

> We are now positioned to successfully do battle in the domestic containerization business. Much of the work Kirk and Dave Proctor have done will accelerate our progress with the new venture. I am extremely excited about the potential of the new venture and over time I believe it will prove to be one of the most significant things we kicked-off in 1987.[713]

Nieman was also provided a "draft list of qualifiers (below) developed for evaluating potential agent affiliates for the domestic containerization program:

> *Draft Qualifiers for Evaluating Potential Domestic Containerization Program Agent Affiliates*[714]
> - *Increased revenue 1987 vs. 1986*
> - *2,000 + Units shipped YTD 1987*
> - *Average revenue per unit exceeds $704*
> - *"Approved" financial standing*
> - *Field sales force*
> - *Top shipper in select lanes*
> - *EDI capability*
> - *Use of partnership advertising*

He added, "Our explicit qualifiers will be further developed in 1988."[715] Additional meetings were held with Gray all day December 29 and 30 to refine the plan.[716]

---

[708] Bill Greenwood interview with Mark Cane, March 19, 2022.

[709] Mark Cane's personal calendar.

[710] Bill Greenwood's personal calendar.

[711] Mark Cane's calendar.

[712] Ibid.

[713] Mark Cane letter to S. C. Nieman, Re: 1987 marketing accomplishments vs. goals, December 22, 1987, *Greenwood Collection*, Barriger Library at UMSL.

[714] Ibid, Attachment 4.

[715] Mark Cane letter to S. C. Nieman, Re: 1987 marketing accomplishments vs. goals, December 22, 1987, *Greenwood Collection*, Barriger Library at UMSL.

[716] Mark Cane's personal calendar.

Former Northern Pacific Railroad Properties are Unencumbered

One of the things BNI Board members, such as the previously mentioned Norton Simon in the mid-1970s, had aggressively promoted was the development of the "Land Grant" properties that BN's predecessor Northern Pacific Railroad received from the U.S. Government to help finance its construction. Northern Pacific had gone through repeated financial difficulties during its early history and, as a result, NP bond buyers placed restrictions on two major bond classes. [717]

> *The Northern Pacific became overextended and fell into bankruptcy again in the Depression of 1893, largely due to the result of too rapid expansion of main and branch lines that had insufficient traffic. As was the case with other railroads, some of the extensions were undertaken not because they were economically justified by traffic but because the company wished to preempt competitors in the expectation that traffic later would grow to justify the construction.*

> *The 1886 reorganization of the Northern Pacific was spurred by the efforts of New York financier J.P. Morgan. The reorganization was to haunt the railroad and its successor, Burlington Northern, for generations. To protect bondholders of the reorganized company and to ensure that the railroad's management would continue to invest in the railroad, the rich natural resources that came to the railroad with its land grant were pledged as collateral for two series of bonds. Bondholders feared that Northern Pacific management might be tempted to focus on exploiting the land grant at the expense of the railroad. For that reason the two bonds issues were structured to prevent milking of the natural resources assets. The two bond issues, one of 100 years and one of 150 years, had no sinking-fund requirement. In addition, they were not callable before their maturity in 1996 and 2046. Under the terms of the indenture, before the company could realize any revenue from timber, mining, or other resource sales, it had to certify to the trustee of the bond issues that an amount of money equal to the resource revenue had been expended on the railroad's property.*

> *In an effort to gain relief from the restrictions of the bonds, the managers of Northern Pacific and, later, of Burlington Northern tried unsuccessfully to get the bonds called in or otherwise paid off, including an ill-fated attempt to persuade the U.S. treasury to issue very long-term bonds to replace the Northern Pacific bonds.*

The encumbrances affected "approximately 2,398 miles of the former Northern Pacific Railway Company's ("NP") main lines and 1,360 miles of NP's branch lines, together with substantially all of Railroad's natural resources properties." [718] "Under terms of these mortgages, Railroad is permitted to sell timber, land and minerals and to lease mineral interests. However, the proceeds from such sales and leases, net of expenses and taxes, must be deposited with the trustees under such mortgages. Except for $500,000 of such proceeds annually, which must be applied to the purchase on the open market of bonds outstanding under such mortgages, such proceeds are available for withdrawal by Railroad upon certification to the mortgage trustees of additions and betterments to Railroad properties subject to those mortgages." [719] BNI Holding Company had salivated over this encumbered property and finally got the break it sought. The 1987 Annual Report Form-10K stated:

---

[717] Kaufman, pp. 26-27.
[718] Burlington Northern Inc, 1986 Annual Report Form 10-K, p. 11.
[719] Ibid.

On November 25, 1987, Judge Robert Carter of the United States District Court for the Southern District of New York approved a settlement in <u>Rievman v. Burlington Northern Railroad Company</u>, a class action that had been pending since May 15, 1985. Under terms of the settlement, holders of approximately $69.9 million of the former Northern Pacific Railroad Company ("NP") 4% prior lien bonds, due January 1, 1997, and approximately $47.8 million of NP 3% general lien bonds, due January 1, 2047, will receive approximately $14.75, plus interest, and $45.625, plus interest, per $100 bond, respectively. On January 12, 1988, the settlement became final and no longer subject to judicial review. The payment was made to the bondholders on February 1, 1988. Also, on that date, certain oil, and natural gas, timber, coal and real estate properties that comprised a portion of the collateral securing the bonds were released from the liens of the bonds' mortgages. Railroad is the successor obligor of the NP of the two series of bonds.[720]

This was the key to the lock that would allow the complete separation of BN Railroad from BN Railroad properties/resources to fully feed BNI's Resources businesses. It would prove to have a monumental impact on BNRR and the IBU.

1987 Comparative Intermodal Load Originations

In 1981 when BN's IBU was formed, BN intermodal's 339 thousand loads handled were the lowest among the major United States railroads. In 1987, total loads handled had grown 162% to 887 thousand. Loads originated at BN Hubs were 693 thousand which was the fourth highest in the industry as shown below:[721]

Railroad	1987 Originated Loads
Conrail	810,000
Santa Fe	719,000
CSX	708,000
Burlington Northern	693,000
Union Pacific	551,000
Southern Pacific	537,000
Norfolk Southern	513,000
Others	869,000

1987 BNI, BNRR and BN Intermodal Financial Performance

BN Inc. financial performance improved in 1987 with the help of improved BN Railroad performance:

The 1987 financial and operating performance of Burlington Northern Inc., improved significantly. Earnings per share were $4.93 compared to the pro forma $3.46 recorded in 1986. Free cash flow (funds provided by operations less capital expenditures) was $691 million in 1987

---

[720] Burlington Northern Inc., 1987 Annual Report Form 10-K, p. 11.

[721] Burlington Northern Railroad, Intermodal Hit Squad, Final Report, February 24, 1992, *Greenwood Collection*, Barriger Library at UMSL.

versus $644 million the previous year. In October, the Board of Directors increased the annual common dividend by 10% to $2.20 per share.

Burlington Northern Railroad achieved record traffic volumes in 1987 and contributed 57% of BNI's consolidated operating income. All major commodity groups showed gains, with the agricultural, food and forest products groups each recording increases of greater than 15% over 1986 revenue –ton-miles. The railroad's continuing efforts to reduce costs resulted in better profit margins in 1987. The attendant productivity gains have enabled the company to compete effectively with other carriers by providing improved service and saving to our shippers.[722]

Unfortunately, "record traffic volumes" in 1987 did not coincide with record BNRR revenue or operating income. BNRR capital expenditures fell to $280.6 million from $312.2 million in 1986 and $650.6 million in 1985.

Intermodal revenue grew $62 million (almost 12%). Ag revenue grew 11%. Coal revenue grew a reported 6.6%. Adjusted for the $122 million 1986 coal litigation reserve, coal revenue actually fell 2.7% primarily due to added share loss and rate reductions to secure long term contracts and stop UP/C&NW market share gains. With an increase of 10.2%, for the first time since 1981 BNRR's non coal/Ag/ Intermodal businesses achieved year-to-year revenue growth.

This table reflects the performance of the IBU relative to BNRR overall:

Burlington Northern Railroad 1981-1987 Financial Performance ($ millions) [723]

	IML Rev.	BNRR Rev.	BNRR Op. Inc.	BNRR OR	BNI LT Debt	Pref. Stock	Int. Exp.	Div. Exp.	Debt/ Cap.
1981	$267	$4,088	$527	87.1%	$1,330	$105	$140	$58	29%
1982	273	3,773	457	87.9%	1,333	105	136	71	27%
1983	335	4,058	734	81.9%	2,930	709	142	87	41%
1984	443	4,490	980	78.2%	2,454	697	310	130	35%
1985	485	4,098	822	79.9%	3,118	519	312	184	41%
1986	523	3,801	506[a]	86.7%	3,394	62	389	123	49%
1987	585	4,038	602	85.1%	3,001	57	372	155	44%

[a] Reported Operating Income was $152.8 mm, including approximately $20 million (pre-tax) of IBU driven Trailer Train dividends. It would have been a rounded $506 mm without the special non-cash charge of $352 mm, and $628 mm without that plus a coal rate litigation reserve.

BNI's long term debt fell almost $400 million and the debt to capitalization ratio fell to 44% but combined interest and dividend expense increased to $527 million from $512 million in 1986.

---

[722] Richard Bressler, To Our Stockholders, Burlington Northern Inc., 1987 Annual Report Form 10-K.
[723] Burlington Northern Inc., 1981-1987 Annual Reports and 10-Ks.

Chapter 15 - 1988 Brings Major Disruptions Setting the Stage for Future Challenges

Steve Nieman's Fate is Sealed

The year 1988 would be tumultuous for BN Railroad and BN Intermodal. By November of 1987, Bill Greenwood had Darius Gaskins' support to replace Steve Nieman as the IBU's leader. Nieman's fate was sealed on the evening of December 13, 1987. That evening the IBU celebrated its Annual Christmas dinner at the Worthington Hotel in Downtown Ft. Worth. Neiman handled arrangements for the event including the post-meal entertainment. Darius Gaskins and his wife Stephanie as well as Bill Greenwood and his wife Colleen were invited. Greenwood had a close affinity with the IBU given that he was its founding-father and Gaskins had a good relationship with the group because of the number of initiatives he helped the IBU pioneer. In addition, after another year of solid intermodal growth and continued innovation there was a lot to celebrate.

It turned out that Nieman had arranged for a burlesque-type performer to provide the post-meal "entertainment." Her act made the vast majority of the attendees very uncomfortable and it got worse when she started to make Gaskins the butt of her jokes and even sat on his lap. The only people laughing were Nieman and his wife who clearly thought it was hilarious. Darius and Mrs. Gaskins happened to be sitting next to the Greenwoods and after the performer left Darius Gaskins' lap he leaned over to Bill Greenwood and whispered, "You're going to fire him, right?" Greenwood whispered back, "Yes I am."[724] Greenwood added, "Nieman was a smart and personable person but he would say the right things and just not take action. The experience surrounding domestic containerization was a good example of that."[725]

1988 IBU Strategic Direction as the Nieman Era Closes

Nieman had asked each of his direct reports to provide write-ups for their area of responsibility. The only write-up that survives is Mark Cane's for Intermodal Marketing. Although parts of it repeat earlier themes, it is included to provide a fuller perspective for the major issues and focal areas of the time:[726]

Burlington Northern Intermodal
1988 Strategic Plan
Marketing Issues Review

Product Strategy

In 1987, "Service by design" became BN's operating and marketing theme. The spirit of this theme has been the foundation of Intermodal's product strategy for several years and will continue to be so. In addition, Intermodal is a firm adherent to the concept of "quality is free." Not only does quality result in lower total cost, it also gives you the opportunity to differentiate

---

[724] Bill Greenwood interview with Mark Cane, March 22, 2022.
[725] Ibid.
[726] Cane, Mark, Burlington Northern Intermodal 1988 Strategic Plan, Marketing Issues Review, December, 1987, *Greenwood Collection*, Barriger Library at UMSL.

yourself from the competition and capture the added quality by charging and getting more for your service, thereby increasing return.

BN's Intermodal product consists of several elements. The following is a summary of BN Intermodal's strategy regarding these product elements:

Train Service

For too long, the railroad industry has operated under the principle of "get the business first and then we'll run the train." Intermodal has tried to make service a function of customer needs rather than a function of operating convenience. This has meant initiating new services with little to no freight in-hand and experiencing the classic new product life cycle common to all industries. Because of past industry practices of starting new services and discontinuing them after, say, a week of light business, customers have been wary of adjusting their routing guidelines and shifting business to rail. Such was the experience we encountered with the first Expediters, where business was much less than forecasted during start-up. BN's Expediter performance, wherein commitments have been firmly adhered to, has gained BN substantial market credibility. This has significantly shortened the time period of loss for subsequent new services.

Rail Intermodal service can be characterized as a batch business rather than a piece business. That is, given the operating characteristics and economics of rail service where the product is transportations of many trailers or containers, the more freight you put on the train, the more profit you tend to generate. This is unlike Intermodal's prime competition, the irregular route motor carrier business which is more of a piece business in which the product is transportation of a single trailer or container. This has significant ramifications for Intermodal competitiveness, especially in light density shorter haul markets. In such markets, trainload intermodal quantities may be difficult to obtain and time needed to batch loads into trainload quantities may make intermodal service non-competitive compared to a truck which can head for destination immediately after loading.

Given this competitive disadvantage, Intermodal's service strategy is to run multiple schedules in a lane, with train lengths as short as financially practical in order to meet required service standards. This strategy is also appropriate when Intermodal's two basic target market segments are considered. The LTL motor carrier segment, in which Intermodal is used as a linehaul substitute, needs late pm or early am availabilities and late am or early pm cutoffs. The TL segment, where intermodal generally competes with irregular route carriers, needs late PM cutoffs and early AM availabilities. Intermodal's strategy has been to tailor multiple frequencies to these market segments' needs. Another benefit of this strategy is a reduction in the severity of damage created by a service failure or missed gate cutoff in that the shipment is only delayed until the next frequency rather than the next day's train.

Because not all current and prospective service lanes have sufficient density to justify single or multiple dedicated train service schedules, Intermodal has and will continue to rely on a network of train schedules with frequent swaps of business blocks. The intermodal network has already grown to such a sophisticated level that additional information system support is required to manage and plan optimally. The level of network sophistication will only increase over time. This will increase the need for IS support and even more-so increase the need for error free service as any service failure within the network Impacts service on all connecting services.

Another feature of Intermodal's product strategy is to schedule service to be only as fast as required to be competitive rather than as fast as possible. Customer service requirements generally fall into day slots, such as first am, second pm, third am, etc. To attempt to provide faster service than is required would entail unnecessary expense (locomotives, right of way) and would reduce service reliability because of the loss of any allowable cushion. Customers requiring the fastest service possible will utilize air freight or team drivers which intermodal has trouble competing against under the best of circumstances, anyway.

As previously mentioned, Intermodal's prime competition comes from the Irregular Route motor carrier. When utilizing truck, shippers spend less for load securement than they do for conventional Intermodal. Intermodal's strategy has been to build a level of service quality into the system that will require no more load securement of the customer than is required for over the road transportation. This has been accomplished with Expediter with tremendous success, primarily due to restricted train lengths. Improved train handling combined with utilization of articulated car technologies are expected to open other trains to relaxed loading guidelines.

Hub Service

BN Intermodal has tried to make train service schedules invisible to the customer. The customer is purchasing transportation from Hub to Hub, or Door-to-door, or some variation, which makes train service incidental. Since BN is primarily a provider of Hub to Hub service today, advertised service standards are published for cutoff to availability. This makes Hub ramping and grounding just as important to the service package as train service.

As with train service, BN's Hub service strategy is to provide the level of service required, and as best as possible, no more and no less. Therefore, service standards for ramping and grounding must accommodate estimated train volumes. In order to appropriately measure and manage Hub ramping and grounding performance, Intermodal has developed a Service Performance Measurement System.

For several reasons, a major BN service strategy is to become a large scale provider of door-to-door service. First, one of the most frequent Intermodal weaknesses cited by current and prospective customers is fragmentation. Agents were expected to bridge the Intermodal service links but have not done the job to the degree required. We cannot mortgage our future waiting for this to happen. Second, Intermodal profitability can be a make or break proposition because of equipment and drayage economies. Since all of drayage and much of equipment expense is incurred between hub and door, BN cannot effectively manage its economic destiny without controlling this aspect of Intermodal service. Transition from being in the Hub to Hub to being in the Door-to-door business will put significant additional responsibilities on Hubs for selection of drayage companies and management of their service. Intermodal information systems are currently being geared up to assist this effort. The importance of information system support to effectively make the transition and profitably do business door-to-door cannot be overstated.

Information Accuracy

Information is a frequently forgotten element of service. We can provide impeccable transit service but if inaccurate tracing information is conveyed or if the freight bill contains an error, we experience a service failure. Because information accuracy depends so heavily on accurate and timely data entry, significant resources will be required to assure that this end is met.

Even if we possess perfect information, improper or non-conveyance of information also constitutes a service failure. Therefore, additional resources are required for EDI transmission and telephone management (timely, courteous, complete and accurate response).

<u>*Offline Market Opportunities*</u>

Significant untapped business opportunity is known to exist between markets within 350-400 miles on each side of the Mississippi River. The fragmented rail industry meets within this zone. Because rail carriers on each side have viewed haul lengths shorter than 400 miles as unattractive, little or no Intermodal service has been provided within this zone. When viewed from the standpoint of a single line carrier, these markets become 600-800 mile haul opportunities.

With this view, Intermodal has identified offline BN hubs as a significant opportunity. The Detroit Hub on the GTW was the first opportunity capitalized on. Other potential Class I partners have not been so willing but they will remain targets for additional such ventures. In addition to penetration of the Mississippi watershed market, this approach can also be a viable way to serve California.

Newly created short lines railroads also present similar opportunities. Because they do not tend to serve high density markets, the market opportunity with them is less but their lower cost structures increase potential economic opportunity.

Fragmentation remains one of the most critical weaknesses of Intermodal nationwide. Establishment of an offline hub network linked into the existing BN system by Expediter type trains carries significant potential to reduce fragmentation. Considerable thought has also been given to the establishment of an Intermodal railroad consortium, managed by a single entity that would deliver comprehensive single line service capability to a majority of the nation's markets, thereby eliminating fragmentation on a large scale.

<u>*Pricing Strategy*</u>

<u>*Pricing Philosophy*</u>

Intermodal has evolved from a share driven business philosophy to one driven by margin and return on assets (ROA) employed. As capacity is filled, it is imperative that the capacity is filled with the best possible business. This can be managed with price.

<u>*Pricing Management Constraints*</u>

BN Intermodal is not in a position to effectively manage capacity with price primarily because of a lack of knowledge of what business is being carried (actual commodity, beneficial owner, actual receiver, true origin and destination), and lack of information system support to differentiate price based on various variables.

In order to gain required market knowledge, beginning in 1988, complete billing information is being required for every domestic shipment. This is a long term strategic action to position BN to both price more intelligently and plan services better.

Price differentiation is feasible conceptually today but is not feasible operationally. Current systems do not allow differentiation according to variables such as service levels, season, day of week, or time of day. Even if the systems could accommodate these multiple levels of price, there is a lack of system support for the field so that they know what level of service to provide.

Another critical element of ROA driven pricing is quick response to changing market conditions. Lack of electronically stored and transmitted prices reduces the ability to effect timely changes.

In addition to lack of adequate system support to change, as required, our strategic price management direction, we face resistance from the market. It is unlikely either our intermodal rail competitors or our selling agents are yet of the mindset necessary to bring about this change. Therefore, significant training will be required of agents, significant changes must be made in the channel relationship (see Channel Management), and a strong market leadership position must be established with competitors.

<u>Pricing Authority Delegation</u>

Two prime pricing objectives are optimization and responsiveness. In order to provide responsiveness, BN Intermodal has delegated limited pricing authority to National Marketing Executives (NMEs) and the National Marketing Center (NMC). In an attempt to optimize, price setting authority rests at various levels with as many stakeholders as practical involved. These include Hub Managers who watch out for their Hub's interest, Lane Market Managers who watch out for their trains' and lanes' interest, NMEs' and the NMC who watch out for their customers' interest and Segment Market Managers who watch out for the system interests of their market segment. What may appear to be cumbersome has proven to be extremely effective and is a strategic strength BN will continue to capitalize on in the future.

<u>Promotion Strategy</u>

In the domestic United States market, Intermodal service carries an image of being poor quality and low priced. As such, Intermodal has historically appealed, in general, to shippers of relatively low value, time insensitive, and therefore very price competitive commodities.

Unfortunately, this image has, on the whole, been justified. Using BN as an example, up to the early 1980s good quality intermodal service was only available in the Chicago – PNW and Chicago – Denver lanes. Only within the last year has BN provided comprehensive high quality Intermodal service. Equally unfortunate is the fact that few rail carriers other than BN provide comprehensive quality service.

As a result, BN has two major promotion challenges. The first is to communicate the message that Intermodal doesn't necessarily mean poor service (that Intermodal isn't what it used to be).

The second is to convincingly differentiate BN's Intermodal service from the rest of the industry. That is, BN Intermodal provides quality service, competitive and in many cases more reliable than that provided over the road, at a competitive but not a cheap price, which makes it qualified as a viable transportation mode for business not traditionally carried (more margin potential).

To accomplish this, BN's promotion efforts have focused on improving the image of Intermodal overall and differentiating BN as better. Target markets for media advertising are motor carriers to attract line-haul conversion and beneficial owners of freight to interest them in Intermodal first, and then to get them to specify BN Intermodal to agents through a demand-pull approach. Media utilized are primarily trade journals read by transportations and materials management decision makers of beneficial owners.

Direct mail promotion has been and will continue to be utilized to inform agents and beneficial owners of new service offerings. A critical direct mail item developed in 1987 which will be a key strategic promotion item for the future is the BN Intermodal Product Manual. This manual, which will be updated quarterly, is a "how to" and "what is" for BN Intermodal. In that so much promotion emphasis is being placed on service competitiveness of BN, it is important to note that prices are not quoted in the manual.

For years, BN has been extremely tight lipped with the media. In 1987, a strategic shift in BN Intermodal's relationship with the press began. In recognition of the fact that well managed Public Relations is one of the cheapest and most effective forms of advertising, press releases and media interviews were utilized extensively and the plan is to continue to do so. This has been accomplished without compromising BN's policies regarding non-disclosure of sensitive operating and financial statistics.

The same open approach has applied to internal promotion, within BN. Commitment to and support of BN's employees is facilitated by an understanding of the competitive environment, how BN is doing, what BN needs to accomplish to be successful, and what level of commitment is required of employees to bring success. Promotion efforts on this front include the monthly Intermodal Newsletter whose audience includes agents, members of the media, and key BN employees. Selected stories from the newsletter appear in BN News and the employee newsletter mailed to all employees homes. Intermodal intends to continue active participation at Division, Region and System Operating employees' staff meetings, and every other staff meeting we become aware of, in order to spread the Intermodal story.

<u>*Marketing Channels*</u>

BN currently markets its Domestic Intermodal service through transportation agents, directly to motor carriers, and directly to a small minority of beneficial owners who refuse to do business with an agent. This channel approach has proven successful to BN with regard to the historical drive for market share. In that BN's strategic drive has shifted to quality service, margin and ROA, the channel approach is evolving, primarily in the relationship with agents.

BN has utilized agents to sell its service for several major reasons. First, given the fact that BN serves a limited market (geographically), agents can sell more economically in that they sell multiple lines (greater chance of a successful call because of broader coverage and more options)

294

and are not directly compensated by BN (more people selling for you with no additional cost). Second, BN has not had the infrastructure to provide effective door-to-door service while some agents have (some better than others). Third, use of agents has shielded BN from claims liability. Fourth, because of stringent credit guidelines, use of agents has shielded BN from bad debt liability and improved cash flow.

Major weaknesses with this relationship from BN's standpoint include isolation of BN from the beneficial owner (lack of market knowledge), downward price pressure in that the agent has just as much incentive to make it on the buy rather than the sell (pressure costs down, including line haul rail and drayage, rather than price up), poor product knowledge on the part of agents which has resulted in sale of price and not service, and relatively little brand loyalty for BN. Consistent with a market share driven strategy, BN has rather freely allowed new agent entrants which has compounded the effects of the above.

Consistent with a margin/return/quality service strategy, BN is modifying its approach to the agent channel. First, qualifications for new agent agreement holders have been tightened which will increase the overall quality of representation and help lessen pressure on prices. Second, qualifications and contribution of existing agreement holders are being reevaluated which is resulting in many agreement cancellations. Third, complete billing information including beneficial owner, commodity, true origin and true destination have been required of all shipments as of January 1, 1988 (see Pricing Strategy), which will give BN significantly better market intelligence to permit far more effective channel, price and service management. Fourth, an agent training program is being formulated to convey BN product knowledge to agents, teach how to sell value, and hopefully generate greater BN brand loyalty. These steps are positioning BN to play a far bigger role in the management of the agent channel.

For the longer term, BN Intermodal is investigating the concepts of exclusive agency for accounts or geographic areas and direct compensation of agents through either flat fees or commissions. Several needs are driving these actions. First, there is a strong need to have the agent be the agent of BN rather than the shipper's agent. While BN has its prime interest in meeting the needs of the shipper, BN must have the agent working equally in its interest from a service design and profitability standpoint. Second, major shippers are putting more and more of their business up for competitive bidding among a multitude of agents. This puts significant price pressure on the railroad as each agent attempts to get price reductions to give it a bidding advantage. This pressure will continue until carriers designate agents to represent their services in such bidding processes. Third, as BN continues its drive for quality service, the agent can be the weak link in the service chain if not effectively managed. In addition, the value created by capital investments made to improve service quality will not be captured if the agent is unaware of or fails to sell it. Fourth, as BN evolves into a door-to-door provider of Intermodal service (see Product Strategy), some of the duties traditionally performed by agents will now be performed by BN. In order to attract and retain the best agents for representation of BN's services, BN must compensate them with both parties benefiting from making it on the sell rather than on the buy.

As BN begins to perform more and more of the functions traditionally performed by agents, a logical question is why utilize them at all. In that much of effective selling still depends on personal relationships (and is expected to continue to do so), BN can capitalize on the strong relationships selected agents already have. In addition, utilization of agents shelters BN from Railroad Retirement, pension fund, and other fringe benefit liabilities while still retaining an *entrepreneurial sales force which is easier to selectively add to or prune, if need be, than a direct BN sales force.*

Regarding direct sales, BN's Commodity Business Units are a relatively untapped Intermodal sales force. Through capture of complete billing information, the intent is to credit commodity market managers for Intermodal business so that they consider it a part of their product package rather than the competition, thereby promoting more balanced decisions.

Asset Utilization

Lane Management

In late 1986, BN established three Lane Management groups within the Marketing section of Intermodal. Each group was assigned specific geographic territory within which they have responsibility and accountability for BN's Intermodal service and financial performance. In the spirit of "service by design'" these groups have responsibility to assure that BN's Intermodal service is addressing market needs, balancing service provided with financial opportunity.

Lane Management groups are responsible for seeking out new service opportunities, evaluating their viability, developing and implementing new product plans, and managing the service and financial performance of ongoing services. In that they have service and P&L accountability, they watch for opportunities to improve both rather than one at the expense of the other which has been more typical in the railroad industry, historically. This puts them in a position to better allocate resources such as hub, train, locomotive and right of way capacity. Since they feel a sense of ownership for "their" lane and monitor the pulse closely, they are in a position to react faster to changing business conditions, through price, service, or equipment supply adjustments.

The effectiveness of the lane groups will improve significantly when the new Intermodal information systems tools, such as the new Service Performance Measurement and Intermodal Profitability systems are fully operational.

Bob Ingram Replaces Steve Nieman

By January 18, 1988, Bob Ingram had been hired as BN's Vice President Intermodal. After CSX purchased Sea-Land, Ingram was recruited by the Soo Line Railroad to be its leader of Marketing and Sales, replacing Ken Hoepner. He was with the Soo Line when Greenwood first inquired about his interest in BN's IBU leadership position.

Brooks Bentz recalled that he learned Greenwood interviewed three candidates for the job leading the IBU, including Ingram. The others were Doug Hagestad who was at the time running the intermodal business on the Illinois Central Railroad, and Bentz who had been CEO of IU International's Ameritrans Division.[727] Another person Greenwood considered was Bob Lake who at the time was President, Ryder Freight System, a nationwide truckload carrier operating under the Ryder name. Prior to that Lake had been Executive Vice President, General Manager Commercial Transport Division of North American Van

---

[727] Brooks Bentz email to Mark Cane, March 10, 2022.

Lines. [728] He was not in a position to leave Ryder at the time and later in 1988 he wrote to Greenwood, "I am sorry my availability did not coincide with your need in the intermodal organization because I would sure like to be a part of BN."[729]

Given the strategic imperative to act on domestic containerization, the BN Worldwide start-up, and the need to respond to the APL challenge, Ingram was a logical choice the lead the IBU:

- He had significant international container business experience
- He had built networks of railroads to support Sea-Land's contract-train inland services
- He was one of the originators of double stack technology.

Greenwood said he had concerns about how Ingram would fit into the BN culture and wanted to consider more candidates but, as was the case when Nieman was hired, he was urged by Darius Gaskins to just hire him and move on. [730]   As important as the above qualifications were, Greenwood's concern about Ingram was ultimately overcome and he hired him because of one more factor which was the most critical.

Bob Ingram Shared the IBU Strategic Vision

Supported by the strength of Ingram's background, Greenwood bet on his leadership of the IBU primarily because he shared the IBU's strategic vision in several key areas that were critical for the IBU to significantly improve customer service and profitability. BN had to:[731]

- Strengthen its Intermodal franchise by broadening its rail-based geographic footprint
- Accelerate its use of double stack technology and domestic containerization
- Continue its pursuit of prudent RoadRailer applications
- Bridge the fragments in the intermodal product offering by restructuring its domestic marketing channel relationship through migration to retail and/or carrier agents who were incented to "make it on the sell"
- Migrate toward domestic door-to-door service in the non-carrier market segment, taking control over drayage
- Gain tighter control over its equipment through increased (lower cost) ownership over its base car fleet and tighter control over its trailer and container fleet
- Assist international steamship customers with their dilemma of empty containers needing to return westbound by establishing a domestic ISO container reload capability

Whereas Nieman was slow to act, Ingram was the opposite. He took no time to establish his position and communicate what he would be focusing on. Nieman had just issued an organization chart on January 11[732] that included Murry Watson and BN Worldwide reporting to him as well as Ralph Muellner as Vice President International. A week later, on January 18, Ingram issued a new Intermodal

---

[728] Robert D. Lake resume.

[729] Robert D. Lake letter to Mr. William E. Greenwood, September 19, 1988, *Greenwood Collection*, Barriger Library at UMSL .

[730] Mark Cane interview with Bill Greenwood, March 19, 2022.

[731] Ibid.

[732] Burlington Northern Railroad Intermodal/International Organization Chart, January 11, 1988, *Greenwood Collection*, Barriger Library at UMSL.

organization chart that was identical to Nieman's except for two new and very significant features. Ingram's included a vacant position for President—BN Intermodal Services, and a dotted line position reporting to him that was occupied by R.C. Matney as President—Mark VII Transportation. His intent was to establish the new Domestic Containerization business under the BN Intermodal Services banner. The desire within the IBU was to create this new business outside of BN's Railroad bureaucracy to give it more operating cost and service flexibility, similar to BN Worldwide and Winona Bridge. Ingram understood the rationale for organizing it that way and initially supported that desire.

What was immediately clear is that working with Ingram would be diametrically unlike working with Bill Greenwood or Steve Nieman. While also aggressive, Bill Greenwood's approach to leading the IBU was collaborative and inclusive. Neiman had difficulties making tough decisions but he valued the input of the team he was leading and didn't obstruct. Greenwood and Nieman were quite predictable but Ingram was mercurial and very much a "Lone Ranger."

Steve Nieman Shifts to Winona Bridge, but is Soon Replaced by Bill DeWitt

When Nieman was informed of his replacement as IBU leader he was asked if he would take responsibility for getting Winona Bridge off the ground and leading it. Nieman had been involved in the work surrounding Winona Bridge since the idea was conceived and had consistently given it his verbal support. He accepted the position and became its president, reporting to Greenwood.

On February 2, 3 and 4 Bill Greenwood assembled his Business Unit leaders for a Sales and Marketing Strategic Management and Planning Conference. Nieman briefed all of the business unit leaders on what the initial WBRC plan was related to the Minneapolis/St. Paul—Seattle corridor and the possibility of utilizing the strategy elsewhere.

Nieman did not thrive in the unstructured, start-up, WBRC environment and chose to leave BN by April. He was replaced by Bill DeWitt (who left his Asst. VP Marketing Resources position) as the new Winona Bridge President. Gay Minnich—Olson was assigned by the IBU to assist DeWitt. They did a great deal of work developing business opportunities, an operating plan and establishing labor representation. Because the UTU threatened to strike over WBRC, BN pursued a Federal Court injunction. DeWitt kept working on a successful service initiation while the WBRC initiative worked its way through the courts. At an offsite BN Strategic Marketing Vision Conference held outside of Austin, TX, he had the following comments to all of BN's Business Unit Heads about WBRC:[733]

- WBRC would initially focus on BN's Northern Tier.
- It was striving to generate at least 50 trailers per train and at that volume the wage related train operating labor cost would be reduced from $26 to $7.85 per trailer. Higher volume would increase the cost differential.
- The time for BN to collect payment for freight bills related to the service would be only 17 days compared to an average of 68 days for Intermodal overall which was significant in a high interest rate environment.

---

[733] Mark Cane personal calendar and notes related to Bill DeWitt's WBRC Presentation, Lakeway Resort, TX, October 3-6, 1988, *Greenwood Collection*, Barriger Library at UMSL .

- While at that time it was primarily a low-cost labor strategy there was capability to utilize it to pursue other strategic initiatives
- If it successfully overcame court challenges WBRC could be expanded to other service corridors.

The Court ruled late in the year against BN. Gaskins said:[734]

> *That died because we tried that and the court said, No, no, no, no. You're not going to get rid of your labor contracts through a double-breasting operation. We see our way through that. That's not going to happen.*

The WBRC initiative was terminated in January, 1989. BN's 1987 Annual Report Form 10-K said:

> *During 1987, Railroad granted its wholly-owned subsidiary, Winona Bridge Railway Company, trackage rights over 1,860 miles of Railroad's lines from Seattle to Winona Junction (Wisconsin). This arrangement would have operated new-business intermodal trains with reduced crew sizes over Railroad's northern main line between Seattle and Minneapolis – St. Paul. The plan was dropped because of adverse court actions in 1988.*[735]

R.C. Matney/RoadRailer and Domestic Containerization Related Organization Restructuring

Mark Cane provided a status update on the domestic containerization effort to Gaskins, Greenwood and Nieman on January 11, 1988 which included a review of what the IBU team believed were the strategic imperatives related to expanding BN's geographic footprint and changing the way it did business through the effort. Ingram was briefed on the vision for the effort and the elements of the project plan after he arrived.

Until December of 1987, the IBU did not devote the focus to the Matney/RoadRailer initiative that the domestic containerization and Winona Bridge efforts had received. On January 22, Caroline Dewhirst, the IBU point person for the RoadRailer effort received a detailed legal opinion from Art Zaegel, BN's primary business venture legal counsel, that discussed possible options for a structuring of a joint venture company with Matney and Mark VII, the BN and the Santa Fe, also independent of BN's Railroad bureaucracy.[736]

After his January 18 arrival, Ingram immediately picked up on the proposal Matney had given Greenwood to advance RoadRailer technology on BN. He and Mark Cane had meetings to discuss the proposed venture on January 28 and they had a meeting with Matney on January 29. A meeting was held in Chicago with Norfolk Southern (who was running RoadRailer trains) to discuss the venture on February 24. [737]

---

[734] National Railroad Hall of Fame, Darius W. Gaskins, Jr., Interview Transcript, November 5, 2020, Accessed from: https://www.nrrhof.org/darius-w-gaskins-jr, on March 20, 2023.

[735] Burlington Northern Inc., 1987 Annual Report Form 10-K, p. 5.

[736] Arthur R. Zaegel letter to Ms. C.C. Dewhirst, Re: Mark VII / RoadRailer Project, January 22, 1988, *Greenwood Collection*, Barriger Library at UMSL.

[737] Mark Cane personal calendar.

Meanwhile, The IBU lacked organizational alignment for these efforts. On March 18 Ingram met with Bill Greenwood to discuss the IBU's organization and his ideas for a restructuring in order to get aligned. On April 15 Ingram announced a major IBU organizational restructuring. In a letter to the Intermodal Department Ingram wrote:[738]

> *I am pleased to announce that effective Monday, April 18 the following reporting relationship changes and promotions will be made within the Intermodal organization. They include:*
> - *Mark Cane promoted to General Manager – RoadRailer Systems*
> - *Axel Holland promoted to General Manager – Hub Operations*
> - *William Berry promoted to AVP – Intermodal Lane Management*
> - *Gary Agnew promoted to Director – Intermodal Group Planning*
> - *David Burns, General Manager Hub Operations with expanded responsibility to include interline relations and operational research and engineering*
> - *Thomas Doty, Market Manager – Agents will report directly to me along with existing direct reports Kathy Louth, Jack Round, Marv Dowell and Ralph Muellner.*
>
> *This modified organization will expand the lane management concept to include both Marketing and equipment control; provide an increased focus on hub terminal operations and marketing; a functional group to deal with the multi-faceted aspects of our RoadRailer Systems development and a closer link between our interline rail planning functions and the Intermodal operational groups.*

Prior to this restructuring Axel Holland reported to Dave Burns and BN's 26 Hub managers reported jointly to them. Following this restructuring, Dave Burns not only assumed responsibility for interline intermodal service with other railroads; he also assumed responsibility for Operations Research and retained reporting responsibility for only the nine largest Hubs. Axel Holland assumed the same title as Dave Burns (GM Hub Operations) and reported directly to Ingram. He had authority for the remaining seventeen Hubs plus responsibility for Hub administration and lift device maintenance. Bill Berry retained responsibility for equipment management and maintenance as well as Lane Management. Tom Doty assumed responsibility for marketing through agents, motor carriers and interline railroads.

On April 22 he sent out the following letter concerning another organizational change:[739]

> *I am pleased to announce that Brooks A. Bentz has accepted the position of AVP Domestic Container Systems reporting to me in Ft. Worth. Brooks' responsibility will include the development of an organization to manage the Domestic Container Program which will include the westbound loading of marine containers with domestic cargos and the widespread introduction of doublestack container services throughout Burlington Northern's system.*
>
> *Brooks' past experience includes operations management positions with both the Norfolk and Western Railway and the Delaware and Hudson Railway, intermodal management with the Boston Maine Railway, and most recently nationwide domestic experience with Ameritrans, a subsidiary of PIE.*

---

[738] Robert S. Ingram letter to the Intermodal Department subject: Intermodal Organization, April 15, 1988, *Greenwood Collection*, Barriger Library at UMSL.
[739] Robert S. Ingram letter to the Intermodal Department subject: Intermodal Organization, April 22, 1988, *Greenwood Collection*, Barriger Library at UMSL.

The Domestic Container Systems group will be located at our Fort Worth headquarters on the 35th floor.

On April 26, 1988 Ingram sent a letter to all of BN's Marketing and Sales business unit heads informing them of the IBU's organization changes. It included the following which gave more insight into his strategic intent: [740]

Mark Cane has been appointed General Manager of RoadRailer Systems – with the return of the 240 Mark IV units from the Norfolk Southern and our further involvement with R.C. Matney in the development of the Mark VII Corporation, a joint project between Norfolk Southern, BN and the Santa Fe – it was necessary to create an independent organization to deal outside of the normal Intermodal channels with this highly specialized project while still maintaining the specialized knowledge and relationship with the existing Intermodal network.

I have asked Mark to insure that each of the commodity groups has a full understanding of the Mark VII concept and additionally suggested that he review RoadRailer potentials identified within the marketing sectors.

Brooks Bentz has joined the company as AVP, Domestic Container Systems – Brooks will be heavily involved in the marketing of international containers predominantly in the westbound direction, the introduction of domestic 45 and 48-foot containers within the existing Intermodal structure and the development of specialized container moves of commodities not heretofore handled in domestic container programs.

This latter area is of particular importance since APL/APD has indicated a long-term objective to penetrate the U.S. domestic scene utilizing their infrastructure of doublestack trains and specialized container equipment. At the Atlanta Intermodal Expo, they displayed approximately 10 container types and various doublestack configurations. Included in the containers were 48-foot, high-cube refrigerated units; 53-foot dry vans; a 53-foot dry van with an autorack assembly installed for setup vehicles and lastly, adjacent to their area was a newly developed domestic flatbed container provided by SCI which was loaded with lumber.

On April 27 Ingram published a new IBU organization chart that had Cane in his new position with Caroline Dewhirst and a vacant position authority reporting to him, and Brooks Bentz in his new position with Kirk Williams and Dave Proctor reporting to him. [741]

Comparative BNRR/Intermodal Pricing Performance

The IBU Lane Management structure was announced on August 1, 1986. It took a while for the teams to get staffed and for rudimentary systems support to be established to help them and the segment

---

[740] Robert S. Ingram letter to William E. Greenwood, Donald W. Scott, William J. DeWitt, R. Richard Carter, T. Daniel Flood, Kenneth L. Hagen, Don D. Meyer, Nicholas P. Moros, Gary D. Schlaeger, Sharon S. White, Subject: Intermodal Organization, April 26, 1988, *Greenwood Collection*, Barriger Library at UMSL.

[741] Burlington Northern Intermodal Organization Chart, April 27, 1988, *Greenwood Collection*, Barriger Library at UMSL.

marketing teams with better information to manage prices more effectively. Meanwhile, international intermodal prices were falling due to the introduction of double stack competition and that also impacted westbound domestic lane prices as APL's Liner Train domestic containerization influence grew. On May 9, 1987, Mark Cane put out the letter to the Marketing, Sales and Hub teams related to a stronger emphasis that would be placed on raising prices while filling excess capacity. The table below reflects the relative degree of success of these efforts compared to the pricing behavior of other BN business units between January of 1987 and April of 1988. The source of this information was a new Price Measurement System that Bill Greenwood had been pushing for.[742] Internal and external critics of BN and its Marketing group would focus on revenue per revenue-ton-mile as a proxy for price performance but it reflected changes in business mix as well as prices. This system compared actual revenue from comparable shipments in origin/destination pairs with like-equipment-types between time periods.

BUSINESS UNIT DETAIL	1987 Q1	1987 Q2	1987 Q3	1987 Q4	1988 Q1	PERIOD ENDING 4/30/88
AGRICULTURAL	-5.8	-1.9	-0.1	4.6	14.4	15.1
FOOD & CONSUMER	-3.4	-4.6	-5.2	-3.4	0.8	3.1
INDUSTRIAL	-4.2	-5.5	-3.1	-0.2	2.3	3.3
FOREST	-3.9	-3.8	-2.2	-0.3	3.4	3.1
AUTOMOTIVE	-0.7	-2.4	-2.9	-3.3	1.9	3.6
INTERMODAL	-2.5	-1.5	0.1	-0.2	1.2	1.3
COAL & TACONITE	-9.6	-6.7	-2.9	-2.8	2.0	3.5
BNRR	-3.8	-3.2	-1.6	-0.2	3.7	4.4

The chart showed that the IBU had maintained price levels through 1987, in spite of the influence of aggressive motor carrier competition with 48' X 102' trailers (vs. mostly 45' X 96" rail trailers) and aggressive and disruptive double stack competition, more effectively than the other business units. It shows the influence of efforts to raise domestic intermodal prices initiated in May of 1987. In addition, the IBU had grown 1987 revenue 11.9% so this showed that it was not "buying market share." Other business units increased prices more than the IBU during the first four months of 1987 from more depressed 1986 levels. The significant 1987 coal decreases were due to PRB competition from the C&NW-UP. The significant Ag increases in 1988 were due to the installation of leaders in the Ag Commodities Business Unit from the grain industry. They understood how to let the market's supply and demand dynamics determine a market-clearing price for BN's grain transportation services, especially through the implementation of the auction-driven Certificate of Transportation Service (COTS) program.

RoadRailer / Mark VII Initiative

Ingram's people-approach was counter to the strong and inclusive team culture that had been the hallmark of the IBU since its founding as was stressed in the previously cited *The Wisdom of Teams*.[743] Mark Cane related:[744]

> My appointment to the RoadRailer initiative by Bob Ingram wasn't put to me as a matter of choice but as a directive. Over the years I turned down inquiries from recruiters for positions in other companies. My new relationship with Ingram was awkward at-best.

[742] William E. Greenwood letter to Richard Bressler, June 8, 1988, *Greenwood Collection*, Barriger Library at UMSL.
[743] Katzenbach and Smith, Chapter 2.
[744] Mark Cane's personal recollection.

Since Ingram's arrival, a recruiter for APL had contacted me and I believed I had to explore the opportunity. I traveled to Tucson on Saturday, April 23 and interviewed with a partner from the corporate recruiter Ward Howell. His description of the APL opportunity sounded intriguing and, given the presence APL was establishing in the market, I said I would be interested in a next step if APL felt likewise. Over May 5 and 6 I interviewed with six APL executives in Oakland.[745]

During this time I was working with R.C. Matney on a refinement of the RoadRailer plan. We met in Indianapolis all day on May 4 and developed initial plans for a June 8 demonstration event at the Birmingham Hub for prospective customers. The demo included a RoadRailer/stack car connector designed by Bill Berry that would allow RoadRailers to run behind stack cars. Customers invited to the demonstration included representatives from UPS because their endorsement of joint BN-Santa Fe service between the Southeast and California would be a major market coup. We also believed it would be essential for solidifying the participation of the Santa Fe. It was so important that I arranged for BN's corporate jet to transport the UPS executives. I gave a project update to Darius Gaskins and Bill Greenwood on May 25 and it was well-received.[746]

I received a very attractive job offer from APL on May 30 and asked for a few days to consider it. I was told that was fine. Meanwhile, my wife was expecting our third child on June 4. I had a meeting with Ingram to review the demonstration train plans and told him that I would not be at the demonstration if my wife had not delivered our baby by June 8. I said I promised my wife I would be present for the delivery. Ingram became apoplectic and said I had to be there. I told him everything was totally under control and that Dave Albright and Caroline Dewhirst would be capably handling everything on-site. Ingram insisted that I be there on June 8 and if I wasn't there he would fire me. I said my family came first and if Ingram insisted on that I would resign. Given that dilemma and feeling a sense of obligation to Bill Greenwood I called and set up an appointment to talk with him. We met on Saturday, June 4 and I told him that things were not going well with Ingram.[747] I explained the circumstances and, believing my relationship with Ingram was irreparably broken, I told him I planned to resign and accept the job offer from APL. I added that out of loyalty I did not want Greenwood to be blindsided by my resignation. He asked me to reconsider and offered me the job Bill DeWitt vacated when he was appointed President of Winona Bridge. I said I would accept that job. I called APL, thanked them for considering me for their team, and informed them I was declining the job offer. Effective June 13, I left the IBU and was BN's Asst. VP - Marketing Resources. Our healthy baby was born the morning of June 8 and right after the delivery I was working over the phone from the delivery room with Dave Albright (in Birmingham) to confirm that everything related to the demonstration train was in order. The event went off as-designed without any problems.[748]

As indicated above, among the things demonstrated at Birmingham was a double stack car modified with a RoadRailer hitch on one end that would allow RoadRailer trailers to be coupled onto the end of a double stack train. The stack-RoadRailer hitch had been designed and patented by Bill Berry.[749]

---

[745] Mark Cane's personal calendar.

[746] Ibid.

[747] Mark Cane personal calendar.

[748] Bill Greenwood and Mark Cane personal calendars.

[749] Bill Berry interview with Mark Cane, April 24, 2022.

Ingram proceeded with the Mark VII venture. He met with Tom Fitzgerald (VP Traffic) of the Santa Fe on June 9 and followed it with a letter on June 10 that stated:[750]

> *Attached is a copy of the memorandum I have sent to Bill Greenwood and Darius Gaskins outlining our conversations.*
>
> *Later today I will forward two individual letters covering the development of the RoadRailer/ Stack Car Service from southeastern points over Avard and the development of a coordinated service eastward from Chicago via Conrail.*

The Fitzgerald letter included documents that described the ATSF/BN Relationship as one involving:

- Joint Line Services with revenue and profits for each carrier reflecting their portion of the linehaul and their capital participation
- Service scope of both companies is required by marketplace

It outlined features of the "original plan" and a modified one from May 1988 that compared as follows:

	Original Plan	*May 1988*
Scope	*3 Year*	*3 Year*
	1,680 units each	*1,680 units each*
Capital	*R.C. Provide*	*Rail Supplied*
	Total $140 million	
Line Haul	*Rail transport*	*$.30 per mile*
	$.28 per mile	
Revenue	*Min. 40 Units*	*Min. 40 Units*
	Per Train	*Per Train with Stack Option*
Service	*Door-to-Door*	*Door-to-Door*
	Truck Competitive	*Truck Competitive*
Sales	*Retail Sales*	*50% retail*
		Balance 3rd party
Revenue Split	*Profit Split*	*Profit Split*
	R.C. 50%	*R. C. Reduced share*
	Rail Prorate	*Rail prorate*

The original plan was consistent with BN's vision for how the domestic intermodal business needed to be operated. This venture provided the perfect opportunity to run it that way from the start. Having R.C. Matney's Mark VII sell the service was not an issue. He would be a carrier-agent with a vested interest in "making it on the sell" because of the capital stake he would have in it. In addition, his

---

[750] Robert S. Ingram letter to Mr. Tom Fitzgerald, June 10, 1988, *Greenwood Collection*, Barriger Library at UMSL.

compensation would have been based on the profitability of the operation (profit split) to reinforce an incentive to "make it on the sell." Santa Fe's traditional thinking, and risk-averse nature, drove the venture back toward the same industry business model that was not working effectively.

Outstanding issues related to Mark VII involvement were identified. They included their scale of operation, their capitalization, and their involvement in door-to-door retail. Outstanding rail issues were Santa Fe two-man crews, capitalization, and the scope of the service – whether it would only cover the Avard Gateway, Chicago, or both.

Ingram laid out six possible options that included:

1. Proceed with Mark VII with rail provided capital, a restructured profit sharing, a realigned sales effort (not exclusively Mark VII) but with Mark VII as the contract sales / marketing organization
2. Proceed with limited deployment of 2,000 units with rail capital, a restructured profit sharing, a realigned sales force and Mark VII as the contract sales / marketing organization
3. Limit Mark VII to Avard / Southeast with rail capital, restructured profit sharing, realigned sales effort and Mark VII as the contract sales / marketing organization
4. Combine BN Expediter and Mark VII with BN supplying capital, ATSF only providing rail transport, with a combination stack and RoadRailer services over the Avard Gateway
5. Terminate study and have Mark VII find other rail transportation
6. Develop a combined rail / truck service and exclude the ATSF with BN infrastructure used to Oklahoma City or Amarillo on the west end with truck beyond for truck pick-up or delivery at the shippers' door in the west and reefer capability added

Ingram asked a rhetorical question, "Does R.C. bring market strength? His conclusion was that "most likely did." His preferred solution was to start with a 2,000 unit service with a reduction of Mark VII profits to reflect a reduction in their capital contribution, to focus on selling both through retail and a coordinated third party network, with the option of using COFC/Stack using the ATSF "Q" labor agreement. (The "Q" agreement was what Santa Fe had negotiated with their labor organizations to run their Expediter-type trains.)

He cited the reaction he received to his preferred option as:

1. Internal ATSF concerns that BN and R.C. would access ATSF's Chicago – LA corridor
2. A public perception of immediate full service ATSF/BN coordination
3. The ATSF would have a labor issue that would force 3-man RoadRailer crews on them
4. A perception of an overpowering BN commercial role
5. Concern that BN would be forfeiting the Avard Gateway

His proposed solution was to have Mark VII market and operate the service with a combination of RoadRailer and stack capability via Southeast BN points including St. Louis via Avard with the ATSF using their "Q" agreement on combined service with the stage set for further service expansion.[751]

---

[751] Attachments to Robert S. Ingram letter to Mr. Tom Fitzgerald, June 10, 1988, *Greenwood Collection*, Barriger Library at UMSL.

Ingram Proposes Another RoadRailer Venture

On July 12, 1988 Ingram sent a more detailed proposal for a joint venture to Fitzgerald.[752] In it he proposed the formation of a new jointly-owned venture for the Avard Gateway RoadRailer initiative called BSF AMERICA. With the full support of Darius Gaskins and Bill Greenwood, it would be outside of the Railroad bureaucracy and purchase underlying transportation service from the two owning carriers.

It would have:
- Single line marketing capability over Avard route for pricing to customers, billing and tracing
- Railroad would be responsible for door-to-door transportation with motor carriers acting as railroad's agent in performing drayage service
- Continued good relations with third party intermodal customers.

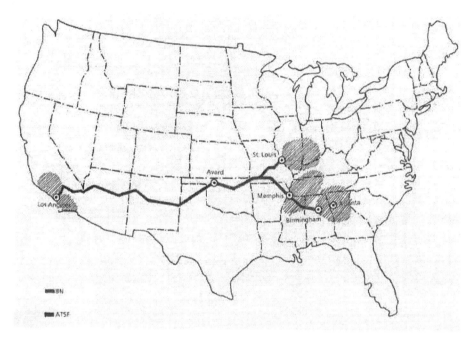

The proposal included a swap of Intermodal Marketing Franchises with BN (or its subsidiary) having single line marketing rights for RoadRailer service over ATSF's lines between Avard or Tulsa and Los Angeles and Stockton. ATSF or its subsidiary would have single line marketing rights for double stack intermodal service over BN's lines between Avard or Tulsa and Memphis and St. Louis. Earnings would go entirely to the railroads with no outside party participating. The proposal went so far as to include a draft of a press release announcing the BSF AMERICA joint venture that would be issued on August 10, 1988 entitled, "Burlington Northern Railroad and Atchison, Topeka & Santa Fe Railway Announce Joint Intermodal Marketing Venture," that included quotes from Darius Gaskins and John Swartz, President of the ATSF Railway Company. (See Appendix 4.)

A joint BN–ATSF meeting to discuss the JV opportunity was attended by three of Santa Fe's McKinsey representatives (John Russell, JP Ruiz-Funes, and Bill Spencer) as well as the Santa Fe's Don McInnes, Carl Ice, Ron Lane and Rich Weicher. Another attendee was John Gray who had been contracted by Santa Fe CEO Rob Krebs (at the request of Santa Fe Pacific shareholder and Board member Sam Zell) to assist McKinsey in their effort of helping the Santa Fe Railroad figure out what to do with their intermodal business to maximize shareholder value.[753]

---

[752] Robert Ingram letter to Mr. Thomas J. Fitzgerald, July 12, 1988, *Greenwood Collection*, Barriger Library at UMSL.
[753] John Gray interview with Mark Cane, April 21, 2022.

Ingram persisted with a letter to Fitzgerald on August 23 that told him about a testing program BN was conducting at the Association of American Railroads' (AAR's) research and development testing operation in Pueblo, Colorado. Ingram said: [754]

> *Bill Berry has advised me that sometime in late September we are planning on taking the modified equipment (stack car plus 40 RoadRailers) up to a test speed of 80 miles per hour.*
>
> *During the past month, there have been numerous modifications including stack car truck bracing to significantly reduce hunting at high speed. We anticipate having the modified braking systems available for tests and review.*

He proposed a joint BN/SF meeting at Pueblo during the week of September 26 to observe the tests and learn their implications. One of the things that had been impeding RoadRailer adoption is the 75 trailer length limit imposed on RoadRailer trains. Understanding that double stack technology would be a prime component of the future of the intermodal business, Ingram and Bill Berry worked to have a stack car modified with a RoadRailer hitch on one end so that combined stack / RoadRailer trains could be operated, thereby complementing the profitability RoadRailers would generate with double stack container business profitability. (This modified stack car connected with RoadRailers was demonstrated in Birmingham.) Santa Fe's willingness to promote stack technology and the Avard gateway was also inhibited by the way they operated their trains between Chicago and Los Angeles. They maintained their track to FRA Class 5 standards (as opposed to BN's FRA Class 4) which allowed top passenger train speeds of 90 mph and freight train speeds of 79 mph. Double stack cars were limited to 60 mph so there was a desire to modify them to allow safe and faster operation. FRA approval was necessary to operate the cars at speeds consistent with Santa Fe's operating practices which they desired to minimize the effect double stack trains had on their high priority trailer trains in their prime corridor.

Yet, Santa Fe remained unresponsive.

BN Domestic Containerization Moves to the Launching Pad

Concurrent with Ingram's work to bring RoadRailer and the Avard Gateway to a new life on the BN, he was also working to get BN aggressively into the domestic containerization business. As described above, he hired Brooks Bentz to run the new venture. In Bentz's words: [755]

> *I received a telephone call from Bob Ingram in March of 1988 saying he wanted to discuss me joining him at Burlington Northern, where he had recently become Vice President – Intermodal, taking over as Steve Neiman's successor. In particular, he wanted to talk about a "domestic container program."*
>
> *There were a couple of issues at stake. One was what to do with the excess of empty marine containers, the other was how to make use of domestic doublestack technology beyond handling steamship boxes.*

---

[754] Bob Ingram letter to Thomas J. Fitzgerald, August 23, 1988, *Greenwood Collection*, Barriger Library at UMSL.
[755] Brooks Bentz email to Mark Cane, November 15, 2022.

During our earliest discussions, Bob and I spoke about establishing a stand-alone business. At the time BN already had a precedent with BN Worldwide, for which Bob served as Chairman. Using this model, we talked about a new subsidiary that would focus on developing a doublestack network encompassing both a new domestic container business using BN boxes as well as a program for making use of surplus empty marine containers.

When I joined BN as AVP-Domestic Container Systems in early 1988 it was with the idea that we would take the small team already in place (Kirk Williams and David Proctor) and develop the business plan for the new operation, which subsequently be incorporated as a BN subsidiary, with me serving as its president, still reporting to Bob and ultimately to Bill. Shortly after my arrival we began to add staff. Tom Perdue joined us from Soo Line with responsibility for operations and systems and Don Werby came on board to work with the steamship lines on utilization of ocean containers.

*The long-term vision we discussed was twofold: on the commercial front, **BN AMERICA** would eventually absorb BN's Intermodal Group, shifting functions out of the railroad and away from its inherent constraints and to a more flexible, broad-based operating subsidiary. On the personal/professional front, Bob eventually expected to succeed Bill, who was then EVP-Marketing & Sales and I expected to assume Bob's responsibilities as the railroad's intermodal functions were shifted to BNA. In practice, of course, it did not unfold that way.*

*The concept for **BN AMERICA** was an outgrowth of my past experience at Boston & Maine and Ameritrans, an early 3rd-party logistics subsidiary of IU International (which owned the largest trucking operation in North America at the time). In reality, it was a fairly simple idea. One of the things that struck me was that railroads had trouble getting past the parochial view of their service territory; meaning not being able to see beyond the end of their track. The upshot of this, in part, was the view on the part of customers that railroads were much more difficult to deal with than truck lines and that intermodal service was overly complex.*

On the other hand, Don Orris had created what amounted to the first transcontinental railroad with the APL stacktrain network. This network transcended the artificial borders each carrier erected at interchange points and terminals and offered a truly truck competitive, seamless, door-to-door service. In what became a trend, the railroads universally ceded the 'equity' in the customer relationships to outside parties. Following, J. B. Hunt and Schneider developed national truckload networks with an intermodal line-haul component. But, these were just more instances of 3rd parties carving out a piece of what might otherwise be handled by the railroad. The bottom line is none of the Class-1 carriers wanted to undertake the heavy lifting required to deal directly with BCOs (Beneficial Cargo Owners).

*So, what were we going to do? I wanted to come up with a moniker that was new, catchy and connoted a service that extended significantly beyond the borders of BN and eradicated the perceived restriction of operating only where our tracks went. **BN AMERICA** also lent itself to the theme of a nationwide carrier, akin to J.B. Hunt or Schneider. BNA came to me, popping out of the steam in the shower one morning and I felt it suited the concept perfectly. This, then, was the core of the idea: Create a new business, owned and operated by the railroad that provided a nationwide, door-to-door truckload service using the newest, lightest, highest-cube boxes and stacktrain linehaul economics to deliver the lowest possible rates.*

We envisioned and began the process of negotiating wholesale rates over Conrail, CSX and NS to reach eastern markets and intended to establish our own off-line terminals in places like north Jersey, Philadelphia, Baltimore, Charlotte, Atlanta (where one already existed) and others, as market demand dictated. This would give us the nationwide network we were seeking, covering all major markets on the continent.

*One particularly important problem was how the new service would be sold. I felt it was critical that the **BN AMERICA** brand identity be held to the highest standards and be constantly, and directly, in front of the customer. At the same time, the traditional sales channel through 3rd party shipper agents was not to be discarded, but rather used to leverage the new brand through a modified contractual arrangement.*

*Under the new arrangement, **BN AMERICA** would use a select number of 3rd party agents who would sell the service to customers. These agents would be carefully chosen for their depth and breadth of skills and ability to grow with the business as a partner, not an independent entity.*

Clearly this would engender controversy, because it would change the relationship between the railroad and the agent, as well as the relationship with the customer. We anticipated that many, if not all, agents would view this new business as a threat. Some would view it as a threat because they would not be invited to participate. Some would view it as a threat because the railroad would have direct access to customers and customer information. And, some would view it as a threat because of the way we intended to set rates, fees, and the billing and collection of charges.

I also felt that consolidation in the industry would continue to be a major commercial force and that requiring 3rd parties to "choose up sides" might actually result in creating long-term competitive advantage. We actually held preliminary discussions with ATSF concerning a de facto merger of our respective intermodal groups (whether in whole or in part was never determined) under the name BSF AMERICA, whereby we would jointly own and operate a much larger enterprise using the BNA model. We could not convince ATSF this was a viable path and abandoned the effort.

Another critical part of the business conceptual design was what I called the "Delta Model," after the Delta Airlines Customer Service Center concept. What this meant was a centralized customer service function that would leverage current technology to provide the finest in customer service. In the "Delta Model" example I was referring to the airline's ability to answer virtually every customer inquiry concerning rates, service and equipment. This was envisioned to include assignment of equipment, advance reservations and on-the-spot pricing. We also developed a mechanism for the customer to self-price service through "Price Perfect", which was an electronic catalog of book rates based on zip codes.

Operationally we had conceived a somewhat different approach for train operations. This involved what amounted to fixed or semi-fixed consists in major lanes. For example, in the Chicago-PNW corridor we would operate trains of 100 platforms (200 boxes) in each direction. Clearly, this was not a balanced lane in terms of shipment volume, but the analogy was much like operation of a 400-TEU ship: The capacity is fixed; it typically operates fully loaded in the head-haul direction and the challenge is in selling to fill capacity in the back-haul direction.

Under this concept, we would sell slots on a pre-reserved basis at a price that was lower than the spot market price that would be offered on the day of "sailing." This would ensure a couple of things: [1] We would always know our capacity in advance; [2] We would have a pretty good idea of the number of empty slots we were going to need to fill on a continuing basis, based upon traffic balance history. This approach would also give direction to the sales force on where we needed to focus marketing, sales and pricing efforts in order to improve balance.

Coupling this strategy with a strategy for box management, which included assignment of boxes to key accounts, would enable us to clearly define and understand what our sales and marketing mission was. For example, if Boise Cascade contracted for 10 48-footers from Seattle to Chicago each week, we would assign a specific pool of containers to them. This would also then generate 10 empties per week in the Chicago area. This would mean the sales force would have a defined goal of loading these specific boxes back to Seattle (or at least closer proximity) to minimize empty movements. This strategy would apply for the core base of business in each major lane. Extra trains and spot market pricing would also be used to handle overflow business.
What we were striving for was a measure of predictability in demand for boxes and slots, which we would use to maximize utilization of assets and earnings. Our ability to provide a reliable service was also enhanced markedly.

Some of the other things we wanted to accomplish were an improved system of managing and controlling surplus empty steamship boxes and clearing up some difficulties with the existing BN intermodal contract, the most onerous of which was the so-called Quick-Pay discount.

The issue with empty ISO 20s and 40s was the large imbalance, something like 5-t0-1 inbound v. outbound. Rather than hauling empties all over the place, our objective was to augment the domestic container program by either finding export loads or loads that were destined for an area close to the ports served by the owning liner companies.

Don Werby was a veteran of the container business and Bob suggested bringing him aboard to lead this aspect of the program. Don started by reaching out to his contacts in the ocean carrier business. This shortly brought down the wrath of Ralph Muellner, who was the head of international. He confronted me in the aisle of a flight we were both on and told me very forcefully how he wanted Don to stay away from his f-ing customers! Rather than get into a debate in a public place when he was clearly agitated, I acknowledged his issue and said I would speak with Don about how to proceed. I do not how this was resolved after I departed, but it was something sorely needed to help build the network and reduce empty box-miles.

The issue with the so-called Quick-Pay discount was related to interest rates. When I was running Ameritrans, between 1984-1987, we were introduced to the Quick-Pay discount. My recollection was that UP was first with this, but perhaps it was BN. In any event, the prime rate at the time was at an all-time high. Commercial rates had gotten as high as 18% - 20%, as I recall. The Quick Pay deals were pretty simple: pay fast, get a break on the price. We, as a 3rd party took advantage of this because our cash flow permitted it. This became onerous for the railroad when interest rates dropped back down to 8% - 9%. The discounts didn't change, so in effect the railroad was paying us 18% when the best we could do elsewhere was less than half of that.

Clearly this was not equitable, nor was it how these deals were supposed to work. The problem was, as usual, the system designed by the carriers had been co-opted by the 3rd parties. What was designed as a mechanism to incent people to pay quickly and reward them when they did, actually became a competitive tool for one 3rd party to hit another over the head by taking the discount and using it to reduce rates to customers to steal business. The upshot of this was the discounts became an entrenched practice with no easy way out. So, the carriers were stuck in a difficult spot – the deal was no good, but if it were changed, their customers (the 3rd parties) would be hurt with their customers.

Our approach was to expunge the Quick Pay discount by "including it in the price." This meant a short-term hit on the rate we would charge, but no contractual commitment for a discount that could bite us when interest rates became volatile.

Of course, the whole issue of how to sell the product and the relationship with 3rd parties was problematic. I felt we came up with a reasonable and attractive solution. Some of the responses to what we did remind me of what happens during election campaigns: no matter what we said, a few people spread misinformation because they felt it was in their interest to do so. Others, like D. F. Reeves, figured out how to work the program effectively. The conundrum concerning marine containers was certainly not new, but no one had ever effectively sorted out how to solve the problem. One of the key elements of our approach was the integration of the management of empty marine container hauling capacity with that of the capacity management of our own domestic boxes. This, alone, was a big step in terms of reconfiguring the distribution of equipment to maximize utilization and minimize empty repositioning. The basic idea was to manage all containers (marine and domestic) as one large, integrated pool, with smaller sub-pools assigned to major accounts.

*Another facet of **BN AMERICA** that went in concert with equipment management was equipment maintenance. My view was the average railroad trailer from the national pool was much like the company auto one gets from the general office pool v. an assigned vehicle: always dirty, beat-up, out of fuel and looking neglected. Rail trailers were hardly ever a good advertisement to shippers of the virtues of intermodal transportation.*

Our aim was to change that by having a prescribed preventive maintenance program and a network of contract maintenance and repair facilities. Since BNA was essentially a closed loop system, this was much more practical than with general pool vehicles and AAR billing practices.

We began implementation of the BNA program with institution of service between Denver and Dallas. This was a weak corridor and suffered from volume imbalances. We developed a strong promotional campaign and selected Greater South Traffic as the 3rd party we would pilot the program with. We did the research to determine the highway competitive information and based our directional pricing on this knowledge. We also tested the negotiated fee strategy, which led us to have differing levels of fees depending upon traffic balance and pricing constraints. Our initial establishment of the rates and fees was done concurrently with GST, so that we were all in agreement before we started. During the start-up phase I do not recall the volume and revenue figures, but I know we were satisfied with the way the program got underway.

> *I really wanted to keep the **BN AMERICA** brand identity in front of the customer, but we needed to be sensitive to past relationships. The solution we reached was a gradual migration to what we were seeking. I felt we should have a relationship with 3rd party agents similar to that had by airlines with travel agents. This would give us equity with the customer and allow us to be more proactive in managing the relationship with both the customer and the 3rd party, including having all of the relevant and important customer data and intelligence.*
>
> *I also wanted to do two things with agent fees. One was to make them flexible and the other was to make sure they were reasonable. These are related: We wanted agents to make money where there was money to be made. In many instances, fees were simply too low. On the other hand, in extremely competitive markets, we wanted to share the pain, rather than have us take the hit while the agent maintained their fees.*
>
> *Summarizing, **BN AMERICA** was designed to look and operate like a truckload motor carrier in the eyes of the true customer (beneficial owner) and to gain market share by providing superior customer service and equipment at the best possible prices.*
>
> *The broad objective was creating an overall perceptual change in the eyes of the customer that would move intermodal business from a second service to parity with over-the-road transportation.*

The vision articulated by Bentz was consistent with the vision that had existed within the IBU before his arrival. Since the days of the original 1981 Intermodal Task Force there had been a belief that BN's Intermodal business would not achieve its full domestic truckload customer service and profit potential until it controlled door-to-door service, pricing, and sales channel management. It also recognized synergies that existed with the international container business. Another critical element, like BN Worldwide and Winona Bridge, was an organization structure independent of BN's innovation-stifling Railroad bureaucracy. Such aggressive and innovative thinking was easier to articulate than fully implement. This was especially so under a leader, Bob Ingram, who did not understand how to navigate internal company politics, who did not completely trust his team, did not pay attention to details, and who felt insecure in his relationship with those he reported to.

BN Double Stack Clearance Improvements for Domestic Containerization

Part of the preparation work that was done to make it possible for BN to compete in the double stack domestic containerization business was accomplished in conjunction with BN's Engineering Department starting in 1987. The IBU team asked for a survey of clearance restrictions on intermodal routes that would not allow for the passage of two stacked 9'6" high domestic containers and capital authority was secured to fix clearance obstructions. In total, "thirty-one tunnels were slated for clearance improvements on the Pacific Division to accommodate domestic double-stack trains." [756] BN's System Chief Engineer, Bill Glavin, said: [757]

---

[756] Burlington Northern Railroad, *BN News*/1988 Annual Report, Summer 1989, *Greenwood Collection*, Barriger Library at UMSL.
[757] Glavin, William E., BN Becomes Roadway Innovator, *Progressive Railroading*, March, 1989, p. 30, *Greenwood Collection*, Barriger Library at UMSL.

To improve its service capability further, BN has embarked on a clearance improvement program to accommodate stack trains of the largest shipping containers now in use. This program involves modification of the five through truss bridges and 26 tunnels, and undercutting the track under about 20 overhead structures. The truss alterations range from minor adaptations to the portal knee braces, to a complete redesign of the portal and sway bracing on such major structures as the Mississippi River crossing at Burlington, Iowa. The Burlington project alone involves alterations to 60 overhead frames, and the work will require ten months, including design time, to complete.

Tunnel clearance improvements are being made by track location or crown removal. We had considered lowering the track through several tunnels to gain additional clearance, but the typical large vertical correction needed made this procedure too disruptive to traffic and too costly. Crown removal is a proven technique, but it requires considerable preliminary geological investigation to determine the feasibility of this procedure at every location. Methods of crown removal employed thus far include saw cutting, which generally is most effective in notching, and excavation by road header, which is most effective in unreinforced concrete.

Clearance improvements between Seattle and Chicago via Vancouver, Wash., were completed in 1988.

Santa Fe's Internal 1988 Challenges

While Ingram was pushing the Santa Fe to act on an innovative BSF AMERICA Avard Gateway venture, Santa Fe's parent Santa Fe Southern Pacific (SFSP) was going through its own internal challenges that radiated into the railroad. Since the ICC had rejected a reconsideration of the proposed SF-SP merger one of the railroads had to be divested. SFSP decided the SP would go.[758] It was sold to Philip Anschutz who combined it with his DRGW railroad. That transaction was approved by the ICC on August 9, 1988 and the deal closed on October 13, 1988. SFSP CEO Robert Krebs still had to fend-off hostile investors including Olympia and York, and Sam Zell and his Itel Corporation. Olympia and York's Reichmann brothers retained McKinsey and Company to advise it on the viability of the Santa Fe Railroad and survey "other railroads about the Santa Fe's attractiveness as a potential merger partner."[759]

McKinsey agreed with the Reichmann brothers that the railroad seemed the least desirable part of SFSP. But when this conclusion was brought to the board, Krebs convinced directors to have McKinsey do a deeper dive on the railroad, this time with SFSP as its client. Thus began a relationship that would continue until just about the last days of the Santa Fe.[760]

Because of Santa Fe's intense internal focus on how to survive as a stand-alone railroad and the initiation of a total strategic review with McKinsey, Ingram's overtures related to BSF America went nowhere.

---

[758] Bryant and Frailey, pp. 357-361.

[759] Ibid, p. 360.

[760] Ibid, p. 361.

Why Not a BN/Southern Pacific Intermodal Marriage?

While Bentz and his small team were working to establish BN's novel domestic container business, and the Santa Fe would not respond to BN overtures, Ingram pursued a working relationship with the Southern Pacific Railroad. BN's inferior intermodal franchise had to be addressed to optimally implement its strategic initiatives. SP also accessed California although its route from Chicago to LA over BN's Kansas City gateway. It was inferior to Santa Fe's but it was better than nothing. In addition, with its consolidation with the DRGW railroad, a combination with BN over the Denver gateway provided a route competitive with the Union Pacific to the Bay Area. With a linkage to BN's Expediter service between Portland and Seattle, coverage along the Interstate 5 corridor between Seattle and Los Angeles would also be opened up. The SP had also opened the International Container Transfer Facility (ICTF) in 1987. It was located four miles from the Ports of Los Angeles / Long Beach which gave it a competitive advantage for international container shipments. Overall the condition of, and service levels provided by, the SP were inferior to the Santa Fe, but again something workable was better than nothing.

The BN had previous discussions about general interline/VCA opportunities with the SP but nothing significant in the intermodal area had born fruit. On October 5, 1988 Ingram met with SP's VP Marketing & Sales Craig Philip about the formation of a BN-SP intermodal relationship. On October 7 he sent Phillip a letter[761] stating:

> *The following is a recap of our discussion last Wednesday night in San Francisco outlining one possible avenue in establishing an Intermodal relationship between BN and SP.*
>
> *In discussing our meeting with Bill Greenwood, I characterized it as an outgrowth of the meeting at National Freight and our initial conversations at the Greenbrier following up on that Sunday discussion.*
>
> *Reflecting on our objective, BN feels that our control of a door-to-door intermodal system through a single entity is a requirement to insure long-term viability in the marketplace. In reviewing the options, we discussed approaches. They are:*
>
> - *Creation of a joint venture marketing company to provide an umbrella over multiple rail segments providing a single point of customer contact while maintaining ownership by the participating railroads.*
> - *Establishment of large scale wholesaling agreements with major intermodal operators that meet entry tests for capitalization and commitment to service.*
>
> *Our discussion last week centered around the differences in philosophies of both our companies in approaching the solution. Essentially, Burlington Northern prefers to have direct BN participation in the management of the intermodal product while maintaining a limited or restrictive relationship with the domestic and international intermodal operators. You expressed an intent on your company's behalf to identify major intermodal companies that have made commitments in container, car or terminal facilities and have committed to a long-term market presence as the vehicle to market a major segment of your intermodal activity.*

---

[761] Robert S. Ingram letter to Mr. Craig Phillip, Vice President Marketing and Sales, October 7, 1988, *Greenwood Collection*, Barriger Library at UMSL .

We concluded that while both approaches on the surface are quite different, they do not mutually exclude or preclude the possibility of our companies establishing a relationship that could fit each other's long-term requirements. The following is a summary of a proposal.

- *For Southern Pacific to view BN AMERICA (our domestic container operation) as a rail intermodal operator and contract with BN AMERICA to move its transportation product on Southern Pacific's rail system.*
- *For Burlington Northern to grant SP direct access to Chicago via Kansas City and Denver to allow SP to move traffic of other intermodal operators under single railroad control to and from West Coast origins. In a nut shell, BN would be granting SP intermodal operating rights from our Western Gateways to California points.*

As a practical matter, we would envision re-establishing the relationship on several existing intermodal operators' traffic from a joint line representation to a single line SP control. In essence, we can see a single set of tracks supporting competing intermodal container and trailer services, some marketed by existing off-shore operators and their domestic subsidiaries, others marketed by BN AMERICA, a railroad subsidiary, and possibly other domestic entrants into the market.

From our perspective, the benefit is that the BN would receive revenue through a transportation charge paid by the Southern Pacific for the movement of this traffic over BN lines while, on the other hand, SP would benefit from BN payment of transportation charges for traffic over SP's lines. In the real world, each company would control its own marketing, equipment, and possibly terminal services which satisfies our requirement, while at the same time allowing you to maintain a position as a wholesale provider of intermodal transportation services focusing multiple operators on your system.

I think the above captures the essence of our conversation and would appreciate your review and thoughts on this issue.

Phillip was non-responsive to Ingram's proposals. At the Lakeway Strategic Vision Staff Conference Ingram reported that he had come to the conclusion that George Woodward, Executive VP Marketing & Sales of the SP, "wants to jump in bed with APL and Sea-Land. [762] Railroads like the UP, SP, Santa Fe and Conrail had little trouble yielding the commercial leverage of their intermodal franchises to others such as the inland arms of the steamship companies, especially APL, Sea-Land, Maersk and K-Line. They were willing wholesalers of their capacity to these players. BN's problem was that it did not have the clout with connecting railroads that many tens of millions of dollars worth of international container business brought. Ingram had that working for him in his former life at Sea-Land, but not at BN. In addition, what BN was proposing to do in the market from the standpoint of a value-added marketing orientation was relatively hard to do compared to having an operating orientation and just basically providing hook-and-haul train services while the parties providing the services accessorial to the rail line-haul service captured the bulk of the value.

---

[762] Mark Cane personal calendar and notes related to Bob Ingram's Intermodal Presentation, Lakeway Resort, TX, October 3-6, 1988, *Greenwood Collection*, Barriger Library at UMSL.

The Only Santa Fe Joint-Venture Progress Before Year-End

The only thing accomplished between BN and the Santa Fe before the end of the year was summarized in a letter Bob Ingram sent to the Santa Fe's John Grygiel.[763] It was a follow-up to a meeting Ingram had with Grygiel in Chicago on November 10. The main points were:

- BN and Santa Fe would agree to upgrade their respective bi-directional service between BN points of St. Louis and Birmingham and Santa Fe points in California.
- BN would be responsible for westbound, Santa Fe eastbound
- The interchange point would continue to be Avard
- BN would provide haulage service for westbound Santa Fe business originating in Tulsa and Oklahoma City and sourced from points as far east as the Fort Smith, Arkansas area.

Ingram also promised Grygiel that he would encourage Bill Greenwood to discuss carload business issues with Tom Fitzgerald in December.

Bill Greenwood sent Fitzgerald a letter on December 12 congratulating him on "a successful VCA our two companies put together in Kansas City last week. I believe both Santa Fe and Burlington Northern are going to benefit in 1989 from increased volume and margin."[764]

The Steamship Size Evolution Accelerates

In 1988, the stakes to establish a strong double stack / domestic containerization capability got even higher because of the strategic direction containerized steamship companies were taking related to ship sizes. Prior to 1988 the lines were content to build the ships as large as they could be and still pass through the Panama Canal so that they could access the United States East Coast via water. The canal's locks, at 110 feet wide and 1,000 feet long, had been designed to be large enough to allow the passage of United States Navy's largest future battleships which also allowed passage of World War II Essex Class aircraft carriers.[765] Given the explosion of trade between the United States and Far East nations, steamship companies sought to expand their capacity and lower their costs through the utilization of larger ships.

As with the rail industry's conversion to double stack intermodal technology, new generation ships allowed for significant improvements in labor and port productivity. The prices obtained from railroads for double stack service were low enough to make it much more compelling to utilize rail transportation for even the least time sensitive container business from the Far East to the U.S. East Coast. In 1988, APL was the first water carrier to build and deploy container ships that would not fit through the Canal because their length was longer, their beam was wider, and their draft was deeper than what the Canal and its locks could accommodate. These ships were called Post-Panamax Class and the volume of containers they could carry was basically two-to-four times what they could handle up to 1980.

The following table illustrates the containership size evolution through 1989:

---

[763] Robert S. Ingram letter to John Grygiel, November 22, 1988, *Greenwood Collection*, Barriger Library at UMSL.
[764] William E. Greenwood letter to Mr. Thomas J. Fitzgerald, December 12, 1988, *Greenwood Collection*, Barriger Library at UMSL.
[765] Sheffi, Yossi, *Logistics Clusters, Delivering Value and Driving Growth*, The MIT Press, Cambridge, MA, 2012, p.72.

Containership Size Evolution through 1988[766]

Generation	Class	Length	Beam	Draft	TEU Capacity
First (1956-1970)	Converted	135-200 meters		Under 9 meters	500-800
Second (1970-1980)	Cellular Containership	215 meters		10 meters	1,000-2,500
Third (1980-1988)	Panamax Class	250-290 meters	32 meters	11-12 meters	3,000-4,000
Fourth (1988-)	Post-Panamax Class	275-305 meters	49 meters	11-13 meters	4,000-5,000

The growth in containership capacity had far-reaching implications for rail intermodal service. A double stack train could typically carry around 200-240 forty foot containers. A Post-Panamax ship loaded to capacity of even 2,000 forty foot containers (4,000 TEUs) with 70% destined for inland points would discharge 1,400 containers for rail shipment – seven full trainloads at one time. The impact of that many trains hitting the railroad at one time was similar to the experience of a pig passing through a snake. It also raised the stakes for on, and near-dock, intermodal facilities such as SIG because of the impact such a large volume of containers being discharged placed on demand for drayage services.

APL's Competitive Intermodal Market Impact

In 1992, Michael Burke sent Bill Greenwood his resume.[767] He had operating experience with Southern Pacific and joined APL in 1985 as Vice President Operations for their US land based business. In the resume he claimed that between 1985 and the end of 1988 APL had increased weekly liner train frequency from 14 trains per week to 150 and their volume from 92,236 containers to 386,001. They increased their annual land-based revenue from $94 million to $463 million and had increased their ownership of double stack wells to 2,500.

BN Worldwide Update

Murry Watson continued to build up his capability to execute his vision. In January, BNWW bought an NVOCC, Worldwide Logistics. At the Lakeway Conference[768] he related a number of observations that had significant implications for the IBU:

- He was working on providing worldwide door-to-door capabilities supported by state-of-the-art computer support capabilities.
- The ship is not important – cargo is.
- The current steamship system is designed backwards with ships running weekly while inland ran 24 hours a day, 7 days a week

---

[766] Courtesy of Dr. Jean-Paul Rodrigue, Dept. of Global Logistics & Geography, Hofstra University, New York.

[767] Michael L. Burke letter to Mr. William E. Greenwood, January 28, 1992, *Greenwood Collection*, Barriger Library at UMSL.

[768] Mark Cane's personal calendar and notes related to Murry Watson's BNWW Presentation, Lakeway Resort, TX, October 3-6, 1988, *Greenwood Collection*, Barriger Library at UMSL.

- As a Non Vessel Owning Common Carrier (NVOCC) that charters space on ships, BNWW can effectively provide daily ship service
- Customers want worldwide logistics, not transportation, and APL and Sea-Land can't provide that.
- That BNWW can be the logistics manager for the customer
- APL and Sea-Land consider BNWW one of their prime competitors
- BNWW type capability was being developed within APL and Sea-Land
- BNWW was dependent on excellent affiliations with high quality communications
- Other containership lines were trying to follow APL and Sea-Land with Maersk doing it low-key
- The swing in Asian production to Southeast Asia would favor California ports over the PNW and Malaysian production could route to the United States East Coast effectively eastbound through the Suez Canal with the ability to drop European bound cargo and pick-up United States bound cargo there which was a threat the US West Coast ports and railroads
- North/South trade between the United States, Mexico and South America could explode

In September, Watson hired Mic Dinsmore from the Port of Seattle (POS) to join BNWW as Vice President – Pacific. This did not sit well with the POS and harmed an already stressed relationship between the Port and BN, and especially the IBU. What inflamed the situation is that Dinsmore allegedly "brought with him" to BNWW 60,000 units per year of business from a company called AOMI that the POS had been handling through their own brokerage operation.[769]

At the October 3, 1988 BNWW Board meeting, of which Bob Ingram was Chairman, Watson reported a year-to-date BNWW loss of $1.3 million on revenue of $3.3 million. He then made a request that BNWW be granted authority to enter into the "slot charter" business. That would change the nature of BNWW from being a Non-Vessel Owning Common Carrier to a Vessel Owning Common Carrier (VOCC). The Board expressed concern that such a venture would be contrary to Watson's Board-approved business plan. He then submitted a proposed 1989 budget that included VOCC operation with a 1989 revenue projection of $91 million.[770]

In late 1988 Watson arranged a meeting with Darius Gaskins to discuss his plan and organization needs. Since he was going to be talking about his hiring plan he asked Alan Speaker to join the meeting. Speaker was BN's AVP Human Resources responsible for, among other things, recruiting, HR administration and compensation policy. This is how Speaker remembered the meeting:[771]

> Watson and I met with Gaskins in his office. For a half hour Watson presented elements of his plan and the human resources implications. Throughout the presentation Gaskins would fire his "thousand questions" like a machine gun. I thought Watson handled himself pretty well and that he told a compelling story. When Watson was finished he left. That left me alone with Gaskins and I said, "Wow. That was impressive." Gaskins looked back at me with a grin and said, "Do you believe all that shit?" I wasn't sure how to take it but I later learned that Gaskins had good intuition.

---

[769] Murry Watson letter to Bill Greenwood, Subject: Article in the *Seattle Times* Regarding Mic Dinsmore's Leaving the Port, Joining BNW and Bringing AOMI With Him, September 6, 1988, *Greenwood Collection*, Barriger Library at UMSL.

[770] Burlington Northern Worldwide, Inc., Minutes of Meeting of the Board of Directors, October 3, 1988, *Greenwood Collection*, Barriger Library at UMSL.

[771] Mark Cane interview with Alan Speaker, April 21, 2022.

For the year 1988, BNWW's plan was to generate revenue of $65 million and income before income taxes of $2.5 million. Actual results were revenue of $5.8 million and a loss before income taxes of $2.9 million.[772]

BN Railroad Labor Action Without a Northern Lines UTU Section 6 Notice

The 1988 BNI 10-K[773] noted:

> *During 1988, a new round of labor negotiations began. Labor organizations representing 88 percent of Railroad's union-represented employees served notices under section 6 of the Railway Labor Act ("RLA") to change collective bargaining agreements. The remaining 12 percent of union employees (from the United Transportation Union representing employees of the former Great Northern Railway Company and Northern Pacific Railway Company) did not serve notice. Railroad has reserved the right to serve counter-proposals, and Railroad held initial conferences under the RLA with all but one of the unions.*
>
> *In addition to negotiations under the RLA process, three unions accepted Railroad's offer to enter into informed problem-solving discussions regarding issues of joint interest between Railroad and unions. Railroad did not join multi-employer industry bargaining, but reserved the right to participate in industry bargaining at a later date. Railroad is unable to predict the outcome of the informed discussions or subsequent negotiations.*

Darius Gaskins took an aggressive approach to doing what could be done to address labor costs and work rules that harmed BN's competitiveness. Through 1986 and 1987 he drove the pursuit of BN's innovative "short-line" partnership program of sales or leases of light density lines to entrepreneurs who could run train operations without the burden of archaic labor rules and compensation rates. That strategy went so far as to spawn the creation of Montana Rail Link (MRL), willingness to support the creation of the BN-Santa Fe BSF AMERICA joint venture, BN AMERICA, and even the pursuit of Winona Bridge and totally revitalized business development and production of business fed to BN on formerly underutilized lines. Grinstein, who would go out of his way to avoid confrontation, shut down the "short line" effort in 1988 as part of his "kinder and gentler" approach to addressing BN's labor cost dilemma. Recall that Grinstein was brought in to lead BN Railroad by Richard Bressler primarily due to his supposed labor relations expertise.

The "kinder and gentler" tone was reflected in the 1988 Annual Report and the internal employee communications magazine: [774]

> *One major 1989 challenge is to successfully conclude negotiations with our labor unions with the goal of forming a long-term partnership between management and union employees, which will*

---

[772] David R. Boehm (Manager Corporate Audit) letter to Mr. Murry Watson, February 24, 1989, *Greenwood Collection*, Barriger Library at UMSL.

[773] Burlington Northern Inc., 1988 Form 10-K, pp. 5-6.

[774] Burlington Northern Railroad, *BN News*/1988 Annual Report, Summer 1989, *Greenwood Collection*, Barriger Library at UMSL.

yield substantial gains in both the company's productivity and the quality of life for our employees.[775]

In past years BN and other Class I carriers have negotiated as a group with the rail unions and have developed agreements that have covered the entire industry. In September, BNI Chairman Gerald Grinstein proposed a new approach and invited the unions to meet independently with BN to develop agreements tailored to the specific needs of BN and its employees. Several unions agreed to pursue this joint problem-solving approach and began informal discussions in late 1988.

Darius Gaskins added:[776]

Tom Matthews was our head of Human Resources and Labor Relations when Grinstein came into the picture. Tom was even more aggressive than I was in wanting to take on the labor dilemma. He wanted to file Section 6 notices. Grinstein intervened and said he could deal with these people. He said, "There will be no confrontation in our labor strategy." He said he could deal with these people by just wining and dining them. He literally took over the labor strategy and outright refused to file Section 6 notices. It was too bad because I believe we were in a strong position with the United Transportation Union (UTU). We had just done the MRL deal and the Brotherhood of Locomotive Engineers (BLE) had won the right to represent both the engineers and conductors on MRL. The UTU got shut out and I really believe they would have worked with us in spite of Mel Winter (Northern Lines UTU General Chairman). When it was clear that Grinstein was going to directly run labor relations in a way he disagreed with, Tom Matthews decided to resign. I helped him get a job with Frank Lorenzo at Continental Airlines.

Grinstein promoted his Western Airlines associate Joe Hilly to VP Labor Relations in September reporting to Jim Dagnon who had been promoted to Sr. VP Labor Relations in May of 1987.[777] The failure of Grinstein's, Dagnon's and Hilly's leadership to address the lack of a Section 6 notice for the Northern Lines UTU territory would come to haunt BN, and especially the IBU, eventually subjecting it to a damaging non-competitive labor cost situation. Grinstein declined to file a Section 6 notice on behalf of the Railroad because of his belief that his "joint problem-solving" idea would work better.[778]

BNRR Operations Department Reorganization

In mid-July the Operations Department under Joe Galassi was restructured to eliminate layers and align operations closer to a corridor orientation such as the IBU had done with Lane Management. The six Region structure was reduced to two – a Northern Region and a Southern Region, and the number of operating Divisions was reduced to nine. As part of this reorganization, Hunter Harrison moved from the former Chicago Region to Overland Park to lead a new Service Design initiative. His new team was the focal point for the BN's Service by Design effort that focused on scheduling all car movements. This was intended to do for carload business what the IBU had done with its focus on cutoff-to-availability

---

[775] Burlington Northern Inc., 1988 Annual Report.

[776] Darius Gaskins interview with Mark Cane, May 26, 2022.

[777] Burlington Northern Inc., 1991 Form 10-K, p. 9.

[778] Burlington Northern Railroad, *Burlington Northern News*, Summer 1989, p. 13, *Greenwood Collection*, Barriger Library at UMSL.

standards and service measurement and improve asset utilization. It was also applied to maintenance planning so that track work productivity would improve while minimizing service interruptions.

By this time, Harrison's brash management style and other issues had put him "on thin ice" within the company. His "Frisco-like" style totally conflicted with Grinstein's "kinder and gentler" approach. An incident that went a long way to seal his fate with BN occurred shortly before the Operations Dept. reorganization. As Chicago Region VP he independently undertook an effort to reduce sections of the underutilized BN main line between Galesburg and Eola, outside of Chicago, from two main lines to single track to reduce maintenance costs. Initiatives like this were undertaken immediately after the BN – Frisco merger under the Operating Department reign of Grayson protégé (and Harrison mentor) William F. Thompson. According to Earl Currie:[779]

> *Instead of analyzing the proposal with a line capacity simulation model (he made) an attempt to validate the concept by simply telling Dispatchers not to use the second main track where it was proposed to be removed.*

When it became clear in Overland Park and Ft. Worth how badly service was being impacted it was seismic. Steve Bobb, who at the time was a relatively new Marketing Department employee from Ft. Worth happened to be in Overland Park when the news hit. He had a meeting scheduled with Joe Galassi and was waiting outside his office:

> *I was sitting in the waiting area and all of a sudden I hear Galassi screaming into the phone, "Hunter, you don't just start removing main line track without consulting anyone. You can't do that!*[780]

While he had other strikes against him, this was a pivotal event that pulled Harrison out of the running for one of the two remaining Regional VP positions and led to his move to Service Design in Overland Park.

BN Motor Carriers is Sold

In September, 1988, the Mike Lawrence led Burlington Northern Motor Carriers was sold.[781] BNI incurred a loss of $20 million on the sale.[782] The $20 million loss was charged by BNI to BN Railroad. That ended the era of BN's ownership of a motor carrier.

BN's ETSI Anti-trust Lawsuit Settlement

Another Coal business related sword that had been hanging over BN's head was an antitrust suit brought against a number of railroads, including BN, by Energy Transportation Systems, Inc. (ETSI). As previously explained, ETSI was formed to create a pipeline that would carry slurried coal from the Powder River Basin to electric utilities – especially Arkansas Power & Light. BN and other railroads

---

[779] Currie, Earl J., *BN-Frisco, A Tough Merger*, Self-Published, January 2010, p. 68.
[780] Mark Cane interview with Steve Bobb, May 3, 2022.
[781] Burlington Northern Inc., 1988 Form 10-K, p. 5
[782] Ibid, p. 11.

refused to grant ETSI's pipeline authority to cross their tracks. ETSI alleged collusion and charged railroads with an antitrust violation of the Sherman Act, seeking an award in excess of $940 million plus injunctive relief.[783] This occurred after the C&NW/UP won a long-term contract AP&L's PRB coal from BN in 1984 at a deep discount. This killed the pipeline's future even if it could get the water it needed. BN was one of four railroads that settled the suit out of court for a total of $350 million between them (the ATSF was the exception and it would come to haunt them):[784]

> In November, 1988 the Company and Railroad reached an agreement to settle an antitrust action filed by Energy Transportation Systems, Inc. (ETSI). The terms of the settlement involved a $100 million cash payment on December 1, 1988 and deferred payments of $25 million plus interest on December 1, 1989, 1990 and 1991. The entire amount of the settlement, $108.5 million ($1.45 per share) net of $66.5 million in income taxes has been included in the 1988 Consolidated Statement of Income. The settlement also included future rate adjustments for Houston Light and Power with a NPV of $58 million over a 12 year period. In addition, an antitrust suit with Lower Colorado River Authority related to the ETSI matter was settled for $6 million.

Bill Greenwood commented:[785]

> Union Pacific was the first railroad to settle in late 1987 and it really upset Ed Burke who was our chief legal officer. When his UP counterpart called and told him he threw his phone against the wall and demolished it. We believed we had to settle too because the risk grew. The ETSI pipeline's backers made more money through the anti-trust suit against the railroads than they ever would have made if the pipeline had been constructed. If you add the impact of BN's lost profits after the C&NW-UP got into the PRB with the cost of the ETSI settlement, the obstruction strategy was very damaging to BN as well as Santa Fe. A viable ETSI threat might not have prevented the ICC from opening the PRB to the C&NW-UP but the loss of more than $175 million over it for decisions that were made a decade earlier really stung.

Darius Gaskins added:[786]

> I had a chance to look at the video depositions of Lou Menk and Dick Grayson in 1987 and they put BN in a really bad position. The case was going to be heard in Beaumont, Texas which I knew would be a hostile venue for us. I thought it was best to try to settle. Ed Burke and I met with the plaintiffs and Union Pacific. They said they would settle the case for $39 million. UP said no but Ed and I thought it would be a smart to settle. I called Dick Bressler and suggested that we take the $39 million offer and settle. Bressler told me to stand down as this was a Board matter and hence above my pay grade.

UP allegedly settled for something more than $40 million. KCS settled for $82 million and the C&NW settled in late 1987 for $15 million to ETSI, $9 million to Houston Power and Light, and with a $29 million

[783] Burlington Northern Inc., 1986 Annual Report Form 10-K, p. 13.
[784] Burlington Northern Inc., 1988 Annual Report.
[785] Bill Greenwood interview with Mark Cane, November 7, 2022.
[786] Darius Gaskins interview with Mark Cane, May 1, 2023.

rate reduction to Arkansas Power and Light.[787] The combined cost to BN and UP was approximately $215 million which was more than 5 times more than Gaskins would have been able to settle it for. Santa Fe was the last remaining railroad in the conflict.

Grinstein's "No-Show" in the Contentious Burlington Northern Railroad/Burlington Resources Assets Distribution Fight

Because of what it enabled, what would prove to be the most fateful event in 1988 for BN Railroad, and long-term for its Intermodal business, was the successful defeasance of the old Northern Pacific bonds. That event broke the handcuffs that tied former NP land and resources to the railroad. It was the event that Richard Bressler (and Norton Simon before him) had been striving for since he joined Burlington Northern. BNI stated in its 1987 Annual Report Form 10-K:

> On January 12, 1988, the settlement became final and no longer subject to judicial review. The payment was made to the bondholders on February 1, 1988. Also, on that date, certain oil, and natural gas, timber, coal and real estate properties that comprised a portion of the collateral securing the bonds were released from the liens of the bonds' mortgages. Railroad is the successor obligor for the NP of the two series of bonds.[788]

Putting salt in the wound, BN Railroad was assessed the $35 million bond premium that went to the bondholders which allowed the land and resources to be stripped from the railroad:

> In January 1988, a settlement became final between Railroad and holders of Prior Lien Bonds and General Lien Bonds which modified the terms of the two series of bonds. Under the terms of the settlement, Railroad paid a cash premium in 1988 of approximately $35 million to the bondholders for the release of certain properties from the mortgage liens.[789]

This event triggered the break-up of Burlington Northern Inc. Darius Gaskins described how his view of BN Railroad, and the event, contrasted with Bressler's:

> I saw it as an opportunity. He saw it as just something to get rid of and to drain a cow. So his view was, "You guys generate the cash. We're going to invest it in oil and gas." That was his call. I don't have a quarrel with that.[790]

And did BN Railroad "generate the cash." In 1988, BNI planning analyst Jim Evans wrote a White Paper that assessed BN Railroad. It was submitted to Bressler and Grinstein (who copied it to Bill Greenwood). In the introduction he said: [791]

---

[787] Expensive Defeat for Santa Fe, Chicago Tribune, March 14, 1989, accessed from: https://www.chicagotribune.com/news/ct-xpm-1989-03-14-8903260754-story.html, on March 23, 2023.

[788] Burlington Northern Inc., 1987 Annual Report Form 10-K, p. 11.

[789] Burlington Northern Inc., 1988 Form 10-K, p. 21.

[790] Kaufman, p. 244.

[791] Evans, Jim, White Paper – Burlington Northern Railroad, 1988, p. 1, *Greenwood Collection*, Barriger Library at UMSL.

The railroad business is a fundamentally sound business for several reasons. The transportation service provided is basic, and it will survive despite the form of ownership. Each of the major railroads existing today is a treasure chest of assets which can be used as seed capital for new businesses or as sources of cash flow for non-operating purposes. Finally, if properly managed, almost any railroad can be a generator of excess cash.

He pointed out how much free cash flow BNRR had generated for, and distributed to, BNI between 1981 and 1987, largely attributed to Louis Menk's and Robert Downing's instincts and courage, for a business Richard Bressler had told his board in 1980, "I see zero return on this enormous investment ":

BNRR Cash Distributed to BN Inc., 1981-1987 ($millions) [792]

	1981	1982	1983	1984	1985	1986	1987	1981-87
Free cash ($mm)	$139	$41	$319	$587	$363	$415	$598	$2,462

Evans added: [793]

It is interesting to note that even in a period when capital was not rationed, BNRR still generated excess cash from operations (a steady level of debt and consolidated tax returns are assumed in the above calculations.) In most of the years enough was left for a healthy dividend and more. From 1981 through 1987 over $2.4 billion in discretionary cash was generated for the owner of BNRR.

Gaskins elaborated on the events that led to the break-up of BN Railroad from the Holding Company:[794]

There [were] a lot of attempts to do some financial engineering to improve shareholder return. One of the first attempts was, they were talking about doing a buyout, a leveraged buyout. (Tom) O'Leary was running that proposal, and he had hired an investment banker and studied the feasibility of it, and they called all the heads of the operating units into a meeting and said, What do you guys think? It was the strangest meeting because I'm sitting there and everybody's looking around, and they're looking at me because they expect me to say...and I put my hand up, and I said, This is the dumbest idea I've ever heard. We're talking about having a national railroad strike, and you want to load up debt on the railroad to pay some new investors? This is craziness! So, I threw up on it and the other Vice Chairmen and operating cats sort of followed along. So, we said, thumbs down. O'Leary was not willing to take it on his own initiative, and it died. So that was the first attempt. You could tell it was one of those things that comes up, people get ideas when they're trying to financially engineer. Some of them make sense, some of them don't. That one didn't make sense.

The next one was, we split the company in separate parts. Railroad would be standalone, trucking company would be standalone, oil and gas would be standalone, real estate would be standalone, and El Paso will go back to being a gas pipeline standalone. That's eventually what we did.

---

[792] Ibid, p. 3.

[793] Ibid.

[794] National Railroad Hall of Fame, Darius W. Gaskins Interview Transcript, November 5, 2020, Accessed from: https://www.nrrhof.org/darius-w-gaskins-jr, on March 21, 2023.

There was an episode in there that I consider unfortunate. In order for this transaction to work for the real estate company, they were told by their investment bankers that they needed a billion dollars' worth of land to be a credible market presence in real estate. They had arguably $800 million's worth of land that had been owned by the railroad but was peripheral. It was in industrial parks and stuff like that. So, they came to the railroad and they said, We want more. I said, Well, hey guys, I can't agree with that. It doesn't make sense. Because their proposal was, they wanted to take control of the land that the railroad operated on and lease it back to us. That didn't make any sense because we were trying to separate these two things apart and we needed our right of way, we needed to monetize that, we needed the benefit from it, we needed to manage it. So, I said, We can't go along with it. There was a meeting in Dick Bressler's office, where I was there and Tom O'Leary was there and Chris Bailey was there, who was a real estate guy, and Bressler heard the arguments and said, I agree with you Darius, that's fine. You can keep your land under the railroad. Well, that's what I thought was the answer. Well, it wasn't the answer because then when the deal got ready to get done, we look at the documents and they have a bunch of land under the railroad included in going to the real estate company to get to their target of a billion dollars. I said, Uh-uh, not going to sign these documents. Bressler was confused, he said, Well, I thought we had an agreement! And we did, but it was not the agreement they asked me to sign. So, I just said no. I got my way, but it was ... not a pleasant situation.

Larry Kaufman interviewed Darius Gaskins about the break-up. Gaskins said: [795]

Grinstein was bitching because Grinstein loves the notion of a railroad the way it used to be. He thought it was wrong to take all the money out of the railroad ... He thought it was wrong to take the land away from the railroad when we're splitting up ...

Gaskins said Grinstein's resistance didn't go much beyond complaining.[796]

Worst thing was that Grinstein was supposed to be backing me up, but he sent me to the meeting by myself, so what's that all about? If you really think I'm on the right course, where are you? He wasn't there. He's not into confrontation, I guess.

Gaskins explained how the event led to his resignation:[797]

When I had gone to the railroad, I told them I'd stay seven years. I went in '82. I told them I'd stay seven years. I didn't have a contract, but I just said, I owe it to you to stay seven years. After that, I'm not sure what I'm going to do. And I really wasn't sure what I wanted to do. So, time was ticking along and Gerry, when he came in, we had a conversation and he said, I hope you'll consider staying longer than seven years. I said, Well, we'll cross that bridge when we get to it. By the time my seventh year was in, he was glad to see the back of me, I'll tell you that, so it was clear he wanted to take control of this. He kind of liked it. His labor strategy wasn't going real well, but he didn't know that yet. He and Lyn really enjoyed the life as CEO of the railroad, so they were the toast of the town. ... he was happy when I left. He was so happy, he put me on

---

[795] Kaufman, p. 245.
[796] National Railroad Hall of Fame, Darius W. Gaskins Interview Transcript, November 5, 2020, Accessed from: https://www.nrrhof.org/darius-w-gaskins-jr, on March 21, 2023.
[797] Ibid.

the board, which was very awkward. I didn't want to be on the board, and he said, Well, you really should be on the board. Well, he was being careful about things because he didn't want it to be an overt breach, so he put me on the board.

Put into perspective, the degree to which the BN Railroad "contributed" to the formation of Burlington Resources is stunning. The following is an account of the value BN Railroad shed:

- BNRR distributed $2.4 billion in free cash flow to the Holding Company between 1981 and 1987.
- In 1988 the Railroad contributed an additional $496 million in cash to Burlington Resources.[798]
- BNRR got charged $20 million for the loss the Holding Company incurred on the BN Motor Carriers investment to that point. Additional losses associated with BNT and SFT would follow in later years.
- BNRR got charged the $35 million premium that went to the holders of old Northern Pacific Railroad bonds to break their link that kept resources tied to the railroad, enabling the stripping of land and resources for BR.
- BNRR was stripped of 1.8 million acres of fee interest property (less $43 million in return for industrial land sales to Glacier Park) the railroad had legal title to (mostly former NP land grants that had been encumbered by the NP bonds). The property and mineral rights went to BR subsidiaries.[799]
- It assumed $2.7 billion of long term debt in the break-up, much of which had been secured to purchase El Paso Natural Gas and Southland. Of the total, $1.1 billion of long term debt was strictly Holding Company related. Only $1.2 billion of the long-term debt was tied to Railroad mortgage and equipment bonds and capitalized Railroad equipment leases.[800]
- BNRR assumed $292 million of 1988 interest expense as well as subsequent interest expenses related to the debt (inherited by the independent railroad) used to finance energy investments.
- It assumed responsibility to pay common stock shareholders $165 million per year in dividends.[801]

More specifically on the land front, a March 6, 1989 letter from Meredith McManus, Sr. VP Administration to Galassi, Bill Francis, Bob Howery and the Division GMs with copies to Grinstein, Greenwood and the other Executive staff summarized the BN Railroad property transfers associated with the BRI spinoff:[802]

Plum Creek Timber Company, Inc.	*2,470 parcels*	*1,140,324 acres*
Glacier Park Company	*1,351 parcels*	*694,342 acres*
Meridian Minerals Company	*4,831 parcels*	*2,414,531 acres*
Meridian Oil Inc.	*4,789 parcels*	*2,462,807 acres*

The value placed on this transferred rail property was $424 million. The letter also pointed out that following the asset transfer, BNRR had leased back from Glacier Park the Hoyt Street Yard in Portland, Pier 88 in Seattle and the East False Creek Yard in Vancouver, BC, among other rail properties.

---

[798] Burlington Northern Inc., 1988 Annual Report Form 10-K, p. 17.

[799] Ibid, pp. 5, 13.

[800] Ibid, p. 20.

[801] Ibid, p. 17.

[802] Meredith McManus letter to Messrs. Galassi, Howery, Francis, et. al., Subject: Property Transfers Associated with BRI Spinoff, March 6, 1989, *Greenwood Collection*, Barriger Library at UMSL.

It left BNRR with a very weak balance sheet with a long term debt to total capitalization ratio of 75.5% compared to an historic pre-Bressler BNI high of 36% during the cash-strapped year of 1980 when rail operating income was weak and Powder River Basin investments were so intense. It strapped the Railroad with $457 million per year of long term debt and common equity financing costs in 1988. BN Railroad was put into a position where it was unable to finance any meaningful strategic initiatives. Larry Kaufman mentioned how Jerry Grinstein and BNI's directors stood aside and let it happen.

> *Grinstein, who now headed the Burlington Northern Railroad, told Forbes magazine after the spin-off, "The standing joke was that they (Burlington Resources) got the gold and we (the railroad) got the shaft." Grinstein, who was the one officer who got a choice of which company he would join, chose the railroad. Several members of the board also chose to remain with the railroad, somewhat to Bressler's surprise.*[803]

Gaskins added: [804]

> *One thing that did irritate me is that the same board members who voted to dividend all that cash … and that voted for all those oil and gas acquisitions, the day Jerry came over, they were wringing their hands and saying, "We've got too much debt on this property." I said, "Wait a minute. I never voted for those debts."*

BNI directors aside from Bressler, O'Leary and Grinstein who stayed with the Railroad following the BR split were Richard Cooley, Daniel Davison, Charles Harper, and Arnold Weber.[805] O'Leary actually came to BNI from the railroad industry. He was hired by Missouri Pacific Corporation in 1965 as an Assistant Treasurer and was appointed President in 1974.[806] After Union Pacific acquired MP, Bressler hired him as Vice Chairman of BNI and appointed him to BNI's board in 1982.[807] Bressler made him President and CEO of Burlington Resources when the BN/BR breakup occurred and kept him on Burlington Northern's board.

Gaskins' description of Grinstein's behavior through the entire break-up of BNI, and his lack of courage in defending the best interest of BN Railroad's customers, employees and shareholders, was typical of what the IBU and the rest of the railroad would experience and have to work around and through for the next seven years. He lacked any semblance of operating expertise or skill. His lack of strategic vision, such as not realizing how handicapped a stripped and debt-laden railroad would be, his unwillingness to step-up and confront what was wrong and defend what was right, such as his decision/desire to leave Gaskins alone on the front line of an existential intra-corporate financial battle, and his overriding political rather than business nature would handicap BN Railroad through 1995. The way the directors who decided to remain with the Railroad handled the situation was also a sign of trouble to come in relation to their oversight of Grinstein. They displayed their own lack of strategic vision, lack of business knowledge, and a failure to realize the ways Grinstein handicapped the business.

---

[803] Kaufman, pp. 246-247.

[804] Ibid, pp. 246-247.

[805] Burlington Northern Inc., Notice of Annual Meeting of Stockholders to be Held April 5, 1990, pp. 2-3.

[806] Thomas H. O'Leary obituary, Seattle Times, May 3, 2009, Accessed from: https://www.legacy.com/us/obituaries/seattletimes/name/thomas-o-leary-obituary?id=28596751, on March 22, 2023.

[807] Burlington Northern Inc., 1985 Annual Report Form 10-K, p. 14.

Larry Kaufman interviewed Grinstein's politician friend Daniel Evans who joined BN's board in 1991. Evans was a former governor and senator from Washington State who had known, "Grinstein from their years in Seattle public life," and told Kaufman:[808]

> *Jerry is an unusual guy. He has superb human skills. He gets along well with virtually anybody and really uses those skills in his management style to really coalesce the railroad and its people.*

The BN Railroad owed a tremendous debt of gratitude to Gaskins for exercising his courage to the point of his willingness to resign over the harsh treatment of the railroad in the spin-off transaction. As bad as it was, it could have been much worse.

This is how BNI described the transaction:

> *Burlington Resources Inc. (BR) was created in May 1988 to function as a holding company for the Company's natural resource operations, including the exploration, development and production of oil, gas, coal and other minerals, the transportation and sale of natural gas, the sale of timber and logs, the manufacture of and sale of forest products, and the development and management of real estate. In July 1988 an IPO of BR reduced company ownership to 87%. On October 20, 1988 the Board decided to distribute the 130 million BR shares owned by BNI to shareholders on December 31, 1988.[809]*

BN's Remanufactured Locomotive Initiative

Following up on the success of the Power –by-the-Hour initiative, before Darius Gaskins left BN he inspired another "out-of-the-box" effort related to locomotive power. Given the degree to which the BNI Holding Company was restricting railroad capital, it was difficult for BN to renew its aging road-switcher/local train locomotive fleet. When it was suggested that BN investigate the opportunity to utilize remanufactured locomotives, Gaskins gave it his full support.

The 1988 BNI Annual Report Form 10-K stated:[810]

> *During 1988, Railroad signed agreements to lease or purchase 250 re-manufactured locomotives to be delivered over the next five years. The agreements are contingent upon the availability of locomotive hulks as well as certain locomotive performance criteria.*

Former BN CMO Ed Bauer commented:[811]

> *Our road-switching, regional-local, locomotive fleet was really aging and service reliability was deteriorating. We worked with EMD, Morrison Knudson (MK), and Lawrence Beal's National Railway Equipment.   We retired old GP9, GP30 and GP35 locomotives and turned them over to the manufacturers to give us back basically new, GP39-2 units. They came with full warranties*

---

[808] Kaufman, p. 272.
[809] Burlington Northern Inc., 1988 Annual Report Form 10-K, p. 1.
[810] Ibid, p. 29.
[811] Ed Bauer Interview with Mark Cane, October 5, 2022.

and modern technology at a cost of only about 60% of what a new locomotive would have cost us. The GP39-2s came with four year warranties compared to only two year warranties for new locomotives. The old locomotives would be stripped to their frames. The trucks would be rebuilt and modern electrical and air brakes would be installed. The cabs were new. It was such a good program that after we ran out of BN hulks we acquired more on the open-market. The performance of the locomotives was outstanding. They were maintained by BN's workforce and had mean-time-between-failure rates higher than 92 days.

The addition of these locomotives also helped improve the quality of BN's intermodal train service by freeing up capacity. As of the end of 1988, 17 of these locomotives had been delivered.[812]

Coal Litigation Saga

The footnotes accompanying the 1988 financials, below, referred to coal litigation settlements. The $175 million ETSI settlement was the most prominent but utility rate litigation settlements were also material. These settlements were significant to BN's Intermodal business because the IBU was in a constant fight for growth capital. The PRB coal-share losses and deterioration of coal margins for retained business that accompanied the loss of BN's PRB monopoly in 1984 were bad enough. The loss of BNRR cash to the holding company and ongoing interest expenses related to assumption of debt to finance BNI's energy industry acquisitions made it even more difficult. Losses associated with coal rate litigations made it worse. Here are three examples from the saga that also illustrate the frustrations that politically motivated regulation brought:

One of BN's first PRB coal customers was the City of San Antonio. Their coal moved from the Cordero Mine to the Elmendorf, TX power plant in conjunction with Southern Pacific. In 1976 BN set a rate of $10.93 per ton. It proved to be non-compensatory. In conformance with the regulatory process BN justified a rate of $23.05 and it was approved by the ICC In 1980.[813] Mark Cane recalled:[814]

> *When I was in Alliance in 1979-1980 we knew we were on thin ice with the San Antonio-Elmendorf trains. We treated those V-93 trains like hot shots across our Division like we treated UPS trains elsewhere across BN's system. We tried to take away any reasons for them to criticize BN and make more trouble for us.*

In 1980, Congress gave San Antonio special treatment (mentioned earlier) with a special rate cap legislated into the Staggers Act. In 1981 the ICC ruled BN and SP actually undercharged San Antonio by $19 million between 1980 and 1981. Then the ICC changed course in 1986 and ordered a $38 million refund for overcharges between 1980 and 1984. After fights through the District Court, two Appeals Courts and the Supreme Court, BN and SP were ordered to refund an additional $70 million for overcharges between 1976 and 1980. C&NW/UP won this business from BN in 1985.[815]

A second case was Arkansas Power and Light for shipment to their Newark, AR plant via interchange with MP (UP in 1982 via merger). In 1979 BN/MP charged $12.78 per ton. In 1981 the ICC approved an

---

[812] Burlington Northern Inc., 1988 Annual Report Form 10-K, p. 29.

[813] Frailey, Fred W., Powder River Country, *Trains Magazine*, November, 1989, p. 51-52.

[814] Mark Cane's personal recollection, March 22, 2023.

[815] Frailey, Fred W., Powder River Country, *Trains Magazine*, November, 1989, p. 52.

increase to $18.75 and another in 1982 to $22.62.[816] In 1987 the ICC ordered BN to refund $22 million to AP&L. This was one of the first contracts the C&NW/UP won from BN in 1984. Because it was the business ETSI depended on, it was the final blow for their pipeline effort.

A third was Omaha Public Power who appealed to the ICC for relief in 1982 after BN raised the rate by 53% to their Arbor, NE plant with the approval of the ICC. After a long battle, BN agreed to refund $21.5 million in 1988 as part of a contract renewal negotiation. BN's decision was triggered by a new ICC decision described by Fred Frailey:[817]

> ... the ICC invoked a new policy for fixing maximum coal rates in the absence of competition: It said to imagine there were another railroad and to calculate what costs this efficiently run competitor would incur handling coal for several shippers. What rate, asked the ICC, would a competing railroad then offer? That, in essence, would be a fair price. By the time the ICC's decision came out there was competition, and to keep the business, BN cut its rate to OPP by 40 percent, according to reports.

This helps to explain the coal business dilemma BN would continue to face. It also helps explain why BN's IBU struggled so much to obtain growth capital. In a business with such a massive shared fixed-cost and fixed-plant infrastructure, any difficulty experienced in one business has an effect on others. Each line of business is like a cylinder in an engine. The engine works best when all cylinders are firing efficiently. This concept, and the importance of the BN Intermodal business "cylinder "within the overall BN Railroad business "engine," was completely understood by Darius Gaskins and Bill Greenwood. It would not be understood or appreciated during the Grinstein era after 1988.

1988 BNI, BR and BN Intermodal Performance

In 1988, Burlington Northern Inc.'s total revenue grew 10.6% and operating income (OI) grew 15.7%. Burlington Resources revenue fell 8.6% and BR operating income fell 72.8% as indicated below ($ Billions):[818]

Comparative 1988 vs. 1987 BN Railroad vs. Burlington Resources Performance

	1988		1987	
	BNRR	**BR**	**BNRR**	**BR**
Total Revenue	4.700	2.167	4.250	2.371
Operating Income	.679[a]	.101	.587	.371
Net Income	.179[a]	.072	.255	.231

[a] Includes ETSI suit settlement cost

Unlike the 1970s when BN's resources businesses vastly outperformed, and fed capital to, the railroad, BNRR again significantly outperformed the Resources business in 1988. This occurred in spite of all of the new Burlington Resources investments that were financed at the expense of the Railroad. It did not matter however. The Railroad's lot was cast and looking back was worthless.

The new BNI only included the BN Railroad. The 1988 annual Report From 10-K stated:

---

[816] Ibid.

[817] Ibid.

[818] Burlington Northern Inc., 1988 Annual Report.

While 1988 was a year of transition, it was also a year of excellent performance. Burlington Northern Inc. reported revenues of $4.7 billion, up almost 11 percent from 1987. Net income from continuing operations increased almost 16 percent to $207 million or $2.73 per share. The impact of the ETSI antitrust litigation settlement reduced total net income to $156 million or $2.04 per share.

Burlington Northern Railroad achieved recorded traffic volumes in 1988, with total revenue ton-miles increasing 8 percent to 224 billion. All major commodity groups reported volume gains.

Our Industrial Products unit increased by 20 percent due in part to substantial strength of the U.S. industrial sector.

Agricultural Products revenues increased $172 million or 30 percent from 1987 levels on a 7 percent increase in volume. Improvements in export volume and innovations such as the Certificate of Transportation program were major ingredients in this remarkable revenue growth. The COTs program allows the market to bid for future grain hauling capacity and thereby sets an appropriate market-based price for this service.

Coal, our largest volume and revenue producer. Also experienced strong growth in 1988 with revenues up by $147 million or 11 percent from 1987. High electrical demands brought on by last summer's drought, new export shipments for test burns in the Far East and increased offline sales due to aggressive marketing efforts all played a part in this success story.[819]

This table shows the revenue performance of the IBU relative to BNRR overall:

Burlington Northern Railroad 1981-1988 Financial Performance ($ millions)[820]

	IML Rev.	BNRR Rev.	BNRR Op. Inc.	BNRR OR	BNI LT Debt	Pref. Stock	Int. Exp.	Div. Exp.	Debt/ Cap.
1981	$267	$4,088	$527	87.1%	$1,330	$105	$140	$58	29%
1982	273	3,773	457	87.9%	1,333	105	136	71	27%
1983	335	4,058	734	81.9%	2,930	709	142	87	41%
1984	443	4,490	980	78.2%	2,454	697	310	130	35%
1985	485	4,098	822	79.9%	3,118	519	312	184	41%
1986	523	3,801	506[a]	86.7%	3,394	62	389	123	49%
1987	585	4,038	602	85.1%	3,001	57	372	155	44%
1988	615	4,541	679[b]	85.0%	2,723	14	292	165	76%

[a] Reported Operating Income was $152.8 mm, including approximately $20 million (pre-tax) of IBU driven Trailer Train dividends. It would have been a rounded $506 mm without the special non-cash charge of $352 mm, and $628 mm without that plus a coal rate litigation reserve.

[b] 1988 earnings included an ETSI related special charge of $175 million, after-tax $108 million ($1.45 per share). Without the special charge, operating income and operating ratio would have been $854 million and 81.2, respectively.

---

[819] Burlington Northern Inc., 1988 Annual Report.
[820] Burlington Northern Inc., 1981-1988 Annual Reports and Forms 10-K.

The incredible increase in Ag performance, in which revenue grew at a pace more than 4 times faster than volume, was enabled by the joint vision of Darius Gaskins and Bill Greenwood. They strove to put industry experts (including Rich Carter, Phil Weaver and J.B. Elliot) in charge of business units and the Ag Unit was a shining example of that. Just as the IBU was striving/struggling to capture value, over an industry-worst franchise, that was accruing to others in the intermodal value chain, the Ag unit was successfully doing it in a big way in the Ag market value chain, over an industry-best franchise, by letting the market drive the prices that were charged. Another initiative pushed by Gaskins, Greenwood and the Ag team was to secure short-term grain cars from equipment supplies through a market-oriented Dutch-Auction that significantly brought down car lease rates. Again, while the IBU struggled with a very weak franchise the Ag team had the strongest grain franchise in the railroad industry. They capitalized on it and proved that BN and the railroad industry had been leaving incredible amounts of value on the table just as the IBU believed was happening in the intermodal business.[821]

Intermodal revenue grew 5.1% in 1988 to $615 million, topping $600 million for the first time. Volume grew 12.5% to an industry leading 998 thousand revenue shipments as the growth in expanded network and, lower revenue-per-unit, Expediter shipments made up a larger proportion of total volume. The 1989 Annual Report featured BN AMERICA with two-page center photo of BNA containers (below) and a caption that said:[822]

> *Domestic container shipping is considered to be the future of the intermodal market. BN AMERICA, with the industry's largest fleet of new domestic containers, is ready to capitalize on this opportunity.*

In this last year of Darius Gaskins' leadership, BN Railroad Operating Income grew 45.5% to $854 million, excluding the ETSI settlement expense. Under the innovative and dynamic leadership of Darius Gaskins and Bill Greenwood, BN Railroad freight revenue grew 20% and adjusted Operating Income grew 69% between 1986 and 1988 despite the coal volume and yield impact of Union Pacific's entry into the PRB. Gaskins came to BN without any practical railroad background but he aggressively dug into the details of the business to accommodate for his lack of railroad experience. He trusted his people and encouraged them to take prudent risks. He encouraged taking another swing if one swung and missed. He provided unqualified support for BN's IBU and the development of BN AMERICA. Due to the loss of Gaskins, ineffective leadership by an unknowledgeable Jerry Grinstein, and Grinstein's unwillingness to give Bill Greenwood unobstructed freedom to run BN Railroad, 1988 would prove to be the peak year for BNRR profitability through the time of the Santa Fe merger in 1995.

Comparative 1988 Originated Intermodal Loads

In 1988, BN handled 998 thousand total Intermodal loads, up 12.5% from 887 thousand in 1987 and 194% from 1981 when the IBU was formed. Loads originated at BN Hubs grew 11.1% to 770 thousand

---

[821] See National Railroad Hall of Fame interview with Darius Gaskins for more details: https://www.nrrhof.org/darius-w-gaskins-jr.

[822] Burlington Northern Inc., Annual Report 1989, p. 6-7.

compared to 693 thousand in 1987. BN's industry position grew from last place in 1981 among the major Class I's to the third highest in the industry as shown below:[823]

Railroad	1988 Originated Loads
Conrail	825,000
Santa Fe	805,000
Burlington Northern	770,000
CSX	640,000
Southern Pacific	600,000
Union Pacific	596,000
Norfolk Southern	550,000
Others	912,000

BN Employee and Locomotive Productivity, 1978-1988

As stated earlier, in the last year of Darius Gaskins' leadership, BN Railroad Operating Income grew 45.5% to $854 million, excluding the ETSI settlement expense. As stated above, BN Railroad freight revenue grew 20% and adjusted Operating Income grew 69% between 1986 and 1988 despite the coal volume and yield impact of Union Pacific's entry into the PRB. There was more to the story than revenue. Steady improvements continued for two of the prime drivers of railroad production – people and locomotives. The drive to simultaneously improve service while improving productivity accelerated after Gaskins took the helm from Drexel and former Frisco operating executives in 1984.

BN Railroad Employee and Locomotive Productivity, 1978-1988[824]

	RTMs (B)	Avg. Employees	RTMs per Employee (mm)	Freight Locomotives	RTMs per Frt. Loco. (mm)
1978	116.3	46,684	2.491	1,860	62.5
1979	135.0	49,559	2.724	2,039	66.2
1980	170.6	58,965	2.893	2,856	59.7
1981	174.9	55,347	3.160	2,606	67.1
1982	157.9	46,015	3.431	2,200	71.8
1983	172.3	40,914	4.211	2,088	82.5
1984	200.6	39,791	5.041	2,310	86.8
1985	184.1	37,885	4.860	2,080	88.5
1986	187.2	35,109	5.332	2,106	88.9
1987	206.3	32,810	6.288	2,104	98.1
1988	223.6	32,402	6.816	2,252	99.3

BN's employee count fell 18.6% and RTMs per employee grew 11.5% through 1988 despite the C&NW/UP entry into the PRB which contributed to an 8.2% drop in BN's RTMs in 1985. While freight locomotive count was only 2.5% less in 1988 than 1984, RTMs per freight locomotive grew 14.4% even

---

[823] Burlington Northern Railroad, Intermodal Hit Squad, Final Report, February 24, 1992, *Greenwood Collection*, Barriger Library at UMSL.

[824] Burlington Northern Inc., 1979-1988 Railway Financial and Operating Statistics, CS 14.1 Reports, *Greenwood Collection*, Barriger Library at UMSL.

though the proportion of coal to total revenue fell from the record pre-C&NW/UP high of 41.4% to 33.0% and the proportion of revenue from lighter density Intermodal grew from 9.9% to 13.5%.[825]

Such significant productivity improvements were critical to survival in a deregulated environment where price competition was so severe. That price competition helped create internal animosity between Operations/Finance and Marketing/Sales because Operations would say they were continually cutting costs but Marketing gave all of the cost-cuts away. Yet, that was the nature of the market if you were perceived to be a commodity and could/would not differentiate your service levels.

The struggles of BN's IBU to improve its geographic franchise and capture more of the value within the Intermodal supply chain would grow even further in 1989.

---

[825] See *Against All Odds*, Volume III, Appendix 1.

Appendix 1 – October, 1981, BN Railroad's Motor Carrier Divertible Carload Business[826]

Exhibit 1

TASK FORCE DIVERTABLE TRAFFIC
SUMMARY TOTALS
REPORT DATE: 10/14/81

FCST_GROUP	EST RAIL CARS	EST TRAILERS	EST TONS	EST RTM	EST REVENUE	EST LRIC COST	EST LRIC CONTRIB	LRIC RATIO
05 POTATOES	10,661	21,630	469,165	484,315,571	16,825,269	12,273,678	4,551,591	1.37
06 FRUIT	8,468	17,062	365,898	475,034,838	14,197,164	11,515,699	2,681,465	1.23
07 MISC FARM PROD	1,447	2,597	52,332	37,589,324	1,504,535	1,516,323	-11,788	.99
09 OTHR METALLIC ORE	214	493	10,668	7,032,579	192,958	160,762	32,196	1.20
11 SAND & GRAVEL	4,477	10,705	231,347	163,662,093	4,298,854	3,618,234	680,620	1.19
12 NON METALLIC ORES	1,461	3,283	71,076	56,669,367	1,825,097	1,304,180	520,917	1.40
15 CANNED GOODS	38,480	84,816	1,807,359	1,333,786,836	45,404,052	34,187,169	11,216,883	1.33
16 FROZEN FOODS	18,636	37,705	813,657	1,019,229,412	33,543,722	24,617,149	8,926,573	1.36
17 SUGAR	2,121	5,036	108,749	73,803,420	3,360,802	1,774,598	1,586,204	1.89
18 BEVERAGES	37,535	103,326	2,234,865	1,275,606,896	49,985,482	30,925,460	19,060,022	1.62
19 MISC FOODS	37,648	71,056	1,252,495	791,951,120	37,904,956	25,142,992	12,761,964	1.51
21 PLYWOOD	4,205	9,009	194,746	238,213,935	8,116,709	4,878,720	3,237,939	1.66
22 LUMBER	13,379	28,500	616,310	742,100,975	22,679,381	15,689,984	6,990,397	1.45
23 PANELBOARD	2,490	5,879	123,132	116,634,625	3,934,381	2,406,454	1,527,927	1.63
24 MISC WOOD	3,283	5,188	104,060	184,593,377	3,760,167	3,000,179	759,988	1.25
25 WOOD PULP	2,979	8,221	177,660	144,808,184	4,215,752	2,673,422	1,542,330	1.58
26 PAPER	23,064	49,477	916,268	617,395,944	23,025,809	15,765,806	7,260,003	1.46
27 FERTILIZER	1,248	3,015	65,057	34,375,256	981,875	797,194	184,681	1.23
28 CHEMICALS	5,341	11,977	257,980	159,425,773	5,621,187	3,867,254	1,753,933	1.45
29 PETRO PRODUCTS	534	890	16,607	13,780,757	584,107	446,842	137,265	1.31
30 COKE	2,253	4,596	99,655	94,950,590	3,137,849	2,218,933	918,916	1.41
31 CEMENT	705	1,377	29,697	16,319,302	641,377	464,149	177,228	1.38
32 BENTONITE	3,759	8,708	188,552	211,218,738	7,049,430	4,639,703	2,409,727	1.52
33 GYPSUM	30,307	65,687	1,269,398	891,276,734	36,031,030	22,939,949	13,092,081	1.57
34 STEEL	24,551	61,432	1,381,231	894,724,096	34,920,147	19,713,659	15,206,488	1.77
35 ALUMINUM	8,971	25,985	562,065	639,054,181	21,235,761	11,107,622	10,128,139	1.91
36 NON FERROUS METAL	3,263	10,995	237,037	210,595,819	6,448,205	3,500,603	2,947,602	1.84
37 FABRICATED METAL	9,518	16,739	312,087	268,908,505	15,455,667	7,816,735	7,638,932	1.98
38 MACHINERY	11,022	16,085	225,477	168,906,101	13,220,506	8,065,607	5,154,899	1.64
39 APPLIANCE & FURN	27,452	39,226	279,733	187,453,249	23,504,711	16,270,359	7,234,352	1.44
42 WASTE & SCRAP	19,300	35,526	726,402	434,459,876	15,382,266	11,841,552	3,540,714	1.30
44 ALL OTHER	35,173	55,645	764,321	515,418,856	31,760,041	21,413,113	10,346,928	1.48
TOTAL	393,945	821,866	15,985,076	12,479,096,349	490,749,249	326,552,083	164,197,166	1.50

Source: Burlington Northern Intermodal Task Force, Exhibit 1, Divertible Traffic Summary Totals, 10/14/81.

---

[826] *Greenwood Collection*, Barriger Library at UMSL.

Appendix 2 – Circa 1983-1986 BN *Innovative Intermodal Service* Print Advertisements[827]

"When you asked for better intermodal facilities, we gave you results. Not excuses." Bill Greenwood, Senior Assistant Vice President, Intermodal

Last year, we spent more than $8 million upgrading intermodal hub facilities in Cicero, Memphis, Portland and Naperville. We've added new lift devices to move containers and trailers on and off flatcars more quickly. We've added truck receiving lanes. We've continued to update our computerized systems to keep track of your shipments from origin to destination. And this year we're making similar improvements at other locations across the country.

Why do we do it? Because we want your business. And we think efficient, competitively-priced intermodal service is one way to get it. But BN service is more than tracks and trains. It's people. People in each community we serve, working hard at putting the railroad to work for you. We're the new Burlington Northern. Give us a call. We're in the white pages.

BURLINGTON NORTHERN RAILROAD

The better we get, the better it gets for you.

---

[827] *Greenwood Collection*, Barriger Library at UMSL.

BN innovations make intermodal work for you.

HUB CENTERS MAKE YOUR SHIPMENTS MOVE MORE EFFICIENTLY.

The Hub Center is just one Burlington Northern innovation that is making intermodal work harder for you. Throughout the U.S., BN Hub Centers are ready to move your intermodal shipments quickly and efficiently.

At BN, we know the trucking side of intermodal as well as the rail side. In fact, most of our Hub Center managers have years of experience in the motor-carrier industry. They run our Hub Centers much like truck terminals — with the emphasis on customer service.

BN Hub Centers handle only intermodal traffic. Most of your shipments move on dedicated trains that don't stop at classification or hump yards. So you get faster, safer service and consistent deliveries. We have the equipment and the know-how to handle your shipments efficiently. Truck drivers don't wait long to drop off or pick up loads. And trailers and containers are loaded and unloaded quickly. Both your trucks and your shipments get in and out of the Hub Center faster.

BN's commitment to efficient service is making intermodal faster, more economical and more reliable. That means better service for your customers and increased profitability for you.

To find out how BN innovations can make intermodal work harder for you, call 1-800-545-0600.

B Innovative Intermodal Service

338

WHILE MOST FREIGHT CARRIERS ARE MAKING SHIPPERS FIT THEIR SERVICE, BURLINGTON NORTHERN IS TAILORING A SERVICE TO FIT ITS CUSTOMERS.

At BN's new Memphis Hub Center we offer a rare commodity in the transportation business: *innovative intermodal service.* That means we'll work with you to determine your top priority needs. Then, we'll analyze the kind of freight you ship...its dimensions, weight, value, and any special bracing or loading requirements necessary. We'll look at your loss and damage concerns and recommend solutions. In short, we'll tailor a package that perfectly fits your needs. And we'll offer it to you at a very reasonable price.

You get peace-of-mind.
Call our Memphis Hub Center and we'll not only take a load of freight off your hands, we'll take a load off your mind, too.

If you're within a 200 mile radius of the Hub, we can arrange to pick up the freight right at your dock. Then we'll move it across the country quickly and economically by rail. Finally, we can arrange delivery to the receiver's dock. One phone call, one bill of lading, and no hassles.

The secret is simple: Innovative intermodal.

At BN, intermodal means creatively working with you on a package that combines the economies of low-cost long-distance rail transport with the convenience and flexibility of truck pick-up and delivery. The result: a package that fits your needs and your pocketbook.

We're as close as 1-800-HUB-2345. Just call and we'll take it from there. But, just for your information, BN's Memphis Hub Center is located at 2440 Dunn Cove with access to major freeways. It covers 14 acres with parking space for 300 trailers and containers. It has a mobile loader to lift trailers and containers on and off railcars. We're open 7 days a week under a 24-hour security force. Call us today and let us tailor a package for you.
PHONE, TOLL FREE:
1-800-HUB-2345

To trace a trailer or container, phone 1-800-342-5123.
For sales and service, phone 1-901-369-6138.

BN innovations make intermodal work for you.

DEDICATED SERVICE MEANS DELIVERY TIMES YOU CAN RELY ON.

Dedicated service is another innovation that makes Burlington Northern intermodal work for you. When your shipments travel on BN's dedicated trains, you get faster, safer service and delivery times you can rely on.

Dedicated trains handle only intermodal traffic. Instead of stopping at classification or hump yards, they're handled at BN Hub Centers so your shipments move faster and more securely.

BN Hub Centers are run like truck terminals, by managers with years of experience in the motor-carrier industry. The bottom line is service. We have the equipment and the know-how to handle your shipments efficiently—every mile of the way.

Dedicated trains, efficient Hub Centers and skilled transportation specialists are making BN intermodal faster, more economical and more reliable. That means

better service for your customers and increased profitability for you.

To find out how BN innovations can make intermodal work for you, call 1-800-545-0600.

Innovative Intermodal Service

BN innovations make intermodal work for you.

NEW HANDLING TECHNIQUES KEEP YOUR SHIPMENTS SECURE.

Innovative handling techniques from Burlington Northern are making intermodal work for you. BN gives your shipments special care every mile of the way, so they arrive securely at your final destination.

Dedicated trains handle only intermodal traffic—they don't stop at classification or hump yards. Your shipments are handled at BN Hub Centers, so you get faster, safer service. And BN's new tie-down system

(in our 102"-wide trailers) gives you another way to secure loads that need extra protection. Our transportation experts invented this easy-to-use system to help speed loading, reduce secure-ment costs and cut damage losses. It even lets you ship less than full trailer loads more safely than ever before.

BN is always looking for new ways to make your shipments move faster, more efficiently, more safely. That dedication pays

off in better service for your customers and increased profit-ability for you.

To find out how BN innovations can make intermodal work for you or for information on securing your shipments, call 1-800-545-0600.

BN innovations make intermodal work for you.

BN 600 SAVES YOU TIME AND MONEY ON THE LONG HAULS.

BN 600 is a Burlington Northern innovation that is making intermodal work for you. BN 600 saves you time and money on shipments of 600 miles or more. With trucks and trains working together, you get reliable, efficient service.

BN 600 dedicated trains handle only intermodal traffic. They don't stop at classification or hump yards, so they move faster and more safely. Pickup and delivery are available within a radius of up to 250 miles of each convenient Hub Center.

BN 600 means more than saving money—it means better service for your customers and increased profitability for you. The partnership of trucks with trains gives you the best combination of reliability, economy, safety and speed.

To find out how BN innovations can make intermodal work for you, call 1-800-545-0600.

Innovative Intermodal Service

BN 600: Trucks and trains together.

SAVE MORE THAN MONEY WHEN YOU SHIP MORE THAN 600 MILES.

For shipments of 600 miles or more, Burlington Northern's Innovative Intermodal Service can save you time and money. With trucks and trains working together, you get reliable, more efficient service. We call it BN 600.

BN 600 trains are dedicated only to intermodal shipments. They don't stop at classification or hump yards, so they move down the line faster and more safely.

Pickup and delivery are available within a 250-mile radius of each convenient Hub Center.

BN 600 helps you help your customers in fewer man-hours and at better prices. That means more than saving money — it means better service for your customers and increased profitability for you. The partnership of trucks with trains gives you the best combination of reliability,

economy, safety and speed.

To find out how BN 600 can help you improve efficiency and increase profits for shipments more than 600 miles, call 1-800-545-0600.

BN innovations make intermodal work for you.

NEW BN EXPEDITER CUTS YOUR COSTS ON SHORT-HAUL SHIPMENTS.

Burlington Northern's new BN Expediter service gives you a cost-competitive alternative for trailer shipments between our hubs at Dallas, St. Louis, Birmingham, Kansas City, Tulsa, Memphis and Springfield. BN Expediter offers you a consistent, reliable, profitable way to handle short-haul intermodal shipments in this territory.

Recently, BN introduced lower rates systemwide. BN Expediter reflects this change with a rate structure that can cut your overall shipping costs and help you make better use of your assets.

BN Expediter service has been streamlined to give you dependable, daily service and consistent availability times. The trains are dedicated to intermodal traffic to meet the needs of trailer shippers with fast, efficient service.

With BN 600, we brought you efficient, reliable, economical service on intermodal shipments over 600 miles. Now, with new BN Expediter, we give you those same benefits for short-haul shipments. Find out what BN Expediter can do for you. Call 1-800-545-0600, and ask for your free BN Expediter brochure.

Appendix 3 – May, 1987 BN Intermodal Service Map[828]

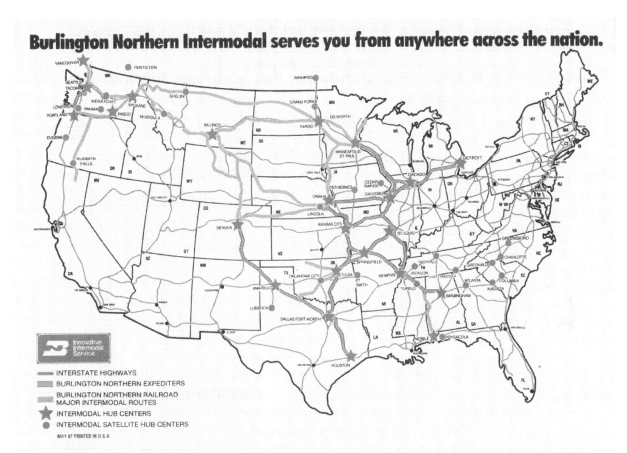

---

[828] *Greenwood Collection*, Barriger Library at UMSL.

Appendix 4: Unissued August 10, 1988 Draft Press Release Announcing the Formation of the BN/Santa Fe "BSF AMERICA" Joint Venture[829]

BURLINGTON NORTHERN RAILROAD AND
ATCHISON, TOPEKA & SANTA FE RAILWAY
ANNOUNCE JOINT INTERMODAL MARKETING VENTURE

August 10, 1988 -- Darius Gaskins, Jr., President of Burlington Northern Railroad Company("BN"), and W. John Swartz, President of the Atchison, Topeka and Santa Fe Railway Company ("ATSF"), today announced they are planning to form a jointly-owned intermodal marketing venture to handle the full scope of marketplace activities for intermodal traffic moving on joint service routes of the two lines. The companies intend to focus initially on intermodal traffic moving between the Southeast and California via Avard.

The decision to form a venture was reached after extensive discussions between marketing and intermodal executives of both companies.

The new venture, to be named Burlington Santa Fe America ("BSF AMERICA"), will enhance the existing marketing strategies of both companies. Its primary objective will be to work with existing third parties and other intermodal customers to strengthen the parent companies' respective positions in the intermodal marketplace.

It is anticipated that senior management of BSF AMERICA will be comprised of executives familiar with the intermodal business environment. In addition, BN and ATSF will each designate a senior executive for a key management position in the new venture. Those appointments are expected to be made in September.

John Grygiel, Vice President Traffic of the Santa Fe and Robert Ingram, Vice President Intermodal of the Burlington Northern, said the new venture's marketing strategies will include the maintenance of both companies' existing sales representation through third parties and other intermodal customers. The new venture's objective will be to expand the existing intermodal traffic base by employing new technologies which provide operating economies. This will allow BSF AMERICA to be competitive over a wide range of traffic situations.

- more -

---

[829] *Greenwood Collection*, Barriger Library at UMSL.

First add: BSF AMERICA

BSF AMERICA's intermodal transportation and terminal services will be provided by the existing intermodal organizations of BN and ATSF. However, all marketing activities and customer interface in the designated joint line service areas will be conducted by BSF AMERICA. Both executives expect a closer and more responsive relationship to develop between the new company and existing customers. It is anticipated that BSF AMERICA's full marketing organization will be in place by the end of this year, so that intermodal marketing activities can begin as soon as possible.

BSF AMERICA will seek any necessary government approvals or exemptions before the new company commences marketing operations.

#

For more information, contact:

John Grygiel
Vice President Traffic
Santa Fe Railroad
312/347-3070

Steve Forsberg
Director, Marketing Communications
Burlington Northern Railroad
817/878-2308

Bibliography

Armstrong, John H., *The Railroad – What It Is, What It Does*, Simmons-Boardman Publishing Corp., Omaha, 1977.

Bryant Jr., Keith L., and Frailey, Fred W., *History of the Atchison, Topeka and Santa Fe Railway, New Edition*, University of Nebraska Press, Lincoln, 2020.

Collins, James C., *Good to Great: Why Some Companies Make the Leap ... and Others Don't*, HarperCollins, New York, 2001.

Comfort, Mildred Houghton, *James Jerome Hill - Railroad Pioneer*, T.S. Denison & Company, Inc. Minneapolis, 1973.

Currie, Earl J., *BN-Frisco, A Tough Merger*, Self Published, 2010.

Currie, Earl J., *Burlington Northern, A Great Adventure, 1970-1979*, WSU Press, Pullman, WA, 2019.

Currie, Earl J., *Transformation of a Railroad Company, Burlington Northern, 1980-1995*, WSU Press, Pullman, WA , 2019.

David, Pierre A. & Stewart, Richard D., *International Logistics – The Management of International Trade Operations*, Cengage Learning, Mason, OH, 2010.

DeBoer, David J., *Piggyback and Containers – A History of Rail Intermodal on America's Steel Highway*, Golden West Books, San Marino, CA, 1992.

Donald G. McInnes Collection B-147, John W. Barriger III National Railroad Library, St. Louis Mercantile Library, University of Missouri - St. Louis (UMSL), 1 University Blvd., St; Louis, MO 63121-4400.

Glischinski, Steve, *Burlington Northern and Its Heritage*, Andover Junction Publications, Andover, New Jersey, 1992.

Great Northern Railway Company, Public Relations Department, *A Condensed History of The Great Northern Railway*, St. Paul, MN, 1953.

Green, Howard, *Railroader – The Unfiltered Genius and Controversy of Four-Time CEO Hunter Harrison*, Page Two Books, 2018.

Hidy, Ralph W., Hidy, Muriel E., and Scott, Roy V. with Hofsommer, Don L., *The Great Northern Railway, A History*, Harvard Business School Press, Boston, 1988.

Holck, Alfred J.J., *The Hub of Burlington Lines West*, South Platte Press, David City, Nebraska, 1991.

Katzenbach, John R., Smith, Douglas K., *The Wisdom of Teams – Creating the High-Performance Organization*, Harvard Business School Press, Boston, 1993.

Kaufman, Lawrence H., *Leaders Count – The Story of the BNSF Railway*, Texas Monthly Custom Publications, Austin, TX, 2005.

Loving Jr., Rush, *The Well Dressed Hobo: The Many Wondrous Adventures of a Man who Loved Trains*, Indiana University Press, Bloomington & Indianapolis, 2016.

Mark S. Cane Collection, John W. Barriger III National Railroad Library, St. Louis Mercantile Library, University of Missouri - St. Louis (UMSL), 1 University Blvd., St; Louis, MO 63121-4400.

Mattingly, Garrett, *The Armada*, Houghton Mifflin, Boston, 1959.

Morgan, David P., *The Evolution of Power on the Burlington*, Chicago, Burlington & Quincy Railroad Company, 1963.

Overton, Richard C., *Burlington Route – A History of the Burlington Lines*, University of Nebraska Press, Lincoln, Nebraska, 1965.

Panza, James D., Dawson, Richard W., Sellberg, Ronald P., *The TTX Story, Volume 1*, The Pennsylvania Railroad Technical & Historical Society, Allentown, Pennsylvania, 2018.

Panza, James D., Dawson, Richard W., Sellberg, Ronald P., *The TTX Story, Volume 2*, The Pennsylvania Railroad Technical & Historical Society, Allentown, Pennsylvania, 2018.

Persico, Joseph E., *Roosevelt's Secret War*, Random House, New York, 2002.

Rodengen, Jeffrey L., *Innovation and Integrity – The Story of Hub Group*, Write Stuff Enterprises, 2007.

Sermak, Robert M., *History of Alliance Division of the Burlington Northern, 1978-1982*, A Research Paper Presented to the Faculty of the Graduate School, Chadron State College, November 1983.

Sheffi, Yossi, *Logistics Clusters, Delivering Value and Driving Growth*, The MIT Press, Cambridge, MA, 2012.

Spoor, Michael J., *Chicago, Burlington & Quincy In Color*, Volume I, Morning Sun Books, Edison, NJ, 1994.

William Greenwood Collection, John W. Barriger III National Railroad Library, St. Louis Mercantile Library, University of Missouri - St. Louis (UMSL), 1 University Blvd., St; Louis, MO 63121-4400.

Yenne, Bill, *The History of the Burlington Northern*, Bonanza Books, New York, 1991.

Volume I Index

"Black Hole" Zone ... 146, 245

"Flexi-Van" service 23

1893 Northern Pacific bonds 67, 69

1893 Northern Pacific Bonds 37

1973 Energy Crisis 34

A.T. Kearney 147

ACF Industries 147, 148

Advisory Committee on a National Highway Program 15

Agnew, Gary 228, 300

Alaska Hydro-Train 208

Albright, Dave 303

Allen, Bill 116, 127

Alliance Shippers 152

Amarillo Hub 172

Amax 34

American Freightways 186

American President Lines 315, 317, 318

American President Lines - Disrupts industry 154

American President Lines (APL) ... 148, 153, 174, 201, 237, 267

American Trucking Association (ATA) 16

Ameritrans 300

Amtrak 52, 87, 163

Anschutz, Philip 313

AOMI 318

APL / American President Domestic 301

APL Buys National Piggyback 175

APL Linertrain 155, 185

ARCO ... *See* Atlantic Richfield Company

Argo (UP Seattle terminal) 157

Arkansas Power and Light 323, 329

Armstrong, Bernie 154

Arthur Anderson 223

Association of American Railroads 17, 145, 307

Atchison, Topeka & Santa Fe early intermodal history 29

Atchison, Topeka and Santa Fe Railroad 29

Atlanta Intermodal Expo . 301

Atlantic Richfield Company (ARCO) 40

ATSF .... *See* Santa Fe

Atwell, Bob 228

Avard Gateway 215, 248

Avard Gateway - another 1987 marketing and bridge operating rights 272

Avard Gateway marketing and bridge rights proposal - 1987 268

Babb, Doug 93, 203

BAH study (Booz Allen) - 1981 ...... 79, 117, 120, 207

Baker, Don 203

Bauer, Ed 247, 328

Bauer, Tom 59

Beal, Lawrence 328

Bechtel 40

Beck, David 18

Behling, Burton N. 17

Bentz, Brooks - BN IBU Domestic Containerization/BN AMERICA tart 307

Bentz, Brooks – Joins BN's IBU 300

Bergeland, Paul 163

Berry, William ... 60, 109, 113, 140, 149, 153, 162, 185, 191, 226, 228, 239, 244, 282, 283, 300, 303, 307

Berry, William - Pre-Intermodal experience 109

Billings Hub 143

Bi-Modal Corporation..... 145, 159

Binger, Robert 38, 69, 87

Birmingham Hub 142, 172

Black Mesa coal slurry pipeline 40

BLE .... *See* Brotherhood of Locomotive Engineers

BN - Santa Fe merger overture - 1982 113

BN "750-mile Rule" 176

BN / Roadrailer Southwest Express - 1983 159

BN 364 day trailer leases. 149

BN 600 project 188

BN Airfreight (BNAFI) 85, 107

BN AMERICA 308, 315

BN Business Unit Price Performance - 1987-1988 302

BN Green 45X102 Trailers - 1983 148

BN Hub Manager Profile . 129

BN IBU - 1984 Organization Realignment 171

BN Innovative Intermodal Service Brand 128

BN Intermodal "White Paper" - 1984 165

BN Intermodal competitive situation - 1981 92

BN Intermodal corridor management - 1986 225

BN Intermodal Detroit Hub Genesis 231

BN Intermodal vision/objective - 1981 .. 91

BN Intermodal White Paper (1984) Outcome 170

BN land and resource holdings - 1977 36

BN Motor Vehicle Action Group - 1982 105

BN Organization Study - 1982 116

BN Railroad Employee and Locomotive Productivity, 1978-1988 333

BN Railroad -Headquarters relocation to Ft. Worth 162

BN Railroad vs. Resources Performance 1973-1980 67

BN Sales and Service reorganization - 1984 .. 172

BN Short Line sales 245

BN Transport 85, 94, 95, 107, 141, 208

BN Worldwide 274, 297, 308, 317

BN/CSX Voluntary Cooperation Agreement (VCA) 245

BN/IBU Performance - 1982 138

BN/IBU Performance - 1983 163

BN/IBU Performance - 1985 219

BN/IBU Performance - 1986 252

BN/IBU Performance - 1987 286

BN/IBU Performance - 1988 330

BNI -1986 Asset and Accounting Charge Write-off 250

BNRR business component performance 1986 vs. 1981 253

Bobb, Steve 321

Boggs, Hale 19

Boise Cascade Company ... 39

Booz Allen Hamilton (BAH) 75

Booz Allen Hamilton Study - 1981 75

Brady, Emmett 89, 163

Brehm, Norm 257

Bresnahan, William A........ 16

Bressler, Richard .. 46, 67, 68, 70, 181, 182, 251, 323, 327

Bressler, Richard - Joins Burlington Northern 68

Brotherhood of Locomotive Engineers (BLE) 195, 320

Brotherhood of Railway and Airline Clerks (BRAC) .. 141, 199

Bruce, Harry 145

Bruce, Seaton 175

Bryan, Charlie 203

Bryant, Keith..................... 29

BSF America 306, 309, 313

Buchanan, Roy................. 203

Buchholz, Don 228

Budd Company 148

Buffet, Warren 1

Burk, Lyle 190, 233

Burke, Ed 322

Burke, Michael 317

Burlington Northern "Piggyback" Performance 1970-1979 56

Burlington Northern "piggyback" situation in early 1981 85

Burlington Northern and Its Heritage.................. 5, 349

Burlington Northern Holding Company justification - 1981 75

Burlington Northern Inc. break-up - 1988 325

Burlington Northern intermodal history, 1970-1979 51

Burlington Northern Motor Carriers (BNMC) 321

Burlington Northern Motor Carriers Inc. (BNMC).... 209

Burlington Northern-Frisco Merger.......................... 46

Burlington Resources (BR) 326

Burlington Resources Inc. (BR)............................. 328

Burlington Route – A History of the Burlington Lines ...5, 350

Burns, David ... 57, 89, 90, 95, 105, 106, 107, 111, 115, 127, 129, 134, 143, 206, 227, 228, 263, 300

Burns, David - Pre-Intermodal experience 106

Burton, Ray................ 42, 269

C&NW .... 48, *See* Chicago & North Western Railway

Cane, Mark 108, 121, 174, 204, 228, 233, 247, 259, 270, **283**, 297, 299, 301, 306

Cane, Mark - 1978 BN Shareholders' Meeting .. 44

Cane, Mark - 1987 IBU Marketing Goals 256

Cane, Mark - 1987 Pricing philosophy guidance ... 264

Cane, Mark - 1988 IBU Strategic Marketing Issues 289

Cane, Mark - Leaves IBU, 1988............................. 303

Cane, Mark - pre-Intermodal background.................... 86

Carnahan, John............... 236

Carr, Paul V..................... 255

Carroll, Phil 203

Carter, Judge Robert 286

Carter, President Jimmy ... 63, 72

Carter, Rich...................... 332

Cascade Tunnel 161, 219

CB&Q - Early Piggyback History 25

CB&Q Train No. 14 27

CB&Q Train No. 61 27

Cena, Larry...................... 238

Central Motor Freight Association 19

Central Pacific Railroad 8

Certificate of Transportation Service (COTS) 302, 331

Channel policy statement - 1987 260
Chessie Railroad 66
Chicago & Northwestern Railroad (C&NW). 135, 201
Chicago neutral chassis pool 206
Chicago Tunnel Company . 26
Chicago, Burlington & Quincy In Color 25, 350
Chicago, Burlington & Quincy Railroad (CB&Q) 5
Chrysler 207, 231
Cicero Hub...... 115, 128, 137, 142, 206, 227
Cicero Hub buildout - 1983 143
Cicero Hump Yard construction - 1958....... 27
Cicero Yard 25
Circus Ramps 57
Circus Train.................... 57
City of San Antonio 329
City Public Service Board of San Antonio................ 250
Clay, General Lucius D....... 15
Clean Air Act of 1974 42
Clipper EXXPRESS 152
Cochran, Earle 192, 216
Cockrell, Lila 74
Collins, Mike.................... 206
Colorado & Southern Railroad (C&S) 231
Columbia River 161
Columbia University............xi
Common User Stack Train 157, 234
Comparative intermodal loadings - 1987............ 286
Comparative Intermodal Loadings - 1988 332
Competitive service profiles - 1987 264
Conrail...... 86, 101, 107, 148, 155, 158, 227, 231, 236, 238, 240, 245, 268, 286, 304, 309, 315, 333

Consolidated Freightways (CF) 224
Cook, Tom 236
Corps of Engineers 10
COSCO 202
Cox, Terry 8
Coyne, Fran (BN Human Resources)....... 84, 88, 108
Coyne, Frank (CFO)........... 69
Crane, Stanley 240
Craven, Dave 225
Crighton, Jim 259
CSX............ 66, 126, 286, 333
CSX Corporation - Buys Sea-Land............................ 224
CSX/Sea-Land Intermodal (CSXI) established........ 267
Cumberland Road (aka National Road) 7
Dagnon, Jim............. 266, 276
Dallas Smith Engineering Corp............................ 207
Dallas Smith Trailer - lawsuit 268
Dallas Smith Trailers....... 160, 207, 225, 238
Dan Flood 239
Dave DeBoer 187
Davidson, Dick................ 240
Davies, Gerald 94, 96, 116, 126
Dawson, Richard xii
DeBoer, David J. xii, 5, 28, 55, 187, 281, 349
Decker Coal 34
Dell'Osso, Lou.. 170, 178, 181
Delta Airlines 249
Delta Model.................... 309
Denver Hub 142, 234
Department of Justice (DOJ) - Trailer Train pooling authority...................... 270
Detroit Hub and Expediter established 259
Dewhirst, Caroline.......... 299
DeWitt, William..xi, 106, 111, 113, 114, 115, 121, 122, 129, 140, 151, 174, 190,

198, 203, 210, 225, 226, 228, 298, 301, 303
DeWitt, William – Assumes Winona Bridge, replacing Steve Nieman 298
DeWitt, William - BNI Holding Company 85
DeWitt, William - Pre-Intermodal experience 107
Differential prices - 1987. 264
Dinsmore, Mic 318
Domestic containerization 237
Domestic containerization development - 1987 281
Domestic containerization program – draft agent affiliate qualifiers 284
Domestic containerization vision and dilemma - 1987 283
Donahue, Michael .. 117, 162, 177, 278, 279
Dopp, Bert 134
Doty, Tom 186, 257, 300
Double stack - relative economics (1987)........ 282
Double stack cars - first BN acquisition 185
Double stack clearance improvements - 1988.. 312
Dowell, Marv ... 226, 228, 300
Downing, Robert 181
Drexel, Walter 107, 110, 112, 116, 125, 127, 136, 142, 159, 162, 165, 185, 191, 202, 210, 211, 249, 262
Drexel, Walter - appointed President and COO of BN Railroad 110
DRGW Railroad................ 268
Duchossois Industries...... 203
Dutch-Auction 332
Egan, Bill .. 100, 125, 172, 213
El Paso Natural Gas 178, 250, 251, 326
Electro-Motive Division (EMD) 328

Elliot, J.B. 332
Elrick and Lavidge - Market
    Research..................... 198
Empire State Xpress 159
Energy Transportation
    Systems, Inc. (ETSI) 40
Energy Transportation
    Systems, Inc. (ETSI) – 1988
    BN Litigation Settlement
    321
Environmental Protection
    Agency.......................... 33
Ethington, Ivan 93, 100
ETSI 49, 329, 331
Evans, Daniel 66, 328
Evans, Jim 323
Evergreen 202
Expediter
    Chicago-Kansas City 249
Expediter 700-mile length-of-
    haul restriction removal
    233
Expediter trains 216
Expediter Trains - Genesis
    187
Expediters - Aggressive 1987
    expansion 258
Fallon, George H................ 16
Farmer, Katie....................... 2
Federal Highway Act of 1956
    23
Federal Railroad
    Administration (FRA).... 46,
    187
Federal-Aid Highway Act of
    1938 11
Federal-Aid Highway Act of
    1944 13
Federal-Aid Highway Act of
    1956 20
Federal-Aid Highway
    Amendments of 1974 ... 61
Finkbiner, Thomas............. 86
Fitzgerald, Tom 316
Flood, Dan 255
Flying Tiger Line 203
FMC 147

FMC Marine and Rail Division
    146
Ford Motor Company....... 10,
    160, 231, 238
Ford, Henry 10
Fort Worth and Denver
    Railroad (FW&D) 231
Frailey, Fred....xii, 29, 48, 329
Francis, Bill 225, 326
Frick, Dick 202
Frisco First Mortgage line
    sale impediment.......... 234
Frisco Transportation (FT)208
Fry, Nick.............................xii
Ft. Union Geologic Formation
    33
Galassi, Joe 117, 172, 213,
    229, 262, 266, 320, 326
Galesburg Hub......... 142, 165
Garland, Robert 94, 100, 117,
    119, 162, 177
Garst, Mary 249
Gaskins, Darius ..... x, 72, 114,
    122, 124, 125, 126, 127,
    128, 129, 136, 137, 142,
    160, 165, 170, 171, 177,
    185, 188, 202, 205, 210,
    211, 212, 242, 246, 250,
    262, 269, 271, 280, 283,
    289, 297, 299, 303, 304,
    306, 318, 319, 323, 325,
    327, 328, 332
Gaskins, Darius - "Plant a
    thousand flowers"
    philosophy.................. 160
Gaskins, Darius - Pre-BN
    experience................... 124
Gaskins, Darius - promoted
    to BNRR president and
    COO 211
Gaskins, Darius - supporting
    the Intermodal BU....... 128
Gearbulk Container Services
    235
General Dam Act of 1906.. 10
General Motors 22, 147, 203,
    225, 226, 249
Gillespie, Beth 154

Gillette-Orin Line ... 39, 46, 48
Glacier Park Company 326
Glavin, Bill...................... 312
Gleason, Richard ..55, 84, 85,
    86, 93, 94, 96, 100, 111,
    112, 117, 125, 127, 136,
    177, 212
Glischinski, Steve......... 5, 349
Gore, Sr., Senator Albert ...15
Grand Trunk Western (GTW)
    Railroad 226, 231
Gray, John.............. 223, 306
Gray, John - Domestic
    containerization guidance
    283
Gray, John - Seattle
    International Gateway 199
Grayson, Richard ..70, 93, 95,
    100, 102, 103, 105, 110,
    111, 112, 113, 116, 137,
    141, 142, 162, 208, 211,
    249, 321, 322
Grayson, Richard -
    Authorizes 1981
    Intermodal Task Force... 94
*Great Northern Pacific
    Steamship Company*........7
Great Northern Railway (GN)
   5
Great Northern Steamship
    Company 6
Greeling, Jake 108
Greenwood, William x, xi, 68,
    92, 93, 103, 107, 116, 120,
    122, 125, 126, 127, 129,
    140, 142, 149, 154, 162,
    175, 177, 181, 185, 187,
    190, 192, 195, 203, 204,
    209, 210, 212, 213, 223,
    225, 226, 229, 235, 248,
    249, 255, 266, 269, 271,
    273, 278, 280, 283, 284,
    289, 296, 297, 298, 299,
    301, 302, 303, 304, 314,
    316, 317, 323, 326, 332
    Alliance Division
        Experience................ 84

pre-BN Intermodal
    experience................ 83
Greenwood, William - 1981
    Intermodal Task Force .. 95
Greenwood, William - 1982
    Task Force
    implementation meeting
    with Grayson and Drexel
    111
Greenwood, William - First
    Intermodal experiences 88
Greenwood, William - Initial
    Intermodal focus........... 92
Greenwood, William - post
    Task Force PR efforts .. 101
Greenwood, William -
    promoted to Executive VP
    Marketing and Sales.... 262
Greenwood, William -
    Promoted to SVP
    Marketing and Sales.... 212
Greenwood, William -
    promoted to VP
    Intermodal 177
Greenwood, William -
    recruits Bill DeWitt...... 107
Greenwood, William -
    recruits Dave Burns..... 106
Greenwood, William -
    Recruits Ken Hoepner ... 89
Greenwood, William -
    Recruits Mark Cane....... 86
Greenwood, William - saves
    Gordon Trafton for BN and
    the IBU 108
Grinstein, Gerald 320, 323,
    327
Grinstein, Gerald - elected
    BNI vice chair and moves
    to Ft. Worth................. 267
Grinstein, Gerald - Joins BN
    Inc. Board 249
Grinstein, Gerald - Winona
    Bridge 276
Gross, Larry 203, 227
Grygiel, John................... 316
Gulf Interstate Pipeline 41
Gunderson....... 201, 234, 270

Gustin, Dennis 102, 103, 141,
    163
Hall, John 228
Hanjin 202, 234, 267
Hanson, Bob 205
Harrison Street Freight
    House 26
Harrison, Hunter 130, 131,
    133, 162, 171, 172, 229,
    230, 236, 243, 320
Hawaiian Marine Lines...... 55
Hayford, Warren 79
Hepburn Act 22
Herndon, Bruce 171, 228
Hertog, John.................... 211
Hidy, Muriel E.............. 5, 349
Hidy, Ralph W.............. 5, 349
High Country News........... 41
Highway Cost Allocation
    Report 13, 20
Highway Trust Fund 19, 20
Hill, James J. 5
Hilly, Joe 272, 276, 320
History of the Atchison,
    Topeka and Santa Fe
    Railway... ii, xii, 30, 31, 349
Hitz, George.................... 203
Hoepner, Kenxi, 94, 107, 109,
    116, 120, 122, 140, 150,
    153, 163, 269, 296
Hoepner, Ken – Background
    & First Intermodal
    experiences 89
Holck, Alfred J.J. 25, 349
Holland, Axel .. 102, 109, 127,
    129, 228, 300
Honda...................... 202, 207
Horwitz, Wayne.............. 277
Houston Hub ... 142, 159, 165
Houston Light and Power 322
Houston Power and Light 322
Howery, Bob.... 190, 233, 326
Howland, David...........xii, 57
Hub Group...... 2, 3, 102, 152,
    197, 350
Hub start-up schedule - 1983
   142
Humphrey, George........... 18

Hyundai 202, 207, 235
IBU - 1982 promotion and
    advertising.................. 115
IBU "Must Do Wells" - 1986
   222
IBU buys BN's first personal
    computer..................... 133
IBU highway satellite hubs
   215
IBU organizational
    restructuring - April 1988
   300
IBU reorganization - 1983140
IBU reorganization - 1986228
IBU Strategy #1 - Convert
    from a network of ramps
    to a network of hubs ... 140
IBU Strategy #2 - New
    technology equipment in
    dedicated trains 145
IBU Strategy #3 - customer
    oriented marketing
    packages..................... 151
ICC approves the Union
    Pacific / Missouri Pacific /
    Western Pacific merger
   135
Ice, Carl........................... 306
Illinois Central.................. 145
Illinois Central Railroad 8
Illinois Central-Gulf (ICG)
    Railroad 158, 187
IMC Sight Drafts 153
Indiana Harbor Belt (IHB)
    Railroad 236
Ingram, Bob.... 136, 147, 206,
    284, 318
Ingram, Bob – Proposed
    Santa Fe / Mark VII
    venture – June 1988....304
Ingram, Bob - Replaces Steve
    Nieman 296
Ingram, Bob - Revised Santa
    Fe / Mark VII venture –
    July 1988 -.................... 306
Innovative Intermodal
    Service Brand...... 129, 149,
    151

Intercity Freight Market
    Share - 1929-1955......... 13
Intermodal Container
    Transfer Facility (ICTF). 241
Intermodal Marketing
    Company (IMC) incentives
    153
Intermodal P&L System -
    1987 263
Intermodal Reporter........ 266
Intermodal Service
    Performance
    Measurement.............. 232
Intermodal Service
    Performance
    Measurement System. 263
Intermodal Task Force - 1981
    Vulnerable business
    identified................... 96
Intermodal Task Force of
    1981 95
International Container
    Transfer Facility (ICTF) 234,
    314
International Harvester
    Company 79
Interregional Highways 12
Interstate Commerce Act of
    1887 73
Interstate Commerce
    Commission...... 22, 23, 72,
    124, 241, 270, 279
Interstate Highway System 20
Iowa Public Service Company
    250
Irving (DFW) Hub.... 142, 159,
    165, 205, 234
Itel Corporation....... 146, 313
ITOFCA........................... 152
J.B. Hunt ...308, *See* J. B. Hunt
    Transport, Inc.
J.B. Hunt Transport, Inc....... 1
JARAX International 211
Jensen, Bob 197
Jesuit principle of
    management.............. 134
John Gray 200

John W. Barriger III National
    Railroad Library..............xii
Johnson, Dave 129, 172
Journal of Commerce 266
K Line............................. 234
Kalabus, Andy.......... 231, 259
Kansas City Hub 114, 142, 234
Kansas-Nebraska Natural Gas
    Co. 40
Karl, Mike 274
Kath, Cliff........................ 171
Katzenbach, Jon xi
Kehr, Curt 116
Kellogg's - 1983-1986 Modal
    shift 266
Kelly, Jim...........................xii
Kelly, Jim - Background ... 235
Kenefick, John 46
King, Julie....................ii, xii
Klemett, Jim 190
K-Line.............................. 315
Kotler, Phil...................... 122
Krebs, Robert.....xii, 272, 306,
    313
Kreyling, Ed..................... 227
Krismer Ken 154
Lamphier, Thomas............. 70
Land Grant System 8
Lander Line - C&NW.......... 39
Larson, Dennis......... 154, 228
Lawrence, Mike 209
Leachman, Rob........... 52, 94
Lehman Brothers Kuhn Loeb
    40
Levitt, Theodore.............. 122
Lewis and Clark.................. 7
Lewis, Dick......... 96, 225, 273
Liner Train (APL)...... 148, 302
Long Island Railroad........... 9
Lorentzsen, Norman... 47, 67,
    70, 79
Louth, Kathy 300
Loving Jr., Rush................. 74
Lower Colorado River
    Authority 322
MacDonald, Thomas H...... 10
Madison Formation Aquifer
    41

Maersk..... 234, 236, 315, 318
Magnuson, Senator Warren
    249
Mandel, Alex 267
Mark VII Transportation. 298,
    301
Marketing Myopia... 121, 122
Master Plan for Free
    Highway Development.. 11
Matney, R.C..... 93, 158, 175,
    298, 301
Matney, RC - Mark VII 271
Matson Shipping Lines 28
Matthews, Tom 181, 277, 320
Mattingly, Garrett xi
Mazda...................... 208, 231
Mazda/Ford Flat Rock
    assembly plant 259
McCormack, John W. 18
McInnes, Don 306
McKinsey & Company xi, 306,
    313
McLean, Malcom.............. 136
McManus, Meredith 326
Media image improvement
    campaign - 1987.......... 266
Memphis Hub.......... 137, 142
Menk, Lou....................... 322
Menk, Louis 47, 66, 70, 79,
    181
Meridian................... 250, 251
Meridian Minerals Company
    326
Meridian Oil Inc.............. 326
Meyer, Don...... 190, 225, 228
Micro-bridge.................... 54
Mid-South Railroad 269
Midway (Minneapolis / St.
    Paul) Hub.... 109, 112, 113,
    114, 119, 127, 128, 129,
    132, 140, 141, 162, 163,
    165
Midway Hub conversion
    experience.................. 140
Miller, Ed 186
Milwaukee Road..... 9, 53, 62,
    102, 187
Mini-bridge.......... 53, 54, 147

Minnich-Olson, Gay. 228, 298
Missouri Pacific Railroad .. 65,
    135, 178, 179, 199
Mitsubishi........................ 231
Mobile Hub 171
MOL................................ 202
Montana Rail Link 320
Montana Rail Link (MRL) -
    1987 Formation.......... 279
Morgan, J.P. 36, 285
Morrison Knudson (MK).. 328
Motor Carrier Act of 1935. 23
Motor Carrier Industry
    Regulatory Relief - 1970s-
    1982 61
Muellner, Ralph...... 157, 172,
    231, 235, 241, 297, 300
Muellner, Ralph - Common
    User Stack Train 202
Nankivell, James.... 52, 53, 55
National Ambient Air Quality
    Standards (NAAQS) 33
National Association of
    Commerce Attorneys.. 101
National Piggyback. 152, 175,
    224, 237
National Piggyback - 1983 BN
    acquisition?................ 158
National Railroad Hall of
    Fame...... ii, xii, 84, 88, 101,
    111, 124, 126, 162, 173,
    192, 211, 212, 213, 267,
    269, 276, 278, 299, 324,
    332
National Railroad Passenger
    Service Act..................... 62
National Railway Equipment
    328
Neswick, Gerald L............ 218
New York Central Railroad 23
Newman, Ron................. 283
Nieman, Steve 225, 283, 284,
    289
Nieman, Steve - "Bad rates
    but not bad freight" 263
Nieman, Steve - promoted to
    Group VP Intermodal .. 255

Nieman, Steve - Recruited to
    lead BN IBU 224
Nieman, Steve - Shifts to
    Winona Bridge............. 298
Nimer, Dan 122, 150, 265
Nippon Yusen Kaisha (NYK). 6
Nissan 207
NOL................................ 202
Nolan, Norton & Co........ 174,
    204, 222
Noorlag, Jr., William 19
Norfolk Southern...... 86, 210,
    226, 227, 260, **268**, 286,
    299, 301, 333
Norfolk Southern assumes
    BN RoadRailer service -
    1986 226
North American Car (NAC)
    .... 145, 159, 203
North American Van Lines
    .... 210, 260
Northern Lines merger..... 51,
    262
Northern Pacific bond
    defeasance - 1988 323
Northern Pacific Railroad –
    Bond encumbrance history
    285
Northern Pacific Railway (NP)
    .... 5, 35
Northwestern University 150,
    249, 265
Novas, Peter 143
NYK 202, 235
Odasz, Frank.................... 40
Ohanian, Lee E................. 80
Olympia and York............ 313
Omaha Hub 165, 171
Omaha Public Power....... 330
OOCL 202
Operating Department
    Overland Park relocation
    137
Organization of the
    Petroleum Exporting
    Countries (OPEC)........... 34
Orris, Don 155, 156, 175, 308
Overland Mail.................. 52

Overnite Transportation
    Company - Union Pacific
    Acquisition................... 242
Overton, Richard C. 5, 350
Pacella Western Electric
    facility......................... 236
Pacific Intermountain
    Express (PIE) 300
Pacific Northwest Perishable
    Shippers Association .. 152,
    264
Pacific Rail Services 199
Pacific Zip........................... 52
Palm Springs Staff
    Conference - 1981......... 79
Panama Canal.................. 316
Panza, James xii
Pasco Hub....................... 172
Paul Roberts - Transmode
    198
Penn Central Railroad.. 37, 62
PepsiCo........................... 210
Perdue, Tom 308
Philip, Craig..................... 314
*Piggyback and Containers – A
    History of Rail Intermodal
    on America's Steel
    Highway*..... ii, xii, 5, 28, 55,
    187, 349
Piggyback Blues See Simpson,
    Red
Plum Creek Timber
    Company, Inc............... 326
Port of Seattle 135, 136, 175,
    200, 318
Port of Seattle -
    Development of
    containerization 136
Port of Tacoma 137, 185
Port of Tacoma - Sea-Land
    200
Porter, McNeil 267
Portland Hub .. 113, 114, 119,
    127, 128, 129, 131, 132,
    140, 163, 172, 259
Portland Hub conversion
    experience................... 142
Post-Panamax ships......... 316

Powder River Basin 5, 37, 178, 201, 221, 246, 321, 327

Powder River Basin coal build-up history 33

Power by the Hour Locomotives 246

Pratt, Jim 154

PRB 329

President Carter 72

President Dwight Eisenhower 15

President Thomas Jefferson 7

Proctor, David 283, 308

Promotion and advertising strategy - 1987 265

Provo, Larry 40

Pullman 147

R.J. Reynolds (RJR) 200

Railroad Act of 1864............ 9

Railroad Industry regulatory relief - 1970s - 1982 62

Railroad Revitalization and Reform (4R) Act of 1976 62

Railway Labor Act (RLA) .. 319

Rayburn, Sam 16

Reckinger, Duane 226

Reebie Associates' Transearch 198

Reebie, Robert .. 93, 145, 158

Reed, John 113

Reed, Lyle 116, 127, 177, 211, 225

Regional Railroad Reorganization (3R) Act 62

Reichmann brothers 313

Reilly, William 108

Remanufactured locomotives initiative 328

Reynolds, John 190, 196

Richards, Curt xii

Riding the Rails – Inside the Business of America's Railroads .... ii, xii

Rievman v. Burlington Northern Railroad Company 286

RoadRailer 93, 106, 145, 203, 221, 225, 260

RoadRailer - Background. 158

RoadRailer – Mark IV vs. Mark V 271

RoadRailer / Mark VII , Matney venture - 1988 299

Roadway Express............. 134

Robinson, Ray................. 228

Rock Island Railroad .. 62, 124

Rodel, Doug 129, 141, 163

Rose, Mark H. 18

Round, Jack 226, 263, 300

Russell, John 306

Rust Belt 22, 35, 80

Ryder, James A. 211

Sanders, Malcolm........... 101

Santa Fe - follows BN's Expediter strategy 258

Santa Fe Fuel Foiler car ... 146

Santa Fe Railway 215, 238, 241, 258, 286, 301, 304, 315, 333

Santa Fe Southern Pacific Corp 241

Schlaeger, Gary 96

Schneider National 1, 209, 210, 308

Schramm, Ken 28

Schwarz, Larry 95

Scott, Don....................... 212

Scott, Roy V. 5, 349

Seaboard Coast Line.......... 66

Sea-Land - BN recaptures business - 1985............ 200

Sea-Land business - BN loses, 1983 135

Sea-Land Services... 101, 135, 147, 148, 153, 154, 156, 163, 175, 185, 200, 201, 202, 206, 219, 224, 227, 234, 235, 237, 241, 257, 260, 296, 315, 318

Seatbelts for Your Shipments advertising theme - 1983 149

Seattle International Gateway (SIG).............. 199

Section 6 notices 320

Sellberg, Ron xii

Sermak, Robert........... 39, 49

Service by Design............. 232

Service Failure Notification System 263

Shum, Don 156

Shurstad, Tom 175

Silverman, Gary 75, 79

Simon, Norton 35, 39, 40, 285, 323

1973 statement to BN shareholders............ 37

Simon, Roger .. 121, 140, 149, 153, 239, 270

Simpson, Red.............. 30, 31

Single trailer rates 101

Slingshot trains 187

Soo Line Railroad..... 102, 163

Sorrow, Ron..................... 267

South Seattle Hub ... 114, 142

Southern Pacific Railroad ... 8, 52, 86, 114, 147, 173, 185, 202, 237, 241, 255, 258, 268, 286, 314, 317, 329, 333

Southern Railroad 58, 173

Southland Royalty Company 326

Southland Royalty Company - BNI buys, 1985............. 219

Southwest Express 203

Speaker, Alan.................. 318

Spokane Hub 114, 142

Spoor, Michael J 25, 350

Sprau, David 218

Springer, Lee................... 228

Springfield Hub............... 165

Sprint trains 187

St. Louis – San Francisco (Frisco) Railroad 46

St. Louis Hub................... 142

Stack car/RoadRailer hitch test - 1988 307

Stack cars - bulkheads, yes or no?............................ 282

Stacy Street - BN Seattle International Hub 157

Staggers Rail Act of 1980 . 67, 73, 83, 329
Stampede Pass 161, 218, 244
Stampede Tunnel 218, 219
Standard and Poor's Corp. 251
Stanzel, Volker 21
Starling, Dave 236
Stern, Louis..................... 122
Stevedoring Services of America (SSA)...... 200, 284
Stevens Pass................... 161
Stiles, Roger 157
Suez Canal 318
Super C 29
Surface Transportation Assistance Act of 1982 . 61, 91
SW^{2}C = So What, Who Cares? 123
Swartz, John 272, 306
Teamster's National Master Freight labor agreement 224
Teamsters Union....... 18, 199
Temple, Nick 244
Texas Christian University225
Texas Eastern Pipeline 41
The El Paso Company...... 183
The Energy Crisis of 1973.. 37
The Great Northern Railway, A History................. 5, 349
The Hub of Burlington Lines West 25, 349
The Prospect Group - Trailer Train acquisition proposal 269
The Santa Fe Trail Transportation Company 209
The Story of the BNSF Railway...... 16, 29, 40, 350
The Streamliner.......... 52, 94
The TTX Story ii, xii, 104, 145, 350
The United States Clean Air Act 33

The Wisdom of Teams....xi, 5, 83, 302
Thomas, Bud................... 109
Thompson, Andy 190, 233
Thompson, Bill (Trailer Train) 201
Thompson, William F. 70, 71, 84, 116, 138, 321
Thrall Car 147, 148, 203
Tierney, John 117, 262
Tolan, Fred 264
Toll Roads and Free Roads 11
Toyota 207, 231
Trafton, Gordon 106, 130, 131, 133, 190, 225, 229
Trafton, Gordon - Pre-Intermodal experience 107
Trailer Train.... 147, 185, 201, 235, 239, 257
Trailer Train - 1986 Dividend Payment 240
Trailer Train - 1987 Stock Transfer Plan 270
Trailer Train - Financial Performance 1981-1986 239
Train #106 58
Train #24 132
Train #3 .... 52, 133
Train #63 .... 130, 182
Trains #7, 8, 9, and 10 200
Transamerica................... 154
Transport Topics............... 18
Treat, Ned 189, 228
Trinity Industries 147
Triple Crown.... 203, 260, 271
Tulsa Hub................ 172, 234
U. S. Customs Service 236
U.S. Bureau of Public Roads 10
U.S. Highway Trailer Length Limits 1930-present.............. 103
U.S. Postal Service (USPS) 53, 187, 263
U.S. Railway Association (USRA) 62
U.S. Steel 22

Union Pacific.......... 46, 48, 65
Union Pacific Historical Society 52, 94
Union Pacific Railroad . 8, 242
Union Pacific Railroad (UP) .. 30, 52, 53, 54, 76, 86, 94, 102, 112, 131, 135, 137, 147, 148, 155, 156, 157, 174, 181, 185, 199, 200, 201, 207, 221, 229, 234, 236, 238, 240, 252, 253, 257, 260, 271, 286, 287, 302, 314, 315, 333
United Auto Workers .. 22, 80
United Energy Resources ..40
United Parcel Service . 29, 55, 101, 110, 111, 130, 131, 134, 162, 171, 187, 210, 230, 242, 258, 264, 303
United States freight share 1955-1980 65
United Steel Workers.. 22, 80
United Transportation Union 195, 204, 275, 319, 320
UTU..................... *See* United Transportation Union
Vaden, Jerry K................218
VCA BN and Santa Fe Intermodal, 1986 proposal 248
Vertical integration - lack of 257
Volume is Vanity and Margin is Sanity - 1987 263
Wackstein, Eli 177, 204
Wallner, Doc................... 259
Walpert, Bill.................... 196
Washington Central Railroad (WCRC) 244
Watson, Murry212, 222, 255, 274, 297, 317
Weaver, Phil 332
Weber, Arnold................. 249
Weeks, Sinclair 18
Wegler, D.E..................... 275
Weicher, Rich 306
Weingroff, Richard F. ... 7, 10, 15

Werby, Don 308

Western Airlines.............. 249

Western Avenue 200, 206, 227, 267

Western Pacific Railroad .. 66, 135, 199, 223

Western Rail Properties (WRPI) 48

Westwood Shipping 202, 235

Weyerhaeuser Corporation 67

Whitacre, Tom 119, 279

White, Theodore H............ 16

Whitehead and Kales 147

Wholesale vs. retail issue - 1987 260

Wilkins, Chuck 208, 238

Williams, Kirk... 258, 283, 308

Wilson, Robert 67

Winona Bridge................. 298

Winona Bridge Railroad - labor and competitive background, 1987 275

Winter, Mel 190, 275, 320

Wood, Don 162, 165, 177, 211, 262

Woodward, George......... 315

Woolford, Julian 129, 228

World War I 21

World War II 21, 35

Worldwide Logistics - BNWW NVOCC acquisition 317

Yeager, Phil..................... 102

Yom Kippur War 34

Youngstown Steel Door... 148

Zachau, Jim 204

Zadnichek, M.L. 28

Zaegel, Art 299

Zarembski, Alan.............. **283**

Zell, Sam 306, 313

Zero Sum Game - Intermodal Industry relationships.. 245

Zero-Sum-Game - 1987 ... 274

ZETA-TECH Associates 283

Made in the USA
Columbia, SC
05 October 2024

43659647R00204